ESSENTIAL ECONOMICS FOR BUSINESS

Pearson

At Pearson, we have a simple mission: to help people make more of their lives through learning.

We combine innovative learning technology with trusted content and educational expertise to provide engaging and effective learning experiences that serve people wherever and whenever they are learning.

From classroom to boardroom, our curriculum materials, digital learning tools and testing programmes help to educate millions of people worldwide – more than any other private enterprise.

Every day our work helps learning flourish, and wherever learning flourishes, so do people.

To learn more, please visit us at **www.pearson.com/uk**

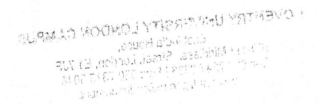

ESSENTIAL ECONOMICS FOR BUSINESS

Fifth edition

John Sloman

Economics Network
Visiting Professor, University of the West of England

Elizabeth Jones

Principal Teaching Fellow and Dean of Students,
University of Warwick

 Pearson

Harlow, England • London • New York • Boston • San Francisco • Toronto • Sydney
Auckland • Singapore • Hong Kong • Tokyo • Seoul • Taipei • New Delhi
Cape Town • São Paulo • Mexico City • Madrid • Amsterdam • Munich • Paris • Milan

Pearson Education Limited
Edinburgh Gate
Harlow CM20 2JE
United Kingdom
Tel: +44 (0)1279 623623
Web: www.pearson.com/uk

First published 2005 (print)
Second edition 2008 (print)
Third edition 2011 (print)
Fourth edition published 2014 (print and electronic)
Fifth edition published 2017 (print and electronic)

© Pearson Education Limited 2005, 2011 (print)
© Pearson Education Limited 2014, 2017 (print and electronic)

ISBN: 978-1-292-15127-4 (print)
      978-1-292-15129-8 (PDF)
      978-1-292-15131-1 (eText)

British Library Cataloguing-in-Publication Data
A catalogue record for the print edition is available from the British Library

Library of Congress Cataloging-in-Publication Data
A catalog record for the print edition is available from the Library of Congress

10 9 8 7 6 5 4 3 2 1
20 19 18 17

Print edition typeset in 8/12pt Stone Serif ITC Pro -Medium by iEnergizer Aptara® Ltd
Print edition printed in in Slovakia by Neografia.

NOTE THAT ANY PAGE CROSS REFERENCES REFER TO THE PRINT EDITION

Brief Contents

Contents

PART D THE MACROECONOMIC ENVIRONMENT OF BUSINESS

Preface

TO THE STUDENT

Welcome to the fifth edition of *Essentials Economics for Business* (previously called *Economics and the Business Environment*). If you are a student on a business or management degree or diploma course and taking a module which includes economics, then this text is written for you. Such modules may go under the title of Business Environment or Business Context, or they may simply be called Introduction to Economics or Introduction to Business Economics. Alternatively, you may be studying for an MBA and need a grounding in basic economic concepts and how they apply to the business environment.

The text covers the core economics that you will need as a business student, but it also covers various business-related topics not typically covered in an introductory economics textbook. These topics include elements of business organisation and business strategy.

As well as making considerable use of business examples throughout the text, we have included many case studies in boxes (62 in all). These illustrate how economics can be used to understand particular business problems or aspects of the business environment. Many of these case studies cover issues that you are likely to read about in the newspapers. Some cover general business issues; others look at specific companies. There are also an additional 107 case studies on the text's companion website. These, along with references to various useful websites, are listed at the end of each of the four parts of the text.

We hope that, in using this text, you will share our fascination for economics. It is a subject that is highly relevant to the world in which we live. You only have to look at global events and the news since the onset of the financial crisis of 2008 to see its importance. Many of our needs are served by business – whether as employers or as producers of the goods and services we buy. After graduating, you will probably take up employment in business. A grounding in economic principles and how they relate to the world of business should prove invaluable in the business decisions you may well have to make.

The aim throughout the text is to make this intriguing subject clear for you to understand and as relevant as possible to you as a student of business.

The written style is direct and straightforward, with short paragraphs to aid rapid comprehension. Definitions of all key terms are given in the margin, with defined terms appearing in bold. We have highlighted 29 Key Ideas, which are fundamental to 'thinking like an economist'. We refer back to these every time they recur throughout the text. This helps you to see how the subject ties together, and also helps you to develop a toolkit of concepts that can be used in a whole host of different contexts.

Summaries ('Recaps') are given at the end of each section of each chapter. These should help you in reviewing the material you have just covered and in revising for exams. Each chapter finishes with a series of questions, as does each of the boxes. These can be used to check your understanding of the chapter and help you to see how its material can be applied to various business problems.

There are also questions interspersed throughout the text in 'Pause for Thought' panels. These encourage you to reflect on what you are learning and to see how the various ideas and theories relate to different issues. Answers to these questions are given on the companion website.

We hope you enjoy the text and come to appreciate the crucial role that economics plays in all our lives and, in particular, in the practice of business.

Good luck and enjoy. Perhaps this will be just the beginning of a life-long interest in economic issues and how they apply to the world of business – and in your own personal life too!

TO LECTURERS AND TUTORS

The aim of this text is to provide a short course in economic principles as they apply to the business environment. It is designed to be used by first-year undergraduates on business studies degrees and students on diplomas where economics is taught from the business perspective, either as a separate one-semester module or as part of a business environment module. It is also suitable for students studying economics on MBA, CMS, DMS and various professional courses.

In addition to covering core economic principles, various specialist business topics are also covered that do not appear in conventional introductory economics textbooks. The following are some examples of these additional topics:

- Business organisations
- Industrial structure
- STEEPLE analysis (as an extension of PEST analysis)
- The structure–conduct–performance paradigm and its limitations
- The control of prices (new to this edition)
- The multinational corporation
- Globalisation and business
- Marketing the product
- Strategic analysis and choice
- Principal–agent analysis and the problem of asymmetric information as applied to various business situations
- The problems of adverse selection and moral hazard
- Application of game theory to business situations
- Porter's five forces model
- Growth strategy
- Business strategy in a recession
- Transactions cost analysis
- Ratio analysis to measure firms' success (new to this edition)
- Alternative aims of firms
- Pricing in practice
- The product life cycle
- The small-firm sector
- Flexible labour markets and firms

- The economics of entrepreneurship
- Business ethics and corporate social responsibility
- Government and the firm, including competition policy and regulation
- The macroeconomic environment of business, including the impact of macroeconomic policy on business
- Analysis of global policy responses to the credit crunch and the impact on business (new to this edition)
- The competitive advantage of nations
- Trading blocs including the effect of the single European market on business
- Monetary union, the crisis in the eurozone and its impact on business
- The implications of exchange rate movements and international capital flows for business.

The text is split into four parts containing a total of 13 chapters. Each chapter could be covered in a week, giving enough material for a semester. Each chapter is divided into discrete sections, each with its own summary, providing ideal coverage for a single study session for a student. Chapters finish with review questions, which can be used for seminars or discussion sessions.

The first nine chapters cover microeconomics and its relation to business. The final four cover the macroeconomic environment of business, both national and international. This higher weighting for microeconomics reflects the structure of many economics for business or business environment modules.

SPECIAL FEATURES

The text contains the following special features:

- *A direct and straightforward written style*, with short paragraphs to aid rapid comprehension. The aim all the time is to provide maximum clarity.
- *Attractive full-colour design*. The careful and consistent use of colour and shading makes the text more attractive to students and easier to use by giving clear signals as to the structure.
- *Figures with captions*. Most diagrams have captions to explain their properties and to highlight key features.
- *Key Ideas* are highlighted and explained where they first appear. There are 29 of these ideas, which are fundamental to the study of economics on business courses. Students can see them recurring throughout the text. Showing how ideas can be used in a variety of contexts helps students to 'think like an economist' and to relate the different parts of the subject together. All 29 Key Ideas are defined in a special section at the end of the text.
- *Pause for Thought* questions integrated throughout the text. These encourage students to reflect on what they

have just read and make the learning process a more active one. Answers to these questions appear on the companion website. This new edition contains additional Pause for Thought questions.
- *Part opening sections* for each of the four parts of the text, setting the scene and introducing the material to be covered.
- *Chapter opening sections* that identify key business issues to be covered in that chapter.
- *All technical terms are highlighted and clearly defined in the margin* on the page they appear. This feature is especially useful for students when revising.
- *A comprehensive index*, including reference to all defined terms. This enables students to look up a definition as required and to see it used in context.
- *Many boxes with additional applied material*. All boxes include questions so as to relate the material back to the chapter in which the box is located. The extensive use of applied material makes learning much more interesting for students and helps to bring the subject alive. This is particularly important for business students who need to

relate economic theory to their other subjects and to the world of business generally. There are many new and updated boxes in this edition to provide additional case study material.

■ *Additional case studies appearing on the companion website.* These are referred to at the end of each of the four Parts of the text. Most of these cases contain questions for the students to reflect on and answers can be found on the lecturer site.

■ *Detailed summaries appear at the end of each section.* These allow students not only to check their comprehension of a section's contents, but also to get a clear overview of the material they have been studying.

■ *Review questions at the end of each chapter.* These are designed to test students' understanding of the chapter's salient points. These questions can be used for seminars or as set work to be completed in the students' own time. Answers can be found on the lecturer site.

■ *A list of relevant websites given at the end of each part.* Details of these websites can be found in the Web Appendix at the end of the text. You can easily access any of these sites from the Economics News website (at **www.pearsoned.co.uk/sloman**). When you enter the site, click on Hotlinks. You will find all the sites from the Web Appendix listed. Click on the one you want and the 'hotlink' will take you straight to it.

SUPPLEMENTS

Economics News Site

■ Search 'Sloman Economics News' and visit the news blog site. This contains around 10 new posts per month. Each post considers a topic in the news that relates to economics, with an introduction to and description of the news item, links to newspaper articles from around the world, videos, podcasts and data. There are questions on each item and references to the relevant chapter(s) of the text.

■ There are also hotlinks to a range of websites, including each of those referred to at the end of each of the four Parts of the text.

Student Website

The text's companion website provides a comprehensive set of online resources **at www.pearsoned.co.uk/sloman.** Access is provided with every new purchase of this text. Resources on the website include

■ Animations of key models with audio explanations ('audio animations').

■ 107 case studies with questions for self-study, ordered part-by-part and referred to in the text.

■ Updated list of over 250 hotlinks to sites of use for economics.

■ Answers to all in-chapter (pause for thought) questions.

■ Hotlinks to the websites referred to at the end of each Part of the text.

■ Glossary.

■ Flashcards of key terms.

■ Access to articles from the News site relevant to any given chapter.

Instructor Resources

There are many resources for lecturers and tutors that can be downloaded from the Instructor Resource Centre. These have been thoroughly revised for the fifth edition. These include:

■ *PowerPoint® slide shows* in full colour for use with a data projector in lectures and classes. These can also be made available to students by loading them on to a local network. There are several types of slideshows:

– All figures from the text and most of the tables. Each figure is built up in a logical sequence, thereby allowing tutors to show them in lectures in an animated form. There is also a static version for printing onto acetate for use with a conventional OHP.

– Customisable lecture plans. These are a series of bullet-point lecture plans. There is one for each chapter. Each one can be easily edited, with points added, deleted or moved, so as to suit particular lectures. A consistent use of colour is made to show how the points tie together. They come in various versions:

• Lecture plans with integrated diagrams. These lecture plans include animated diagrams, charts and tables at the appropriate points.

• Lecture plans with integrated diagrams and questions. These are like the above but also include multiple-choice questions, allowing lectures to become more interactive. They can be used with or without an audience response system (ARS). ARS versions are available for InterWrite PRS® and TurningPoint® and are ready to use with appropriate 'clickers'. There is also a 'show of hands' version for use without clickers.

• Lecture plans without the diagrams. These allow you to construct your own diagrams on the blackboard or whiteboard or use an OHP.

- *Case studies*. These, also available on the companion website for students, can be reproduced and used for classroom exercises or for student assignments. Answers are also provided (not available on the student site).
- *Workshops*. There are 13 of these – one per chapter. They are in Word® and can be reproduced for use with large groups (up to 200 students) in a lecture theatre or large classroom. Suggestions for use are given in an accompanying file. Answers to all workshops are given in separate Word® files.
- *Economic experiments*. These are simulations that can be used in class and cover topics such as markets, price controls, taxes and public goods.

- *Business videos:* interviews with senior managers in a number of firms and other organisations discussing various economic issues that affect them. Accompanying questions test students' understanding of the topics covered.
- *Teaching/learning case studies*. There are 20 of these. They examine various approaches to teaching introductory economics and ways to improve student learning of introductory economics.
- *Answers to:*
  - all end-of-chapter questions
  - pause for thought questions
  - questions in boxes
  - questions in the case studies
  - the 13 workshops.

ACKNOWLEDGEMENTS

First, many thanks to Elizabeth for all her work in helping to prepare this new edition and for adding lots of new content. Many thanks too to all the reviewers of the text, who, as with the previous edition, have given us valuable advice for improvements. Thanks also to the team at Pearson, and especially Natalia Jaszczuk, Caitlin Lisle and Andrew Muller.

Finally, thanks to all my family and especially, as always, to my wife Alison for her continued patience, love and support.

John Sloman

Once again, my thanks go to John Sloman for giving me this wonderful opportunity to co-author my second edition of this text and to the team at Pearson for their continued support. I am forever grateful to my family and in particular my parents, whose unfailing love and support have made this possible.

Elizabeth Jones

Publisher's acknowledgements

We are grateful to the following for permission to reproduce copyright material:

Figures

Figure 1.5 adapted from *The structure–conduct–performance paradigm—Industrial Market Structure and Economic Performance*, 3.ed, Houghton Mifflin Company (Scherer, Frederic M.; Ross, David 1990) © South-Western, a part of Cengage Learning, Inc. reproduced by permission, From SCHERER. SPB - SCHERER IND MKT STR&ECONPERF, 3E. © 1990 South-Western, a part of Cengage Learning, Inc. Reproduced by permission. www.cengage.com/permissions; Figure 2.1 from The Financial Times Stock Exchange Index (FTSE), London Stock Exchange Group companies and is used by FTSE International Limited under licence. All rights in the FTSE indices and / or FTSE ratings vest in FTSE and/or its licensors. Neither FTSE nor its licensors accept any liability for any errors or omissions in the FTSE indices and / or FTSE ratings or underlying data. No further distribution of FTSE Data is permitted without FTSE's express written consent"; Figure 2.2 adapted from Based on data in Halifax House Price Index, administered by Markit.; Figures 7.1, 7.2 from Based on data in UNCTAD FDI database (UNCTAD); Figures 7.1a, 7.1b from Cross Border Mergers & Acquisitions', World Investment Report Annex Tables, UNCTAD (June 2015); Figures 7.4a from Based on data in UNCTAD Stat and World Economic Outlook (IMF).; Figure 7.4b from Based on data in UNCTAD Stat, FDI (UNCTAD); Figure 9.3 after Stern Review: Executive Summary, Prepared by Stern Review, from data drawn from World Resources Institute Climate; Analysis Indicators Tool (CAIT) on-line database version 3.0. Contains public sector information licensed under the Open Government Licence (OGL) v3.0.http://www.nationalarchives.gov.uk/doc/open-government-licence.

Text

Extract 3. from The triumph of unreason? Why you are not always rational with your credit card, *The Economist* 11/01/2007 (From the print edition), http://www.economist.com/node/8516366, The Economist by ECONOMIST NEWSPAPER LTD. Reproduced with permission of ECONOMIST NEWSPAPER LTD in the format Book via Copyright Clearance Center; Extract 3. from Why a nudge from the state beats a slap, *The Guardian*, 20/07/2008 (Richard Reeves), https://www.theguardian.com/books/2008/jul/20/politics.society1; Extract 3. from Own-label steamroller rumbles on, *Marketing Week* 06/12/1996 (Alan Mitchell); Extract 3. from http://www.ipa.co.uk/, 2006 IPA Effectiveness Awards: the winners', Institute of Practitioners in Advertising; Extract 3.5 from Supermarket own-brands generate more than half of UK grocery sales *Marketing Magazine*, 27/11/2014 (Ben Bold), Campaign, Reproduced from Campaign Magazine with the permission of the copyright owner, Haymarket Media Group Limited.; Extract 6. from 'Suck it and see': The hazards of being an entrepreneur, *The Economist* 01/02/2007, The Economist by ECONOMIST NEWSPAPER LTD. Reproduced with permission of ECONOMIST NEWSPAPER LTD in the format Book via Copyright Clearance Center; Extract 6.1 from http://www.rankingthebrands.com/PDF/Interbrand%20Best%20Global%20Brands%202012.pdf, "Interbrand's Best Global Brands 2012 report is a look at financial performance of the brand, role of brand in the purchase decision process and the brand strength. Go to www.bestglobalbrands.com for more information."; Extract 6.3 from Domino's Pizza sees customers rise as recession keeps people at home, *The Guardian*, 01/10/2009 (Abhinav Ramnarayan), https://www.theguardian.com/business/2009/oct/01/dominos-pizza-sales-recession; Extract 6.3 from Training in the recession: winner or loser?', Institute of Directors Survey Report (November 2008)., © 2017 Institute of Directors. All rights reserved; Extract 6.3 from Mobile will turn internet into world's biggest advertising medium by 2017, says report, *Campaign* 22/06/2015 (Omar Oakes), http://www.campaignlive.co.uk/article/mobile-will-turn-internet-worlds-biggest-advertising-medium-2017-says-report/1352438, Reproduced from Campaign Magazine with the permission of the copyright owner, Haymarket Media Group Limited; Extract 6.3 from Business profile: San Carlo, *Big Hospitality* 31/07/2009 (Paul Wooton), Restaurant Magazine; Extract 7.4 from Mapping China's middle class, *McKinsey Quarterly* 01/06/2013 (Dominic Barton, Yougang Chen, Amy Jin), Excerpt from "Mapping China's middle class", June 2013,

McKinsey & Company, www.mckinsey.com. Copyright (c) 2016 McKinsey & Company. All rights reserved. Reprinted by permission.; Extract 7.4 from Xu Ping, 19/04/2010, Partner, King & Wood Mallesons, www.kwm.com; Extract 8.1 from Telecommuting: The Work-From-Home Option, *http://www.dqchannels.com/*, 18/02/2005 (DQC BUREAU); Extract 10.5 from China's economy: Exercising its pricing power, *The Economist* 22/06/2006, The Economist by ECONOMIST NEWSPAPER LTD. Reproduced with permission of ECONOMIST NEWSPAPER LTD in the format Book via Copyright Clearance Center.

Photographs

John Sloman : 1, 2, 23, 24, 51, 74, 101, 102, 133, 160, 180, 203, 229, 230, 260, 289, 312

All other images © Pearson Education

Introduction

In this text we will be looking at the economic environment in which firms operate and how economic analysis can be used in the process of business decision taking. In doing so, you will gain an insight into how economists think and the sorts of concepts they use to analyse business problems.

But what particular aspects of business does the economist study? Firms are essentially concerned with using inputs to make output. Inputs cost money and output earns money. The difference between the revenue earned and the costs incurred constitutes the firm's profit. Firms will normally want to make as much profit as possible, or at the very least to make satisfactory profits and certainly to avoid a decline in profits.

In order to meet these and other objectives, managers must make choices: choices of what types of output to produce, how much to produce and at what price; choices of what techniques of production to use; what types and how many workers to employ; what suppliers to use for raw materials, equipment, etc. In each case, when weighing up alternatives, managers will want to make the best choices for their firm. Business economists study these choices. They study economic decision making by firms.

All these choices will be affected by the environment in which the firm operates. If the firm is in a stable market with a well-established customer base, the choices may be relatively simple. The choices will be very different if firms are in a rapidly changing market, with lots of competition and new products and processes being developed.

The decisions of the firm are also affected by the much broader national and international environment. Is the economy expanding or contracting? What is happening to interest rates and taxes? Is there competition from other countries? Are there opportunities for expanding abroad? At the time of writing, the terms under which the UK will leave the EU are under discussion. The nature of Brexit and the UK's future relations with the EU will affect the choices that firms make.

The local, national and international economic and political environments all crucially influence a firm's decisions. We will be looking at these influences as the text progresses.

Business and the economic environment

Business issues covered in this chapter

- Which factors influence a firm's behaviour and performance?
- How are businesses organised and structured?
- What are the various legal categories of business and how do different legal forms suit different types of business?
- What are the aims of business?
- Will owners, managers and other employees necessarily have the same aims? How can the decision makers in a firm be persuaded to achieve the objectives of the owners and hence their employers?
- How are businesses influenced by their national and global market environment?
- How are different types of industry classified in the official statistics?
- How do economists set about analysing business decision taking?

What are the core economic concepts that are necessary to understand the economic choices that businesses have to make, such as what to produce, what inputs and what technology to use, where to locate their production and how best to compete with other firms?

The business environment has been somewhat uncertain since the financial crisis of 2008/9. Uncertainty has come from many quarters: how much Chinese economic growth will slow; what will happen to the price of oil and various other commodities; the future of the EU and the euro; the UK's relationship with the EU; the ability of the global banking system to withstand various shocks. These uncertainties affect business confidence and business plans.

What is more, the world economy has undergone many other changes in recent decades, and these changes have had profound effects on businesses across the world.

For a start, most countries have increasingly embraced the 'market' as the means of boosting prosperity. You can see this in the abandonment of state planning in former communist countries, the privatisation of state industries around the world, the dismantling of barriers to international trade, the development of global financial markets, the use of government policies to promote competition and reductions in government regulation of business in order to attract inward investment. A consequence has been the growth of multinational businesses seeking the best market opportunities and the cheapest sources of supply. This has also contributed to increasing interdependence between nations, which has both good and bad consequences, as we will discuss in part D.

Other important influences on businesses around the world have included the development of computers and IT, improvements in transport and communications and, more recently, a rapid growth in the use of the Internet, including e-commerce and social media. These technological advances have provided both opportunities and threats to businesses. Firms have had to adapt to them to maintain their competitiveness, but these developments have also allowed businesses to take advantage of growing market opportunities.

Today, for many firms the world is their market. Their business environment is global. This is obviously the case with large multinational companies, such as McDonald's, Sony, VW, HSBC, Nestlé and Shell. But many small and medium-sized enterprises (SMEs) also have global reach, selling their products in various countries, often via the Internet, and buying their supplies from wherever in the world they get the best deal. Clearly the terms of access to such markets is crucial. For example, for companies based in the UK or trading with the UK, economic relations between the UK and the rest of the EU may be key to determining the success of their business.

For other firms, however, their market is much more local. Take a restaurant or firm of heating engineers – in fact, look in the Yellow Pages and you will see a host of companies serving a market whose radius is no more than a few miles. But these firms can also be affected by the global environment, either in terms of where their supplies are sourced and/or if they face competition from global companies. A local shop is likely to face competition from a supermarket, such as Tesco or Wal-Mart, both of which have shops around the world and source their supplies from across the globe.

In this chapter, we take an overview of the types of environment in which firms operate and of the role of the economist in business decision taking. We start by looking at the internal environment of the firm – the organisation and aims of the business. We then look at the external environment in which the firm operates – the nature of competition it faces, the type of industry in which it operates, the prices of its inputs, the general state of the economy (e.g. whether growing or in recession), the actions of the government and other authorities that might affect the firm (e.g. changes in taxes or interest rates, or changes in competition legislation) and the global environment (e.g. the extent to which the company operates internationally and how it is influenced by global market opportunities and the state of the world economy). Finally we look at the approach of the economist to analysing the business environment and business decision taking.

Box 1.1 introduces many of the topics that you will be covering in this book by taking the case of John Lewis and seeing how it is affected by its environment.

BOX 1.1   A PERFECT PARTNERSHIP

Making the best of your business environment

John Spedan Lewis created John Lewis in 1864 with the opening of a single shop on Oxford Street, London. In 1937, it bought Waitrose, which at the time had 10 shops. However, prior to this, in 1929, the first Trust Settlement was created making the John Lewis Partnership legal. Since then the Partnership has grown to include 46 John Lewis shops across the UK, 32 department stores, 12 John Lewis at home, shops at Heathrow Airport Terminal 2 and at St Pancras International and Birmingham New Street stations, 346 Waitrose supermarkets, an online and catalogue business, a production unit and a farm.[1]

The John Lewis Partnership has over 91 000 permanent staff and it is they who own the business. The interests of these employees are the first priority of the John Lewis Partnership and they benefit if the company does well. They share in the profits and their opinions are taken into account in decision making, creating a democratic and transparent business. The Partnership has annual gross sales of £11.0 billion and provides a wide range of goods and services. John Lewis itself has over 350 000 lines available in store and more than 280 000 lines available online. In addition, it offers other services, such as credit cards, insurance and broadband, to name a few.

The John Lewis Partnership is a unique one, with an organisational structure that puts its employees at its heart. Despite this very different focus, the Partnership has been a success, expanding its reach over the past century. But how

has it continued to be successful? What lessons are there for other businesses? How has its performance been affected by its business environment – by consumer tastes, by the actions of its rivals, by the state of the national and world economies and by government policy?

In particular, how would an economist analyse the Partnership's performance so as to advise it on its best strategy for the future? This is the sort of thing that business economists do and the sort of thing we will be doing throughout this text. We will also look at the impact of the behaviour of businesses on their customers, on employees, on competitors and on society in general. So let's take a closer look at the John Lewis Partnership and relate its business in general to the topics covered in this book.

The market environment

To be successful, it is important for the John Lewis Partnership to get its product right. This means understanding the markets that it operates in and how consumer demand responds to changes in prices and to the other services being offered. For example, in 2008, John Lewis responded to challenging conditions by increasing the number of products available for national delivery, prioritising customer service and introducing free delivery across the UK. Its investment in customer service clearly achieved its goal, helping John Lewis to rank as the best company in the 2009 UK Customer Satisfaction Survey.

[1] All figures refer to the financial year 2015/16.

▶

It has maintained good customer service since then and in the 2014 Verdict Customer Satisfaction Awards it won various awards, including Best Overall Retailer. It continued its success in the 2015 Awards, winning Best Retailer for Electricals, Homewares and Clothing. Waitrose was also recognised in these 2015 Awards, being awarded the Best Food & Grocery Retailer. Waitrose also won 'Favourite Supermarket' in the Which? 2015 Customer Survey, with John Lewis placed second in the 'best shops' category.[2]

John Lewis also enforced its commitment to being 'Never Knowingly Undersold', which helped the company to maintain its market share. It also added lines such as Jigsaw to its fashion ranges to continue to meet customer demand and keep up with the fast-moving women's fashion industry.

We look at how markets work in general in Chapter 2 and then look specifically at consumer demand and methods of stimulating it in Chapter 3.

To stay successful, the Partnership must respond to changes in the global economic environment, to changing tastes and fashions and must, to some extent, set fashion. Given the legal structure of its business, it must also balance its competitive position with its objective of 'giving every Partner a voice in the business they co-own'. To quote from the John Lewis Partnership website, 'We build relationships with our customers, suppliers and each other based on honesty, respect and encouragement.'[3]

The store 'John Lewis' operates in a highly competitive market, facing competition in its fashion departments from firms such as Debenhams, Selfridges and Next, and in other departments from firms such as Currys and DFS. The products it sells are crucial for its success, but the prices charged are equally important. Consumers will not be willing to pay any price, especially if they can buy similar products from other stores. Thus, when setting prices and designing products, consideration must be given to what rival companies are doing. John Lewis' prices must be competitive to maintain its sales, profitability and position in the global market.

With the emergence of the Internet and online shopping, John Lewis has had to adapt its strategy and consider which markets to target. Back in 2011, John Lewis expanded its online market to continental Europe, as part of a £250 million investment programme. This decision to expand was partly influenced by record Christmas sales in 2010/11, which were up by 8.9 per cent to £545 million in the five weeks to 1 January compared to the previous year. Online sales were also significantly higher in 2010, justifying this online investment.

Over the past few years, John Lewis has added to its online presence and online sales have expanded rapidly, recorded at £1.5 billion for 2015/16, with Click & collect overtaking home delivery.[4] Reflecting the changing national and global market environment, where consumers are increasingly shopping online, John Lewis has invested more money to improve its online experience through Oracle Commerce. This new platform produces more relevant results and makes it easier for customers to search, which has led to improved conversion rates. David Hunn, Director of IT Delivery at John Lewis said:

Our on-going customer commitment includes adopting new technology to enable us to better serve customer

needs and meet their expectations for convenience, choice and experience . . . This latest Oracle deployment is driving growth online and supporting our aim to deliver a true omni-channel experience.[5]

The John Lewis Partnership has typically been UK based, but Waitrose ventured into the Channel Islands in 2011, following approval by the Jersey Competition Regulatory Authority (JCRA) in August 2010 for it to purchase five Channel Island supermarkets.[6] If the Partnership were to think about expanding further into the global marketplace, such as into the USA and Asia, careful consideration would need to be given to the competitors in these nations and to the tastes of consumers. Tesco, for example, had little success in its foray into the United States. The factors behind this would be something that the Partnership would need to consider before making any significant global move.

Strategic decisions such as growth by expansion in the domestic and global economy are examined in Chapters 6 and 7, respectively.

Production and employment

Being a profitable business depends not just on being able to sell a product, but on how efficiently the product can be produced. This means choosing the most appropriate technology and deploying the labour force in the best way. John Lewis and Waitrose, as with other companies, must decide on how many workers to employ, what wage rates to pay and what the conditions of employment should be. We explore production and costs in Chapter 4 and the employment of labour in Chapter 8.

Despite rising sales in difficult trading conditions, in 2013 John Lewis cut over 300 managerial positions, the biggest cut seen since 2009 when hundreds of call-centre workers lost their jobs. Workers typically have involvement in decisions due to the nature of the organisational structure, but these enforced job cuts came as a shock, especially given the good Christmas trading when sales were 13 per cent up on the same period the previous year. However, it appears as though much of these sales came from its online trading, further suggesting a change in the way we shop and a need for companies to adapt. This is reinforced by the collapse of companies such as HMV, which are facing increased competition from online companies, including Amazon.

On the production side, the Partnership is a vertically integrated company, with a production unit and a farm. John Lewis makes its own-brand textiles in Lancashire and also has a small fabric-weaving operation creating thousands of products for its stores every week. Its efficient operations also allow John Lewis to operate a seven-day delivery system on orders of products such as curtains. However, the growth in this area has required changes, as the Managing Director, Ron Bartram pointed out:

To support that growth we've had to change the way we work . . . We need to expand our output in every area but our factory is very tight for space . . . We have to be flexible to handle the peaks and troughs of demand, and many Partners have been cross-trained so they can help out in different areas of the factory.[7]

[2] www.johnlewispartnership.co.uk/about/john-lewis.html

[3] www.johnlewispartnership.co.uk/about/the-partnership-spirit.html

[4] www.johnlewispartnership.co.uk/content/dam/cws/pdfs/financials/interim%20reports/john_lewis_partnership_interim_report_2015.pdf

[5] 'John Lewis improves online customer experience with Oracle Commerce', press release

[6] John Whiteaker, 'Waitrose invades Channel Islands', Retail Gazette, 26 August 2010.

[7] Katy Perceval, 'Material world', JLP e-Zine, 21 May 2010.

In addition to selling its own-brand items in both John Lewis and Waitrose, numerous other brands are sold. As an organisation which prides itself on its ethical stance, this does create a need for an awareness of how its suppliers treat the environment, their employees, their own suppliers and their customers. This is an example of a more general point about the Partnership's 'corporate social responsibility'. We examine these broader social issues in Chapter 9, along with government policies to encourage, persuade or force firms to behave in the public interest.

The Partnership has been active in diversifying its suppliers and creating opportunities for small and medium-sized enterprises (SMEs) to access its supply chain, creating wider social benefits. In addition, Waitrose became the first supermarket to commit to stocking 100 per cent own-label British dairy and, as stated on the website, Waitrose 'looks to buy local with buyers seeking out the finest local and regional products, helping to boost the economy in many rural areas and enabling customers to sample the very best foods made locally.'[8]

Its championing of British produce and its position as a farmer helped Waitrose win the 'Best Buy' Award in 2015, with almost 50 per cent of the tested products being worthy of the Best Buy award, ahead of all other competitors.[9] Given the growing awareness of the sources of products and their ingredients, being able to advertise the local side of its business has big benefits.

The members of the John Lewis Partnership remain a success story of Britain's high streets and the Partnership has been hailed by the government as a 'model of responsible capitalism'.

The economy

So do the fortunes of the John Lewis Partnership and other companies depend solely on their policies and those of their competitors? The answer is no. One important element of a company's business environment is largely beyond its control:

the state of the national economy and, for internationally trading companies, of the global economy. When the world economy is booming, sales and profits are likely to grow without too much effort by the company. However, when the global economy declines, as we saw in the economic downturn from 2008, trading conditions will become much tougher. In the years since the financial crisis, the global economy has remained in a vulnerable position and this has led to many companies entering administration, such as Woolworths, Jessops, HMV, Comet, Blockbuster and Peacocks.

In the Annual Report by the John Lewis Partnership from 2009, its Chairman said:

> As the economic downturn gained momentum, the focus of the Partnership has been to achieve the right balance between continuing to meet the needs and expectations of our customers and Partners while making sufficient profit to support our growth plans, by controlling our costs tightly and managing our cash efficiently.[10]

John Lewis experienced a slowdown in its sales of large purchases in its home market as the financial crisis began to spread. This decline in sales was largely driven by the collapse of the housing market, which has remained weak ever since. Operating profit for the Partnership (excluding property profits) was down 17.7 per cent in April 2009 (compared to the same time the year before) at £316.8 million. For John Lewis itself, gross sales fell by 0.1 per cent and this pushed its operating profit down by £54.6 million from April 2008 to April 2009. Like-for-like sales were also down 3.4 per cent. Due to the nature of the products being sold, Waitrose was somewhat more insulated against the financial crisis and in the same tax year experienced a 5.2 per cent increase in gross sales; a like-for-like sales growth of 0.4 per cent, but a fall in operating profit (excluding property profits) of 3.4 per cent.

In the past few years, the supermarket industry has become increasingly competitive, with low-cost retailers such as Aldi

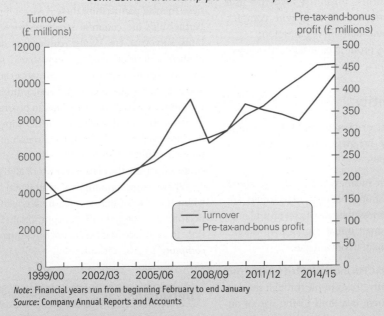

John Lewis Partnership plc sales and profit

Note: Financial years run from beginning February to end January
Source: Company Annual Reports and Accounts

---

[8] www.johnlewispartnership.co.uk/about/waitrose/products-and-services.html
[9] 'Waitrose is the 2015 supermarket best buy champion'; 28 December 2015.

[10] 'The John Lewis Partnership Annual Report and Accounts 2009'.

and Lidl posing a very real threat to the major supermarkets. Consumers have tended to become more willing to shop around, getting different products in different supermarkets. Thus, people who previously would do all their shopping in Waitrose may now just use it for more speciality products and buy the more basic lines in a cheaper supermarket.

As more difficult conditions have prevailed in the economy, the Partnership has nevertheless continued to increase its market share and deliver healthy profits.[11]

Prior to 2009, John Lewis' advertising investment seemed largely ineffective and part of its strategy to boost demand was the use of a new approach to advertising. The company's highly emotive TV advertising campaigns stimulated interest in the brand and led to increased numbers of shoppers visiting its stores and increased sales. According to the Institute of Practitioners in Advertising (IPA), the campaign generated £1074 million of extra sales and £261 million of extra profit in just over two years. In 2012, John Lewis was the Grand Prix winner, receiving the Gold Award in the IPA's Effectiveness Awards.

Gross sales have continued to grow over the years, as the chart shows. Pre-tax-and-bonus profits too have generally risen, but dipped in the direct aftermath of the financial crisis.[12] However, they fell in 2011/12, 2012/13 and 2013/14 as Waitrose responded to competition by cutting prices on many of its more basic lines. Nevertheless, in 2014/15 and 2015/16 pre-tax-and-bonus profits grew once more.[13]

So, there are perhaps signs that companies like the John Lewis Partnership, which are responsive to consumer demand and to the changing economic environment, can record healthy growth and profit despite challenging trading conditions. Whether this continues will depend on the Partnership's internal organisation and, crucially, on the external environment.

We examine the national and international business environment in Part D. We also examine the impact on business of government policies to affect the economy – policies such as changes in taxation, interest rates, exchange rates and customs duties. We also look at the impact of the UK's decision to leave the EU.

 Choose a well-known company that trades globally and do a web search to find out how well it has performed in recent years and how it has been influenced by various aspects of its business environment.

---

[12] 'The John Lewis Partnership Annual Report and Accounts 2011'.

[13] www.johnlewispartnership.co.uk/media/press/y2015/press-release-10-september-2015-john-lewis-partnership-plc-interim-results-for-the-half-year-ended-1-August-2015.html

---

[11] www.johnlewispartnership.co.uk/content/dam/cws/pdfs/financials/annual%20reports/John_Lewis_plc_annual_report_and_accounts_2009.pdf

---

1.1 THE BUSINESS ORGANISATION

There are many factors that affect the behaviour of firms, and here we focus on three key things:

- the legal status of the business;
- the way in which the firm is organised – whether as a simple top-down organisation or as a more complex multi-department or multi-division organisation;
- the aims of the firm – is profit maximisation the objective of the firm, or are there other aims?

The firm as a legal entity

In a small firm, the owner or owners are likely to play a major part in running the business. Such businesses will normally be one of two types.

The sole proprietor. Here, the business is owned by just one person. Owners of small shops, builders and farmers are typical examples. Such businesses are easy to set up and may require only a relatively small initial capital investment. However, they suffer two main disadvantages:

- *Limited scope for expansion.* Finance is limited to what the owner can raise personally, for example through savings or a bank loan. Also there is a limit to the size of an organisation that one person can effectively control.
- *Unlimited liability.* The owner is personally liable for any losses that the business might make. This could result in the owner's house, car and other assets being seized to pay off any outstanding debts, should the business fail.

The partnership. This is where two or more people own the business. In most partnerships there is a legal limit of 20 partners. Partnerships are common structures for solicitors, accountants, surveyors, etc. Whilst partnerships do mean a loss of control, as decision making is now shared, with more owners there is scope for expansion. Extra finance can usually be raised and as partners can specialise in and control different areas of the business, a larger organisation can become more viable.

Since 2001 limited liability partnerships have been possible. However, many firms still retain unlimited liability. This problem could be very serious, as the mistakes of one partner could jeopardise the personal assets of all the other partners.

Where large amounts of capital are required and/or when the risks of business failure are relatively high, partnerships are not generally an appropriate form of organisation. In such cases it is best to form a company (or *joint-stock company*, to give it its full title).

> ### Definition
>
> **Joint-stock company** A company where ownership is distributed between shareholders.

Companies

A company is legally separate from its owners. This means that it can enter into contracts and own property. Any debts are its debts, not the owners'.

The owners are the shareholders. Each shareholder receives his or her share of the company's distributed profit: these payments are called 'dividends'. The owners have only *limited liability*. This means that, if the company goes bankrupt, the owners will lose the amount of money they have invested in the company, but no more – their cars, houses, etc. belong to them and not to the company. This has the advantage of encouraging people to become shareholders, thereby providing more finance to businesses and creating greater scope for expansion.

Shareholders often take no part in the running of the firm. They may elect a board of directors which decides broad issues of company policy. The board of directors in turn appoints managers who make the day-to-day decisions. This can create problems in terms of the divorce of ownership (by shareholders) from control (by managers), as we will see on page 9.

There are two types of company: public and private.

Public limited companies (plc). These are companies that can offer new shares publicly: by issuing a prospectus, they can invite the public to subscribe to a new share issue. In addition, many public limited companies are quoted on the Stock Exchange (see section 6.4), where existing shares can be bought and sold. A public limited company must hold an annual shareholders' meeting. Examples of well-known UK public limited companies are Marks & Spencer, BP, Barclays, BSkyB and Tesco.

Private limited companies (Ltd). Private limited companies cannot offer their shares publicly. Shares have to be sold privately. This makes it more difficult for private limited companies to raise finance, and consequently they tend to be smaller than public companies. However, they are easier to set up than public companies. One of the most famous examples of a private limited company is Manchester United Football Club, which, until it was bought out by the Glazer family in 2005, was a public limited company. It then became a public limited company again in August 2012 when 10 per cent of its shares were floated on the New York Stock Exchange.

Co-operatives

There are also two types of co-operatives.

Consumer co-operatives. These are officially owned by the consumers, although they play no part in running the business.

Producer co-operatives. These are owned by the firm's workers, who share in the firm's profits. John Lewis is a prime example of such an organisation, as we discussed in Box 1.1.

The internal organisation of the firm

The internal operating structures of firms are frequently governed by their size. Small firms tend to be centrally managed, with decision making operating through a clear managerial hierarchy. In large firms, however, the organisational structure tends to be more complex, although technological change is forcing many organisations to reassess the most suitable organisational structure for their business.

U form

In small to medium-sized firms, the managers of the various departments – marketing, finance, production, etc. – are normally directly responsible to a chief executive, whose function is to co-ordinate their activities: relaying the firm's overall strategy to them and being responsible for interdepartmental communication. We call this type of structure *U (unitary) form* (see Figure 1.1).

When firms expand beyond a certain size, a U-form structure is likely to become inefficient. This inefficiency arises from difficulties in communication, co-ordination and control, as the Chief Executive's office receives too much information to make efficient decisions and so it becomes too difficult to manage the whole organisation from the centre.

Definitions

Limited liability Where the liability of the owners for the debts of a company is limited to the amount they have invested in it.

U-form business organisation One in which the central organisation of the firm (the chief executive or a managerial team) is responsible both for the firm's day-to-day administration and for formulating its business strategy.

Figure 1.1   U-form business organisation

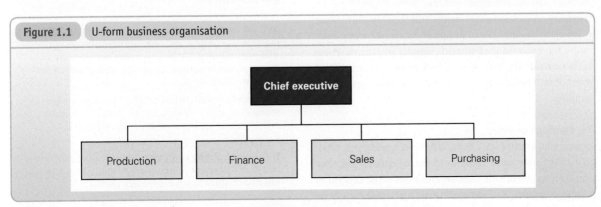

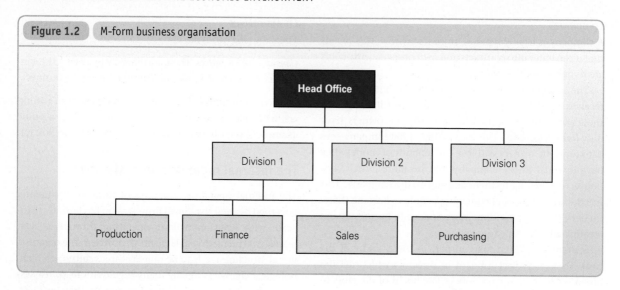

Figure 1.2 M-form business organisation

M form

To overcome these organisational problems, the firm can adopt an *M (multi-divisional) form* of managerial structure (see Figure 1.2).

This suits larger firms. The firm is divided into a number of 'divisions'. Each division could be responsible for a particular stage of production, a particular product or group of products, or a particular market (e.g. a specific country). The day-to-day running and even certain long-term decisions of each division would be the responsibility of the divisional manager(s). This leads to the following benefits:

- reduced length of information flows;
- the chief executive being able to concentrate on overall strategic planning;
- an enhanced level of control, with each division being run as a mini 'firm', competing with other divisions for the limited amount of company resources available.

The flat organisation

One of the major problems with M-form organisations is that they can become very bureaucratic with many layers of management. Recent technological innovations, however, especially in respect to computer systems such as e-mail and management information systems, have enabled senior managers to communicate easily and directly with those lower in the organisational structure. As a result, some companies have moved back towards simpler structures. These *flat organisations*, as they are called, dispense with various layers of middle management and so can speed up communication.

The holding company

As many businesses have expanded their operations, often on a global scale, more complex forms of business organisation have evolved. One such organisation is the *H-form* or *holding company*. A holding company (or parent company) is one that owns a controlling interest in other subsidiary companies. These subsidiaries, in turn, may also have controlling interests in other companies. There may thus be a complex web of interlocking holdings. While the parent company has ultimate control over its various subsidiaries, typically both tactical and strategic decision making is left to the individual companies within the organisation. A good example of such an organisation would be the Walt Disney Company.

The aims of the firm

Economists have traditionally assumed that firms want to maximise profits. The 'traditional theory of the firm', as it is called, shows how much output firms should produce and at what price in order to make as much profit as possible. But do firms necessarily want to maximise profits?

One question arises over the time period in which they may want to maximise profits. For example, if a business adopts a strategy of growth, more must be spent on investment in machinery and advertising to increase both production and sales. These large expenditures will reduce the

Definitions

M-form business organisation One in which the business is organised into separate departments, such that responsibility for the day-to-day management of the enterprise is separated from the formulation of the business's strategic plan.

Flat organisation One in which technology enables senior managers to communicate directly with those lower in the organisational structure. Middle managers are bypassed.

H-form or holding company A business organisation in which the parent company holds interests in a number of other companies or subsidiaries.

profit in the short run, but profits in the long run may be maximised. In this case, what is inconsistent with short-run profit maximisation may be wholly consistent with long-run profit maximisation.

A more fundamental criticism of the assumption of profit maximisation, however, is that in large companies it is not the owners that make the decisions about how much to produce and at what price. In such cases other objectives may be pursued by these decision makers.

The divorce of ownership from control

As we saw in our discussion of public limited companies, the shareholders are the owners and they elect directors. Directors in turn employ professional managers who often have considerable discretion in making decisions on things such as pricing, advertising, costing, etc. There is therefore a separation between the ownership and control of a firm.

The owners (shareholders) may want to maximise profits to increase their dividends, but what are the objectives of the managers? They will probably want to pursue their own interests, such as a higher salary, greater power or prestige, greater sales, better working conditions or greater popularity with their subordinates. Indeed, different managers in the same firm may well pursue different aims. The point is that these aims may conflict with the aim of maximum profit.

> ### Pause for thought
>
> Make a list of four possible aims that a manager of a McDonald's restaurant might have. Which of these might conflict with the interests of McDonald's shareholders?

Managers will still have to ensure that *sufficient* profits are made to keep shareholders happy, but that may be very different from maximising profits. Alternative theories of the firm to those of profit maximisation, therefore, tend to assume that large firms are profit 'satisficers'. That is, managers strive hard for a minimum target level of profit, but are less interested in profits above this level.

The principal–agent relationship

Can the owners of a firm ever be sure that their managers will pursue the business strategy most appropriate to achieving the owners' goals (i.e. profit maximisation)? This is an example of the *principal–agent problem*. One of the features of a complex modern economy is that people (principals) have to employ others (agents) to carry out their wishes. If you want to go on holiday, it is easier to go to a travel agent to sort out the arrangements than to do it all yourself. Likewise, if you want to sell a house, it is more convenient to go to an estate agent.

The crucial advantage that agents have over their principals is specialist knowledge and information. This is usually why we employ agents. For example, owners employ managers for their specialist knowledge of a market or their understanding of business practice. But this situation of *asymmetric information* – that one party (the agent) knows more than the other (the principal) – means that it will be very difficult for the principal to judge in whose interest the agent is operating. Are the managers pursuing their own goals, rather than the goals of the owner? It is the same in other walks of life. The estate agent may try to convince you that it is necessary to accept a lower price, while the real reason may be to save the agent time, effort and expense.

 KEY IDEA 1 *The principal–agent problem.* Where people (principals), as a result of a lack of knowledge (asymmetric information), cannot ensure that their best interests are served by their agents. Agents may take advantage of this situation to the disadvantage of the principals.

Principals may attempt to reconcile the fact that they have imperfect information, and are thus in an inherently weak position, in the following ways.

- *Monitoring* the performance of the agent. Shareholders could monitor the performance of their senior managers through attending annual general meetings. The managers could be questioned by shareholders and ultimately replaced if their performance is unsatisfactory.
- Establishing a series of *incentives* to ensure that agents act in the principals' best interest. For example, managerial pay could be closely linked to business performance, through schemes such as profit sharing. Although this can be useful in encouraging managers (agents) to act in the owners' (principals') interests, this is likely to be more effective the larger the incentive: e.g. the larger the share in company profits. But this could prove costly from the owners' point of view.

Within any firm there will exist a complex chain of principal–agent relationships – between workers and managers, between junior managers and senior managers, between senior managers and directors, and between directors and shareholders. All groups will hold some

> ### Definitions
>
> **Principal–agent problem** One where people (principals), as a result of lack of knowledge, cannot ensure that their best interests are served by their agents.
>
> **Asymmetric information** A situation in which one party in an economic relationship knows more than another.

specialist knowledge which they may use to further their own distinct goals. Predictably, the development of effective monitoring and evaluation programmes and the creation of performance-related pay schemes have been two central themes in the development of business practices in recent years – a sign that the principal is looking to fight back!

> ### Pause for thought
>
> *Identify a situation where you, as a consumer, are in a principal–agent relationship with a supplier. How can you minimise the problem of asymmetric information in this relationship?*

Staying in business

Aiming for profits, sales, salaries, power, etc. will be useless if the firm does not survive! Trying to *maximise* any of the various objectives may be risky. For example, if a firm tries to maximise its market share by aggressive advertising or price cutting, it might invoke a strong response from its rivals. The resulting war may drive it out of business. Concern with survival, therefore, may make firms cautious.

However, being cautious does not guarantee survival and could even lead to the demise of a business, as market share may be lost to more aggressive competitors. Ultimately, if a firm is concerned with survival, it must be careful to balance caution against keeping up with competitors, ensuring that the customer is sufficiently satisfied and that costs are kept sufficiently low by efficient management and the introduction of new technology.

RECAP

1. There are several types of legal organisation of firms: the sole proprietorship, the partnership, the private limited company, the public limited company and co-operatives. In the first two cases, the owners have unlimited liability. With companies, however, shareholders' liability is limited to the amount they have invested. This reduced risk encourages people to invest in companies, providing scope for expansion.

2. As firms grow, so they tend to move from a U-form to an M-form structure. In recent years, however, with the advance of information technology, many firms have adopted a flatter organisation – a return to U-form structure. Multinational companies often adopt relatively complex forms of organisation. Many multinationals adopt a holding company (H-form) structure.

3. Typically, owners of firms will seek to maximise profits. With large companies, however, there is a divorce of ownership from control. Control is by managers, who might pursue goals other than profit.

4. The problem of managers not pursuing the same goals as the owners is an example of the *principal–agent problem*. Agents (in this case the managers) may not always carry out the wishes of their principals (in this case the owners). Because of asymmetric information, managers can pursue their own aims, as long as they produce results that satisfy the owners. The solution for owners is for there to be a better means of monitoring the performance of managers, and incentives for the managers to behave in the owners' interests.

1.2 THE EXTERNAL BUSINESS ENVIRONMENT

The decisions and performance of a firm are affected not just by its internal organisation and aims; they are also affected by the external environment in which the firm operates.

Dimensions of the external business environment

It is normal to identify various dimensions to the external business environment. These include political, economic, social/cultural and technological factors.

Political factors. Firms are directly affected by the actions of government and other political events. These might be major events affecting the whole of the business community, such as the collapse of communism, the Iraq War or a change of government. Alternatively, they may be actions affecting just one part of the economy. For example, the ban

on smoking in pubs and restaurants has affected the tobacco industry; a minimum price on alcohol will affect restaurants, pubs, the supermarket industry, etc.

Economic factors. Businesses are affected by a whole range of economic factors, such as a rise in the cost of raw materials, or a price cut by a rival firm, or new taxes, or movements in interest rates or exchange rates. A firm must constantly take such factors into account when devising and implementing its business strategy.

It is normal to divide the economic environment in which the firm operates into two levels:

■ *The microeconomic environment.* This includes all the economic factors that are *specific* to a particular firm operating in its own particular market. Thus one firm may be operating in a highly competitive market, whereas another may not; one firm may be faced by rapidly changing consumer tastes (e.g. a designer clothing manufacturer), while another may be faced with a virtually constant consumer demand (e.g. a potato merchant); one firm may face rapidly rising costs, while another may find that costs are constant or falling.

■ *The macroeconomic environment.* This is the *national* and *international* economic situation in which a business as a whole operates. Business in general will fare much better if the economy is growing than if it is in a recession, like that following the financial crisis of 2008. In examining the macroeconomic environment, we will also be looking at the policies that governments adopt in their attempt to steer the economy, since these policies, by affecting things such as taxation, interest rates and exchange rates, will have a major impact on firms.

Social/cultural factors. This aspect of the business environment concerns social attitudes and values. These include attitudes towards working conditions and the length of the working day, equal opportunities for different groups of people (whether by ethnicity, gender, physical attributes, etc.), the nature and purity of products, the use and abuse of animals, and images portrayed in advertising. The social/cultural environment also includes social trends, such as an increase in the average age of the population, or changes in attitudes towards seeking paid employment while bringing up small children. In recent times, various ethical issues, especially concerning the protection of the environment, have had a big impact on the actions of business and the image that many firms seek to present.

Technological factors. Over the past 25 years, there has been rapid technological change. This has had a huge impact not only on how firms produce and sell products, but also on how their business is organised. The use of robots and other forms of computer-controlled production has changed the nature of work for many workers. It has also created a wide range of new opportunities for businesses, many of which have yet to be realised. The information technology revolution is also enabling much more rapid communication and making it possible for many workers to do their job from home, while travelling, or from another country. The growth in online shopping has enabled firms to reach truly global markets, creating many opportunities, but it has also presented problems for other high-street retailers.

The division of the factors affecting a firm into political, economic, social and technological is commonly known as a *PEST analysis*. More recently, three more elements of the business environment have been added to give what is known as *STEEPLE analysis*. The extra elements are:

Environmental (ecological) factors. The environment has become an increasingly important issue in politics and business. The government has adopted a policy of 'naming and shaming' large polluters. Firms are therefore taking a greener approach to their activities and trying to find ways of minimising adverse effects on the environment, whether through cleaner technologies, or better waste management and recycling, or through greener products. This might create extra costs for firms, but a greener image can also help to drive sales as consumers have become more environmentally aware. It can also provide more finance for firms from the government and those investors seeking to improve their image. Business attitudes towards the environment are examined in section 9.4.

Legal factors. Businesses are affected by the legal framework in which they operate. Examples include industrial relations legislation, product safety standards, regulations governing pricing in the privatised industries and laws preventing collusion between firms to keep prices up. We examine some of these laws in sections 9.3–9.6.

Ethical factors. Firms are increasingly under pressure to adopt a more socially responsible attitude towards business. Corporate responsibility is a major concern for many firms, whether in terms of working conditions, the safety and quality of their products, truthful advertising, their attitudes towards the environment, concern for local residents and the general avoidance of what might be seen as 'suspect' business practices. Business ethics and corporate responsibility are examined in section 9.2.

The PEST or STEEPLE framework is widely used by organisations to audit their business environment and to help them establish a strategic approach to their business activities. It is nevertheless important to recognise that there is a great overlap and interaction among these sets of factors. Laws and government policies reflect social attitudes; technological factors determine economic ones, such as costs and productivity; technological progress often reflects the desire of researchers to meet social or environmental needs; and so on.

To be successful, a business needs to adapt to changes in its business environment and, wherever possible, take advantage of them. Ultimately, the better business managers understand the environment in which they operate, the more likely they are to be successful, either in exploiting everchanging opportunities or in avoiding potential disasters.

 KEY IDEA 2 *The behaviour and performance of firms is affected by the business environment.* The business environment includes social/cultural (S), technological (T), economic (E), ethical (E), political (P), legal (L) and environmental (E) factors. The mnemonic STEEPLE can be used to remember these.

Definition

PEST (or STEEPLE) analysis Where the political, economic, social and technological factors shaping a business environment are assessed by a business so as to devise future business strategy. STEEPLE analysis also takes into account ethical, legal and environmental factors.

Although we will be primarily concentrating on the economic environment, we will also look at the other dimensions in PEST and STEEPLE analysis at various points in the text, especially where they impact on the economic environment. Examples include competition legislation, the effect of social factors on consumer demand, changing business attitudes towards pollution and social responsibility, and the effects of technology on costs, sales and the ways in which businesses meet the changing needs of customers.

Pause for thought

1. *Under which heading of a PEST or STEEPLE analysis would you locate training and education?*
2. *Identify at least one factor under each of the STEEPLE headings facing an electricity generating company.*

Globalisation and the changing business environment

The external business environment of many firms is becoming increasingly global. International trade has grown much faster than countries' output, and so too has cross-border investment grown much faster than investment by companies within their home market. Many companies now see the world as their market and source their supplies from wherever in the world they can buy most cheaply. For some this simply means importing their inputs and exporting their products. Increasingly, however, companies set up their own factories or branches abroad.

The world economy is becoming much more integrated and interdependent. This process of *globalisation*, as it is called, has been hastened by various social/cultural, technological, economic, environmental, political and ethical factors (STEEPLE).

■ Social/cultural factors include the growing influence of Western consumerist culture as companies such as Nike, Levi, McDonald's and Disney sell their products around the world.
■ Technological factors include the communications revolution which, through the Internet, e-mails, Skype and computer linking, has allowed companies to communicate with their customers, suppliers and subsidiaries as easily halfway round the world as in the next town. Another key technological advance has been the reduction in size or weight of many products. The use of plastics rather than metals and the use of ever smaller and more powerful computer chips are just two examples of why it has become cheaper to transport goods long distances.

Definition

Globalisation The process whereby the economies of the world are becoming increasingly integrated.

■ Economic factors include the globalisation of markets and production, as firms' activities spread across the globe. Markets around the world have tended to become more competitive as domestic firms increasingly face competition from abroad. Then, at a macroeconomic level there is increasing convergence of economies, as interest rates, inflation rates and tax rates become more similar from one country to another.
■ Environmental and ethical factors include growing concerns worldwide over the burning of fossil fuels, the depletion of fish stocks, the pollution of land, sea and air, the cutting down of rainforests and the decline in biodiversity. Increasingly these are seen as global rather than national problems. Another example is the growing worldwide concern for human rights and decent employment conditions.
■ Political and legal factors include the development of trading blocs such as the North America Free Trade Association (NAFTA) (consisting of the USA, Canada and Mexico) and the EU. Within the context of the EU, the future exit of Britain may have significant implications for businesses across the world. These factors also include international agreements to dismantle barriers to trade and the international movement of finance and labour – and here the migration crisis is very relevant. We can also consider the growing influence of international bodies such as the World Trade Organization (WTO) and the International Monetary Fund (IMF) to influence global events; and also meetings of the Group of Seven (G7) major industrialised countries (Canada, France, Germany, Italy, Japan, the UK and the USA) or the G20 countries of major developed and newly industrialised countries to agree on means of harmonising their policies.

Pause for thought

Using the STEEPLE categories, in what ways has the USA influenced the business environment in countries outside the USA?

We explore the microeconomic effects of globalisation in detail in Chapter 7 and the macroeconomic effects in Chapters 12 and 13.

Classifying industries

One of the most important elements of the economic environment of a firm is the nature of the industry in which it operates and the amount of competition it faces. Knowledge of the structure of an industry is therefore crucial if we are to understand business behaviour and its likely outcomes.

In this section we will consider how the production of different types of goods and services is classified and how firms are located in different industrial groups.

BOX 1.2 THE BIOTECHNOLOGY INDUSTRY

Its business environment

There are few areas of business that cause such controversy as biotechnology. It has generated new medicines, created pest-resistant crops, developed eco-friendly industrial processes and, through genetic mapping, is providing incalculable advances in gene therapy. These developments, however, have raised profound ethical issues. Many areas of biotechnology are uncontentious, but genetic modification and cloning have met with considerable public hostility, colouring many people's views of biotechnology in general.

Biotechnology refers to the application of knowledge about living organisms and their components to make new products and develop new industrial processes.

A growing sector

It has been one of the most rapidly growing sectors in recent years and has contributed significantly to the development of the knowledge-based economy. In 2014, established biotechnology centres generated revenues of $123 billion (a growth of 24 per cent over the previous year), employed 183 000 staff and had a market capitalisation of $1063 billion.[1] Growth in the sector is expected to continue.

This growth is driven primarily by high levels of research and development (R&D) both by large companies and by non-commercial organisations, such as universities. R&D across all sectors declined following the financial crisis of 2008, but recovered more quickly in the biotech sector than in most other sectors. In 2013, biotech R&D spending increased by 14 per cent; however, this included a 20 per cent increase in the USA, but a 4 per cent decline in Europe. In 2014, global R&D spending increased by an impressive 20 per cent and this time the growth was solid in both the USA (22 per cent) and the EU (14 per cent).[2]

In global terms, the USA dominates this sector. Data from the OECD shows that in 2013 (the latest year available) the USA had 11 387 biotechnology firms, of which 1165 were dedicated biotechnology firms, and between 2010 and 2013 these firms accounted for 37 per cent of worldwide patent applications. Spain remains the European leader with 2831 biotechnology firms, followed by France with 1950, although France continues to have a very high percentage of dedicated biotechnology firms at 65.8 per cent. However, Spain only accounted for 1.21 per cent of patent applications, with France at 5.23 per cent. In this area, Germany leads the EU, accounting for 7.92 per cent of all patent applications.[3] When compared to Europe as a whole, the biotechnology sector in the USA continues to spend more than twice as much on research and development and generates twice as much in revenues. The UK was sixth in the rankings, with 614 biotechnology firms, accounting for 4.11 per cent of all patent applications, which is a high percentage, given the number of specialist firms. Some experts have suggested that industrial biotechnology could become a £12 billion industry in the UK by 2025, but only if sufficient investment is found.

The industry is dominated by small and medium-sized businesses. For example, of the 614 biotechnology firms in the UK, 491 have fewer than 50 employees (80 per cent). In the USA, 72 per cent of its 11 387 biotech firms are classed as being small.

However, most of the R&D expenditure comes from larger firms, including 91 per cent in the USA and 84.4 per cent in France.

A key characteristic of this industry is that biotech firms tend to form geographical clusters, typically around key universities and research institutes. In the UK, clusters can be found in Cambridge, Oxford and London. The link with universities and research institutes taps into the UK's strong science base.

Funding for the industry

The UK biotech industry is well supported by the government and other charitable organisations such as the Wellcome Trust. Such support helps to fund what is a highly research-intensive sector. The UK government not only provides finance, but encourages firms to form collaborative agreements, and through such collaboration hopes to encourage better management and use of the results that research generates. It also offers help for biotechnology business start-ups, and guidance on identifying and gaining financial support.

The EU too provides a range of resources to support business within the biotech sector. The EUREKA programme attempts to help create pan-EU partnerships, and Horizon 2020 is providing almost €80 billion of EU funding for R&D over the seven years 2014–20, much of which is expected to go to the biotechnology sector. Such support by governments is seen as a crucial requirement for the creation of a successful biotechnology sector, as product development within the industry can take up to 12 years.

The majority of funding for the industry comes from 'venture capital' (investment by individuals and firms in new and possibly risky sectors). Even though the UK is Europe's largest venture capital market, such funding is highly volatile. Many of the biotech companies that are listed on the stock market, after significant share price rises in 1999 and 2000, then saw their share prices collapse, along with those of various high-tech companies. With a depressed stock market, raising finance becomes much more difficult.

Consolidation within the industry

Both public and private biotech companies in Europe have shown an increase in merger and acquisition (M&A) activity. 2014 was a very active year for M&As, driven by 'booming stock market valuations', which meant that biotech companies had strong bargaining power. There was a 46 per cent increase from 2013, with 68 biotechnology M&A deals, valued at $49 billion.[4]

High growth in this sector is expected to continue and forecasts suggest an annual growth of 10.8 per cent per year for the 10 years until 2019.[5] Indeed, Jonathon Porritt, a leading environmentalist in the UK, estimates that the global market for biotechnology could lie somewhere between £150 billion and £360 billion by 2025. The differential between these estimates is substantial, but nevertheless it gives some indication as to the likely trend for this industry and where significant job creation might arise.

 From the brief outline above, identify the social/cultural, technological, economic, ethical, political, legal and environmental dimensions shaping the biotechnology industry's business environment.

---

[1] 'Beyond borders: reaching new heights', *Biotechnology Industry Report 2015* (EY, 2015).

[2] Ibid.

[3] *Key biotechnology indicators* (OECD, July 2015).

[4] 'Beyond borders: reaching new heights'.

[5] Global Technology Market Research Report; IBIS World (January 2015).

| Figure 1.3 | Output of industrial sectors (as a percentage of GDP) |

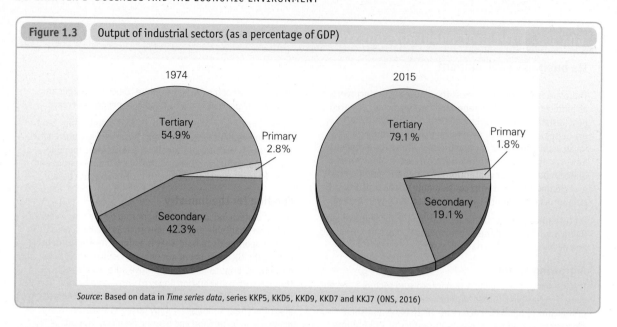

Source: Based on data in *Time series data*, series KKP5, KKD5, KKD9, KKD7 and KKJ7 (ONS, 2016)

| Figure 1.4 | Employment by industrial sector (% of total employees) |

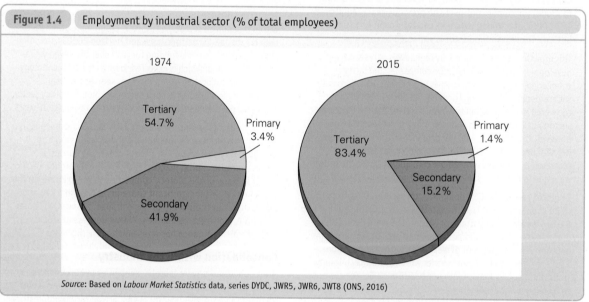

Source: Based on *Labour Market Statistics* data, series DYDC, JWR5, JWR6, JWT8 (ONS, 2016)

Classifying production

When analysing production it is common to distinguish three broad categories.

- *Primary production*. This refers to the production and extraction of natural resources such as minerals and sources of energy. It also includes output from agriculture.
- *Secondary production*. This refers to the output of the manufacturing and construction sectors of the economy.
- *Tertiary production*. This refers to the production of services, and includes a wide range of sectors such as finance, the leisure industry, retailing, tourism and transport.

Figures 1.3 and 1.4 show the share of output (or *gross domestic product (GDP)*) and employment of these three sectors in 1974 and 2015. They illustrate how the tertiary sector has expanded rapidly. In 2015, it contributed 79.1

per cent to total output (up from 54.9 per cent in 1974) and employed 83.4 per cent of all workers (up from 54.7 per cent). By contrast, the share of output and employment of the secondary sector has declined. In 2014, it accounted for

Definitions

Primary production The production and extraction of natural resources, plus agriculture.

Secondary production The production from manufacturing and construction sectors of the economy.

Tertiary production The production from the service sector of the economy.

Gross domestic product (GDP) The value of output produced within the country over a 12-month period.

only 19.1 per cent of output (down from 42.3 per cent in 1974) and 15.2 per cent of employment (down from 41.9 per cent).

This trend is symptomatic of a process known as *deindustrialisation* – a decline in the share of the secondary sector in GDP. Many commentators argue that this process of deindustrialisation is inevitable and that the existence of a large and growing tertiary sector in the UK economy reflects its maturity. As people become richer, so a growing proportion of their consumption is of services such as leisure activities.

It is possible to identify part of the tertiary sector as a fourth or 'quarternary' sector. This refers to the knowledge-based part of the economy and includes services such as education, information generation and sharing, research and development, consultation, culture and parts of government. This sector tends to grow as a proportion of the tertiary sector (see Box 1.3, page 18).

Pause for thought

Into which of the three sectors would you put (a) the fertiliser industry; (b) a marketing agency serving the electronics industry?

The classification of production into primary, secondary and tertiary (or even quarternary) sectors allows us to consider broad changes in the economy. However, if we require a more comprehensive analysis of the structure of industry and its changes over time, then such a general classification is of little value. What we need to do is to classify firms into particular industries.

Classifying firms into industries

An *industry* refers to a group of firms that produce a particular category of product. Thus we could refer to the electrical goods industry, the tourism industry, the aircraft industry or the insurance industry. Industries can then be grouped together into broad *industrial sectors*, such as manufacturing industry, or mining and quarrying, or construction, or transport.

Classifying firms into industrial groupings and sub-groupings has a number of purposes. It helps us to analyse various trends in the economy and to identify areas of growth and areas of decline. It helps to identify parts of the economy with specific needs, such as training or transport infrastructure. Perhaps most importantly, it helps economists and businesspeople to understand and predict the behaviour of firms that are in direct competition with each other. In such cases, however, it may be necessary to draw the boundaries of an industry quite narrowly.

To illustrate this, take the case of the vehicle industry. The vehicle industry produces cars, lorries, vans and coaches. The common characteristic of these vehicles is that they are self-propelled road transport vehicles. In other words, we could draw the boundaries of an industry in terms of the broad physical or technical characteristics of the products it produces. However, the problem with this type of categorisation is that these products may not be substitutes in an *economic* sense. If you need to buy a new vehicle to replace your car, you're hardly likely to consider buying a coach or a lorry! Lorries are not in competition with cars. If we are to group together products which are genuine competitors for each other, we will want to divide industries into more narrow categories. For example, we could classify cars into several groups according to size, price, function, engine capacity, etc.: e.g. luxury, saloon (of various size categories), estate (again of various size categories), seven seater and sports.

On the other hand, if we draw the boundaries of an industry too narrowly, we may end up ignoring the effects of competition from another closely related industry. For example, if we are to understand the pricing strategies of electricity supply companies in the household market, it might be better to focus on the whole domestic fuel industry.

Thus how narrowly or broadly we draw the boundaries of an industry depends on the purposes of our analysis. If the issue is one of *consumer demand* we might want to focus on the market and group goods together that are in direct competition with each other (e.g. particular types of car). If, however, the issue is one of *supply* – of *production* and *costs* – we might want to group products that are produced in the same companies (e.g. vehicle manufacturers).

Standard Industrial Classification

The formal system under which firms are grouped into industries is known as the *Standard Industrial Classification (SIC)*. The most recent revision in 2007 brought the UK and EU systems of industry classification largely into alignment with each other and this is a crucial part of monitoring business within the internal market. SIC (2007) is divided into

---

Definitions

Deindustrialisation The decline in the contribution to production of the manufacturing sector of the economy.

Industry A group of firms producing a particular product or service.

Industrial sector A grouping of industries producing similar products or services.

Standard Industrial Classification (SIC) The name given to the formal classification of firms into industries used by the government in order to collect data on business and industry trends.

Table 1.1	Standard Industrial Classification, 2007

Section

A	Agriculture, forestry and fishing
B	Mining and quarrying
C	Manufacturing
D	Electricity, gas, steam and air conditioning supply
E	Water supply, sewerage, waste management
F	Construction
G	Wholesale and retail trade, repair of motor vehicles
H	Transport and storage
I	Accommodation and food service activities
J	Information and communication
K	Financial and insurance activities
L	Real estate activities
M	Professional, scientific and technical activities
N	Administrative and support service activities
O	Public administration and defence; compulsory social security
P	Education
Q	Human health and social work activities
R	Arts, entertainment and recreation
S	Other service activities
T	Activities of households as employers, and producers of goods and services for own use
U	Extra-territorial organisations and bodies

Source: Based on *Standard Industrial Classification 2007* (Office for National Statistics)

Table 1.2	The classification of the manufacture of a tufted carpet

Section C	Manufacturing (comprising divisions 10 to 33)
Division 13	Manufacture of textiles
Group 13.9	Manufacture of other textiles
Class 13.93	Manufacture of carpets and rugs
Subclass 13.93/1	Manufacture of woven or tufted carpets and rugs

Source: Based on *Standard Industrial Classification 2007* (Office for National Statistics)

Table 1.3	UK output and employment by industry in 2014 (1990 = 100)

Industry	Output in 2014 (1990 = 100)	Employment in 2014 (1990 = 100)
A	97.5	88.0
B	61.7	40.3
C	102.1	52.8
D, E	144.9	92.7
F	100.4	95.0
G, I	162.8	112.6
J – L	212.5	131.7
M – N	287.2	181.8
O – Q	142.6	131.1
R – S	173.6	127.1

Source: Based on data in UK National Accounts and Labour Market Statistics (ONS)

21 sections (A–U), each representing a production classification (see Table 1.1). These 21 sections in SIC (2007) are in turn divided into a total of 88 divisions; these are then divided into 272 groups, which are divided into 615 classes and then 191 subclasses. Table 1.2 gives an example of how a manufacturer of a tufted carpet would be classified according to this system.

Changes in the structure of the UK economy

Given such a classification, how has UK industry changed over time? Table 1.3 shows the changes in output and employment of the various sectors identified by the SIC between 1990 and 2014 with 1990 as the base year (1990 = 100).

You can see from the table that the biggest increases in output have been in the service industries (sectors G to S). If we examine the subsections and divisions within the SIC, we can get a more detailed picture of how the structure of industry has changed. For example, we find that the process of deindustrialisation has not been experienced by all manufacturing industries. Certain divisions, such as instrument and electrical engineering, are in fact among the fastest growing in the whole UK economy. It is

the more traditional manufacturing industries, such as metal manufacturing, that have experienced a substantial decline.

In respect to employment, there are again substantial variations between divisions. Thus whereas the financial services sector has seen a rapid growth in employment (at least up to the financial crisis of 2008), there has been a decline in employment in parts of the retail banking sector as a result of technological advances (fewer counter staff are required in high street banks, given the growth in cash machines, direct debits, debit cards, etc.). And whereas there has been a decline in employment in primary industries (such as agriculture and mining) and in traditional manufacturing industries (such as shipbuilding and metal manufacturing), there has been a growth in employment in some of the more 'high-tech' industries.

Structure–conduct–performance

As we shall see throughout the book, business performance is strongly influenced by the market structure within which

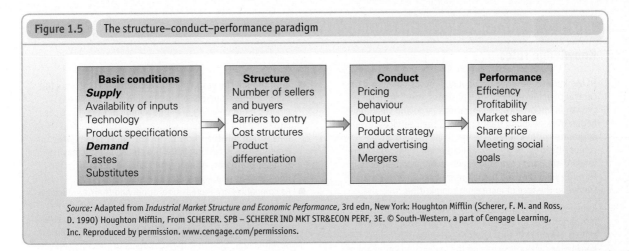

Figure 1.5 The structure–conduct–performance paradigm

Source: Adapted from *Industrial Market Structure and Economic Performance*, 3rd edn, New York: Houghton Mifflin (Scherer, F. M. and Ross, D. 1990) Houghton Mifflin, From SCHERER. SPB – SCHERER IND MKT STR&ECON PERF, 3E. © South-Western, a part of Cengage Learning, Inc. Reproduced by permission. www.cengage.com/permissions.

the firm operates. This is known as the *structure–conduct–performance paradigm* and is illustrated in Figure 1.5.

The structure of an industry depends on a number of basic conditions – some concerning production (supply) and some concerning consumer demand. For example, the availability of inputs and technology will influence whether it is more efficient to produce on a large scale or on a small scale. The nature of consumer tastes and whether there are close alternative products ('substitutes') available will influence the range of products produced and whether these should be highly differentiated from one producer to another or very similar across the industry. Such conditions will influence whether the market structure is highly competitive or dominated by just a few producers who are able to erect various barriers to the entry of competitors into the market.

A business operating in a highly competitive market structure will conduct its activities differently from a business in a market with relatively few competitors. For example, the more competitive the market, the more aggressive the business may have to be in order to sell its product and remain competitive. The less competitive the market structure, the greater the chance that collusion between producers might be the preferred strategy, as this reduces the excesses and uncertainties that outright competition might produce.

Such conduct will in turn influence how well businesses perform. Performance can be measured by several different indicators, such as efficiency in terms of cost per unit of output, current or long-term profitability, market share or growth in market share, changes in share prices or share prices relative to those of other firms in the industry or to other firms in general, to name some of the most commonly used.

Throughout the text, and particularly in Chapter 5, we shall see how market structure affects business conduct, and how business conduct affects business performance. It would be wrong, however, to argue that business performance is totally shaped by external factors such as market structure. In fact, the internal aims, organisation and strategy of business may be very influential in determining success. We examine business strategy and the factors determining business competitiveness in Chapter 6.

> ### Pause for thought
>
> *Why is a firm facing little competition from rivals likely to have higher profits, but also higher costs, than a firm facing intense competition?*

RECAP

1. The external business environment is commonly divided into four dimensions: political, economic, social and technological (PEST analysis); or into seven dimensions, where the additional three are environmental, legal and ethical (STEEPLE analysis).

2. The economic dimension of the business environment is divided into two: the microeconomic environment and the macroeconomic environment. The microenvironment refers to the particular market in which the firm operates. The macroenvironment refers to the national and international economy in which all firms operate.

3. The process of globalisation has meant that for many companies their external environment has an important international dimension.

4. Production is divided into primary, secondary and tertiary sectors. The contribution to output of these different sectors of production has changed over time. Over the years the tertiary sector has grown, while the secondary sector has contracted.

5. Firms are classified into industries and industries into sectors. Such classification enables us to chart changes in industrial structure over time and to assess changing patterns of industrial concentration.

BOX 1.3 **THE CHANGING NATURE OF BUSINESS**

Knowledge rules

In the knowledge-driven economy, innovation has become central to achievement in the business world. With this growth in importance, organisations large and small have begun to re-evaluate their products, their services, even their corporate culture in the attempt to maintain their competitiveness in the global markets of today. The more forward-thinking companies have recognised that only through such root and branch reform can they hope to survive in the face of increasing competition.[1]

Knowledge is fundamental to economic success in many industries and, for most firms, key knowledge resides in skilled members of the workforce. The result is a market in knowledge, with those having the knowledge being able to command high salaries and often being 'head hunted'. The 'knowledge economy' is fundamentally changing the nature, organisation and practice of business.

The traditional limited company was based around five fundamental principles:

■ Individual workers needed the business and the income it provided more than the business needed them. After all, employers could always find alternative workers. If a worker loses his job, the opportunity cost to that worker is much bigger than the opportunity cost to the firm. As such, the company was the dominant partner in the employment relationship.

■ Employees tended to be full time and depended upon this work as their sole source of income.

■ The company was integrated, with a single management structure overseeing all the various stages of production. This was seen as the most efficient way to organise productive activity.

■ Suppliers, and especially manufacturers, had considerable power over the customer by controlling information about their product or service.

■ Technology relevant to an industry was often developed within the industry.

In more recent times, with the advent of the knowledge economy, the principles above have all but been turned on their heads.

■ The key resource in a knowledge economy is knowledge itself, and the workers that hold such knowledge. Without such workers, the company is unlikely to succeed. As such, the balance of power between the business and the specialist worker in today's economy is far more equal.

■ Even though the vast majority of employees still work full time, the development of the flexible firm, which has created more diversity in employment contracts, such as part-time and short-term contracts and consultancy, means that full-time work is not the only option. (We examine this in section 8.5.) The result is an increasing number of workers offering their services to business in non-conventional ways: e.g. as consultants.

■ As companies are increasingly supplying their products to a complex global marketplace, so many find they do not have the necessary expertise to do everything themselves – from production through all its stages, research and development, adapting their products to specific markets, to marketing and sales. With communication costs that have become insignificant, businesses are likely to be more efficient and flexible if they outsource and de-integrate. Not only are businesses outsourcing various stages of production, but many are employing specialist companies to provide key areas of management, such as HRM (human resource management) – hiring, firing, training, benefits, etc.

■ Whereas in the past businesses controlled information given to their customers, today access to information via sources such as the Internet means that power is shifting towards the consumer.

■ Today, unlike in previous decades, technological developments are less specific to industries. Knowledge developments are diffused and cut across industry boundaries. What this means for businesses, in a knowledge-driven economy, is that they must look beyond their own industry if they are to develop and grow. We frequently see partnerships and joint ventures between businesses that cut across industry types and technology.

What is clear from the above is that the dynamics of the knowledge economy require a quite fundamental change in the nature of business. Organisationally it needs to be more flexible, helping it to respond to the ever-changing market conditions it faces. Successful companies draw upon their core competencies to achieve market advantage, and thus ultimately specialise in what they do best. For other parts of their business, companies must learn to work with others, either through outsourcing specialist tasks, or through more formal strategic partnerships.

Within this new business model the key assets are the specialist people in the organisation – its 'knowledge workers'.

 How is the development of the knowledge economy likely to affect the distribution of income in the economy? Will it become more equal or less equal? (Clue: think about the effects of specialist knowledge on the wage rates of specialists.)

---

[1] *Innovation management and the knowledge-driven economy*, European Commission, Directorate-general for Enterprise (ECSC-EC-EAEC Brussels-Luxembourg, 2004).

1.3 **THE ECONOMIST'S APPROACH TO BUSINESS**

Tackling the problem of scarcity

We have looked at various aspects of the business environment and the influences on firms. We have also looked at some of the economic problems that businesses face. But what contribution can economists make to the analysis of these problems and to recommending solutions?

To answer this question we need to go back one stage and ask what it is that economists study in general. What is it that makes a problem an *economic* problem? The answer is that there is one central problem faced by all individuals and all societies. This is the problem of *scarcity*.

We define *scarcity* as 'the excess of human wants over what can actually be produced'.

Of course, we do not all face the problem of scarcity to the same degree. A poor person unable to afford enough to eat or a decent place to live will hardly see it as a 'problem' that a rich person cannot afford a second Ferrari. But economists do not claim that we all face an *equal* problem of scarcity. The point is that people, both rich and poor, want more than they can have and this will cause them to behave in certain ways. Economics studies that behaviour.

Two of the key elements in satisfying wants are *consumption* and *production*. As far as consumption is concerned, economics studies how much the population spends; what the pattern of consumption is in the economy; and how much people buy of particular items. The business economist, in particular, studies consumer behaviour; how sensitive consumer demand is to changes in prices, advertising, fashion and other factors; and how the firm can seek to persuade the consumer to buy its products.

As far as production is concerned, economics studies how much the economy produces in total; what influences the rate of growth of production; and why the production of some goods increases and that of others falls. In order to produce, inputs (or 'factors of production') are required and we can identify three main types: human resources (labour); natural resources (land and raw materials); manufactured resources (capital). The business economist tends to focus on the role of the firm in the production process: what determines the output of individual businesses, the range of products they produce, the techniques and inputs they use and why, the amount they invest and how many workers they employ.

Demand and supply

We said that economics is concerned with consumption and production. Another way of looking at this is in terms of *demand* and *supply*. It is quite likely that you already knew that economics had something to do with demand and supply. In fact, demand and supply and the relationship between

them lie at the very centre of economics. But what do we mean by the terms, and what is their relationship with the problem of scarcity?

Demand is related to wants. If goods and services were free, people would simply demand whatever they wanted. Such wants are virtually boundless: perhaps only limited by people's imagination. *Supply*, on the other hand, is limited. It is related to resources. The amount that firms can supply depends on the resources and technology available.

Given the problem of scarcity, and that human wants exceed what can actually be produced, *potential* demands will exceed *potential* supplies. Society therefore has to find some way of dealing with this problem. Somehow it has to try to match demand and supply. This applies at the level of the economy overall: *aggregate* demand will need to be balanced against *aggregate* supply. In other words, total spending in the economy must balance total production. It also applies at the level of individual goods and services. The demand and supply of cabbages must balance, and so must the demand and supply of laptops, books, cars and houses.

But if potential demand exceeds potential supply, how are *actual* demand and supply to be made equal? Either demand has to be curtailed, or supply has to be increased, or a combination of the two. Economics studies this process. It studies how demand adjusts to available supplies, and how supply adjusts to consumer demands.

The business economist studies the role of firms in this process: how they respond to demand, or, indeed, try to create demand for their products; how they combine their inputs to achieve output in the most efficient way; how they decide the amount to produce and the price to charge their customers; and how they make their investment decisions. In this, firms are affected by the economic environment in which they operate. In section 1.2, we saw how we can divide the economic environment into microeconomics and macroeconomics. At a *microeconomic* level, firms are affected by their competitors, by technology and by changing consumer tastes. At a *macroeconomic* level they are affected by the state of the economy, by government macroeconomic policies and by the global economy.

> ### Pause for thought
>
> *When you go into a supermarket, the shelves are normally well stocked. Does this mean that the problem of scarcity has been solved?*

Making choices

Resources are scarce and so choices must be made. There are three main categories of choice that must be made in any society.

- *What* goods and services are going to be produced and in what quantities, given that there are not enough resources to produce all the things that people desire? How many

> ### Definitions
>
> **Scarcity** The excess of human wants over what can actually be produced to fulfil these wants.
>
> **Consumption** The act of using goods and services to satisfy wants. This will normally involve purchasing the goods and services.
>
> **Production** The transformation of inputs into outputs by firms in order to earn profit (or meet some other objective).

cars, how much wheat, how much insurance, how many pop concerts, etc. will be produced?

■ *How* are things going to be produced, given that there is normally more than one way of producing things? Which resources will be used and in what quantities? What techniques of production are going to be adopted? Will cars be produced by robots or by assembly-line workers? Will electricity be produced from coal, oil, gas, nuclear fission, renewable resources or a mixture of these?

■ *For whom* are things going to be produced? In other words, how is the nation's income going to be distributed? After all, the higher your income, the more you can consume of the nation's output. What will be the wages of farm workers, printers, cleaners and accountants? How much will pensioners receive? How much profit will owners of private companies receive or state-owned industries make?

All societies have to make these choices, whether they are made by individuals, by business or by the government.

Choice and opportunity cost

Choice involves sacrifice. The more food you choose to buy, the less money you will have to spend on other goods. The more food a nation produces, the fewer resources there will be for producing other goods. In other words, the production or consumption of one thing involves the sacrifice of alternatives. This sacrifice of alternatives in the production (or consumption) of a good is known as its *opportunity cost*.

> **KEY IDEA 3**
>
> **Opportunity cost.** The opportunity cost of something is what you give up to get it/do it. In other words, it is cost measured in terms of the best alternative forgone.

If a tailor can produce either 100 jackets or 200 pairs of trousers, then the opportunity cost of producing one jacket is the two pairs of trousers forgone. The opportunity cost of you buying this textbook is the new pair of jeans you also wanted that you have had to go without! The opportunity cost of working overtime is the leisure you sacrifice.

Rational choices

Economists often refer to *rational choices*. This simply means the weighing up of the *costs* and *benefits* of any activity, whether it be firms choosing what and how much to produce, workers choosing whether to take a particular job or to work extra hours, or consumers choosing what to buy.

Imagine you are doing your shopping in a supermarket and you want to buy some baked beans. Do you buy expensive Heinz baked beans or do you buy the cheap alternatives, such as the supermarket's own 'value' brand? To make a rational (i.e. sensible) decision, you will need to weigh up the costs and benefits of each alternative. Heinz baked beans may taste better to you and thus will give you a lot of enjoyment, but they have a high opportunity cost: because they are expensive, you will need to sacrifice quite a lot of consumption of other goods if you decide to buy them. If you buy the cheaper alternatives, although you may not enjoy them as much, you will have more money left over to buy other things: they have a lower opportunity cost.

Thus rational decision making, as far as consumers are concerned, involves choosing those items that give you the best value for money, i.e. the *greatest benefit relative to cost*. One person's choice of which product to buy may not be the same as another's, yet both decisions could still be rational.

The same principles apply to firms when deciding what to produce. For example, should a car firm open up another production line? A rational decision will again involve weighing up the benefits and costs. The benefits are the revenues that the firm will earn from selling the extra cars. The costs will include the extra labour costs, raw material costs, costs of component parts, etc. It will be profitable to open up the new production line only if the revenues earned exceed the costs entailed: in other words, if it earns a profit.

In the more complex situation of deciding which model of a mobile phone to produce, or how many of each model, the firm must weigh up the relative benefits and costs of each: i.e. it will want to produce the most profitable product mix.

Marginal costs and benefits

In economics we argue that rational choices involve weighing up *marginal costs* and *marginal benefits*. These are the costs and benefits of doing a little bit more or a little bit less of a given activity. They can be contrasted with the *total* costs and benefits of the activity. For example, the mobile phone manufacturer we were considering just now will weigh up the marginal costs and benefits of producing mobiles – in other words, it will compare the costs and revenue of producing *additional* mobile phones. If additional phones add more to the firm's revenue than to its costs, it will be profitable to produce them.

> ### Definitions
>
> **Opportunity cost** The cost of any activity measured in terms of the best alternative forgone.
>
> **Rational choices** Choices that involve weighing up the benefit of any activity against its opportunity cost.
>
> **Marginal costs** The additional cost of doing a little bit more (or 1 unit more if a unit can be measured) of an activity.
>
> **Marginal benefits** The additional benefits of doing a little bit more (or 1 unit more if a unit can be measured) of an activity.

KEY IDEA 4

Rational decision making involves weighing up the marginal benefit and marginal cost of any activity. If the marginal benefit exceeds the marginal cost, it is rational to do the activity (or to do more of it). If the marginal cost exceeds the marginal benefit, it is rational not to do it (or to do less of it).

Pause for thought

1. Assume that you have an assignment to write. How would you make a rational choice about whether to work on it today or whether to do something else?
2. Assume that you are looking for a job and are offered two. One is more pleasant to do, but pays less. How would you make a rational choice between the two jobs?

Choices and the firm

All economic decisions made by firms involve choices. The business economist studies these choices and their results.

We will look at the choices of how much to produce, what price to charge the customer, how many inputs to use and in what combination. Firms must also make decisions that have longer-term effects, such as whether to expand the scale of their operations, merge with or take over another company, diversify into other markets or export more. The right choices (in terms of best meeting the firm's objectives) will vary according to the type of market in which the firm operates, its predictions about future demand, its degree of market power, the actions and reactions of competitors, the degree and type of government intervention, the current tax regime, the availability of finance, and so on. In short, we will be studying the whole range of economic choices made by firms and in a number of different scenarios.

In all these cases, the owners of firms will want the best possible choices to be made, i.e. those choices that best meet the objectives of the firm. As we have seen, making the best choices will involve weighing up the marginal benefits against the marginal opportunity costs of each decision.

RECAP

1. The central economic problem is that of scarcity. We have endless wants, but there is a limited supply of resources. As such, it is impossible to provide everybody with everything they want. Potential demands exceed potential supplies.

2. Because resources are scarce, people have to make choices. Society has to choose by some means or other *what* goods and services to produce, *how* to produce them and *for whom* to produce them. Microeconomics studies these choices.

3. Rational choices involve weighing up the marginal benefits of each activity against its marginal opportunity costs. If the marginal benefit exceeds the marginal cost, it is rational to choose to do more of that activity.

4. Businesses are constantly faced with choices: how much to produce, what inputs to use, what price to charge, how much to invest, etc. We will study these choices.

QUESTIONS

1. Compare and contrast the relative strengths and weaknesses of unlimited liability partnerships with public limited companies.

2. Explain why the business objectives of owners and managers are likely to diverge. How might owners attempt to ensure that managers act in their interests and not in the managers' own interests?

3. Assume you are a UK car manufacturer and are seeking to devise an appropriate business strategy. Conduct a STEEPLE analysis of the UK car industry and evaluate the various strategies that the business might pursue.

4. What is the Standard Industrial Classification (SIC)? In what ways might such a classification system be useful? Can you think of any limitations or problems such a system might have over time?

5. Outline the main determinants of business performance. In each case, explain whether it is a micro- or macroeconomic issue.

6. Virtually every good is scarce in the sense we have defined it, but are water and air exceptions? If they are *not* scarce, explain whether it would be possible to

charge for them. Does the way in which you define water and air determine whether they are scarce or abundant?

7. Which of the following are macroeconomic issues, which are microeconomic ones and which could be either depending on the context?
   (a) Inflation.
   (b) Low wages in certain service industries.
   (c) The rate of exchange between the pound and the euro.
   (d) Why the price of cabbages fluctuates more than that of cars.
   (e) The rate of economic growth this year compared with last year.
   (f) The decline of traditional manufacturing industries.
   (g) Britain's referendum about whether to exit the EU.

8. Make a list of three things you did yesterday. What was the opportunity cost of each?

9. How would you use the principle of weighing up marginal costs and marginal benefits when deciding whether to (a) buy a new car; (b) study for an extra hour? How would a firm use the same principle when deciding whether to (a) purchase a new machine; (b) offer overtime to existing workers?

ADDITIONAL PART A CASE STUDIES ON THE *ESSENTIAL ECONOMICS FOR BUSINESS* WEBSITE (www.pearsoned.co.uk/sloman)

A.1 **Minding the Gap.** An investigation into Gap and the business and economic issues it faces.

A.2 **The UK defence industry.** A PEST analysis of the changes in the defence industry in recent years.

A.3 **Downsizing and business reorganisation.** Many companies in recent years have 'downsized' their operations and focused on their core competences. This looks particularly at the case of IBM.

A.4 **Scarcity and abundance.** If scarcity is the central economic problem, is anything truly abundant?

A.5 **Global economics.** This examines how macroeconomics and microeconomics apply at the global level and identifies some key issues.

A.6 **The opportunity cost of studying at university.** An examination of the costs of being a student, using the concept of opportunity cost.

WEBSITES RELEVANT TO PART A

Numbers and sections refer to websites listed in the Web Appendix and hotlinked from this book's website at **www.pearsoned. co.uk/sloman/**

■ For a tutorial on finding the best economics websites see site C8 (Internet for Economics).

■ For news articles relevant to Part A, Google the Sloman Economics News site.

■ For general economics news sources see websites in section A of the Web Appendix at the end of the text, and particularly A1–5, 7–8, 11, 12, 18–25, 35 and 36. See also links to newspapers worldwide in A38, 39, 43 and 44 and the news search feature in Google at A41.

■ For business news items, again see websites in section A of the Web Appendix at the end of the text, and particularly A1–3, 20–25, 35, 36.

■ For sources of economic and business data, see sites in section B and particularly B1–5, 27, 33, 34, 35, 38 and 47.

■ For general sites for students of economics for business, see sites in section C and particularly C1–7.

■ For sites giving links to relevant economics and business websites, organised by topic, see section I and particularly sites I47, 8, 11, 12, 14, 18.

Markets, demand and supply

One of the key determinants of a business's profitability is the price of its products. Many firms have the option of changing their prices in order to increase their profits. Sometimes, a cut in price might be in order, if the firm anticipates that this will generate a lot more sales. At other times, a firm may prefer to raise its prices, believing there will be little effect on sales – perhaps it believes that its competitors will follow suit; or perhaps there are no close competitors, making it easy for the firm to get away with raising prices.

For some firms, however, the prices of the products they sell are determined not by them, but by the market. The 'market' is the coming together of buyers and sellers – whether in a street market, a shop, an auction, a mail-order system, the Internet or whatever. Thus we talk about the market for apples, the market for oil, for cars, for houses, for televisions and so on. As we shall see, market prices are determined by the interaction of demand (buyers) and supply (sellers).

When the price is determined by the market, the firm is called a *price taker*. It has to accept the market price as given. If the firm attempts to raise the price above the market price, it will simply be unable to sell its product; it will lose all its sales to its competitors. Take the case of farmers selling wheat. They have to accept the price as dictated by the market. If individually they try to sell above the market price, no one will buy from them.

Competitive markets also imply that consumers are price takers. In fact, this is typically the case when you buy things, whether or not the seller is operating in a competitive market. For example, when you get to the checkout at a supermarket, you don't start negotiating with the member of staff over the price of the products in your trolley. Instead, you take the prices as given.

So how does a competitive market work? How are prices determined in such markets? We examine this question in Chapter 2.

In Chapter 3 we look more closely at demand and at firms' attempt to understand demand and the behaviour of consumers. Then in Chapter 4 we look at supply and ask how much a profit-maximising firm will produce at the market price.

The working of competitive markets

Business issues covered in this chapter

- How do markets operate?
- How are market prices determined and when are they likely to rise or fall?
- Under what circumstances do firms have to accept a price given by the market rather than being able to set the price themselves?
- What are the influences on consumer demand?
- How responsive is consumer demand to changes in the market price? How responsive is it to changes in consumer incomes and to the prices of competitor products?
- How is a firm's sales revenue affected by a change in price?
- What factors determine the amount of supply coming onto the market?
- How responsive is business output to changes in price?

2.1 BUSINESS IN A PERFECTLY COMPETITIVE MARKET

The price mechanism under perfect competition

In a *free market* individuals can make their own economic decisions. Consumers are free to decide what to buy with their incomes: free to make demand decisions. Firms are free to choose what to sell and what production methods to use: free to make supply decisions.

For simplicity we will examine the case of a *perfectly competitive market*. This is where both producers and consumers are too numerous to have any control over prices: a situation where everyone is a *price taker*. In such markets, the demand and supply decisions of consumers and firms are transmitted to each other through their effect on *prices*: through the *price mechanism*. The prices that result are the prices that firms have to accept.

Definitions

Free market One in which there is an absence of government intervention. Individual producers and consumers are free to make their own economic decisions.

Perfectly competitive market A market in which all producers and consumers of the product are price takers. (There are other features of a perfectly competitive market; these are examined in Chapter 4.)

Price taker A person or firm with no power to be able to influence the market price.

Price mechanism The system in a market economy whereby changes in price, in response to changes in demand and supply, have the effect of making demand equal to supply.

The working of the price mechanism

We now look at how the price mechanism works to eliminate *shortages* and *surpluses*. A shortage of a product causes its market price to rise and this, as we shall see, eliminates the shortage. A surplus causes price to fall and this eliminates the surplus. Let us see why.

If consumers decide they want more of a good at the current price or if producers decide to cut back supply, demand will exceed supply. (This is exactly what happened in the case of pencils following a 'craze' for adult colouring; you can read about it in an article in the Independent.[1]) The resulting *shortage* will encourage sellers to *raise* the price of the good. This will act as an incentive for producers to supply more, since production of each unit will now be more profitable. On the other hand, it will discourage consumers from buying so much. *The price will continue rising until the shortage has thereby been eliminated.*

If, on the other hand, consumers decide they want less of a good at the current price (or if producers decide to produce more), supply will exceed demand. The resulting *surplus* will cause sellers to *reduce* the price of the good. This will act as a disincentive to producers, who will supply less, since production of each unit will now be less profitable. At the same time, it will encourage consumers to buy more. *The price will continue falling until the surplus has thereby been eliminated.*

This price, where demand equals supply, is called the *equilibrium price*. By *equilibrium* we mean a point of balance or a point of rest, i.e. a point towards which there is a tendency to move. It is the price mechanism that works to find this equilibrium price.

The same analysis can be applied to labour (and other input) markets, except that here the demand and supply roles are reversed. Firms are the demanders of labour; individuals are the suppliers.

If an industry expands so that the demand for a particular type of labour exceeds its supply, the resulting shortage will drive up the wage rate (i.e. the price of labour) as employers compete with each other for labour. The rise in the wage rate will have the effect of curbing firms' demand for that type of labour and encouraging

more workers to take up that type of job. Wages will continue rising until demand equals supply, thereby eliminating the shortage.

If an industry declines, so that there is a surplus of a particular type of labour, the wage rate will fall until demand equals supply. As with price, the wage rate where the demand for labour equals the supply is known as the *equilibrium* wage rate.

Pause for thought

Explain how wages will adjust if (a) demand for a particular type of labour exceeds its supply and (b) supply for a particular type of labour exceeds its demand.

The response of demand and supply to changes in price illustrates a very important feature of how economies work.

KEY IDEA 5 *People respond to incentives, such as changes in prices or wages.* It is important, therefore, that incentives are appropriate and have the desired effect.

The effect of changes in demand and supply

How will the price mechanism respond to changes in consumer demand or producer supply? After all, the pattern of consumer demand changes over time. For example, people may decide they want more holidays abroad and fewer at home. Likewise the pattern of supply also changes. For example, changes in technology may allow the mass production of microchips at lower cost, while the production of hand-built furniture becomes relatively expensive. As demand and supply change, prices will be affected and these act as signals and incentives.

A change in demand

A rise in demand causes a shortage and hence a rise in price, which acts as an *incentive* for businesses to supply more, as it is more profitable. They divert resources from products with lower prices relative to costs (and hence lower profits) to the higher priced and hence more profitable product.

A fall in demand causes a surplus and hence a fall in price. This then acts as an incentive for businesses to supply less. These goods are now less profitable to produce.

A change in supply

A rise in supply (e.g. as a result of improved technology) causes a surplus and hence a fall in price. This then acts as an incentive for consumers to buy more. A fall in supply causes a rise in price. This then acts as an incentive for consumers to buy less.

Definitions

Equilibrium price The price where the quantity demanded equals the quantity supplied; the price where there is no shortage or surplus.

Equilibrium A position of balance. A position from which there is no inherent tendency to move away.

---

[1] Alexandra Sims, 'Adult colouring book craze prompts global pencil shortage', *Independent* (21 March 2016).

KEY IDEA 6
Changes in demand or supply cause markets to adjust. Whenever such changes occur, the resulting 'disequilibrium' will bring an automatic change in prices, thereby restoring 'equilibrium' (i.e. a balance of demand and supply).

Let us now turn to examine each side of the market – demand and supply – in more detail.

RECAP

1. A firm is greatly affected by its market environment. The more competitive the market, the less discretion the firm has in determining its price. In the extreme case of a perfect market, the price is entirely outside the control of the firm and consumers. The price is determined by demand and supply in the market, and both sides of the market have to accept this price: they are price takers.

2. In a perfect market, price changes act as the mechanism whereby demand and supply are balanced.

3. If there is a shortage, price will rise until the shortage is eliminated. If there is a surplus, price will fall until that is eliminated.

2.2 DEMAND

The relationship between demand and price

The headlines announce, 'Major crop failures in Brazil and East Africa: coffee prices soar.' Shortly afterwards you find that coffee prices have doubled in the shops. What do you do? Presumably you will cut back on the amount of coffee you drink. Perhaps you will reduce it from, say, six cups per day to two. Perhaps you will give up drinking coffee altogether.

This is simply an illustration of the general relationship between price and consumption: *when the price of a good rises, the quantity demanded will fall.* This relationship is known as the *law of demand* and there are two reasons behind it:

■ People feel poorer. They are not able to afford to buy so much of the good with their money. The purchasing power of their income (their *real income*) has fallen. This is called the *income effect* of a price rise.

■ The good is now dearer relative to other goods. People thus switch to alternative or 'substitute' goods. This is called the *substitution effect* of a price rise.

In our example of the increase in the price of coffee, we will not be able to afford to buy as much as before (the income effect), and we will probably drink more tea, hot chocolate, cola, fruit juices or even water instead (the substitution effect).

Similarly, when the price of a good falls, the quantity demanded will rise. People can afford to buy more (the income effect), and they will switch away from consuming alternative goods (the substitution effect).

A word of warning: be careful about the meaning of the words *quantity demanded.* They refer to the amount consumers are willing and able to purchase at a given price over a given time period (e.g. a week, or a month). They do *not* refer to what people would simply *like* to consume. You might like to own a luxury yacht, but your demand for luxury yachts will almost certainly be zero at current prices!

The demand curve

Consider the hypothetical data in Table 2.1. The table shows how many kilos of potatoes per month would be purchased at various prices.

Columns (2) and (3) show the *demand schedules* for two individuals, Tracey and Darren. Column (4), by contrast,

Definitions

Law of demand The quantity of a good demanded per period of time will fall as the price rises and rise as the price falls, other things being equal (*ceteris paribus*).

Income effect The effect of a change in price on quantity demanded arising from the consumer becoming better or worse off as a result of the price change.

Substitution effect The effect of a change in price on quantity demanded arising from the consumer switching to or from alternative (substitute) products.

Quantity demanded The amount of a good that a consumer is willing and able to buy at a given price over a given period of time.

Demand schedule for an individual A table showing the different quantities of a good that a person is willing and able to buy at various prices over a given period of time.

Table 2.1	The demand for potatoes (monthly)			
	Price (pence per kg) (1)	Tracey's demand (kg) (2)	Darren's demand (kg) (3)	Total market demand (tonnes: 000s) (4)
A	20	28	16	700
B	40	15	11	500
C	60	5	9	350
D	80	1	7	200
E	100	0	6	100

Figure 2.1 Market demand curve for potatoes (monthly)

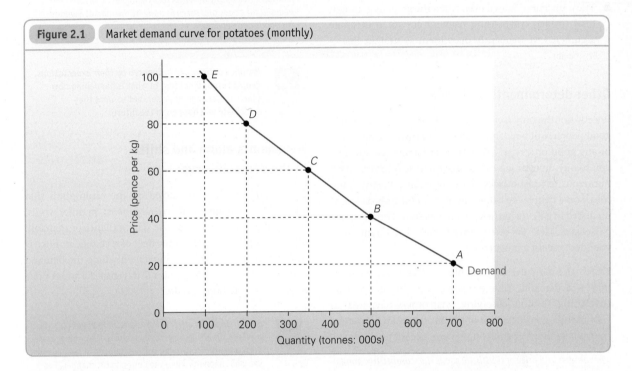

shows the total *market demand schedule*. This is the total demand by all consumers. To obtain the market demand schedule for potatoes, we simply add up the quantities demanded at each price by *all* consumers, i.e. Tracey, Darren and everyone else who demands potatoes. (This is known as horizontal summation.) Notice that we are talking about demand *over a period of time* (not at a *point* in time). Thus we would talk about daily demand or weekly demand, etc.

The demand schedule can be represented graphically as a *demand curve*. Figure 2.1 shows the market demand curve for potatoes corresponding to the schedule in Table 2.1. The price of potatoes is plotted on the vertical axis. The quantity demanded is plotted on the horizontal axis.

Point *E* shows that at a price of 100p per kilo, 100 000 tonnes of potatoes are demanded each month. When the price falls to 80p we move down the curve to point *D*. This shows that the quantity demanded has now risen to 200 000 tonnes per month. Similarly, if the price falls to 60p, we move down the curve again to point *C*: 350 000 tonnes are now demanded. The five points on the graph (*A*–*E*) correspond to

the figures in columns (1) and (4) of Table 2.1. The graph also enables us to read off the likely quantities demanded at prices other than those in the table.

Pause for thought

Referring to Figure 2.1, what tonnage of potatoes would be purchased per month if the price were 70p per kg?

Definitions

Market demand schedule A table showing the different total quantities of a good that consumers are willing and able to buy at various prices over a given period of time.

Demand curve A graph showing the relationship between the price of a good and the quantity of the good demanded over a given time period. Price is measured on the vertical axis; quantity demanded is measured on the horizontal axis. A demand curve can be for an individual consumer or a group of consumers, or more usually for the whole market.

A demand curve could also be drawn for an individual consumer. As with market demand curves, individuals' demand curves generally slope downward from left to right: the lower the price of the product, the more a person is likely to buy.

Two points should be noted at this stage:

- In textbooks, demand curves (and other curves too) are only occasionally used to plot specific data. More frequently they are used to illustrate general theoretical arguments. In such cases the axes will simply be price and quantity, with the units unspecified.
- The term 'curve' is used even when the graph is a straight line! In fact, when using demand curves to illustrate arguments we frequently draw them as straight lines – it's easier.

Other determinants of demand

Price is not the only factor that determines how much of a good people will buy. Think about your own consumption of any good or service – which other factors would cause you to buy more or less of it? Take the case of travel. With numerous terrorist attacks taking place in different countries, some people are being put off travelling abroad, as is discussed in a Reuters article,[2] which looks at Thomas Cook passengers. Here are some other factors that might affect your demand for a product:

Tastes. The more desirable people find the good, the more they will demand. Your tastes are probably affected by advertising, fashion, observing what others buy, such as your friends, considerations of health and your experiences from consuming the good on previous occasions.

The number and price of substitute goods (i.e. competitive goods). The higher the price of *substitute goods*, the higher will be the demand for this good as people switch from the substitutes. For example, the demand for coffee will depend on the price of tea. If tea goes up in price, the demand for coffee will rise.

The number and price of complementary goods. *Complementary goods* are those that are consumed together: coffee and milk, cars and petrol, shoes and polish. The higher the price of complementary goods, the fewer of them will be bought and hence the less the demand for this good. For example, the demand for electricity depends on the price of electrical goods. If the price of electrical goods goes up, so that fewer are bought, the demand for electricity will fall.

Income. As people's incomes rise, their demand for most goods will rise. Such goods are called *normal goods*. There are exceptions to this general rule, however. As people get richer, they spend less on *inferior goods* such as supermarkets' value lines and switch to better quality goods.

Expectations of future price changes. If people think that prices are going to rise in the future, they are likely to buy more now before the price does go up and so demand will increase. Think about the housing market. If people expect the price of houses to increase, they try to buy now before that happens.

> ### Pause for thought
>
> *Can you think of any other factors that affect (a) your demand for goods and services and (b) the market demand for goods and services?*

 KEY IDEA 7 *People's actions are influenced by their expectations.* People respond not just to what is happening now (such as a change in price), but to what they anticipate will happen in the future.

Movements along and shifts in the demand curve

A demand curve is constructed on the assumption that 'other things remain equal' (*ceteris paribus*). In other words, it is assumed that none of the determinants of demand, other than price, change. The effect of a change in price is then simply illustrated by a movement along the demand curve, e.g. from point *B* to point *D* in Figure 2.1 when price rises from 40p to 80p per kilo.

 KEY IDEA 8 *Partial analysis: other things remaining equal (ceteris paribus).* In economics it is common to look at just one determinant of a variable such as demand or supply and see what happens when the determinant changes. For example, if price is taken as the determinant of demand, we can see what happens to quantity demanded as price changes. In the meantime, we have to assume that other determinants remain unchanged. This is known as the 'other things being equal' assumption (or, using the Latin, the '*ceteris paribus*' assumption). Once we have seen how our chosen determinant affects our variable, we can then see what happens when another determinant changes, and then another, and so on.

> ### Definitions
>
> **Substitute goods** A pair of goods which are considered by consumers to be alternatives to each other. As the price of one goes up, the demand for the other rises.
>
> **Complementary goods** A pair of goods consumed together. As the price of one goes up, the demand for both goods will fall.
>
> **Normal goods** Goods whose demand rises as people's incomes rise.
>
> **Inferior goods** Goods whose demand falls as people's incomes rise.

[2] Sarah Young, 'Thomas Cook holiday demand falls as wary customers delay booking', *Reuters* (22 March 2016).

| Figure 2.2 | An increase in demand for good X |

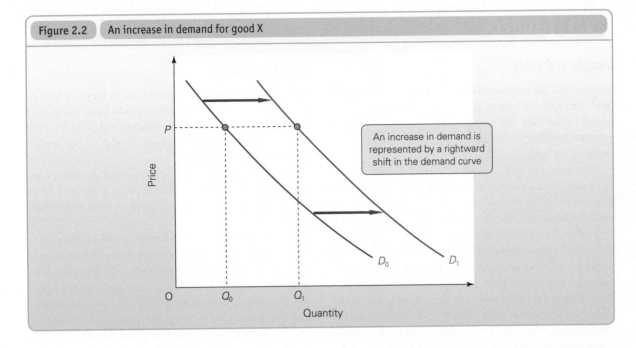

An increase in demand is represented by a rightward shift in the demand curve

What happens, then, when one of these other determinants changes? The answer is that we have to construct a whole new demand curve; the curve shifts. Consider a change in one of the determinants of your demand for books, excluding price: say your income rises. Assuming books are a normal good, this increase in income will cause you to buy more at any price: the whole curve will shift to the right. Thus in Figure 2.2 at a price of P, a quantity of Q_0 was originally demanded. But now, after the increase in demand, Q_1 is demanded. (Note that D_1 is not necessarily parallel to D_0.)

If a change in a determinant other than price causes demand to fall, the whole curve will shift to the left. Less will be demanded at each price than before.

To distinguish between shifts in and movements along demand curves, it is usual to distinguish between a change in *demand* and a change in the *quantity demanded*. A shift in demand is referred to as a *change in demand*, whereas a movement along the demand curve, as a result of a change in price, is referred to as a *change in the quantity demanded*.

Pause for thought

The price of cinema tickets rises and yet it is observed that cinema attendance increases. Does this mean that the demand for cinema tickets is upward sloping?

Definitions

Change in demand The term used for a shift in the demand curve. It occurs when a determinant of demand *other* than price changes.

Change in the quantity demanded The term used for a movement along the demand curve to a new point. It occurs when there is a change in price.

RECAP

1. When the price of a good rises, the quantity demanded per period of time will fall. This is known as the 'law of demand'. It applies both to individuals' demand and to the whole market demand.

2. The law of demand is explained by the income and substitution effects of a price change.

3. The relationship between price and quantity demanded per period of time can be shown in a table (or 'schedule') or as a graph. On the graph, price is plotted on the vertical axis and quantity demanded per period of time on the horizontal axis. The resulting demand curve is downward sloping (negatively sloped).

4. Other determinants of demand include tastes, the number and price of substitute or complementary goods, income and expectations of future price changes. You are a consumer, so anything that influences the goods you buy and how much of them, will be a determinant of demand.

5. If price changes, the effect is shown by a movement along the demand curve. We call this effect 'a change in the quantity demanded'.

6. If any other determinant of demand changes, the whole curve will shift. We call this effect 'a change in demand'. A rightward shift represents an increase in demand; a leftward shift represents a decrease in demand.

2.3 SUPPLY

Supply and price

Imagine you are a farmer deciding what to do with your land. Part of your land is in a fertile valley. Part is on a hillside where the soil is poor. Perhaps, then, you will consider growing vegetables in the valley and keeping sheep on the hillside.

Your decision will depend to a large extent on the price that various vegetables will fetch in the market, and likewise the price you can expect to get from sheep and wool. As far as the valley is concerned, you will plant the vegetables that give the best return. If, for example, the price of potatoes is high, you will probably use a lot of the valley for growing potatoes. If the price gets higher, you may well use the whole of the valley, perhaps being prepared to run the risk of potato disease. If the price is very high indeed, you may even consider growing potatoes on the hillside, even though the yield per hectare is much lower there. In other words, the higher the price of a particular crop, the more you are likely to grow it in preference to other crops.

This illustrates the general relationship between supply and price: *when the price of a good rises, the quantity supplied will also rise*. There are three reasons for this.

■ As firms supply more, they are likely to find that, beyond a certain level of output, costs rise more and more rapidly. Only if price rises will it be worth producing more and incurring these higher costs.

In the case of the farm we have just considered, once potatoes have to be grown on the hillside, the costs of producing them will increase. Also if the land has to be used more intensively, say by the use of more and more fertilisers, again the cost of producing extra potatoes is likely to rise quite rapidly. It is the same for manufacturers. Beyond a certain level of output, costs are likely to rise rapidly as workers have to be paid overtime and as machines approach their full capacity. If higher output involves higher costs of production, producers will need to get a higher price if they are to be persuaded to produce extra output. This concept is considered further in Chapter 4.

■ The higher the price of the good, the more profitable it becomes to produce. Firms will thus be encouraged to produce more of it by switching from producing less profitable goods.

■ Given time, if the price of a good remains high, new producers will be encouraged to set up in production. Total market supply thus rises.

The first two determinants affect supply in the short run. The third affects supply in the long run. We distinguish between short-run and long-run supply at the end of section 2.5 (see page 45).

The supply curve

The amount that producers would like to supply at various prices can be shown in a *supply schedule*. Table 2.2 shows a hypothetical monthly supply schedule for potatoes, both for an individual farmer (farmer X) and for all farmers together (the whole market).

The supply schedule can be represented graphically as a *supply curve*. A supply curve may be an individual firm's supply curve or a market supply curve (i.e. that of the whole industry).

Figure 2.3 shows the *market* supply curve of potatoes. As with demand curves, price is plotted on the vertical axis and quantity on the horizontal axis. Each of the points *a–e* corresponds to a figure in Table 2.2. Thus, for example, a price rise from 60p per kilogram to 80p per kilogram causes a movement along the supply curve from point *c* to point *d*: total market supply rises from 350 000 tonnes per month to 530 000 tonnes per month.

Not all supply curves are upward sloping (positively sloped). Sometimes they are vertical, or horizontal, or even downward sloping. This depends largely on the time period over which the response of firms to price changes is considered. (This question is examined on page 45.)

Pause for thought

1. How much would be supplied at a price of 70p per kilo?
2. Draw a supply curve for farmer X. Are the axes drawn to the same scale as in Figure 2.3?

Other determinants of supply

As with demand, supply is not determined simply by price. The other determinants of supply are as follows.

The costs of production. The higher the costs of production, the less profit will be made at any price. As costs rise, firms will cut back on production, probably switching to alternative products whose costs have not risen so much. As

Definitions

Supply schedule A table showing the different quantities of a good that producers are willing and able to supply at various prices over a given time period. A supply schedule can be for an individual producer or group of producers, or for all producers (the market supply schedule).

Supply curve A graph showing the relationship between the price of a good and the quantity of the good supplied over a given period of time.

Table 2.2	The supply of potatoes (monthly)		
	Price of potatoes (pence per kg)	Farmer X's supply (tonnes)	Total market supply (tonnes: 000s)
A	20	50	100
B	40	70	200
C	60	100	350
D	80	120	530
E	100	130	700

time. These are said to be *goods in joint supply*. An example is the refining of crude oil to produce petrol. Other grade fuels will be produced as well, such as diesel and paraffin. If more petrol is produced, due to a rise in demand, then the supply of these other fuels will rise too.

Nature, 'random shocks' and other unpredictable events. In this category we would include the weather and diseases affecting farm output, wars affecting the supply of imported raw materials, the breakdown of machinery, industrial disputes, earthquakes, floods, fire, and so on.

The aims of producers. A profit-maximising firm will supply a different quantity from a firm that has a different aim, such as maximising sales. We considered the aims of the firm in section 1.1.

Expectations of future price changes. If price is expected to rise, producers may temporarily reduce the amount they sell. Instead they are likely to build up their stocks and only release them on to the market when the price does rise. At the same time they may plan to produce more, by installing new machines, or taking on more labour, so that they can be ready to supply more when the price has risen. Consider

such, less will be supplied at any price. Costs could change as a result of changing input prices, changes in technology, organisational changes within the firm, changes in taxation, etc.

The profitability of alternative products (substitutes in supply). Many firms produce a range of products and will move resources from the production of one good to another as circumstances change. If some alternative product (a *substitute in supply*) becomes more profitable to supply, perhaps due to a rise in its price or a fall in its production costs, producers are likely to switch from the first good, thus cutting its supply, to this alternative. For example, if the price of carrots goes up, or the cost of producing carrots comes down, farmers may decide to cut down potato production in order to produce more carrots. The supply of potatoes is therefore likely to fall.

The profitability of goods in joint supply. Sometimes when one good is produced, another good is also produced at the same

Definitions

Substitutes in supply These are two goods where an increased production of one means diverting resources away from producing the other.

Goods in joint supply These are two goods where the production of more of one leads to the production of more of the other.

Figure 2.3	Market supply curve of potatoes (monthly)

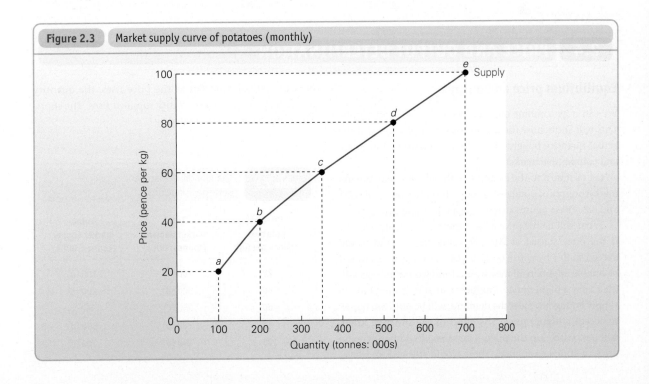

the housing market again. If you are thinking of selling your house, but expect that house prices will soon be higher, it would be rational to wait and put your house on the market only when prices have risen.

Movements along and shifts in the supply curve

The principle here is the same as with demand curves. The effect of a change in price is illustrated by a movement along the supply curve: e.g. from point *d* to point *e* in Figure 2.3 when price rises from 80p to 100p. Quantity supplied rises from 530 000 to 700 000 tonnes.

If any other determinant of supply changes, the whole supply curve will shift. A rightward shift illustrates an

increase in supply. More will be supplied at any given price. A leftward shift illustrates a decrease in supply. A movement along a supply curve is often referred to as a *change in the quantity supplied*, whereas a shift in the supply curve is simply referred to as a *change in supply*.

Definitions

Change in the quantity supplied The term used for a movement along the supply curve to a new point. It occurs when there is a change in price.

Change in supply The term used for a shift in the supply curve. It occurs when a determinant other than price changes.

RECAP

1. When the price of a good rises, the quantity supplied per period of time will usually also rise. This applies both to individual producers' supply and to the whole market supply.
2. There are two reasons in the short run why a higher price encourages producers to supply more: (a) they are now willing to incur the higher costs per unit associated with producing more; (b) they will switch to producing this product and away from now less profitable ones. In the long run there is a third reason: new producers will be attracted into the market.
3. The relationship between price and quantity supplied per period of time can be shown in a table (or schedule) or as a graph. As with a demand curve, price is plotted on the vertical axis and quantity per period of time on the

horizontal axis. The resulting supply curve is upward sloping (positively sloped).
4. Other determinants of supply include the costs of production, the profitability of alternative products, the profitability of goods in joint supply, random shocks and expectations of future price changes.
5. If price changes, the effect is shown by a movement along the supply curve. We call this effect 'a change in the quantity supplied'.
6. If any determinant other than price changes, the effect is shown by a shift in the whole supply curve. We call this effect 'a change in supply'. A rightward shift represents an increase in supply; a leftward shift represents a decrease in supply.

2.4 PRICE AND OUTPUT DETERMINATION

Equilibrium price and output

We can now combine our analysis of demand and supply. This will show how the actual price of a product and the actual quantity bought and sold are determined in a free and competitive market.

Let us return to the example of the market demand and market supply of potatoes, and use the data from Tables 2.1 and 2.2. These figures are given again in Table 2.3.

What will be the price and output that actually prevail? If the price started at 20p per kilogram, demand would exceed supply by 600 000 tonnes (*A* – *a*). Consumers would be unable to obtain all they wanted and would thus be willing to pay a higher price. Producers, unable or unwilling to supply enough to meet the demand, will be only too happy to accept a higher price. The effect of the shortage, then, will be to drive up the price. The same would happen at a price of 40p per kilogram. There would still be a shortage;

price would still rise. But as the price rises, the quantity demanded falls and the quantity supplied rises. The shortage is progressively eliminated.

Table 2.3	The market demand and supply of potatoes (monthly)	
Price of potatoes (pence per kg)	Total market demand (tonnes: 000s)	Total market supply (tonnes: 000s)
20	700 (*A*)	100 (*a*)
40	500 (*B*)	200 (*b*)
60	350 (*C*)	350 (*c*)
80	200 (*D*)	530 (*d*)
100	100 (*E*)	700 (*e*)

Figure 2.4 The determination of market equilibrium (potatoes: monthly)

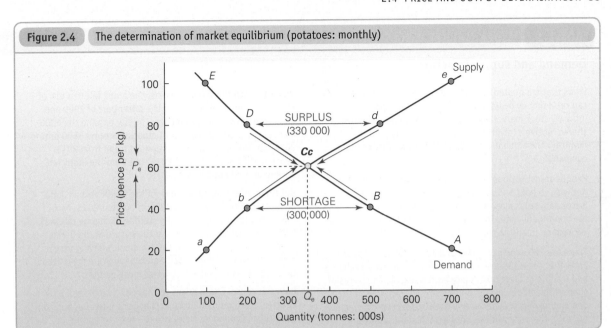

What would happen if the price started at a much higher level: say at 100p per kilogram? In this case supply would exceed demand by 600 000 tonnes (e – E). The effect of this surplus would be to drive down the price as farmers competed against each other to sell their excess supplies. The same would happen at a price of 80p per kilogram. There would still be a surplus; price would still fall.

In fact, only one price is sustainable. This is the price where demand equals supply: namely 60p per kilogram, where both demand and supply are 350 000 tonnes. When supply matches demand the market is said to *clear*. There is no shortage and no surplus.

As we saw at the beginning of the chapter, the price where demand equals supply is called the *equilibrium price*. This is the same as the market clearing price. In Table 2.3, if the price starts at other than 60p per kilogram, there will be a tendency for it to move towards 60p. The equilibrium price is the only price at which producers' and consumers' wishes are mutually reconciled, where the producers' plans to supply exactly match the consumers' plans to buy.

KEY IDEA 9

Equilibrium is the point where conflicting interests are balanced. Only at this point is the amount that demanders are willing to purchase the same as the amount that suppliers are willing to supply. It is a point which will be automatically reached in a free market through the operation of the price mechanism.

Definition

Market clearing A market clears when supply matches demand, leaving no shortage or surplus. The market is in equilibrium.

Demand and supply curves

The determination of equilibrium price and output can be shown using demand and supply curves. Equilibrium is where the two curves intersect.

Figure 2.4 shows the demand and supply curves of potatoes corresponding to the data in Table 2.3. Equilibrium price is P_e (60p) and equilibrium quantity is Q_e (350 000 tonnes).

At any price above 60p, there would be a surplus. Thus at 80p there is a surplus of 330 000 tonnes (d – D). More is supplied than consumers are willing and able to purchase at that price. Thus a price of 80p fails to clear the market. Price will fall to the equilibrium price of 60p. As it does so, there will be a movement along the demand curve from point D to point C, and a movement along the supply curve from point d to point c.

At any price below 60p, there would be a shortage. Thus at 40p there is a shortage of 300 000 tonnes (B – b). Price will rise to 60p. This will cause a movement along the supply curve from point b to point c and along the demand curve from point B to point C.

Point Cc is the equilibrium: where demand equals supply.

Movement to a new equilibrium

The equilibrium price will remain unchanged only so long as the demand and supply curves remain unchanged. If either of the curves shifts, a new equilibrium will be formed.

A change in demand

If one of the determinants of demand changes (other than price), the whole demand curve will shift. This will lead to a movement *along* the *supply* curve to the new intersection point.

BOX 2.1   STOCK MARKET PRICES

Demand and supply in action

Firms that are quoted on the stock market (see pages 153–4) can raise money by issuing shares. These are sold on the 'primary stock market' (see section 6.4). People who own the shares receive a 'dividend' on them, normally paid six-monthly. The amount varies with the profitability of the company.

People or institutions that buy these shares, however, may not wish to hold on to them for ever. This is where the 'secondary stock market' comes in. It is where existing shares are bought and sold. There are stock markets, primary and secondary, in all the major countries of the world.

There are 2292 companies (as of October 2016) whose shares and other securities are listed on the London Stock Exchange and trading in them takes place each weekday. The prices of shares depend on demand and supply. For example, if the demand for Tesco shares at any one time exceeds the supply on offer, the price will rise until demand and supply are equal. Share prices fluctuate throughout the trading day and sometimes price changes can be substantial.

To give an overall impression of share price movements, stock exchanges publish share price indices. The best known one in the UK is the FTSE 100, which stands for the 'Financial Times Stock Exchange' index of the 100 largest companies' shares. The index represents an average price of these 100 shares. The chart shows movements in the FTSE 100 from 1995 to 2016. The index was first calculated on 3 January 1984 with a base level of 1000 points. It reached a peak of 6930 points on 30 December 1999 and fell to 3287 on 12 March 2003, before rising again to a high of 6730 on 12 October 2007.

However, with the financial crisis, the index fell to a low of 3512 on 3 March 2009. During the latter part of 2009 and 2010, the index began to recover, briefly passing the 6000 mark at the end of 2010, but fluctuating around 5500 during 2011/12. The index was on an upward trend from 2013, peaking at 7104 on 27 April 2015, but then the index fell back to around 6000 in early 2016.

But then, after the initial shock of the Brexit vote in June 2016, it rose again to above 7000 in October 2016. Part of the reason for this was that the sterling exchange rate was falling with the uncertainty over the nature of the Brexit deal. With many of the FTSE 100 companies having assets denominated in dollars, a falling exchange rate meant that these dollar assets were now worth more pounds.

But what causes share prices to change? Search for a blog entitled 'The Shanghai Stock Exchange: a burst bubble?' on the Sloman Economics News site to see how changes in supply and demand caused share prices quoted on that exchange to decline dramatically in 2015. On the London Stock Exchange, why were prices so high in 1999, but only just over half that value just three years later? Why did this trend occur again in the late 2000s and what is likely to happen to share prices as the time for the UK's leaving the EU approaches? The answer lies in the determinants of the demand and supply of shares.

Demand

There are five main factors that affect the demand for shares.

The dividend yield. This is the dividend on a share as a percentage of its price. The higher the dividend yields on

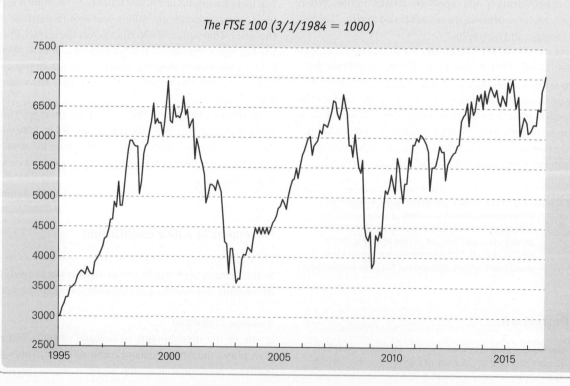

The FTSE 100 (3/1/1984 = 1000)

shares the more attractive they are as a form of saving. One of the main explanations of rising stock market prices from 2003 to 2007 was high profits and resulting high dividends. The financial crisis and slowdown in the world economy can explain the falling profits and dividends of companies from 2007 and the subsequent gradual recovery in the global economy was reflected by recovering dividends.

The price of and/or return on substitutes. The main substitutes for shares in specific companies are other shares. Thus if, in comparison with other shares, Tesco shares are expected to pay high dividends relative to the share price, people will buy Tesco shares. As far as shares in general are concerned, the main substitutes are other forms of saving. Thus if the interest rate on savings accounts in banks and building societies fell, people with such accounts would be tempted to take their money out and buy shares instead.

Another major substitute is property. If house prices rise rapidly, as they did from the late 1990s to 2007, this will reduce the demand for shares as many people switch to buying property in anticipation of even higher prices. If house prices level off, as they did in 2005/6, this makes shares relatively more attractive as an investment and can boost the demand for them. However, with the global slowdown pushing both house prices and share prices downwards, investors looked for other substitutes. Investments such as gold and government debt became more popular, as they were seen as safer bets.

Incomes. If the economy is growing rapidly and people's incomes are thus rising rapidly, they are likely to buy more shares. Thus in the mid-to-late 1990s, when UK incomes were rising at an average annual rate of over 3 per cent, share prices rose rapidly (see chart). As growth rates fell in the early 2000s, so share prices fell. The trend then repeated itself with growth rates picking up from 2003 to 2007 and then declining once again with the onset of the recession from 2007. With signs of a global economic recovery, albeit a relatively weak one, share prices rose between 2012 and mid-2015. However, they have fallen since with slowing growth of the Chinese and other Asian economies.

Wealth. 'Wealth' is people's accumulated savings and property. Wealth rose in the 1990s and many people used their increased wealth to buy shares. It was a similar picture in the mid-2000s. Much of the wealth worldwide was in relatively 'liquid' form – i.e. in a form that can easily be turned into cash (and hence used to buy shares).

Expectations. From 2003 to 2007, people expected share prices to go on rising. They were optimistic about continued growth in the economy and that certain sectors, such as leisure and high-tech industries, would grow particularly strongly. Looking at the graph, you can clearly see why this expectation emerged. But as people bought shares, this pushed their prices up even more, thereby fuelling further speculation that they would go on rising and encouraging further share buying.

With the financial crisis and fears of recession, we saw a dramatic fall in share prices, as confidence was shaken. As people anticipated further price falls, so they held back from buying, thereby pushing prices even lower. Prices remained volatile after the financial crisis, as uncertainty remained about the global economy and only when it appeared as though the world was in recovery did share prices begin to rise consistently once more. However, uncertainty has once again emerged and share prices have fallen back. Concerns have centred on the sluggish recovery in Europe, falling growth in China and many other developing countries, and the consequences of the UK's exit from the EU.

Supply

The factors affecting supply are largely the same as those affecting demand, but in the opposite direction.

If the return on alternative forms of saving falls, people with shares are likely to hold on to them, as they represent a better form of saving. The supply of shares to the market will fall. If incomes or wealth rises, people again are likely to want to hold on to their shares.

As far as expectations are concerned, if people believe that share prices will rise, they will hold on to the shares they have. Supply to the market will fall, thereby pushing up prices. If, however, they believe that prices will fall, as they did in 2008, they will sell their shares now before prices do fall. Supply will increase, driving down the price.

Share prices and business

Companies are crucially affected by their share price. If a company's share price falls, this can indicate that 'the market' is losing confidence in the company, as we saw with Tesco during the latter part of 2014. This will make it more difficult to raise finance, not only by issuing additional shares in the primary market, but also from banks.

It will also make the company more vulnerable to a takeover bid. This is where one company seeks to buy out another by offering to buy all its shares. A takeover will succeed if the owners of more than half of the company's shares vote to accept the offered price. Shareholders are more likely to agree to the takeover if the company's shares have not been doing very well recently.

Other factors too may cause share prices to fall, such as changes in the price of key commodities. With oil prices on a downward trajectory since 2014, companies such as BP saw their share prices decline from 519.20 on 4 July 2014 to 328.7 on 8 January 2016.

1. *If the rate of economic growth in the economy is 3 per cent in a particular year, why are share prices likely to rise by more than 3 per cent that year?*
2. *What has happened to the FTSE 100 index over the past 12 months? Can you explain the reasons behind the data?*

> **Figure 2.5** The effect of a shift in the demand or supply curve: (a) effect of a shift in the demand curve; (b) effect of a shift in the supply curve

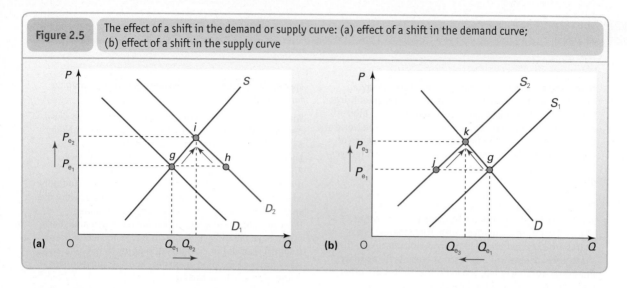

(a)   **(b)**

> ### Pause for thought
>
> *What would happen to price and quantity if the demand curve shifted to the left? Draw a diagram to illustrate your answer.*

For example, in Figure 2.5(a), if a rise in consumer incomes led to the demand curve shifting to D_2, there would be a shortage of $h - g$ at the original price P_{e1}. This would cause price to rise to the new equilibrium P_{e2}. As it did so there would be a movement along the supply curve from point g to point i, and along the new demand curve (D_2) from point h to point i. Equilibrium quantity would rise from Q_{e1} to Q_{e2}.

The effect of the shift in demand, therefore, has been a movement *along* the supply curve from the old equilibrium to the new: from point g to point i.

A change in supply

Likewise, if one of the determinants of supply changes (other than price), the whole supply curve will shift. This will lead to a movement *along* the *demand* curve to the new intersection point.

For example, in Figure 2.5(b), if costs of production rose, the supply curve would shift to the left: to S_2. There would be a shortage of $g - j$ at the old price of P_{e1}. Price would rise

from P_{e1} to P_{e3}. Quantity would fall from Q_{e1} to Q_{e3}. In other words, there would be a movement along the demand curve from point g to point k, and along the new supply curve (S_2) from point j to point k.

To summarise: a shift in one curve leads to a movement along the other curve to the new intersection point.

Sometimes a number of determinants might change. This may lead to a shift in *both* curves. When this happens, equilibrium simply moves from the point where the old curves intersected to the point where the new ones intersect. If this is the case, it is a good idea to consider each effect separately, rather than immediately trying to find the new equilibrium.

> ### Pause for thought
>
> *Referring to Figure 2.4 and Table 2.3, what would happen to the equilibrium price of potatoes if there were a good harvest and the monthly supply of potatoes rose by 300 000 tonnes at all prices?*

Search for the following blogs on the Sloman Economics News site for some examples of supply and demand in action: 'One little piggy went to market . . .' (pork markets), '£1 per litre' (the price of petrol) and 'When will wine run out?' (the market for fine wine).

RECAP

1. If the demand for a good exceeds the supply, there will be a shortage. This will result in a rise in the price of the good.
2. If the supply of a good exceeds the demand, there will be a surplus. This will result in a fall in the price.
3. Price will settle at the equilibrium. The equilibrium price is the one that clears the market, such that demand

equals supply. This is shown in a demand and supply diagram by the point where the two curves intersect.

4. If the demand or supply curves shift, this will lead either to a shortage or to a surplus. Price will therefore either rise or fall until a new equilibrium is reached at the position where the supply and demand curves now intersect.

2.5 ELASTICITY OF DEMAND AND SUPPLY

Price elasticity of demand

When the price of a good rises, the quantity demanded will fall. That much is fairly obvious. But in most cases firms and economists want to know just *how much* the quantity demanded will fall. In other words, we want to know how *responsive* demand is to a rise (or fall) in price.

Take the case of two products: petrol and broccoli. In the case of petrol, a rise in price is likely to result in only a slight fall in the quantity demanded. If people want to continue driving, they have to pay the higher prices for fuel. A few may turn to riding bicycles, and some people may try to make fewer journeys, but for most people, a rise in the price of petrol and diesel will make little difference to how much they use their cars.

In the case of broccoli, however, a rise in price may lead to a substantial fall in the quantity demanded. The reason is that there are alternative vegetables that people can buy. Many people, when buying vegetables, are very conscious of their prices and will buy whatever is reasonably priced.

We call the responsiveness of demand to a change in price the *price elasticity of demand*. If we know the price elasticity of demand for a product, we can predict the effect on price and quantity when the *supply* curve for that product shifts.

KEY IDEA 10

Elasticity. The responsiveness of one variable (e.g. demand) to a change in another (e.g. price). This concept is fundamental to understanding how markets work. The more elastic variables are, the more responsive is the market to changing circumstances.

Figure 2.6 shows the effect of a shift in supply with two quite different demand curves (*D* and *D'*). Curve *D'* is more elastic than curve *D* over any given price range. In other words, for any given change in price, there will be a larger change in quantity demanded along curve *D'* than along curve *D*.

Assume that initially the supply curve is S_1, and that it intersects with both demand curves at point *a*, at a price of P_1 and a quantity of Q_1. Now supply shifts to S_2. What will happen to price and quantity? In the case of the less elastic demand curve *D*, there is a relatively large rise in price (to P_2) and a relatively small fall in quantity (to Q_2): equilibrium is at point *b*. In the case of the more elastic demand curve *D'*, however, there is only a relatively small rise in price (to P_3) but a relatively large fall in quantity (to Q_3): equilibrium is at point *c*.

Defining price elasticity of demand

What we want to compare is the size of the change in quantity demanded of a given product with the size of the change in its price. Price elasticity of demand does just this. It is defined as follows:

$$P\varepsilon_D = \frac{\text{Proportionate (or percentage)}}{\text{change in quantity demanded}}{\text{Proportionate (or percentage) change in price}}$$

Definition

Price elasticity of demand A measure of the responsiveness of quantity demanded to a change in price.

Figure 2.6 Market supply and demand

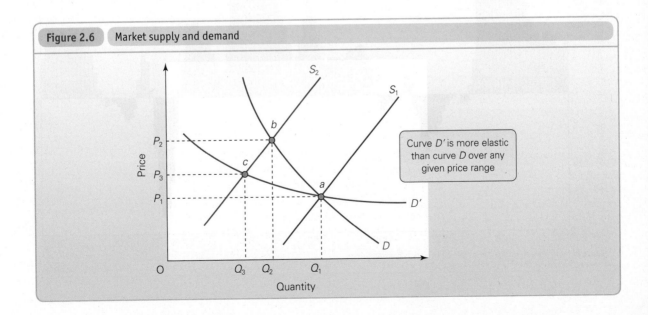

Curve *D'* is more elastic than curve *D* over any given price range

BOX 2.2   UK HOUSE PRICES

The ups and downs of the housing market

If you are thinking of buying a house sometime in the future, then you may well follow the fortunes of the housing market with some trepidation. This market is very important to consumers, firms and government, with households spending more on housing as a proportion of their income than on anything else.

The chart shows what has happened to annual house price inflation since 1984. In the late 1980s there was a housing price explosion in the UK, with house prices *doubling* between 1984 and 1989. This caused a rush to buy houses, with people expecting further rises and hence borrowing increased significantly, with many taking out exceptionally large mortgages. By the end of 1988 (the peak of boom), house prices were rising at an annual rate of 34 per cent.

However, from 1990 to 1995 house prices fell by 12.2 per cent and this sent many households into *negative equity*. This occurs when the size of a household's mortgage is greater than the value of their house, meaning that if they sold their house, they would still owe money. Many people therefore found themselves in a situation where they were unable to move house.

Following this decline, there was another boom from 1996 to 2007, with house prices rising by 26 per cent per year at the peak (in the 12 months to January 2003). For many, especially low income households, owning a home of their own was becoming increasingly difficult – the average price of a house was more than five times the size of a first-time buyer's income in 2007, compared to just twice the size in the mid-1990s.

With the financial crisis of 2007–8 and subsequent recession, house prices started to decline. By early 2009, they were falling at an annual rate of 17.5 per cent. With the expectation of further decreases in house prices, many households postponed buying. These lower prices did give first-time buyers a greater chance of getting onto the property ladder, if they could find the finance, but many still remained reluctant, fearing a return of the problem of negative equity.

House prices began to rise once again in late 2013 and by July 2014 the UK's annual house price inflation rate was 11.7 per cent, but with significant variation across the UK (see the blog, 'House price variations: a regional story', on the Sloman Economics News site). House prices have

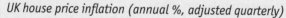

UK house price inflation (annual %, adjusted quarterly)

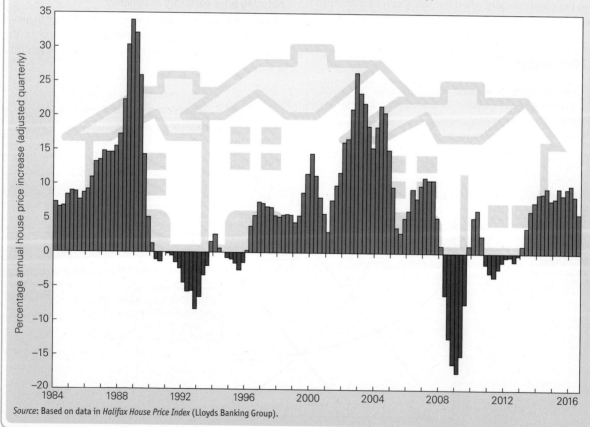

Source: Based on data in *Halifax House Price Index* (Lloyds Banking Group).

continued to rise and in 2015 annual house price inflation was 4.5 per cent, but still with significant variation between regions. These higher house prices have also affected the rental sector (see the blog, 'The rental sector', on the Sloman Economics News site).

House prices are determined by demand and supply. If demand rises (i.e. shifts to the right) or if supply falls (i.e. shifts to the left), the equilibrium price of houses will rise. Similarly, if demand falls or supply rises, the equilibrium price will fall.

So why did house prices rise so rapidly in the 1980s, late 1990s, 2000s and from 2014, but fall in the early 1990s and late 2000s? The answer lies primarily in changes in the *demand* for housing. Let us examine the various factors that affected the demand for houses.

Incomes (actual and anticipated). The second half of the 1980s, 1996 to 2007 and 2013 to the current date (late 2016) were periods of rising incomes. The economy was experiencing an economic 'boom' or recovery as in the latter case. Many people wanted to spend their extra incomes on housing, either buying a house for the first time, or moving to a better one. What is more, many people thought that their incomes would continue to grow, and were thus prepared to stretch themselves financially in the short term by buying an expensive house, confident that their mortgage payments would become more and more affordable over time.

The early 1990s and late 2000s, by contrast, were periods of recession or low growth, with rising unemployment and flat or falling incomes. People had much less confidence about their ability to afford large mortgages.

The cost of mortgages. Most people need a mortgage to buy a house. If mortgages become more affordable, people tend to borrow more and this fuels the demand for houses and drives up their prices. Mortgages become more affordable if either the rate of interest falls or people are given longer to repay the loan.

During the second half of the 1980s, mortgage interest rates were generally falling. Although they were still high compared with rates today, in *real* terms they were negative! In other words, even if you paid back none of the mortgage and simply accumulated the interest owed, your house would be rising faster in price than your debt; your 'equity' in the house (i.e. the value of the house minus what you owe on it) would be rising.

In 1989, however, this trend was reversed. Mortgage interest rates were now rising. Many people found it difficult to maintain existing payments, let alone to take on a larger mortgage. From 1996 to 2003 mortgage rates were generally reduced again, once more fuelling the demand for houses. Even with gently rising interest rates from 2003 to 2007, mortgages were still relatively affordable. Between 2009 and 2016 interest rates remained at an all-time low, which has reduced the cost of mortgage repayments. However, due to continued uncertainty following the financial crisis and lenders remaining

cautious, housing demand did not start to increase significantly until around 2013.

The availability of mortgages. In the late 1980s and early-to-mid 2000s, mortgages of several times a person's annual income were readily available and only small deposits were required. Indeed, in the mid-2000s, some mortgage lenders were willing to lend more than 100 per cent of the value of the property. By contrast, in the early 1990s and late 2000s banks and building societies were much more cautious about granting mortgages. They were aware that with the banking crisis and a global recession contributing to rising unemployment, as well as falling house prices and hence a growing problem of negative equity, there was a growing danger that borrowers would default on payments.

Between 2008 and 2012, many mortgage lenders were asking for significant deposits (25 per cent), which prevented many from entering the property market. This was then relaxed from 2013, also helped by government-backed 'Help to Buy' schemes, and borrowers were more able to access mortgages with smaller deposits (5 per cent). This greater ease of access to finance contributed to rises in house prices.

Speculation. In the 1980s and from 1997 to 2007, people generally believed that house prices would continue rising. This encouraged people to buy as soon as possible, and to take out the biggest mortgage possible, before prices went up any further. There was also an effect on supply. Those with houses to sell held back until the last possible moment in the hope of getting a higher price. The net effect was a rightward shift in the demand curve for houses and a leftward shift in the supply curve. The effect of this speculation, therefore, was to help bring about the very effect that people were predicting (see Box 2.4, page 46).

In the early 1990s and late 2000s, the opposite occurred. People thinking of buying houses held back, hoping to buy at a lower price. People with houses to sell tried to sell as quickly as possible before prices fell any further. Again the effect of this speculation was to aggravate the change in prices – this time a fall in prices.

Demographics. The general rise in house prices over the whole period since 1984 has been compounded by demographics: population has grown more rapidly than the housing stock. There are also more single households and more workers coming to the UK and these factors have caused demand to grow more rapidly than supply over the long term.

1. Draw supply and demand diagrams to illustrate what was happening to house prices (a) in the second half of the 1980s, from 1997 to 2007 and since 2013; (b) in the early 1990s and 2008–13.
2. Are there any factors on the supply side that contribute to changes in house prices? If so, what are they?
3. Find out what has happened to house prices over the past three years. Attempt an explanation of what has happened.

If, for example, a 20 per cent rise in the price of a product causes a 10 per cent fall in the quantity demanded, the price elasticity of demand will be:

$$-10\%/20\% = -0.5$$

Three things should be noted about the figure that is calculated for elasticity.

The use of proportionate or percentage measures. Elasticity is measured in proportionate or percentage terms because this allows comparison of changes in two qualitatively different things, which are thus measured in two different types of unit, i.e. it allows comparison of quantity changes (quantity demanded) with monetary changes (price).

It is also the only sensible way of deciding *how big* a change in price or quantity is. Take a simple example. An item goes up in price by £1. Is this a big increase or a small increase? We can answer this only if we know what the original price was. If a can of beans goes up in price by £1, that is a huge price increase. If, however, the price of a house goes up by £1, that is a tiny price increase. In other words, it is the percentage or proportionate increase in price that we look at in deciding how big a price rise it is.

The sign (positive or negative). If price increases (a positive figure), the quantity demanded will fall (a negative figure). If price falls (a negative figure), the quantity demanded will rise (a positive figure). Thus price elasticity of demand will be negative: a positive figure is being divided by a negative figure (or vice versa).

The value (greater or less than 1). If we now ignore the sign and just concentrate on the value of the figure, this tells us whether demand is elastic or inelastic.

- *Elastic demand* ($\varepsilon > 1$). This is where a change in price causes a proportionately larger change in the quantity demanded. In this case the price elasticity of demand will be greater than 1, since we are dividing a larger figure by a smaller figure.
- *Inelastic demand* ($\varepsilon < 1$). This is where a change in price causes a proportionately smaller change in the quantity demanded. In this case the price elasticity of demand will be less than 1, since we are dividing a smaller figure by a larger figure.
- *Unit elastic demand* ($\varepsilon = 1$). This is where the quantity demanded changes proportionately the same as price. This will give an elasticity equal to 1, since we are dividing a figure by itself.

The determinants of price elasticity of demand

The price elasticity of demand varies enormously from one product to another. But why do some products have a highly elastic demand, whereas others have a highly *inelastic* demand? What determines price elasticity of demand?

The number and closeness of substitute goods. This is the main determinant of price elasticity of demand. The more substitutes there are for a good and the closer they are as substitutes, the greater will be the price elasticity of demand. The reason is that people will be able to switch to the substitutes when the price of the good rises. The more numerous the substitutes and the closer they are, the more people will switch: in other words, the bigger will be the substitution effect of a price rise.

For example, the price elasticity of demand for a particular brand of a product will probably be fairly high, especially if there are many other, similar brands. If the price of a brand of washing powder goes up, people can simply switch to another brand; there is a large substitution effect. By contrast, the demand for a product in general will normally be pretty inelastic. If the price of food in general goes up, demand for food will fall only slightly. People will buy a little less, since they cannot afford so much; this is the *income* effect of the price rise. But there is no alternative to food that can satisfy our hunger; there is therefore virtually no *substitution* effect.

The proportion of income spent. The higher the proportion of our income we spend on a good, the more we will have to reduce our consumption of it following a rise in price: the more elastic will be the demand. Think about salt – the amount we spend on it accounts for a tiny proportion of our income and so if its price doubles, it makes little difference to our overall expenditure: the income effect of a price rise is very small. However, a car accounts for a much larger proportion of our income and so if the price of cars double, there would be a larger income effect.

The time period. Another important determinant is the time period. When price rises, people may take time to adjust their consumption patterns and find alternatives. The longer the time period after a price change, the more elastic the demand is likely to be.

Pause for thought

Think of two products and estimate which is likely to have the higher price elasticity of demand. Explain your answer.

Definitions

Elastic demand If demand is (price) elastic, then any change in price will cause the quantity demanded to change proportionately more. (Ignoring the negative sign) it will have a value greater than 1.

Inelastic demand If demand is (price) inelastic, then any change will cause the quantity demanded to change by a proportionately smaller amount. (Ignoring the negative sign) it will have a value less than 1.

Unit elasticity When the price elasticity of demand is unity, this is where quantity demanded changes by the same proportion as the price. Price elasticity is equal to –1.

Price elasticity of demand and consumer expenditure

One of the most important applications of price elasticity of demand concerns its relationship with the total amount of money consumers spend on a product. *Total consumer expenditure (TE)* is simply price multiplied by quantity purchased:

$$TE = P \times Q$$

For example, if consumers buy 3 million units (*Q*) at a price of £2 per unit (*P*), they will spend a total of £6 million (*TE*).

Total consumer expenditure is the same as the *total revenue (TR)* received by firms from the sale of the product (before any taxes or other deductions).

What will happen to consumer expenditure, and hence firms' revenue, if there is a change in price? The answer depends on the price elasticity of demand.

Elastic demand. As price rises, so quantity demanded falls, and vice versa. When demand is elastic, quantity changes proportionately more than price. Thus the change in quantity has a bigger effect on total consumer expenditure than does the change in price. This is summarised in Figure 2.7. In other words, total expenditure and total revenue change in the same direction as quantity.

This is illustrated in Figure 2.9(a). The areas of the rectangles in the diagram represent total expenditure (and total revenue). Why? The area of a rectangle is its height multiplied by its length. In this case, this is price multiplied by

quantity purchased, which is total expenditure. Demand is elastic between points *a* and *b*. A rise in price from £4 to £5 (25 per cent) causes a proportionately larger fall in quantity demanded: from 20m to 10m units (−50 per cent). Total expenditure *falls* from £80m (the shaded area) to £50m (the striped area).

When demand is elastic, then, a rise in price will cause a fall in total expenditure and hence the total revenue earned by the firms selling the product. A reduction in price, however, will result in consumers spending more, and hence firms earning more. Two cases where the elasticity of demand has been important are discussed on the Sloman Economics News site in the blogs: 'Price changes for travellers in Bristol' and 'Morrisons Brand: 'Milk for Farmers''.

So far we have been looking at the *market* demand curve. If we take the demand curve for a single firm, however, which is also a price taker, its demand curve will be perfectly elastic (i.e. horizontal). The price elasticity of demand is −∞. In other words, being a price taker, it can sell as much as it likes at the given market price. Any increase in its output and sales necessarily results in an increase in its total revenue, since it is selling a higher quantity at the *same* price. (When firms are not price takers, they face a downward-sloping demand curve. We consider such firms in Chapter 5.)

Inelastic demand. When demand is inelastic, price changes proportionately more than quantity. Thus the change in price has a bigger effect on total expenditure than does the change in quantity. This is summarised in Figure 2.8. In other words, total expenditure changes in the same direction as price.

This effect is illustrated in Figure 2.9(b). Demand is inelastic between points *a* and *c*. A rise in price from £4 to £8 (100 per cent) causes a proportionately smaller fall in quantity demanded: from 20m to 15m units (−25 per cent). Total revenue *rises* from £80m (the shaded area) to £120m (the striped area). In this case, firms' revenue will increase if there is a rise in price, and fall if there is a fall in price.

In the extreme case of a totally inelastic demand curve, this would be represented by a vertical straight line. No

Figure 2.7	Effects of a change in price on total expenditure: price elastic demand

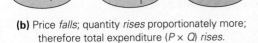

(a) Price *rises*; quantity *falls* proportionately more; therefore total expenditure (*P* × *Q*) falls.

(b) Price *falls*; quantity *rises* proportionately more; therefore total expenditure (*P* × *Q*) rises.

Figure 2.8	Effects of a change in price on total expenditure: price inelastic demand

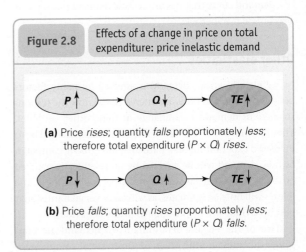

(a) Price *rises*; quantity *falls* proportionately less; therefore total expenditure (*P* × *Q*) rises.

(b) Price *falls*; quantity *rises* proportionately less; therefore total expenditure (*P* × *Q*) falls.

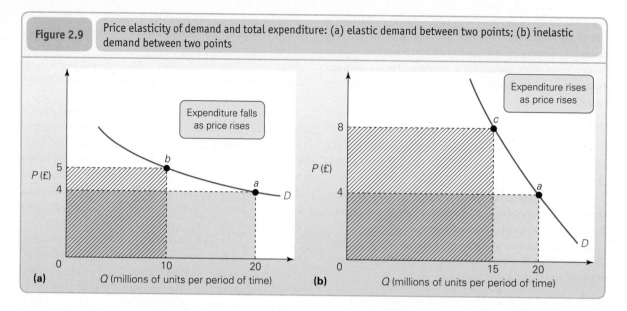

Figure 2.9 Price elasticity of demand and total expenditure: (a) elastic demand between two points; (b) inelastic demand between two points

matter what happens to price, quantity demanded remains the same and so the price elasticity of demand will be zero. It is obvious that the more the price rises, the bigger will be the level of consumer expenditure.

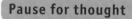

Pause for thought

1. *If the price of petrol goes up, what will happen to a firm's total revenue? Does your answer change if it is only the price of Esso petrol that increases?*
2. *Can we determine the impact on a firm's profits following a price fall if it faces (a) an elastic demand and (b) an inelastic demand? Explain.*

Unit elastic demand. With unitary elastic demand (where the value for elasticity $= -1$), the proportionate changes in price and quantity are equal. Any rise in price will be exactly offset by a fall in quantity, which means that total revenue and total expenditure will remain unchanged. In Figure 2.10 the striped area is exactly equal to the shaded area: in both cases total revenue and expenditure are £800 million. The shape of a demand curve that has unit elastic demand is known as a rectangular hyperbola.

Other elasticities

As we already know, demand is affected by many factors besides price and so firms are interested to know the responsiveness of demand to a change in these other variables. They might want to know how responsive demand will be to increased expenditure on a particular advertising campaign or how demand will be affected by more ethically sourced products. Of course, as with many aspects of business, the figures will only be estimates, as we can never guarantee that past behaviour will be the same as future behaviour.

Two of the biggest determinants of demand are consumer incomes and the prices of substitute or complemen-

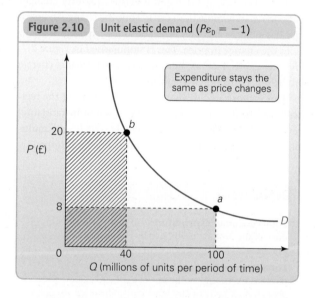

Figure 2.10 Unit elastic demand ($P\varepsilon_D = -1$)

tary goods. Firms will want to know just how responsive demand will be if these factors change. That is: they will want to know the *income elasticity of demand* – the responsiveness of demand to a change in consumers' incomes (Y) – and the *cross-price elasticity of demand* – the responsiveness of demand for their good to a change in the price of another good (whether a substitute or a complement).

Definitions

Income elasticity of demand The responsiveness of demand to a change in consumer incomes: the proportionate change in demand divided by the proportionate change in income.

Cross-price elasticity of demand The responsiveness of demand for one good to a change in the price of another: the proportionate change in demand for one good divided by the proportionate change in price of the other.

BOX 2.3 SHALL WE PUT UP OUR PRICE?

Competition, price and revenue

When you buy a can of drink on a train, or an ice cream in the cinema, or a bottle of wine in a restaurant, you may well be horrified by its price. How can they get away with it?

The answer is that these firms are *not* price takers. They can choose what price to charge. We will be examining the behaviour of such firms in Chapter 5, but here it is useful to see how price elasticity of demand can help to explain their behaviour.

Take the case of the can of drink on the train. If you are thirsty, and if you haven't brought a drink with you, then you will have to get one from the train's bar, or go without. There is no substitute. What we are saying here is that the demand for drinks on the train is inelastic at the normal shop price. This means that the train operator can put up the price of its drinks, and food too, and earn *more* revenue, because demand will be relatively unresponsive.

Generally, the less competition a firm faces, the lower will be the elasticity of demand for its products, since there will be fewer substitutes (competitors) to which consumers can turn.

The lower the price elasticity of demand, the higher is likely to be the price that the firm charges.

When there is plenty of competition, it is quite a different story. Petrol stations in the same area may compete fiercely in terms of price. One station may hope that by reducing its price by 1p or even 0.1p per litre below that of its competitors, it can attract customers away from them. With a highly elastic demand, a small reduction in price may lead to a substantial increase in their revenue. The problem is, of course, that when they *all* reduce prices, no firm wins. No one attracts customers away from the others! In this case it is the customer who wins.

1. *Why might a restaurant charge very high prices for wine and bottled water and yet quite reasonable prices for food?*
2. *Why are clothes with designer labels so much more expensive than similar 'own brand' clothes from a chain store, even though they may cost a similar amount to produce?*

Income elasticity of demand (Yε_D)

We define the income elasticity of demand for a good as follows:

$$Y\varepsilon_D = \frac{\text{Proportionate (or percentage)}}{\text{Proportionate (or percentage) change in income}}$$

For example, if a 2 per cent rise in consumer incomes causes an 8 per cent rise in a product's demand, then its income elasticity of demand will be:

8%/2% = 4

Note that in the case of a normal good, the figure for income elasticity will be positive: a *rise* in income leads to a *rise* in demand (a positive figure divided by a positive figure gives a positive answer).

The major determinant of income elasticity of demand is the degree of 'necessity' of the good. Typically, the demand for luxury goods expands rapidly as people's incomes rise, whereas the demand for more basic goods such as bread will only rise a little. If your income rises, you are unlikely to buy a lot more bread or milk, but you may buy more football tickets or foreign holidays. Thus items such as foreign holidays or cars have a high income elasticity of demand, whereas items such as potatoes and bus journeys have a low income elasticity of demand.

In the case of inferior goods such as many of the 'value' products in supermarkets, as income rises, demand *falls*. As people earn more, they switch to the supermarket's superior lines or to branded products and hence the demand for the 'value' product falls. Unlike **normal goods**, which have a positive income elasticity of demand, **inferior goods** have a negative income elasticity of demand: a *rise* in income leads

to a *fall* in demand (a negative figure divided by a positive figure gives a negative answer).

Income elasticity of demand is an important concept to firms considering the future size of the market for their product. If the product has a high income elasticity of demand, sales are likely to expand rapidly as national income rises, but may also fall significantly if the economy moves into recession.

Firms may also find that some parts of their market have a higher income elasticity of demand than others, and may thus choose to target their marketing campaigns on this group. For example, middle income groups may have a higher income elasticity of demand for high-tech products than lower income groups (who are unlikely to be able to afford such products even if their incomes rise somewhat) or higher income groups (who can probably afford them anyway, and thus would not buy much more if their incomes rose). For this reason, changes in the distribution of income can be an important factor for firms to consider when making decisions about what to sell.

Cross-price elasticity of demand (Cε_{Dab})

This is often known by its less cumbersome title of *cross elasticity of demand*. It is a measure of the responsiveness of

Definitions

Normal goods Goods whose demand increases as consumer incomes increase. They have a positive income elasticity of demand. Luxury goods will have a higher income elasticity of demand than more basic goods.

Inferior goods Goods whose demand decreases as consumer incomes increase. Such goods have a negative income elasticity of demand.

demand for one product to a change in the price of another (either a substitute or a complement). It enables us to predict how much the demand curve for the first product will shift when the price of the second product changes. For example, knowledge of the cross elasticity of demand for Coca-Cola with respect to the price of Pepsi would allow Coca-Cola to predict the effect on its own sales if the price of Pepsi were to change.

We define cross-price elasticity as follows:

$$C\varepsilon_D = \frac{\text{Proportionate (or percentage) change in quantity demand for good A}}{\text{Proportionate (or percentage) change in price of good B}}$$

If good B is a *substitute* for good A, A's demand will *rise* as B's price rises. For example, the demand for bicycles will rise as the price of public transport rises. In this case, cross elasticity will be a positive figure. If B is *complementary* to A, however, A's demand will *fall* as B's price rises and thus as the quantity of B demanded falls. For example, the demand for petrol falls as the price of cars rises. In this case, cross elasticity will be a negative figure.

The major determinant of cross elasticity of demand is the closeness of the substitute or complement. The closer it is, the bigger will be the effect on the first good of a change in the price of the substitute or complement, and hence the greater will be the cross elasticity – either positive or negative.

Pause for thought

If Good A had a cross-price elasticity of demand of zero with respect to good B, would good B be a substitute or a complement for good A, or neither?

Firms will wish to know the cross elasticity of demand for their product when considering the effect on the demand for their product of a change in the price of a rival's product (a substitute). If firm B cuts its price, will this make significant inroads into the sales of firm A? If so, firm A may feel forced to cut its prices too; if not, then firm A may keep its price unchanged. The cross-price elasticities of demand between a firm's product and those of each of its rivals are thus vital pieces of information for a firm when making its production, pricing and marketing plans.

Similarly, a firm will wish to know the cross-price elasticity of demand for its product with any complementary good. Car producers will wish to know the effect of petrol price increases on the sales of their cars.

Price elasticity of supply (Pεs)
Just as we can measure the responsiveness of demand to a change in a determinant of demand, we can also measure the responsiveness of supply to a change in a determinant

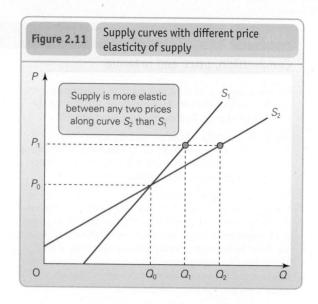

Figure 2.11 Supply curves with different price elasticity of supply

of supply. The *price elasticity of supply* refers to the responsiveness of supply to a change in price. We define it as follows:

$$P\varepsilon_S = \frac{\text{Proportionate (or percentage) change in quantity supplied}}{\text{Proportionate (or percentage) change in price}}$$

Thus if a 15 per cent rise in the price of a product causes a 30 per cent rise in the quantity supplied, the price elasticity of supply will be:

30%/15% = 2

In Figure 2.11 curve S_2 is more elastic between any two prices than curve S_1. Thus, when price rises from P_0 to P_1 there is a larger increase in quantity supplied with S_2 (namely, Q_0 to Q_2) than there is with S_1 (namely, Q_0 to Q_1).

There are two main determinants of the price elasticity of supply.

The amount that costs rise as output rises. The less the additional costs of producing additional output, the more firms will be encouraged to produce for a given price rise, and the more elastic will supply be.

Supply is thus likely to be elastic if firms have plenty of spare capacity, if they can readily get extra supplies of raw materials, if they can easily switch away from producing alternative products and if they can avoid having to introduce overtime working (at higher rates of pay). If all these

Definition

Price elasticity of supply The responsiveness of quantity supplied to a change in price: the proportionate change in quantity supplied divided by the proportionate change in price.

conditions hold, costs will be little affected by a rise in output and supply will be relatively elastic. The less these conditions apply, the less elastic will supply be.

Time period.

■ Immediate time period. Firms are unlikely to be able to increase supply by much immediately. Think about a market stall selling fresh vegetables: supply is virtually fixed, or can vary only according to available stocks. Supply is highly inelastic.

■ Short run. If a slightly longer time period is considered, some inputs can be increased (e.g. raw materials), while others will remain fixed (e.g. heavy machinery). Supply can increase somewhat and so is more elastic.

■ Long run. In the long run, there will be sufficient time for all inputs to be increased and for new firms to enter the industry. Supply, therefore, is likely to be highly elastic. In some circumstances the supply curve may even slope downwards. (See the section on economies of scale in Chapter 4, pages 82–4.)

RECAP

1. Price elasticity of demand measures the responsiveness of the quantity demanded to a change in price. It is defined as the proportionate (or percentage) change in quantity demanded divided by the proportionate (or percentage) change in price.

2. Given that demand curves are downward sloping, price elasticity of demand will be negative.

3. If quantity demanded changes proportionately more than price, the figure for elasticity will be greater than 1 (ignoring the sign): it is elastic. If the quantity demanded changes proportionately less than price, the figure for elasticity will be less than 1: it is inelastic. If they change by the same proportion, the elasticity has a value of 1: it is unit elastic.

4. Demand will be more elastic the greater the number and closeness of substitute goods, the greater the proportion of income spent on the good and the longer the time period that elapses after the change in price.

5. When the demand for a firm's product is price elastic, a rise in price will lead to a reduction in consumer expenditure on the good and hence to a reduction in the total revenue of producers.

6. When demand is price inelastic, however, a rise in price will lead to an increase in total expenditure and revenue.

7. Income elasticity of demand measures the responsiveness of demand to a change in income. For normal goods it has a positive value. Demand will be more income elastic the more luxurious the good.

8. Cross-price elasticity of demand measures the responsiveness of demand for one good to a change in the price of another. For substitute goods the value will be positive; for complements it will be negative. The cross-price elasticity will be greater the closer the two goods are as substitutes or complements.

9. Price elasticity of supply measures the responsiveness of supply to a change in price. It has a positive value. Supply will be more elastic the less costs per unit rise as output rises and the longer the time period.

| BOX 2.4 | SPECULATION |

Taking a gamble on the future

In a world of shifting demand and supply curves, prices are constantly moving.

If prices are likely to change in the foreseeable future, this will affect the behaviour of buyers and sellers *now*. If, for example, it is now December and you are thinking of buying a new winter coat, you might decide to wait until the January sales, and in the meantime make do with your old coat. If, on the other hand, when January comes you see a new summer jacket in the sales, you might well buy it now and not wait until the summer for fear that the price will have gone up by then. Thus a belief that prices will go up will cause people to buy now; a belief that prices will come down will cause them to wait.

The reverse applies to sellers. If you are thinking of selling your house and prices are falling, you will want to sell it as quickly as possible. If, on the other hand, prices are rising sharply, you will wait as long as possible so as to get the highest price. Thus a belief that prices will come down will cause people to sell now; a belief that prices will go up will cause them to wait.

This behaviour of looking into the future and making buying and selling decisions based on your predictions is called *speculation*. Speculation is often based on current trends in price behaviour. If prices are currently rising, people may try to decide whether they are about to peak and go back down again, or whether they are likely to go on rising. Having made their prediction, they will then act on it. This speculation will thus affect demand and supply, which in turn will affect price. Speculation is commonplace in many markets: the stock exchange (see Box 2.1), the foreign exchange market and the housing market (see Box 2.2) are three examples. Large firms often employ specialist buyers who choose the right time to buy inputs, depending on what they anticipate will happen to their price.

Speculation tends to be *self-fulfilling*. In other words, the actions of speculators tend to bring about the very effect on prices that speculators had anticipated. For example, if speculators believe that the price of BP shares is about to rise, they will buy more of them. The demand curve for BP shares shifts to the right. Those owning BP shares and thinking of selling will wait until the price has risen. In the meantime, the supply curve shifts to the left. The result of these two shifts is that the share price rises. In other words, the prophecy has become self-fulfilling.

Speculation over commodity prices

The prices of two commodities, oil and copper, illustrate the process of speculation and how it can make price changes larger. Figure (a) shows changes in the prices of these two commodities from 2002 to 2016. As you can see, they rose dramatically from 2002 to 2008, only to fall back significantly and then pick up again, stabilising somewhat throughout 2012 and into 2013. From 2014, the price of both

commodities fell, with oil falling particularly sharply in the latter part of 2014 and 2015. Why did this happen, and what part did speculation play in the process?

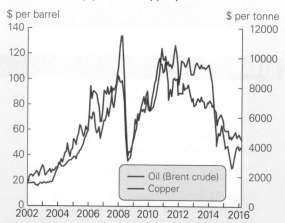

(a) Oil and copper prices

Oil prices. Between 2002 and 2008 there was a significant increase in the demand for oil. This was partly the result of increased world economic growth after a slowdown in 2001/2 and partly the result of the massive growth in demand from China and India as their economies powered ahead and their populations grew. Their income elasticity of demand for oil is high, reflecting their high income elasticity of demand for manufacturing, transport and power.

There were also growing problems with supply throughout the 2000s. The war in Iraq and disruptions in supply in other oil-producing countries meant that supply could not match the growth in demand without substantial price increases.

Speculation compounded this process. As oil prices rose, governments and oil companies increased demand so as to build up stocks (or 'inventories') ahead of any further price increases. At the same time, holders of oil stocks released less onto the market, waiting for the price to rise further.

This is illustrated in Figure (b). A rise in demand from D_1 to D_2 caused by the underlying increase in demand for oil, plus a fall in supply from S_1 to S_2 caused by disruptions in supply, would have resulted in a price rise from P_1 to P_2. But speculation compounded this effect. A further rise in demand to D_3 caused by speculative building of stocks, plus a fall in supply to S_3 as a result of the speculative holding back of supplies, meant that price rose to P_3.

Oil prices reached a peak at over $140 per barrel in July 2008. Then things changed dramatically. Investment in new oil wells, stimulated by earlier rises in prices, was beginning to increase supply. At the same time, stocks were near maximum and hence this reduced the demand for further stock building.

The resulting fall in prices put speculation into reverse. Oil stocks were reduced as more oil was released onto the market before prices fell any further. Meanwhile, with growing concerns about the world banking system and fears of a

Definitions

Speculation This is where people make buying or selling decisions based on their anticipations of future prices.

Self-fulfilling speculation The actions of speculators tend to cause the very effect that they had anticipated.

(b) Speculation compounding a price increase

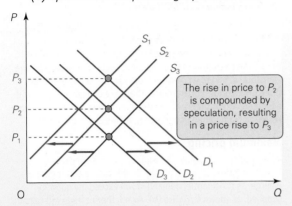

The rise in price to P_2 is compounded by speculation, resulting in a price rise to P_3

credit shortage, it became clear that the world was heading for recession. This reduced the demand for oil and with stocks being run down as oil purchasers waited for the price to fall further, this speculation did cause further falls in price. By the end of December 2008, oil was trading at around $34 per barrel, a fall in price of 76 per cent in just over five months.

This is illustrated in Figure (c). A fall in demand from D_1 to D_2, plus a rise in supply from S_1 to S_2, would have caused price to fall from P_1 to P_2. But again, speculation compounded this effect, resulting in a further fall in demand to D_3 and a rise in supply to S_3. Price fell to P_3.

(c) Speculation compounding a price fall

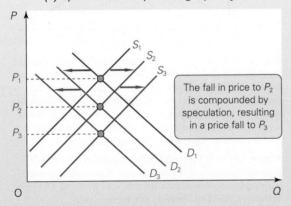

The fall in price to P_2 is compounded by speculation, resulting in a price fall to P_3

As the global economy began to recover in the late 2000s, oil prices steadily increased, reaching $128 per barrel in early 2011. Prices then stabilised at just over $100 per barrel through to June 2014, reaching peaks in August 2013 and June 2014 of $114 and $112 per barrel, respectively. Since that point, prices have fallen sharply. In August 2014, prices were just above $100 per barrel, but by January 2015 they had fallen to under $50 per barrel. Prices fluctuated around that level for some months but towards the end of 2015, the downward trajectory continued, leaving prices at a low of $30 in January 2016.

The underlying causes of the fall in prices were three-fold. First, the supply from shale oil deposits in North America and elsewhere rapidly increased. Second, OPEC announced that it would not cut back supply to compensate for the increased supply of shale oil. It hoped to make many shale oil wells unprofitable and discourage investment in new shale wells,

but in the meantime this merely compounded the problem of excess supply. Third, continuing weakness in the global economy was suppressing demand. These factors are considered on the Sloman Economics News site in the following blogs, 'A crude indicator of the economy (Part 2)', 'An oil glut', and 'Will there be an oil price rebound?' This combination of factors, together with speculation that prices will continue to fall, shifted demand to the left and supply to the right, thus keeping prices low. They will not remain as low as this for ever, but as long as supply remains sufficiently high, they could stay below $80 per barrel for some time.

Copper prices. A similar picture of underlying changes in demand and supply, amplified by speculation, can be seen in the case of copper (see Figure (a)). Surging demand from China and India, with supply unable to keep pace, pushed up prices from 2004. This trend was exaggerated by speculation, as stocks were built in anticipation of further rises.

The trend was temporarily reversed in late 2006. Increased mining output, prompted by the earlier price increases, coupled with slowing worldwide demand and the perception that copper stocks were unnecessarily large, saw copper prices fall by some 35 per cent between June 2006 and February 2007. But then the continuing growth in the world economy caused the copper price to rise again.

The financial crisis and global recession caused copper prices to plummet – from $8.5 per tonne in July 2008 to $2.9 in December. Once the fall had begun, it was compounded by speculation that it would fall further.

Then throughout 2009 and into 2010 the price steadily rose, first because speculators believed that the price had fallen too low to reflect underlying supply and demand, and later as the recovery began to gather pace and speculators anticipated resulting further rises in raw material prices. The price became more stable throughout the latter part of 2012 and 2013 as the recovery remained weak. Then with economic uncertainty throughout 2015 and into 2016, slowing demand from China and speculation that prices would continue to fall, copper prices did indeed fall once more. You can read about the price of copper in a Financial Times article[1] and how it has been influenced by various factors.

These speculative trends in both oil and copper prices were exaggerated by another factor. Financial investors, such as investment banks and insurance companies, have increasingly held commodities in addition to shares, bonds and other assets.[2] They have done so as a means of 'diversifying their portfolios' (their asset holdings) and thereby spreading their risks. This has increased the amount of speculative buying or selling of copper, oil, gold, etc.

1. *Under what circumstances are people engaging in speculation likely to (a) gain, (b) lose from doing so?*
2. *Find out what has happened to the price of (a) oil and (b) copper over the past 12 months and give an explanation. To what extent have the price changes been influenced by speculation?*

[1] Henry Sanderson, 'China demand for copper forecast to slow', *Financial Times* (21 March 2016).

[2] Note that if you buy copper, say, in this way, you don't physically take ownership of the copper, but acquire a paper or electronic asset denoting your ownership.

BOX 2.5 **MARKET INTERVENTION**

How might governments set about changing the price of a product?

Over the decades, there has been a general shift across the world to free markets. However, sometimes the free-market price may not be seen as the 'best' price and governments may wish to adjust that price. Here, we look at some ways in which governments around the world have intervened either to lower the price of a particular product or to raise it.

Minimum pricing

If the government feels that the current price is too low, it may set a *minimum price* (or price floor) *above* the equilibrium price. This will create a surplus, as illustrated in Figure (a). Normally, a surplus would be eliminated by a fall in price, but with the price not allowed to fall, the surplus remains.

(a) Minimum price: price floor

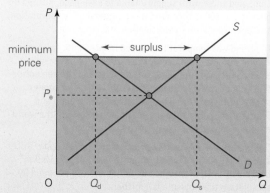

One market where a system of minimum price controls has been extensively discussed is that of alcohol, but few countries have implemented one. A country that has is Canada and although different provinces have different policies, the empirical evidence from this minimum pricing policy is very positive. In Saskatchewan, evidence suggests that a 10 per cent rise in alcohol prices leads to an 8 per cent fall in consumption.[1] Tim Stockwell and Gerald Thomas reviewed eight years of data from British Columbia on price rises, alcohol consumption and health effects. They came to some key conclusions:

> A 10 per cent increase in average minimum prices across all beverage types would result in a 3.4 per cent decrease in total alcohol consumption . . . [It was] significantly associated with a 32 per cent reduction in wholly-alcohol caused deaths . . . a 9 per cent drop in alcohol-related hospital admissions and significant delayed effects on deaths from alcohol-related diseases, such as liver cirrhosis and various cancers, after two years.[2]

More recent research from Canada has also found that the 10 per cent rise in the price of alcohol over nine years in British Columbia led to a 9.2 per cent reduction in violent assaults and an 18.8 per cent reduction in alcohol-based motoring offences.[3] Similar policies have been discussed elsewhere, including in the UK and particularly Scotland, as estimates by the Royal College of Physicians suggest that the total cost of

excessive drinking is £6 billion, half of which is directly related to higher costs for the NHS.

Critics of the minimum price, however, argue that it will be ineffective, because those at whom it is primarily aimed (binge drinkers) will be largely unresponsive to the higher price, due to their inelastic demand. Instead, it would be the 'sensible' drinkers who suffer from having to pay a higher price on alcohol. Furthermore, there are concerns that it will adversely affect pubs and small supermarkets. However, the research from Canada suggests that this is not the case.

Maximum pricing

When a price is set below the equilibrium, it is known as a *maximum price* (or price ceiling). In this case, a shortage will emerge, as the quantity demanded will exceed the quantity supplied, as shown in Figure (b). Again, the shortage will remain, as the price is not allowed to rise to eliminate the shortage.

(b) Maximum price: price ceiling

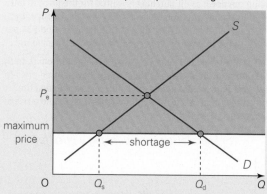

One market where we have seen maximum prices is housing and particularly in the rental sector, where governments intervene to keep rents below a particular level. In 1943, New York City introduced rent controls and although the number of properties where this policy still applies has fallen, it remains the longest running rent control policy in the USA, with approximately 38 000 apartments and 2 million residents affected.

A key objective of this policy is to ensure that the stock of affordable housing is maintained and to prevent landlords from exploiting low-income tenants. Carl Weisbrod, Chairman of the New York City planning commission, said:

> [rent regulation] is essential for the future of the city, for its economic goals, for social equality to make a city attractive and available for all, rich, poor and middle class.[4]

Berlin has become the first city in Germany to make rent controls a reality for new and existing tenants. Landlords are not permitted to charge more than 10 per cent above the local average rental value. This policy is aimed at addressing housing shortages in the market and keeping the city affordable for low-income households.[5]

Critics of such rent controls argue that they interfere with the efficient allocation of resources by reducing the quantity and

[1] Nick Triggle, 'The battle over alcohol pricing', *BBC News* (30 January 2013).
[2] Denis Campbell, 'Canada is proof that state-controlled drinking is good for health', *The Guardian* (30 April 2013).
[3] Denis Campbell, 'Minimum alcohol pricing cuts serious crime, study reveals', *The Observer* (28 June 2015).
[4] Rupert Neate and Lisa O'Carroll, 'New York's rent controls: essential for the future of the city', *The Guardian* (19 August 2015).
[5] Ruby Russell, 'Berlin becomes first German city to make rent cap a reality', *The Guardian* (1 June 2015).

quality of housing and removing the incentive for landlords to make improvements. In terms of Figure (b), keeping the rent below the equilibrium creates a shortage of rental accommodation.

Fat taxes

If governments want to increase prices, another option is to impose a tax. When a tax is imposed it shifts the supply curve upwards by the amount of the tax, since the tax is a cost to the producers. This, in turn, causes a movement up along the demand curve, pushing up price. This is illustrated in Figure (c).

(c) A tax on a product

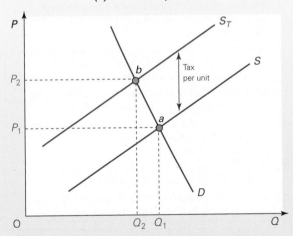

Assume that the tax is of a fixed amount per unit. This is shown by the vertical distance between the original supply curve (S) and the supply curve after the imposition of the tax (S_T). The tax pushes the price up from P_1 to P_2. Notice, however, that the price does not rise by the full amount of the tax, because the demand curve is downward sloping. In other words, not all of the tax will be passed on to consumers – the producers will have to absorb some of it. The more elastic the demand, the less the price will rise, and the more producers will have to absorb the tax.

With the growing problem of obesity and over-consumption of fatty and sugary products, Denmark introduced a 'fat tax' in October 2011, aiming to increase the cost of products high in saturated fat and hence encourage consumers to reduce their consumption of them (see the blog post, 'Taxing fatty products', on the Sloman Economics News site). The tax did raise more revenue than expected, but the implication of this is that consumption of fatty products continued and the tax was administratively very costly.

Polls suggested that 80 per cent of Danish consumers did not adjust their consumption habits following the tax and many simply continued to buy the same quantity, but purchased the products from Germany and Sweden. One impact of this was the loss of approximately 1300 Danish jobs.

Furthermore, the tax was 'regressive' – hurting the poor more than the rich – and so after just 15 months, and having weighed up the 'negligible health benefits against the demonstrable social and economic costs', Danish politicians abandoned the controversial policy.[6]

Despite the evidence from Denmark, calls still remain in other countries for similar taxes on fatty products and on sugary drinks to try to combat unhealthy consumption habits. In the 2016 UK Budget, the Chancellor, George Osborne, set out measures to introduce a tax on sugary drinks, as a measure to tackle childhood obesity (see the blog, 'A soft target for a tax', on the Sloman Economics News site). This tax will be at a rate of 18p per litre on drinks containing between 5g and 8g of sugar per 100ml and 24p per litre for drinks with more than 8g per 100ml. According to the Office for Budget Responsibility, the measure could lead to a price rise of as much as 80 per cent on a typical two-litre bottle of own-brand cola.[7]

As expected, the drinks manufacturers that will be affected are unhappy with this policy, indicating that it is consumers who will suffer from higher prices. Just how much the price hikes will deter parents and children from purchasing the drinks will only be known after the policy has been in force for some months.

Buffer stocks

In some markets, government controls may be felt to be necessary if the market suffers from price volatility and that is certainly the case with agricultural markets. Consumers can face very high or low prices and farmers' incomes are likely to fluctuate.

One way in which governments can intervene is to fix prices. In years of good harvests, there will be a surplus at the fixed prices (as in Figure (a)). To deal with this, the government could buy up the surpluses and store them. These *buffer stocks*, as they are called, could then be released back onto the market in years when harvests are bad.

The scheme will help to stabilise prices. However, if the price is relatively high so that over the years more is bought into the stocks than released from them, there will be a problem of what to do with the growing surpluses. This was a problem faced by the EU, when, under its Common Agricultural Policy, it fixed prices above the long-term free-market average. The result was 'food mountains' that either had to be destroyed or dumped onto world markets at low prices.

1. What methods could be used by the government to deal with:
   (a) the surpluses that result from minimum price controls?
   (b) the shortages that result from maximum price controls?
2. How are price elasticity of demand and supply relevant in the context of minimum/maximum price controls and taxes?
3. Why are agricultural prices subject to greater fluctuations than those of manufactured products?

Definitions

Minimum price A price floor set by the government or some other agency. The price is not allowed to fall below this level (although it is allowed to rise above it).

Maximum price A price ceiling set by the government or some other agency. The price is not allowed to rise above this level (although it is allowed to fall below it).

Buffer stocks Stocks of a product used to stabilise its price. In years of abundance, the stocks are built up. In years of low supply, stocks are released onto the market.

[6] Christopher Snowdon, 'Denmark's fat tax disaster – the proof of the pudding', *Institute of Economic Affairs* (25 May 2013).

[7] 'Sugar tax surprise in Budget, but growth forecasts cut', *BBC News* (16 March 2016).

QUESTIONS

1. Referring to Table 2.1 (page 27), assume that there are 200 consumers in the market. Of these, 100 have schedules like Tracey's and 100 have schedules like Darren's. What would be the total market demand schedule for potatoes now?

2. Refer to the list of determinants of demand (see page 28). For what reasons might the demand for sofas from a particular outlet, such as DFS, fall? Is the slow recovery from recession relevant here?

3. Refer to the list of determinants of supply (see pages 30–1). For what reasons might (a) the supply of potatoes fall; (b) the supply of leather rise?

4. This question is concerned with the supply of oil for central heating. In each case consider whether there is a movement along the supply curve (and in which direction) or a shift in it (and whether left or right):
   (a) new oil fields start up in production;
   (b) the demand for central heating rises;
   (c) the price of gas falls;
   (d) oil companies anticipate an upsurge in the demand for central heating oil;
   (e) the demand for petrol rises;
   (f) new technology decreases the costs of oil refining;
   (g) all oil products become more expensive.

5. The price of cod is much higher today than it was 30 years ago. Using demand and supply diagrams, explain why this should be so.

6. What will happen to the equilibrium price and quantity of butter in each of the following cases? You should state whether demand or supply or both have shifted and in which direction:
   (a) a rise in the price of margarine;
   (b) a rise in the demand for yoghurt;
   (c) a rise in the price of bread;
   (d) a rise in the demand for bread;
   (e) an expected increase in the price of butter in the near future;
   (f) a tax on butter production;
   (g) the invention of a new, but expensive, process of removing all cholesterol from butter, plus the passing of a law which states that butter producers must use this process. In each case assume that other things remain the same.

7. Why does price elasticity of demand have a negative value, whereas price elasticity of supply has a positive value?

8. Rank the following in ascending order of elasticity: jeans, black Levi jeans, black jeans, black Levi 501 jeans, trousers, outer garments, clothes.

9. Will a general item of expenditure like food or clothing have a price elastic or inelastic demand? Explain.

10. Explain which of these two pairs are likely to have the highest cross-price elasticity of demand: two brands of coffee, or coffee and tea?

11. Would a firm want demand for its brand to be more or less elastic? How might a firm achieve this?

12. Why are both the price elasticity of demand and the price elasticity of supply likely to be greater in the long run?

Demand and the consumer

Business issues covered in this chapter

■ What determines the amount of a product that consumers wish to buy at each price?

■ How are purchasing patterns dependent on human psychology?

■ Why are purchasing decisions sometimes risky for consumers and how can insurance help reduce or remove the level of risk?

■ How do businesses set about gathering information on consumer attitudes and behaviour, and what methods can they use to forecast the demand for their products?

■ How can firms differentiate their products from those of their rivals?

■ What strategies can firms adopt for gaining market share, developing their products and marketing them?

■ What are the effects of advertising and what makes a successful advertising campaign?

■ How has the growth of the Internet affected businesses' approach to advertising?

If a business is to be successful, it must be able to predict the strength of demand for its products and be able to respond quickly to any changes in consumer tastes. It will also want to know how its customers are likely to react to changes in its price or its competitors' prices, or to changes in income. In other words, it will want to know the price, cross-price and income elasticities of demand for its product. The better the firm's knowledge of its market, the better will it be able to plan its output to meet demand, and the more able it will be to choose its optimum price, product design, marketing campaigns, etc.

3.1 DEMAND AND THE FIRM

In Chapter 2 we examined how prices are determined in perfectly competitive markets: by the interaction of market demand and market supply. In such markets, although the *market* demand curve is downward sloping, the demand curve faced by the individual firm will be horizontal. This is illustrated in Figure 3.1.

The market price is P_m. The individual firm can sell as much as it likes at this market price, but it is too small to have any influence on the market – it is a price taker. It will not force the price down by producing more because, in terms of the total market, this extra output would be an infinitesimally small amount. If an individual farmer

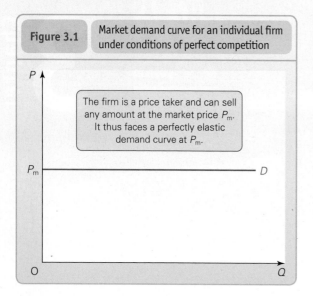

| Figure 3.1 | Market demand curve for an individual firm under conditions of perfect competition |

The firm is a price taker and can sell any amount at the market price P_m. It thus faces a perfectly elastic demand curve at P_m.

doubled the output of wheat sent to the market, it would be far too tiny an increase to affect the world price of wheat!

In practice, however, most firms are not price takers; they have some discretion in choosing their price. Such firms face a downward-sloping demand curve. If they raise their price, they will sell less; if they lower their price, they will sell more, as we saw in section 2.2. But firms don't just want to know in which direction quantity will move; they want to know just *how much* the quantity demanded will change and hence they want to know the price elasticity of demand, as we considered in the previous chapter.

In general, the less price elastic the demand, the better it will be for firms, because this will give them more power over prices. It is thus clearly in firms' interests to try to make the demand for their product less elastic. Firms will generally try to do this by attempting to differentiate their product from those of their rivals. If they can produce a product that consumers feel does not have a close substitute, then demand will be relatively inelastic. Success here will depend partly on designing and producing a product that is clearly different, and partly on achieving an effective marketing and advertising programme.

3.2 UNDERSTANDING CONSUMER BEHAVIOUR

In this section we examine the nature of consumer behaviour and in particular relate consumer demand to the amount of satisfaction that consumers get from products.

Marginal utility

When you buy something, it is normally because you want it. You want it because you expect to get pleasure, satisfaction or some other sort of benefit from it. This applies to everything from chocolate bars, to bus journeys, to calculators, to jeans, to insurance. Economists use the term 'utility' to refer to the benefit or satisfaction we get from consumption. As an illustration, you can read about the utility from watching football in the following blog, 'The Leicester effect: the impact on the preparedness to pay to watch the EPL', on the Sloman Economics News Site.

An important concept for helping understand the nature of demand is *marginal utility* (*MU*). This is the additional utility you get from consuming an *extra* unit of a product. For example, we might refer to the marginal utility (or extra satisfaction) that a consumer gains from a second slice of pizza or a fifth slice. Clearly, the nature and amount of utility that people get varies from one product to another, and from one person to another, but there is a simple rule that applies to virtually all people and all products: *the principle of diminishing marginal utility* (Key idea 11). For example, the second cup of tea in the morning gives you less additional satisfaction than the first cup. The third cup gives less still.

> **KEY IDEA 11**
>
> *The principle of diminishing marginal utility.* As you consume more of a product, and thus become more satisfied, so your desire for additional units of it will decline.

> **Pause for thought**
>
> *Are there any goods or services where consumers do not experience diminishing marginal utility? If so, give some examples. If not, then explain why.*

This rule states that the marginal utility will fall as we consume more of a product over a given period of time. This doesn't mean that the *total utility* (*TU*) you get from consuming all units of a commodity falls, but that each *additional* unit adds less and less to your total satisfaction.

However, there is a problem with the concept of marginal utility. How can we measure utility? After all, we

> **Definitions**
>
> **Marginal utility (*MU*)** The extra satisfaction gained from consuming one extra unit of a good within a given time period.
>
> **Total utility (*TU*)** The total satisfaction a consumer gets from the consumption of all the units of a good consumed within a given time period.

cannot get inside each other's heads to find out just how much pleasure we are getting from consuming a product!

One way round the problem is to measure marginal utility in money terms, i.e. the amount that a person would be prepared to pay for one more unit of a product. Thus if you were prepared to pay 70p for an extra packet of crisps per week, then we would say that your marginal utility from consuming it is 70p. As long as you are prepared to pay more or the same as the actual price, you will buy an extra packet. If you are not prepared to pay that price, you will not.

Consumer surplus

The demand curve shows how much consumers are prepared to pay for a given quantity of a good. Yet, quite often, we do not have to pay that full amount. For example, if a packet of crisps costs 60p, but you were prepared to pay 70p, you don't offer the shopkeeper 70p, but pay the 60p to buy the crisps. You then benefit from having 10p left in your pocket! The difference between what you were willing to pay (70p) and the price you actually paid (60p) is known as the *consumer surplus* (10p, in this case).

Marginal utility and the demand curve for a good

We can now see how marginal utility relates to a downward-sloping demand curve. As the price of a good falls, it will be worth buying extra units. You will buy more because the price will now be below the amount you are prepared to pay, i.e. price is less than your marginal utility. But as you buy more, your marginal utility from consuming each extra unit will get less and less. How many extra units do you buy? You will stop when the marginal utility has fallen to the new lower price of the good: when $MU = P$. Beyond that point it is not worth buying any more. This represents the optimal consumption point, as *rational* consumers will aim to maximise their consumer surplus. Many factors will affect an individual's utility, as is discussed in the blog from the Sloman Economics News Site: 'Peak stuff'.

Definitions

Consumer surplus The difference between how much a consumer is willing to pay for a good and how much they actually pay for it.

Rational consumer behaviour When consumers weigh up the marginal utility they expect to gain from a product they are considering purchasing against the product's price (i.e. the marginal cost to them). By buying more of a product whose marginal utility exceeds the price and buying less of a product whose price exceeds marginal utility, the consumer will maximise consumer surplus.

An individual's demand curve

Individual people's demand curves for any good are the same as their marginal utility curves for that good, measured in money.

This is demonstrated in Figure 3.2, which shows the marginal utility curve for a particular person and a particular good. The downward-sloping nature of the curve illustrates diminishing marginal utility.

If the price of the good were P_1, the person would consume Q_1: where $MU = P$. Thus point a would be one point on that person's demand curve. If the price fell to P_2, consumption would rise to Q_2, since this is where $MU = P_2$. Thus point b is a second point on the demand curve. Likewise if price fell to P_3, Q_3 would be consumed. Point c is a third point on the demand curve.

Thus, as long as individuals aim to maximise consumer surplus and so consume where $P = MU$, their demand curve will be along the same line as their marginal utility curve.

The firm's demand curve

The firm's demand curve will simply be the (horizontal) sum of all individuals' demand curves for its product.

The shape of the demand curve. The price elasticity of demand will reflect the rate at which MU diminishes. If there are close substitutes for a good, it is likely to have an elastic demand, and its MU will diminish slowly as consumption increases. The reason is that increased consumption of this product will be accompanied by decreased consumption of the alternative product(s). Since total consumption of this product plus the alternatives has increased only slightly (if at all), the marginal utility will fall only slowly.

For example, the demand for a given brand of petrol is likely to have a fairly high price elasticity, since other brands are substitutes. If there is a cut in the price of Esso petrol (assuming the prices of other brands stay constant), consumption of Esso will increase a lot. The *MU* of Esso petrol will fall slowly, since people consume less of other

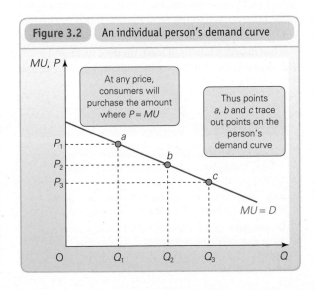

Figure 3.2 An individual person's demand curve

At any price, consumers will purchase the amount where $P = MU$

Thus points a, b and c trace out points on the person's demand curve

$MU = D$

brands. Petrol consumption *in total* may be only slightly greater and hence the *MU* of petrol only slightly lower.

Shifts in the demand curve. How do *shifts* in demand relate to marginal utility? For example, how would the marginal utility of (and hence demand for) margarine be affected by a rise in the price of butter? The higher price of butter would cause less butter to be consumed. This would increase the marginal utility of margarine, since if people are using less butter, their desire for margarine is higher. The *MU* curve (and hence the demand curve) for margarine thus shifts to the right.

The problem of imperfect information

So far we have assumed that when people buy goods and services, they know exactly what price they will pay and how much utility they will gain. In many cases this is a reasonable assumption. When you buy a bar of chocolate, you clearly do know how much you are paying for it and have a very good idea how much you will like it. But what about a television, medicine, a car, a washing machine, or any other *consumer durable*? In each of these cases you are buying something that will last you a long time and/or that you only buy occasionally; and the further into the future you look, the less certain you will be of its costs and benefits to you. The problem of imperfect information is considered in the blog, 'When it's a pain choosing the right painkiller' on the Sloman Economics News site.

Take the case of a washing machine costing you £400. If you pay cash, your immediate outlay involves no uncertainty: it is £400. But washing machines can break down. After two years you could find yourself with a repair bill of £100. This cannot be predicted and yet it is a price you will have to pay, just like the original £400. In other words, when you buy the washing machine, you are uncertain as to the full 'price' it will entail over its lifetime.

The costs of the washing machine are uncertain, but so too are the benefits. You might have been attracted to buy it by the manufacturer's glossy brochure, or by the look of it, or by adverts on TV, in magazines, etc. When you have used it for a while, however, you will probably discover things you had not anticipated. The spin dryer does not get your clothes as dry as you had hoped; it is noisy; it leaks; the door sticks; and so on. The market does work to provide information, for example through customer feedback on websites, but while this can help to reduce customer uncertainty, it will not eliminate it.

Buying consumer durables thus involves uncertainty. So too does the purchase of assets, whether a physical asset such as a house or financial assets such as shares. In the case of assets, the uncertainty is over their future *price*. If you buy shares in a currently profitable company, what will happen to their price in the future? Will they shoot up in price, thus enabling you to sell them at a large profit, or will they fall? You cannot know for certain. A lot depends on the company's future performance and what other people think that performance is likely to be.

At this point it is useful to distinguish between uncertainty and risk. *Risk* is where an outcome may or may not occur, but where the *probability* of it occurring is known. *Uncertainty* is where the probability is not known.

Insurance: a way of removing risks

Insurance is a means of eliminating, or at least reducing, risk for people. If, for example, you could lose your job if you are injured, you can remove the risk of loss of income by taking out an appropriate insurance policy. Typically, people don't like risk and so most people are willing to pay to take out insurance.

But why is it that the insurance companies are prepared to shoulder the risks that their customers were not? Do they simply love risk? Definitely not! The answer is that the insurance company is able to *spread its risks*.

The spreading of risks

If there is a one in 10 000 chance of your house burning down each year, although it is only a small chance it would be so disastrous that you are simply not prepared to take the risk. You thus take out house insurance and are prepared to pay a premium of *more than* 0.01 per cent (one ten thousandth) of the value of your house.

The insurance company, however, is not just insuring you. It is insuring many others at the same time. If your house burns down, there will be approximately 9999 others that do not. The premiums the insurance company has collected will be more than enough to cover its payments. The more houses it insures, the smaller will be the variation in the proportion that actually burn down each year.

Definitions

Consumer durable A consumer good that lasts a period of time, during which the consumer can continue gaining utility from it.

Risk This is when an outcome may or may not occur, but where the probability of its occurring is known.

Uncertainty This is when an outcome may or may not occur and where the probability of its occurring is not known.

Spreading risks (for an insurance company) The more policies an insurance company issues and the more independent the risks of claims from these policies are, the more predictable will be the number of claims.

Law of large numbers The larger the number of events of a particular type, the more predictable will be their average outcome.

This is an application of the *law of large numbers*. What is unpredictable for an individual becomes highly predictable in the mass. The more people the insurance company insures, the more predictable is the total outcome.

What is more, the insurance company will be in a position to estimate just what the risks are. It can thus work out what premiums it must charge in order to make a profit. With individuals, however, the precise risk is rarely known. Do you know your chances of living to 80? Almost certainly you do not. But a life assurance company will know precisely the chances of a person of your age, sex and occupation living to 80! It will have the statistical data for an average person to show this information. In other words, an insurance company will be able to convert your *uncertainty* into their *risk*.

The spreading of risks does not just require that there should be a large number of policies. It also requires that the risks should be *independent*. If any insurance company insured 1000 houses *all in the same neighbourhood*, and then there was a major fire in the area, the claims would be enormous. The risks of fire were not independent. The company would, in fact, have been taking a gamble on a single event. If, however, it provides fire insurance for houses scattered all over the country, the risks *are* independent.

An example of the problem presented by risks which are *not* independent is the widespread flooding in the UK in recent years, as we discuss in this blog: 'Flooding the insurance market'. In 2012 and again in 2015, the UK experienced record insurance payouts for flood and storm damage

totalling £1 billion and £1.5 billion, respectively. The total cost of flood damage in 2015 reached £5 billion. Flooding had previously caused severe damage in many parts of the country and this led to house insurance premiums increasing to cover the rapidly rising costs of flooding. The 2012 and 2015 floods affected many of the same homes, further increasing premiums; in some cases insurance companies were simply not willing to insure homeowners or were charging huge compulsory excesses. One such insurance policy had an excess of £10 000 and many homes were left underinsured. The problem is that the risks of flood damage are *dependent*: if one household in an area prone to flooding claims for flood damage, the probability of all other houses in that area also claiming is pretty high, if not certain.

Insurance companies also tend to offer a diverse range of insurance (houses, cars, travel, health, life) and this *diversification* allows the company to spread its risk: this time across many products. The more types of insurance a company offers, the greater is likely to be the independence of the risks.

Definitions

Independent risks Where two risky events are unconnected. The occurrence of one will not affect the likelihood of the occurrence of the other.

Diversification Where a firm expands into new types of business.

BOX 3.1 ROGUE TRADERS

Buyer beware!

Markets are usually an efficient way of letting buyers and sellers exchange goods and services. However, this does not stop consumers making complaints about the quality of the goods or services they receive.

It is impossible to get a true measure of customer dissatisfaction because aggrieved consumers do not always complain and data are collected by a number of separate agencies. Particular sectors though seem to be more vulnerable to 'rogue traders' than others.

There are many companies providing dispute resolution services. The complaints cover a broad range of areas, with a significant number concerning charges and the quality of service. Perhaps this is evidence that customers are not willing to be taken advantage of and are now expecting more.

Ombudsman Services, a UK organisation, exists to resolve such complaints, which tend to be most common in home maintenance/repairs/installations; doorstep selling of gas and electricity contracts; the mis-selling of PPI (payment protection insurance); and second-hand motor vehicles and vehicle repairs.

According to the Ombudsman Services 2014/15 Annual Report, it resolved 62 806 complaints throughout the year of the 215 969 initial contacts. In April 2014, it recorded a 191

per cent increase in energy complaints and in January 2015, communications complaints increased by 16 per cent compared to the same time the previous year. Of the complaints resolved by the Ombudsman, 62 per cent came to a mutually acceptable settlement, while 27 per cent required a final decision by the Ombudsman.

Consumer complaints are also of concern over cross-border sales, as the growth of buying over the Internet has blossomed in recent times (see Box 4.6, page 96). Data gathered by econsumer.gov covering 30 countries show that in the final quarter of 2015, the most complained about product/service was shop-at-home and catalogue services with 2086 complaints. This was followed by prizes/sweepstakes/lotteries and unsolicited emails with 238 and 218 complaints respectively. Other products/services in the top 10 were Internet information services, spyware, travel/vacations and romance scams. Consumers located in the USA were most likely to lodge a complaint and it is companies located in China that received the most complaints, followed by the USA and UK.

The chart shows the types of consumer complaints about e-commerce. The percentages are based on the 23 608 e-consumer law violations during 2014, not the total number of complaints; one complaint may have multiple law violations.

▶

Adverse selection and moral hazard

But why does a market, which you would think would respond to consumer wishes, give rise to consumer complaints? Why is it that rogue traders can continue in business? The answer can be found in the concepts of adverse selection and moral hazard. In both cases, the problem is essentially one of 'information asymmetries' and is an example of the 'principal–agent problem' (see pages 9–10). The buyer (the 'principal') has poorer information about the product than the agent (the 'seller').

Information asymmetries. Complaints by consumers are likely to be few if the product is fairly simple and information about the exchange process is publicly available. For example, if I buy apples from a market trader but subsequently return them because some are damaged, they are likely to exchange the apples, or offer a full refund, because failure to do so would lead to the trader's sales falling as information gets out that they sell poor-quality fruit. Here information asymmetries are minimal.

However, where the product is more complex, perhaps with consumers making large outlays, and information is more private, the situation can be very different. The greater the information 'gap' between sellers and consumers, the greater the scope for deception and fraud and the more likely are rogue traders to thrive. In these situations the number of consumer complaints increases.

Consider the sale of a conservatory, a large extension to a house usually comprising a number of various building products, including double-glazed windows and doors. A product such as this involves an expensive outlay for consumers, but they may have very limited information about the price of materials and labour, as well as the method of building a conservatory.

Assume that there is a standard-sized conservatory and that a high-quality seller would be prepared to supply this product at a price of £10 000. Such a price would reflect the quality of

their work and would keep them in the business of selling high-quality products. On the other hand, assume that a poor-quality supplier, a 'rogue trader', could provide this conservatory at £5000.

Given information asymmetry, let us assume that consumers are not aware of who is a high-quality or low-quality seller. As a result, rogue traders offer to supply a standard conservatory for, say, £9000.

Adverse selection. This price of £9000, however, is not enough to cover the costs of high-quality sellers, and so they will not want to offer their services to build high-quality conservatories. On the other hand, 'rogue traders' will find this price very profitable and it will attract a higher than normal number of such sellers into the market. Of course, if consumers know that the only sellers in the market are likely to be 'rogue traders', they will not buy conservatories and the market will collapse.

The problem just described is an example of *adverse selection*. In this case a group of sellers ('rogue traders') have been attracted to the market by prices considerably greater than their costs even before any transactions have taken place.

 Adverse selection. Where information is imperfect, high-risk/poor-quality groups will be attracted to profitable market opportunities to the disadvantage of the average buyer (or seller). **KEY IDEA 12**

Although information is imperfect, things aren't as bad as the above suggests. Consumers do try to find out about sellers before they buy and most consumers get a good product. However, 'rogue traders' also make sales. The poorer the information on the part of consumers, the more adverse will be their selection: the worse the likely quality of the products they buy.

George Akerlof published a paper in the 1970s that considered the problem of asymmetric information in the market for used cars in his paper entitled 'The Market for

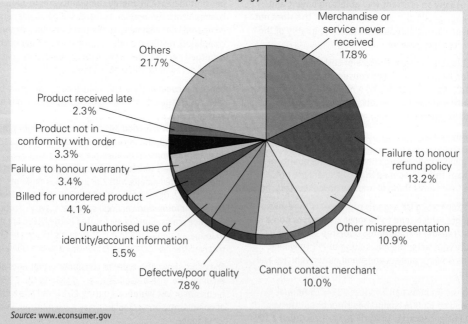
E-consumer complaints by type of product, 2014

Source: www.econsumer.gov

Lemons'.[1] In this paper, he set out the problem that asymmetric information presents to consumers. He demonstrated how it can, in extreme circumstances, lead to the total unravelling of a market, as second-hand car dealers consistently try to sell poor-quality cars (or 'lemons') as 'reliable' ones and as consumers, unable to distinguish poor-quality cars from good ones, become increasingly mistrustful.

Moral hazard. This is another problem that arises from asymmetric information. This occurs once a contract has been signed and is known as *moral hazard*. In our example, the rogue trader might initially agree to supply and install the conservatory to meet particular high standards of quality for a particular price. However, unless the buyer has full information about the construction of conservatories or can keep a constant watch over the work, defective materials or poor-quality workmanship may be supplied. But the buyer will not know this until a later date when problems start to appear with the conservatory!

Moral hazard results because the seller has acted inappropriately (immorally) and to the detriment of the buyer. The 'hazard' arises because of imperfect information on the part of the consumer. Rogue traders are tempted to supply an inferior product, believing that they can get away with it.

KEY IDEA 13 — *Moral hazard.* Following a deal, if there are information asymmetries (see page 9), it is likely that one party will engage in problematic (immoral and/or hazardous) behaviour to the detriment of the other. In other words, lack of information by one party to the deal may result in the deal not being honoured by the other party.

Usually, the process of law would work in favour of the buyer because a contract had been established, but in many cases involving rogue traders the business has been declared bankrupt or the costs to buyers of pursuing a legal case are too great.

Solutions

So how can sellers signal to buyers that they offer high-quality products? And how can consumers trust this information? A number of methods exist.

Establishing a reputation. A single firm can establish a reputation for selling high-quality goods, usually over a

number of years, or perhaps it has created a valued brand name through advertising. Alternatively, firms can offer guarantees and warranties on their products, such as Kia's seven-year guarantee. Although this guarantee, or a ten-year guarantee on the building work associated with a conservatory, is of no use if the firm has gone bankrupt!

Trade associations and other third parties. Firms can also band together collectively and establish a trade association. Examples include the Federation of Master Builders or the Association of British Travel Agents (ABTA). The trade association may provide guarantees for consumers. For example, if one firm provides a poor-quality product, then consumers may get compensation via the association. ABTA, for example, guarantees to make sure customers will complete their holiday, or obtain a refund, if they have purchased it from a member that has gone bankrupt. By encouraging consumers to purchase from member firms, both consumers and firms gain.

Trade associations are a means by which firms can demonstrate that they regulate themselves rather than have governments impose rules on them.

Sometimes third parties can help firms to signal high quality. The online auction site eBay, for example, provides a feedback system for buyers and sellers so they can register their happiness or otherwise with sales. It also provides a complaint resolution service. However, there has been much criticism of eBay's mechanisms to monitor the quality of sellers, with indications that eBay tries to protect some high-powered sellers, by making it difficult for buyers to provide negative feedback. Likewise, the Competition and Markets Authority (CMA), under the auspices of the Enterprise Act (2002), has created an Approved Codes of Practice scheme whereby trade associations and their members will guarantee that customers will receive high-quality service. Successful associations can display a CMA Approved Codes logo.

Government intervention. On the whole, recent governments have not liked to intervene in particular industries, preferring a sector to regulate itself. However, in the case of the financial services industry, the government has directly intervened because the impact of the industry on consumers in recent times has been widespread and financially devastating. Following a number of financial scandals, including the mis-selling of pensions and mortgages, the government replaced ineffective self-regulation in 2000 with the Financial Services Authority (FSA), an independent industry regulator with statutory powers, whose Board was appointed by and accountable to the Treasury. In this instance the level of product complexity and information asymmetry between buyer and seller was viewed to be too great for the industry to control itself.

However, the FSA was widely criticised for failing to do anything to curb the lending boom which led to the financial crisis in 2007 and it was abolished in April 2013. Its replacement, the Financial Conduct Authority (FCA), has greater powers. (See section 9.5 for a more general discussion of competition policy and regulation.)

1. *What are the disadvantages of trade associations?*
2. *The communications sector is one area that receives a high number of complaints. Can we use the concepts of moral hazard and adverse selection to explain why this might be the case?*

Definitions

Adverse selection Where information is imperfect, high-risk/poor-quality groups will be attracted to profitable market opportunities to the disadvantage of the average buyer (or seller).

Moral hazard Following a deal, if there are information asymmetries (see page 9), it is likely that one party will engage in problematic (immoral and/or hazardous) behaviour to the detriment of the other. In other words, lack of information by one party to the deal may result in the deal not being honoured by the other party.

[1] G. Akerlof, 'The Market for "Lemons": Quality, Uncertainty and the Market Mechanism', *Quarterly Journal of Economics* Vol. 84, No. 3. (August 1970)

BOX 3.2 PROBLEMS FOR UNWARY INSURANCE COMPANIES

'Adverse selection' and 'moral hazard'

In Box 3.1, we saw how consumers may suffer from adverse selection and from moral hazard on the part of suppliers. Adverse selection and moral hazard can also apply the other way round. Insurance companies may incur higher costs from adverse selection and moral hazard on the part of certain policyholders. These higher costs are then likely to be passed on to other policyholders.

Adverse selection

This occurs where the people taking out insurance are those who pose the highest risk.

For example, suppose that a company offers medical insurance. It surveys the population and works out that the average person requires £200 of treatment per year. The company thus sets the premium at £250 (the extra £50 to cover its costs and provide a profit). But it is probable that the people most likely to take out the insurance are those most likely to fall sick: those who have been ill before, those whose families have a history of illness, those in jobs that are hazardous to health, etc. These people on average may require £500 of treatment per year, but the insurance company doesn't know this. The insurance company would soon make a loss.

But cannot the company then simply raise premiums to £550 or £600? It can, but the problem is that it will thereby be depriving the person of *average* health of reasonably priced insurance and thus may discourage some people from taking out insurance.

The answer is for the company to discriminate more carefully between people. You may have to fill out a questionnaire so that the company can assess your own particular risk and set an appropriate premium. There may need to be legal penalties for people caught lying!

Moral hazard

This occurs where having insurance makes you less careful and thus increases your risk to the insurance company. For example, if your bicycle is insured against theft, you may be less concerned to go through the hassle of chaining it up each time you leave it.

Again, if insurance companies work out risks by looking at the *total* number of bicycle thefts, these figures will understate the risks to the company because they will include thefts from *uninsured* people who are likely to be more careful.

1. What details does an insurance company require to know before it will insure a person to drive a car?
2. How will the following reduce moral hazard?
   (a) A no-claims bonus.
   (b) Having to pay the first so much of any claim.
   (c) Offering lower premiums to those less likely to claim (e.g. lower house contents premiums for those with burglar alarms).

The problem of moral hazard occurs in many other walks of life. A good example is that of debt. If someone else is willing to pay your debts (e.g. your parents) it is likely to make you less careful in your spending! This argument has been used by some rich countries for not cancelling the debts of poor countries.

RECAP

1. Economists call consumer satisfaction 'utility'. Marginal utility diminishes as consumption increases over any given period of time.

2. People will consume more of a good as long as its marginal utility to them (measured in terms of the price they are prepared to pay for it) exceeds its price. They will stop buying additional amounts once MU has fallen to equal the price. The difference between what they are willing to pay for a product and what they actually pay for it is called the consumer surplus.

3. An individual's demand curve lies along the same line as the individual's marginal utility curve, when a consumer maximises consumer surplus. The market demand curve is the sum of all individuals' marginal utility curves.

4. When people buy consumer durables they may be uncertain of their benefits and any additional repair and maintenance costs. When they buy financial assets they may be uncertain of what will happen to their price in the future. Buying under these conditions of imperfect knowledge is therefore a form of gambling. When we take such gambles, if we know the odds we are said to be operating under conditions of *risk*. If we do not know the odds we are said to be operating under conditions of *uncertainty*.

5. Insurance is a way of eliminating risks for policyholders. In order to avoid risks, people are prepared to pay premiums in order to obtain insurance. Insurance companies are prepared to take on these risks because they can spread them over a large number of policies. According to the law of large numbers, what is unpredictable for a single policyholder becomes highly predictable for a large number of them provided that their risks are independent of each other.

3.3   BEHAVIOURAL ECONOMICS

Up to now we have assumed that consumers behave rationally – trying to get best value for money by making choices between products that will maximise their consumer surplus (see page 53). However, a moment's thought leads to examples of behaviour that do not appear 'rational'. For example, have you ever bought something simply because a lot of other people were buying it? The answer is probably 'yes'! 'Behavioural economics' relaxes the rationality assumption and looks at the way people *actually* behave.

Behavioural economics recognises that people are subject to emotions and impulses, which can result in 'errors' and biases in their decision making. By understanding how people actually behave, firms can target their marketing strategies to influence this behaviour. Irrational shopping is discussed in the blog, 'Are impulses irrational?', on the Sloman Economics News site.[1]

Explaining 'irrational' consumer choices

How options are framed

The choices people make are influenced by the context in which they are made; people will often make different choices when they are presented, or framed, in different ways. For example, people will buy more of a good when it is flagged up as a special offer than they do if there is no mention of an offer, even though the price is the same. This principle has led to the development of 'nudge' theory, which underpins many marketing techniques. We look at it in more detail in Box 3.3 (page 61).

Too much choice

Choice is generally thought to be a good thing. But can we have too much choice? Choice should allow us to maximise our utility by making 'better' decisions. Yet this does not always seem to be the case. Experiments have been conducted which appear to show that, in certain circumstances, consumers are more likely to buy when presented with less choice. Too much choice can be confusing and hinder decision making, thereby reducing consumers' utility.

Bounded rationality

A person might want to maximise consumer surplus, but faces complex choices and imperfect information. Sometimes it *would* be possible to obtain better information, but the individual decides it is not worth the time and effort, and perhaps expense, of getting more information.

People's ability to be 'rational' is thus limited or *bounded* by the situation in which they find themselves. So they may resort to making the best guess, or to drawing on past experiences of similar choices that turned out to be good or bad. It is important for firms to understand the different assumptions people make and their different responses in situations of bounded rationality.

This use of past experience, or rules of thumb or trial and error, is known as *heuristics*. The decision is not guaranteed to be optimal, but it might be the best bet given the limited information or time available.

Pause For Thought

Why might different people respond differently from each other in otherwise similar circumstances?

Relativity matters

If I am making a choice about buying a car, traditional economics says my demand will derive from a number of factors: my income; my tastes for driving and for particular cars; the prices of the car I am considering and of the alternatives; and the associated costs of motoring. Yet I might also be highly influenced by the car my sister drives; if she chooses an Audi, perhaps I would like a more expensive car – a Mercedes possibly. If she switches to a Jaguar, then perhaps I will opt for a Porsche. I want a better (or faster or more expensive) car than my sister; I am concerned not only with my choice of car but with my *relative* choice.

This does not disprove that our choices depend on our perceived utility. But it does demonstrate that our satisfaction often depends on our consumption *relative* to that of other people, such as our peers. This is something that the advertising industry is only too well aware of. Adverts often try to encourage you to buy a product by showing that *other* people are buying it.

Definitions

Bounded rationality When the ability to make rational decisions is limited by lack of information or the time necessary to obtain such information.

Heuristics People's use of strategies that draw on simple lessons from past experience when they are faced with similar, although not identical, choices.

---

[1] See also, Neil Ranadé, 'Behavioural Economics – why the way you shop is irrational', CapacityGrid (29 May 2013).

Herding and 'groupthink'

Being influenced by what other people buy, and thus making relative choices, can lead to herd behaviour. A fashion might catch on; people might grab an item in a sale because other people seem to be grabbing it as well; people might buy a particular share on the stock market because other people are buying it.

Now part of this may simply be bounded rationality. Sometimes it may be a good rule of thumb to buy something that other people want, as they might know more about it than you do. But there is a danger in such behaviour: other people may also be buying it because other people are buying it, and this builds momentum. Sales may soar and the price may be driven well above a level that reflects the utility that people will end up gaining.

Sunk costs

When buying products, 'rational' consumers will weigh up the *additional* benefits and costs of their purchases (i.e. the utility gained against the money spent on the products). This must imply that costs already incurred in the past are irrelevant. These are called sunk costs. Yet when we look at how people actually behave, they do seem to be influenced by sunk costs.

Take the case of a person who spends a lot on a car, which subsequently turns out to be unreliable and requires a lot spending on it to keep it on the road. The rational person would ask whether the large amount spent on repairs and maintenance is worth it and whether it would be better to sell it and buy a new car. But many people would decide not to sell it as they had paid a lot in the first place (a sunk cost) and would rather spend money keeping it on the road.

The point is, if consumers were behaving rationally, they would ignore these sunk costs. They cannot be recouped. Yet many people do behave as if they were *continuing* to pay these costs.

When emotions take over

In many cases, the experience of the emotion of desire when contemplating buying something, such as a bar of chocolate, is merely an aid to rational behaviour. You imagine the pleasure you will receive, something that is borne out when you do actually eat the chocolate. Similarly, the emotion of displeasure at the thought of paying for the product helps you to be cautious and think of the opportunity cost of buying the product: what will you have to sacrifice?

Sometimes, however, the emotion is misplaced. People may be lured by the packaging and the pleasure they imagine they will gain, rather than the pleasure they actually will gain. Advertisers know this well! To them, perceived pleasure at the time of purchase is more important than actual pleasure at the time of consumption.

Research suggests that consumers can be 'nudged' into changing their behaviour by some rather simple tactics (see Box 3.3). Product placement can be highly influential in encouraging consumers to buy something spontaneously that they otherwise would not have bought. When you go to the checkout in a supermarket, chocolate bars, crisps and other unhealthy products are prominently displayed and many shoppers will simply pick one up without weighing up the marginal costs and benefits. Perhaps this is something that could be used to encourage consumers to eat healthier products, by displaying fruit at the checkouts! Some supermarkets are beginning to make this change, but it is not universal.

In another departure from rationality, people may downplay the costs of a purchase. Research into the brain activity of consumers by George Loewenstein, an economist at Carnegie Mellon University in Pittsburgh suggests that 'rather than weighing the present good against future alternatives, as orthodox economics suggests happens, people actually balance the immediate pleasure of the prospective possession of a product with the immediate pain of paying for it'.[2]

This has profound implications for buying on credit. The abstract nature of credit cards and the fact that payment is deferred until some later date means that many people downplay the costs of the items they buy. No wonder many shops like to offer credit. Not only does it encourage people to buy things now rather than waiting, it may encourage them to buy things they would never otherwise have bought – either now or later!

Relevance to economic policy

Governments, in designing policy, will normally attempt to change people's behaviour – both consumers and producers. They might want to encourage people to choose to work harder, to save more, to recycle rubbish, to use their cars less, to eat more healthily, and so on. If the policy is to be successful, it is vital for the policy measures to contain appropriate incentives: whether it be a tax rise, a grant or subsidy, a new law or regulation, an advertising campaign or direct help.

But whether the incentives are appropriate depends on how people will respond to them, and to know that, the policy makers will need to understand people's behaviour. This is where behavioural economics comes in. People might respond as rational maximisers; but they may not. It is thus important to understand how context affects behaviour and adjust policy incentives appropriately.

---

[2] Quoted in 'The triumph of unreason', *The Economist* (11 January 2007).

| BOX 3.3 | NUDGING PEOPLE |

How to change behaviour

One observation of behavioural economics is that people make many decisions out of habit. They use simple rules, such as: 'I'll buy the more expensive item because it's bound to be better'; or 'I'll buy this item because it's on offer'; or 'I'm happy with Brand X, so why should I change brands?'; or 'Other people are buying this, so it must be worth having'.

Given that people behave like this, how might they be persuaded to change their behaviour? Governments might want to know this. What policies will encourage people to stop smoking, or save energy, or take more exercise or eat more healthy food? Firms too will want to know how to sell more of their products or to motivate their workforce.

According to Richard Thaler and Cass Sunstein,[1] people can be 'nudged' to change their behaviour. For example, healthy food can be placed in a prominent position in a supermarket or healthy snacks at the checkout. Often it is the junk foods that are displayed prominently and unhealthy, but tasty, snacks are found by the checkout. If fashion houses ceased to use ultra-thin models, it could reduce the incentive for many girls to under-eat. If kids at school are given stars or smiley faces for turning off lights or picking up litter, they might be more inclined to do so.

Another example concerns 'opting in' versus 'opting out'. With organ donor cards, or many company pension schemes or charitable giving, people have to opt in. In other words, they have to make the decision to take part. Many as a result do not, partly because they never seem to find the time to do so, even though they might quite like to. With the busy lives people lead, it's too easy to think, 'Yes, I'll do that some time', but never actually get round to doing it.

With an 'opt-out' system, people are automatically signed up to the scheme, but can freely choose to opt out. Thus it would be assumed that organs from people killed in an accident who had not opted out could be used for transplants. If you did not want your organs to be used, you would have to join a register. It could be the same with charitable giving. Some firms add a small charitable contribution to the price of their products (e.g. airline tickets or utility bills), unless people opt out. Similarly, firms could automatically deduct pension contributions from employees' wages unless they opted out of the scheme.

> Opt-in schemes have participation rates of around 60 per cent, while otherwise identical opt-out funds retain between 90 and 95 per cent of employees. It is no wonder that Adair Turner, in his report on pensions, urged legislation to push pension schemes to an opt-out default position and that policy is moving in this direction.[2]

Understanding people's behaviour and then adjusting incentives, often only very slightly, can nudge people to behave differently. Politicians are increasingly looking at ways of nudging people to behave in ways that they perceive as better, whether socially, environmentally or simply personally.

In the UK, the Coalition government formed in 2010 set up a dedicated 'nudge' unit, officially known as the Behavioural Insights Team, for this purpose. Subsequently, it became independent of the UK government, operating as a social purpose company to help organisations to apply behavioural insights in support of 'social purpose goals'.

Some examples of the way the team has influenced policy certainly appear impressive. A trial with HMRC was carried out, informing people who failed to pay their tax that most other people had already paid. This increased payment rates by over 5 percentage points!

1. How would you nudge members of a student household to be more economical in the use of electricity?
2. How could the government nudge people to stop dropping litter?
3. In the 2011 UK Budget, George Osborne announced that charitable giving in wills would be exempt from inheritance tax. Do you think this will be an effective way of encouraging more charitable donations?

[1] Richard H. Thaler and Cass R. Sunstein, *Nudge: Improving Decisions about Health, Wealth, and Happiness* (Yale University Press, 2008).

[2] Richard Reeves, 'Why a nudge from the state beats a slap', *Observer* (20 July 2008).

RECAP

1. Traditional economics is based on the premise that consumers act rationally, weighing up the costs and benefits of the choices open to them. Behavioural economics acknowledges that real-world decisions do not always appear rational; it seeks to understand and explain what economic agents actually do.

2. A number of effects can explain why rational decision making may fail to predict actual behaviour. These include: the roles of framing and relativity; individuals failing to disregard sunk costs and being confused by too many choices. Research undertaken by behavioural economists is bringing together aspects of psychology and economics, in order to understand fully how we behave.

3.4 ESTIMATING AND PREDICTING DEMAND

If a business is to be successful, it must have a good understanding of its market. How might a business set about discovering the wants of consumers and hence the intensity of demand? The more effectively a business can identify such wants, the more likely it is to increase its sales and be successful. The clearer idea it can gain of the rate at which the typical consumer's utility will decline as consumption increases, the better estimate it can make of the product's price elasticity. Also, the more it can assess the relative utility to the consumer of its product compared with those of its rivals, the more effectively it will be able to compete by differentiating its product from theirs.

In this section we first examine methods for gathering data on consumer behaviour and then see how firms set about forecasting changes in demand over time.

Methods of collecting data on consumer behaviour

There are three general approaches to gathering information about consumers. These are: *observations of market behaviour*, *market surveys* and *market experiments*.

Market observations

The firm can gather data on how demand for its product has changed over time. Virtually all firms will have detailed information on their sales broken down by week, month, year, etc. They will also tend to have information on how sales have varied from one part of the market to another.

In addition, the firm will need to obtain data on how the various determinants of demand (such as price, advertising and the price of competitors' products) have themselves changed over time. Firms are likely to have much of this information already, e.g. the amount spent on advertising and the prices of competitors' products. Other information might be relatively easy to obtain by paying an agency to do the research.

Having obtained this information, the firm can then use it to estimate how changes in the various determinants have affected demand in the past, and hence what effect they will be likely to have in the future.

Even the most sophisticated analysis based on market observations, however, will suffer from one major drawback. Relationships that held in the past will not necessarily hold in the future. Consumers are human, and humans change their minds. Their perceptions of products change (something that the advertising industry relies on!), tastes change and technology changes. It is for this reason that many firms turn to market surveys or market experiments to gather more information about the future.

Market surveys

It is not uncommon to be stopped in a city centre, or to have a knock at the door, a postal questionnaire or a phone call, and be asked whether you would kindly answer the questions of some market researcher. A vast quantity of information can be collected in this way. It is a relatively quick and cheap method of data collection. Questions concerning all aspects of consumer behaviour might be asked, such as those relating to present and future patterns of expenditure, or how people might respond to changing product specifications or price, both of the firm in question and of its rivals.

A key feature of the market survey is that it can be targeted at distinct consumer groups, thereby reflecting the specific information requirements of a business. For example, businesses selling luxury goods will be interested only in consumers falling within higher income brackets. Other samples might be drawn from a particular age group or gender, or from those with a particular lifestyle, such as eating habits.

The major drawback with this technique concerns the accuracy of the information acquired. Accurate information requires various conditions to be met.

A random sample. If the sample is not randomly selected, it may fail to represent a cross-section of the population being surveyed and so the results may be biased.

Clarity of the questions. It is important for the questions to be phrased in an unambiguous way, so as not to mislead the respondent.

Avoidance of leading questions. It is very easy for the respondent to be led into giving the answer the firm wants to hear. For example, when asking whether the person would buy a new product that the firm is thinking of launching, the questionnaire might make the product sound really desirable. The respondents might, as a result, say that they would buy the product, but later, when they see the product in the shops, decide they do not want it.

Truthful response. It is very tempting for respondents who are 'keen to please' to give the answer that they think the

Definitions

Observations of market behaviour Information gathered about consumers from the day-to-day activities of the business within the market.

Market surveys Information gathered about consumers, usually via a questionnaire, that attempts to enhance the business's understanding of consumer behaviour.

Market experiments Information gathered about consumers under artificial or simulated conditions. A method used widely in assessing the effects of advertising on consumers.

questioner wants, or for other somewhat reluctant respondents to give 'mischievous' answers. In other words, people may lie!

Stability of demand. By the time the product is launched, or the changes to an existing product are made, time will have elapsed. The information may then be out of date. Consumer demand may have changed, as tastes, fashions and technology have shifted, or as a result of the actions of competitors.

Market experiments

Rather than asking consumers questions and getting them to *imagine* how they *would* behave, the market experiment involves observing consumer *behaviour* under simulated conditions. It can be used to observe consumer reactions to a new product or to changes in an existing product and so this method is particularly useful when information is scarce.

A simple experiment might involve consumers being asked to conduct a blind taste test for a new brand of toothpaste. The experimenter will ensure that the same amount of paste is applied to the brush, and that the subjects swill their mouths prior to tasting a further brand. Once the experiment is over, the 'consumers' are quizzed about their perceptions of the product.

More sophisticated experiments could be conducted. For example, a *laboratory shop* might be set up to simulate a real shopping experience. People could be given a certain amount of money to spend in the 'shop' and their reactions to changes in prices, packaging, display, etc. could be monitored.

The major drawback with such 'laboratories' is that consumers might behave differently because they are being observed. For example, they might spend more time comparing prices than they would otherwise, simply because they think that this is what a *good*, rational consumer should do. With real shopping, however, it might simply be habit, or something 'irrational' such as the colour of the packaging, that determines which product they select. If you are in a rush, you may simply grab the first brand of orange juice you find, irrespective of its price (see Box 3.3).

> #### Pause for thought
>
> *Identify some other drawbacks in using market experiments to gather data on consumer behaviour.*

Another type of market experiment involves confining a marketing campaign to a particular town or region. The campaign could involve advertising, or giving out free samples, or discounting the price, or introducing an improved version of the product, but each confined to that particular locality. Sales in that area are then compared with sales in other areas in order to assess the effectiveness of the various campaigns.

Forecasting demand

Businesses are not just interested in knowing the current strength of demand for their products and how demand is likely to be affected by changes in its determinants, such as product specifications and the price of competitors' products. They are also interested in trying to predict *future* demand. After all, if demand is going to increase, they may well want to invest *now* so that they have the extra capacity to meet the extra demand. But it will be a costly mistake to invest in extra capacity if demand is not going to increase.

We now, therefore, turn to examine some of the forecasting techniques used by business.

Simple time-series analysis

Simple time-series analysis involves directly projecting from past sales data into the future. Thus if it is observed that sales of a firm's product have been growing steadily by 3 per cent per annum for the past few years, the firm can use this to predict that sales will continue to grow at approximately the same rate in the future. Similarly, if it is observed that there are clear seasonal fluctuations in demand, as in the case of holidays, ice cream or winter coats, then again it can be assumed that fluctuations of a similar magnitude will continue into the future.

Using simple time-series analysis assumes that demand in the future will continue to behave in the same way as in the past. The problem is that it may not. Just because demand has followed a clear pattern in the past does not necessarily mean that it will continue to exhibit the same pattern in the future. After all, the determinants of demand may have changed: consumers do change their minds! Successful forecasting, therefore, will usually involve a more sophisticated analysis of trends.

The decomposition of time paths

One way in which the analysis of past data can be made more sophisticated is to identify different elements in the time path of sales. Figure 3.3 illustrates one such time path, the (imaginary) sales of woollen jumpers by firm X. It is shown by the continuous green line, labelled 'Actual sales'. Four different sets of factors normally determine the shape of a time path like this.

Trends. These are increases or decreases in demand over a number of years. In our example, there is a long-term decrease in demand for this firm's woollen jumpers up to year seven and then a recovery in demand thereafter.

Trends may reflect factors such as changes in population structure, or technological innovation or longer-term changes in fashion. Thus if wool were to become more expensive over time compared with other fibres, or if there were a gradual shift in tastes away from woollen jumpers and towards acrylic or cotton jumpers, or towards sweatshirts, this could explain the long-term decline in demand up to year seven. A gradual shift in tastes back towards natural fibres, and to wool in particular, or a gradual reduction in

Figure 3.3 (Imaginary) sales of woollen jumpers

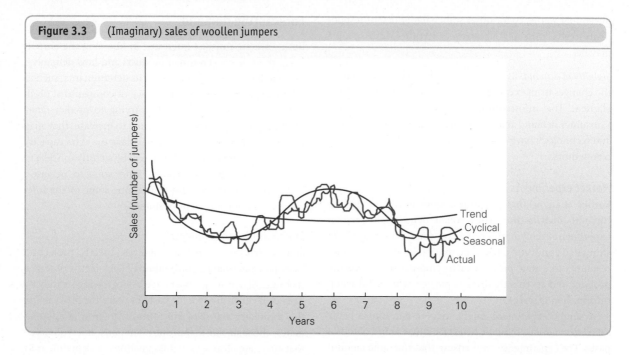

the price of wool, could then explain the subsequent recovery in demand.

Alternatively, trends may reflect changes over time in the structure of an industry. For example, an industry might become more and more competitive, with new firms joining. This would tend to reduce sales for existing firms (unless the market was expanding very rapidly).

Cyclical fluctuations. In practice, the level of actual sales will not follow the trend line precisely. One reason for this is the cyclical upswings and downswings in business activity in the economy as a whole. In some years incomes are rising rapidly and thus demand is buoyant. In other years, the economy will be in recession, with incomes falling. In these years, demand may well also fall. In our example, in boom years people may spend much more on clothes (including woollen jumpers), whereas in a recession, people may make do with their old clothes. The cyclical variations line is thus above the trend line in boom years and falls below the trend line during a recession.

Seasonal fluctuations. The demand for many products also depends on the time of year. In the case of woollen jumpers, the peak demand is likely to be as winter approaches or just before Christmas. Thus the seasonal variations line is above the cyclical variations line in winter and below it in summer.

Short-term shifts in demand or supply. Finally, the actual sales line will also reflect various short-term shifts in demand or supply, causing it to diverge from the smooth seasonal variations line.

There are many reasons why the demand curve might shift. A competitor might increase its price, or there may be a sudden change in fashion, caused, say, by a pop group

deciding to wear woollen jumpers for their new video: what was once seen as unfashionable by many people now suddenly becomes fashionable! Alternatively, there may be an unusually cold or hot, or wet or dry spell of weather. This was the case in January 2010, where UK shoppers were prompted to buy scarves, boots and coats as a result of the extremely cold weather.

Likewise there are various reasons for sudden shifts in supply conditions. For example, there may be a sheep disease which ruins the wool of infected sheep. As a result, the price of wool goes up, and sales of woollen jumpers fall.

These sudden shifts in demand or supply conditions are often referred to as 'random shocks' because they are usually unpredictable and temporarily move sales away from the trend. (Note that *long-term* shifts in demand and supply will be shown by a change in the trend line itself.)

Even with sophisticated time-series analysis, which breaks time paths into their constituent elements, there is still one major weakness: time-series analysis is merely a projection of the *past*. Most businesses will want to anticipate *changes* to sales trends – to forecast any deviations from the current time path. One method for doing this is *barometric forecasting*.

Barometric forecasting

Assume that you are a manager of a furniture business and are wondering whether to invest in new capital equipment. You would only want to do this if the demand for your product was likely to rise. You will probably, therefore, look for some indication of this. A good barometer of future demand for furniture would be the number of new houses being built. People will tend to buy new furniture some months after the building of their new house has commenced.

Barometric forecasting involves the use of *leading indicators*, such as housing starts, when attempting to predict the future. In fact some leading indicators, such as increased activity in the construction industry, rises in Stock Exchange prices, a rise in the rate of exchange and a rise in industrial confidence, are good indicators of a general upturn in the economy. In other words, firms use these indicators to predict what is likely to happen to their own demand.

Barometric forecasting suffers from two major weaknesses. The first is that it only allows forecasting a few months ahead –

as far ahead as is the time lag between the change in the leading indicator and the variable being forecast. The second is that it can give only a general indication of changes in demand. It is simply another form of time-series analysis. Just because a relationship existed in the past between a leading indicator and the variable being forecast, it cannot be assumed that exactly the same relationship will exist in the future.

Normally, firms use barometric forecasting merely to give them a rough guide as to the likely changes in demand for their product, i.e. whether it is likely to expand or contract, and by how much. Nevertheless, information on leading indicators is readily available in government or trade statistics.

Definitions

Barometric forecasting A technique used to predict future economic trends based upon analysing patterns of time-series data.

Leading indicators Indicators that help predict future trends in the economy.

Pause for thought

What might be a good leading indicator of the demand for a particular brand of printer ink?

RECAP

1. Businesses seek information on consumer behaviour so as to predict market trends and improve strategic decision making.

2. One source of data is the firm's own information on how its sales have varied in the past with changes in the various determinants of demand, such as consumer incomes and the prices of competitors' products.

3. Another source of data is market surveys. These can generate a large quantity of cheap information. Care should be taken, however, to ensure that the sample of consumers investigated reflects the target consumer group.

4. Market experiments involve investigating consumer behaviour within a controlled environment. This method is particularly useful when considering new products where information is scarce.

5. It is not enough to know what will happen to demand if a determinant changes. Businesses will want to forecast what will actually happen to demand.

6. Time-series analysis bases future trends on past events. Time-series data can be decomposed into different elements: trends, seasonal fluctuations, cyclical fluctuations and random shocks.

7. Barometric forecasting involves making predictions based upon changes in key leading indicators.

3.5 STIMULATING DEMAND

For most firms, selling their product is not simply a question of estimating demand and then choosing an appropriate price and level of production. In other words, they do not simply take their market as given. Instead they will seek to *increase* demand. They will do this by developing their product and differentiating it from those of their rivals, and then marketing it by advertising and other forms of product promotion. This will make their product more price inelastic.

What firms are engaging in here is *non-price competition*. In such situations the job of the manager can be quite complex, involving strategic decisions about product design and quality, product promotion and the provision of various forms of after-sales service.

Product differentiation

Central to non-price competition is *product differentiation*. Most firms' products differ in various ways from those of their rivals. Take the case of washing machines. Although

all washing machines wash clothes, and as such are close substitutes for each other, there are many differences between brands. They differ in price, in their capacity, their styling, their range of programmes, their economy in the use of electricity, hot water and detergent, their reliability, their noise, their after-sales service, etc.

Definitions

Non-price competition Competition in terms of product promotion (advertising, packaging, etc.) or product development.

Product differentiation Where a firm's product is in some way distinct from its rivals' products. In the context of growth strategies, this is where a business upgrades existing products or services so as to make them different from those of rival firms.

Firms attempt to design their product so that they can emphasise its advantages (real or imaginary) over the competitor brands. By doing this, a firm is advertising its product's unique selling point (USP): what it is that makes the product different from competitors' products. Just think of the specific features of particular models of car, tablet computers or brands of cosmetic, and then consider the ways in which these features are stressed by advertisements. In fact, think of virtually any advertisement and consider how it stresses the features of that particular brand. It doesn't even have to be a high-tech product: look at men's razors. This is a product that undergoes constant innovation, whereby each competitor aims to advertise any new feature that differentiates their product from those of its rivals.

Features of a product

A product has many dimensions, and a strategy to differentiate a product may focus on one or more of these. Dimensions include:

- *Technical standards.* These relate to the product's level of technical sophistication: how advanced it is in relation to the current state of technology. This would be a very important product dimension if, for example, you were purchasing a laptop or tablet.
- *Quality standards.* These relate to aspects such as the quality of the materials used in the product's construction and the care taken in assembly. These will affect the product's durability and reliability. The purchase of consumer durables, such as televisions, furniture and toys, will be strongly influenced by quality standards.
- *Design characteristics.* These relate to the product's direct appeal to the consumer in terms of appearance or operating features. Examples of design characteristics are colour, style and even packaging. The demand for fashion products such as clothing will be strongly influenced by design characteristics.
- *Service characteristics.* This aspect is not directly concerned with the product itself, but with the support given to the customer after the product has been purchased. Servicing, product maintenance and guarantees would be included under this heading. When purchasing a new car, the quality of after-sales service might strongly influence the choice you make.

Market segmentation

Different features of a product will appeal to different consumers. Where features are quite distinct, and where particular features or groups of features can be seen to appeal to a particular category of consumers, it might be useful for producers to divide the market into segments. Taking the example of cars again, the market could be divided into luxury cars, large, medium and small family cars, sports cars, multi-terrain vehicles, seven-seater people carriers, etc. Each type of car occupies a distinct market segment and each segment will have cars that are of a different quality and that cater to differing tastes.

When consumer tastes change over time, or where existing models do not cater for every taste, a firm may be able to identify a new segment of the market – a *market niche*. Having identified the appropriate market niche for its product, the marketing division within the firm will then set about targeting the relevant consumer group(s) and developing an appropriate strategy for promoting the product.

Marketing the product

There is no universally accepted definition of marketing, but it is generally agreed that it covers the following activities: establishing the strength of consumer demand in existing parts of the market, and potential demand in new niches; developing an attractive and distinct image for the product; informing potential consumers of various features of the product; fostering a desire by consumers for the product; and, in the light of all these, persuading consumers to buy the product.

Product/market strategy

Once the nature and strength of consumer demand (both current and potential) have been identified, the business will set about meeting and influencing this demand. In most cases it will be hoping to achieve a growth in sales. To do this, one of the first things the firm must decide is its *product/market strategy*. This will involve addressing two major questions:

- Should it focus on promoting its existing product, or should it develop new products?
- Should it focus on gaining a bigger share of its existing market, or should it seek to break into new markets?

These choices can be shown in a *growth vector matrix*. This is illustrated in Figure 3.4. The four cells show the possible combinations of answers to the above questions: cell A – *market penetration* (current product, current market); cell B – *product development* (new product, current market); cell C – *market development* (current product, new market); cell D – *diversification* (new product, new market).

Market penetration. In the market penetration strategy, the business will seek not only to retain existing customers, but to expand its customer base with current products in current markets. Of the four strategies, this is generally the least risky: the business will be able to play to its product's strengths and draw on its knowledge of the market. The business's marketing strategy will tend to focus upon aggressive product promotion and distribution. Such a strategy, however, is likely to lead to fierce competition from existing business rivals, especially if the overall market is not

---

> ### Definitions
>
> **Market niche** A part of a market (or new market) that has not been filled by an existing brand or business.
>
> **Growth vector matrix** A means by which a business might assess its product/market strategy.

Figure 3.4	Growth vector components

Product

	Current	New
Current	**A** Market penetration	**B** Product development
New	**C** Market development	**D** Diversification

Market

expanding and if the firm can therefore gain an increase in sales only by taking market share from its rivals.

Product development. Product development strategies will involve introducing new models and designs in current markets. It could include the introduction of an upgrade or a completely new model. This strategy may be adopted in fast-moving markets where competitors frequently launch new products.

Market development. With a market development strategy the business will seek increased sales of current products by expanding into new markets. These may be in a different geographical location (e.g. overseas), or new market segments. Alternatively, the strategy may involve finding new uses and applications for the product. Such a strategy is likely if the current market has become saturated and hence sales are beginning to slow.

Diversification. A diversification strategy will involve the business expanding into new markets with new products. This strategy can prove to be highly profitable, but of all the strategies, this is the most risky given the unknown factors that the business is likely to face.

Pause for thought

What unknown factors is the business likely to face following a diversification strategy?

Once the product/market strategy has been decided upon, the business will then attempt to devise a suitable *marketing strategy*. This will involve looking at the marketing mix.

The marketing mix

In order to differentiate the firm's product from those of its rivals, there are four variables that can be adjusted. These are as follows:

- product;
- price;

- place (distribution);
- promotion.

The particular combination of these variables, known as 'the four Ps', represents the business's *marketing mix*, and it is around a manipulation of them that the business will devise its marketing strategy.

Product considerations. These involve issues such as quality and reliability, as well as branding, packaging and after-sales service.

Pricing considerations. These involve not only the product's basic price in relation to those of competitors' products, but also opportunities for practising price discrimination (the practice of charging different prices in different parts of the market; see section 5.6), offering discounts to particular customers, and adjusting the terms of payment for the product.

Place considerations. These focus on the product's distribution network, and involve issues such as where the business's retail outlets should be located, what warehouse facilities the business might require, and how the product should be transported to the market.

Promotion considerations. These focus primarily upon the amount and type of advertising the business should use. In addition, promotion issues might also include selling techniques, special offers, trial discounts and various other public relations 'gimmicks'.

Every product is likely to have a distinct marketing *mix* of these four variables. Thus we cannot talk about an ideal value for one (e.g. the best price) without considering the other three. What is more, the most appropriate mix will vary from product to product and from market to market.

What the firm must seek to do is to estimate how sensitive demand is to the various aspects of marketing. The greater the sensitivity (elasticity) in each case, the more the firms should focus on that particular aspect. It is important for a firm to make sure that the four Ps do not come into conflict with each other, which is possible when one element of the marketing mix is adjusted.

Pause for thought

Give an example of how changing one of the four Ps might conflict with another of them.

Definition

Marketing mix The mix of product, price, place (distribution) and promotion that will determine a business' marketing strategy.

BOX 3.4 BRANDS AND OWN BRANDS

What's in a name?

Supermarkets have been involved in price wars for many years (as we discuss in Box 5.3, page 115), but here we focus on one particular aspect of this competitive industry: the battle of the Own-brands labels. If you walk into a supermarket, you will be faced with shelves stacked full of well-known brands, such as Heinz and Kellogg's. However, you will also see a variety of own-brand items, be it Tesco 'Finest' or Sainsbury's 'Taste the Difference', or a whole host of own-label brands in Aldi or Lidl.

Prior to the 1990s, supermarket sales were dominated by well-known brands, with the profits of companies such as Kellogg's and Heinz increasing by as much as 15 per cent per year. Own brands accounted for only around one quarter of sales.

Branded products are produced in large volumes and this enabled economies of scale to be exploited, giving the big brands a cost advantage over own brands. However, with the development of new technologies and closer working relationships between retailers and suppliers, own-brand manufacturers became able to produce smaller batches at lower costs while saving on marketing and distribution costs.

> Own-label products also lay claim to cost advantages, both on marketing and distribution – a few dedicated trucks from factory to retailer regional distribution centre are nothing compared with the cost of a fleet serving every retailer, wholesaler, and convenience shop.

> This means all the paraphernalia of advertising, distribution, and new product development that made the brand manufacturing model so powerful decades ago is unravelling, and becoming an enormous cost burden instead – a burden that adds up to 50 per cent on to the final consumer price and allows retailers to undercut brands while creaming off higher margins. The virtuous cycle goes into reverse, and becomes a vicious circle.[1]

The early 1990s saw the market share of own brands soar, helped by a rise in their quality. By the mid-1990s, they accounted for 54.5 per cent of supermarket sales. Yet this majority share did not last and during the boom years of the late 1990s and early 2000s, the market share of these 'own brands' began to decline.

However, with the onset of the financial crisis in 2008 and falling consumer incomes, this trend reversed, with many consumers opting for the cheaper own-brand alternatives. Research by Mintel found that the market for own-brand food and drink increased by 24 per cent between 2006 and 2011 and sales of own-brand food and drink alone have increased from £40.6 billion in 2009 to £48.3 billion in 2014, with further rises expected.[2]

One thing we can identify from past trends in own-brand sales is how they tended to fluctuate with the state of the economy and hence consumer incomes. During periods of recession consumers became more price conscious and looked for cheaper substitutes, while in booms the popularity of brands revived as consumers become more concerned about quality.

A question of quality

With technological advance and increased investment by supermarkets, we have also seen improvements in the quality of own brands, such that they are no longer seen just as the cheap substitute, but now as a feasible alternative to the more expensive brands during both recessions and booms. In 2014, the Nielsen Global Survey of Private Label found that 71 per cent of respondents thought the quality of own-brand products had improved.[3] Nielsen's UK Head of Retailer and Business Insight, Mike Watkins said:

> The perception of own-label products has improved dramatically in recent years. As with manufacturer brands, retailers have, over time, successfully built equity into their own-brand products by investing in product innovation, further developing ranges and increasing marketing activity.[4]

In the UK, throughout 2015, Aldi led the way in promoting its own brands as a cheaper but equally tasty version of the premium brands. Through its TV advertising campaigns, we saw numerous blind taste tests being conducted and consumers shown to be selecting Aldi's brand as the expensive premium brand, due to its better taste.

As the quality of own brands has improved, so consumer perceptions have changed.

> More shoppers than ever are choosing own brands from supermarket shelves over name brands, with own labels accounting for 54 per cent of UK supermarket sales, according to research from Nielsen.

---

[1] Alan Mitchell, 'Own-label steamroller rumbles on', *Marketing Week* (6 December 1996).
[2] Mintel Press Release, 'Own label food and drink NPD overtook branded for the first time in 2011 (54–46%)' (May 2012).

[3] 'Global perceptions about store brands improve, but share of basket varies by country', *Nielsen Global Survey of Private Label* (18 November 2014).
[4] Ibid.

The research group's data found that 71 per cent of UK consumers think that the quality of own brands has improved, while 50 per cent said they would buy more if greater variety was on offer.

The research is potentially bad news for brand owners, with 60 per cent of shoppers saying the quality of most own-label brands is as good as that of name brands, nearly double the proportion of consumers who thought that four years ago.

Over two-fifths (42%) reckoned that some own-label brands were better quality than name brands and only 26 per cent thought that own brands were not suitable when quality was a consideration.

The total own-label sales in the UK is nearly three times that of the global average.[5]

However, there are still significant numbers of consumers who do not see own-brand products as suitable quality substitutes. Mintel found that branded goods are seen as being more trustworthy, authentic and traditional than their own-brand equivalents. For some, own brands are still seen as being for those on a budget and it is own brands that have seen the most intense price competition between the supermarkets.

Given the trends in the brand versus own-brand competition, we might be expecting to see a revival of the brands if the economy strengthens. But if economic uncertainty remains and supermarkets continue their investment in their own-brand quality, then these items might continue with their upward trajectory, being seen by many as offering value for money. The key to success for the supermarkets might then lie in whose own brand is best.

Waitrose was awarded the Which? 'Best Buy' for its own-brand goods (as we saw in Box 1.1), but opinions are wide-ranging when it comes to which supermarket brand is best. The book and website Supermarket Own Brand Guide has proven successful, offering consumers a chance to view comparisons on all of the own-brand products, suggesting that despite slightly happier economic times, consumers remain price conscious and are always on the look-out for a bargain.

Diversification

With the emergence of own-brand products, manufacturers of brands have focused on the high-quality nature of their products, but as we have seen, quality improvements in own-brand items has had an effect on the quality differential.

Another way in which brand manufacturers were able to maintain their success was to extend their brand to new products and, in doing so, use the brand image to promote them. This not only generated revenue, but also reduced the producer's reliance on a single product. Take the case of Virgin. The brand originally applied to record stores, but it now embraces airlines, trains, finance, soft drinks, mobile phones, holidays, bridal wear, cinemas, radio, virtual car showrooms, online books, an online wine store, an Internet service provider, cable television, cosmetics, health clubs, balloon rides, gift 'experiences' and stem cell banks. With the launching of Virgin Galactic in 2004 and orders for five 'spaceliners', it now even includes space tourism! This is a prime example of diversification.

A mixed picture

Although there have been overall movements in the market shares of branded and own-label products, there are big differences in own-label penetration from one product to another. Some market segments are dominated by the supermarkets' own-label products, such as fresh fruit and vegetables, whereas for other segments, such as chocolate and cereal bars, the brands continue to dominate.

Where products are viewed as fairly homogenous, at least in the eyes of the consumer (e.g. petrol, milk and frozen peas), product differentiation by brand is difficult to achieve. There are no real cost advantages and prices are more competitive. On the other hand, where products are more differentiated, consumers may identify their particular product by branding. Examples include products targeted at a particular group (defined by gender, age or socioeconomic status), products that reflect a certain style of living (e.g. healthy eating), products that embody high quality or innovative characteristics, or have a long history. With these products, pricing is not the only competitive variable; actively differentiating and promoting the product is crucial.

Own-label products and brands have something to offer the consumer and the existence of both is definitely beneficial. The emergence of own-label products has therefore given consumers much more choice by innovating, keeping quality high and forcing branded products to compete on price.

1. *How has the improvement in the quality of own brands affected the price elasticity of demand for branded products? What implications does this have for the pricing strategy of brand manufacturers?*
2. *Do the brand manufacturers have any actual or potential cost advantages over own-brand manufacturers?*

[5] Ben Bold, 'Supermarket own-brands generate more than half of UK grocery sales', *Marketing Magazine* (27 November 2014).

Advertising

One of the most important aspects of marketing is advertising. The major aim of advertising is to sell more products, and businesses spend a vast quantity of money on advertising to achieve this goal. Through advertising, a business is not only making consumers aware of the product and its features, but is purposefully trying to persuade the consumer to buy the good.

In fact, there is a bit more to it than this. Advertisers are trying to do two things:

- Shift the product's demand curve to the right.
- Make it less price elastic.

This is illustrated in Figure 3.5. D_1 shows the original demand curve with price at P_1 and sales at Q_1. D_2 shows the curve after an advertising campaign. The rightward shift allows an increased quantity (Q_2) to be sold at the original price. If, at the same time, the demand is made less elastic, the firm can also raise its price and still experience an increase in sales. Thus, in the diagram, price can be raised to P_2 and sales will be Q_3 – still substantially above Q_1. The total gain in revenue is shown by the shaded area.

How can advertising bring about this new demand curve?

Shifting the demand curve to the right. This will occur if the advertising brings the product to more people's attention and if it increases people's desire for the product, such that they want to purchase more at any given price.

Making the demand curve less elastic. This will occur if the advertising creates greater brand loyalty. People must be led to believe (rightly or wrongly) that competitors' brands are inferior. This will allow the firm to raise its price above that of its rivals with no significant fall in sales. There will be only a small substitution effect of this price rise because consumers have been led to believe that there are no close substitutes.

Pause for thought

How would you expect a successful advertising campaign to affect the product's cross-price elasticity of demand?

The more successful an advertising campaign is, the more it will shift the demand curve to the right and the more it will reduce the price elasticity of demand.

We often see some of the most well-known brands being advertised in the middle of big sporting events and the impact on sales of such products is clearly affected by the success of the host nation, as we discuss in the blog, 'The economic downs of rugby', on the Sloman Economics News site.

Advertising and the state of the economy

One final thing to consider is the impact of booms and recessions on marketing and advertising, a topic discussed in the blog, 'Advertising's role in the economy'. Marketing expenditure can be a huge expense for a firm, and so varying the amount spent on advertising as the state of the economy changes can be a sensible strategy. According to the Advertising Association, advertising expenditure was fairly stable between 2010 and 2014 at between £14.5 billion and £16 billion. Since then it has increased to a record high of £9.4 billion in the first half of 2015, with expectations that it will reach £20 billion in 2016.

Conversely, in the economic downturn following the financial crisis, firms were able to reduce their costs significantly by cutting back on advertising. Spending fell from £18.6 billion in 2004 to £14.2 billion in 2009 in constant 2008 prices.

However, is cutting back on marketing in a recession the right thing to do? Maintaining, or even increasing, expenditure on marketing during a recession might enable a firm to take advantage of weaker competitors. Increasing market share during a downturn may mean higher profits when demand recovers.

According to research from the Open University that looked at previous recessions, advertising during unfavourable economic times can increase sales, market share and brand reputation in the long run, as Domino's UK, the pizza company, found when its advertising during 2009–10 led to excellent sales and profits growth. This included using social media and launching a smartphone app. Other media-savvy companies also maintained their advertising, despite the recession. But in many cases they switched to the Internet, as a cheaper and perhaps more far-reaching means of promoting their product. One prime example of this is Cadbury's Dairy Milk, with the famous 'drumming gorilla'!

From the above, you may think that the only link between recession and advertising is that the former causes a fall in the latter. However, a three-year study launched in January 2011 by the Advertising Association and Deloitte suggests that advertising could be the stimulant an economy needs to move out of a recession. In the report published in

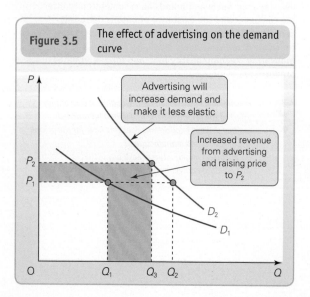

| Figure 3.5 | The effect of advertising on the demand curve |

2014, they claim that for every £1 spent on advertising in the UK, £6 is generated for the wider economy. If we look at the figure for 2011, approximately £16 billion was spent on ad campaigns, which, based on the study's estimates, implies advertising added some £100 billion to the UK's gross domestic product (GDP) and over 550 000 high-quality jobs. Perhaps adverts are key contributors to economic growth.

> **Pause for thought**
>
> *Assume that the government runs an advertising campaign to encourage people to stop smoking. How will this affect the position of the demand curve and the price elasticity of demand for cigarettes?*

BOX 3.5	ADVERTISING AND THE LONG RUN

Promoting quality

It is relatively straightforward to measure the short-term impact of an advertising campaign; a simple before and after assessment of sales will normally give a good indication of the advertising's effectiveness. But what about the medium- and longer-term effects of an advertising campaign? How will sales and profits be affected over, say, a five-year period?

The typical impact of advertising on a product's sales is shown in Figure (a). Assume that there is an advertising campaign for the product between time t_1 and t_2. There is a direct effect on sales while the advertising lasts and shortly afterwards. Sales rise from S_1 to S_2. After a while (beyond time t_3), the direct effect of the advertising begins to wear off, and wears off completely by time t_4. This is illustrated by the dashed line. But the higher level of sales declines much more slowly, given that many of the new customers continue to buy the product out of habit. Sales will eventually level off (at point t_5). It is likely, however, that sales will not return to the original level of S_1; there will be some new customers who will stick with the product over the long term. This long-term effect is shown by the increase in sales from S_1 to S_3.

But just what is this long-term effect? One way to explore the impact of advertising over the long run is to evaluate how advertising and profitability in general are linked. Figure (b) shows how advertising shapes the image of the product and its perceived quality, which the customer then compares with price to determine the product's value. The more that advertising can enhance the perceived quality of a product, the more it will increase the product's profitability.

How this benefits the business over the longer term can be illustrated by the cases of VW Golf and the Famous Grouse whisky, winners of a Gold and Silver awards of the Institute of Practitioners in Advertising, the UK professional institute. To quote from the IPA website:

> Thirty years ago, a small car called Golf was born. . . . Communications helped create, nourish and nurture the genuinely loved and financially valuable brand Golf is today. The story includes some of the UK's most famous ads – from 'Casino' and 'Changes' in the 1980s, to 'Singing in the Rain' in 2005 – but this is not just about them. It's about how Golf communications have become increasingly sophisticated, based on new thinking about the car buying process, and about the role of communications within it. Golf is now not just a much loved and enduring icon, it has also become the third biggest selling car in UK history.

The Famous Grouse was stuck in the middle of the whisky market in the UK; with its sector (Blended Scotch) declining while single malts and own-label brands experienced strong growth. It was a small Perthshire company with global ambitions, but without the scale of its global competitors. With the help of AMV BBDO, they overcame this and built a brand-centric advertising

(a) Advertising and the long run

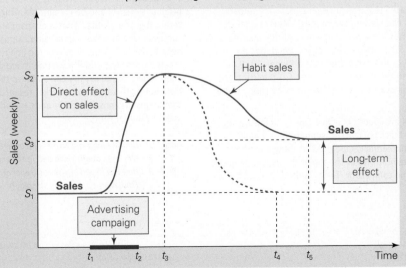

▶

(b) Advertising, profit margins and company growth

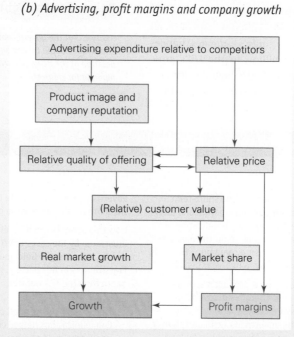

platform – one that engaged the consumer, made them love the brand and helped The Famous Grouse stand out from the crowd. They invested in their brand equity in the UK while other brands retreated, and developed a campaign that more than returned their investment, producing a retail sales value in excess of over £513m in the UK.[1]

The UK tea market

PG Tips, launched in 1930, is another brand that leads its respective market. The UK tea market has been dominated by PG Tips since 1958, when it became market leader, a position it still holds today, with over 25 per cent of the 'traditional' tea market in 2015 and sales of £149 million. The 'chimp' adverts, the Aardman T-Birds and more recently Monkey and Johnny Vegas, have established a clear brand image, enabling PG Tips to hold its ground in a highly competitive market and charge a price premium. (Blind tests have revealed that consumers cannot distinguish between any of the leading tea brands!) Market analysis shows that PG Tips has a price elasticity of demand of −0.4 compared with its nearest rival, Tetley, which has an elasticity of −1.4. It is estimated that between 1980 and 2000 advertising the PG Tips brand cost £100 million but generated in the region of £2 billion in extra sales. Not a bad return!

In 2013, PG Tips introduced the 'New Ones', an innovation focusing on the black tea market, supported by a multi-million pound marketing campaign. This innovation has helped to maintain PG Tips at the top of the market segment, with its long-time competitor, Tetley, suffering a decline in market share to just 12.2 per cent.

However, the tea market is changing; research from Mintel indicates that the traditional teabag is in decline, with sales falling by 22 per cent between 2010 and 2015.[2] At the same time, the popularity of fruit and herbal teas is growing and Twinings is now challenging PG Tips to become the market leader. This change in the market has led to significant innovation in speciality teas, partly driven by health, as they are typically not taken with milk and sugar and partly driven by being a more exciting alternative to regular black tea!

Another example of an advert that led to a fantastic return on investment is Foster's, the IPA Effectiveness Awards Grand Prix Winner in 2014.[3] The advert, featuring Brad and Dan as agony uncles, led to the biggest return on investment of any beer campaign. It generated £32 of revenue per £1 spent on advertising and returned Foster's to the position of market leader.

The message is that advertising should seek to promote a product's quality and be memorable. This is the key to long-term sales and profits. What is also apparent is that successful brands have advertising campaigns which have been consistent over time. A brand image of quality is not created overnight and if investment and innovation are not maintained, brand loyalty can suffer in the long run. However, with continuous market research and innovative campaigns it is possible for brands to endure and yield profits over the longer term.

1. *How are long-run profits and advertising linked?*
2. *Why does quality 'win out' in the end?*
3. *How would you advise the owner of the PG Tips brand (Unilever) on a pricing strategy?*

[1] '2006 IPA Effectiveness Awards: the winners', Institute of Practitioners in Advertising (28 October 2014)
[2] Mintel Report (2015)
[3] 'Foster's campaign wins Grand Prix at 2014 IPA Effectiveness Awards', *IPA News item* (28 October 2014).

RECAP

1. When firms seek to differentiate their products from those of their competitors, they can adjust one or more of four dimensions of the product: its technical standards, its quality, its design characteristics, and the level of customer service.

2. Marketing involves developing a product image and then persuading consumers to purchase it.

3. A business must choose an appropriate product/market strategy. Four such strategies can be identified: market penetration (focusing on existing product and market);

   product development (new product in existing market); market development (existing product in new markets); diversification (new products in new markets).

4. The marketing strategy of a product involves the manipulation of four key variables: product, price, place and promotion. Every product has a distinct marketing mix.

5. The aims of advertising are to increase demand in the short and long run and make the product less price elastic.

QUESTIONS

1. How would marginal utility and market demand be affected by a rise in the price of (a) a substitute good, (b) a complementary good?

2. How can marginal utility be used to explain the price elasticity of demand for a particular brand of a product?

3. Why are insurance companies unwilling to provide insurance against losses arising from war or 'civil insurrection'? Name some other events where it would be impossible to obtain insurance.

4. What has happened to premiums for home insurance for those houses in areas that are at risk of flooding? Which factors have caused this change? Is there a role for the government to intervene in this market?

5. What are the relative strengths and weaknesses of using (a) market observations, (b) market surveys and (c) market experiments as a means of gathering evidence on consumer demand?

6. You are working for a recording company which is thinking of signing up some new bands. What market observations, market surveys and market experiments could you conduct to help you decide which bands to sign?

7. You are about to launch a new range of cosmetics, but you are still to decide upon the content and structure of your advertising campaign. Consider how market surveys and market experiments might be used to help you assess consumer perceptions of the product. What limitations might each of the research methods have in helping you gather data?

8. Imagine that you are an airline attempting to forecast demand for seats over the next two or three years.

   What do you think could be used as leading indicators?

9. How might we account for the growth in non-price competition within the modern developed economy?

10. Consider how the selection of the product/market strategy (market penetration, market development, product development and diversification) will influence the business's marketing mix. Choose a particular product and identify which elements in the marketing mix would be most significant in developing a successful marketing strategy for it.

11. Think of some advertisements that deliberately seek to make demand less price elastic. How do they do this?

12. Imagine that 'Sunshine' sunflower margarine, a well-known brand, is advertised with the slogan, 'It helps you live longer' (the implication being that butter and margarines high in saturates shorten your life). What do you think would happen to the demand curve for a supermarket's *own* brand of sunflower margarine? Consider both the direction of shift and the effect on elasticity. Will the elasticity differ markedly at different prices? How will this affect the pricing policy and sales of the supermarket's own brand? Could the supermarket respond other than by adjusting the price of its margarine?

13. There are many methods of advertising, from newspapers to television to the Internet. What trends can you identify for the amount of spending on the various methods of advertising as a percentage of total advertising expenditure?

14. How can advertising help a nation recover from an economic downturn?

Supply decisions in a perfectly competitive market

In this chapter we turn to supply. In other words, we focus on the amount that firms produce at different prices. In Part C we shall see how the supply decision is affected by the microeconomic environment in which a firm operates, and in particular by the amount of competition it faces. However, in this chapter, we assume that the firm is a price taker. This means that it has to accept the price as given by the market. We also assume that the firm seeks to maximise profits.

Profit is made by firms earning more from the sale of goods than the goods cost to produce. A firm's total profit ($T\Pi$) is thus the difference between its total sales revenue (TR) and its total costs of production (TC).

In order, then, to discover how a firm can maximise its profit, or even make a profit at all, we must first consider what determines costs and revenue. Sections 4.1 and 4.2 examine costs. Section 4.3 considers revenue, and then section 4.4 puts costs and revenue together to examine profit.

4.1 PRODUCTION IN THE SHORT RUN

The cost of producing any level of output depends on the amount and mix of inputs used and the price that the firm must pay for them. Let us first focus on the quantity and mix of inputs used.

Short-run and long-run changes in production

If a firm wants to increase production, it will need more inputs, but how easy and quick is it to acquire them? This will vary from input to input. For example, a manufacturer can increase output by switching on spare machines and hence using more electricity, but it might take a long time to increase output further by obtaining and installing more machines, and longer still to build a second or third factory.

If, then, the firm wants to increase output in a hurry, it will only be able to increase the quantity of certain inputs and so the input mix will be adjusted. It can use more raw materials, more fuel, more tools and possibly more labour (by hiring extra workers or offering overtime to its existing workforce). But it will have to make do with its existing buildings and most of its machinery.

The distinction we are making here is between *fixed inputs* and *variable inputs*. A *fixed* input is an input that cannot be increased within a given time period (e.g. buildings). A *variable* input is one that can.

The distinction between fixed and variable inputs allows us to distinguish between the short run and the long run.

The short run
The *short run* is a time period during which at least one input is fixed. This means that in the short run output can be increased only by using more variable inputs. For example, if a shipping line wanted to carry more passengers in response to a rise in demand, it could accommodate more passengers on existing sailings if there was space. It could increase the number of sailings with its existing fleet, by hiring more crew and using more fuel. But in the short run it could not buy more ships; there would not be time for them to be built.

The long run
The *long run* is a time period long enough for all of a firm's inputs to be varied. Thus in the long run, the shipping company could have a new ship built to cater for the increase in demand.

The short run and long run are not set periods of time and they will be different from firm to firm. Thus if it takes a farmer a year to obtain new land, buildings and equipment, the short run is any time period up to a year and the long run is any time period longer than a year. But if it takes a shipping company three years to obtain an extra ship, the short run is any period up to three years and the long run is any period longer than three years.

For this section we will concentrate on *short-run* production and costs. We will look at the long run in section 4.2.

> **Pause for thought**
>
> *How will the length of the short run for the shipping company depend on the state of the shipbuilding industry?*

Production in the short run: the law of diminishing returns

Production in the short run is subject to *diminishing returns*, which is a concept we first alluded to in section 2.3 (page 30). You may well have heard of 'the law of diminishing returns'; it is one of the most famous of all 'laws' of economics. To illustrate how this law underlies short-run production, let us take the simplest possible case where there are just two inputs: one fixed and one variable.

Take the case of a farm. Assume the fixed input is land and the variable input is labour. Since the land is fixed in supply, output per period of time can be increased only by employing extra workers. But imagine what would happen as more and more workers crowded on to a fixed area of land. Workers will begin to get in each other's way and the land simply cannot go on yielding more and more output indefinitely. After a point, the additions to total output from each extra worker will begin to diminish.

We can now state the *law of diminishing (marginal) returns*.

 KEY IDEA 14
The law of diminishing marginal returns. When increasing amounts of a variable input are used with a given amount of a fixed input, there will come a point when each extra unit of the variable input will produce less extra output than the previous unit.

> **Definitions**
>
> **Fixed input** An input that cannot be increased in supply within a given time period.
>
> **Variable input** An input that can be increased in supply within a given time period.
>
> **Short run** The period of time over which at least one input is fixed.
>
> **Long run** The period of time long enough for all inputs to be varied.
>
> **Law of diminishing (marginal) returns** When one or more inputs are held fixed, there will come a point beyond which the extra output from additional units of the variable input will diminish.

BOX 4.1 DIMINISHING RETURNS AND BUSINESS

What can managers do?

Everywhere you look in business you can see diminishing returns. It applies to both giant multinational corporations and the corner shop; to manufacturing, farming, mining and services. Let us take some examples.

A car manufacturer. In the short run, a company such as Toyota or Ford will have a particular number of factories. If it wants to increase output in the short run, there will not be enough time to build a new one. So what does it do? The answer is that it will have to use its existing plants more intensively. For example, it could increase the length of shifts. But as it does so, output per worker is likely to fall as workers become more tired or fed up. It could use its machines more intensively. But as it does so, breakdowns or maintenance problems are likely to increase and at some point the machine will simply not be able to produce any more.

Eventually, no matter how many extra people are employed, the factory will reach full capacity. At this point any additional workers would produce no extra output whatsoever. Returns from additional labour have diminished to zero.

The convenience store. Go into a shop and see what fixed inputs you can see. There will be the shelving, the tills, the warehouse space at the back and the floor space itself. At busy times the shop may take on more workers, but will each additional worker be able to serve the same number of customers? Probably not. Assume, for example, that there are two tills. Once they are fully in use, taking on more workers will not allow more customers to be served. True, additional workers can make sure the shelves are stocked, collect the trolleys, and so on; but diminishing returns to labour are obvious. Each additional worker is permitting fewer and fewer *extra* customers to be served.

The problem applies similarly to supermarkets. At busy times, queues at the tills get longer and crowding in the shop slows down your progress around it.

The arable farm. In the short run, farmers have a fixed amount of land. They can increase crop yields by applying more fertiliser. However, beyond a certain quantity of fertiliser per hectare, diminishing returns to fertiliser will set in. Additional bags will yield less and less additional output. Case B.13 on the website looks at some evidence on diminishing returns to the application of nitrogen fertiliser on farmland.

The firm of solicitors. In the case of professional practices such as this, the number of partners will be fixed in the short run, along with the premises and much of the equipment. It might be possible to hire additional secretarial support or other office staff at short notice, but not another partner. But partners are only human. They get tired and less efficient as the work expands. Each additional hour they work beyond a certain level is likely to result in lower productivity.

The student. Which brings us to you! You have no doubt experienced diminishing returns to study time. Working that extra hour late at night may result in little if any extra learning!

1. Give some other examples of diminishing returns to inputs other than labour (such as the fertiliser example above).
2. If all inputs were variable (as they are in the long run), would expanding output result in diminishing marginal returns? (We examine this question later when we consider the long run.)

A good example of the law of diminishing returns is given in Case Study B.19 on the website. The case looks at diminishing returns to the application of nitrogen fertiliser on farmland. There is also an article on the Sloman Economics News site titled 'Tackling diminishing returns in food production' which provides another good application of this core concept.

Opportunity cost

When measuring costs, economists always use the concept of *opportunity cost.* opportunity cost is the cost of any activity measured in terms of the sacrifice made in doing it, i.e. the cost measured in terms of the opportunities forgone (as we saw in section 1.3). If a car manufacturer can produce ten small saloon cars with the same amount of inputs as it takes to produce six large saloon cars, then the opportunity cost of producing one small car is 0.6 of a large car. If a taxi and car hire firm chooses to use all of its cars as taxis, then the opportunity cost includes not only the cost of employing taxi drivers and buying fuel, but also the sacrifice of rental income from hiring its vehicles out.

Measuring a firm's opportunity costs

To measure a firm's opportunity cost, we must first discover what inputs it has used. Then we must measure the sacrifice involved in using them. To do this it is necessary to put inputs into two categories.

Inputs not owned by the firm: explicit costs. The opportunity cost of those inputs not already owned by the firm is simply the price that the firm has to pay for them. Thus if the firm uses £100 worth of electricity, the opportunity cost is £100. The firm has sacrificed £100 which could have been spent on something else.

These costs are called *explicit costs* because they involve direct payment of money by firms.

Inputs already owned by the firm: implicit costs. When the firm already owns inputs (e.g. machinery) it does not as a rule

Definition

Explicit costs The payments to outside suppliers of inputs.

have to pay out money to use them. Their opportunity costs are thus *implicit costs*. They are equal to what the inputs could earn for the firm in some alternative use, either within the firm or hired out to some other firm.

Here are some examples of implicit costs:

- Say you own a house. The opportunity cost of living in your house is the rental income you could have earned had you chosen to rent it out to a tenant.
- A firm draws £100 000 from the bank out of its savings in order to invest in a new plant and equipment. The opportunity cost of this investment is not just the £100 000 (an explicit cost), but also the interest it thereby forgoes (an implicit cost).
- The owner of the firm could have earned £30 000 per annum by working for someone else. This £30 000 is the opportunity cost of the owner's time.

If there is no alternative use for an input, as in the case of a machine designed to produce a specific product, and if it has no scrap value, the opportunity cost of using it is *zero*. In such a case, if the output from the machine is worth more than the cost of all the *other* inputs involved, the firm might as well use the machine rather than let it stand idle.

What the firm paid for the machine – its *historic cost* – is irrelevant. Not using the machine will not bring that money back. It has been spent. These are sometimes referred to as 'sunk costs'.

 KEY IDEA 15 | *Sunk costs and the bygones principle.* The principle states that sunk (fixed) costs should be ignored when deciding whether to produce or sell more or less of a product. Only variable costs should be taken into account.

Likewise, the *replacement cost* is irrelevant. That should be taken into account only when the firm is considering replacing the machine.

Costs and inputs

As a firm changes its output, its costs will change. We can look at the growth of a company, such as Google, and see how its costs have varied as the company has grown. A firm's costs of production will depend on the inputs it uses. The more inputs it uses, the greater will its costs be. More precisely, this relationship depends on two elements:

Pause for thought

Assume that a farmer decides to grow wheat on land that could be used for growing barley. Barley sells for £100 per tonne. Wheat sells for £150 per tonne. Seed, fertiliser, labour and other costs of growing crops are £80 per tonne for both wheat and barley. What are the farmer's costs and profit per tonne of growing wheat?

- The productivity of the inputs. The greater their physical productivity, the smaller will be the quantity of them that is needed to produce a given level of output, and hence the lower will be the cost of that output.
- The price of the inputs. The higher their price, the higher will be the costs of production.

In the short run, some inputs are fixed in supply. Therefore, the total costs (*TC*) of these inputs are fixed and thus do not vary with output. Consider a piece of land that a firm rents: the rent it pays will be a *fixed cost*. Whether the firm produces a lot or a little, its rent will not change.

The cost of variable inputs, however, does vary with output. The cost of raw materials is a *variable cost*. The more that is produced, the more raw materials are used and therefore the higher is their total cost. *Total cost* is thus total fixed cost (*TFC*) plus total variable cost (*TVC*).

Average and marginal cost

In addition to the total cost of production (fixed and variable) there are two other measures of cost which are particularly important for our analysis of profits. These are average and marginal cost.

Average cost (AC) is cost per unit of production:

$$AC = TC/Q$$

Thus if it costs a firm £2000 to produce 100 units of a product, the average cost would be £20 for each unit (£2000/100).

As with total cost, average cost can be divided into the two components, fixed and variable. In other words, average cost equals *average fixed cost* (*AFC = TFC/Q*) plus *average variable cost* (*AVC = TVC/Q*):

$$AC = AFC + AVC$$

Definitions

Implicit costs Costs which do not involve a direct payment of money to a third party, but which nevertheless involve a sacrifice of some alternative.

Historic costs The original amount the firm paid for inputs it now owns.

Replacement costs What the firm would have to pay to replace inputs it currently owns.

Fixed costs Total costs that do not vary with the amount of output produced.

Variable costs Total costs that do vary with the amount of output produced.

Total cost (*TC*) **(per period)** The sum of total fixed costs (*TFC*) and total variable costs *(TVC)*: $TC = TFC + TVC$.

Average (total) cost (*AC*) Total cost (fixed plus variable) per unit of output: $AC = TC/Q = AFC = AVC$.

Average fixed cost (*AFC*) Total fixed cost per unit of output: $AFC = TFC/Q$.

Average variable cost (*AVC*) Total variable cost per unit of output: $AVC = TVC/Q$.

Table 4.1	Costs for firm X						
Output (Q) (£000) (1)	TFC (£000) (2)	TVC (£000) (3)	TC (TFC + TVC) (£000) (4)	AFC (TFC/Q) (£000) (5)	AVC (TVC/Q) (£000) (6)	AC (TC/Q) (£000) (7)	MC (ΔTC/ΔQ) (£000) (8)
0	12	0	12	–	–	–	
1	12	10	22	12	10	22	10
2	12	16	28	6	8	14	6
3	12	21	33	4	7	11	5
4	12	28	40	3	7	10	7
5	12	40	52	2.4	8	10.4	12
6	12	60	72	2	10	12	20
7	12	91	103	1.7	13	14.7	31

Marginal cost (MC) is the *extra* cost of producing *one more unit*, i.e. the rise in total cost per one unit rise in output:

$$MC = \frac{\Delta TC}{\Delta Q}$$

where Δ means 'a change in'.

For example, assume that a firm is currently producing 1 000 000 boxes of matches a month. It now increases output by 1000 boxes (another batch): $\Delta Q = 1000$. Assume that as a result its total costs rise by £30: $\Delta TC = £30$. What is the cost of producing *one* more box of matches? It is:

$$MC = \frac{\Delta TC}{\Delta Q} = \frac{£30}{1000} = 3p$$

(Note that all marginal costs are variable, since, by definition, there can be no extra fixed costs as output rises.)

Table 4.1 shows costs for an imaginary firm, firm X, over a given period of time (e.g. a week). The table shows how average and marginal costs can be derived from total costs. It is assumed that total fixed costs are £12 000 (column 2) and that total variable costs are as shown in column 3.

The figures for *TVC* have been chosen to illustrate the law of diminishing returns. Initially, *before* diminishing returns set in, *TVC* rises less and less rapidly as more variable factors are added. For example, in the case of a factory with a fixed supply of machinery, initially as more workers are taken on, the workers can do increasingly specialist tasks and make a fuller use of the capital equipment. Extra workers are producing more and more extra output. However, above a certain output (3 units in Table 4.1), diminishing returns set in. Given that extra workers (the extra variable factors) are producing less and less extra output, the extra units of output they do produce will be costing more and more in terms of wage costs. Thus *TVC* rises more and more rapidly. You can see this by examining column 3.

Pause for thought

Use the figures in the first three columns of Table 4.1 to plot TFC, TVC and TC curves (where costs are plotted on the vertical axis and quantity on the horizontal axis). Mark the point on each of the TVC and TC curves where diminishing returns set in. What do you notice about the slope of the two curves at this output?

The figures in the remaining columns in Table 4.1 are derived from columns 1 to 3. Look at the figures in each of the columns and check how the figures are derived. Note the figures for marginal cost are plotted between the lines to illustrate that marginal cost represents the increase in costs as output increases from one unit to the next.

We can use the data in Table 4.1 to draw *MC*, *AFC*, *AVC* and *AC* curves (see Figure 4.1).

Marginal cost (MC). The shape of the *MC* curve follows directly from the law of diminishing returns. Initially, in Figure 4.1, as more of the variable input is used, extra units of output cost less than previous units. This means that *MC* initially falls.

Figure 4.1 Average and marginal costs

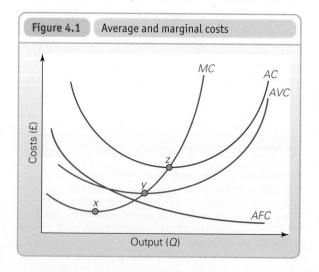

Beyond a certain level of output, however, diminishing returns set in. This is shown as point *x*. Thereafter *MC* rises. Additional units of output cost more and more to produce, since they require ever-increasing amounts of the variable input.

Average fixed cost (AFC). This falls continuously as output rises, since total fixed costs are being spread over a greater and greater output. If a firm finds that its fixed costs represent a large proportion of its total costs, expanding output can be a good strategy to adopt, as average fixed costs will begin to fall.

Average (total) cost (AC). This is the vertical sum of the average fixed cost and the average variable cost curves. As you can see from Figure 4.1, as *AFC* falls, the gap between *AVC* and *AC* decreases.

The relationship between average cost and marginal cost. The shape of the *AC* curve depends on the shape of the *MC* curve. As long as new units of output cost less than the average, their production must pull the average cost down. That is, if *MC* is less than *AC*, *AC* must be falling. Likewise, if new units cost more than the average, their production must pull the average up. That is, if *MC* is greater than *AC*, *AC* must be rising. Therefore, the *MC* curve crosses the *AC* curve at its minimum point (point *z* in Figure 4.1). If you find this concept difficult, then try inserting some data for *AC*, *MC* and *TC* at different levels of output.

Pause for thought

Before you read on can you explain why the marginal cost curve will always cut the average cost curve at its lowest point?

For example, say 4 units of output cost £5 each to produce. Total cost = £20 (4×5) and average cost = £5(20/4). If output is increased by 1 unit and this unit costs an extra £5 to produce, (the same as the average cost) then the average cost simply remains at £5 (Average cost = $TC/Q = 25/5 = $ £5). However, now assume that the marginal cost of this fifth unit is £6 ($MC > AC$). Total costs for 6 units are now £26 and the average cost is: $AC = TC/Q = 26/5 = $ £5.20. The average cost has been pulled up by the higher marginal cost. The opposite will happen if marginal cost is lower than average cost.

Average variable cost (AVC). Since $AVC = AC - AFC$, the *AVC* curve is simply the vertical difference between the *AC* and the *AFC* curves. Again, note that as *AFC* falls, the gap between *AVC* and *AC* narrows. Since all marginal costs are variable (by definition, there are no marginal fixed costs), the same relationship holds between *MC* and *AVC* as it did between *MC* and *AC*. That is, if *MC* is less than *AVC*, *AVC* must be falling, and if *MC* is greater than *AVC*, *AVC* must be rising. Therefore, as with the *AC* curve, the *MC* curve crosses the *AVC* curve at its minimum point (point *y* in Figure 4.1).

RECAP

1. Production in the short run is subject to diminishing returns. As greater quantities of the variable input(s) are used, so each additional unit of the variable input will add less to output than previous units, i.e. output will rise less and less rapidly.

2. When measuring costs of production, we should be careful to use the concept of opportunity cost. In the case of inputs not owned by the firm, the opportunity cost is simply the explicit cost of purchasing or hiring them: it is the price paid for them. In the case of inputs already owned by the firm, it is the implicit cost of what the factor could have earned for the firm in its best alternative use.

3. As some factors are fixed in supply in the short run, their total costs are fixed with respect to output. In the case

of variable factors, their total cost increases as more output is produced and hence as more of them are used. Total cost can be divided into total fixed and total variable cost.

4. Marginal cost is the cost of producing one more unit of output. It will probably fall at first but will start to rise when diminishing returns set in.

5. Average cost, like total cost, can be divided into fixed and variable costs. Average fixed cost will decline as more output is produced. The reason is that the total fixed cost is being spread over a greater and greater number of units of output. Average variable cost will tend to decline at first, but once the marginal cost has risen above it, it must then rise. The same applies to average cost.

BOX 4.2   **UNDERSTANDING YOUR FIXED COSTS**

The effect of changing output

The distinction between fixed and variable costs has profound implications for the behaviour of any business. In the short run, if a firm increases its output, total variable costs will increase; total fixed costs will not. Put another way, average variable costs may well rise, but average fixed costs will fall (as Figure 4.1 illustrates).

So why is this so important for business? The answer is that no firm will want to have its fixed inputs underused, except for short periods of time. After all, using more of them incurs no extra fixed costs – by definition. The larger the proportion of fixed costs to variable costs, the more important this becomes. It becomes especially important when a business has more than one production plant and where the ratio of fixed and variable costs vary between them.

The case of electricity generation

Let's take the example of electricity generation and compare a gas-fired power station with a nuclear one. There is a similar average cost of generating electricity from each type of station (around £80 to £100 per megawatt/hour), yet the proportion of fixed and variable costs is very different. A nuclear power station has low variable costs (mainly fuel), but is very expensive to build, maintain and decommission and so has very high fixed costs; average fixed cost at full capacity is around 91 per cent of average cost. In comparison, gas-fired power stations are relatively cheap to build, but more expensive to run, such that average fixed cost at normal capacity account for only around 16 per cent of average cost.

The implication of these differences is that nuclear power stations should be kept working near to full capacity, because when output increases, average fixed costs are spread over more units and so the lower average fixed cost pulls down average costs. However, if less output is produced in a gas-fired power station with its lower fixed costs, this will not significantly increase its average fixed cost.

As electricity cannot be stored and demand fluctuates with the time of day, it is necessary to have spare capacity to meet surges in demand and so gas-fired power stations with their lower fixed costs can fill this role. Thus, the output of nuclear power stations is virtually constant, while the output of gas-fired stations fluctuates with demand.

Economic vulnerability

Type 1 vulnerability: to changes in demand. Although many firms have a U-shaped average cost curve, the rate at which average costs fall and then rise as output increases will vary between firms. This explains why some firms are more vulnerable than others to changes in demand.

Consider two firms, A and B. Each firm's average cost curve is shown in Figure (a). Assume, for simplicity, that each firm achieves minimum average cost at point x, namely at the same output Q_0 and at the same average cost, AC_0. But now consider what would happen if there was a recession, as we saw across the world following the financial crisis of 2007–8. Assume that both firms experience a fall in demand and, as a result, cut output to Q_1.

With a U-shaped AC curve, both firms see per-unit costs begin to rise, but firm A's costs rise significantly faster than firm B's, because firm A has a very steep AC curve. The same fall in quantity pushes firm A's average costs up from AC_0 to AC_1 (point a) but only causes firm B's costs to increase to AC_2 (point b) as firm B's AC curve is very flat. There is thus a more significant effect on A's profit margin and profits than on B's.

The following are factors that create a steeper AC curve and hence greater economic vulnerability:

■ If a firm has high ratio of fixed factors to variable factors then it is likely to face a steep AC curve. Total fixed costs do not change with output and hence, if output falls, it implies that its high fixed costs are being spread over fewer and fewer units of output and this causes average costs to rise rapidly.

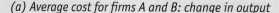

(a) Average cost for firms A and B: change in output

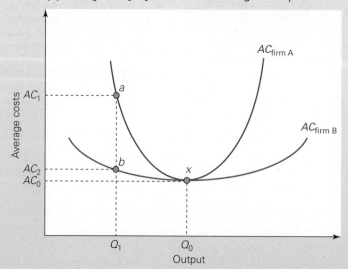

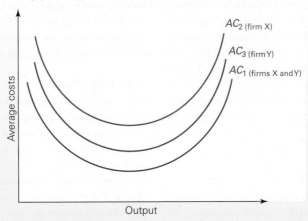

(b) Average cost for firms X and Y: change in costs

If a firm is relatively inflexible in its use of inputs, it may find that a cut in production means that efficiency goes down and average cost rises rapidly. Similarly if it wishes to expand output beyond Q_0, it may find it difficult to do so without incurring considerable extra costs, for example by employing expensive agency staff or hiring expensive machinery.

Type 2 vulnerability: to changes in input prices. Another way in which firms can be vulnerable is due to heavy reliance on external or bought-in inputs. For example, some firms may be heavily dependent on oil and so if the price of oil changes, it can have a very big effect on the firm's costs of production, its profit margins and profit. During an economic boom or a period of high growth, production tends to increase, as does the demand for oil and its price. A firm that is very dependent on oil will, therefore, see a significant effect on its costs of production and its *AC* curve will shift vertically upwards. However, for a firm that does not use much oil during production, or has alternative inputs, changes in the global price of oil (or another input) may cause only a very small shift in the *AC* curve.

In Figure (b), both firms X and Y have the same shaped *AC* curve, which we will assume is initially the same (i.e. AC_1). But let us also assume that firm X is very dependent on oil, whereas firm Y is not.

Assume that oil prices now rise. This will lead to a large upward shift in firm X's *AC* curve from AC_1 to AC_2, but a smaller upward shift in firm Y's *AC* curve from AC_1 to AC_3. There is a much larger cost penalty imposed on firm X than on firm Y, due to X's reliance on oil as a factor of production.

In 2010, oil prices rose significantly, so firms which were big users of oil, either directly into the production process or for transporting their inputs and produce, saw their costs rise and their profits eroded. However, from late 2014 oil prices fell considerably and so those firms which were heavily dependent on oil saw their *AC* curves shift downwards significantly, thereby helping to increase their profits. Other firms which were less reliant on oil, however, did not benefit so much from low global prices for oil.

Both type 1 and type 2 vulnerability. If a firm is vulnerable to a change in output due to both its fixed costs and its reliance on external inputs, then any change in economic circumstances can cause serious problems.

A good example of such a firm is the Japanese steel producer, Nippon Steel and Sumitomo Metal Corporation NSSMC. This firm's fixed costs are high as a percentage of internal costs, implying a steep *AC* curve and a vulnerability to a fall in output. This was visible in 2009 when, in response to the recession, NSSMC was forced to reduce its output to just above 50 per cent of its maximum capacity.

But, in addition, NSSMC's external costs account for a high percentage of its total costs, such that many of the firm's costs are beyond its control. This was observed during 2008 when the price of oil and other raw materials increased again. This imposed a severe cost penalty on the firm.

The structure of the firm is thus a key determinant of how vulnerable it is to reductions in demand or increases in input prices. Understanding this can help managers devise strategies to insulate themselves from such fluctuations.

1. *On a diagram similar to Figure 4.1, sketch the AFC, AVC, AC and MC curves for (a) a nuclear power station and (b) a gas-fired power station. For simplicity assume that both stations would produce the same amount of electricity at full capacity.*
2. *Conduct some research on a firm of your choice, looking into its data on costs and decide whether or not you think this firm would be economically vulnerable due to its fixed costs.*
3. *Now look at some data on a firm of your choice and decide whether or not you think this firm would be vulnerable from too much reliance on bought-in or external inputs. Is it the same firm as you discussed in the previous question? If your data suggests the firm would be vulnerable in both ways, what might this mean for the firm?*

4.2 PRODUCTION AND COSTS: LONG RUN

In the long run *all* inputs are variable. There is time for the firm to install new machines, to use different techniques of production or to build a new factory (maybe in a different part of the country), and in general to combine its inputs in whatever proportion and in whatever quantities it chooses.

Therefore, when planning for the long run, a firm will have to make a number of decisions about the scale of its operations and the techniques of production it will use. These decisions will affect the firm's costs of production and can be completely irreversible, so it is important to get them right.

The scale of production

If a firm were to double all of its inputs – something it could only do in the long run – would it double its output? Or would output more than double or less than double? We can distinguish three possible situations.

Constant returns to scale. This is where a given percentage increase in inputs will lead to the same percentage increase in output.

Increasing returns to scale. This is where a given percentage increase in inputs will lead to a larger percentage increase in output.

Decreasing returns to scale. This is where a given percentage increase in inputs will lead to a smaller percentage increase in output.

Notice the terminology here. The words 'to scale' mean that *all* inputs increase by the same proportion. Decreasing returns to *scale* are therefore quite different from *diminishing* marginal returns (where only the *variable* input increases). The differences between marginal returns to a variable input and returns to scale are illustrated in Table 4.2.

In the short run, input 1 is assumed to be fixed in supply (at 3 units). Output can be increased only by using more of the variable input (input 2). In the long run, however, both inputs are variable.

In the short-run situation, diminishing returns can be seen from the fact that as input 2 is increased, output increases at a decreasing rate (25 to 45 to 60 to 70 to 75). In the long-run situation, the table illustrates increasing returns to scale. As both inputs are increased, output increases at an *increasing* rate (15 to 35 to 60 to 90 to 125).

Economies of scale

The concept of increasing returns to scale is closely linked to that of *economies of scale*. A firm experiences economies of scale if costs per unit of output fall as the scale of production increases. Clearly, if a firm is getting increasing returns to scale from its inputs, then as it produces more, it will be using smaller and smaller amounts of inputs per unit of output. Other things being equal, this means that it will be producing at a lower unit cost.

There are several reasons why firms are likely to experience economies of scale. Some are due to increasing returns to scale, some are not:

Specialisation and division of labour. In large-scale plants, workers can do more simple repetitive jobs. With this *specialisation and division of labour*, less training is needed; workers can become highly efficient in their particular job, especially with long production runs; there is less time lost in workers switching from one operation to another; each worker only needs one set of tools, thereby cutting costs; supervision is easier. Workers and managers who have specific skills in specific areas can be employed and this may improve productivity.

Indivisibilities. Some inputs are of a minimum size. They are indivisible. The most obvious example is machinery. Take the case of a combine harvester. A small-scale farmer could not make full use of one. They only become economical to use, therefore, on farms above a certain size. The problem of *indivisibilities* is made worse when different machines, each of which is part of the production process, are of a different size. Consider a firm that uses two different machines at different stages of the production process: one produces a maximum of 6 units a day, the other can package a maximum of 4 units a day. Therefore, if all machines are to be

Table 4.2	Short-run and long-run increases in output				

	Short run			Long run	
Input 1	Input 2	Output	Input 1	Input 2	Output
3	1	25	1	1	15
3	2	45	2	2	35
3	3	60	3	3	60
3	4	70	4	4	90
3	5	75	5	5	125

Definitions

Economies of scale When increasing the scale of production leads to a lower cost per unit of output.

Specialisation and division of labour Where production is broken down into a number of simpler, more specialised tasks, thus allowing workers to acquire a high degree of efficiency.

Indivisibilities The impossibility of dividing an input into smaller units.

fully utilised, a minimum of 12 units per day will have to be produced, involving two production machines and three packaging machines.

The 'container principle'. Any capital equipment that contains things (blast furnaces, oil tankers, pipes, vats, etc.) will tend to cost less per unit of output the larger its size. This is due to the relationship between a container's volume and its surface area. A container's cost will depend largely on the materials used to build it and hence roughly on its *surface area*. Its output will depend largely on its *volume*. Large containers have a bigger volume relative to surface area than small containers. For example, a container with a bottom, top and four sides, with each side measuring 1 metre, has a volume of 1 cubic metre and a surface area of 6 square metres (6 surfaces of 1 square metre each). If each side were now to be doubled in length to 2 metres, the volume would be 8 cubic metres and the surface area 24 square metres (6 surfaces of 4 square metres each). Therefore a fourfold increase in the container's surface area, and thus an approximate fourfold increase in costs, has led to an eightfold increase in capacity.

Greater efficiency of large machines. Large machines may be more efficient, in the sense that more output can be gained for a given amount of inputs. For example, whether a machine is large or small, only one worker may be required to operate it. Also, a large machine may make a more efficient use of raw materials.

By-products. With production on a large scale, firms may produce sufficient waste products to enable them to make some by-product, thereby spreading costs over more units of output.

Multi-stage production. A large factory may be able to take a product through several stages in its manufacture. This saves time and cost moving the semi-finished product from one firm or factory to another. For example, a large cardboard-manufacturing firm may be able to convert trees or waste paper into cardboard and then into cardboard boxes in a continuous sequence.

All the above are examples of *plant economies of scale*. They are due to an individual factory or workplace or machine being large. There are other economies of scale that are associated with the business itself being large – perhaps with many factories.

Organisational. With a large business, individual plants can specialise in particular functions. There can also be centralised administration of the plants. Often, after a merger between two firms, savings can be made by *rationalising* their activities in this way.

Spreading overheads. Some expenditures are economic only when the *business* is large, such as research and development; only a large business can afford to set up a research laboratory. Think back to Box 1.2, where we considered the biotechnology industry and how in the USA and France over

80 per cent of R&D comes from larger companies. This is another example of indivisibilities, only this time at the level of the whole business rather than the plant. The greater the business's output, the more these *overhead costs* are spread.

Financial economies. Large businesses may be able to obtain finance at lower interest rates than small ones, as they are seen as a lower risk or have the power to negotiate a better deal. Indeed, during the financial crisis many small businesses did find that banks were unwilling to lend to them at competitive rates of interest. You can read about the finance of small firms in an article from the Financial Times.[1] Larger firms may also be able to obtain certain inputs more cheaply, by purchasing in bulk. This relates to the concept of opportunity cost. The larger a business's order of raw materials, the more likely it is that the supplier will offer a discount, as the opportunity cost of losing the business is relatively high. This helps to reduce the cost per unit.

Economies of scope. Often a business is large because it produces a range of products. This can result in each individual product being produced more cheaply than if it was produced in a single-product firm. The reason for these *economies of scope* is that various overhead costs and financial and organisational economies can be shared between the products. For example, a firm that produces a whole range of CD players, receivers, amplifiers and tuners can benefit from shared marketing and distribution costs and the bulk purchase of electronic components. Producing a range of products also allows a business to spread its risks and hence insulate itself against a fall in demand for one of its products.

Many companies will experience a variety of economies of scale and you can find examples in practice from a variety of sources. On the Sloman Economics News site, you will find blogs that discuss economies of scale, such as those experienced by companies using cloud computing ('Operating in a cloud'), the possibility of achieving economies of scale through takeovers ('Taking over?') and whether big

---

Definitions

Plant economies of scale Economies of scale that arise because of the large size of the factory.

Rationalisation The reorganising of production (often after a merger) so as to cut out waste and duplication and generally to reduce costs.

Overheads Costs arising from the general running of an organisation, and only indirectly related to the level of output.

Economies of scope When increasing the range of products produced by a firm reduces the cost of producing each one.

---

[1] Andrew Bounds, 'SME lending grows for first time since financial crisis', *Financial Times* (2 February 2016).

supermarkets can use economies of scale to their advantage ('Supermarket wars: a pricing race to the bottom'). The economies of scale for large cloud providers is also discussed in numerous articles, including an article by Randy Bias[2] and another that considers the case of Microsoft.[3]

Diseconomies of scale

When businesses get beyond a certain size, costs per unit of output may start to increase and in this article from Ship & Bunker,[4] there is an interesting analysis of the problem of diseconomies of scale in the case of large vessels. There are several reasons for such *diseconomies of scale*:

- Management problems of co-ordination may increase as the business becomes larger and more complex, and as lines of communication get longer. There may be a lack of personal involvement by management. We saw the emergence of this problem with growing U-form organisations in section 1.1.
- Workers may feel 'alienated' if their jobs are boring and repetitive, and if they feel an insignificantly small part of a large organisation. Poor motivation may lead to shoddy work.
- Industrial relations may deteriorate as a result of these factors and also as a result of the more complex interrelationships between different categories of worker.
- Production line processes and the complex interdependencies of mass production can lead to great disruption if there are hold-ups in any one part of the business.

> **Pause for thought**
>
> *Which of the economies of scale we have considered are due to increasing returns to scale and which are due to other factors?*

Whether businesses experience economies or diseconomies of scale will depend on the conditions applying in each individual business.

The size of the whole industry

As an *industry* grows in size, this can lead to *external economies of scale* for its member firms. This is where a firm, whatever its own individual size, benefits from the *whole industry* being large. For example, the firm may benefit from having access to specialist raw material or component suppliers, labour with specific skills, firms that specialise in marketing the finished product, sharing research and development, and banks and other financial institutions with experience of the industry's requirements. What we are referring to here is the *industry's infrastructure*: the

---

facilities, support services, skills and experience that can be shared by its members. This is one of the reasons why firms engaging in biotechnology R&D tend to locate in clusters around top UK universities, as we saw in Box 1.2.

> **Pause for thought**
>
> *Would you expect external economies of scale to be associated with the concentration of an industry in a particular region? Explain.*

When industries form a cluster in an area, external economies are likely to be experienced. We examine such industrial clusters in Box 4.3 (pages 86–7).

The member firms of a particular industry might, however, experience *external diseconomies of scale*. For example, as an industry grows larger, this may create a growing shortage of specific raw materials or skilled labour. This will push up their prices, and hence the firms' costs. If the industry grows larger in a particular region, the price of land could increase and there may be increased pollution and congestion in the surrounding area.

Long-run average cost

We turn now to *long-run* cost curves. Since there are no fixed inputs in the long run, there are no long-run fixed costs. For example, a firm may rent more land in order to expand its operations. Its rent bill will therefore rise as it expands its output. All costs, then, in the long run are variable costs.

Although it is possible to draw long-run total, marginal and average cost curves, we will concentrate on *long-run average cost* (*LRAC*) *curves*. These can take various shapes, but a typical one is shown in Figure 4.2.

It is often assumed that as a firm expands, it will initially experience economies of scale and thus face a downward-sloping *LRAC* curve. But while it is possible for a firm to

> **Definitions**
>
> **Diseconomies of scale** Where costs per unit of output increase as the scale of production increases.
>
> **External economies of scale** Where a firm's costs per unit of output decrease as the size of the whole industry grows.
>
> **Industry's infrastructure** The network of supply agents, communications, skills, training facilities, distribution channels, specialised financial services, etc. that support a particular industry.
>
> **External diseconomies of scale** Where a firm's costs per unit of output increase as the size of the whole industry increases.
>
> **Long-run average cost curve** A curve that shows how average cost varies with output on the assumption that all factors are variable.

---

[2] Randy Bias, 'Understanding Cloud datacenter economies of scale', *Cloudscaling Blog* (4 May 2010).

[3] Charles Babcock, 'Microsoft: "Incredible economies of scale" await Cloud users', *InformationWeek* (11 May 2011).

[4] 'Drewry warns mega ships could diminish economies of scale', *Ship & Bunker* (10 March 2016).

| Figure 4.2 | A typical long-run average cost curve |

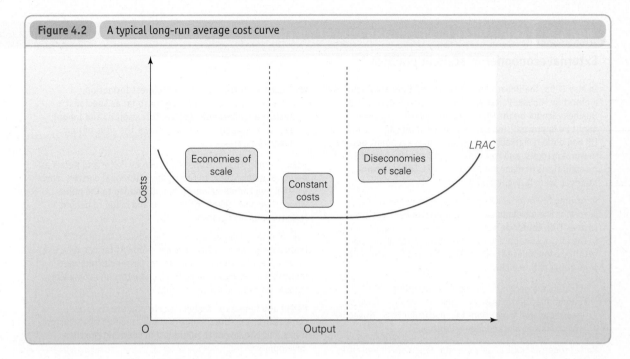

experience a continuously decreasing *LRAC* curve, in most cases, after a certain point, all such economies will have been achieved and thus the curve will flatten out. Then (possibly after a period of constant *LRAC*), the firm will get so large that it will start experiencing diseconomies of scale and thus a rising *LRAC*. At this stage, production and financial economies begin to be offset by the managerial problems of running a giant organisation. There is evidence to show that this is the case within growing businesses, but there is less evidence to indicate that technical diseconomies of scale exist.

Assumptions behind the long-run average cost curve
We make three key assumptions when constructing long-run average cost curves:

Input prices are given. At each output, a firm will face a given set of input prices. If input prices *change*, therefore, both short- and long-run cost curves will shift. Thus an increase in wages would shift the curves upwards.

However, input prices might be different at *different* levels of output. For example, one of the economies of scale that many firms enjoy is the ability to obtain bulk discount on raw materials and other supplies. In such cases the curve does *not* shift. The different input prices are merely experienced at different points along the curve, and are reflected in the shape of the curve. Input prices are still given for any particular level of output.

The state of technology and input quality are given. These are assumed to change only in the *very* long run. If a firm gains economies of scale, it is because it is able to exploit *existing* technologies and make better use of the existing availability of inputs, thus shifting the curve downwards.

Firms operate efficiently. The assumption here is that firms operate efficiently: that they choose the cheapest possible way of producing any level of output. If the firm did not operate efficiently, it would be producing at a point above the *LRAC* curve.

Transactions costs

So far we have concentrated largely on production costs: the cost of the inputs used in the production process. There is another category of costs, however, that businesses will need to take into account when considering the scale and scope of their organisation. These are *transactions costs*: costs associated with the process of buying or selling. There are four main categories of transactions costs:

Search costs. In many cases, inputs can be obtained from a large number of suppliers and a firm will incur costs in searching out the best supplier in terms of price and/or quality. The problem here is that the firm starts with imperfect information and it takes time and money to obtain that information. It may employ a *logistics* company to seek out the best sources of supply, but obviously the logistics

> ### Definitions
>
> **Transactions costs** The costs associated with exchanging products. For buyers it is the costs over and above the price of the product. For sellers it is the costs over and above the costs of production.
>
> **Logistics** The business of managing and handling inputs to and outputs from a firm.

BOX 4.3 INDUSTRIAL CLUSTERS AND COMPETITIVENESS

External economies of scale in practice

In May 2003, the Department of Trade and Industry published a report by Michael Porter and Christian Ketels of Harvard Business School on the UK's competitiveness and how it might be improved.[1] The authors declared that since 1980 the UK had done remarkably well in halting its economic decline in world markets, and had in fact matched and even bettered its main rivals in many industrial sectors. Other sectors, however, were faring less well.

According to Porter and Ketels, a key part in any country's success is the development of successful industrial clusters, such as IT in California's Silicon Valley and financial services in the City of London. Such clusters can bring substantial external economies of scale, with individual firms benefiting from being part of a cluster.

> Clusters are geographically proximate groups of interconnected companies, suppliers, service providers, and associated institutions in a particular field, linked by commonalties and complementarities.[2]

Porter suggests that clusters are vital for competitiveness in three crucial respects:

- Clusters improve productivity. The close proximity of suppliers and other service providers enhances flexibility.
- Clusters aid innovation. Interaction among business within a cluster stimulates new ideas and aids their dissemination.

- Clusters contribute to new business formation. Clusters are self-reinforcing, in so far as specialist factors such as dedicated venture capital, and labour skills, help reduce costs and lower the risks of new business start-up.

The UK's industrial clusters were seen by Porter and Ketels as being relatively weak. In fact, many traditional clusters, such as steel and car manufacturing, had thinned to the point where they now lacked critical mass and failed to benefit from the clustering effect.

The UK mainly had strengths in the services sector, such as financial services, media, defence, products for personal use, healthcare and telecommunications. Lesser clusters were identified in entertainment, semiconductors and computers, transportation and office products.

Porter and Ketels concluded that, to improve its competitiveness, the UK must not only support what clusters it has, but endeavour to upgrade and contribute to their development.

> The UK needs to mount a sustained programme of cluster development to create a more conducive environment for productivity growth and innovation through the collective action of companies and other institutions . . . It will be essential to mobilise businesses and business institutions that are willing and able to engage in the upgrading of their clusters.[3]

---

[1] Michael E. Porter and Christian H. M. Ketels, *UK competitiveness: moving to the next stage* (DTI and ESRC, May 2003).
[2] Ibid., p. 27.

[3] Ibid., p. 46.

---

company will charge for its services. What is more, the firm may well run into the principal–agent problem unless it can monitor the behaviour of the logistics company – i.e. its agent (see pages 9–10).

Contract costs. When a supplier is found, time and effort may be incurred in bargaining over price and quality. If the supplier is to continue supplying over a period of time, then a contract will probably be negotiated. There will be costs in drawing up such contracts, including legal costs and the time of specialists to ensure that specifications are correct.

Monitoring and enforcement costs. When a contract has been drawn up, it is unlikely to cover every eventuality. To use the jargon, it is 'incomplete'. For example, if a logistics company is contracted to provide transportation of a manufacturing firm's products, the contract may specify maximum times for delivery. The manufacturing firm is then likely to incur costs in ensuring that the logistics firm sticks to the contract – and in taking action if it does not. What is more, there is a moral hazard involved (see pages pages 56–8). If the logistics firm *could* deliver items more quickly than specified in the contract, it will have no incentive to do so, even though it would have been in the manufacturer's interests.

Transport and handling costs. The more firms rely on buying components from other firms, rather than making them in-house, the greater will be the costs of transporting and handling these materials.

 KEY IDEA 16 *Transactions costs.* The costs associated with exchanging products. For buyers it is the costs over and above the price of the product. For sellers it is the costs over and above the costs of production. Transactions costs include search costs, contract costs, monitoring and enforcement costs, and transport and handling costs.

Pause for thought

What transactions costs do you incur when (a) going to the supermarket to do a regular shop; (b) buying a new laptop?

Transactions costs and the scale and scope of the firm

One way of reducing transactions costs is for the firm to produce more *within* the firm rather than buying inputs from other firms or supplying to other firms. What we

In 2012, the UK government took further steps to support cluster developments, including through the creation of Enterprise Zones. These zones aim to create jobs and boost business in 24 areas across England and, according to the Department of Communities and Local Government, since their foundation in April 2012, they have 'laid down the foundations for success for 540 businesses, attracting over £2.2 billion of private sector investment, building world class business facilities and transport links and attracting 19 000 jobs'.[4] Members of these zones benefit from lower business rates and more flexible planning regulations and cluster development has become an integral part of the remit of other policy areas, including science and innovation, export and foreign investment promotion and small- and medium-sized enterprise policies.

However, according to Porter and Ketels, the onus should not just be on government: businesses themselves need to take a more active role in developing clusters.

> Business leaders must take a more prominent role in cluster development and other efforts to upgrade UK and regional competitiveness. Without improvements in their business environments, companies' investments will otherwise be less profitable and effective.[5]

Also, more research needs to be conducted to understand the process of development of clusters and how best to exploit them.

Cluster development and upgrading needs to be based on a more rigorous understanding of emerging or established clusters in the UK. Past efforts have been incomplete and rigorous data to support cluster development is not yet available. The UK needs to mount a new, more comprehensive statistical effort on clusters at the national and regional level. New data requirements for companies may be needed to support the new economy.[6]

Over the next few decades, we are likely to see the development of clusters in emerging economies. Indeed, some industries have already begun the process, such as the migration of the automotive assembly industry to Asian economies. In the pharmaceutical industry, clusters in London and New York are expected to remain the leaders, but an existing cluster in Shanghai is expected to grow very quickly. PWC expects Hollywood and Los Angeles to remain dominant in the film industry until 2040, but suggests that competition from Mumbai and Shanghai is likely to emerge.[7]

 What policies or initiatives might a 'programme of cluster development' involve? Distinguish between policies that government and business might initiate.

[4] HM Government, Enterprise Zones.
[5] Porter and Ketels, *UK competitiveness*, p. 46.
[6] Ibid., p. 47.
[7] PwC, *Future industry clusters*.

---

are describing here is a ***vertically integrated firm***. This is where a firm is involved in several stages of the production of a good, such as component production, assembly and wholesale and retail distribution. The energy sector is an example of an industry with a considerable degree of vertical integration and you can read some of the articles concerning this in this first and second blog titled 'The Big Six: for how much longer?' on the Sloman Economics News site.

Firms may expand their operations vertically by integrating backwards down the *supply chain* or forwards up it. *Backward integration* is where a firm itself produces the inputs it needs. Thus a car manufacturer may itself produce components such as body panels, engines and trimmings. *Forward integration* is where a firm itself moves into producing stages closer to the end consumer. Thus a manufacturer of building materials may move into construction or become a builder's merchant.

Through vertical integration, a firm is able to avoid many of the costs discussed above. For example, a firm will not need to compare different suppliers, so will not incur search costs. As components are produced in-house, they do not need to be transported from one location to another and so transport and handling costs will fall. As no contracts exist between the firm and any supplier, legal fees will not be an issue and nor will the problem of monitoring and enforcing any contract. We return to this in section 6.2, where we will take a closer look at some other reasons why firms may vertically integrate, as well as the disadvantages of it.

Definitions

Vertically integrated firm A firm that produces at more than one stage in the production and distribution of a product.

Supply chain The flow of inputs into a finished product, from the raw materials stage, through manufacturing and distribution, right through to the sale to the final consumer.

Backward integration Where a firm expands backwards down the supply chain to earlier stages of production.

Forward integration Where a firm expands forward up the supply chain towards the sale of the finished product.

BOX 4.4 **MINIMUM EFFICIENT SCALE**

The extent of economies of scale in practice

Two of the most important studies of economies of scale have been those made by C. F. Pratten[1] in the late 1980s and by a group advising the European Commission[2] in 1997. Both studies found strong evidence that many firms, especially in manufacturing, experienced substantial economies of scale.

In a few cases, long-run average costs fell continuously as output increased. For most firms, however, they fell up to a certain level of output and then remained constant.

The extent of economies of scale can be measured by looking at a firm's *minimum efficient scale* (*MES*). The *MES* is the size beyond which no significant additional economies of scale can be achieved; in other words, the point where the *LRAC* curve flattens off. In Pratten's studies he defined this level as the minimum scale above which any possible doubling in scale would reduce average costs by less than 5 per cent (i.e. virtually the bottom of the *LRAC* curve). In the diagram *MES* is shown at point *a*.

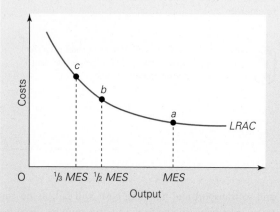

The *MES* can be expressed in terms either of an individual factory or of the whole firm. Where it refers to the minimum efficient scale of an individual factory, the *MES* is known as the *minimum efficient plant size* (*MEPS*).

The *MES* can then be expressed as a percentage of the total size of the market or of total domestic production. Table (a), based on the Pratten study, shows *MES* for plants and firms in various industries. The first column shows *MES* as a percentage of total UK production. The second column shows *MES* as a percentage of total EU production. Table (b), based on the 1997 study, shows *MES* for various plants as a percentage of total EU production.

Expressing *MES* as a percentage of total output gives an indication of how competitive the industry could be. In some industries (such as footwear and carpets), economies of scale were exhausted (i.e. *MES* was reached) with plants or firms that were still small relative to total UK production and even smaller relative to total EU production. In such industries there would be room for many firms and thus scope for considerable competition.

In other industries, however, even if a single plant or firm were large enough to produce the whole output of the industry in the UK, it would still not be large enough to experience the full potential economies of scale; the *MES* is greater than 100 per cent. Examples from Table (a) include factories producing cellulose fibres, and car manufacturers. In such industries there is no possibility of competition. In fact, as long as the *MES* exceeds 50 per cent there will not be room for more than one firm large enough to gain full economies of scale. In this case the industry is said to be a *natural monopoly*. As we shall see in the next few chapters, when competition is lacking consumers may suffer by firms charging prices considerably above costs.

A second way of measuring the extent of economies of scale is to see how much costs would increase if production were reduced to a certain fraction of *MES*. The normal fractions used are 1/2 or 1/3 *MES*. This is illustrated in the diagram. Point *b* corresponds to 1/2 *MES*; point *c* to 1/3 *MES*. The greater the percentage by which *LRAC* at point *b* or *c* is higher than at point *a*, the greater will be the economies of scale to be gained by producing at *MES* rather than at 1/2 *MES* or 1/3 *MES*. For example, in the table there are greater economies of scale to be gained from moving from 1/2 *MES* to *MES* in the production of electric motors than in cigarettes.

The main purpose of the studies was to determine whether a single EU market is big enough to allow both economies of scale and competition. The tables suggest that in all cases, other things being equal, the EU market is large enough for firms to gain the full economies of scale *and* for there to be enough firms for the market to be competitive.

The second study also found that 47 of the 53 manufacturing sectors analysed had scope for further exploitation of economies of scale.

With the EU having expanded significantly since these two studies and with the use of the Internet growing all the time, firms across the EU are part of an increasingly large market. Further studies that consider the MES across different

[1] C. F. Pratten, 'A survey of the economies of scale', in *Research on the 'Costs of Non-Europe'*, Volume 2 (Luxembourg: Office for Official Publications of the European Communities, 1988). Copyright © 1988 European Communities.
[2] European Commission/Economists Advisory Group Ltd, 'Economies of scale', in *The Single Market Review*, Subseries V, Vol. 4 (Luxembourg: Office for Official Publications of the European Communities, 1997). Copyright © 1997 European Communities.

Table (a)

Product	MES as % of production		% additional cost at half MES
	UK	EU	
Individual plants			
Cellulose fibres	125	16	3
Rolled aluminium semi-manufactures	114	15	15
Refrigerators	85	11	4
Steel	72	10	6
Electric motors	60	6	15
TV sets	40	9	9
Cigarettes	24	6	1.4
Ball-bearings	20	2	6
Beer	12	3	7
Nylon	4	1	12
Bricks	1	0.2	25
Tufted carpets	0.3	0.04	10
Shoes	0.3	0.03	1
Firms			
Cars	200	20	9
Lorries	104	21	7.5
Mainframe computers	>100	n.a.	5
Aircraft	100	n.a.	5
Tractors	98	19	6

Sources: see footnote 1

Table (b)

Plants	MES as % of total EU production
Aerospace	12.19
Tractors and agricultural machinery	6.57
Electric lighting	3.76
Steel tubes	2.42
Shipbuilding	1.63
Rubber	1.06
Radio and TV	0.69
Footwear	0.08
Carpets	0.03

Source: see footnote 2

industries, especially in the EU, are vital to determine whether continued expansion will bring benefits in terms of falling *LRAC* and thus economies of scale or if continued enlargement could lead to diseconomies of scale. *MES* studies could be used to address the question: how big is too big when it comes to the EU? The European Commission has agreed to fund such investigations, but no research is available at present.

1. Why might a firm operating with one plant achieve MEPS and yet not be large enough to achieve MES? (Clue: are all economies of scale achieved at plant level?)
2. Why might a firm producing bricks have an MES which is only 0.2 per cent of total EU production and yet face little effective competition from other EU countries?

RECAP

1. In the long run, a firm is able to vary the quantity of all its inputs. There are no fixed inputs and hence there are no fixed costs.

2. If it increases all inputs by the same proportion, it may experience constant, increasing or decreasing returns to scale.

3. Economies of scale occur when costs per unit of output fall as the scale of production increases. This can be due to a number of factors, some of which are directly caused by increasing (physical) returns to scale. These include the benefits of specialisation and division of labour, the use of larger and more efficient machines, and the ability to have a more integrated system of production. Other economies of scale arise from the financial and administrative benefits of large-scale organisations.

4. Typically, *LRAC* curves are drawn as L-shaped or as saucer-shaped. As output expands, initially there are economies of scale. When these are exhausted, the curve will become flat. When the firm becomes very large, it may begin to experience diseconomies of scale. If this happens, the *LRAC* curve will begin to slope upwards again.

5. Transactions costs are the costs associated with exchanging products. They include search costs, the costs of drawing up and monitoring contracts and transport and handling costs. The more firms rely on other firms as suppliers or buyers, the larger these costs are likely to be. Vertical integration is one way of reducing such transactions costs.

4.3 REVENUE

Remember that we defined a firm's total profit as its total revenue minus its total costs of production. In the last two sections we have examined costs. We now turn to revenue.

As with costs, we distinguish between three revenue concepts: total revenue (*TR*), average revenue (*AR*) and marginal revenue (*MR*).

Total, average and marginal revenue

Total revenue (TR)
Total revenue is the firm's total earnings per period of time from the sale of a particular amount of output (*Q*).

For example, if a firm sells 1000 units (*Q*) per month at a price of £5 each (*P*), then its monthly total revenue will be £5000: in other words, £5 × 1000 (*P* × *Q*). Thus:

$$TR = P \times Q$$

Average revenue (AR)
Average revenue is the amount the firm earns per unit sold. Thus:

$$AR = TR/Q$$

So if the firm earns £5000 (*TR*) from selling 1000 units (*Q*), it will earn £5 per unit. But this is simply the price! Thus:

$$AR = P$$

Marginal revenue (MR)
Marginal revenue is the extra total revenue gained by selling one more unit (per time period). So if a firm sells an extra 20 units this month compared with what it expected to sell, and in the process earns an extra £100, then it is getting an extra £5 for each extra unit sold: *MR* = £5. Thus:

$$MR = \Delta TR / \Delta Q$$

We now need to see how revenue varies with output. We concentrate on average and marginal revenue. We can show this relationship graphically in the same way as we did with costs.

The relationship will depend on the market conditions under which a firm operates. The revenue curves we look at in this section are for a price-taking firm: a firm that faces a horizontal demand curve (see section 3.1). When firms face a downward-sloping demand curve and thus have some choice in setting price, they will face different revenue curves. We look at such curves in the next chapter.

Average and marginal revenue curves

Average revenue. We are assuming in this chapter that the firm has such a small share of the market that it is a price taker. That is, it has to accept the price given by the intersection of demand and supply in the whole market. At this price, it can sell as much as it is capable of producing, but if it increases the price, it would lose all its sales to competitors. Furthermore, it would be irrational to reduce price below the equilibrium. This is illustrated in Figure 4.3.

Definitions

Total revenue (*TR*) **(per period)** The total amount received by firms from the sale of a product, before the deduction of taxes or any other costs. The price multiplied by the quantity sold: $TR = P \times Q$.

Average revenue (*AR*) Total revenue per unit of output. When all output is sold at the same price, average revenue will be the same as price: $AR = TR/Q = P$.

Marginal revenue (*MR*) The extra revenue gained by selling one or more units per time period: $MR = \Delta TR/\Delta Q$.

| Figure 4.3 | Deriving a firm's AR and MR: price-taking firm |

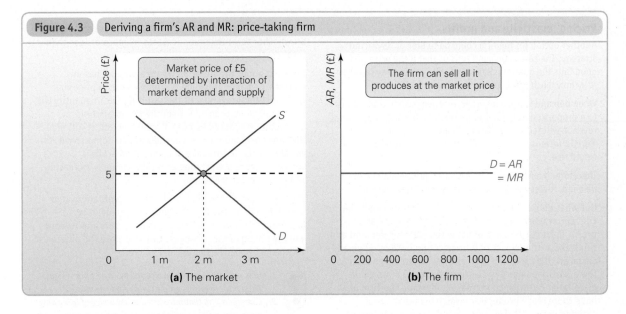

(a) The market   **(b)** The firm

Figure 4.3(a) shows market demand and supply. Equilibrium price is £5. Figure 4.3(b) looks at the demand for an individual firm which is tiny relative to the whole market. (Look at the difference in the scale of the horizontal axes in the two diagrams.)

Being so small, any change in the firm's output will be too insignificant to affect the market price. The firm thus faces a horizontal demand 'curve' at this price. It can sell any output up to its maximum capacity without affecting this £5 price.

Average revenue is thus constant at £5. The firm's average revenue curve must therefore lie along exactly the same line as its demand curve.

Marginal revenue. In the case of a horizontal demand curve, the marginal revenue curve will be the same as the average revenue curve, since selling one more unit at a constant price (*AR*) merely adds that amount to total revenue. If an extra unit is sold at a constant price of £5, an extra £5 is earned.

BOX 4.5 COST, REVENUE AND PROFITS

Strategies to increase total revenue

A firm's profit depends on two key factors: costs and revenue. If a firm's costs increase, while its revenue remains constant, then profits will fall. Whereas if a firm can increase its total revenue without incurring a rise in costs then profits will rise. If both total revenue and total costs change in the same direction, then we are unable to determine the impact on profits, unless we know the amount by which they each change. In this box, we consider some strategies to increase revenue, while also considering the potential effect of such strategies on costs and, in turn, on profits.

Total revenue is determined by price and quantity, so a change in either factor will affect total revenue. How might a firm go about boosting sales at the current price? Firms may look to find new markets for their products, as we have seen with companies such as Apple, which have expanded into Asian markets.

Another strategy used by firms is product differentiation. This aims to distinguish their product from others and encourage consumers to switch to it. Alternatively, a firm may engage in advertising to try to persuade consumers to buy the product.

With successful implementation of these strategies, at any given price, quantity should now rise and hence so will total revenue. But does this mean that profits increase?

Advertising, product innovation and market research require time, resources and money and so can be very expensive. While the outcome of such investment might be an increase in total revenue, the means of achieving it will be an increase in total costs. This means that unless we know the relative increase in total revenue and total costs, the impact on profits will be unknown.

Furthermore, the increase in costs will occur as soon as work starts on the process of product differentiation or market research, or at the beginning of an advertising campaign. The increase in revenue may not be felt for some time, as advertising campaigns, entrance into a new market and a differentiated product can take many months before having the anticipated effect. Any firm engaging in such a strategy may therefore experience a time period in which its costs are rising while revenue is remaining fairly constant. In other words, profits decline, until the sales figures respond to the firm's strategy. In 2013, Starbucks implemented a strategy to boost profits, as is discussed in an article by Tucker Dawson.[1]

---

[1] Tucker Dawson, 'How Starbucks uses pricing strategy for profit maximization', *Price Intelligently* (30 June 2013).

▶

Pricing, elasticity and profits

Another option for the firm could be to look at its pricing strategy. The Law of Demand tells us that if the price of a good falls the quantity demanded will rise. The key question is by how much will quantity demanded rise?

When demand is price inelastic, any decrease in price leads to a proportionately smaller increase in demand and so total revenue will fall (as we saw in Chapter 2). But if the firm were to *increase* the price of such a product, total revenue would rise.

Therefore, if a firm knows its product's price elasticity of demand, it can use this to help it increase total revenue.

But what about the impact on profits? Let us revisit the concept of elasticity and its relation to revenue and profit. Consider now a product with an *elastic* demand and think about the impact of a price cut on both revenue and costs. In this case, a cut in price will boost revenue, as the quantity demand rises proportionately more than price falls. But with an increase in demand the firm may have to increase production, which means its total variable costs will rise, and possibly its average variable costs too (although average fixed costs will fall). If, however, the firm has sufficient stocks to satisfy the higher demand, then the impact on costs may be less

severe. With elastic demand, the impact on profit depends on whether total revenue increases by more or less than total costs.

But what about the situation where a product has an inelastic demand? This time it is an *increase* in price that will boost total revenue, as the resulting fall in quantity will be proportionately smaller than the rise in price. If production is reduced by even a small amount, it will reduce the firm's demand for raw materials and in doing so cut its variable costs. In this case, the impact on profit is somewhat more predictable, as total revenue is increasing, while total costs are falling.

There are many factors that can influence profitability and whenever a firm considers a change in strategy, it is important to consider the impact on both costs and revenue and the timing of such changes. This may make the difference between a company's success and failure.

1. How will total revenue be affected by (a) a price rise and (b) a price fall if the product was relatively elastic?
2. Consider a firm that introduced a new policy of using only environmentally friendly inputs and locally sourced products in its production process. Analyse the impact of this strategy on the firm's costs and revenue. How do you think profits will be affected?

RECAP

1. Total revenue (*TR*) is the total amount a firm earns from its sales in a given time period. It is simply price multiplied by quantity: $TR = P \times Q$.

2. Average revenue (*AR*) is total revenue per unit: $AR = TR/Q$. In other words, $AR = P$.

3. Marginal revenue is the extra revenue earned from the sale of one more unit per time period: $MR = \Delta TR/\Delta Q$.

4. The *AR* curve will be the same as the demand curve for the firm's product. In the case of a price taker, the demand curve and hence the *AR* curve will be a horizontal straight line and will also be the same as the *MR* curve.

4.4 PROFIT MAXIMISATION

We are now in a position to put costs and revenue together to find the output at which profit is maximised, and also to find out how much that profit will be. At this point, you may find an article by Renee O'Farrell[5] interesting: it considers the advantages and disadvantages of pursuing a strategy of profit maximisation. First we need to look a little more precisely at what we mean by the term 'profit'.

The meaning of 'profit'

One element of cost is the opportunity cost to the owners of the firm incurred by being in business. This is the minimum return that the owners must make on their capital in order to prevent them from eventually deciding to close down and

perhaps move into some alternative business. It is a *cost* since, just as with wages, rent, etc., it has to be covered if the firm is to continue producing. This opportunity cost to the owners is sometimes known as *normal profit*, and is included in the cost curves.

What determines this normal rate of profit? It has two components. First, someone setting up in business invests capital in it. There is thus an opportunity cost, which is the interest that could have been earned by lending the capital

> **Definition**
>
> **Normal profit** The opportunity cost of being in business. It consists of the interest that could be earned on a riskless asset, plus a return for risk taking in this particular industry. It is counted as a cost of production.

---

[5] Renee O'Farrell, 'Advantages & disadvantages of profit maximization', *Small Business*Chron.com* (Houston Chronicle, 24 June 2011).

Figure 4.4 Short-run equilibrium of industry and firm under perfect competition

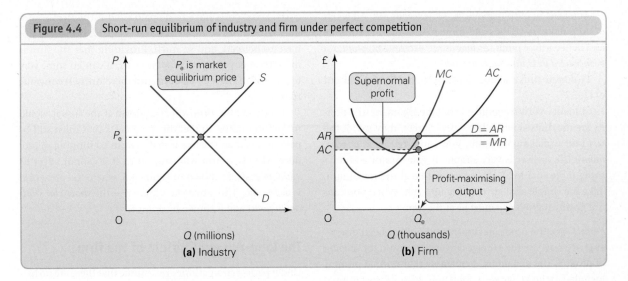

(a) Industry   **(b)** Firm

---

in some riskless form (e.g. by putting it in a savings account in a bank). Nobody would set up a business unless they expected to earn at least this rate of profit. Running a business is far from riskless, however, and hence a second element is a return to compensate for risk. Thus:

Normal profit (%) = rate of interest on a riskless loan + a risk premium

The risk premium varies according to the line of business. In those with fairly predictable patterns, such as food retailing, it is relatively low. Where outcomes are very uncertain, such as mineral exploration or the manufacture of fashion garments, it is relatively high. Thus if owners of a business earn normal profit, they will (just) be content to remain in that industry.

Any excess of profit over normal profit is known as *supernormal profit*. If firms earn supernormal profit, they will clearly prefer to stay in this business. Such profit will also tend to attract new firms into the industry, since it will give them a better return on capital than elsewhere. If firms earn *less* than normal profit, however, then after a time they will consider leaving and using their capital for some other purpose. The article 'Milk prices: who gets the cream?', from the Sloman Economics News site, considers profitability in the milk industry.

Short-run profit maximising

In the *short run under perfect competition*, we assume that the number of firms in an industry cannot be increased: there is simply not time for new firms to enter the market.

Figure 4.4 shows short-run equilibrium for an industry and the profit-maximising position for a firm under perfect competition. Both parts of the diagram have the same scale for the vertical axis. The horizontal axes have totally different scales, however. For example, if the horizontal axis for the firm were measured in, say, thousands of units, the

horizontal axis for the whole industry might be measured in millions or tens of millions of units, depending on the number of firms in the industry.

Let us examine the determination of price, output and profit in turn.

Price. The price is determined in the industry by the intersection of demand and supply. The firm faces a horizontal demand (or average revenue) 'curve' at this price. It can sell all it can produce at the market price (P_e), but nothing at a price above P_e and we know it would not be rational to sell at a price below P_e.

Output. The firm will maximise profit where marginal cost equals marginal revenue ($MR = MC$), at an output of Q_e. In fact this *profit-maximising rule* will apply to firms in all types of market, as long as we assume that the objective of the firm is to maximise profits, so it is very important to understand.

But why are profits maximised when $MR = MC$? The simplest way of answering this is to see what the position would be if MR did not equal MC.

Referring to Figure 4.4, at a level of output below Q_e, MR exceeds MC. This means that by producing more units there will be a bigger addition to revenue (MR) than to cost (MC). Total profit will *increase. As long as MR exceeds MC, profit can be increased by increasing production.*

Definitions

Supernormal profit The excess of total profit above normal profit.

Short run under perfect competition The period during which there is too little time for new firms to enter the industry.

Profit-maximising rule Profit is maximised where marginal revenue equals marginal cost.

At a level of output above Q_e, MC exceeds MR. All levels of output above Q_e thus add more to cost than to revenue and hence *reduce* profit. *As long as MC exceeds MR, profit can be increased by cutting back on production.*

Profits are thus maximised where $MC = MR$: at an output of Q_e.

Students worry sometimes about the argument that profits are maximised when $MR = MC$. Surely, they say, if the last unit is making no profit, how can profit be at a *maximum*? The answer is very simple. If you cannot add anything more to a total, the total must be at the maximum. Take the simple analogy of going up a hill. When you cannot go any higher, you must be at the top.

Profit. Once the profit-maximising output has been discovered, we now use the average curves to measure the *amount* of profit at the maximum. Remember that normal profit is included in the AC curve. If, therefore, $AC = AR$, just normal profit will be made. For example, if the price (AR) were £8 and AC were also £8, then the firm would be earning enough revenue to cover all its costs and still earn normal profit, but no supernormal profit.

If the firm's average cost (AC) curve dips below the average revenue (AR) 'curve', as in Figure 4.4, the firm will earn supernormal profit. Supernormal profit per unit at Q_e is the vertical difference between AR and AC at Q_e. So if AR (= P) were £10 and AC were £8, then supernormal profit per unit would be £2.

Total supernormal profit at Q_e is found by multiplying supernormal profit per unit (AR – AC) by the total number of units sold (Q_e). This is given by the area of the shaded rectangle in Figure 4.4. The reason is that the area of a rectangle is found by multiplying its height (AR – AC) by its width (Q_e).

Loss minimising. Sometimes there may be no output at which the firm can make even normal profit. Such a situation is illustrated in Figure 4.5. With the average revenue 'curve' given by AR_1, the AC curve is above the AR curve at all levels of output.

> ### Pause for thought
>
> 1. If the industry under perfect competition faces a downward-sloping demand curve, why does an individual firm face a horizontal demand curve?
> 2. What will be the effect on a firm's profit-maximising output of a rise in fixed costs?

In this case, the output where $MR = MC$ will be the loss-minimising output. The amount of loss at the point where $MR = MC$ is shown by the shaded area in Figure 4.5.

Whether or not to produce. If a firm is making a loss, however, should it shut down? To answer this we need to return to our distinction between fixed and variable

costs. Fixed costs have to be paid even if the firm is producing nothing at all. Rent has to be paid, business rates have to be paid, and so forth. Providing that the firm is more than covering its *variable* costs, it can go some way to paying off these fixed costs and therefore will continue to produce.

Therefore, the firm will shut down if the loss it would make from doing so (i.e. the fixed costs that must still be paid) is less than the loss it makes from continuing to produce. That is, a firm will shut down if it cannot cover its variable costs, as shown in Figure 4.5, where the price (AR) is below AR_2. This situation is known as the **short-run shutdown point** and is shown by point S.

The long-run equilibrium of the firm

Under perfect competition, we assume that there are no barriers to entry for new firms and in the long run we assume that there is time for firms to enter the industry. This will occur if typical firms are making supernormal profits. Likewise, if existing firms can make supernormal profits by increasing the scale of their operations, they will do so, since all inputs are variable in the long run.

The effect of the entry of new firms and/or the expansion of existing firms is to increase industry supply. This is illustrated in Figure 4.6.

The industry supply curve shifts to the right. This in turn leads to a fall in price. Supply will go on increasing, and price falling, until firms are making just normal profits. This will be when price has fallen to the point where the demand 'curve' for the firm just touches the bottom of its long-run average cost curve. This is shown as curve D_L. Q_L is thus the long-run equilibrium output of the firm, with P_L the long-run equilibrium market price. This long-run equilibrium is productively efficient, as the firm is producing at the minimum average cost. If the firm is unable to cover its long-run average costs, it will shut down and exit the industry.

> ### Pause for thought
>
> Consider a perfectly competitive market where losses are being made in the short run by a given firm. By drawing a diagram to illustrate this, use the same analysis as we used above to explain what will happen in this market such that we arrive at a long-run equilibrium.

> ### Definition
>
> **Short-run shut-down point** This is where the AR curve is tangential to the AVC curve. The firm can only just cover its variable costs. Any fall in revenue below this level will cause a profit-maximising firm to shut down immediately.

Figure 4.5 Loss-minimising under perfect competition

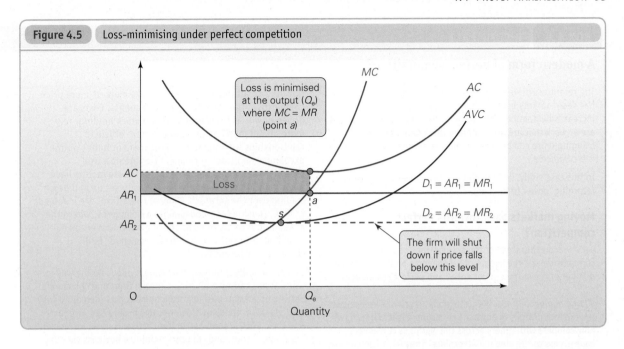

Figure 4.6 Long-run equilibrium under perfect competition

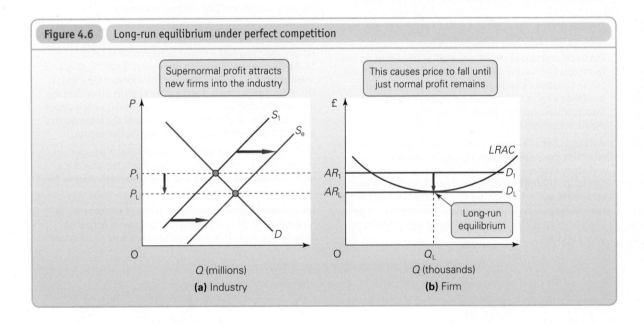

Do firms and consumers benefit from perfect competition?

Under perfect competition the firm faces a constant battle for survival. In the long run, firms produce at minimum average cost and hence are productively efficient. If it becomes less efficient than other firms, it will make less than normal profits and be driven out of business. If it becomes more efficient, it will earn supernormal profits. But these supernormal profits will not last for long. Soon other firms, in order to survive themselves, will be forced to copy the more efficient methods

of the new firm or other firms will enter, pushing down the market price.

It is the same with the development of new products. If a firm is able to produce a new product that is popular with consumers, it will be able to gain a temporary advantage over its rivals. But again, any supernormal profits will last only as long as it takes other firms to respond. Soon the increase in supply of the new product will drive the price down and eliminate these supernormal profits. Similarly, the firm must be quick to copy new products developed by its rivals. If it does not, it will soon make a loss and be driven out of the market.

BOX 4.6 **E-COMMERCE**

A modern form of perfect competition?

The relentless drive towards big business in recent decades has seen markets become more concentrated and increasingly dominated by large producers. However, forces are at work that are undermining this dominance, and bringing more competition to markets. One of these forces is *e-commerce*.

In this case study, we consider just how far e-commerce is returning 'power to the people'.

Moving markets back towards perfect competition?

Let us reconsider three of the assumptions of perfect competition and the impact of e-commerce on them: a large number of firms; freedom of entry; and perfect knowledge.

A large number of firms. With the global reach of the Internet, the number of firms in any market has increased. Firms must now compete with others across the world, as consumers have access to the global marketplace. They must keep an eye on the prices and products of competitors worldwide and be aware of the continual emergence of new, smaller businesses.

Freedom of entry. The Internet has had a key role to play here, reducing the costs of business start-ups.

The traditional idea of rented office space, large start-up and fixed costs is no longer the only way to run a business. Small online companies have been created from home, with little more than a computer, and many companies are transferring their purchases to the Internet, finding that prices can be significantly cheaper.

Marketing costs for small Internet-based companies can be relatively low, especially with powerful search engines, and many of these new online companies are more specialist, relying on interest 'outsourcing' (buying parts, equipment and other supplies through the Internet) rather than making everything themselves. They are also more likely to use delivery firms rather than having their own transport fleet.

Not only do all the above factors make markets more price competitive, they also bring other benefits. Costs are driven down, as firms economise on stock holding, rely more on outsourcing and develop more efficient relationships with suppliers. 'Procurement hubs', online exchanges and trading communities are now well established in many industries. All of these factors have made it relatively cheap for new firms to set up and begin trading over the Internet. Many of these firms are involved in 'B2C' (business-to-consumers) e-commerce, where they are selling directly to us as consumers. However, many have begun to sell to other firms, known as 'B2B' (business-to-business).

One particularly interesting example is eBay and the way in which it has caused a blurring between firms and consumers. Setting up a small business from home is now incredibly easy and, via eBay, consumers can become businesses with just one click. With around 160 million active users worldwide and hundreds of thousands of users running a business via eBay in the UK, buying and selling 'junk' has become a viable source of income. Estimates suggest that at any one time, there are over 800 million 'listings' on eBay.

eBay itself is an example of a business that expanded with the growth of the Internet. Founded in 1995, eBay grew rapidly, reaching half a million users and revenues of $4.7 billion in the USA within three years. In 2015, eBay's revenue was $8.6 billion. However this represented a slight fall of $0.2 billion from a year earlier as many other sites are increasingly offering similar services. However, eBay's global reach and volume of customers, courtesy of the Internet, has enabled it to maintain a position of market dominance.

Although it is just one company, the fact that it has millions of users, acting as businesses, means that it has provided a highly competitive environment, despite its dominance as the main provider of such a service.

The increase in competition from the rise of e-commerce, in whatever form, has led to firms' demand curves becoming more price elastic. This is especially the case for goods which

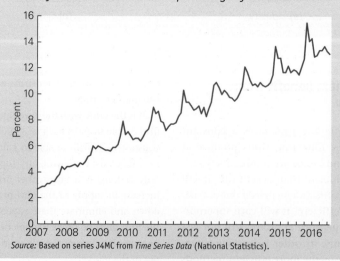

Value of Internet retail sales as a percentage of total retail sales

Source: Based on series J4MC from *Time Series Data* (National Statistics).

are cheap to transport or for services, such as travel agents, insurance and banking. While some large firms, such as Amazon, do provide competition for the more traditional firms, the greater freedom of entry for new firms that has been created by the Internet is providing an ever-increasing degree of competition, as more and more small businesses are set up every day. This has also created a more innovative environment, where the quality and range of products is also growing daily.

Perfect knowledge. The Internet has also added to consumer knowledge. There are some obvious ways, e.g. facts and figures through sites such as Wikipedia, information on where to eat or stay through sites such as TripAdvisor and technical information on products on sites such as Amazon. However, it has also improved consumer knowledge through greater transparency. Online shopping agents such as Kelkoo and Google and online comparison sites such as GoCompare and MoneySupermarket can quickly locate a list of alternative suppliers and their prices. There is greater information on product availability, quality and consumer feedback. Virtual shopping malls, full of e-retailers, place the high-street retailer under intense competitive pressure.

We have seen evidence of this online competition, with the decline or downfall of some well-known high-street retailers, such as HMV, Comet, Peacocks and Borders. Although the weak trading conditions following the economic downturn after 2007 were partly to blame, it has also been the sheer volume of competition these companies face from the Internet. HMV faces steep competition from companies like Amazon, as DVDs, BluRay and CDs can be sold much more cheaply online. LoveFilm and Netflix also provide a new way of watching films.

Google shopping allows consumers to compare prices on larger consumer durables such as fridges, cookers and washing machines, and with the large supermarkets offering such items online and price comparisons being so easy, consumers are finding bargains on the Internet. These competitive pressures from online retailing certainly added to the woes of Comet and other companies that collapsed.

It is not just the traditional consumer that has benefited from greater and better information. Many firms are also consumers, purchasing inputs from other firms. It is now commonplace for firms to use the Internet to search for cheaper sources of supply. This is even more relevant now that many firms face a worldwide marketplace and can source their supplies from across the globe.

The limits to e-commerce

In 20 years, will we be doing all our shopping on the Internet? Will the only shopping malls be virtual ones? Although e-commerce is revolutionising some markets, it is unlikely that things will go anything like that far.

One benefit of 'shop shopping' is that you get to see the good, touch it and use it, and can buy the good there and then. Although you can order things online and get next-day or even same-day delivery, it's still not quite instant

possession. Furthermore, people like wandering round the shops, meeting friends, seeing what takes their fancy, trying on clothes, browsing through DVDs and so on. 'Retail therapy' is an enjoyable experience for many and they are prepared to pay for it.

Online shopping can be limited by technology and infrastructure as, although the quality and speed of the Internet has improved, purchases can be hampered by busy sites and slow connections. Online shopping means you have to wait for your purchases to be delivered and, as noted above, most people much prefer to have goods today rather than tomorrow! Also, what if deliveries are late or fail completely? In the run-up to Christmas, Internet shopping is at its highest and one of the biggest problems is parcels going missing. In 2011, Yodel failed to deliver around 15 000 parcels per day as Christmas approached, as discussed in a Financial Times article.[1] Similar problems occurred in 2014 when, 10 days before Christmas, Yodel announced that it was no longer collecting parcels for delivery due to a backlog. You can read about this in the Guardian[2] and Mail Online.[3] Their delivery infrastructure simply could not cope with the increase in demand from online shopping. Many consumers remain concerned with the security of Internet shopping, as credit/debit cards must be used and this, in itself, means that Internet shopping is not available to everyone.

Also, costs might not be as low as expected. How efficient is it to have many small deliveries of goods? How significant are the lost cost savings from economies of scale that larger producers or retailers are likely to generate?

Nevertheless, new markets have been created by e-commerce and it has made many existing markets, both retail and B2B, more competitive. This is especially so for services and for goods whose quality is easy to identify online. Many firms are being forced to face up to having their prices determined by the market.

1. *Give three examples of products that are particularly suitable for selling over the Internet and three that are not. Explain your answer.*
2. *Before reading ahead, consider your own shopping and buying habits – how much shopping do you do online? What do you think are the limits to e-commerce? Compare your answers with a friend and try to determine the key factors that explain any differences and what, then, are the limits to e-commerce?*
3. *Why may the Internet work better for replacement buys than for new purchases?*
4. *Explain how eBay can both increase competition across the economy and simultaneously acquire very substantial monopoly power.*

---

[1] Claer Barrett, 'Surge in online orders hits deliveries', *Financial Times* (23 December 2011).

[2] Gwyn Topham, 'Yodel warns of parcel backlog as Christmas deliveries face delay', *The Guardian* (12 December 2014).

[3] Ben Wilkinson, 'Deliver firm Yodel's boss forced into apology after delays mean thousands of customers may not receive parcels in time for Christmas' *Mail Online* (24 December 2014).

As far as consumers are concerned, they benefit from perfect competition, as prices are as low as they can be – at minimum average cost. We therefore see consumer surplus at its maximum.

However, consumers have no choice, as products are homogenous and firms have no funds available for research and development, quality improvements or product innovation. Finally, perfectly competitive firms are unable to exploit economies of scale, as by definition economies of scale occur as firms expand output, but perfect competition requires firms to be small.

Pause for thought

Why is it highly unlikely that an industry where firms can gain substantial economies of scale can also be perfectly competitive?

Perfect competition is often used as a benchmark to assess the effectiveness of actual markets. However, we should be careful when talking about a 'perfectly' competitive market, as it would not necessarily be an ideal environment for promoting new products and new technologies, as an article from Mises Institute, a pro-free-market organisation, argues.[6]

[6] Friedrich A. Hayek, 'The Meaning of Competition', *Mises Daily Articles*, Mises Institute (15 March 2010) (an excerpt from Hayek's *Individualism and Economic Order*, Mises Institute (originally published 1947)

RECAP

1. Normal profit is the minimum profit that must be made to persuade a firm to stay in business in the long run. It is counted as part of the firm's costs. Supernormal profit is any profit over and above normal profit.

2. The maximum profit output is where marginal revenue equals marginal cost. Having found this output, the level of maximum (supernormal) profit can be found by finding the average (supernormal) profit ($AR - AC$) and then multiplying it by the level of output.

3. For a firm that cannot make a profit at any level of output, the point where $MR = MC$ represents the loss-minimising output. In the short run, a firm will close down if it cannot cover its variable costs. In the long run, it will close down if it cannot make normal profits.

4. In the short run, there is not time for new firms to enter the market, and thus supernormal profits can persist. In the long run, however, any supernormal profits will be competed away by the entry of new firms.

QUESTIONS

1. Are all explicit costs variable costs? Are all variable costs explicit costs?

2. Up to roughly how long is the short run in the following cases?

   (a) A mobile karaoke firm.
   (b) Electricity power generation.
   (c) A small grocery retailing business.
   (d) 'Superstore Hypermarkets plc'.

   In each case, specify your assumptions.

3. The following are some costs incurred by a shoe manufacturer. Decide whether each one is a fixed cost or a variable cost or has some element of both.

   (a) The cost of leather.
   (b) The fee paid to an advertising agency.
   (c) Wear and tear on machinery.
   (d) Business rates on the factory.
   (e) Electricity for heating and lighting.
   (f) Electricity for running the machines.
   (g) Basic minimum wages agreed with the union.
   (h) Overtime pay.
   (i) Depreciation of machines as a result purely of their age (irrespective of their condition).

4. Why does the marginal cost curve pass through the bottom of the average cost curve and the average variable cost curve?

5. Does the marginal value of a variable (such as cost, revenue or profit) determine the average value of the variable, or does the average value of the variable determine the marginal value? Explain your answer.

6. What economies of scale is a large department store likely to experience?

7. Why are many firms likely to experience economies of scale up to a certain size and then diseconomies of scale after some point beyond that?

8. Normal profits are regarded as a cost (and are included in the cost curves). Explain why.

9. What determines the size of normal profit? Will it vary with the general state of the economy?

10. A firm will continue producing in the short run even if it is making a loss, providing it can cover its variable costs. Explain why. Just how long will it be willing to continue making such a loss?

11. Would it ever be worthwhile for a firm to try to continue in production if it could not cover its *long-run* average (total) costs?

12. The price of tablet computers and digital cameras fell significantly in the years after they were first introduced and at the same time demand for them increased substantially. Use cost and revenue diagrams to illustrate these events. Explain the reasoning behind the diagram(s) you have drawn.

13. Illustrate on a diagram similar to Figure 4.6 what would happen in the long run if price were initially below P_L.

ADDITIONAL PART B CASE STUDIES ON THE *ESSENTIAL ECONOMICS FOR BUSINESS* WEBSITE (www.pearsoned.co.uk/sloman)

B.1 The interdependence of markets. A case study of the operation of markets, examining the effects on a local economy of the discovery of a large shale oil deposit.

B.2 Coffee prices. An examination of the coffee market and the implications of fluctuations in the coffee harvest for growers and coffee drinkers.

B.3 The measurement of elasticity. This examines how to work out the value for elasticity using the 'mid-point' method.

B.4 Any more fares? Pricing on the buses: an illustration of the relationship between price and total revenue.

B.5 Shall we put up our price? Some examples of firms charging high prices in markets where demand is relatively inelastic.

B.6 Elasticities of demand for various foodstuffs. An examination of the evidence about price and income elasticities of demand for food in the UK.

B.7 Adjusting to oil price shocks. A case study showing how demand and supply analysis can be used to examine the price changes in the oil market since 1973.

B.8 The role of the speculator. This assesses whether the activities of speculators are beneficial or harmful to the rest of society.

B.9 The demand for butter. An examination of a real-world demand function.

B.10 Markets where prices are controlled. This examines what happens if price is set either above or below the equilibrium.

B.11 Rent control. This shows how setting (low) maximum rents is likely to lead to a shortage of rented accommodation.

B.12 Agriculture and minimum prices. This shows how setting (high) minimum prices is likely to lead to surpluses.

B.13 The fallacy of composition. An illustration from agricultural markets of the fallacy of composition: 'what applies in one case will not necessarily apply when repeated in all cases'.

B.14 What we pay to watch sport. Consideration of the demand for season tickets to watch spectator sports such as football.

B.15 The characteristics approach. An approach to analysing consumer behaviour and how consumers choose between products.

B.16 Diminishing returns in the bread shop. An illustration of the law of diminishing returns.

B.17 Dealing in futures markets. How buying and selling in futures markets can reduce uncertainty.

B.18 Short-run production. An analysis of how output varies with increases in the quantity of variable inputs used.

B.19 Diminishing returns to nitrogen fertiliser. This case study provides a good illustration of diminishing returns in practice by showing the effects on grass yields of the application of increasing accounts of nitrogen fertiliser.

B.20 The fallacy of using historic costs. A demonstration of how it is important to use opportunity costs and not historic costs when working out prices and output.

B.21 The relationship between averages and marginals. An examination of the rules showing how an average curve relates to a marginal curve.

B.22 Short-run cost curves in practice. Why *AVC* and *MC* curves may have a flat bottom.

B.23 Deriving cost curves from total physical product information. This shows how total, average and marginal costs can be derived from a total product information and the price of inputs.

B.24 Division of labour in a pin factory. This is the famous example of division of labour given by Adam Smith in his *Wealth of Nations* (1776).

B.25 The logic of logistics. How efficient logistics can drive down a firm's costs and increase its revenue.

WEBSITES RELEVANT TO PART B

Numbers and sections refer to websites listed in the Web Appendix and hotlinked from this book's website at **www.pearsoned.co.uk/sloman/**

- For news articles relevant to Part B, Google the Sloman Economics News site.

- For general news on markets, demand and supply, see websites in section A of the Web Appendix, and particularly sites A1–5, 7–8, 11, 12, 18–25, 35 and 36. See also links to newspapers worldwide in A38, 39, 43 and 44 and the news search feature in Google at A41.

- For links to sites on markets, see section I, the relevant parts of I7, 11, 13 and 14.

- For data on commodities, see site 29.

- For data on advertising, see site E37.

- For data on stock markets, see section B, sites B14, 27 and 32; see also sites A1 and F18.

- For data on the housing market, see section B, sites B7–11.

- For a case study examining costs, see site D2.

- For student resources relevant to Part B, see section C, sites C1–7, 9, 10, 14 and 19; see also, site B6.

- For games and simulations, see section D, sites D3, 6–9, 12–14, 16–20.

- For sites favouring the free market, see site E34.

The microeconomic environment
of business

Whatever the aims of firms, they must take account of the environment in which they operate if they are to be successful. In Part C we look at the microeconomic environment of firms, i.e. the market conditions that firms face in their particular industry.

Most firms are not price takers; they can choose the prices they charge. But in doing so they must take account of the reactions of their rivals. We look at pricing and output decisions in Chapter 5 and see how the aims of a firm affect these decisions.

Firms must also take account of rivals in planning their longer-term strategy – in making decisions about developing and launching new products, how quickly and how much to expand, the methods of production to use, their supply chain, the balance of what should be produced in-house and what should be 'outsourced' (i.e. bought in from other firms), their sources of finance, and whether to target international markets or to confine themselves to producing and selling domestically. These strategic decisions are the subject of Chapters 6 and 7.

In Chapter 8, we turn to the labour market environment of business. What power does the firm have in setting wages; what is the role of trade unions; how flexibly can the firm use labour? These issues all affect the profitability of business, its organisation and its choice of techniques.

Finally, in Chapter 9 we look at the impact of government policy towards business and how this in turn affects firms' decision making. How much does government legislation constrain business activity? Do we need governments to force firms to behave in the interests of society or will firms choose to take a socially responsible attitude towards things such as ethical trading, the environment, product standards and conditions for their workforce?

Pricing and output decisions in imperfectly competitive markets

5.1 ALTERNATIVE MARKET STRUCTURES

In the previous chapter we looked at price-taking firms, which face a perfectly elastic demand curve. In this chapter we examine firms that face a downward-sloping demand curve, which gives them some 'market power', such that they can raise their price without losing *all* of their customers.

The degree of market power that firms have affects the competitiveness of an industry. This, in turn, can affect the prices charged to consumers and paid to suppliers, how much profit firms make, and the incentives to invest and innovate. In particular, it affects firms' behaviour and sometimes that may be against the public interest. In such cases, governments or regulators may wish to intervene.

Factors affecting the degree of competition

So what influences the degree of competition in an industry? There are four key determinants:

■ The number of firms.
■ The freedom of entry and exit of firms into the industry.
■ The nature of the product.
■ The shape of the demand curve.

The number of firms

The more firms there are competing against each other, the more competitive any market is likely to be, with each firm trying to steal customers from its rivals. Though there are many ways by which this can be done, one strategy will be to keep prices low. This will generally be in the consumer's interest.

If, however, there are only a few firms in the market, there may be less intense price competition, though as we shall see, this is not always the case. Sometimes, there may be only two or three firms in the industry and yet they are constantly trying to undercut each other's prices to gain greater market share.

The freedom of entry and exit of firms into the industry

A key factor that will affect the number of firms in an industry is how easy it is for a new firm to set up in competition. In some markets, there may be barriers to entry (see pages 106–7) which prevent new firms from entering and this then acts to restrict the number of competing firms in the market. A key question here is, just how great are the barriers to the entry of new firms?

There is also the question of how costly it is to leave an industry. If the costs of exit are low, firms may be more willing to enter in the first place.

Pause for thought

1. *Consider a situation where you have set up a business selling a brand new product, which is not available anywhere else. As the only seller of this product, what could you do in terms of price?*
2. *Why could the ease with which a firm can leave an industry be a factor that determines the degree of competition within that industry?*

The nature of the product

If firms produce an identical product – in other words, if there is no product differentiation within the industry – there is little a firm can do to gain an advantage over its rivals. If, however, firms produce their own particular brand or model or variety, this may enable them to charge a higher price and/or gain a larger market share from their rivals.

The shape of the demand curve

Finally, the degree of competition is related to the price elasticity of demand. The less elastic is the demand for a firm's product, the greater will be its control over the price it charges – the less will sales fall as it raises its price. Thus the less elastic the demand for its product, the greater will be a firm's market power.

 KEY IDEA 17 *Market power benefits the powerful at the expense of others.* When firms have market power over prices, they can use this to raise prices and profits above the perfectly competitive level. Other things being equal, the firm will gain at the expense of the consumer. Similarly, if consumers or workers have market power they can use this to their own benefit.

Market structures

Traditionally, we divide industries into categories based on the factors above, which determine the degree of competition that exists between the firms. There are four such categories.

At the most competitive extreme is *perfect competition*, which we examined in the last chapter. Each firm is so small relative to the whole industry that it has no power to influence market price. It is a price taker.

At the least competitive extreme is *monopoly*. This is where there is just one firm in the industry, and hence no competition from within the industry. Normally the monopolist will have effective means of keeping other firms out of the industry. We look at monopoly in section 5.2.

In the middle there are two forms of *imperfect competition*: monopolistic competition and oligopoly. Under imperfect competition firms still face a downward-sloping demand curve, but have varying degrees of market power. The vast majority of firms in the real world operate under imperfect competition.

The more competitive of the two is *monopolistic competition* (not to be confused with monopoly). This involves quite a lot of firms competing and there is freedom for new firms to enter the industry in the long run, if for example they see that existing firms are making supernormal profits. Thus, as under perfect competition, this will have the effect of driving down profits to the normal level.

Examples of monopolistic competition can be found by flicking through the *Yellow Pages*. Taxi companies, restaurants, small retailers, small builders, plumbers, electrical contractors, etc. all normally operate under monopolistic competition – as does busking, which is discussed on the Freakonomics blog.[1] As a result of the high degree of competition, firms' profits are kept down. However, competition is not perfect, as the firms are all trying to differentiate their product or service from their rivals'. They have *some* power over prices: their demand curve, while relatively elastic, is not horizontal.

Definitions

Monopoly A market structure where there is only one firm in the industry.

Imperfect competition The collective name for monopolistic competition and oligopoly.

Monopolistic competition A market structure where, like perfect competition, there are many firms and freedom of entry into the industry, but where each firm produces a differentiated product and thus has some control over its price. (Not to be confused with a monopoly or monopolist!)

---

[1] Daniel Hamermesh, 'The Economics of Busking', *Freakonomics* (21 May 2012)

Table 5.1	Features of the four market structures			
Type of market	**Number of firms**	**Freedom of entry**	**Examples of product**	**Implication for demand curve for firm's product**
Perfect competition	Very many	Unrestricted	Fresh fruit and vegetables, shares, foreign exchange (approximately)	Horizontal. The firm is a price taker
Monopolistic competition	Many/several	Unrestricted	Builders, restaurants, hairdressers	Downward sloping, but relatively elastic. The firm has some control over price
Oligopoly	Few	Restricted	Cars, petrol, banking, razors	Downward sloping, relatively inelastic, but depends on reactions of rivals to a price change
Monopoly	One	Restricted or completely blocked	Local water company, many prescription drugs	Downward sloping; more inelastic than oligopoly. Firm has considerable control over price

The other type of imperfect competition is *oligopoly*, where there are only a few firms and where the entry of new firms is difficult. Some or all of the existing firms will be dominant – that is, they will tend to have a relatively high market share and can influence prices, advertising, product design, etc. As under monopoly, the entry of new firms is restricted. We examine oligopoly in section 5.3.

Table 5.1 summarises the features of the four different types of market structure.

Pause for thought

Give one more example in each of the four market categories in Table 5.1.

Market structure and the conduct and performance of firms

The market structure under which a firm operates will determine its behaviour. Firms under perfect competition behave quite differently from firms that are monopolists, which behave differently again from firms under oligopoly or monopolistic competition.

This behaviour (or 'conduct') will in turn affect the firm's performance: its prices, profits, efficiency, etc. In many cases it will also affect other firms' performance: their prices, profits, efficiency, etc. The collective conduct of all the firms in the industry will affect the whole industry's performance.

Definition

Oligopoly A market structure where there are few enough firms to enable barriers to be erected against the entry of new firms.

Some economists thus see a causal chain running from market structure to the performance of that industry. This paradigm was first considered in section 1.2:

Structure → Conduct → Performance

This does not mean, however, that all firms operating in a particular market structure will behave in exactly the same way. For example, some firms under oligopoly may be highly competitive, whereas others may collude with each other to keep prices high. This conduct may then, in turn, influence the development of the market structure. For example, the interaction between firms may influence the development of new products or new production methods, and may encourage or discourage the entrance of new firms into the industry.

It is also important to remember that some firms with different divisions and products may operate in more than market structure. As an example, consider the case of Microsoft. Its Internet Explorer competes with more successful rivals, such as Chrome and Firefox and, as a result, has little market power in the browser market. Its Office products, by contrast, have a much bigger market share and dominate the word processor, presentation and spreadsheet markets.

Also, some firms under oligopoly are highly competitive and may engage in fierce price cutting, while others may collude with their rivals to charge higher prices. It is for this reason that government policy towards firms – known as 'competition policy' – prefers to focus on the *conduct* of individual firms, rather than simply on the market structure within which they operate. Regulators focus on aspects of conduct such as price fixing and other forms of collusion. Indeed, competition policy in most countries accepts that market structures evolve naturally (e.g. because of economies of scale or changing consumer preferences) and do not necessarily give rise to competition problems.

Nevertheless, market structure still influences firms' behaviour and the performance of the industry, even though it does not, in the case of oligopoly and monopoly, rigidly determine it.

BOX 5.1 CONCENTRATION RATIOS

Measuring the degree of competition

5-firm and 15-firm concentration ratios for various industries (by output)

Industry	5-firm ratio	15-firm ratio	Industry	5-firm ratio	15-firm ratio
Sugar	99	99	Alcoholic beverages	50	78
Tobacco products	99	99	Soap and toiletries	40	64
Oils and fats	88	95	Accountancy services	36	47
Confectionery	81	91	Motor vehicles	34	54
Gas distribution	82	87	Glass and glass products	26	49
Soft drinks, mineral water	75	93	Fishing	16	19
Postal/courier services	65	75	Advertising	10	20
Telecommunications	61	75	Wholesale distribution	6	11
Inorganic chemicals	57	80	Furniture	5	13
Pharmaceuticals	57	74	Construction	5	9

Source: Based on data in United Kingdom Input–Output Analyses, Table 8.31 (Office of National Statistics). Reproduced under terms of the click-use licence

We can get some indication of how competitive a market is by observing the number of firms; the more firms there are, the more competitive the market would seem to be. However, this does not tell us anything about how *concentrated* the market might be. There may be *many* firms (suggesting a situation of perfect competition or monopolistic competition), but the largest two firms might produce 95 per cent of total output. This would make these two firms more like oligopolists.

Thus, even though a large number of producers may make the market *seem* highly competitive, this could be deceiving. Another approach, therefore, to measuring the degree of competition is to focus on the level of concentration of firms.

The simplest measure of industrial concentration involves adding together the market share of the largest so many firms: e.g. the largest 3, 5 or 15. This gives the '3-firm', '5-firm' or '15-firm concentration ratios'. There are different ways of estimating market share: by revenue, by output, by profit, etc. By using concentration ratios we can get a picture of just how dominant the largest firms in any industry are.

The table shows the 5-firm and 15-firm concentration ratios of selected industries in the UK by output. As you can see, there is an enormous variation in the degree of concentration from one industry to another.

One of the main reasons for this is differences in the percentage of total industry output at which economies of

scale are exhausted (see Box 4.4 on page 88). If this occurs at a low level of output, there will be room for several firms in the industry which are all benefiting from the maximum economies of scale. If it occurs at a higher level of output, then it may be more efficient for only a small number of firms to be in the industry, each having a position of market dominance, or possibly even just one firm.

The degree of concentration will also depend on the barriers to entry of other firms into the industry (see pages 106–7) and on various factors such as transport costs and historical accident. It will also depend on how varied the products are within any one industrial category. For example, in categories as large as furniture and construction there is room for many firms, each producing a specialised range of products.

So is the degree of concentration a good guide to the degree of competitiveness of the industry? The answer is that it is *some* guide, but on its own it can be misleading. In particular it ignores the degree of competition from abroad, and from other industries within the country.

1. *What are the advantages and disadvantages of using a 5-firm concentration ratio rather than a 15-firm, 3-firm or even a 1-firm ratio?*
2. *Why are some industries like bread baking and brewing relatively concentrated, in that a few firms produce a large proportion of total output (see web cases C.4 and C.5), and yet there are also many small producers?*

RECAP

1. The structure of an industry will affect the way in which firms behave and this in turn will affect the performance of that industry. This is known as the structure–conduct–performance paradigm.

2. There are four market structures. In ascending order of firms' market power, they are: perfect competition, monopolistic competition, oligopoly and monopoly.

5.2 MONOPOLY

What is a monopoly?

This may seem a strange question because the answer seems obvious. A monopoly exists when there is only one firm in the industry.

But whether an industry can be classed as a monopoly is not always clear. It depends on how narrowly the industry is defined. For example, a textile company may have a monopoly on certain types of fabric, but it does not have a monopoly on fabrics in general. The consumer can buy fabrics other than those supplied by the company. A rail company may have a monopoly over rail services between two cities, but it does not have a monopoly over public transport between these two cities. People can travel by coach or air, or use private transport. When you went to an adventure playground as a child, your parents may have refused to buy you an ice cream, because they were too expensive. The ice cream seller had a local monopoly, but it was obviously not the only seller of ice creams in the UK! Consider the following blog from the Sloman Economics News site, which asks: 'Is Amazon a monopolist?'

To some extent, the boundaries of an industry are arbitrary. What is more important for a firm is the amount of market power it has, and that depends on the closeness of substitutes produced by rival industries. Before 2006, Royal Mail had a monopoly over the delivery of letters in the UK, but still faced competition in communications from telephone, faxes and e-mail (and more recently from social media). Since the government opened the market to competitors, Royal Mail has complained about the 'unfair' competition it faces from other firms, such as Whistl, which delivers mail, packets and parcels but only in certain areas. An article from Post&Parcel[2] considers this competition to Royal Mail.

Barriers to entry

For a firm to maintain its monopoly position, there must be barriers to the entry of new firms. Barriers also exist under oligopoly, but in the case of monopoly they must be high enough to block the entry of new firms. Barriers can take various forms:

Economies of scale. If the monopolist's costs per unit go on falling significantly up to the output that satisfies the whole market, the industry may not be able to support more than one producer. This case is known as **natural monopoly**. It is particularly likely if the market is small. For example, two bus companies might find it unprofitable to serve the same routes, each running with perhaps only half-full buses, whereas one company with a monopoly over the routes could make a profit. Electricity transmission via a national grid is another example of a natural monopoly. The following blogs: 'Fair Fares?' and 'BT, Openreach and Ofcom' from the Sloman Economics News site consider the bus and communications industry respectively.

Even if a market could support more than one firm, a new entrant is unlikely to be able to start up on a very large scale. Thus the monopolist, which is already experiencing economies of scale, can charge a price below the cost of the new entrant and drive it out of business. If, however, the new entrant is a firm already established in another industry, it may be able to survive this competition.

Economies of scope. These are the benefits in terms of lower average costs of production, because a firm produces a range of products. For example, a large pharmaceutical company producing a range of drugs and toiletries can use shared research, marketing, storage and transport facilities across its range of products. These lower costs make it difficult for a new single-product entrant to the market, since the large firm will be able to undercut its price and drive it out of the market.

Product differentiation and brand loyalty. If a firm produces a clearly differentiated product, where the consumer associates the product with the brand, it will be very difficult for a new firm to break into that market. Rank Xerox invented and patented the plain paper photocopier. After this legal monopoly (see below) ran out, people still associated photocopiers with Rank Xerox. It was not unusual to hear someone say that they are going to 'Xerox the article' or, for that matter, 'Hoover their carpet'. Other examples of strong brand image include Guinness, Kellogg's Cornflakes, Coca-Cola, Nescafé and Sellotape.

Lower costs for an established firm. An established monopoly is likely to have developed specialised production and marketing skills. It is more likely to be aware of the most efficient production and marketing techniques and the most reliable and/or cheapest suppliers. It is likely to have access to cheaper finance, as we saw with larger companies in section 1.1, and is thus likely to be operating on a lower cost curve. New firms would therefore find it hard to compete and, with their higher average costs, would be likely to lose any price war.

Ownership of, or control over, key inputs or outlets. If a firm governs the supply of vital inputs (say by owning the sole supplier of some component part, through 'backward

---

> ### Definition
>
> **Natural monopoly** A situation where long-run average costs would be lower if an industry were under monopoly than if it were shared between two or more competitors.

[2] 'Royal Mail's challenger, TNT Post UK, to rebrand as "whistl"', *Post&Parcel* (15 September 2014)

vertical integration'), it can deny access to these inputs to potential rivals. On a world scale, the de Beers company has a monopoly in fine diamonds because all diamond producers market their diamonds through de Beers.

Similarly, if a firm controls the outlets through which the product must be sold (through 'forward vertical integration'), it can prevent potential rivals from gaining access to consumers. For example, Birds Eye Wall's used to supply freezers free to shops on the condition that they stocked only Wall's ice cream in them. On the Sloman Economics News site, how vertical and horizontal integration act as a barrier to entry in the energy market is discussed in the blogs 'The Big Six: for how much longer?' and 'Making UK energy supply more competitive'.

Legal protection. The firm's monopoly position may be protected by patents on essential processes, by copyright, by various forms of licensing (allowing, say, only one firm to operate in a particular area) and by tariffs (i.e. customs duties) and other trade restrictions to keep out foreign competitors. Examples of monopolies protected by patents include most new medicines developed by pharmaceutical companies (e.g. anti-AIDS drugs), Microsoft's Windows operating systems and agro-chemical companies, such as Monsanto, with various genetically modified plant varieties and pesticides. While patents do help monopolists to maintain their market power, they are also essential in encouraging new product innovation, as R&D is very expensive. Patents allow firms that engage in R&D to reap the rewards of that investment.

Mergers and takeovers. The monopolist can put in a takeover bid for any new entrant. The sheer threat of takeovers may discourage new entrants.

Retained profits and aggressive tactics. An established firm is likely to have some retained profits behind it. If a new firm enters the market, the established firm could reduce prices and thus start a price war, or start a massive advertising campaign, knowing that it could sustain losses until the new entrant leaves the market. The threat of this can act as a barrier to entry.

Profit maximising under monopoly

The rule for profit maximisation is the same under any market structure. It should produce the output where marginal cost equals marginal revenue. The cost curves for a monopolist will look similar to those for a firm under perfect competition, although, due to economies of scale, they could be lower. The revenue curves, however, will look different, as the firm is no longer a price taker.

Average and marginal revenue
Compared with other market structures, demand under monopoly will be relatively inelastic at each price. The monopolist can raise its price and consumers have no alternative supplier to turn to within the industry. They either

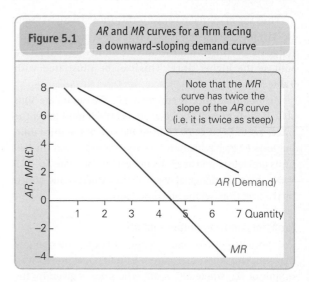

Figure 5.1 *AR* and *MR* curves for a firm facing a downward-sloping demand curve

Note that the *MR* curve has twice the slope of the *AR* curve (i.e. it is twice as steep)

Table 5.2 Revenue for a monopolist

Q (units)	P = AR (£)	TR (£)	MR (£)
1	8	8	8
2	7	14	6
3	6	18	4
4	5	20	2
5	4	20	0
6	3	18	−2
7	2	14	−4

pay the higher price, or go without the good altogether. This price-making power is beneficial for the firm, as is discussed in an article from Harvard Business School.[3]

Because the firm faces a downward-sloping demand curve, its average and marginal revenue curves will also be downward sloping. This is illustrated in Figure 5.1, which is based on Table 5.2.

Note that, as in the case of a price-taking firm, the demand curve and the *AR* curve lie along exactly the same line. The reason for this is simple: *AR* = *P*, and thus the curve relating price to quantity (the demand curve) must be the same as that relating average revenue to quantity (the *AR* curve).

When a firm faces a downward-sloping demand curve, marginal revenue will be less than average revenue, and may even be negative. But why?

Whilst a monopolist can set its price, it is still constrained by its (and hence the industry) demand curve. If a firm wants to sell more per time period, it must lower its price (assuming it does not advertise). This will mean lowering the price not just for the extra units it hopes to sell, but also for those units it would have sold had it not lowered the price.

---

[3] Benson P. Shapiro, 'Commodity Busters: Be a Price Maker, Not a Price Taker', *Working Knowledge* (Harvard Business School, 10 February 2003)

Thus the marginal revenue is the price at which it sells the last unit, minus the loss in revenue it has incurred by reducing the price on those units it could otherwise have sold at the higher price. This can be illustrated with Table 5.2.

Assume that price is currently £7. Two units are thus sold. If the firm wants to sell an extra unit, it must lower the price, say to £6. It gains £6 from the sale of the third unit, but loses £2 by having to reduce the price by £1 on the two units previously sold at £7. Its net gain is therefore £6 − £2 = £4. This is the marginal revenue: the extra revenue gained by the firm from selling one more unit.

Profit-maximising output and price

We can now put cost and revenue curves together on one diagram. This is done in Figure 5.2. Profit is maximised at an output of Q_m, where $MC = MR$. The price is given by the demand curve. Thus at Q_m the price is $AR = P$ (point a on the demand curve). Average cost (AC) is found at point b. Supernormal profit per unit is $AR - AC$ (i.e. a − b). Total supernormal profit is shown by the shaded area.

These profits will tend to be larger the less elastic is the demand curve (and hence the steeper is the MR curve), and thus the bigger is the gap between MR and price (AR). The actual elasticity will depend on whether reasonably close substitutes are available in other industries. The demand for a rail service between two places will be much less elastic (and the potential for profit greater) if there is no bus service running between those same destinations.

Under both monopolistic and perfect competition, any supernormal profits made in the short run will be competed away in the long run, as new firms are able to enter the industry. Significant barriers to entry under monopoly, however, will enable the firm to maintain its supernormal profits in the long run.

Comparing monopoly with perfect competition

Because it faces a different type of market environment, the monopolist will produce a quite different output and at a quite different price from a perfectly competitive industry. Typically a monopolist will charge a price above the market price of an equivalent industry under perfect competition. There are three main reasons for this:

■ Under perfect competition, price equals marginal cost (see Figure 4.4 on page 93). Under monopoly, however, price is above marginal cost (see Figure 5.2). The less elastic the demand curve, the higher will price be above marginal cost.

■ Since there are barriers to the entry of new firms, a monopolist's supernormal profits will not be competed away in the long run. There is no competition to drive down the price. The monopolist is not forced to operate at the bottom of the $LRAC$ curve. Thus, other things being equal, long-run prices will tend to be higher, and hence output lower, under monopoly.

■ The monopolist's cost curves may be higher. The sheer survival of a firm in the long run under perfect competition requires that it uses the most efficient known technique. The monopolist, however, sheltered by barriers to entry, can still make large profits even if it is not using the most efficient technique. It therefore has less incentive to be efficient.

| Figure 5.2 | Profit maximising under monopoly |

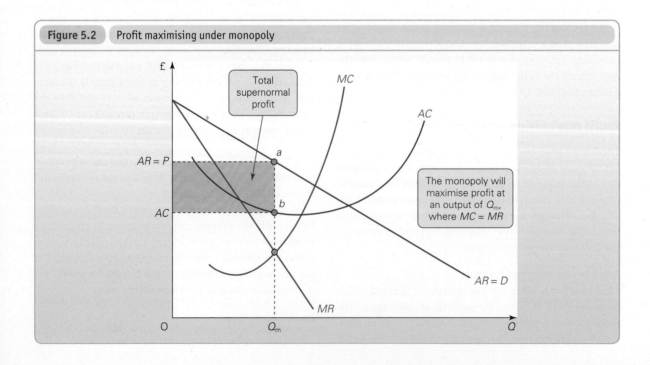

It is possible, however, that a monopolist will operate with lower costs than an equivalent industry under perfect competition. The monopoly may be able to achieve substantial economies of scale due to larger plant size, centralised administration and the avoidance of unnecessary duplication (e.g. a monopoly water company would eliminate the need for several sets of rival water mains under each street). If this results in an *MC* curve substantially below that of the same industry under perfect competition, the monopoly may even produce a higher output at a lower price. However, if the monopolist continues to maximise profits, it will still charge a price above marginal cost and thus be inefficient.

Another reason why a monopolist may operate with lower costs is that it can use part of its supernormal profits for research and development and investment. This may provide the firm with more opportunities to cut its costs relative to a smaller, perfectly competitive firm.

The promise of supernormal profits, protected perhaps by patents, may also encourage the development of new (monopoly) industries producing new products. It is this chance of making monopoly profits that encourages many people to take the risks of going into business.

Although a monopoly faces no competition in the goods market, it may face an alternative form of competition in financial markets. A monopoly, with potentially low costs, which is currently run inefficiently, is likely to be subject to a takeover bid from another company. This *competition for corporate control* may thus force the monopoly to be efficient in order to prevent it being taken over.

Definition

Competition for corporate control The competition for the control of companies through takeovers.

Network effects

Microsoft is a vertically integrated firm (see page 87), with a dominant position in the operating system market (i.e. *Windows*) and in certain application software (*Office* and *Windows Media Player*) markets. It has built this position by creating networks of users, which bring both benefits and costs to society.

Network economies arise when consumers of a product benefit from it being used by *other* consumers. In the case of Microsoft's products, firms benefit from lower training costs because individuals who have learnt to use Microsoft products elsewhere can be readily absorbed into the firm. Individuals benefit too because they do not have to learn to use new software when they move to another organisation and the learning costs are fairly low as a new version of the software is introduced.

The negative aspect of developing strong networks is that users can get 'locked in' to using the software and become reluctant to switch to alternative systems. Protecting the network is vital to Microsoft's competitive edge.

> An operating system attracts software developed around that operating system, thereby discouraging new competition since any alternative faces not only the challenge of creating a better operating system but competing against a whole array of already existing software applications . . . These so-called 'network effects' give an incredible anti-competitive edge to companies like Microsoft that control so many different parts of the network.[1]

It is these negative network effects that have led to Microsoft being under seemingly constant investigation by competition authorities for over two decades. By controlling the *Windows* operating software, Microsoft attempted to force its own Internet browser, *Internet Explorer*, on to consumers and computer manufacturers and this led to Microsoft being accused of abusing its market power and seeking to crush its rivals.

US and EU investigations

Interest in Microsoft's practices began in 1991, with a Federal Trade Commission inquiry into its monopoly abuse of the PC operating system market. However, perhaps the most famous investigation began on 18 May 1998, when the US Justice Department alleged that Microsoft had committed the following anti-competitive actions:

- Microsoft attempted to collude with Netscape Communications to divide the Internet browser market. Netscape Communications refused.
- Microsoft had forced personal computer manufacturers to install *Internet Explorer* in order to obtain a *Windows* operating licence.
- Microsoft insisted that PC manufacturers conformed to a Microsoft front screen for *Windows*. This included specified icons, one of which was Microsoft's *Internet Explorer*.

Definition

Network economies The benefits to consumers of having a network of other people using the same product or service.

---

[1] N. Newman, from 'MS Word to MS world: how Microsoft is building a global monopoly' Net Action (1997).

■ It had set up reciprocal advertising arrangements with America's largest Internet service providers, such as America Online (AOL). Here Microsoft would promote AOL via *Windows*. In return, AOL would not promote Netscape's browsers.

One solution posed by Federal Judge Thomas Penfield Jackson in 2000 was that Microsoft be split into two companies. One would produce and market the *Windows* operating system; the other would produce and market the applications software, such as *Microsoft Office* and the Web browser, *Internet Explorer*.

This was overturned on appeal in June 2001 and Microsoft agreed to provide technical information about *Windows* to other companies to foster competition. Also, Microsoft would not be allowed to retaliate against computer manufacturers that installed rival products or removed icons for Microsoft applications.

Legal action against Microsoft was not confined to the USA. In March 2004, the European Commission fined Microsoft a record €497 million for abusing its monopoly position. It found that Microsoft had harmed competition in the media player market by bundling *Windows Media Player* with its operating system.

Further, Microsoft had refused to supply information about its secret software code to suppliers of alternative network software at reasonable rates. Without it, firms that had purchased *Windows Network* servers would be solely tied in to Microsoft server software, discouraging the development of application software products by Microsoft's rivals.

In April 2006, Microsoft appealed the judgment, claiming that the EU's ruling violated international law by forcing the company to share information with rivals. However, the Court of First Instance found in the Commission's favour. Microsoft complied with the first ruling and un-bundled *Windows Media Player* from its operating systems.

However, until October 2007, Microsoft continued to charge high royalty rates and fees for inter-operability information that would allow competitors to access the secret source code on the *Windows Network System*. As a result, in February 2008 the Commission penalised Microsoft a further €899 million for non-compliance with its 2004 decision and Microsoft became the first company in 50 years of EU competition policy to be fined for non-compliance with a Commission decision.[2] An appeal was made, but Microsoft lost the case in 2012, though it did receive a reduced fine of €860 due to a 'miscalculation'.

Further cases against Microsoft arose in June 2009, when the Commission ordered Microsoft to un-bundle *Internet Explorer* from its new operating system, *Windows 7*. The Commission argued that un-bundling would increase competition and consumers would face more choice between Internet browsers.[3] Microsoft did comply with the Commission,

offering users an option of downloading one browser from a list of 12, including Mozilla *Firefox*, Google's *Chrome*, Apple's *Safari* and *Opera*. However, between May 2011 and July 2012, thousands of customers in Europe did not have this choice and so the European Commission imposed a €561 million fine on Microsoft.[4]

Microsoft was warned by the Commission about anti-competitive behaviour with its *Windows 8* product and was told that severe penalties would be imposed if it broke the 2009 bundling agreement.

Microsoft and the public interest

These lawsuits raise an important issue: is Microsoft acting for or against the public interest? Clearly it has monopoly power and, as we have seen, this suggests an ability to raise prices, limit output and make supernormal profits.

However, the competition authorities have never penalised Microsoft simply for possessing monopoly power. It has been fined when it has *abused* its market power, such as by raising barriers to entry and restricting the opportunities for potential rival firms to offer alternative products to customers, thereby restricting choice. Thus, it is not the monopoly market structure that matters to competition authorities, but the behaviour of the firm once it has monopoly power.

In its defence, Microsoft has argued that it has continually sought to reinvest its profits in new product development and offered a number of innovative solutions over the past 30 years for individuals and businesses alike. Just think of all the versions of *Windows* and the 'free updates' there have been!

Further, in an environment where technology is changing rapidly, Microsoft's control over standards gives the user a measure of stability, knowing that any new products and applications will be compatible with existing ones. In other words, new software can be incorporated into existing systems. In this respect Microsoft can be viewed as operating in society's interest.

Also, Microsoft argues that it has a right to protect its in-house software code from competitors and receive a fair price for it. Indeed, it is a natural response for a firm to protect its intellectual property rights. Failure to do so could lead to the firm's demise and stifle innovation.

Challenges to Microsoft monopoly

Microsoft is facing increasing competitive pressure, helped by the challenges from competition authorities. For example, Microsoft's *Internet Explorer* had a market share of over 80 per cent in the early 2000s, but its desktop *worldwide* market share gradually fell and stabilised at around 50 per cent until falling to 44.8 per cent in February 2016. This happened as first Mozilla's *Firefox* emerged, gaining a market share of 23.7 per cent in 2011, but this has slowly fallen to 11.7 per cent in February 2016, largely replaced by Google's *Chrome*, whose market

---

[2] See: European Commission, 'Antitrust: Commission imposes €899 million penalty on Microsoft for non-compliance with March 2004 Decision', *European Commission Press Release IP/08/318* (27 February 2008).

[3] See: European Commission, 'Antitrust: Commission confirms sending of a Statement of Objections to Microsoft on the tying of Internet Explorer to Windows Reference', *European Commission Press Release MEMO/09/15* (17 January 2009).

---

[4] See: European Commission, 'Commission fines Microsoft for non-compliance with browser choice commitments', *European Commission Press Release IP/13/196* (6 March 2013).

share has increased from 11.2 per cent to 36.6 per cent over the same time period.[5]

There is also a growing challenge from other Internet firms, such as Google and Facebook, which have created enormous networks of users, who are then targeted with tailored adverts paid for by firms which want to reach these vast audiences.

This is a very different business model from that of Microsoft and, as part of the desire to create large networks of users, free products are available that compete with those of Microsoft. For example, Google's *Google Docs* and Apache's *Open Office* both compete with Microsoft's *Office*. Their market shares are growing, but still remain relatively small.

Microsoft's dominance has certainly been tested in many parts of the industry, but its market leading position for its various operating systems is still intact. The only real competitor for a standalone computer is Apple's *Mac* but a

market share of around 10 per cent leaves it significantly behind Microsoft. However, with the rise of tablet computers and smart phones, the market share of Google's Linux open-source operating system, *Android*, is expected to grow significantly over the next few years, especially with the rise of tablets with detachable keyboards that double as a laptop.[6]

You might want to follow subsequent events as the news unfolds (see section A of the Hotlinks section of this book's website for links to newspaper sites).

1. *In what ways was Microsoft's behaviour (a) against the public interest; (b) in the public interest?*
2. *Being locked in to a product or technology is only a problem if such a product can be clearly shown to be inferior to an alternative. What difficulties might there be in establishing such a case?*

---

[5] 'Desktop top browser share trend', *Net Market Share* (2016).

[6] Wikimedia Traffic Analysis Report – Operating Systems (July 2012).

RECAP

1. A monopoly is where there is only one firm in an industry. Whether a monopoly exists depends on how narrowly an industry is defined.

2. Barriers to the entry of new firms will normally be necessary to protect a monopoly from competition. Such barriers include economies of scale (making the firm a natural monopoly or at least giving it a cost advantage over new, smaller, competitors), control over supplies of inputs or over outlets, patents or copyright, and tactics to eliminate competition (such as takeovers or aggressive advertising).

3. The demand curve (*AR* curve) for a monopolist is downward sloping. The *MR* curve is below it and steeper.

4. Profits for the monopolist (as for other firms) are maximised where $MC = MR$.

5. If demand and cost curves are the same in a monopoly and a perfectly competitive industry, the monopoly will produce a lower output and at a higher price than the perfectly competitive industry.

6. Economies of scale for a monopolist may lead to lower prices, and the monopolist's high profits may be used for research and development and investment, which in turn may lead to better products at possibly lower prices.

5.3 OLIGOPOLY

Oligopoly occurs when just a few firms share a large proportion of the industry. Most oligopolists produce differentiated products (e.g. cars, soap powder, soft drinks, electrical appliances), but some may produce almost identical products (e.g. metals, petrol). Much of the competition between such oligopolists is in terms of the marketing of their particular brand. On the Sloman Economics News site, you will find many blogs written about different oligopolies and it is both useful and interesting to compare the conduct and performance of the firms involved. Some examples of powerful oligopolies are the market for toothbrushes ('Wobbly answer to oli-

gopoly'), supermarkets ('An oligopoly price war') and energy ('CMA referral for energy sector').

As with monopoly, there are barriers to the entry of new firms (see pages 106–7). The size of the barriers, however, varies from industry to industry. In some cases entry is relatively easy; in others it is virtually impossible.

Interdependence of the firms

Because there are only a few firms under oligopoly, each firm is likely to have a relatively large market share, and so its actions will affect the other firms in the industry and it, in turn, will be affected by their actions. As such, before a firm makes any decisions, it will have to take account of the behaviour of these other firms. This means that they are mutually dependent: they are *interdependent*. It is this interdependence that differentiates oligopolies from the other market structures.

If a firm changes the price or specification of its product or the amount of its advertising, the sales of its rivals will be affected. The rivals may then respond by changing their price, specification or advertising. A blog on the Sloman Economics News site, 'Pizza price war', illustrates this concept of interdependence under oligopoly.

 People often think and behave strategically. How you think others will respond to your actions is likely to influence your own behaviour. Firms, for example, when considering a price or product change will often take into account the likely reactions of their rivals.

It is impossible, therefore, to predict the effect on a firm's sales of, say, a change in its price without first making some assumption about the reactions of other firms. Different assumptions will yield different predictions. For this reason there is no single generally accepted theory of oligopoly and no common outcome in terms of prices, output and profits. Firms may react differently and unpredictably.

Competition and collusion

Oligopolists are pulled in two different directions:

- The interdependence of firms may make them wish to *collude* with each other. If they can club together and act as if they were a monopoly, they could jointly maximise industry profits.
- On the other hand, they will be tempted to *compete* with their rivals to gain a bigger share of industry profits for themselves.

These two policies are incompatible. The more fiercely firms compete to gain a bigger share of industry profits, the smaller these industry profits will become! For example,

price competition drives down the average industry price, while competition through advertising raises industry costs. Either way, industry profits fall.

Sometimes firms will collude. Sometimes they will not. The following sections examine first *collusive oligopoly*, where we consider both formal agreements and tacit collusion, and then *non-collusive oligopoly*.

Collusive oligopoly

When firms under oligopoly engage in collusion, they may agree on prices, market share, advertising expenditure, etc. Such collusion reduces the uncertainty they face. It reduces the fear of engaging in competitive price cutting or retaliatory advertising, both of which could reduce total industry profits and thus a firm's share of them.

A cartel

A formal collusive agreement is called a *cartel*. The cartel will maximise profits by acting like a monopolist: behaving as if they were a single firm. This is illustrated in Figure 5.3.

The total market demand curve is shown with the corresponding market *MR* curve. The cartel's *MC* curve is the

Definitions

Interdependence (under oligopoly) This is one of the two key features of oligopoly. Each firm is affected by its rivals' decisions and its decisions will affect its rivals. Firms recognise this interdependence and take it into account when making decisions.

Collusive oligopoly When oligopolists agree (formally or informally) to limit competition between themselves. They may set output quotas, fix prices, limit product promotion or development, or agree not to 'poach' each other's markets.

Non-collusive oligopoly When oligopolists make no agreement between themselves – formal, informal or tacit.

Figure 5.3 Profit-maximising cartel

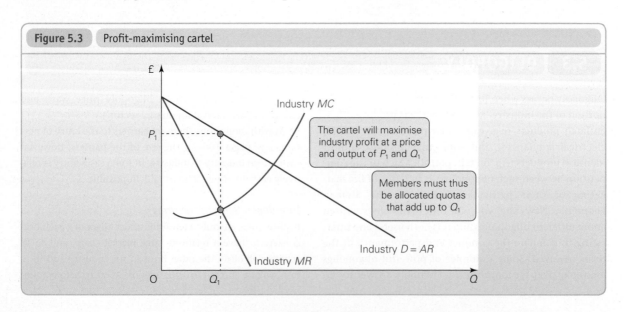

The cartel will maximise industry profit at a price and output of P_1 and Q_1

Members must thus be allocated quotas that add up to Q_1

horizontal sum of the MC curves of its members (since we are adding the output of each of the cartel members at each level of marginal cost). Profit for the whole industry is maximised at Q_1 where $MC = MR$. The cartel must therefore set a price of P_1 (at which Q_1 will be demanded).

But having agreed on price, how will the resulting output (Q_1) be divided between the cartel members? The members may simply compete against each other using non-price competition to gain as big a share of resulting sales (Q_1) as they can.

Alternatively, the cartel members may somehow agree to divide the market between them. Each member would be given a *quota*. These quotas could be the same for every firm, or they might be allocated based on the market share of the firm. Whatever the method of allocation, the sum of all the quotas must add up to Q_1. If the quotas exceeded Q_1, either there would be output unsold if price remained fixed at P_1, or the price would have to fall.

In many countries cartels are illegal, seen by government as a means of driving up prices and profits and acting against the public interest. Government policy towards cartels is examined in section 9.5.

The most famous example of a cartel is OPEC, which was set up in 1960 by the five major oil-exporting countries, Iran, Iraq, Kuwait, Saudi Arabia and Venezuela, and now consists of 13 member countries. You may want to investigate the behaviour of OPEC and how it has influenced oil prices. There are numerous blogs on the Sloman Economics News site that consider this most famous of cartels and how it has managed oil price changes. See, for example the blog from February 2016, 'Will there be an oil price rebound?', another from 2015, 'The price of oil in 2015 and beyond', and another from 2012, 'OPEC cartel faces lawsuit for price fixing'. See also Case Study C.7 on the book's website.

Pause for thought

1. *Which countries are members of the OPEC cartel and what are its objectives?*
2. *How has OPEC's behaviour affected oil prices and have the problems of a typical cartel been experienced by OPEC?*

Tacit collusion

Where open collusion is illegal, firms may simply break the law, or find ways to get round it. Alternatively, firms may stay within the law, but still tacitly collude by watching each other's behaviour. Firms may tacitly 'agree' to avoid price wars or aggressive advertising campaigns.

One form of *tacit collusion* is where firms keep to the price that is set by an established leader. Such *price leadership* is more likely when there is a dominant firm in the industry, normally the largest.

Other forms include having an established set of rules that everyone follows, such as adding a certain percentage on top of average costs for profit. Alternatively, there are certain benchmark prices, which firms follow, such as goods priced at £9.99, rather than at £10.13.

A good example of price fixing can be found in the petrol retailing industry in Melbourne, Australia, in 2009. The ACCC (Australian Competition and Consumer Commission) studied the pricing decisions of a number of petrol stations in the same area and in 49 of the 53 weeks studied, when one of the big three petrol stations changed its price, the industry followed these movements exactly (see the blog on the Sloman Economics News site, 'Price-fixing oligopolies'). Whilst there was no formal collusive agreement in place, this is an example of tacit collusion. Price-fixing agreements of this nature are often very difficult to prosecute, and in this case no action was taken against the petrol stations.

Factors favouring collusion

Collusion between firms, whether formal or tacit, is more likely when firms can clearly identify with each other or some leader and when they trust each other not to break agreements. It will be easier for firms to collude if the following conditions apply:

- There are only very few firms, all well known to each other.
- They are open with each other about costs and production methods.
- They have similar production methods and average costs, and are thus likely to want to change prices at the same time and by the same percentage.
- They produce similar products and can thus more easily reach agreements on price.
- There is a dominant firm.
- There are significant barriers to entry and thus there is little fear of disruption by new firms.
- The market is stable. If industry demand or production costs fluctuate wildly, it will be difficult to make agreements, partly due to difficulties in predicting market conditions and partly because agreements may frequently have to be amended. There is a particular problem in a declining market where firms may be tempted to undercut each other's price in order to maintain their sales.
- There are no government measures to curb collusion.

Definitions

Quota (set by a cartel) The output that a given member of a cartel is allowed to produce (production quota) or sell (sales quota).

Tacit collusion When oligopolists follow unwritten 'rules' of collusive behaviour, such as price leadership. They will take care not to engage in price cutting, excessive advertising or other forms of competition.

Price leadership When firms (the followers) choose the same price as that set by one of the firms in the industry (the leader). The leader will normally be the largest firm.

Elements of competition under collusive oligopoly

Even when oligopolists collude over price, they may compete intensively though product development and marketing. Such 'non-price competition', as we saw in section 3.4, can make the job of the manager quite complex, involving strategic decisions about product design and quality, product promotion and the provision of various forms of after-sales service.

Although non-price competition assumes that price is given in the short run, price may well be affected over the longer term. Industries with intensive non-price competition are likely to face higher marketing costs, and this can result in a higher collusive price.

Even if there is collusion, for example to fix price, firms will always have an incentive to cheat, by undercutting the cartel price or selling more than their allocated quota. Whilst the firm can gain from this action, there is a danger of retaliation, which might lead to a price war, such that in the long run the firm could lose out. However, as long as the firm that undercuts the cartel price is confident of winning any price war, this may be a good strategy to follow. We consider this idea further in section 5.4.

Non-collusive oligopoly

In some oligopolies, there may be only a few (if any) factors favouring collusion. In such cases, the likelihood of price competition is greater.

The kinked demand curve

Economists noted that even when oligopolists did not collude over price, the prices charged across the industry often remained relatively stable. The **kinked demand curve model** was developed to explain this observation and it rests on two key assumptions:

- If a firm cuts its price, its rivals will feel forced to follow suit and cut theirs, to prevent losing customers to the first firm.
- If a firm raises its price, however, its rivals will *not* follow suit since, by keeping their prices the same, they will thereby gain customers from the first firm.

On these assumptions, the oligopolist's perceived demand curve is kinked at the current price and output (see Figure 5.4). It believes that if it raises its price, its rivals will not follow and so there will be a large fall in sales as customers switch to the now relatively lower-priced rivals. With an

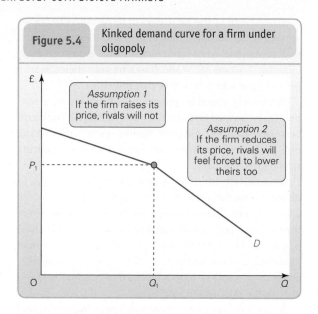

Figure 5.4 Kinked demand curve for a firm under oligopoly

elastic demand above the kink, therefore, the firm will be reluctant to raise its price. On the other hand, it believes that if it reduces its price, its rivals will feel forced to cut their prices too to avoid losing market share, and so few consumers will switch, giving the firm only a modest increase in sales. Therefore, with a relatively inelastic demand below the kink, the firm will also be reluctant to reduce its price.

Oligopoly and the consumer

When oligopolists act collusively and jointly maximise industry profits, they are in effect acting as a monopoly. In such cases, prices may be very high. This is clearly not in the best interests of consumers.

Furthermore, in two respects, oligopoly may be more disadvantageous than monopoly:

- Depending on the size of the individual oligopolists, there may be less scope for economies of scale and hence lower costs to mitigate the effects of market power.
- Oligopolists are likely to engage in much more extensive advertising and marketing than a monopolist. Consumers may benefit from product development and better information about the product's characteristics. However, advertising and marketing are costly and may result in higher prices, so the consumer could lose out.

These problems will be less severe, however, if oligopolists do not collude, if there is some degree of price competition and if barriers to entry are weak.

Indeed, in some respects, oligopoly may be more beneficial to the consumer than other market structures:

- Oligopolists, like monopolists, can use part of their supernormal profit for research and development. Unlike monopolists, however, oligopolists will have a considerable *incentive* to do so. If the product design is improved, this may allow the firm to capture a larger

Definition

The kinked demand curve model The theory that oligopolists face a demand curve that is kinked at the current price: demand being significantly more elastic above the current price than below. The effect of this is to create a situation of price stability.

share of the market, and it may be some time before rivals can respond with a similarly improved product.

■ Non-price competition through product differentiation may result in greater choice for the consumer. Take the case of tablets or mobile phones. Non-price competition has led to a huge range of different products of many different specifications, each meeting the specific requirements of different consumers.

It is difficult to draw any general conclusions about the outcomes in this market structure, since oligopolies differ so much in their behaviour and performance. Although an oligopoly is closer to the non-competitive end of the spectrum, it can still be a highly competitive market structure, as is evident in a blog on the Sloman Economics News site about supermarket price wars, 'An oligopoly price war'.

| BOX 5.3 | OLIGOPOLIES: THE GOOD, THE BAD AND THE UGLY |

Market power in oligopolistic industries

Faced with a choice between competition and collusion, firms under oligopoly can behave very differently in oligopolies. Just how they behave is often of interest to the competition authorities, which are on the look-out for anti-competitive practices. We consider competition policy in section 9.5.

In this box, we consider three oligopolies: supermarkets, energy and auditing. You will find other examples of oligopolies on the Sloman Economics News site.

Supermarkets

In the UK, the largest four supermarkets have a combined market share of approximately 70 per cent, as shown in the chart. Although this has fallen in the past few years, it still represents market dominance by a few firms – a key characteristic of oligopoly.

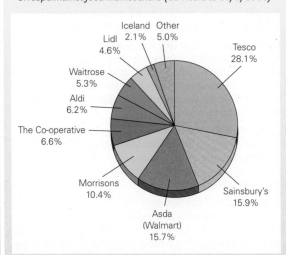

UK supermarket food market share (12 weeks to 11/9/2016)

The industry has faced two major inquiries: first in 2000, concerning relationships with suppliers, and then in May 2006, when the Competition Commission (since replaced by the Competition and Markets Authority (CMA)) said it was 'concerned with whether Tesco, or any other supermarket, can get into such a strong position, either nationally or locally, that no other retailer can compete effectively'.[1]

The big four have been accused of restricting competition and consumer choice at the local and national level, by erecting barriers to entry. These include buying up tracts of land to prevent rival supermarkets setting up there or taking advantage of large economies of scale to make it impossible for new firms to compete on price. To this end, the Commission proposed a 'competition test' in planning decisions and action to prevent land agreements to reduce supermarket dominance in local areas.

Another issue is the 'heavy-handed tactics' used by supermarkets to increase their buying power, driving down costs by forcing suppliers to offer discounts. This may be good if it means lower prices for the final consumer, but these cost savings are not always passed on. While supermarkets' profits increased, there was a detrimental effect on suppliers, whose profit margins were cut to the bone. Attempts to create a voluntary code of practice between supermarkets and their suppliers failed and so in 2013 the UK government set up a Groceries Code Adjudicator to ensure that large supermarkets treat their direct suppliers lawfully and fairly.[2] It investigates complaints and arbitrates in disputes.

Supermarket chains have also been accused of 'shadow pricing', a form of tacit collusion whereby they observe each other's prices and keep them at similar levels – often similarly high levels rather than similarly low levels! This limits true price competition and the resulting high prices have seen profits grow. Nevertheless, in 2008, the Competition Commission reported that it found little evidence of tacit collusion.[3] Furthermore, some price competition does exist and the TV adverts during the recession from 2008 highlighted this. Yet, as we saw in Box 3.4, intense price competition tends to be only over basic items, such as the own-brand 'value' products. To get to them, you normally have to pass the more luxurious ones, which are much more highly priced with higher profit margins. Supermarkets rely on shoppers making impulse buys of these more expensive lines.

1. *In what forms of tacit collusion are supermarkets likely to engage?*
2. *Explain why manufacturers of food products continue to supply supermarkets, despite concerns that they are not always treated fairly.*

---

[1] Peter Freeman, Chairman of the Competition Commission and Inquiry Chairman, 'Grocery enquiry goes local', *Competition Commission News Release* (23 January 2007).

[2] 'Christine Tacon named as supermarket ombudsman', *BBC News* (21 January 2013).

[3] *The supply of groceries in the UK: market investigation*, Competition Commission (2008).

The rapid growth of Aldi and Lidl, explained in a BBC News article[4], is placing more and more demands on the big four to bring their prices down or at least identify their target market.[5] With their current structures and costs, they cannot compete with Aldi and Lidl on price and they are not selling the 'up-market' foods of Marks and Spencer and Waitrose.

Who has the energy to switch?

Another oligopoly investigated by the Competition and Markets Authority (CMA) for breach of a dominant position is the energy sector. The 'Big Six' energy suppliers[6] between them sell to over 90 per cent of UK households. There are many articles on the Sloman Economics News site on the energy market, considering such things as barriers to entry ('Making UK energy supply more competitive'), referral to the CMA ('CMA referral for energy sector'), and the possible savings from switching suppliers ('Do people have the energy to switch?').

The Big Six are vertically and horizontally integrated (see pages 143–6), generating and locally distributing power and offering deals to customers who buy both gas and electricity ('dual-fuel deals'). Vertical integration, in particular, has made it difficult for small suppliers to enter the market, as they had to buy wholesale from one of the big six. Thus a key focus of the industry regulator, Ofgem (the Office of Gas and Electricity markets), has been how to reduce barriers to entry so as to increase suppliers, thereby making the market more competitive and bringing down prices.

3. *Does vertical integration matter if consumers still have a choice of supplier and if generators are still competing with each other?*

In June 2014, Ofgem referred the industry to the CMA to investigate accusations of profiteering by the Big Six and discuss mechanisms to reduce structural barriers that undermine competition. The CMA's report from March 2016 confirmed its preliminary findings of July and December 2015, noting that the structure of the market adversely affects consumers, who pay more than they would in a more competitive market.

Part of the problem is a type of brand loyalty, with customers reluctant to switch suppliers, making it difficult for new entrants to attract customers. One cause is the number of tariffs available, with consumers choosing to stay with their current supplier, unable to determine if cheaper tariffs exist. This was addressed in 2013, when a full set of pricing rules was published, forcing companies to compete on a simple 'per-unit' price, allowing customers to compare tariffs at a glance.

The CMA wants to encourage people to switch to cheaper suppliers by increasing the power of Ofgem and setting up 'an Ofgem-controlled database which will allow rival suppliers to contact domestic and micro business customers who have been stuck on their supplier's default tariff for three years or more with better deals'.[7]

4. *The Big Six have been required to open up their finances to greater scrutiny and publish prices up to two years in advance. How would this help to boost competition?*

In the wholesale and retail sector, Ofgem and the CMA have taken steps to reduce barriers to entry, attempting to make the market genuinely competitive and reduce the Big Six's dominance.

An auditing of competition

Deloitte, Ernst and Young, KPMG and PwC (the 'Big Four') act as auditors for 90 per cent of the UK's stock-market listed companies. They have been criticised for limiting competition, as companies stay with the same auditing firm, which prevents new firms from entering or expanding. A further criticism relates to the relationship between companies and their auditors and a divorce of ownership from control. This feature received particular criticism, with suggestions that this prevented a warning about the financial crisis.

In light of the Big Four's market dominance, an investigation was carried out by the Competition Commission/CMA. Laura Carstensen, the Chair of the CMA's Audit Investigation Group, was quoted in a BBC News article as saying:

> there is dissatisfaction amongst some institutional investors with the relevance and extent of reporting in audited financial reports . . . management may have incentives to present their accounts in the most favourable light, whereas shareholder interests can be quite different.[8]

Despite the Big Four's insistence that the market remains competitive, 'healthy and robust' and that any changes would not be in the public interest, a report was published by the Competition Commission in 2013, suggesting that companies should be forced to rotate auditors.

This was echoed by the European Commission's desire to break up the market dominance of the Big Four.

From June 2016, major UK-listed companies will have to put their auditing work out for tender every ten years and switch auditors, with the bidding process open to more than just the Big Four. The objective is to increase the industry's competitiveness and break the close relationship between companies and auditors.

Furthermore, the powers of the industry regulator, the Financial Reporting Council will be increased and it will be required to review all auditing engagements of the FTSE350 companies every five years on average, as discussed in a Telegraph article.[9]

In anticipation of new European rules, some FTSE100 companies have already changed auditors, including Tesco, which switched from PwC to Deloitte; HSBC replaced KPMG with PwC; RBS moved from Deloitte to Ernst and Young, while Barclays ended its 120-year relationship with PwC, moving to KPMG. But while more companies are changing their auditor, most, like the above, are simply moving from one of the Big Four to another. It appears as though this industry may well remain dominated by a few giants – sound familiar?

5. *What is meant by the divorce of ownership from control in the auditing industry and why might it present a problem?*

---

[4] 'Aldi and Lidl double market share in three years', *BBC News* (17 November 2015).

[5] Sarah Butler, 'Asda suffers unhappy Christmas as shoppers head to Aldi and Lidl', *The Guardian* (12 January 2016).

[6] British Gas, EDF Energy, E.ON UK, npower, Scottish Power and SSE.

[7] Competition and Markets Authority, *Energy market investigation* (March 2016).

[8] 'Competition Commission raps big four accountants', *BBC News* (22 February 2013).

[9] John Ficenec, 'Big Four accountants enjoy record fees despite new rules', *The Telegraph* (16 April 2016).

RECAP

1. An oligopoly is where there are just a few firms in an industry, which has barriers to the entry of new firms. Firms recognise their interdependence.

2. Whether oligopolists compete or collude depends on the conditions in the industry. They are more likely to collude if there are few of them; if they are open with each other; if they have similar products and cost structures; if there is a dominant firm; if there are significant entry barriers; if the market is stable; and if there is no government legislation to prevent collusion.

3. A formal collusive agreement is called a 'cartel'. A cartel aims to act as a monopoly. It can set a price and leave the members to compete for market share, or it can assign quotas. There is always a temptation for cartel members to 'cheat' by undercutting the cartel price if

they think they can get away with it and not trigger a price war.

4. Tacit collusion can take the form of price leadership, or firms can follow an 'agreed' set of rules.

5. When firms do not collude, prices may still be relatively stable. One reason for this is that firms face a kinked demand curve, such that they are reluctant either to raise or to lower prices.

6. Whether consumers benefit from oligopoly depends on the particular oligopoly and how competitive it is; whether the firms engage in extensive advertising and of what type; whether product differentiation results in a wide range of choice for the consumer; and how much of the profits is ploughed back into research and development.

5.4 GAME THEORY

The interdependence between oligopolists requires firms to think strategically and *game theory* was developed by economists to examine the best strategy that a firm can adopt, given the assumptions it makes about its rivals' behaviour.

When considering whether to cut prices, and thereby hopefully gain a bigger market share, a firm will ask: (1) 'How much can we get away with without inviting retaliation?' and (2) 'If a price war does result, will we be the winners?'

The position of rival firms under oligopoly, therefore, is rather like that of generals of opposing armies or the players in a game. It is a question of choosing the appropriate strategy: the strategy that will best succeed in outwitting your opponents. Of course, the strategy that a firm adopts will be concerned not just with price, but also with advertising and product development, amongst other factors.

The firm's choice of strategy will depend on (a) how it thinks its rivals will react to any price changes or other changes it makes; (b) its willingness to take a gamble.

We examine game theory in this section and it will provide some useful insights into firms' behaviour and their strategy on pricing. But game theory can also be applied to a huge range of other areas, as is shown in a BBC News article, 'What exactly is "game theory"?'[4] For example, it is relevant to many international negotiations, such as those on climate change.

In the next chapter we look at other aspects of business strategy, such as whether to expand the business, whether to launch new products or how the business should position itself in the industry relative to its rivals.

Single-move games

The simplest type of 'game' is a *single-move* or *single-period game*. This involves just one 'move' by each firm involved.

For example, two or more firms are considering what price to bid for a contract which will be awarded to the lowest bidder. Each makes its bid by considering what its rivals are likely to do. Once the bids have been made and the contract has been awarded to the lowest bidder, the 'game' is over.

Dominant strategy games

Many single-period games have predictable outcomes, no matter what each firm assumes about its rivals' behaviour. Such games are known as *dominant strategy games*.

A simple example is where there are just two firms with identical costs, products and demand. They are both considering which of two alternative prices to charge. Figure 5.5 shows typical profits they could each make.

Let us assume that at present both firms (X and Y) are charging a price of £2 and that they are each making a profit of £10 million, giving a total industry profit of £20 million. This is shown in the top left-hand cell (A).

Now assume they are both (independently) considering reducing their price to £1.80. In making this decision, they will need to take into account what their rival might do, and

Definitions

Game theory (or the theory of games) The study of alternative strategies that oligopolists may choose to adopt, depending on their assumptions about their rivals' behaviour.

Single-move or single-period game Where each firm makes just one decision without at the time knowing the decision of the other.

Dominant strategy game Where the firm will choose the same strategy no matter what assumption it makes about its rivals' behaviour.

---

[4] 'What exactly is 'game theory'?' *BBC News* (18 February 2015)

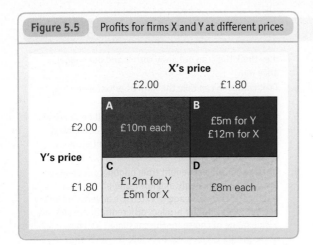

Figure 5.5 Profits for firms X and Y at different prices

how this will affect them. Let us consider X's position. In our simple example there are just two things that its rival, firm Y, might do. Either Y could cut its price to £1.80, or it could leave its price at £2. What should X do?

To answer this question we need to take each of firm Y's two possible actions and look at firm X's best response to each. If we assume that firm Y chooses a price of £2, firm X could keep its price at £2, giving it £10 million in profit. This is shown by cell A. Alternatively, firm X could cut its price to £1.80 and earn £12 million in profit, in cell B. Firm X's best response is therefore to cut price to £1.80, preferring a profit of £12 million to one of £10 million.

What about if we now assume that firm Y charges £1.80 – how should firm X best respond? If firm X charged £2, we would end up in cell C and firm X would earn only £5 million in profits. On the other hand, firm X could also cut its price to £1.80, moving us to cell D and it would earn £8 million in profits. By comparing these two profit outcomes, we can see that firm X's best response is again to cut price to £1.80, preferring a profit of £8 million to a profit of £5 million. Note that firm Y will argue along similar lines, cutting price to £1.80 as well, whatever it assumes firm X will do.

This game is known as a 'dominant strategy game', since both firms' best response is always to play the same (dominant) strategy (namely, cutting price to £1.80), irrespective of what they think the other firm will do, as this will yield the highest possible profits. Both firms do what is best for them, given their assumptions about their rivals' behaviour. The result is that the firms will end up in cell D, with each firm earning a profit of £8 million.

Nash equilibrium. The equilibrium outcome of a game where there is no collusion between the players (cell D in the above game) is known as a *Nash equilibrium*. This occurs when each player does what's best for itself, given the assumptions it makes about its rivals' behaviour. It is named after John Nash, a US mathematician who introduced the concept in 1951. The Oscar-winning film *A Beautiful Mind* depicts the life story of John Nash and you can watch the famous scene where he begins to formulate the famous Nash equilibrium

on YouTube.[5] You may also like to look at the blog on the Sloman Economics News site, 'Death of a Beautiful Mind', following John Nash's death on 23 May 2015.

KEY IDEA 19

Nash equilibrium. **The position resulting from everyone making their optimal decision based on their assumptions about their rivals' decisions. Such an outcome, however, is unlikely to maximise the collective benefit. Nevertheless, without collusion in this 'game', whether open or tacit, there is no incentive to move from this position.**

The prisoners' dilemma. In the previous game in Figure 5.5, a better outcome for the two firms is for them to collude (rather than competing on price) and charge the higher price, each earning £10 million (cell A). However, even if they did collude and charged £2, they would both still be tempted to cheat and cut prices. This is known as the *prisoners' dilemma*: the dilemma faced by suspects of a crime who are in custody and wondering whether to 'shop' their fellow suspects in the hope of getting a lighter sentence. The police rely on the fact that suspects are tempted to own up in case their fellow prisoners do so first. The result is that everyone owns up, even though collusion to keep quiet would have been in all the suspects' interests. The prisoners' dilemma is examined in Box 5.4.

Pause for thought

If firms were to collude, how could they avoid the prisoners' dilemma?

More complex games

More complex 'games' can be devised with more than two firms, many alternative prices, differentiated products and various forms of non-price competition (e.g. advertising). We may also see 'games', where the best response for each firm depends on the assumptions made, meaning there is no dominant strategy. Consider the payoff matrix in Figure 5.6.

Definitions

Nash equilibrium The position resulting from everyone making their optimal decision based on their assumptions about their rivals' decisions. Without collusion, there is no incentive to move from this position.

Prisoners' dilemma Where two or more firms (or people), by attempting independently to choose their best strategy given the assumptions they make about their rivals' behaviour, end up in a worse position than if they had co-operated in the first place.

---

[5] Nash Equilibrium, *YouTube* (available at: https://www.youtube.com/watch?v=2d_dtTZQyUM)

Figure 5.6 Profits for firms X and Y at different prices

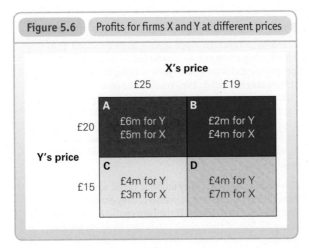

X's price

	£25	£19
£20	**A** £6m for Y £5m for X	**B** £2m for Y £4m for X
£15	**C** £4m for Y £3m for X	**D** £4m for Y £7m for X

Y's price

Pause for thought

What is firm Y's best response to each of firm X's possible choices in the game shown in Figure 5.6? Does it have a dominant strategy in this game?

£3 million in profit (cell C). We no longer have a dominant strategy.

In many situations, firms will have a number of different options open to them and a number of possible reactions by rivals. Such games can become highly complex.

The better the firm's information about (a) its rivals' costs and demand, (b) the likely reactions of rivals to its actions and (c) the effects of these reactions on its own profit, the better the firm's 'move in the game' is likely to be. It is similar to a card game: the more you know about your opponents' cards and how your opponents are likely to react to your moves, and the better you can calculate the effects of their moves on you, the better your moves in the game are likely to be.

If firm X assumes that firm Y will charge £20, then firm X will either earn £5 million in profit if it charges £25 or £4 million in profit if it charges £19. Firm X's best response would be to charge £25. However, if it assumes that firm Y will charge £15, then firm X's best response will now be to charge £19, preferring £7 million in profit (cell D) to

---

BOX 5.4   **THE PRISONERS' DILEMMA**

When confession may be the best strategy

A famous non-economic example of game theory is the origin of the term 'prisoners' dilemma'. Consider Nigel and Amanda who have been arrested for a joint crime of serious fraud. Each is interviewed separately and given the following alternatives:

- If they say nothing, the court has enough evidence to sentence both to a year's imprisonment.
- If either Nigel or Amanda alone confesses, he or she will get only a three-month sentence but the partner would get ten years.
- If both confess, they get three years each.

Let us consider Nigel's dilemma. If he believes that Amanda will confess, then he should also confess, preferring three years in prison to ten years. If he believes that Amanda will not confess, then he should still confess, as by doing so he gets only three months, as opposed to one year. Nigel's best response, then, is always to confess.

Amanda is in the same dilemma and so the result is simple. When both prisoners do what is best for themselves, given how they think the other will behave, they both confess and end up with relatively long prison terms. Only when they collude and both deny will they end up with relatively short sentences, but neither has an incentive to do this, as the more certain they are that their compatriot will deny, the greater the incentive for them to confess!

Of course the police know this and will do their best to prevent collusion, keeping the prisoners separate and trying to persuade each that the other is bound to confess.

1. *Devise a box diagram for the above case, similar to that in Figure 5.5. Why is this a dominant strategy game?*
2. *How would Nigel's choice of strategy be affected if he had instead been involved in a joint crime with Nikki, Kim, Paul and Dave, and they had all been caught?*

The Hunger Games

Suzanne Collins published the first book of the 'The Hunger Games' trilogy in 2008 and it has been made into four films. It follows Katniss Everdeen, living in a future time where a country has been divided into a ruling wealthy Capitol and 12 Districts (plus a secretive 13th District). Each year, a girl and boy from each of the 12 Districts are chosen randomly to compete to the death against each other in The Hunger Games, which is set in a dangerous and very public arena. Katniss volunteers in place of her younger sister and enters the arena with Peeta, the male 'Tribute' and so the use of strategic thinking and game theory begins, until just one 'Tribute' remains.[1]

The Games can last for weeks and so survival relies on avoiding being killed by another 'Tribute' and getting enough sleep to sustain yourself. The problem is, when you are asleep there is the chance of a stealth attack by another competitor, but if you don't sleep, you become more susceptible to future attacks, due to sleep deprivation.

3. *Try constructing a matrix and determine the Nash equilibrium in this game.*

---

[1] See: Samuel Arbesman, 'Probability and game theory in The Hunger Games', *Wired* (4 October 2012).

▶

Many stabs in the dark. In the Games, a coalition is formed between some Tributes, who agree to work together, but still know they are competing against each other and hence, at some point, will have to try to kill their rivals. They are camping together and so, within that group, they know where everyone is.

4. *Does the Nash equilibrium in the game change if we are now thinking about the decision of one member of the Coalition, given the possible responses of the other members of the Coalition?*

Looking at the matrix you constructed and perhaps making some assumptions about the relative value of sleep versus progress, the likely outcome seems to be 'Don't sleep' for everyone. After all, being sleep deprived is better than being dead. So, why do the members of the Coalition get any sleep?

The Hunger Games is a repeated game, where no player knows when their last night will be. The members of the Coalition have to make the sleep decision every night, knowing that every night they don't sleep they may make progress, but will become more vulnerable to other attacks. Furthermore, as there are multiple members of the Coalition, each member will become less trustworthy if others are killed during the night. So perhaps the best response in this infinitely repeated game is for the Coalition to co-operate from the start, so everyone gets some sleep. However, if one night a member is killed, then the next night would probably see each player once again best responding by remaining awake. Perhaps there would be a 'tit-for-tat' strategy, until a winner emerges.

Some other examples of the prisoners' dilemma

Standing at concerts. When people go to a concert or a match, they often stand to get a better view. But once people start standing, everyone is likely to do so: after all, if they stayed sitting, they would not see at all. In this Nash equilibrium, most people are worse off, since, except for tall people, their view is likely to be worse and they lose the comfort of sitting down. But once everyone is standing, nobody has an incentive to sit down, because then you won't see anything. Thus we arrive at a Nash equilibrium.

Too much advertising. Why do firms spend so much on advertising? If they are aggressive, they probably do so to get ahead of their rivals. If they are cautious, they probably do so for fear of their rivals increasing their advertising. Although in both cases it may be in the individual firm's best interests to increase advertising, the resulting Nash equilibrium is likely to be one of excessive advertising: the total spent *on advertising (by all firms) is not recouped in additional sales.*

5. *Give some other examples (economic and non-economic) of the prisoner's dilemma.*
6. *Search for the gameshow 'Golden Balls' on YouTube and watch a clip of the very last part of the game '£66 885 Split or Steal?'. Try constructing a matrix for this game and working out what the Nash equilibrium is.*

Multiple-move games

In many business situations firms will react to what their rivals do. Their rivals, in turn, will react to what they do. In other words, the game goes back and forth from one 'player' to the other, rather like chess or a game of cards. Firms will still have to think strategically (as you do in chess), considering the likely responses of rivals to what they do. These multiple-move games are known as *repeated games* and again there are many applications, including a penalty shoot-out in football.

One of the simplest strategies in a repeated game is *tit-for-tat*. This is where a firm will only cut prices (or make some other aggressive move) if the rival does first. To illustrate this in a multiple-move situation, consider the example we looked at in Figure 5.5, but this time we will extend it beyond one period.

Assume that firm X is adopting the tit-for-tat strategy. If firm Y cuts its price, firm X then responds in round 2 by cutting its price. The two firms end up in cell D – worse off than if neither had cut price. If, however, firm Y had left its price at £2.00, then firm X would respond by leaving its price unchanged too. Both would remain in cell A with a higher profit than in cell D.

As long as firm Y knows that firm X will behave in this way, it has an incentive not to cut its price. To make sure that Y 'understands', X will probably let it be known how it will react if Y cuts its price. In other words, firm X will make a threat.

The importance of threats and promises

There are many situations where an oligopolist will make a threat or promise (either openly or implied) that it will act in a certain way. As long as the threat or promise is *credible* (i.e. its competitors believe it), the firm can gain and it will influence its rivals' behaviour.

> ### Pause for thought
>
> *Assume that there are two major oil companies operating filling stations in an area. The first promises to match the other's prices. The other promises to sell at 1p per litre cheaper than the first. Describe the likely sequence of events in this 'game' and the likely eventual outcome. Could the promise of the second company be seen as credible?*

> ### Definitions
>
> **Repeated games** Where firms decide in turn, in the light of what their rivals do. Such games thus involve two or more moves.
>
> **Tit-for-tat** A strategy where you copy whatever your rival does. Thus if your rival cuts price, you will too. If your rival does not, neither will you.
>
> **Credible threat (or promise)** One that is believable to rivals because it is in the threatener's interests to carry it out.

Figure 5.7 A decision tree

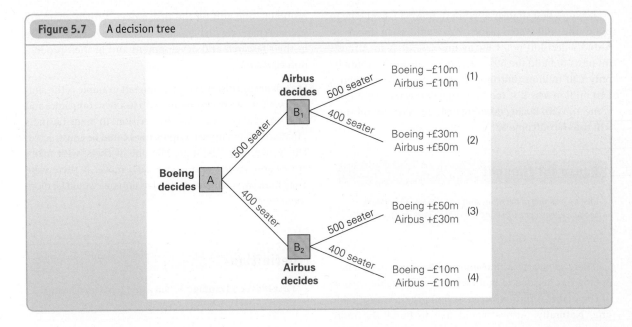

Take the simple situation where a large oil company, such as Esso, states that it will match the price charged by any competitor within a given radius. Assume that competitors believe this 'price promise' but also that Esso will not try to undercut their price. In the simple situation where there is only one other petrol station in the area, what price should it charge? Clearly it should charge the price which would maximise its profits, assuming that Esso will charge the same price. In the absence of other petrol stations in the area, this is likely to be a relatively high price.

Now assume that there are several petrol stations in the area. What should the company do now? Its best response is probably to charge the same price as Esso and hope that no other company charges a lower price and forces Esso to cut its price. Assuming that Esso's threat is credible, other companies are likely to respond in a similar way. Prices will therefore be kept high, because of the credible threat made by Esso.

The economic situation in Greece has seen many applications of game theory, most involving both threats and promises, and you can read about this in articles from The Conversation,[6] Bloomberg[7] and City A.M.[8]

The importance of timing: decision trees
Most decisions by oligopolists are made by one firm at a time rather than simultaneously by all firms. Sometimes a firm will take the initiative. At other times it will respond to decisions taken by other firms. Here we are considering a sequential game.

Take the case of a new generation of large passenger aircraft which can fly further without refuelling. Assume that there is a market for a 500-seater version of this type of aircraft and a 400-seater version, but that the market for each sized aircraft is not big enough for the two manufacturers, Boeing and Airbus, to share it profitably. Let us also assume that the 400-seater market would give an annual profit of £50 million to a single manufacturer and the 500-seater would give an annual profit of £30 million, but that if both manufacturers produced the same version, they would each make an annual loss of £10 million.

Assume that Boeing announces that it is building the 400-seater plane. What should Airbus do? The choice is illustrated in Figure 5.7. This diagram is called a *decision tree* and shows the sequence of events. The small square at the left of the diagram is Boeing's decision point (point A). If it had decided to build the 500-seater plane, we would move up the top branch. Airbus would now have to make a decision (point B_1). If it too built the 500-seater plane, we would move to outcome 1: a loss of £10 million for both manufacturers. Clearly, with Boeing building a 500-seater plane, Airbus would choose the 400-seater plane: we would move to outcome 2, with Boeing making a profit of £30 million and Airbus a profit £50 million. Airbus would be very pleased!

[6] Partha Gangopadhyay, 'How game theory explains Grexit and may also predict Greek poll outcome' *The Conversation* (1 July 2015) (available at http://theconversation.com/how-game-theory-explains-grexit-and-may-also-predict-greek-poll-outcome-44079)

[7] Mohamed A. El-Erian, 'John Nash's Game Theory and Greece', *Bloomberg* (29 May 2015) (available at http://www.bloombergview.com/articles/2015-05-29/john-nash-s-game-theory-and-greece)

[8] Paul Ormerod, 'Against the Grain: What Yanis Varoufakis can learn from a real game theory master - Nicola Sturgeon' *City A.M.* (24 June 2016) (available at http://www.cityam.com/218668/against-grain-what-yanis-varoufakis-can-learn-real-game-theory-master-nicola-sturgeon)

Definition

Decision tree (or game tree) A diagram showing the sequence of possible decisions by competitor firms and the outcome of each combination of decisions.

Boeing's best strategy at point A, however, would be to build the 400-seater plane. We would then move to Airbus's decision point B_2. In this case, it is in Airbus's interests to build the 500-seater plane. Its profit would be only £30 million (outcome 3), but this is better than a £10 million loss if it too built the 400-seater plane (outcome 4). With Boeing deciding first, the Nash equilibrium will thus be outcome 3.

There is clearly a *first-mover advantage* here. Once Boeing has decided to build the more profitable version of the plane, Airbus is forced to build the less profitable one. Naturally, Airbus would like to build the more

profitable one and be the first mover. Which company succeeds in going first depends on how advanced they are in their research and development and in their production capacity.

More complex decision trees. The aircraft example is the simplest version of a decision tree, with just two companies and each one making only one key decision. In many business situations, much more complex trees could be constructed. The 'game' would be more like one of chess, with many moves and several options on each move. If there were more than two companies, the decision tree would be more complex still.

5.5 ALTERNATIVE AIMS OF THE FIRM

The traditional profit-maximising theories of the firm have been criticised for being unrealistic. They assume that it is the *owners* of the firm that make price and output decisions. It is reasonable to assume that owners will want to maximise profits: this much most of the critics of the traditional theory accept. But, as we saw in Chapter 1, in public limited companies there is generally a separation of ownership and control within companies, which creates a principal–agent problem (see pages 9–10). Managers, as agents of the owners (their principals), are the decision makers and may well be motivated by objectives other than maximising profits, such as increasing their own utility by maximising sales or claiming large expenses. Different managers in the same firm may well pursue different aims.

Alternative theories of the firm typically make one or other of two assumptions: either that managers attempt to

maximise some other aim (such as growth in sales); or that they pursue a *number* of aims, which might possibly conflict. In either case, they must still make sufficient profits (the aim of *profit satisficing*) in order to keep shareholders happy. Otherwise they risk being taken over and/or losing their job.

We now examine these two alternative assumptions in turn.

Alternative maximising aims

Sales revenue maximisation

Perhaps the most famous of all alternative theories of the firm is the theory of *sales revenue maximisation*. So why should managers want to maximise their firm's sales revenue? The answer is that the success of managers, and especially sales managers, may be judged according to the level of the firm's sales. Sales figures are an obvious barometer of the firm's health. Managers' salaries, power and prestige may depend directly on sales revenue. The firm's sales representatives may be paid commission on their sales. Thus sales revenue maximisation may be a more dominant aim in the firm than profit maximisation, particularly if it has a dominant sales department.

Total sales revenue (*TR*) will be maximised at a higher output and lower price than will profits. This is illustrated in Figure 5.8. Profits are maximised at output Q_1 and price P_1, where $MC = MR$. Sales revenue, however, is maximised at the higher output Q_2 and lower price P_2, where $MR = 0$. The reason is that if *MR* equals zero, nothing more can be added to total revenue (*TR*) by producing extra and thus *TR* must be at the maximum. Indeed, by producing above Q_2, *MR* would be negative and thus *TR* would fall.

Sales revenue maximisation tends to involve more advertising than an objective of profit maximisation. Ideally the profit-maximising firm will advertise up to the point where the marginal revenue of advertising equals the marginal cost of advertising (assuming diminishing returns to advertising). The firm aiming to maximise sales revenue will go beyond this, since further advertising, although costing more than it earns the firm, will still add to total revenue. The firm will continue advertising until surplus profits above the minimum have been used up.

Growth maximisation

Rather than aiming to maximise short-run revenue, managers may take a longer-term perspective and aim for *growth maximisation* in the size of the firm. They may gain directly from being part of a rapidly growing 'dynamic' organisation; promotion prospects are greater in an expanding organisation, since new posts tend to be created; large firms may pay higher salaries; managers may obtain greater power in a large firm.

Growth is probably best measured in terms of a growth in sales revenue, since sales revenue (or 'turnover') is the simplest way of measuring the size of a business. An alternative would be to measure the capital value of a firm, but this will depend on the ups and downs of the stock market and is thus a rather unreliable method.

If a firm is to maximise growth, it needs to be clear about the time period over which it is setting itself this objective. For example, maximum growth over the next two or three years might be obtained by running factories at maximum capacity, cramming in as many machines and workers as possible, and backing this up with massive advertising campaigns and price cuts. Such policies, however, may not be sustainable in the longer run. The firm may simply not be able to finance them. A longer-term perspective (say, 5–10 years) may therefore require the firm to 'pace' itself, and perhaps to direct resources away from current production and sales into the development of new products that have a potentially high and growing long-term demand.

Equilibrium for a growth-maximising firm. What will a growth-maximising firm's price and output be? Unfortunately, there is no simple formula for predicting this.

In the short run, the firm may choose the profit-maximising price and output, as this will provide the greatest funds for investment. On the other hand, it may be prepared to sacrifice some short-term profits in order to mount an advertising campaign to boost longer-term sales. Thus the price and output depend on the strategy it considers most suitable to achieve growth.

In the long run, prediction is more difficult still. The policies that a firm adopts will depend crucially on the assessments of market opportunities made by managers. Different managers may judge a situation differently.

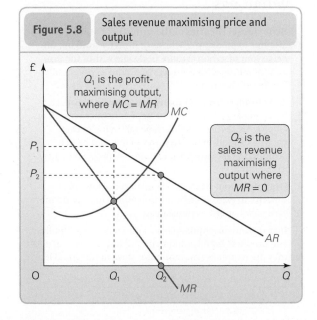

Figure 5.8	Sales revenue maximising price and output

> **Definitions**
>
> **Sales revenue maximisation** An alternative theory of the firm which assumes that managers aim to maximise the firm's short-run total revenue.
>
> **Growth maximisation** An alternative theory which assumes that managers seek to maximise the growth in sales revenue (or the capital value of the firm) over time.

Pause for thought

How will competition between growth-maximising firms benefit the consumer?

One prediction can be made. Growth-maximising firms are likely to diversify into different products, especially if their existing markets become saturated. We considered the Growth Vector Matrix in section 3.4 and will go on to analyse alternative growth strategies in Chapter 6.

Multiple aims

Behavioural theories of the firm: satisficing and the setting of targets

A major advance in alternative theories of the firm has been the development of *behavioural theories*.[9] Rather than setting up a model to show how various objectives could in theory be achieved, behavioural theories of the firm are based on observations of how firms *actually* behave.

Large firms are often complex institutions with several departments (sales, production, design, purchasing, personnel, finance, etc.). Each department is likely to have its own specific set of aims and objectives, which may come into conflict with those of other departments. In such cases all the aims cannot be maximised. Instead a 'satisficing' approach must be taken (see page 122).

These aims in turn will be constrained by the interests of shareholders, workers, customers and creditors (collectively known as *stakeholders*), who will need to be kept sufficiently happy (see Box 5.5).

A satisficing approach will normally involve setting targets for production, sales, profit, stock holding, etc. If, in practice, target levels are not achieved, a 'search' procedure will be started to find what went wrong and how to rectify it. If the problem cannot be rectified, managers will probably adjust the target downwards. If, on the other hand, targets are easily achieved, managers may adjust them upwards. Thus the targets to which managers aspire depend to a large extent on the success in achieving previous targets.

Targets are also influenced by expectations of demand and costs, by the achievements of competitors and by expectations of competitors' future behaviour. For example, if it is expected that the economy is likely to move into recession, sales and profit targets may be adjusted downwards.

If targets conflict, the conflict will be settled by a bargaining process between managers. The outcome of the bargaining, however, will depend on the power and ability of the individual managers concerned. Thus a similar set of conflicting targets may be resolved differently in different firms.

Behavioural theories of the firm: organisational slack

Since changing targets often involves search procedures and bargaining processes and is therefore time-consuming, and since many managers prefer to avoid conflict, targets tend to be changed fairly infrequently. Business conditions, however, often change rapidly. To avoid the need to change targets, therefore, managers will tend to be fairly conservative in their aspirations. This leads to the phenomenon known as *organisational slack*.

When the firm does better than planned, it will allow slack to develop. This slack can then be taken up if the firm does worse than planned. For example, if the firm produces more than it planned, it will build up stocks of finished goods and draw on them if production subsequently falls. It would not, in the meantime, increase its sales target or reduce its production target. If it did, and production then fell below target, the production department might not be able to supply the sales department with its full requirement.

Thus keeping targets fairly low and allowing slack to develop allows all targets to be met with minimum conflict.

Organisational slack, however, adds to a firm's costs. If firms are operating in a competitive environment, they may be forced to cut slack in order to survive. In the 1970s, many Japanese firms succeeded in cutting slack by using *just-in-time methods* of production. These involve keeping stocks to a minimum and ensuring that inputs are delivered as required. Clearly, this requires that production is tightly controlled and that suppliers are reliable. Many firms today

---

Definitions

Behavioural theories of the firm Theories that attempt to predict the actions of firms by studying the behaviour of various groups or people within the firm and their interactions under conditions of potentially conflicting interests.

Stakeholders (in a company) People who are affected by a company's activities and/or performance (customers, employees, owners, creditors, people living in the neighbourhood, etc.). They may or may not be in a position to take decisions, or influence decision taking, in the firm.

Organisational slack When managers allow spare capacity to exist, thereby enabling them to respond more easily to changed circumstances.

Just-in-time methods Where a firm purchases supplies and produces both components and finished products as they are required. This minimises stock holding and its associated costs.

---

[9] A major early work in this field which spawned a lot of further research was: R. M. Cyert and J. G. March, *A Behavioural Theory of the Firm* (Prentice Hall, 1963).

have successfully cut their warehouse costs by using such methods. These methods are examined in section 8.5.

The consumer interest

We've seen how firms that have multiple goals are likely to be satisficers and this can lead to conflicts and organisational slack. But, what does this mean for consumers?

Such firms are less likely to be able to respond to changing market conditions, such as adjustments in consumer demand or in costs. This would then have an adverse effect on their efficiency. However, these firms, unlike profit-maximising firms, will be less concerned with pushing up prices, engaging in aggressive advertising or simply exploiting their market power. This may therefore be in the public interest. The overall impact on consumers will depend on factors such as the extent and type of competition a firm faces and how it responds to its rivals. For example, the more a firm is concerned with its own performance compared to that of its rivals, the more responsive it is likely to be to consumer wishes.

BOX 5.5   STAKEHOLDER POWER?

Who governs the firm?

The concept of the 'stakeholder economy' became fashionable in the late 1990s. Such an economy should serve the interests of everyone. Big business, rather than simply acting in the interests of shareholders, many of whom are big institutions, such as insurance companies and pension funds, should take into account a wider range of stakeholders. But what does this mean for the governance of firms?

Meeting the interests of various stakeholders

The stakeholders of a firm include customers, employees (from senior managers to the lowest paid workers), shareholders, suppliers, lenders and both local and national communities.

The supporters of a stakeholder economy argue that *all* interest groups should have a say in a firm's decisions.

■ Trade unions or workers' councils could be represented on decision-making bodies and perhaps have seats on the board of directors. Alternatively, the workforce might be given the power to elect managers. The John Lewis Partnership is a good example of a company where the workers have a crucial say in the decision-making process (see Box 1.1).
■ Banks or other institutions lending to firms ought to be included in investment decisions. In Germany, where banks finance a large proportion of investment, they are represented on the boards of most large companies.
■ Local communities ought to have a say in any projects (such as new buildings or the discharge of effluent) that affect the local environment, such as new airport terminals or the UK's high-speed rail projects, HS2 and HS3. Customers ought to have more say in the quality of products, for example by being given legal protection against the production of shoddy or unsafe goods. This also concerns poor information about the products being purchased. Recent examples include the mis-selling of payment protection insurance (PPI) in the UK and the horse meat scandal.

Where interest groups cannot be directly represented in decision making, then companies ought to be regulated by the government in order to protect the interests of the various groups. For example, if farmers and other suppliers to supermarkets are paid very low prices, then the purchasing behaviour of the supermarkets could be regulated by some government agency, as we saw in Box 5.3.

Of course, the interests of stakeholders may conflict, which would require businesses to adopt a 'satisficing' approach, aiming for satisfactory levels of each objective with adjustments for any conflicts.

Are businesses becoming more or less responsive to stakeholders' interests?

But is this vision of a stakeholder economy likely to become reality? Trends in the international economy suggest that the opposite might be occurring. The growth of multinational corporations, with their ability to move finance and production to wherever it is most profitable, has weakened the power of employees, local interest groups and even national governments.

Employees in one part of the multinational may have little in the way of common interests with employees in another. In fact, they may vie with each other, for example over which plant should be expanded or closed down. What is more, many firms are employing more casual, part-time, temporary or agency workers and such employees have less say in the company than permanent members of staff, as we will discuss in section 8.5.

Also, the widespread introduction of share incentive schemes for managers (whereby managers are rewarded with shares), has increasingly made profits their driving goal. Finally, the policies of opening up markets and deregulation, policies that were adopted by many governments round the world up to the mid-1990s, have again weakened the power of many stakeholders.

Nevertheless, many companies find themselves under increased pressure to respond to social and environmental concerns and to practise 'corporate social responsibility (CSR)'. An 'irresponsible' firm is likely to attract adverse publicity – which could impact on sales and profit. We examine CSR in section 9.2.

 Are customers' interests best served by profit-maximising firms, answerable primarily to shareholders, or by firms where various stakeholder groups are represented in decision taking?

RECAP

1. In large companies, shareholders (the owners) may want maximum profits, but it is the managers who make the decisions, and managers are likely to aim to maximise their own self-interest rather than that of the shareholders. This leads to profit 'satisficing'. This is where managers aim to achieve sufficient profits to keep shareholders happy, but this is a secondary aim to one or more alternative aims.

2. Managers may seek to maximise sales revenue. The output of a sales-revenue-maximising firm will be higher than that of a profit-maximising one. Its level of advertising will also tend to be higher.

3. Many managers aim for maximum growth of their organisation, believing that this will help their salaries, power, prestige, etc. It is difficult, however, to predict the price and output strategies of a growth-maximising firm.

4. In large firms, decisions are taken or influenced by a number of different people, including various managers and other stakeholders. If interests conflict, a satisficing approach will generally be adopted. This involves setting consistent targets, which will be adjusted in the light of experience and may involve a process of bargaining.

5. Life is made easier for managers if conflict can be avoided. This will be possible if slack is allowed to develop in various parts of the firm. If targets are not being met, the slack can then be taken up without requiring adjustments in other targets.

5.6 SETTING PRICE

How are prices determined in practice? Is there actually an equilibrium price? In many cases, probably not. Do firms construct marginal cost and marginal revenue curves (or equations) and find the output where they are equal? Do they then use an average revenue curve (or equation) to work out the price at that output?

The problem is that firms often do not have the information to do so, even if they wanted to. In practice, firms look for rules of pricing that are relatively simple to apply.

Cost-based pricing

One approach is *average cost* or *mark-up pricing*. Here producers work out the price by simply adding a certain percentage (mark-up) for profit on top of average costs (average fixed costs plus average variable costs).

Choosing the mark-up

The level of profit mark-up on top of average cost will depend on the firm's aims, the likely actions of rivals and their responses to changes in this firm's price and how these responses will affect demand.

Pause for thought

If a firm has a typical-shaped average cost curve and sets prices 10 per cent above average cost, what will its supply curve look like?

Definition

Average cost or mark-up pricing Where firms set the price by adding a profit mark-up to average costs.

If a firm could estimate its demand curve, it could then set its output and profit mark-up at levels to avoid a shortage or surplus. Thus in Figure 5.9 it could choose a lower output (Q_1) with a higher mark-up (*fg*), or a higher output (Q_2) with a lower mark-up (*hj*). If a firm could not estimate its demand curve, then it could adjust its mark-up and output over time by a process of trial and error, according to its success in meeting profit and sales aims.

Pause for thought

If the firm adjusts the size of its mark-up according to changes in demand and the actions of competitors, could its actions approximate to setting price and output where MC = MR?

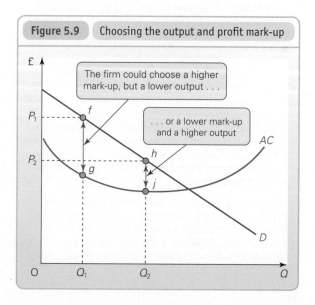

Figure 5.9 Choosing the output and profit mark-up

The firm could choose a higher mark-up, but a lower output . . .

. . . or a lower mark-up and a higher output

Variations in the mark-up

In most firms, the mark-up is not rigid. In expanding markets, or markets where firms have monopoly/oligopoly power, the size of the mark-up is likely to be greater. In contracting markets, or under conditions of rising costs and constant demand, a firm may well be forced to accept lower profits and thus reduce the mark-up.

Firms producing a range of products are likely to apply varying mark-ups to their different products. Those products with inelastic demand can have a higher mark-up imposed on them, as any increase in price will have a relatively small effect on demand. On the other hand, a product with many close substitutes will only have a low mark-up to keep its price competitive. Products with less elastic demand will therefore be expected to make a larger contribution towards a firm's overhead costs.

The firm is likely to take account of the actions and possible reactions of its competitors, as we saw under the model of oligopoly. It may well be unwilling to change prices when costs or demand change, for fear of the reactions of competitors (see the kinked demand curve theory on page 114). If prices are kept constant and yet costs change, either due to a movement along the AC curve in response to a change in demand or due to a shift in the AC curve, the firm must necessarily change the size of the mark-up.

All this suggests that, whereas the mark-up may well be based on a target profit, firms are often prepared to change their target and hence their mark-up.

Price discrimination

Up to now we have assumed that a firm will sell its output at a single price. Sometimes, however, firms may practise *price discrimination*. This is where the firm charges different prices to different customers based on their willingness to pay.

Rather than producing where $MC = MR$ in the market and charging everyone the same profit-maximising price, a firm might be able to charge a higher price to those consumers who place a higher valuation on the product – that is, those who gain a higher utility from the product and hence have a higher willingness to pay for it.

The best scenario for the firm would be to charge every consumer a price equal to their marginal willingness to pay. However, this will be very difficult, if not impossible, to achieve, as normally only the consumer knows this. There is a problem for the firm, therefore, of asymmetric information – the consumer knows more than the firm. However, recent developments in big data may change this as firms gain more and more information about the preferences of individual consumers.[10]

But what if a firm can charge different prices to different *groups* of consumers based on its assumptions about the willingness to pay of each group? For example, airlines may charge much higher ticket prices to late bookers than to early bookers for identical seats on the same flight: see the blog on the Sloman Economics News site, 'Easy or not so easypricing?' Airlines know that late bookers place a higher valuation on the product and hence are willing to pay more for it (see Box 5.6). In the blog 'A sexist surcharge', we consider the differing prices for products for men and women. As we shall see, a firm will be able to increase its profits if it can engage in this form of price discrimination.

Conditions necessary for price discrimination to operate

In order for a firm to charge discriminatory prices, three conditions must be met:

- The firm must be able to set its price, meaning that it must have some degree of market power. Thus price discrimination will be impossible under perfect competition, where firms are price takers.
- It must be possible to split consumers into separate markets and there must not be any possibility of resale between the markets. Consumers in the low-priced market must not be able to resell the product in the high-priced market. For example, children must not be able to resell a half-priced child's cinema ticket for use by an adult.
- Willingness to pay and hence demand elasticity must differ in each market. The firm will charge the higher price in the market where demand is less elastic, and thus less sensitive to a price rise.

Advantages to the firm

Price discrimination allows the firm to earn higher revenue from any given level of sales. This is illustrated in Figure 5.10, which shows a firm's overall demand curve. If it is to sell 200 units without price discrimination, it must charge a price of P_1. The total revenue it earns is shown by the green area. If, however, it can practise price discrimination by selling 150 of those 200 units at the higher price of P_2, it will gain the mauve area in addition to the green area.

Another advantage to the firm of price discrimination is that it may be able to use it to drive competitors out of business. If a firm has monopoly power in one market (e.g. the home market), it may be able to charge a high price due to the relatively inelastic nature of the demand

---

Definition

Price discrimination Where a firm sells the same product at different prices in different markets for reasons unrelated to costs.

---

[10] See: Anna Bernasek and DT Mongan, 'Big data is coming for your purchase history – to charge you more money', *The Guardian* (29 May 2015) (available at http://www.theguardian.com/commentisfree/2015/may/29/big-data-purchase-history-charge-you-more-money)

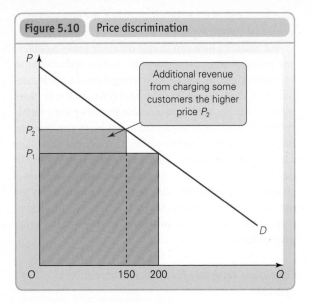

Figure 5.10   Price discrimination

Additional revenue from charging some customers the higher price P_2

way, price discrimination could actually help to increase competition.

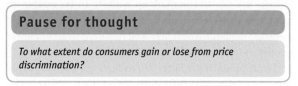

Pause for thought

To what extent do consumers gain or lose from price discrimination?

curve, and thus make high profits. If it is operating under oligopoly conditions in another market (e.g. the export market), it may be able to use the high profits in the first market to subsidise a very low price in the oligopolistic market, thus forcing its competitors out of business. This, of course, could have negative consequences for consumers.

It may also provide the firm with opportunities to enter new markets. Again, if the firm has high profits in its established market, it may be able to use them to cover the costs of entering another market. It could also use them to help it survive a price war with established firms in this new market, should one emerge. In this

Pricing and the product life cycle

New products are launched, become established and then may be replaced by more up-to-date products. Many products go through such a 'life cycle', which typically has four stages (see Figure 5.11):

1. Being launched.
2. A rapid growth in sales.
3. Maturity: a levelling off in sales.
4. Decline: sales begin to fall as the market becomes saturated, or as the product becomes out of date and obsolete.

Analogue televisions, VCR players and traditional mobile phones have all reached stage 4. Writable CDs, many DIY products and automatic washing machines have reached stage 3. Large LED TVs, speed-dating events, herbal treatments, smart phones and tablet computers are probably still in stage 2, but moving towards stage 3. 3D multimedia entertainment devices and biodiesel are probably still in stage 1, but things do change very quickly, especially with high-tech products! An interesting case is the iconic red phone box and you can read about its life cycle in the blog, 'A good or bad call?',

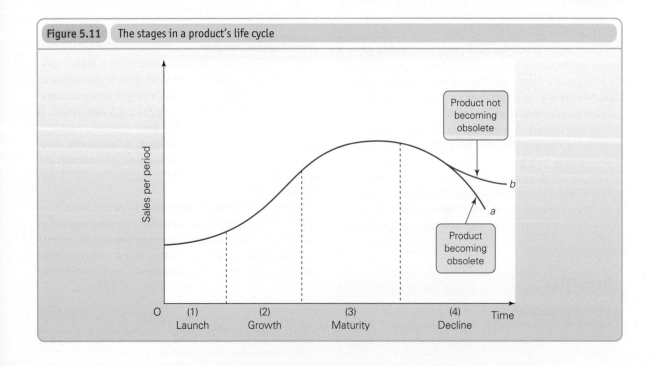

Figure 5.11   The stages in a product's life cycle

Product not becoming obsolete

Product becoming obsolete

Sales per period

Time

(1) Launch   (2) Growth   (3) Maturity   (4) Decline

on the Sloman Economics News site and about a novel innovation in an article from *Business Insider*.[11]

At each stage, the firm is likely to be faced with quite different market conditions: not only in terms of consumer demand, but also in terms of competition from rivals. What does this mean for pricing strategy?

The launch stage

In this stage the firm will probably have a monopoly (unless there is a simultaneous launch by rivals).

Given the lack of substitutes, the firm may be able to exploit its first-mover advantage (see page 122) and charge very high prices, thereby making large profits. This will be especially true if it is a radically new product – like the ball-point pen, the home computer, the mobile phone and the iPod were. Such products are likely to have a rapidly expanding and price-inelastic demand.

The danger of a high-price policy is that the resulting high profits may tempt competitors to break into the industry, even if barriers are quite high. As an alternative, then, the firm may go for maximum 'market penetration' (see the growth vector matrix on pages 66–7): keeping the price low to get as many sales and as much brand loyalty as possible, before rivals can become established.

> ### Pause for thought
>
> *If entry barriers are high, should a firm always charge a high price during this phase?*

Which policy the firm adopts will depend on its assessment of its current price elasticity of demand and the likelihood of an early entry by rivals.

The growth stage

Unless entry barriers are very high, the rapid growth in sales will attract new firms. The industry becomes oligopolistic.

Despite the growth in the number of firms, sales are expanding so rapidly that all firms can increase their sales. Some price competition may emerge, but it is unlikely to be intense at this stage. New entrants may choose to compete in terms of minor product differences, while following the price lead set by the original firm.

The maturity stage

Now that the market has grown large, there are many firms competing. New firms – or, more likely, firms diversifying into this market – will be entering to get 'a piece of the action'. At the same time, the growth in sales is slowing down.

Competition is now likely to be more intense and as such any collusion may well begin to break down. Pricing policy may become more aggressive as businesses attempt to hold on to their market share. Price wars may break out, only to be followed later by a 'truce' and a degree of price collusion returning.

It is in this stage particularly that firms may invest considerably in product innovation in order to 'breathe new life' into old products, especially if there is competition from new types of product. Thus the upgrading of hi-fi cassette recorders, with additional features such as Dolby S, was one way in which it hoped to beat off competition from digital cassette recorders and later minidisc recorders and CD burners.

The decline stage

Eventually, as the market becomes saturated, or as new, superior, alternative products are launched, sales will start to fall. For example, once most households had a fridge, the demand for fridges fell back as people simply bought them to replace worn-out ones, or to obtain a more up-to-date one. Initially in this stage competition is likely to be intense. All sorts of price offers, extended guarantees, better after-sales service, added features, etc., will be introduced as firms seek to maintain their sales. Firms may look for other uses for the product or other markets. These efforts are known as extension strategies. Some firms, however, may be driven out of the market, unable to survive the competition.

After a time, however, the level of sales may stop falling. Provided the product has not become obsolete, people still need replacements. This is illustrated by line b in Figure 5.11. The market may thus return to a stable oligopoly with a high degree of tacit price collusion.

Alternatively, the product becomes obsolete (line a) and sales dry up. Firms will leave the market. It is pointless trying to compete.

The newspaper market is an interesting case where, over recent years, sales have significantly declined with free information becoming increasingly available online. Newspapers have started the move from maturity to decline. However, in reaction to this, all the main newspapers have online websites and in many cases these articles are free to view. By adapting to changing times and tastes, the newspaper sector has found a way into a seemingly new market. However, with declining revenues from their newspaper sales, protecting the industry has now become a concern and this has led to the *Times*, the *Washington Post*, the *Wall Street Journal* and the *Financial Times* implementing a paywall. To access all (or any) of the articles available online, consumers have to take out a subscription. Those newspapers continuing to offer free articles will undoubtedly benefit, but a key question will be how much consumers are willing to pay to access the best journalism. You can read about the changing face of the newspaper industry in the blogs on the Sloman Economics News site, 'Oh, how times are charging' and more recently in 'The decline of the newspaper'.

---

[11] Chloe Pantazi, 'A new London coffee shop is serving drinks out of a red phone box', *Business Insider* (23 February 2016) (available at http://uk.businessinsider.com/red-telephone-box-coffee-shop-in-londons-hampstead-2016-2)

BOX 5.6 PRICING IN PRACTICE

Price is a key variable for all firms, whatever degree of competition they face. Except for firms under perfect competition, they can choose their price. In doing so, there are many pricing strategies they can adopt. This box examines some of them.

Price discrimination

The most common type of price discrimination occurs when a firm separates consumers into two or more markets and charges each group a different price. This is known as *third-degree price discrimination*. Many consumer characteristics can be used to create these separate groups of consumers, with each group being willing and able to pay different prices.

Many of you (the readers!) will have a student identification card and when you go to the cinema or buy a train ticket, or even shop in places like Top Shop, you may get a discount. This is a simple form of price discrimination, where the firm separates consumers into groups, such as students, adults, children and seniors, and charges each a different price. Those with a higher willingness to pay and hence more inelastic demand, such as adults, are charged a higher price. Students, with much tighter incomes on average and more elastic demand, will be charged lower prices and so benefit from price discrimination.

An interesting characteristic that I (Elizabeth) came across was that of nationality, or even language! An archaeological site in India and a museum in Russia had signs outside written in Hindi or Russian and English. However, the instructions in each language were different. In Hindi/Russian, it said the entrance was to the right and in English it directed you to the left. Following the English directions took you to an entrance, but you were charged a much higher price than if you had followed the Hindi/Russian instructions! The sites were operating a tactic of price discrimination, assuming that tourists (many of whom speak English) had a much more inelastic demand and were thus willing to pay a higher price: after all – you're on holiday![1]

Other examples of price discrimination include *inter-temporal pricing* where the price elasticity of demand for a product varies over time. For example, new books are often first published in hardback and at a high price. For those consumers

who are desperate to read it and hence have inelastic demand, they are prepared to pay this high price. After a few months, a paperback edition is released at a much lower price and those with more elastic demand will then buy it. By varying prices over time, the publisher can increase revenue.

Another type of price discrimination is *peak-load pricing*, where consumers are charged a higher price if they travel at peak times. I (Elizabeth) often take the train from Coventry to London. If I need a certain train during peak time, I might have to pay over £100. However, if I am willing to travel at off-peak times, the price I pay can be less than £20 for a return. Commuters who need to travel at peak times have an inelastic demand and with little option but to pay a high price, this is what they are charged. Those with more flexibility benefit from a lower off-peak price.

 1. *Aside from a difference in the price elasticity of demand between those travelling at peak and non-peak times, are there any other factors that may push up the prices of peak travel?*

Full-range pricing

Walking into a supermarket, or indeed most shops, you are often attracted by a product on sale. Rather than just considering the price of each product individually, many stores look at the prices of all products together and devise a pricing strategy to increase profits. By marketing a product with elastic demand at a bargain price, many customers are

---

[1] See, for example: Mark Perry, 'Price discrimination: Russians get a discount', *GET.com* (11 October 2010) and Mark Perry, 'Price discrimination: India and Disney World, *GET.com* (9 October 2012).

Definitions

Third-degree price discrimination When a firm divides consumers into different groups and charges a different price to consumers in each group, but the same price to all consumers within a group.

Inter-temporal pricing This occurs where different groups have different price elasticities of demand for a product at different points in time.

Peak-load pricing The practice of charging higher prices at times when demand is highest because the demand of many consumers (e.g. commuters) is less elastic and the constraints on capacity lead to higher marginal costs.

attracted in to the store to buy this *loss-leader*. Firms hope that customers will then be encouraged to buy higher priced and more profitable items as well. By using a pricing strategy that assesses all products *collectively*, a firm is able to improve its profitability.

How much was it worth?

Another pricing tactic was implemented by Michael Vasos, who owned a French bistro in London. On reading about it you may think it's tantamount to financial suicide! The strategy was simple: pay what you think the meal was worth. Rather than giving customers their bill based on a set of menu prices, the idea was that consumers decide their own bill, by working out how much they thought the meal was worth. Mr Vasos said:

> If you give very good service and very good food, people leave a lot in tips. So I thought why not just leave the whole bill to customers and they can pay what they think it's worth.[2]

Such a strategy certainly has its risks, with the potential for customers to enjoy a three-course meal and leave a mere £1 for the whole bill. However, the strategy seems to have paid off and did lead to other restaurants following suit. Rather than losing money, new customers were attracted and revenues increased.

The honesty box

In some small villages, many of the residents sell eggs, vegetables, fruit and flowers, etc. from outside their front gates and simply leave a box for payment. They rely on people's honesty in paying for the products. In these cases, the cost of having someone actually selling the product would certainly outweigh the revenue earned and so it is a sensible strategy.

However, this idea has been extended. Some WH Smith branches in train stations have used a small container for consumers to pay for their newspapers, trusting in people's

honesty to make the correct payment. Churches, charity shops, bands and even large employers use the concept of the honesty box as it saves costs and, assuming consumers are honest, continues to bring in revenue.

Price wars

Setting a profit-maximising price is not always the best pricing strategy. Instead, it may be better to cut prices below your rivals in order to drive them out of business, allowing you at a later point to raise prices and make more profit.

In early 2012, a pizza price war developed in New York. The 6th Avenue Pizza Company was selling slices for $1.50, but two new competitors (Joey Pepperoni's Pizza and the 2 Bros pizza chain) began pricing a slice at $1. Not to be outdone, the 6th Avenue Company first matched the price and then undercut it to $0.79. 2 Bros then undercut this price to sell at $0.75 and was soon matched by 6th Avenue. Neither was willing to concede, with 6th Avenue suggesting they may begin selling at $0.50 and 2 Bros saying they may begin selling slices for free! In the end, further cuts were not needed, as the chains' imminent demise, together with potential legal problems, encouraged both pizza places to agree to end the price war, with slices returning to $1.50![3]

Budget shops in the UK are commonplace on the high street, in particular those offering products for £1. However, for Poundworld in Poole, Dorset, £1 just wasn't cheap enough. With the credit crunch biting in 2009, customers were looking for any cost savings and according to Poundworld's bosses, 1p was enough of a saving. The opening of the 99p store opposite to it drew customers in and allegedly led to a 70 per cent decline in Poundworld's turnover and eventually forced Poundworld to close the shop.[4]

New pricing tactics are always being developed and when economic times are hard and price is such a key variable, choosing the right price and strategy is crucial.

2. *In a full-range pricing strategy, why does the loss-leader need to have price-elastic demand?*

3. *Are price wars a sensible strategy? Can you find any other cases where price wars have developed?*

4. *Given that consumers switched from Poundworld to the 99p store, what does it suggest about the price elasticity of demand for Poundworld's products?*

Definition

Loss-leader A product whose price is cut by a business in order to attract custom.

---

[2] Nina Goswami, 'You decide how much meals are worth, restaurants tell customers', *The Telegraph* (12 June 2005).

[3] Matt Flegenheimer, '$1 pizza slice is back after a sidewalk showdown ends two parlors' price war', *The New York Times* (5 September 2012).

[4] 'Pound shop forced to close after 99p store opens across the road', *Mail Online* (12 January 2009).

RECAP

1. Traditional economic theory assumes that businesses will set prices corresponding to the output where the marginal costs of production are equal to marginal revenue. They will do so in pursuit of maximum profits. The difficulties that a business faces in deriving its marginal cost and revenue curves suggest that this is unlikely to be a widely practised pricing strategy.

2. Cost-based pricing involves the business adding a profit mark-up to its average costs of production. The profit mark-up set by the business is likely to alter depending upon market conditions.

3. Many businesses practise price discrimination in an attempt to maximise profits from the sale of a product. For a business to practise price discrimination it must be able to set prices, separate markets so as to prevent resale from the cheap to the expensive market, and identify distinct demand elasticities in each market.

4. Products will be priced differently depending upon where they are in the product's life cycle. New products can be priced cheaply so as to gain market share, or priced expensively to recoup cost. Later on in the product's life cycle, prices will have to reflect the degree of competition, which may become intense as the market stabilises or even declines.

QUESTIONS

1. Think of four different products or services and estimate roughly how many firms there are in the market. You will need to decide whether 'the market' is a local one, a national one or an international one. In what ways do the firms compete in each of the cases you have identified?

2. As an illustration of the difficulty in identifying monopolies, try to decide which of the following are monopolies: a train operating company; your local evening newspaper; the village hairdresser; the Royal Mail; Microsoft Office suite of programs; Interflora; the London Underground; ice creams in the cinema; Guinness; food on trains; the board game 'Monopoly'.

3. For what reasons would you expect a monopoly to charge (a) a higher price, and (b) a lower price than if the industry were operating under perfect competition?

4. Will competition between oligopolists always reduce total industry profits?

5. In which of the following industries is collusion likely to occur: bricks, beer, margarine, cement, crisps, washing powder, blank DVD sor Blu-ray disks, carpets? Explain why.

6. Devise a box diagram like that in Figure 5.5, only this time assume that there are three firms, each considering the two strategies of keeping price the same or reducing it by a set amount. Identify the best response for each firm. Is the game still a 'dominant strategy game'?

7. What are the limitations of game theory in predicting oligopoly behaviour?

8. Make a list of six aims that a manager of a high-street department store might have. Identify some conflicts that might arise between these aims.

9. When are increased profits in a manager's personal interest?

10. Since advertising increases a firm's costs, will prices necessarily be lower with sales revenue maximisation than with profit maximisation?

11. A frequent complaint of junior and some senior managers is that they are regularly faced with new targets from above, and that this makes their life difficult. If their complaint is true, does this conflict with the hypothesis that managers will try to build in slack?

12. Outline the main factors that might influence the size of the profit mark-up set by a business.

13. If a cinema could sell all its seats to adults in the evenings at the end of the week, but only a few on Mondays and Tuesdays, what price discrimination policy would you recommend to the cinema in order for it to maximise its weekly revenue?

14. How will a business's pricing strategy differ at each stage of its product's life cycle? First assume that the business has a monopoly position at the launch stage; then assume that it faces a high degree of competition right from the outset.

Business growth and strategy

Business issues covered in this chapter

- What are the objectives of strategic management?
- What are the key competitive forces affecting a business?
- What choices of strategy towards competitors are open to a business?
- What internal strategic choices are open to a business and how can it make best use of its core competences when deciding on its internal organisation?
- By what means can a business grow and how can growth be financed?
- Should businesses seek to raise finance through the stock market?
- Under what circumstances might a business want to merge with another?
- What are the advantages and problems of remaining a small business?
- What issues arise in starting up a business?

6.1 STRATEGIC ANALYSIS

For much of the time most managers are concerned with routine day-to-day activities of the business, such as dealing with personnel issues, checking budgets and looking for ways to enhance efficiency. In other words, they are involved in the detailed operational activities of the business.

Some managers, however, especially those high up in the business, such as the managing director, will be thinking about big, potentially complex issues which affect the whole company. For example, they might be analysing the behaviour of competitors, or evaluating the company's share price or considering ways to expand the business. In other words, these managers are involved in the *strategic* long-term activities of the business. This is known as *strategic management*.

Strategic management involves *analysing* the alternative long-term courses of action for the firm and then *making choices* of what strategy to pursue.

The strategic choices that are made depend on the aims of the firm. Most firms have a 'mission statement' which sets out the broad aims but, as we saw in the last chapter,

Definition

Strategic management The management of the strategic long-term decisions and activities of the business.

with multiple stakeholders the aims in practice might be difficult to establish. It is thus in the *actual* decisions that are taken that the firm's aims can best be judged. In practice these aims are often complex, with economic objectives, such as profit, market share, product development and growth being mixed with broader social, ethical and environmental objectives.

We look at strategic analysis in this section and strategic choices in section 6.2.

Strategic analysis of the external business environment

In Chapter 1 we considered STEEPLE analysis: the various dimensions of the business environment and how they shape and influence business activity. In this section we will take our analysis of the business environment forward and consider more closely those factors that are likely to influence the *competitive advantage* of the organisation.

> ### Definition
>
> **Competitive advantage** The various factors, such as lower costs or a better product, that give a firm an advantage over its rivals.

 KEY IDEA 20

> *Competitive advantage.* The various factors that enable a firm to compete more effectively with its rivals. These can be supply-side factors, such as superior technology, better organisation, or greater power or efficiency in sourcing its supplies – resulting in lower costs; or they could be demand-side ones, such as producing a superior or better-value product in the eyes of consumers, or being more conveniently located – resulting in higher and/or less elastic demand.

The greater the competitive advantage of a firm, whether through lower costs or through less elastic demand for its products, the greater the rate of supernormal profit it will be able to make. In developing their strategy, firms seek to address these two dimensions: costs and demand.

The Five Forces Model of competition

Developed by Professor Michael Porter of Harvard Business School in 1980, the Five Forces Model sets out to identify those factors which are likely to affect an organisation's competitiveness (see Figure 6.1).[1] This then helps a firm choose an appropriate strategy to enhance its competitive opportunities and to protect itself from competitive threats. The five forces that Porter identifies are:

- the bargaining power of suppliers.
- the bargaining power of buyers.

[1] Michael E. Porter, *Competitive Strategy: Techniques for Analyzing Industries and Competitors* (The Free Press, 1980).

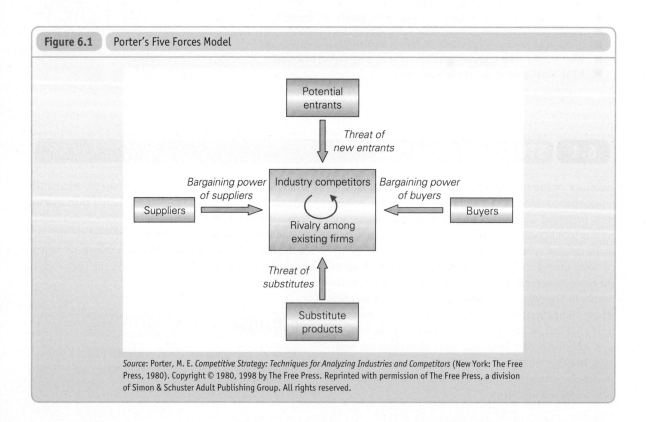

| Figure 6.1 | Porter's Five Forces Model |

Source: Porter, M. E. *Competitive Strategy: Techniques for Analyzing Industries and Competitors* (New York: The Free Press, 1980). Copyright © 1980, 1998 by The Free Press. Reprinted with permission of The Free Press, a division of Simon & Schuster Adult Publishing Group. All rights reserved.

- the threat of potential new entrants.
- the threat of substitute products.
- the extent of competitive rivalry.

The bargaining power of suppliers. Most business organisations depend upon suppliers, whether to provide raw materials or simply stationery. Indeed, many businesses have extensive supply or 'value chain' networks (as we shall discuss below). Such suppliers can have a significant and powerful effect on a business when:

- there are relatively few suppliers in the market, reducing the ability of the business to switch from one supply source to another.
- there are no alternative supplies that can be used.
- the cost of the supplies forms a large part of the firm's total costs.
- a supplier's customers are small and fragmented and as such have little power over the supplying business.

Car dealers often find that car manufacturers can exert considerable pressure over them in terms of pricing, display and after-sales service.

The bargaining power of buyers. The bargaining power of companies that purchase a firm's products will be greater when:

- these purchasing companies are large and there are relatively few of them.
- there are many other firms competing for the purchasing companies' custom, and hence a firm that produces an undifferentiated product (such as vegetables) is likely to be more prone to 'buyer power' than one that produces a unique or differentiated product.
- the costs for the purchasing companies of switching to other suppliers are low.
- purchasing companies could relatively easily produce the good themselves and thereby displace the supplying firm.

The UK grocery retailing sector is dominated by a small number of large supermarket chains, with significant buyer power over farmers and food processors (as we saw in Box 5.3). They often have many alternative supply sources, both domestic and international, and can easily move from one to another with relatively little switching cost. This puts pressure on suppliers to reduce their prices.

This pressure has grown with globalisation. As communication and transport have become easier and cheaper, this has allowed companies to develop lower-cost supply chains in developing countries. This may, however, raise some ethical issues, as we consider in section 9.2.

The threat of potential new entrants. The ability of new firms to enter the market depends largely on the existence and effectiveness of various barriers to entry. These barriers to entry were described in section 5.2 (pages 106–7).

Barriers to entry tend to be very industry, product and market specific. Nevertheless, two useful generalisations can be made. First, companies with products that have a strong brand identity will often attempt to use this form of product differentiation to restrict competition; second, manufacturers will tend to rely on economies of scale and low costs gained from experience as means of retaining a cost advantage over potential rivals.

The threat of substitutes. The availability of substitute products can be a major threat to a business and its profitability, as many close substitutes implies a relatively price-elastic demand. Issues that businesses need to consider in relation to the availability of substitute products are:

- the ability and cost to customers of switching to the substitute.
- the threat of competitors bringing out a more advanced or up-to-date product.
- the impact that substitute products are likely to have on pricing policy.

The makers of games consoles such as Sony, Nintendo and Microsoft have faced the arrival of substitutes, as people can now play games such as *Minecraft* and *Candy Crush* on their Smartphones and tablets instead of using a PlayStation 4 or Xbox One. The Steam download service owned by Valve also means that games such as *Call of Duty* can be downloaded and played on a personal computer as a substitute to using a console. Hence the sale of handheld consoles has fallen sharply. With rapid technological change, it is highly likely that another new substitute will enter this market. So firms operating in the games console market will need to reconsider their strategies as the market continues to change.

The extent of competitive rivalry. As we saw in the previous two chapters, the degree of competition a firm faces is a crucial element in shaping its strategic analysis. Competitive rivalry will be enhanced when there is the potential for new firms to enter the market, when there is a real threat from substitute products and when buyers and suppliers have some element of influence over the firm's performance. In addition to this, competitive rivalry is likely to be enhanced in the following circumstances:

- There are many competitors, each of a similar size. This is a particular issue when firms are competing in a global market.
- Markets are growing slowly. This makes it difficult to acquire additional sales without taking market share from rivals.
- Product differentiation is difficult to achieve; hence switching by consumers to competitors' products is a real threat.

- There are high exit costs. When a business invests in non-transferable fixed assets, such as highly specialist capital equipment, it may be reluctant to leave a market and will compete fiercely to maintain its market position. On the other hand, high exit costs may deter firms from entering a market in the first place and thus reduce the threat of competition.
- There exists the possibility for merger and acquisition. This competition for corporate control may have considerable influence on the firm's strategy.

Porter's model is designed to identify and analyse the competitive factors influencing the firm. Often, however, success might be achievable not via competition but rather through co-operation and collaboration. For example, a business might set up close links with one of its major buyers; or businesses in an industry might collaborate over research and development, thereby saving on costs. Firms have a considerable incentive to collude with their rivals so as to increase their combined profits and avoid damaging competition, as we saw in sections 5.3 and 5.4.

Ideally, in order to plan its strategy, a firm should be able to identify and quantify each of the five forces affecting it. In practice, however, firms often face considerable uncertainty about the market in which they operate. Just how will rivals, suppliers and buyers behave? How will consumer tastes change? What new firms and new products will enter the market?

The actions of complementors. Some economists add a sixth force – that of 'complementors' (a term coined by Andrew Grove of Intel). *Complementors* are firms producing complements. For example, Intel, with its *Celeron*, *Pentium* and *Core i3*, *i5* and *i7* processors, is a complementor to both Microsoft, with its *Windows*, and various computer manufacturers, such as Dell and HP. Where firms are complementors, there is an incentive to form strategic alliances (see pages 143 and 150–1) so as to benefit from co-operation and a reduction in uncertainty.

Porter himself added an alternative sixth force: government. Clearly there are many ways in which government policies impact on business and hence on the strategies that should be adopted, such as tax policy, price controls and regulation, as we discussed in Box 2.5. We examine government policies at a micro level in Chapter 9. Chapter 11 looks at macroeconomic policies.

Pause for thought

1. *Given that the stronger the competitive forces the lower the profit potential for firms, describe what five-force characteristics an attractive and unattractive industry might have.*
2. *Go through each of the five forces and identify to what extent they influence (a) costs and (b) demand elasticity.*

Internal strategic analysis: analysing the value chain

To develop an advantage over its rivals, a business also needs to be organised effectively. Strategic analysis, therefore, also involves managers assessing the internal workings of the business, right from the purchase and delivery of inputs, to the production process, to delivering and marketing the product, to providing after-sales service.

Value-chain analysis, also developed by Michael Porter, is concerned with how each of these various operations adds value to the product and contributes to the competitive position of the business. Ultimately it is these value-creating activities that shape a firm's strategic capabilities. A firm's value chain can be split into two separate sets of activities: primary and support (see Figure 6.2).

Primary activities

Primary activities cover those that involve the product's physical creation or delivery, its sale and distribution and its after-sales service. Such primary activities can be grouped into five categories:

- *Inbound logistics.* Here we are concerned with the handling of inputs, and the storage and distribution of such inputs throughout the business.

Definitions

Complementors Firms producing complementary goods (products that are used together).

Value chain The stages or activities that help to create product value.

Figure 6.2 The value chain

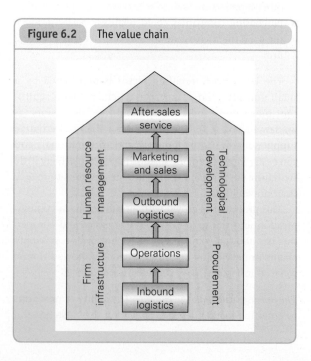

- *Operations.* These activities involve the conversion of inputs into the final product or service. Operations might include manufacturing, packaging and assembly.
- *Outbound logistics.* These are concerned with transferring the final product to the consumer. Such activities would include warehousing and transport.
- *Marketing and sales.* This section of the value chain is concerned with bringing the product to the consumer's attention and would involve product advertising and promotion.
- *After-sales service.* This can include activities such as installation and repair, as well as customer requirements such as training.

A business might attempt to add value to its activities by improving its performance in one or more of the above categories. For example, it might attempt to lower production costs or be more efficient in outbound logistics.

Support activities

Such primary activities are underpinned by support activities. These are activities that do not add value directly to any particular stage within the value chain. They do, however, provide support to such a chain and ensure that its various stages are undertaken effectively. Support activities include:

- *Procurement.* This involves the acquisition of inputs by the firm.
- *Technological development.* This includes activities within the business that support new product and process developments, such as the use of research departments.

- *Human resource management.* Activities in this category include things such as recruitment, training and wage negotiation and determination.
- *Firm infrastructure.* This category includes activities such as financial planning and control systems, quality control and information management.

As well as creating value directly themselves, most firms benefit from outsourcing certain value-chain activities, such as employing an expert firm to do its advertising, or using an external delivery firm for distribution. The companies a firm uses are likely to have economies of scale in their specialist activity (see pages 82–4) and can therefore offer the service at a lower cost than the firm could provide in-house.

Outsourcing, however, involves transactions costs (see pages 85–7) and these must be weighed against the other cost savings. Value-chain analysis, therefore, concerns any business that the firm deals with and hence a value chain can be highly complex.

With the background to strategic analysis defined, we can now shift our focus to consider strategic choice and implementation. What strategies are potentially open to businesses and how do they choose the right ones and set about implementing them?

Pause for thought

Is it possible to add value to the firm by improving any or all of these support activities?

RECAP

1. Strategic management differs from operational management (the day-to-day running of the business) as it focuses on issues which affect the whole business, usually over the long term.
2. In conducting strategic analysis the business should assess its external and internal environment.
3. The Five Forces Model of the external environment identifies those factors that are most likely to influence the competition faced by a business. The five forces are: the bargaining power of suppliers, the bargaining power of buyers, the threat of potential new entrants, the threat of substitutes, and the extent of competitive rivalry.

4. To these five, some economists add a sixth – the actions of complementors. Porter added an alternative sixth factor – the government.
5. The internal environment can be assessed by value-chain analysis. The value chain can be split into primary and support activities. Primary activities are those that directly create value, such as operations, marketing and sales. Support activities are those that underpin value creation in other areas, such as procurement and human resource management.

6.2 STRATEGIC CHOICE

As with strategic analysis, strategic choices fall into two main categories. The first concerns choices to do with the external business environment, e.g. choices of how to compete and what markets to target. The second concerns choices about the internal organisation of the firm and how to use its resources.

Environment- or market-based strategic choices

As with many other areas in this field, our analysis of market-based choices starts with the observations of Michael Porter. As an extension of his Five Forces Model of competition, Porter argued that there are three fundamental (or 'generic') strategies that a business might adopt:

- *cost leadership* – competing through lower costs;
- *differentiation* – competing by producing a product different from rivals' products;
- *focus* – producing a specialised product for a market niche.

In order to identify which of these was the most appropriate strategy, a business would need to establish two things: (a) the basis of its competitive advantage – whether it lies in lower costs or product differentiation; (b) the nature of the target market – is it broad or a distinct market niche?

Cost leadership

A business that is a 'low-cost leader' is able to manufacture and deliver its product more cheaply than its rivals, thereby gaining competitive advantage. The strategic emphasis here is on driving out inefficiency at every stage of the value chain. 'No-frills' budget airlines, such as easyJet and Ryanair, are classic examples of companies that pursue a cost-leadership strategy.

A strategy based upon cost leadership may require a fundamentally different use of resources or organisational structure if the firm is to stay ahead of its rivals. Wal-Mart's hub and spoke distribution system is an example; the company distributes its products to shops from regional depots in order to minimise transport costs.

In addition, firms that base their operations on low costs in order to achieve low prices (although that may not necessarily be the aim of low costs) are unlikely to have a high level of brand loyalty. In other words, if customer choice is going to be driven largely by price, demand is likely to be relatively price elastic. Other virtues of the product that

---

BOX 6.1 **BUSINESS STRATEGY THE SAMSUNG WAY**

Staying ahead of the game

Samsung is a major South Korean conglomerate involved in a number of industries, including machinery and heavy engineering, chemicals, financial services and consumer electronics. In 2014, it had 489 000 employees across its global operations and is a major international investor and exporter.

This box outlines some of the strategic initiatives taken by one of its most successful divisions, Samsung Electronics.

Following the Asian financial crisis in the late 1990s, Samsung faced serious financial concerns, with high debts and poor profitability. Since then, it has managed to reposition itself in the consumer electronics industry and Samsung electronics is now the market leader for 13 of its products, including semi-conductors, TFT-LCDs, monitors and CDMA mobile phones. In 2014, Samsung Electronics had sales of almost £125 billion ($176 billion) and operating profit of £15 billion ($21 billion) and although economic and political uncertainty meant that both these figures were down on 2013, Samsung electronics has strengthened its brand value and corporate rankings.[1]

But how has Samsung become so successful in this highly competitive market?

Strong leadership. This had formerly come from Mr Yoon-Woo Lee and now from Mr Kwon Oh-Hyun, vice-chairman and CEO of Samsung Electronics. He and his management team have a clear vision of the future of the sector and Samsung's role within it. Its vision, 'Inspire the World, Create the Future', reflects its three key strengths: 'New Technology', 'Innovative Products' and 'Creative Solutions'.[2]

They want Samsung to become the leading electronics company in the world, measured by the quantity and quality of the goods it produces. Although it has made significant improvements in its revenue, despite a fall in 2014, data from Forbes shows that in the technology company rankings, it still remains second behind Apple, but ahead of American giants, Microsoft, Google and IBM.[3]

Reorganisation. There has been a dramatic streamlining of the business and the decision-making structure following poor financial performance in the mid-1990s and an association with low-end brands in televisions and air-conditioning units. Aggressive measures were taken to improve the division's finances by cutting jobs, closing unprofitable factories, reducing inventory levels and selling corporate assets. The company was then 'de-layered', ensuring that managers had to go through fewer layers of bureaucracy, thereby speeding up the approval of new products, budgets and marketing plans. A younger management team was introduced, as the market changed and the company aimed to maintain its impressive growth into the future.

New products. Samsung Electronics has been investing heavily in research and development (R&D) to increase its product portfolio and reduce the lead time from product conception to product launch. In 2014 the division invested $13.4 billion in R&D – a 28 per cent increase on the previous year. This made it the second biggest R&D spending company in the world behind Volkswagen. Between 2010 and 2014 it increased its employment of R&D staff by 27 per cent and employed 63 628 people across its 34 R&D units.

It has engaged in a number of strategic alliances with major players such as Sony, IBM and Hewlett Packard to share R&D costs. Samsung leads the global telecommunications industry, offering the widest variety of phones and aims constantly to innovate to maintain its competitive advantage.

---

[1] Samsung Electronics Annual Report, 2014.
[2] www.samsung.com/us/aboutsamsung/samsung_group/values_and_philosophy/

[3] 'The world's largest tech companies: Apple beats Samsung, Microsoft, Google', *Forbes* (11 May 2015).

might tie in buyers, such as quality or after-sales service, are largely absent from such firms' strategic goals.

Differentiation

A differentiation strategy aims to emphasise and promote the uniqueness of the firm's product; to make demand less elastic. Therefore, high rather than low prices are often attached to such products. Product characteristics such as quality, design and reliability are the basis of the firm's competitive advantage. Hence a strategy that adds to such differences and creates value for the customer needs to be identified.

Such a strategy might result in higher costs, especially in the short term, as the firm pursues constant product development through innovation, design and research. However, with the ability to charge premium prices, revenues may increase more than costs, i.e. the firm may achieve higher

profits. Mobile phone handset producers such as Apple and Samsung provide a good example. Even though they are in fierce competition with each other, both firms focus their strategy on product differentiation in terms of features and performance, not price. Screen size and resolution, camera quality, speakers, apps, battery life and overall design are all characteristics used in the competitive battle.

Differentiation in this way, and in fast-changing sectors, can be costly and risky. However, the rewards are potentially large. Differentiated products attract customers, but they tend to be more expensive, which could deter buyers. Firms must weigh up the costs and benefits from such a strategy.

Focus strategy

Rather than considering a whole market as a potential for sales, a focus strategy involves identifying market niches

---

Samsung's investment in research and development has certainly paid off with the company ranking second behind IBM for the number of patents registered every year since 2006. In 2014, it successfully registered 4952 patents. This aggressive innovation strategy, coupled with low inventories and shortening product life cycles, allows Samsung to charge premium prices for state-of-the-art products.

This strategy is important in the rapidly changing world of consumer electronics, where a high-priced new product of today can become a low-priced mass-produced product of tomorrow. Large panel LCD TVs, flash memory chips and mobile phones are all examples. However, Samsung Electronics did suffer in 2014, with a 27 per cent fall in profits on the previous year to $21.3 billion. Much of this decline was driven by increased competition in the mobile handset industry, especially from Apple in the high-end market. With its larger screen, Samsung's Galaxy had a competitive advantage over Apple's iPhone 5, but with Apple's successful launch of the large-screened iPhone 6 in 2014, this contributed to a 21 per cent decline in Samsung's mobile phone sales. Furthermore, competition also increased from lower-priced producers in emerging markets, in particular the Chinese rivals: Huawei, Lenovo and Xiami.

Driving down costs. Samsung invests heavily in modern factories that can cope with large production runs and gain maximum economies of scale. To this end Samsung also supplies components to its competitors as well as making them for its own product range. For example, it sells flash memory chips for Apple's *iPod*, Nokia phones and digital cameras. Further, production systems are flexible enough to allow customisation for individual buyers, ensuring that selling prices are above the industry average. Alongside longer production runs, Samsung is concerned with ensuring that production costs are minimised by making its own business units compete with external rivals.

Developing its brand image. Even though it makes most of its profits on semiconductors, investment in less profitable

consumer products with a clear brand identity helps to raise the profile of all its products. It spends a great deal on sports sponsorship. For example, it sponsored Chelsea football club from 2006 to 2015 and was one of the official sponsors for London 2012 and will continue its deal with the International Olympics Committee until 2020. It also has a $100 million sponsorship deal in the USA with the National Basketball Association (NBA).

When asked about Samsung's brand, Sue Shim, the Executive Vice President and Chief Marketing Officer of Samsung Electronics said:

> A successful brand begins with a clear understanding of the who, what, and why of the company. We at Samsung call it our brand ideal . . . the Samsung brand is on its way to becoming an aspirational brand. The outstanding growth of brand value in 2012 truly demonstrates Samsung's commitment to its brand. Convergence will continue to be a key theme for Samsung in the future. We hope to continue providing value to consumers through new products, services and user experiences.[4]

In March 2015, Samsung launched the new Galaxy 6 Edge handset, with improvements in the design and appearance of the phone. It will be interesting to see if this continued investment in its products and its brand will help it achieve its '2020 Vision' of annual sales of $400 billion and the brand value of Samsung Electronics being in the global top five brands.

1. *What dangers do you see with Samsung's recent business strategy?*
2. *What makes Samsung's policies that we have examined in this box 'strategic' as opposed to merely 'operational'?*

---

[4] www.interbrand.com/en/best-global-brands/2012/articles-and-interviews/sue-shim-samsung.aspx

and designing and promoting products for them. In doing so a business may be able to exploit some advantage over its rivals, whether in terms of costs or product difference. An example is Häagen-Dazs ice cream (a division of General Mills). The mass low-cost ice cream market is served by other large multinational food manufacturers and processors (such as Unilever, with its Wall's brand), and by supermarkets' own brands, but the existence of niche high-quality ice cream markets offers opportunities for companies like Häagen-Dazs and Ben & Jerry's. By focusing on such consumers they are able to sell and market their product at premium prices.

Niche markets, however profitable, are by their nature small and as such limited in their growth potential. There is also the possibility that niches might shift over time or even disappear. This would require a business to be flexible in setting out its strategic position.

Internal resource-based strategic choices

Resource-based strategy focuses on exploiting a firm's internal organisation and production processes in order to develop its competitive advantage. What the firm will seek to exploit or to develop is one or more 'core competencies'.

Core competencies

Core competencies are those skills, knowledge, technologies and product specifications that underpin the organisation's competitive advantage over its rivals. These competencies are likely to differ from one business to another, reflecting the uniqueness of each individual organisation, and ultimately determining its potential for success. The business should seek to create and exploit these competencies, whether in the design of the product or in its methods of production.

 KEY IDEA 21 | *Core competencies.* The areas of specialised expertise within a business that underpin its competitive advantage over its rivals. These competencies could be in production technologies or organisation, in relationships with suppliers, in the nature and specifications of the product, or in the firm's ability to innovate and develop its products and brand image.

Thus Coca-Cola has a core competence in developing an image of a product; Tesco has a core competence in sourcing cheap but reliable supplies; Intel has a core competence in technological research and development that can yield significant continuing advances in the speed and

Definition

Core competencies The key skills of a business that underpin its competitive advantage.

efficiency of memory chips and processor cores; Ikea has a core competence in sourcing low-cost furniture and accessories and selling them at a highly competitive price in low-cost suburban sites where a wide choice is on view and instantly available.

In many cases, however, firms do not have any competencies that give them a distinctive competitive advantage, even though they may still be profitable. In such instances, strategy often focuses either on *developing* such competencies or simply on more effectively using the resources the firm already has.

Can a core competence be sustained?

To sustain a competitive advantage into the *long run*, the competence must satisfy the following four criteria. It must be:

■ *Valuable:* a competence that helps the firm deal with threats or contributes to business opportunities.
■ *Rare:* a competence or resource that is not possessed by competitors.
■ *Costly to imitate:* a competence or resource that other firms find difficult to develop and copy.
■ *Non-substitutable:* a competence or resource for which there is no alternative.

Pause for thought

Referring back to Box 6.1, what core competencies does Samsung have? Remember, you must justify a core competence in terms of all four listed criteria.

Reactions of competitors

The success of a firm's strategic choices depends crucially on the reactions of rival firms. As we saw in the section on game theory (section 5.4), a firm has to be careful that strategic choices, such as developing new product lines or breaking into new markets, do not result in a 'war' with rivals that will end up with all 'players' worse off. The technology to produce a virtually everlasting light bulb has been available for many years, but it has not been in the interests of manufacturers to produce one, as it would force rivals to do the same with a resulting loss of future sales. To avoid this classic prisoners' dilemma (see pages 118–20) there has been tacit collusion between manufacturers not to launch such a product.

Sometimes, it is worth a firm taking the risk of stimulating retaliatory action from its rivals. If it estimates that its market position or core competencies give it a competitive advantage, then it will take the risk of launching a new product, embarking on a marketing campaign, using a new technology or restructuring its organisation. If rivals do retaliate, its core competencies may enable it to do well in any competitive battle.

BOX 6.2 THE RATIOS TO MEASURE SUCCESS

Using numbers to decide

Whenever a firm makes a decision, numerous factors will be considered. Market opportunities will be analysed, the actions of competitors predicted and the economic environment studied. However, crucial to any decision will be the health of the business itself. Owners and managers will need to look at all the firm's numbers before taking any action and there are some ratios that will give a business some key information.

We typically classify ratios into groups based on the information that they show. In this box, we split the ratios into three categories and outline the main ratios within each.

Profitability ratios

These ratios do exactly what they suggest: they provide information about a business's profitability. By measuring a firm's ability to generate earnings and profits, they indicate the success of a firm over time and provide a means of comparison with its competitors. The three main ratios are:

- *Gross Profit Margin:* this measures the ratio of gross profit to sales revenue. Gross profit is calculated by subtracting the variable costs of goods sold from gross revenue and so measures the profitability of a company before fixed costs (overheads) have been taken into account. It is expressed as a percentage and is calculated as:

$$\text{Gross Profit Margin} = \frac{\text{Gross profit}}{\text{Sales turnover}} \times 100$$

- *Net Profit Margin:* this measures the ratio of net profit to sales revenue. Net profit is revenue minus *all* costs: that is, not only the variable costs of production, but also fixed costs, such as rent, insurance, heating and lighting, salaries (unrelated to output) and also taxes. It gives us information about how effective a firm is at turning sales into profits and thus whether or not a business adds value during the production process. Net profit margin is calculated as:

$$\text{Net Profit Margin} = \frac{\text{Net profit}}{\text{Sales turnover}} \times 100$$

It is important that these first two profitability ratios are compared, given their close relationship, as they provide key information about a firm's financial performance.

- *Return on Capital Employed (ROCE):* this measures the efficiency with which a business uses its funds to generate returns. Capital employed refers to the company's total assets minus its current liabilities and the ROCE is calculated as:

$$\text{ROCE} = \frac{\text{Earnings (before interest and taxes)}}{\text{Capital employed}} \times 100$$

High gross and net profit margins are good indicators that a firm is performing effectively, but looking at these two ratios separately can often be misleading. For example, if a firm's gross profit margin is rising, but its net profit margin is falling, then it means that the firm is generating more profit from its sales, but that its costs are increasing at an even faster rate. That is, the company is becoming inefficient.

Just as it is important to examine the trends in profit margins, analysing a firm's ROCE over time is also essential and an upward trend suggests that the firm is earning more in revenue for every £1 of capital employed in the business. Profit margins and ROCE should always be compared between firms within an industry and it is always worth remembering that what is seen as a high profit margin or ROCE in one industry may be a low one in another industry.

1. *What steps might a firm take to improve a) gross profit margin; b) net profit margin; and c) ROCE?*

Financial efficiency ratios

These are ratios that analyse the efficiency with which a business manages its resources and assets. Once again, there are three key ratios:

- *Asset Turnover Ratio:* this ratio looks at the assets (or resources) that a firm has and analyses the amount of sales that are generated from this asset base. Consider a pizza kitchen that has a given level of assets (e.g. work-space, ovens). This ratio will measure the level of sales generated relative to this asset base. The higher the sales, the more efficiently is this firm using its assets; so a higher asset turnover figure is a good indicator of financial efficiency. It is calculated as:

$$\text{Asset Turnover} = \frac{\text{Sales}}{\text{Net assets}} \times 100$$

- *Stock Turnover:* this measures the frequency with which a firm orders in new stock. Holding stock can be extremely costly, as it means that money has already been spent on purchasing or producing the items, but no income has been received from their sale. Thus, a higher figure for stock turnover implies that less money is tied up in stock. This particular ratio will vary significantly from one industry to another and you would expect some industries to have a very high level of stock turnover, due to the nature of the products they are selling. For example, firms whose sales are subject to fluctuation (due, say, to the weather) may need to hold higher stocks. Therefore, although it is suggested that a higher figure for stock turnover is better, this is not always the case. Stock turnover is calculated as:

$$\text{Stock Turnover} = \frac{\text{Cost of sales}}{\text{Average stock held}}$$

- *Debtor and Creditor Days:* these two ratios measure the effectiveness of a firm in collecting payments from and making payments to other traders. Many businesses offer trade credit, where you can buy something today, but pay for it later. Such incentives can be crucial, but it can cause problems when you are the firm offering the trade credit. Debtor days show how long a firm's customers on average take to pay their bill and creditor days show how long a firm takes to pay the bills that it owes. As you will probably realise, comparing these two figures is essential. Ideally, debtor days should be lower than creditor days, as this implies that firm A receives the money it is owed before it has to make payments to those to whom it owes money. They are calculated as follows:

$$\text{Debtor Days} = \frac{\text{Trade debtors}}{\text{Revenue}} \times 365$$

and

$$\text{Creditor Days} = \frac{\text{Trade payables}}{\text{Cost of sales}} \times 365$$

With the business environment under continuing financial pressure, it is vital to use resources efficiently. Businesses in all sectors will want to analyse trends in these financial efficiency ratios, as a means of identifying areas where improvements can be made.

2. *What type of figure would you expect a greengrocer to have for its stock turnover? How might this compare with a furniture store?*

3. *What are the advantages and disadvantages of offering trade credit?*

Liquidity ratios

Many businesses have debts, but the key question is whether they have the ability to repay these debts. Liquidity ratios provide this information and we consider three key ratios below:

- *Current Ratio:* this ratio is a basic measure of how a firm's current assets compare with its current liabilities. If a firm's assets are higher than its liabilities, this suggests that the firm has sufficient funds for the day-to-day running of the business. It is calculated as:

$$\text{Current Ratio} = \frac{\text{Current assets}}{\text{Current liabilities}}$$

- *Acid Test Ratio (or Quick Ratio):* this is very similar to the current ratio. However, instead of comparing all current assets with liabilities, the acid test ratio excludes stocks, sometimes called 'inventories' (e.g. raw materials), as these cannot readily be turned into cash and hence are termed 'illiquid'. They would first have to be made into the finished product before any cash could be earned. The calculation is therefore very similar to the one above:

$$\text{Acid Test Ratio} = \frac{\text{Current assets Stock}}{\text{Current liabilities}}$$

Some businesses will need to carry much higher levels of stocks (or 'inventories') than others and will therefore have a low acid test ratio relative to their current ratio. Thus most manufacturers will need to have a much higher proportion of stocks than most service-sector firms, such as solicitors or accountants. This does not make their businesses necessarily more risky. Ratios need to be judged, therefore, according to what would be expected in a particular industry.

- *Gearing Ratio (or Leverage Ratio):* this is a key ratio for any firm, but also for any individual thinking about investing in it. It shows how much of a firm's finance is

through debt (e.g. long-term borrowing, mortgages or bonds), on which the firm has to pay interest, as opposed to equity (ordinary shares), on which the firm does not pay interest but rather a share of profit. How much profit the firm distributes to shareholders can be adjusted according to what the firm feels it can afford. The higher the gearing ratio the more the business is funded through debt. Gearing is calculated as the percentage of debt to total capital employed (debt and equity capital):

$$\text{Gearing Ratio} = \frac{\text{Debt}}{\text{Capital employed}} \times 100$$

A similar ratio to the gearing ratio is the *Debt-to-Equity* Ratio. In this ratio the numerator is the same, but the denominator is equity capital (i.e. ordinary share capital).

$$\text{Debt/Equity Ratio} = \frac{\text{Debt}}{\text{Equity capital}} \times 100$$

A firm's gearing and debt-to-equity ratios are measures of its financial stability. The higher the ratios, the greater the commitment of the firm to paying interest, and the greater the risk, therefore, if the firm is in financial difficulty, as these commitments have to be met.

With weak trading conditions remaining across the global economy, liquidity is a word that has been used many times in recent years, as all firms need cash to survive. A current ratio of between 1.5 and 2 suggests that a firm has sufficient cash, without having excessive working capital. Again, comparing this ratio over time and with other firms in the same sector is important to give an indication of relative performance. For many people, gearing is the most informative ratio, especially as it provides information about the long-term prospects of the business. As the gearing ratio gets higher (perhaps above 50 per cent), it is a signal that the firm may begin to run into problems when repaying debts. Although sometimes debt can be cheaper than equity finance!

4. *Would you expect the current ratio or the acid test to have a higher figure for any given firm?*

5. *If you were looking to invest in a business, how might you interpret a company that has a gearing ratio of 80 per cent?*

While the ratios discussed should never be analysed independently and can give misleading results if they are not interpreted correctly, they remain a good numerical measure of business performance, as discussed in an article about Fonterra, a New Zealand multinational dairy co-operative.[1] Before undertaking any changes relating to market penetration, scale of operation, diversification etc., the firm will consider the above ratios (and many more) to ensure that it is making the best use of its existing resources and that it has sufficient funds to carry out its plans.

---

1 Keith Woodford, 'Keith Woodford gets under the hood of Fonterra's half year profit announcement and looks at what some of the figures tell us', *interest. co.nz* (23 March 2016).

6.3 GROWTH STRATEGY

The global marketplace has become so competitive and dynamic that simply to remain in the market, many businesses are forced to grow. If a business fails to grow, this could benefit its more aggressive rivals, which may secure a greater share of the market. This could leave the first firm with reduced profits, making it a potential target for acquisition by another firm. Thus business growth is often vital if a firm is to survive.

In this section we consider the various growth strategies open to firms and assess their respective advantages and disadvantages. Growth may be achieved by either *internal* or *external expansion*.

Internal expansion. This is where a business looks to expand its productive capacity by adding to an existing plant or by building a new plant.

External expansion. This is where a business grows by engaging with another. It may do so in one of two ways:

■ The first is to join with another firm to form a single legal identity, through merger or takeover. A *merger* is a situation in which, as a result of mutual agreement, two firms decide to bring together their business operations as one firm. A merger is distinct from a *takeover* in so far as a takeover involves one firm bidding for another's shares – often against the will of the directors of the target firm. One firm thereby acquires another. For simplicity, we will use the term 'merger' to refer to *both* mergers ('mutual agreements') and takeovers ('acquisitions').

■ The second is to form a *strategic alliance* with one or more firms. This is where firms agree to work together but retain their separate identities.

Whether the business embarks upon internal or external expansion, a number of alternative growth paths are open to it. Figure 6.3 shows these various routes, which are considered in the following pages.

Growth by internal expansion

Financing internal growth

Internal growth requires an increase in sales, which in turn requires an increase in the firm's productive capacity. In order to increase its *sales*, the firm is likely to engage in extensive product promotion and may try to launch new products. In order to increase *productive capacity*, the firm will require new investment. Both product promotion and investment require finance and the inability of a firm to access finance may constrain its growth potential.

In the short run, the firm can finance growth by borrowing, by retaining profits or by a new issue of shares. However, there are some constraints.

If a firm borrows money it will have to repay interest and the more it borrows, the more difficult it is to maintain the level of dividends to shareholders. The largest source of finance for investment in the UK is *retained profits*, but if too much of this internal source of finance is used, there will be less available to pay out in dividends. Another option is for a firm to raise capital by a *new issue of shares*, but the problem here is that the distributed profits have to be divided between a larger number of shares, so dividends fall once more. Therefore, whichever way a business finances investment, the more it invests, the more the dividends on shares in the short run will probably fall.

These lower dividends could lead shareholders to sell their shares, unless they are confident that *long-run* profits

Definitions

Internal expansion Where a business adds to its productive capacity by adding to existing or by building new plants.

External expansion Where business growth is achieved by merging with or taking over businesses within a market or industry.

Merger The outcome of a mutual agreement made by two firms to combine their business activities.

Takeover (or acquisition) Where one business acquires another. A takeover may not necessarily involve mutual agreement between the two parties. In such cases, the takeover might be viewed as 'hostile'.

Strategic alliance Where two or more firms work together, formally or informally, to achieve a mutually desirable goal.

| Figure 6.3 | Alternative growth strategies |

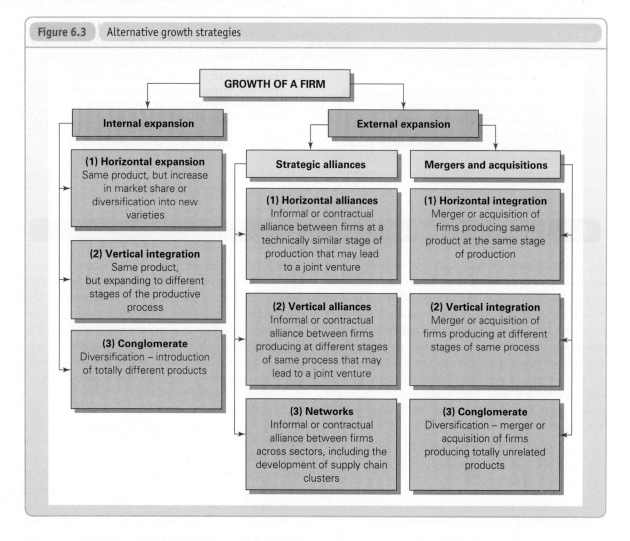

and hence dividends will rise again, thus causing the share price to remain high in the long run. If shareholders do sell their shares, this will cause share prices to fall, as the supply curve of shares will shift to the right. Firms must therefore weigh up the benefits of growth with the potential costs of a falling share price. The problem is that if they fall too far, firms may become susceptible to being taken over and of certain managers losing their jobs. This is known as the *takeover constraint* and to avoid it, growth-maximising firms need to ensure that they have sufficient profits to distribute in the short run. This is the idea of profit 'satisficing': making sufficient profits to keep shareholders happy.

Hence the rate of business growth is influenced by shareholder demands, expectations, market conditions and by the fear of takeover.

In the long run, a rapidly growing firm may find its profits increasing, especially if it can achieve economies of scale and a bigger share of the market. These profits can then be used to finance further growth.

Clearly there is a crucial link between growth and profitability and it works in two ways. First, growth *depends* on profitability, as the more profitable the firm is, the more likely it is to be able to raise finance for investment. Second, as we have

just seen, growth *affects* profitability. In the short run, growth may reduce profits, because of the necessary expenditure on advertising and investment. However, in the long run growth may lead to expansion and hence can increase profits.

Forms of internal expansion

There are three main ways in which a business can grow through internal expansion (see Figure 6.3):

- It can expand or *differentiate its product* within existing markets, by, for example, updating or restyling its product, or improving its technical characteristics. We examined such strategies in Chapter 3.

Definitions

Takeover constraint The effect that the fear of being taken over has on a firm's willingness to undertake projects that reduce distributed profits.

Product differentiation In the context of growth strategies, this is where a business upgrades existing products or services so as to make them different from those of rival firms.

- Alternatively, the business might seek to expand via *vertical integration*. This involves the firm expanding within the same product market, but at a different stage of production. For example, a car manufacturer might wish to produce its own components ('backward vertical integration') or distribute and sell its own car models ('forward vertical integration').
- As a third option, the business might seek to expand outside of its current product range, and move into new markets. This is known as a process of *diversification*.

Growth through vertical integration

If market conditions make growth through increased sales difficult, then a firm may choose to grow through vertical integration. This has a number of advantages:

Economies of scale. These can occur by the business performing *complementary* stages of production within a single business unit. The classic example of this is the steel manufacturer combining the furnacing and milling stages of production, saving the costs that would have been required to reheat the iron had such operations been undertaken by independent businesses. Clearly, for most firms, performing more than one stage on a single site is likely to reduce transport costs, as semi-finished products no longer have to be moved from one plant to another.

Other benefits to the vertically integrated firm may include more favourable borrowing rates from financial institutions, due to its size; the ability to negotiate better deals with suppliers and reduced need for managerial supervision.

Reduced uncertainty. A business that is not vertically integrated may find itself subject to various uncertainties in the marketplace. Examples include uncertainty over future price movements, supply reliability or access to markets.

Backward vertical integration will enable the business to control its supply chain. Without such integration the firm may feel very vulnerable, especially if there are only a few suppliers within the market. In such cases the suppliers would be able to exert considerable control over price. Alternatively, suppliers may be unreliable.

Forward vertical integration creates greater certainty in so far as it gives the business guaranteed access to distribution

and retailing on its own terms. As with supply, forward markets might be dominated by large buyers, which are able not only to dictate price, but also to threaten market foreclosure (being shut out from a market). Forward vertical integration can remove the possibility of such events occurring.

Barriers to entry. Vertical integration may give the firm greater power in the market by enabling it to erect entry barriers to potential competitors. For example, a firm that undertakes backward vertical integration and acquires a key input resource can effectively close the market to potential new entrants, either by simply refusing to supply a competitor, or by charging a very high price for the input such that new firms face an absolute cost disadvantage. The economies of scale discussed earlier may also act as a barrier to entry, as new entrants will find it difficult to compete with established firms that are benefiting from lower average costs.

Reduced transactions costs. Vertical integration allows the firm to avoid the buying, selling and other costs associated with dealing with other firms, whether as suppliers or purchasers.

Consider two firms, one a car manufacturer, the other a supplier of car exhausts. Both manufacturers will be involved in frequent transactions between each other. The car manufacturer sells a lot of cars and so will need a lot of exhausts on a regular basis.

In addition, if the economic environment is uncertain and there is information asymmetry in the exchange, there is then the likelihood of a principal–agent problem, giving rise to a potential for moral hazard (see Boxes 3.1 and 3.2 on pages 55 and 58). One or both of the parties could exploit the situation to their own advantage because they have different sets of information about the markets in which they operate. The exhaust manufacturer could claim that rising steel prices forces it to put up prices. The car manufacturer could argue that poorer than expected sales forces it to reduce the price it can pay for the exhausts. Only if the contract between them is very tightly specified (is 'complete') can situations such as this be avoided.

If there is a binding contract, then this will prevent the car manufacturer from seeking alternative suppliers that could offer the exhausts more cheaply. Renegotiating the contract may be possible, but this too will incur costs. If a firm is free to seek alternative suppliers, then this may be risky (see below).

To avoid these transactions costs, firms may prefer to integrate vertically through internal expansion or merger. However, is vertical integration costless?

Definitions

Vertical integration A business growth strategy that involves expanding within an existing market, but at a different stage of production. Vertical integration can be 'forward', such as moving into distribution or retail, or 'backward', such as expanding into extracting raw materials or producing components.

Diversification A business growth strategy in which a business expands into new markets outside of its current interests

Whilst vertical integration sounds like a good idea and a business will save on transactions costs, it is likely to incur other costs. A large vertically integrated organisation could be more bureaucratic, with the greater difficulties that come with managing more complex tasks. Although the firm is saving on the costs of monitoring contracts with other firms, managers still have to monitor the behaviour of their own internal divisions and employees and so there is a potential for diseconomies of scale.

Managers may set targets for the various divisions, but unless these are both carefully specified and comprehensive, the problem of moral hazard is likely to occur. Employees may meet the targets but may underperform in areas which are not specifically targeted. One response to this problem is to create more and more specific targets. This, however, is likely to remove flexibility and the opportunity for junior managers to take initiative.

Another problem is that by producing components in-house, the firm will not then be able to source them from elsewhere if cheaper suppliers become available (see Case Study 8.25 on the book's website). Thus it may reduce the firm's ability to respond to changing market demands.

Similarly, if a manufacturer buys its components from outside, it could possibly change supplier if the first supplier becomes unreliable. If it produces the components itself, however, switching to an outside supplier may prove more difficult if internal hold-ups occur.

In other words, outsourcing, rather than in-house production, while less secure, can *save* costs by allowing the firm to buy from the cheapest and/or best suppliers. Such suppliers are likely to be in competition with each other and this helps to keep their prices down and quality up. Equally, the ability to shift between retail outlets would allow the firm's products to be sold in the best locations. This may not be possible if it is tied to its own retail network.

Finally, production costs may be higher. Despite the fact that a vertically integrated firm may be large, the *individual* parts of the company may be too small to gain full economies of scale. For example, if a car company produces its own carpets, this carpet production will be on a much smaller scale than if a specialist car carpet manufacturer were to supply *several* car companies.

In deciding its optimum degree of vertical integration, therefore, a firm must weigh up the transactions costs of not integrating against the internal costs of integrating. Many firms are finding that it is better *not* to be vertically integrated but to focus on their core competencies and to outsource their supplies, their marketing and many other functions. That way they put alternative suppliers and distributors in competition with each other.

An alternative is to be *partially* vertically integrated, through a process known as *tapered vertical integration*. To some extent, this enables the firm to receive the benefits of vertical integration without incurring the costs.

Tapered vertical integration. This involves firms making part of a given input themselves and subcontracting the production of the remainder to one or more other firms. For example, Coca-Cola and Pepsi are large vertically integrated enterprises. They have, as part of their operations, wholly-owned bottling subsidiaries. However, in certain markets they subcontract to independent bottlers both to produce and to market their products.

By making a certain amount of an input itself, the firm is less reliant on suppliers and saves on transactions costs, but does not require as much capital equipment as if it produced all the input itself. A policy of tapered vertical integration suits many multinational companies. In certain countries, they produce the inputs themselves; in others, they rely on local suppliers, drawing on the supplier's competitive advantage in that local market.

Of course, tapered vertical integration may not allow the firm to gain such substantial economies of scale and production may thus be less efficient than under vertical integration. It is, therefore, important to realise that for much of the time firms will face a trade-off.

Growth through diversification

An alternative internal growth strategy to vertical integration is that of diversification, where a firm expands to produce a range of products in different markets. A good example of a highly diversified company is Virgin, as we saw in Box 3.4 (page 69).

If the current market is saturated, stagnant or in decline, diversification might be the only avenue open to the business if it wishes to maintain a high growth performance. In other words, it is not only the level of profits that may be limited in the current market, but also the growth of sales.

Diversification also has the advantage of spreading risks. So long as a business produces a single product in a single market, it is vulnerable to changes in that market's conditions. If a farmer produces nothing but potatoes, and the potato harvest fails, the farmer is ruined. If, however, the farmer produces a whole range of vegetable products, or even diversifies into livestock, then he or she is less subject to the forces of nature and the unpredictability of the market.

In some cases, however, diversification may actually be a risky strategy, as a firm might be both developing a new product and entering a new market. But in most cases, diversification should allow the business to use and adapt existing technology and knowledge to its advantage. The experience, skills and market knowledge of the managers of the business will be crucial to ensure that such a strategy is successful.

Definition

Tapered vertical integration Where a firm is partially integrated with an earlier stage of production; where it produces some of an input itself and buys some from another firm.

Growth through merger

Similar growth paths can be pursued via external expansion. However, in this case the business does not create the productive facilities itself, but purchases existing production. As Figure 6.3 identified, we can distinguish three types of merger: horizontal, vertical and conglomerate.

■ A *horizontal merger* is where two firms at the same stage of production within an industry merge. Examples of this are the acquisition of Esporta by Virgin Active in 2011 and the acquisition in 2012 of the photo sharing business Instagram by Facebook.

■ A *vertical merger* is where businesses at different stages of production within the same industry merge. As such we might identify backward and forward vertical mergers for any firm involved. Examples include the merger between TomTom and TeleAtlas in 2008; the purchase of the British software company, Autonomy Corporation, by Hewlett Packard in 2011 and Google's purchase (and subsequent sale) of the mobile device producer, Motorola Mobility, in 2012.

■ A *conglomerate merger* is where firms in totally unrelated industries merge. Many of the big multinational corporations operate in a number of sectors and regularly buy other firms. For example, in 2004 the US conglomerate group General Electric purchased Vivendi, the conglomerate multimedia firm which owned the US media and entertainment firms NBC and Universal. Google has also acquired a large number of firms in a range of different sectors, including a company that makes thermostats (Nest) and one that makes high-altitude drones (Titan).

A further dimension of business growth that we should note at this point is that all of the above-mentioned growth paths can be achieved by the business looking beyond its national markets. In other words, the business might decide to become multinational and invest in expansion overseas. This raises a further set of issues, problems and advantages that a business might face. These will be discussed in Chapter 7 when we consider multinational business.

Why merge?

Why do firms want to merge with or take over others? Is it purely that they want to grow; are mergers simply evidence of the hypothesis that firms are growth maximisers? Or are there other motives that influence the predatory drive?

Merger for growth. Mergers provide a much quicker means to growth than internal expansion. Not only does the firm acquire new capacity, experience and skills, but it also acquires additional consumer demand. Building up this level of consumer demand by internal expansion might have taken a considerable length of time.

Merger for economies of scale. Once the merger has taken place, the constituent parts can be reorganised through a process of 'rationalisation'. The result can be a reduction in costs. For example, only one head office will now be needed. On the marketing side, the two parts of the newly merged company may now share distribution and retail channels, benefiting from each other's knowledge and operation in distinct market segments or geographical locations.

In fact, the evidence on costs suggests that most mergers result in few if any cost savings: either potential economies of scale are not exploited due to a lack of rationalisation, or diseconomies result from the disruptions of reorganisation. New managers installed by the parent company are often seen as unsympathetic, and morale may go down.

Merger for monopoly power. Here the motive is to reduce competition and thereby gain greater market power and larger profits. This applies mainly to horizontal mergers. With less competition, the firm will face a less elastic demand and be able to charge a higher percentage above marginal cost. What is more, the new more powerful company will be in a stronger position to regulate entry into the market by erecting effective entry barriers, thereby enhancing its monopoly position yet further.

Merger for increased market valuation. A merger can benefit shareholders of *both* firms if it leads to an increase in the stock market valuation of the merged firm. If both sets of shareholders believe that they will make a capital gain on their shares then they are more likely to give the go-ahead for the merger.

What is the evidence? In the early stages of a merger boom, such as 2004–6 (see figure in Box 7.1 on page 165), when some good deals may be had, the share price of acquiring firms may rise. However, as the merger boom develops, more marginal firms are acquired. Take the merger boom of the late 1990s. In some 80 per cent of cases there was a significant *fall* in the share value of the acquiring firm.

Merger to reduce uncertainty. Firms face uncertainty at two levels. The first is in their own markets. The behaviour of rivals may be highly unpredictable. Mergers, by reducing the number of rivals, can correspondingly reduce uncertainty. At the same time, they can reduce the *costs* of competition (e.g. reducing the need to advertise).

Definitions

Horizontal merger Where two firms in the same industry at the same stage of the production process merge.

Vertical merger Where two firms in the same industry at different stages in the production process merge.

Conglomerate merger Where two firms in different industries merge.

Pause for thought

Which of the three types of merger (horizontal, vertical and conglomerate) are most likely to lead to (a) reductions in average costs; (b) increased market power?

BOX 6.3   RECESSIONARY STRATEGIES

A testing time for any business is when demand for its products begins to fall and then remains low. This is what has happened to many businesses since the financial crisis of 2007–8. Although the crisis was some years ago, global economic and business trading conditions have remained weak and have not been helped by geopolitical uncertainty, noted by 74 per cent of business leaders as a serious concern.[1]

What then is the best strategy for a business to pursue when faced with this situation? When market demand and hence revenue falls, there will be a big effect on profitability and cash flow, especially for a business operating with low profit margins. Over the past few years, many CEOs have responded by cutting costs, including 96 per cent in 2009 and 77 per cent in 2013. Cost cutting has tended to be in areas such as staff, advertising and marketing, service and training.

Staff. The labour force is a key component of any firm, but at the same time, it represents a significant cost. With falling demand from 2008, firms had surplus staff, and this led to massive job losses across the UK. Unemployment rose from 5.2 per cent (1.6 million) in mid-2008 to 8.4 per cent (2.69 million) by early 2012. In addition, many firms managed to reach agreement with employees for a temporary reduction in hours in an attempt to avoid redundancies. (Unemployment in the UK since declined to a 10-year low of 5.1 per cent in February 2016.)

Whilst cutting back on unneeded staff is a rational and even efficient response for a business, it could mean even lower demand, as a greater percentage of the population see their incomes fall. Such cutbacks, however, may provide a firm with the opportunity to reorganise its business, perhaps through a process of de-layering, to improve the speed and effectiveness of decisions and making a more efficient use of its human resources. The majority of the UK firms that reduced costs did so by cutting back on staff and aiming to improve efficiency.

Training. This is a necessary but costly expenditure for a firm that will often be cut during a period of declining sales. However, training is used to increase productivity, so any cuts could actually reduce the efficiency of staff, and so it may cost a firm more than it saves, especially in the long run. There may also be repercussions in terms of product quality or customer service, which should be two key components of business strategy during a recession. Crucial to success, therefore, could be to invest in training in those areas that generate revenue.

Training is time-consuming and the opportunity cost of it is lost output in the short run. However, in a recession, demand falls and so, rather than laying off workers, it might be a prime opportunity to invest in training staff to increase their productivity, in preparation for the recovery. At the height of the financial crisis, the Institute of Directors surveyed its members, which revealed a strong reluctance to cut training, despite the harsh economic climate. This was supported by research conducted in 2011 at Cardiff University, which seemed to contradict the expectation of huge cuts in training budgets due to the recession.

> The campaign (IoD) encourages employers to maintain investment in training during the recession, both in recognition of the fact that skills have never been more important to the UK's competitiveness in general and also that investing in skills in the downturn can help to put individual businesses in a better position to gain competitive advantage in recovery.[2]

One way in which businesses have maintained their investment in training, while containing costs, is to adapt their methods. This includes in-house training, using more experienced staff to train others, sharing training with other companies and concentrating their training in key areas. This strategy, while viable in a larger company, may not be a suitable strategy for SMEs.

Advertising. As with training, marketing and advertising are extremely costly, hence cutting this budget can be crucial to reducing costs. The Advertising Association confirmed this when it reported that total advertising expenditure in 2009 fell by some 12 per cent.

However, is cutting spending on advertising and marketing the right thing to do? Domino's UK, for example, saw the recession and the subsequent cuts in advertising across other firms as a prime opportunity to increase its share of the pizza market. It was able to gain market share from other pizza companies, which had cut back on advertising expenditure, and also attracted other customers, who began to order cheaper take-aways rather than pay for expensive meals out, as a Guardian article explains.

> The company [Dominos] . . . has taken full advantage of the drop in advertising rates to continue to promote its discounts and deals to a cash-strapped public . . . Our tactical marketing campaigns have played a major role in our success during the period, supported by the firepower of the national advertising fund and the deflationary media market.[3]

We also saw in Chapter 3 how companies such as Cadburys maintained their spending on advertising, but simply changed the method. This is a feature across the advertising industry, with evidence suggesting that the Internet will be the biggest advertising medium in 12 key markets by 2017, representing 28 per cent of global spending on advertising. It has already overtaken television in some markets, including the UK and Canada. Steve King, Chief Executive of ZenithOptimedia said:

> However, [the Internet's dominance over TV] refers only to traditional television viewed on TV sets. The amount of time viewers spend watching online video on their laptops, tablet and smartphones is increasing rapidly, and advertisers are shifting their budgets online to follow them.[4]

The evidence also suggests that mobile advertising will be a key growth sector, increasing its share of global advertising

---

[1] 19th Annual Global CEO Survey, PWC (January 2016).

[2] 'Training in the recession: winner or loser?', *Institute of Directors Survey Report* (November 2008).

[3] Abhinav Ramnarayan, 'Domino's Pizza sees customers rise as recession keeps people at home', *The Guardian* (1 October 2009).

[4] Omar Oakes, 'Mobile will turn internet into world's biggest advertising medium by 2017, says report', *Campaign* (22 June 2015).

expenditure between 2014 and 2017 from 5.1 to 12.9 per cent. If trading conditions do remain weak, these cheaper forms of advertising may prove useful to firms.

Hold on to your customers. Sales may decrease during a recession, but the key thing for a business is to maintain market share, by keeping existing customers. Central to this strategy is maintaining excellent customer service and delivering what the customer wants. Many businesses have focused on this strategy, by adapting products, menus and service to satisfy consumer demands. It may require market research and extra training, both of which are costly, but if it means creating customer loyalty, it is a worthwhile expenditure. This is especially true in the long term, as once the economic recovery starts, a loyal customer base will help a firm grow.

Diversify your product and customer base. In section 3.4, we considered the Growth Vector Matrix, which looks at both of these strategies. If demand in an existing market is stagnant or falling, looking elsewhere for sales may be a crucial strategy for surviving a recession. This could be either through product differentiation, such as a new design/model, or through diversifying the market in which the product is sold. This could involve new geographical locations or simply new market segments.

The coffee industry is one that has not been significantly affected by the recession. Research showed that the six main chains in the UK actually increased the number of outlets by 47 per cent during the 2007/8 period. Since then, the number of outlets has grown significantly and is estimated at 20 728 in 2015, with sales growth of 10 per cent from the previous year and a total turnover of £7.9 billion. Allegra World Coffee Portal predicts that total UK coffee shops will be above 30 000 by 2025, with a turnover of £15 billion (at 2015 prices).[5]

One explanation for this trend is that coffee shops increasingly have everything that businesspeople need, whether it's comfy seats or access to Wi-Fi. As companies were forced to cut costs, hiring out meeting or conference rooms became an unaffordable luxury, and so coffee shops became a substitute meeting place. Furthermore, coffee shops began to sell cheaper lunch options, as eating out also became an expensive luxury and so this industry took advantage of the economic climate, essentially filling a gap in the market with a cheaper substitute.

It is examples like this which demonstrate the importance of responding to customer needs in order to maintain a successful business.

Careful cash-flow management. Putting a business plan in place will go some way to helping a firm manage its organisation in an efficient and successful way. Whatever the state of the global economy, having sufficient working capital is vital. However, in a recession it becomes even more important to manage cash flow. This could involve more accurate financial reporting, a stricter process of credit checking customers and ensuring that products are paid for on time. The 'DNA of an entrepreneur' study reported that a third of SME bosses cut their own salaries in a bid to cut operating costs and improve cash flow.

Pricing and promotions. Prices are central to a consumer's buying decision, as we saw in Chapter 2 and in Box 5.3. Consumers become more price sensitive during recessions and are after value for money. All of the main supermarkets advertise on TV, but from the onset of recession in 2008 these adverts increasingly focused on prices, especially with the growth of the discount retailers, Aldi and Lidl. In response, the big four (Tesco, Sainsbury's, Asda and Morrisons) have cut prices. At the time, Asda cut the price of various staple items. Tesco responded by cutting prices by 50 per cent on thousands of items and Sainsbury's reduced prices on certain items, such as summer groceries.[6] The discount retailers have continued with their strong performance, doubling their combined market share to 10 per cent in the three years to 2015, as consumers continue to look for bargains.

Cutting prices and, crucially, offering promotions were strategies that many businesses adopted during the recession in a bid to retain existing customers and increase sales. The effectiveness of such policies, however, depends on the price elasticity of demand for the products, and on the prices and promotions being offered by competitors. A restaurant manager said:

> They [consumers] still want to go out. But you have to make it affordable for them. You can price yourself out of the market, and then you're in trouble. So keep your prices reasonable, make a little less profit, but make sure you get people through the door.[7]

An optimal solution?

In a recession, there is no one-size-fits-all solution. The strategy that works for one firm will not necessarily be right for another: there is no optimal solution. How a business reacts to a recession, with both low and falling demand, will depend on its product, the size of the firm, the actions of competitors, its organisational structure and, to a large extent, on the culture within the firm. Some businesses will go under, but it is the ones that change their strategy to make it work that will come out of the other side stronger.

For many organisations the downturn should be looked at as an opportunity – those firms that are able to invest now will grow quicker when the market picks up.[8]

1. Are there any other things a business should focus on to help it get through a recession? What are they and why are they important?
2. Select a business. How has it managed to survive the recession? (Hint: use the Internet to help you research its strategy.)
3. Of the strategies considered in this box, which do you think is the most important?

5 'Booming UK coffee shop market outperforms UK retail sector', *Allegra World Coffee Portal* (14 December 2015).

6 'Supermarkets to battle on prices', *BBC News* (27 June 2008).
7 Paul Wootton, 'Business profile: San Carlo, *Big Hospitality* (31 July 2009).
8 'Training in the recession: winner or loser?', *Institute of Directors Survey Report* (November 2008)

The second source of uncertainty is the economic environment. In a period of rapid change, such as often accompanies a boom, firms may seek to protect themselves by merging with others.

Other motives. Other motives for mergers include:

■ Getting bigger so as to become less likely to be taken over oneself.

■ Opportunistic. Firms are presented with an unforeseen opportunity. As you can imagine, mergers based on such a motive are virtually impossible to predict, but firms will always be on the look-out for such opportunities.

■ Merging with another firm so as to defend it from an unwanted predator (the 'White Knight' strategy).

■ Asset stripping. This is where a firm takes over another and then breaks it up, selling off the profitable bits and probably closing down the remainder.

■ Empire building. This is where owners or managers favour takeovers because of the power or prestige of owning or controlling several (preferably well-known) companies.

■ Geographical expansion. The motive here is to broaden the geographical base of the company by merging with a firm in a different part of the country or the world.

Mergers, especially horizontal ones, will generally have the effect of increasing the market power of those firms involved. This could lead to less choice and higher prices for the consumer. For this reason, mergers have become the target for government competition policy. Such policy is the subject of section 9.5.

Growth through strategic alliances

One means of achieving growth is through the formation of strategic alliances with other firms: either horizontally or vertically within an industry or as a network of firms across different industries. They are a means of expanding business operations relatively quickly and at relatively low cost, and are a common way in which firms can deepen their involvement in global markets.

A well-known example of strategic alliances is in the airline industry (see Figure 6.4). Members co-operate over frequent flyer programmes, share business-class airport lounges and code share on various flights.

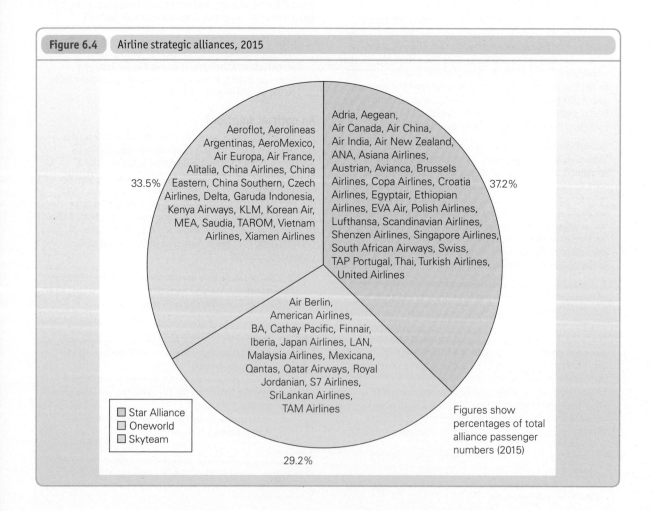

| Figure 6.4 | Airline strategic alliances, 2015 |

What forms can strategic alliances take?

Joint ventures. A **joint venture** is where two or more firms decide to create, and jointly own, a new independent organisation. Joint ventures can be either horizontal or vertical. An example of a horizontal joint venture was when Jaguar Land Rover entered into a deal with Chery Automobile of China in 2012 to manufacture and sell cars in the Chinese market. FilmFlex was an example of a vertical strategic alliance, bringing film and TV makers into the retail sector, but Sony and Disney sold FilmFlex to the US-based company Vubiquity in May 2014.

Consortia. A **consortium** is usually created for very specific projects, such as a large civil engineering work. As such, it has a very focused objective and once the project is completed the consortium is sometimes dissolved. TransManche Link, the Anglo-French company that built the Channel Tunnel, is an example of a defunct consortium. Camelot, by contrast, the company that runs the UK National Lottery, was owned in equal shares by Cadbury Holdings, De La Rue Holdings, Fujitsu Services, Royal Mail Enterprises and Thales Electronics, each of which had particular expertise to bring to the consortium. It was sold to Ontario Teachers' Pension Plan in March 2010.

Franchising and licensing. A less formal strategic alliance is where a business agrees to *franchise* its operations to third parties. McDonald's and Coca-Cola are good examples of businesses that use a franchise network. In such a relationship the franchisee is responsible for manufacturing and/or selling, and the franchiser retains responsibility for branding and marketing. A similar type of arrangement is that of *licensing*. Some lagers and beers sold in the UK, for example, are brewed under licence.

Subcontracting. Like franchising, **subcontracting** is a less formal source of strategic alliance, where companies maintain their independence. When a business subcontracts, it employs an independent business to manufacture or supply some service rather than conduct the activity itself. Car manufacturers are major subcontractors. Given the multitude and complexity of components that are required to manufacture a car, the use of subcontractors to supply specialist items, such as brakes and lights, seems a logical way to organise the business, as Nissan has found.[2]

Networks. **Networks** are less formal than any of the above alliances. A network is where two or more businesses work collaboratively but without any formal relationship binding one to the other. Rather than a formal contract regulating the behaviour of the partners to the agreement, their relationship is based upon an understanding of trust and loyalty. Networks are common in the motor vehicle, electronics, pharmaceutical and other high-tech sectors. Networks can be at both the national and local level and give firms access to technology and resources at lower costs and may also give access to global markets.

Why form strategic alliances?

As a business expands, possibly internationally, it may well be advantageous to join with an existing player in the market. Such a business would have local knowledge and an established network of suppliers and distributors.

In addition, strategic alliances allow firms to share risk. The Channel Tunnel and the consortium of firms that built it is one such example. The construction of the Channel Tunnel was a massive undertaking and far too risky for any single firm to embark upon. With the creation of a consortium, risk was spread, and the various consortium members were able to specialise in their areas of expertise.

They also allow firms to pool capital. Projects that might have prohibitively high start-up costs, or running costs, may become feasible if firms co-operate and pool their capital. In addition, an alliance of firms, with their combined assets and credibility, may find it easier to generate finance, whether from investors in the stock market or from the banking sector.

The past 30 years have seen a flourishing of strategic alliances. They have become a key growth strategy for business both domestically and internationally. They are seen as a way of expanding business operations quickly without the difficulties associated with the more aggressive approach of acquisition or the more lengthy process of merger.

> ### Pause for thought
>
> *Give two reasons why a firm may prefer to form a strategic alliance with another firm rather than merging with it or taking it over.*

> ### Definitions
>
> **Joint venture** Where two or more firms set up and jointly own a new independent firm.
>
> **Consortium** Where two or more firms work together on a specific project and create a separate company to run the project.
>
> **Franchise** A formal agreement whereby a company uses another company to produce or sell some or all of its product.
>
> **Licensing** Where the owner of a patented product allows another firm to produce it for a fee.
>
> **Subcontracting** Where a firm employs another firm to produce part of its output or some of its input(s).
>
> **Network** An informal arrangement between businesses to work together towards some common goal.

[2] Adrian Pearson, '5200 jobs predicted as Sunderland gets Nissan business park', *The Journal* (14 March 2014).

RECAP

1. A business can expand either internally or externally by merging with other firms or by forming strategic alliances. In each case, there are three potential growth strategies open to business: product differentiation, vertical integration and diversification.

2. Growth by internal expansion may be financed by ploughing back profits, by share issue or by borrowing. Whichever method a firm uses, it will require sufficient profits if it is to avoid becoming vulnerable to a takeover.

3. Vertical integration involves remaining in the same market, but expanding into a different stage of production. Vertical integration can reduce a firm's costs through various economies of scale. It can eliminate the various transactions costs associated with dealing with other firms. It can also help to reduce uncertainty, as the vertically integrated business can hopefully secure supply routes and/or retail outlets. This strategy can also enhance the business's market power by enabling it to erect various barriers to entry.

4. Diversification offers the business a growth strategy that not only frees it from the limitations of a particular market, but also enables it to spread its risks and seek profit in potentially fast-growing markets.

5. There are three types of merger: horizontal, vertical and conglomerate. There are various possible advantages of mergers, including growth, economies of scale, market power, increased share values or reduction in uncertainty.

6. One means of achieving growth is through the formation of strategic alliances with other firms. They have the advantage of allowing easier access to new markets, risk sharing and capital pooling.

6.4 FINANCING GROWTH AND INVESTMENT

If businesses are to grow, they will need to invest. In this section we consider the sources of finance for investment, and the roles played by various financial institutions.

Sources of business finance

As mentioned in section 6.3 above, the firm can finance growth by borrowing, by retaining profits or by a new issue of shares.

Many companies rely on their own resources to finance investment and growth. Indeed, the largest source of finance for investment in the UK is firms' own internal funds (i.e. ploughed-back profit).

However, given that business profitability depends in large part on the general state of the economy, internal funds as a source of business finance are likely to show considerable cyclical variation. When profits are squeezed in an economic downturn, as we saw after 2008, this source of investment will decline (but so also will the *demand* for investment; after all, what is the point in investing if your market is declining?).

Other sources of finance, which include borrowing and the issue of shares and debentures, are known as 'external funds'. These are then categorised as short-term, medium-term or long-term sources of finance.

- Short-term finance is usually in the form of a short-term bank loan or overdraft facility, and is used by firms as a form of working capital to aid them in their day-to-day business operations.

- Medium-term finance, again provided largely by banks, is usually in the form of a loan with set repayment targets. It is common for such loans to be made at a fixed rate of interest, with repayments being designed to fit in with the business's expected cash flow. Bank lending tends to be the most volatile source of business finance and is particularly sensitive to the state of the economy.

While part of the reason is the lower demand for loans during a recession, another aspect is the caution of banks in granting loans if prospects for the economy are poor.

- Long-term finance, especially in the UK, tends to be acquired through the stock and bond markets. The proportion of business financing from this source clearly depends on the state of the stock market. In the late 1990s, with a buoyant stock market, the proportion of funds obtained through share issue increased. Then, with a decline in stock market prices from 2000 to early 2003, this proportion fell, only to rise again as the stock market surged ahead after 2004. This pattern was repeated in the financial crisis and its aftermath. From 2007 to 2009 share prices fell and the proportion of investment funding through new issues also fell. With the recovery in stock markets, albeit a patchy one, since then (see figure in Box 2.1 on page 34), funding through new share issue has increased somewhat. But, given the volatility of stock markets as worries about the global economy persist, the scope for funding from new issues has also been variable.

Despite the traditional reliance on the stock market for long-term sources of finance, there has been a growing involvement of banks in recent years, although banks have been criticised for continuing to be too cautious. This can result in a problem of *short-termism*, with bankers often

Definition

Short-termism Where firms and investors take decisions based on the likely short-term performance of a company, rather than on its long-term prospects. Firms may thus sacrifice long-term profits and growth for the sake of quick return.

demanding a quick return on their money or charging high interest rates, and being less concerned to finance long-term investment. This has been a particular problem faced by small and medium-sized enterprises (SMEs).

In many other European countries, such as Germany and France, banks provide a significant amount of *long-term*, fixed interest-rate finance. While this tends to increase companies' gearing ratios and thus increases the risk of bankruptcy, it does provide a much more stable source of finance and creates an environment where banks are much more committed to the long-run health of companies. For this reason the net effect may be to *reduce* the risks associated with financing investment. Nevertheless, with many European banks since the financial crisis facing problems of inadequate finance, many have become more cautious about lending to business in recent years. This has hampered recovery from recession.

Another source of finance is that from outside the country. This might be direct investment by externally based companies in the domestic economy or from foreign financial institutions. In either case, a major determinant of the amount of finance from this source is the current state of the economy and predictions of its future state. One of the major considerations here is anticipated changes in the exchange rate (see Chapter 13). If the exchange rate is expected to rise, this will increase the value of any given profit in terms of foreign currency. As would be expected, this source of finance is particularly volatile.

The stock market

In this section, we will look at the role of the stock market and consider the advantages and limitations of raising capital through it. We will also consider whether the stock market is efficient.

The role of the Stock Exchange

The London Stock Exchange operates as both a primary and secondary market in capital.

As a *primary market* it is where public limited companies (see page 7) can raise finance by issuing new shares, whether to new shareholders or to existing ones. To raise finance on the Stock Exchange a business must be 'listed'. The Listing Agreement involves directors agreeing to abide by a strict set of rules governing behaviour and levels of reporting to shareholders. A company must have at least three years' trading experience and make at least 25 per cent of its shares available to the public. In March 2016, there were 971 UK and 277 international companies on the Official List. These companies in total had an equity market value of £3802.4 billion. During 2015, companies on this list raised £28.3 billion of equity capital, £6.2 billion of which was raised by international companies. This figure was slightly higher than the £26.2 billion for 2014, but significantly lower than the figures for 2008

and 2009, when £66.7 billion and £77.4 billion were raised respectively.

As well as those on the Official List, there are some 1029 companies on the Alternative Investment Market (AIM). Companies listed here tend to be young but with growth potential, and do not have to meet the strict criteria or pay such high costs as companies on the Official List. The market value of these companies as of February 2016 was £68 647.1 million.

As a *secondary market*, the Stock Exchange enables investors to sell existing shares to one another. In 2015, approximately £4.5 billion of trade in UK equities and debt securities took place on an average day.

The advantages and disadvantages of using the stock market to raise capital

As a market for raising capital the stock market has a number of advantages:

- It brings together those that wish to invest and those that seek investment. It thus represents a way that savings can be mobilised to create output, and does so in a relatively low-cost way.
- Firms that are listed on the Stock Exchange are subject to strict regulations. This is likely to stimulate investor confidence, making it easier for businesses to raise finance.
- The process of merger and acquisition is facilitated by having a share system. It enables a business more effectively to pursue this as a growth strategy.

The main weaknesses of the stock market for raising capital are:

- The cost to a business of getting listed can be immense, not only in a financial sense, but also in being open to public scrutiny. Directors' and senior managers' decisions will often be driven by how the market is likely to react, rather by what they perceive to be in the business's best interests. They always have to think about the reactions of those large shareholders in the City that control a large proportion of their shares.
- It is often claimed that the stock market suffers from short-termism. Investors on the Stock Exchange are more concerned with a company's short-term performance and its share value. In responding to this, the business might neglect its long-term performance and potential.

Definitions

Primary market in capital Where shares are sold by the issuer of the shares (i.e. the firm) and where, therefore, finance is channelled directly from the purchasers (i.e. the shareholders) to the firm.

Secondary market in capital Where shareholders sell shares to others. This is thus a market in 'second-hand' shares.

Is the stock market efficient?

One of the arguments made in favour of the stock market is that it acts as an arena within which share values can be accurately or efficiently priced. If new information comes on to the market concerning a business and its performance, this will be quickly and rationally transferred into the business's share value. This is known as the *efficient market hypothesis*. So, for example, if an investment analyst found that, in terms of its actual and expected dividends, a particular share was under-priced and thus represented a 'bargain', the analyst would advise investors to buy. As people then bought the shares, their price would rise, pushing their value up to their full worth. So by attempting to gain from inefficiently priced securities, investors will encourage the market to become more efficient.

 KEY IDEA 22

Efficient capital markets. Capital markets are efficient when the prices of shares accurately reflect information about companies' current and expected future performance.

If the market were perfectly efficient in this sense, then no gain could be made from studying a company's performance and prospects, as any such information would *already* be included in the current share price. In selecting shares, you would do just as well by pinning the financial pages of a newspaper on the wall, throwing darts at them, and buying the shares the darts hit!

If the stock market were perfectly efficient, it would only be unanticipated information that would cause share prices to deviate from that which reflected expected average yields. Such information must, by its nature, be random, and as such would cause share prices to deviate randomly from their expected price, or follow what we call a *random walk*. Evidence suggests that share prices do tend to follow random patterns.

> ### Pause for thought
>
> 1. For what reasons is the stock market not perfectly efficient?
> 2. How might some people gain from the lack of efficiency?

> ### Definitions
>
> **Efficient (capital) market hypothesis** The hypothesis that new information about a company's current or future performance will be quickly and accurately reflected in its share price.
>
> **Random walk** Where fluctuations in the value of a share away from its 'correct' value are random. When charted over time, these share price movements would appear like a 'random walk' – like the path of someone staggering along drunk!

> ### RECAP
>
> 1. Business finance can come from internal and external sources. Sources external to the firm include borrowing and the issue of shares.
> 2. The stock market operates as both a primary and secondary market in capital. As a primary market it channels finance to companies as people purchase new shares. It is also a market for existing shares.
> 3. It helps to stimulate growth and investment by bringing together companies and people who want to invest in them. By regulating firms and by keeping transaction
>
> costs of investment low, it helps to ensure that investment is efficient.
> 4. It does impose costs on firms, however. It is expensive for firms to be listed and the public exposure may make them too keen to 'please' the market. It can also foster short-termism.
> 5. The stock market is relatively efficient. It achieves efficiency by allowing share prices to respond quickly and fully to publicly available information.

6.5 STARTING SMALL

How often do you hear of a small business making it big? Not very often, and yet many of the world's major corporations began life as small businesses. From acorns have grown oak trees! But small and large businesses are usually organised and run quite differently and face very different problems.

Unfortunately, there is no single agreed definition of a 'small' firm. In fact, a firm considered to be small in one sector of business, such as manufacturing, may be considerably different in size from one in, say, the road haulage business. Nevertheless, the most widely used definition is that adopted by the EU for its statistical data. Three categories of small and medium-sized enterprise (SME) are distinguished. These are shown in Table 6.1.

Of the whole UK economy in 2015, micro businesses (between 0 and 9 employees) accounted for 95 per cent of

Table 6.1	EU SME definitions			
Criterion		**Micro**	**Small**	**Medium**
1.	Maximum number of employees	9	49	249
2a.	Maximum annual turnover	€2m	€10m	€50m
2b.	Maximum annual balance sheet total	€2m	€10m	€43m
3.	Maximum % owned by other firms which are large enterprise(s)	25%	25%	25%

Note: to qualify as an SME criteria 1 and 3 must be met and either 2a or 2b

all firms, 18 per cent of turnover and provided 33 per cent of all employment. All SMEs together (fewer than 250 employees) accounted for 99.9 per cent of all firms, 47 per cent of turnover and 60 per cent of employment.[3]

Evidence suggests that a small business stands a significantly higher chance of failure than a large business, and yet many small businesses survive and some grow. What characteristics distinguish a successful small business from one that is likely to fail?

Pause for thought

Before you read on, try to identify what competitive advantages a small business might have over larger rivals.

Competitive advantage and the small-firm sector

The following have been found to be the key competitive advantages that small firms might hold:

Flexibility. Small firms are better able to respond to changes in market conditions and to meet customer requirements effectively. For example, they may be able to develop or adapt products for specific needs. Small firms may also be able to make decisions quickly, avoiding the bureaucratic and formal decision-making processes that typify many larger companies.

Quality of service. Small firms are able to deal with customers in a more personal manner and offer a more effective after-sales service.

Production efficiency and low overhead costs. Small firms can avoid some of the diseconomies of scale that beset large companies. A small firm can benefit from: management that avoids waste; good labour relations; the employment of a skilled and motivated workforce; lower accommodation costs. In a Department for Business, Innovation & Skills (BIS) survey of SME managers, 78 per cent ranked themselves as having strong people management skills.[4]

Product development. Many small businesses operate in niche markets, offering specialist goods or services. The distinctiveness of such products gives the small firm a crucial advantage over its larger rivals. A successful small business strategy, therefore, would be to produce products that are clearly differentiated from those of large firms in the market, thereby avoiding head-on competition – competition which the small firm would probably not be able to survive.

Innovation. Small businesses, especially those located in high-technology markets, are frequently product or process innovators. Such businesses, usually through entrepreneurial vision, manage successfully to match such innovations to changing market needs. Many small businesses are, in this respect, path breakers or market leaders.

Problems facing small businesses

Despite some competitive advantages, there are a number of factors that hinder the success of small firms.

Selling and marketing. Small firms face many problems in selling and marketing their products, especially overseas. Small firms are perceived by their customers to be less stable and reliable than their larger rivals. This lack of credibility is likely to hinder their ability to trade. This is a particular problem for 'new' small firms which have not had long enough to establish a sound reputation. In the BIS survey cited above, only 28 per cent of SME managers ranked themselves as 'strong' at entering new markets.[5]

Funding R&D. Given the specialist nature of many small firms, their long-run survival may depend upon developing new products and processes in order to keep pace with changing market needs. Such developments may require significant investment in research and development. However, the ability of small firms to attract finance is limited, as many of them have virtually no collateral and they are frequently perceived by banks as a highly risky investment. In the same survey, only 27 per cent of SME managers ranked themselves as 'strong' at accessing external finance.[6] As we saw in Chapter 1, this can limit their scope for expansion.

---

[3] See: http://researchbriefings.parliament.uk/ResearchBriefing/Summary/SN06152

[4] Steve Lomax, June Wiseman and Emma Parry, 'Small Business Survey 2014: SME employers', *BIS Research Paper Number 214*, p.4 (Department for Business, Innovation & Skills, March 2015).

[5] Ibid., p.4.

[6] Ibid., p.4.

Management skills. A crucial element in ensuring that small businesses not only survive but grow is the quality of management. If key management skills, such as being able to market a product effectively, are limited, then this will limit the success of the business.

Economies of scale. Small firms will have fewer opportunities and scope to gain economies of scale, and hence their costs may be somewhat higher than their larger rivals. This will obviously limit their ability to compete on price.

The role of the entrepreneur

Crucial to the success and growth of small businesses are the personality, skills and flair of the owner(s). Fostering their entrepreneurial talents has become a key element in government economic strategy around the world. Indeed, the creation of an entrepreneurial culture within society is often considered a prerequisite for economic prosperity.

But what exactly is an entrepreneur? Entrepreneurs are sources of new ideas and new ways of doing things. That is, they are at the forefront of invention and innovation, providing new products and developing markets.

The Global Entrepreneurship Monitor (GEM) provides a framework for analysing entrepreneurship. It suggests that entrepreneurship is a complex phenomenon that can exist at various stages of the development of a business. So someone who is just starting a venture and trying to make it in a highly competitive environment is entrepreneurial. And so

too, but in a different way, are established business owners if they are innovative, competitive and growth-minded.

GEM publishes a total entrepreneurial activity (TEA) index. This shows the proportion of the adult working-age population who, in a given year, are in the process of starting a business and those running a new business less than 3.5 years old. Figure 6.5 shows the TEA for various industrial countries. You can see that in 2015 entrepreneurial activity was extremely high in Sub-Saharan Africa and in the Latin America/Caribbean regions and this has been the case for some years. Within the European countries, the UK appeared midway: above France and Germany, but behind Estonia and the Netherlands. The UK was also ranked below the USA, while the highest figure for TEA occurred in Senegal.

Attitudes towards entrepreneurship in the UK

Attitudes to entrepreneurship are generally positive in the UK, with many creative and imaginative people starting businesses in niche markets, from organic and green products, to specialist computer services, to fashion products, to extreme sports, to painting and decorating, to financial services. A YouGov poll in 2012 found that 49 per cent of people aged 18–24 wanted to run their own business at some point,[7] and in 2014 the record was broken for the largest number of businesses registered.

---

[7] http://yougov.co.uk/publicopinion/

| Figure 6.5 | Total early-stage entrepreneurial activity (TEA) as a percentage of the adult population (2015) |

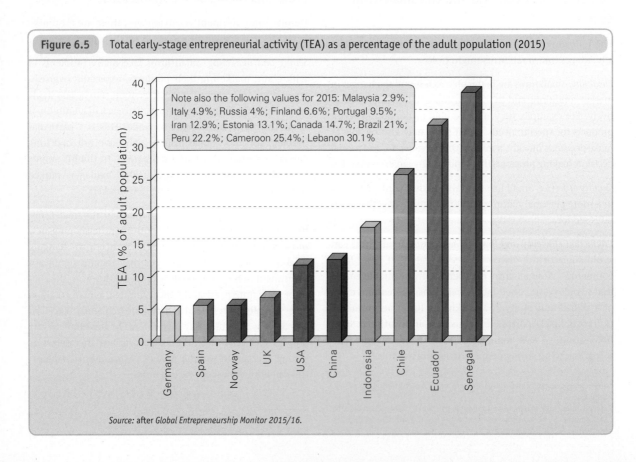

Note also the following values for 2015: Malaysia 2.9%; Italy 4.9%; Russia 4%; Finland 6.6%; Portugal 9.5%; Iran 12.9%; Estonia 13.1%; Canada 14.7%; Brazil 21%; Peru 22.2%; Cameroon 25.4%; Lebanon 30.1%

Source: after *Global Entrepreneurship Monitor 2015/16.*

According to the 2014 GEM UK Report, early-stage entrepreneurial activity in the UK was at 8.6 per cent, above the long-run average, and total entrepreneurial activity remained relatively high, with 8.5 per cent of working-age adults expecting to start a business over the following three years. Furthermore, optimism about opportunities for new businesses has recovered to pre-crisis levels.

Despite the positive data for entrepreneurial activity in the UK, only 58 per cent of the working-age population thought that starting a business was a good career choice and of those who saw good business opportunities, 48 per cent said that they would not start a business because of a fear of failure. This fear was perhaps driven in part by data on survival rates, as the ONS reported in 2015 that the three-year survival rate of UK VAT-registered businesses established in 2009 was 59.6 per cent and had fallen since 2004. The five-year survival rate was also fairly low, with only 41.7 per cent of businesses established in 2009 still active in 2014.[8]

Obtaining finance remained a key concern, as over half of nascent entrepreneurs required external funding. The sources of expected funding between 2008 and 2014 had changed significantly, with the proportion coming from banks/financial institutions and government programmes declining from 18.6 and 17.2 per cent to 8.8 and 7.2 per cent respectively, and more entrepreneurs funding themselves. However, the number of funding requests refused had fallen below pre-crisis levels, including refusal rates of 0.2 and 1.0 per cent for mortgage/secured loans and unsecured loans respectively.

The overall data therefore suggest that the UK continues to have an entrepreneurial spirit and it compares favourably with many other countries. Government support for small businesses has grown, with the UK government recognising their strategic importance. The Department for Business, Innovation and Skills (BIS) was created in June 2009 and part of its role, together with the Treasury, is to provide support, grants and opportunities to small firms.

The government and the EU also offer grants and other forms of assistance through regional, urban, social and industrial policy. In 2013, BIS set up the Start Up Loans Company, which provides start-up support in the form of a repayable loan together with a business mentor for entrepreneurs across the UK. This was in response to relatively low levels of entrepreneurial activity in the UK compared to the USA. The level of small business start-ups in the UK is about three businesses per 100 adults; in the USA, it is over seven businesses per 100 adults.

Various other forms of support exist, including the British Business Bank, opened in 2014, which aims to increase the supply of lending to SMEs. The Coalition government invested £50 million through the 'Smart' scheme to help small firms meet the costs of running R&D projects to develop new products, processes or services. The Business Growth Service provides mentoring and consultancy services to assist SMEs in developing and acting upon growth plans, and in the Budget 2016 the Chancellor announced a permanent increase in the threshold for small business rate relief from £6000 to a maximum of £15 000. The implication of this is that 600 000 small businesses will be relieved of paying business rates from April 2017.

Support in the EU is available with the Competitiveness of Enterprises and Small and Medium-sized Enterprises (COSME) programme, which has a planned budget of €2.3 billion and runs from 2014–20. A new Executive Agency for Small and Medium-sized Enterprises (EASME) was created in January 2014 to manage most parts of COSME on behalf of the EU. Its four objectives are: to improve access to finance for SMEs; to improve access to markets inside the EU and globally; to promote entrepreneurship; and to improve conditions for the competitiveness and sustainability of EU businesses.

This sector therefore remains a vital part of the business environment, with governments placing increased strategic importance on the role of the small firm.

---

[8] 'Statistical Bulletin: Business Demography: 2014', *ONS* (24 November 2015).

Pause for thought

Is business failure necessarily a 'bad thing' for a country?

BOX 6.4   THE DYSON DUAL CYCLONE VACUUM CLEANER

A small business redefining the Hoover

In the 2007 New Years Honours, James Dyson, founder of Dyson Appliances, was knighted. Sir James said that he hoped that the honour would 'encourage other engineers and people who have ideas and inventions to go out and commercialise them and make them international successes'.[1]

The tale of the Dyson Dual Cyclone vacuum cleaner records the successful and dramatic rise of James Dyson. As a budding

entrepreneur, in the early 1980s he invented a revolutionary bagless vacuum cleaner, which worked, in effect, by creating a mini cyclone, whereby a high-speed air vortex pushed dust particles to the side of a collector. Without a bag, the suction power of the cleaner would not diminish over time, unlike conventional vacuums. When he initially developed this product, neither Electrolux nor Hoover was interested – largely because of the profits they made from selling bags!

After an early and unsuccessful attempt to launch the project, Dyson managed to secure a deal with a Japanese company to

---

[1] James Dyson speaking after his knighthood for services to the business world (30 December 2006).

▶

produce and sell the vacuum in Japan. Launched in 1983, the pink-and-lavender 'G-Force' was a hit with Japanese consumers, who fell in love with its revolutionary design and looks. Nevertheless, at the staggering price of £1200, it was unlikely to yield the mass sales Dyson hoped for. Thus Dyson set out to manufacture it himself.

Finding it difficult to raise capital and find backers, Dyson reinvested his profits from the Japanese sales, and in 1993 managed to raise the £4.5 million required to design and patent his product, to establish a network of subcontractor suppliers, and to create an assembly plant near his home in the UK. With his DC01 vacuum cleaner priced at a relatively affordable £200, Dyson hoped to enter the mass market. By the end of the decade the Wiltshire plant was producing some 800 000 machines a year.

Today, Dyson's vacuum cleaner is the market leader in many countries, including the UK, Taiwan, Hong Kong and Australia, with 21 and 18 per cent of the UK and Australian markets respectively, and is the biggest vacuum cleaner brand by value in Japan. It continues to make gains in other key markets, including France, the USA and China, where it has been noted as the most dynamic mover of 2015,[2] and it has tripled its market in China and doubled its South Korean market since 2014. Cordless vacuum cleaners have done particularly well in China and Japan.

The Dyson story is a classic example of how a small business with a revolutionary product can have a massive impact on a market, and within a short period of time become established as a market leader. In 2005, Dyson's salary was £31.5million – more than twice that of any FTSE 100 chief executive! However, his salary saw significant reductions throughout the recession of the late 2000s, falling to £12.5 million in 2007 and then to £457 000 in 2008. During this period, a cost-cutting process was implemented, in particular a 6 per cent cut in R&D. At the same time, pre-tax profits fell by 4 per cent to £85.3 million. However, in 2011, its earnings grew by 30 per cent to £306.3 million and Dyson saw its revenue grow to £1.05 billion, largely driven by sales in the USA and Japan.[3] Dyson has been selling an increasing number of products outside the UK, and in 2012 85 per cent of its products were sold abroad, up from 30 per cent in 2005. Dyson's success has continued with record-breaking profits of £367 million in 2015, up by 13 per cent for the year[4] and his fortune increased in 2015 by £500 million to stand at £3.5 billion.

The Dyson story has not, however, been all good news for the UK: in 2002, Dyson shifted production from the UK plant to Malaysia, with the loss of 560 UK jobs. Dyson countered criticisms of the move by arguing that fierce competition from companies which were selling bagless cleaners for half the price of Dysons forced the company to relocate its manufacturing to a country where labour was much cheaper and which was close to suppliers of parts.

Yet things have turned out just as globalisation advocates would have hoped. Three factories in Malaysia now make 4m vacuum cleaners a year, with all the suppliers within a ten-mile radius, at one-third of the cost in Britain. The Wiltshire factory has become a research and design centre; Dyson employs more people than before, and in more highly skilled jobs. A new phase of R&D has produced a miniature digital motor with a power-to-weight ratio five times that of a Formula 1 racing car, which is being used in a tiny new vacuum cleaner and a super-hygienic, energy-efficient hand drier . . . Innovative firms like Dyson can grow from small beginnings to world-beaters. Global competition is turning many products into commodities, so innovation is essential if companies – and countries – want to stay in business.[5]

Innovative new products include the vacuum that steers on balls instead of wheels (this became Britain's biggest selling vacuum cleaner within a month), a desk fan for greener air-conditioning and the Airblade hand-dryer. There are also suggestions that James Dyson has been asked, and is being funded, by the British government to develop an electric car, investing $1.4 billion in battery technology research, following its purchase of Sakti3.[6] Sir James Dyson has said that 'By investing in long-term research and development, we've been able to keep launching new technologies'.[7]

This drive has continued with significant additions to its staff and a total increase of 1000 new engineers over the four years to 2015, bringing its total number of engineers and scientists to 2000. James Dyson, more than anyone, knows the importance of R&D to business success, having made 5127 prototypes of his first vacuum cleaner before it was launched. In 2014, £160 million was spent on research and development and the company continues to spend £3 million per week on R&D. It is this that has led to such success and will surely continue to give the company, best known for quality, innovation and functionality, a competitive advantage in existing markets and the means to penetrate new ones.

1. *What conditions existed to enable James Dyson's small business to do so well in such a short period of time?*
2. *By 2007, a robotic Dyson vacuum cleaner (the DC06) had been over six years in development, involved several prototypes and cost a considerable amount of money. How would you assess whether the venture should have been scrapped?*

[2] www.euromonitor.com/vacuum-cleaners
[3] 'Dyson sales and profits boosted by US and Japan', *BBC News* (7 September 2012).
[4] David Hellier, 'Rugs to riches: Dyson announces record profits of £367m', *The Guardian* (3 September 2015).
[5] 'Suck it and see', *The Economist* (1 February 2007).
[6] Neil Winton, 'Could the traditional car industry be undone by Dyson, a vacuum cleaner maker?', *Forbes* (25 March 2016).
[7] 'Dyson's pay cut as profits fall', *Times Online* (7 November 2009).

RECAP

1. Small firms survive because they provide or hold distinct advantages over their larger rivals. Such advantages include: greater flexibility, greater quality of service, production efficiency, low overhead costs and product innovation.

2. Small businesses are prone to high rates of failure, however. This is due to problems of credibility, finance and limited management skills.

3. Entrepreneurial activity varies from country to country, but most recognise that is an important ingredient in the health of the economy. Generally, the difficulties and risks of setting up a new business are less than people expect.

QUESTIONS

1. What do you understand by the term 'business strategy'? Explain why different types of business will see strategic management in different ways. Give examples.

2. Outline the Five Forces Model of competition. Identify the strengths and weaknesses of analysing industry in this manner.

3. Investigate a particular industry and assess its competitive environment using the Five Forces approach.

4. Distinguish between a business's primary and support activities in its value chain. Why might a business be inclined to outsource its support activities? Can you see any weaknesses in doing this?

5. What do you understand by the term 'core competence' when applied to a business? What are the arguments for and against a firm narrowly focusing on its core competencies?

6. Explain the two-way relationship between a business's rate of growth and its profitability.

7. Distinguish between internal and external growth strategy. Identify a range of factors which might determine whether an internal or external strategy is pursued.

8. What is meant by the term 'vertical integration'? Why might a business wish to pursue such a growth strategy?

9. A firm can grow by merging with or taking over another firm. Such mergers or takeovers can be of three types: horizontal, vertical or conglomerate. Which of the following is an example of which type of merger (takeover)?

   (a) A soft drinks manufacturer merges with a pharmaceutical company.
   (b) A car manufacturer merges with a car distribution company.
   (c) A large supermarket chain takes over a number of independent grocers.

   To what extent will consumers gain or lose from the three different types of merger identified above?

10. Assume that an independent film company, which has up to now specialised in producing documentaries for a particular television broadcasting company, wishes to expand. Identify some possible horizontal, vertical and other closely related fields into which it may choose to expand.

11. What are the advantages and disadvantages for a company in using the stock market to raise finance for expansion?

12. In what sense can the stock market be said to be efficient? Why is it unlikely to be perfectly efficient?

13. Compare and contrast the competitive advantages held by both small and big business.

14. How has the weak economic climate since 2008 affected small businesses? Do you think it is easier or more difficult to set up a business during a recession? Explain your answer.

Multinational corporations and business strategy in a global economy

Business issues covered in this chapter

- What is the magnitude and pattern of global foreign direct investment and how has it changed?
- What are the key factors that make a nation attractive to foreign investors?
- What forms do multinational corporations take?
- Why do companies become multinational?
- In what ways do multinationals have a cost advantage over companies based in a single country?
- What competitive advantages do multinationals have over companies based in a single country?
- What disadvantages are companies likely to face from having their operations spread over a number of countries?
- What are the advantages and disadvantages of multinational investment for the host state?
- How can the multinational use its position to gain the best deal from the host state?

The world economy has become increasingly interdependent over the past few decades, with improved communications and an increasingly global financial system. This has meant that in many respects a firm's global strategy is simply an extension of its strategy within its own domestic market. However, opening up to global markets can provide an obvious means for a business to expand its markets and spread its risks, especially with the process of globalisation. It also is a means of reducing costs, whether through economies of scale or from accessing cheap sources of supply or low-wage production facilities.

A firm's global growth strategy may involve simply exporting or opening up factories or outlets abroad, or it may involve merging with businesses in other countries or forming strategic alliances. As barriers to trade and the international flow of capital have come down, so more and more businesses have sought to become multinational. The result is that the global business environment has tended to become more and more competitive.

For developing economies, such as India and China, the benefits of this new wave of globalisation are substantial. Foreign companies invest in high value-added, knowledge-rich production, most of which is subsequently exported. Economic growth is stimulated and wages rise. Increased consumption then spreads the benefits more widely throughout the economy, as we will discuss in more detail in Chapter 10. There are, however, costs. Many are left behind by the growth, and inequalities deepen both between and within countries. There are also often significant environmental costs as rapid growth leads to increased pollution, environmental degradation and the depletion of resources.

7.1 MULTINATIONAL CORPORATIONS

There are some 100 000 *multinational corporations* (MNCs) worldwide. Between them they control over 890 000 foreign subsidiaries, which employ some 75 million people. In 2014, the global stock of foreign direct investment (FDI) was $26.0 trillion. The largest MNCs have affiliates in an average of 40 foreign countries each and increasingly it is foreign sales, rather than domestic sales, where growth has occurred. Sales by foreign affiliates accounted for $36.4 trillion in 2014, or around 47 per cent of world GDP and $7.9 trillion in value added. For the top 100 MNCs, foreign sales grew by 1.3 per cent in 2014, whereas domestic sales declined by 5 per cent.

Definition

Multinational corporations Businesses that either own or control foreign subsidiaries in more than one country.

But just what is an MNC? At the most basic level it is a business that either owns or controls subsidiaries in more than one country. It is this ownership or control of productive assets in other countries that makes the MNC distinct from an enterprise that does business overseas by simply exporting goods or services. However, merely to define an MNC as a company with overseas subsidiaries fails to reflect the immense diversity of multinationals.

Diversity among MNCs

Size. Many, if not most, of the world's largest firms – Wal-Mart, Shell, Toyota, etc. – are multinationals. Indeed, the turnover of some of them exceeds the national income of many countries (see Table 7.1).

And yet there are also thousands of very small, often specialist multinationals, which are a mere fraction of the size of the giants. What is more, since the mid-1980s

Table 7.1	Comparison of the ten largest MNCs (by gross revenue) and selected countries (GDP), 2014	
MNC rank	**Country or company (headquarters)**	**GDP ($bn) or gross revenue ($bn)**
	USA	17 968.2
	China	11 384.8
	UK	2 864.9
1	Wal-Mart	485.6
	Belgium	458.7
2	Sinopec Group	446.8
3	Royal Dutch Shell	431.3
4	China National Petroleum	428.6
	Norway	397.6
5	Exxon Mobil	382.5
	Denmark	372.6
6	BP	358.7
7	State Grid	339.4
	Singapore	294.0
8	Volkswagen	268.6
9	Toyota Motor	247.7
	Chile	240.0
	Ireland	227.5
10	Glencore	221.1
	Bangladesh	202.3
	Greece	193.0
	Czech Republic	182.5
	Morocco	103.1
	Afghanistan	19.6
	Sierra Leone	4.3

Note: GDP data are estimates.
Sources: Companies: Fortune Global 500; countries: World Economic Outlook database, IMF.

many large multinational businesses have been downsizing. They have been shrinking the size of their headquarters, removing layers of bureaucracy to speed up decision making, and reorganising their global operations into smaller autonomous profit centres. Gone is the philosophy that big companies will inevitably do better than small ones.

In fact, it now appears that multinationals are seeking to create a hybrid form of business organisation, which combines the advantages of size (i.e. economies of scale) with the responsiveness and market knowledge of smaller firms. The key for the modern multinational is flexibility and to be, at one and the same time, both global and local.

The nature of business. MNCs cover the entire spectrum of business activity, from manufacturing to extraction, agricultural production, chemicals, processing, service provision and finance. There is no 'typical' line of activity of a multinational.

Production locations. Some MNCs are truly 'global', with production located in a wide variety of countries and regions. Other MNCs, by contrast, locate in only one other region, or in a very narrow range of countries.

There are, however, several potentially constraining factors on the location of multinational businesses. For example, businesses concerned with the extraction of raw materials will locate as nature dictates! Businesses that provide luxury services will tend to locate in advanced or emerging countries, where the demand for such services is high or has high growth prospects. Others locate according to the resource intensity of the stage of production. Thus a labour-intensive stage might be located in a developing country where wage rates are relatively low. Another stage, which requires a high level of automation, might be located in an industrially advanced country that has the necessary technology and workforce skills.

Ownership patterns. As businesses expand overseas, they are faced with a number of options. They can decide to go it alone and create wholly owned subsidiaries. Alternatively, they might share ownership, and hence some of the risk, by establishing a joint venture with a foreign company. In such cases the MNC might have a majority or minority stake in the overseas enterprise. In certain countries, where MNC investment is regulated, governments insist on owning or controlling a share in the new enterprise. Much of the time, it will depend on the type of business and how important it is to the host country.

State-owned enterprises (SOEs) account for only about 1 per cent of total MNCs, but they are becoming increasingly important FDI players. They are defined by UNCTAD as MNCs where the government is the single largest shareholder or has at least 10 per cent of the voting power. In 2013 UNCTAD found that there were 550 state-owned

MNCs with more than 15 000 foreign affiliates and foreign assets of over $2 trillion. They mainly operate in capital-intensive industries, such as oil and gas.

The above characteristics of MNCs reveal that they represent a wide and very diverse group of enterprises. Beyond sharing the common link of having production activities in more than one country, MNCs differ widely in the nature and forms of their overseas business, and in the relationship between the parent and its subsidiaries.

> **Pause for thought**
>
> *Given the diverse nature of multinational business, how useful is the definition given on page 161 for describing a multinational corporation?*

Trends in multinational investment

We can estimate the size of multinational investment by looking at figures for foreign direct investment (FDI). FDI represents the finance used either to purchase the assets for setting up a new subsidiary (or expanding an existing one), or to acquire an existing business operation through merger or acquisition.

In 2007 FDI flows reached their peak at just under $2.0 trillion, following a period of global growth and high confidence in the global economy. However, as FDI flows tend to reflect macroeconomic conditions, the onset of recession in 2008 led to companies becoming less aggressive and this caused FDI flows to fall to $1.2 trillion in 2009. They had recovered somewhat by 2011, reaching $1.6 trillion, but had declined by 16 per cent back to $1.2 trillion in 2014. The World Investment Report 2015 states that this decline was down to 'the fragility of the global economy, political uncertainty for investors and elevated geopolitical risks'. However, a recovery was expected for 2015, with global FDI inflows projected to grow by 11 per cent to $1.4 trillion, with the trend expected to continue through 2016 and 2017, when FDI flows are expected to be $1.7 trillion (see Figure 7.1).

FDI has historically been highly concentrated, with most flows going to developed countries, but the proportion going to developing countries has been rising and in 2014 inward FDI flows to developing countries reached their highest level at $681 billion. In 2000, 82.5 per cent of world FDI flows went to developed countries, with only 17 per cent going to developing countries. By 2014, for the first time, more than half the flows of FDI went to developing countries (55 per cent), with developed nations receiving just 40.6 per cent.

Figure 7.1 FDI inflows ($ billions at current prices and exchange rates)

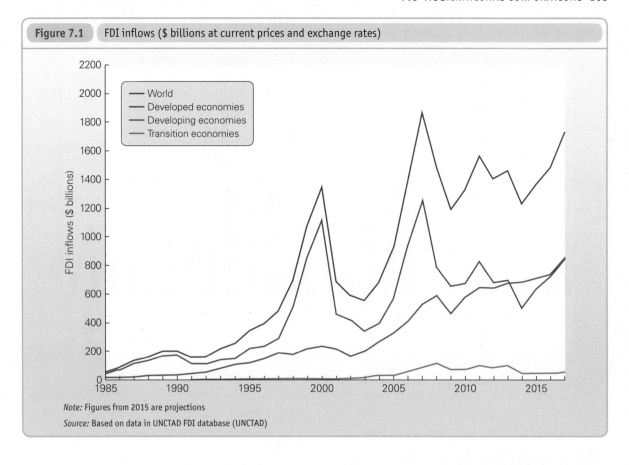

Note: Figures from 2015 are projections

Source: Based on data in UNCTAD FDI database (UNCTAD)

Developing economies in Asia have seen significant growth in their share from 10.5 per cent in 2000 to 37.9 per cent in 2014, but both Latin America and the Caribbean have also seen some growth.

It is a slightly mixed story for transition economies. Growth in their FDI flows until 2008 was impressive, increasing from $5.8 billion in 2000 to $116.3 billion in 2008. However, since the financial crisis, FDI flows to the transition nations have fallen, with a particularly large fall between 2013 and 2014, where they declined from $99.6 billion to $48.1 billion, taking their share of world FDI from just under 8 per cent to 4 per cent in that time period. With sanctions against Russia and lower oil prices causing its economy to decline, inward FDI to Russia was set to remain subdued.

For the poorest countries, the growth in flows is more limited. In 2014, the whole of Africa received just $53.9 billion of FDI inflows, up from $9.6 billion in 2000, but showing little change in the seven years to 2014, where its percentage of world FDI flows has remained between 3 and 4.5 per cent. The least developed countries (LDCs) in 2014 received only 3.6 per cent of total FDI flows to developing countries and this accounted for just 1.5 per cent of world FDI flows. This figure has grown marginally, but the picture of FDI flows still sees the poorest nations receiving very little foreign investment.

FDI and the UK

The UK's share of world FDI has fluctuated considerably, from a high of 19.8 per cent ($184 billion) in 2005 to a low of 2.7 per cent ($42 billion) in 2011. By 2014 its share had risen 5.9 per cent ($72 billion). These percentages are driven mainly by the relative prospects of the UK economy, while the size of the flows also depends on the state of the global economy. Figure 7.2 shows FDI flows to and from the UK in billions of US dollars. It also shows FDI inflows as a percentage of both world FDI inflows and the inflows to the 15 countries ('EU15') that were EU members prior to 2004.

Over the years, outward investment from the UK has tended to exceed inward investment. In 2000, the accumulated stock of investment abroad by the UK was over double the stock of foreign investment in the UK. However, in recent years inflows have tended to exceed outflows. Indeed, in 2013, 2014 and 2015 outflows were negative, with sales of existing investments abroad exceeding new investments abroad. As a result, by 2015 the accumulated stock of foreign investment in the UK ($1783 billion) had overtaken the stock of investment abroad by the UK ($1538 billion). Investment yields income to the investing company. Because the stock of UK investment abroad is now less than that of foreign investment in the UK, inflows of income earned from abroad are likely to be less than outflows of income from the UK.

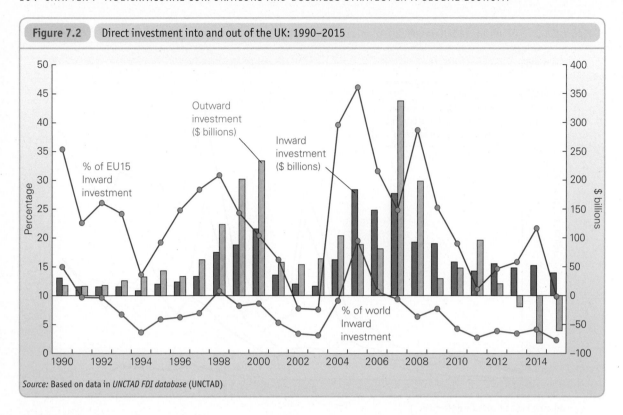

Figure 7.2   Direct investment into and out of the UK: 1990–2015

Source: Based on data in *UNCTAD FDI database* (UNCTAD)

Pause for thought

With the emergence of China, India and the CEECs, the UK's position as an attractive place for FDI has been under threat. What do you think the UK government might do either to minimise FDI outflows or to attract a greater volume of FDI inflows?

Other countries

Other notable countries with regard to high FDI flows as a percentage of world FDI in 2014 are the USA with a 7.5 per cent share, although this figure had decreased significantly from 2013, when its share was 15.7 per cent, following Vodafone's divestment of Verizon. Singapore received 5.5 per cent of world FDI flows; Brazil received 5.1 per cent; Australia 4.2 per cent; Canada 4.4 per cent; and British Virgin Islands 4.6 per cent (as companies sought to take advantage of its tax haven status). The biggest recipient of world FDI flows was China with 10.5 per cent.

Countries that have a large foreign multinational sector, such as the UK, are significantly affected by foreign business actions and their decisions about where to locate and invest. MNCs generally have higher rates of productivity than domestic firms, and this puts competitive pressure on domestic firms to increase their productivity. In the UK, approximately 50 per cent of R&D expenditure is by foreign affiliates.

RECAP

1. There is great diversity among multinationals in respect to size, nature of business, size of overseas operations, location, ownership and organisational structure.

2. Foreign direct investment (FDI) tends to fluctuate with the ups and downs of the world economy. Over the years, however, FDI has accounted for a larger and larger proportion of total investment.

3. The UK was traditionally a net investor overseas and hence inflows of income earned from abroad were generally greater than outflows of income from the UK. However, this position has reversed in recent years.

4. Inflows of FDI were traditionally highly concentrated in the developed world, but the share received by developing economies has been increasing and overtook that of developed countries in 2014.

BOX 7.1   MERGER ACTIVITY

An international perspective

With increased globalisation, cross-border M&As are becoming more common and data indicate that in some countries these deals are now more frequent than internal deals, where one company merges with another domestic company. In the mid-1990s cross-border M&As accounted for about 16 per cent of all deals; now they account for over 40 per cent.

According to data from the ONS, in 2015 there were 447 acquisitions involving UK companies. Of these, 197 were acquisitions of UK companies by UK companies and the remaining 250 were acquisitions by UK companies abroad or by foreign companies into the UK.[1]

Cross-border M&As can be crucial for a firm looking to gain rapid entry into an overseas market and there is increased activity both within and between developed and developing economies. But, what have been the trends, patterns and driving factors in mergers and acquisitions (M&A) around the world in recent years? Chart (a) provides an overview of the trends since 1990.

The 1990s

The early years of the 1990s saw relatively low M&A activity as the world was in recession, but as world economic growth picked up, so worldwide M&A activity increased. Economic growth was particularly rapid in the USA, which became the major target for acquisitions.

With the dismantling of trade barriers and increased financial deregulation, globalisation accelerated and with this came

increased competition. Companies felt the need to become bigger in order to compete more effectively.

In Europe, M&A activity was boosted by the development of the Single Market, which came into being in January 1993. Companies took advantage of the abolition of trade barriers in the EU, which made it cheaper and easier for them to operate on an EU-wide basis. As 1999 approached, and with it the arrival of the euro, so European merger activity reached fever pitch, stimulated also by the strong economic growth experienced throughout the EU.

By 2000, annual worldwide M&A activity was some three times the level of the beginning of the 1990s. Around this time there were some very large mergers indeed. These included a $67 billion marriage of pharmaceutical companies Zeneca of the UK and Astra of Sweden in 1998, a $183 billion takeover of telecoms giant Mannesmann of Germany by Vodafone of the UK in 1999 and a $40.3 billion takeover of Orange of the UK by France Telecom in 2000.

Other sectors in which merger activity was rife included financial services and the privatised utilities sector. In the UK in particular, most of the privatised water and electricity companies were taken over, with buyers attracted by the sector's monopoly profits. French and US buyers were prominent.

The period since 2000

The period from 2000 to 2015 saw fluctuations in the value and number of mergers and acquisitions as the state of the economy changed, but in particular this period saw a change

[1] *Mergers and Acquisitions involving UK companies*, ONS (8 March 2016).

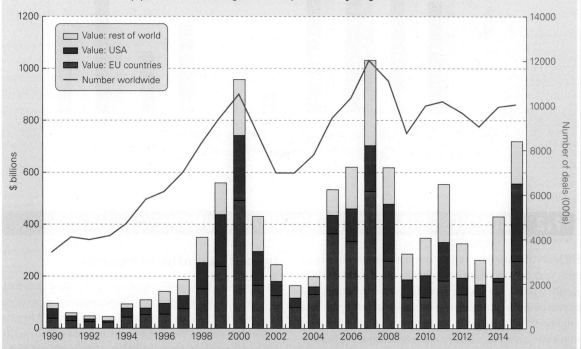

(a) Cross-border mergers and acquisitions by target: 1990–2015

Note: The data cover only those deals that involve an acquisition of an equity of more than 10%.

Source: 'Cross Border Mergers & Acquisitions', *World Investment Report Annex Tables*, UNCTAD (June 2016)

in the worldwide pattern of M&A activity. Whilst this predominantly involved a company in a neighbouring country, or a country that is a traditional trading partner, increasingly both European and US companies have looked to other parts of the world to expand their activities.

In 2000, there were 10 517 cross-border deals, with a total value of over $950 billion. An economic slowdown from 2000 reduced the number and value of worldwide mergers, which fell by 82.6 per cent to $165 billion in 2003. As the economic recovery began, M&A activity also increased over the next four years, reaching a new peak in 2007 of 12 044 deals, with a combined total value of over $1 trillion.

As the financial crisis and recession hit the world economy, however, there was a significant fall in cross-border M&As, with many deals breaking down when one of the merging firms pulled out. Between 2007 and 2009, there was a 72 per cent fall in the value of cross-border M&As to just $288 billion. Even when the worst of the crisis was over, the global economy remained vulnerable and, as you can see from chart (a), between 2009 and 2011 there was only a modest

recovery, as some firms restructured and some large firms attempted to acquire weakened competitors or purchase undervalued complementary businesses.

However, with concerns about the USA's public finances and the eurozone crisis, M&A activity once again slowed, with only a small recovery in 2014, when the value of deals increased to $399 billion. Despite the geopolitical uncertainty, UNCTAD expects growth in M&A activity to continue in 2016.

A changing pattern of M&As

We have a seen a big change in the pattern of cross-border M&A activity since the 1990s and in chart (b) you can see a comparison of the trends in regional M&A activity during the 1990s and in the period 2007 to 2015. Three interesting points can be identified:

- North America saw a fall in its global share of cross-border M&As from 25.3 per cent in the 1990s to 20.2 per cent between 2007 and 2014; and its share measured by value fell from 34.6 per cent to 28.6 per cent.

(b) Cross-border mergers and acquisitions by target region (% of total number and value)

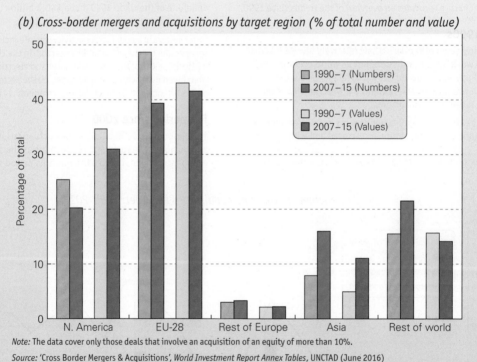

Note: The data cover only those deals that involve an acquisition of an equity of more than 10%.

Source: 'Cross Border Mergers & Acquisitions', *World Investment Report Annex Tables*, UNCTAD (June 2016)

7.2 BUSINESS STRATEGY IN A GLOBAL ECONOMY

The global marketplace can provide massive opportunities for firms to expand: access to new markets, new customers, new supply sources, new ideas and skills. At the same time, the growth of multinationals presents major competitive threats to domestic firms, as new market entrants from abroad arrive with lower costs, innovative products and marketing, or some other core competence which the domestic firm finds difficult to match. In this section we explore the strategic implications for business in facing up to the global economic system.

Types of multinational expansion

As we saw in section 6.3, businesses can look to expand in one of two ways: through either internal or external expansion. MNCs are no exception to this rule. They can expand overseas, either by creating a new production facility from scratch (such as Nissan in the North East of England), or by merging with or taking over existing foreign producers (such as the acquisition of Asda by

- Asian countries saw a dramatic increase in their share of the number of cross-border M&As from 7.8 per cent in the 1990s to 15.9 per cent from the period 2007 to 2014. There was also an increase in their share of the value from 4.8 per cent to 11.6 per cent. China and India have been particularly attractive places due to fast-growing economies, lower costs, including cheaper labour and tax rates, and these countries have become more receptive to all forms of FDI, including M&As.
- EU countries have seen a reduction in the share of the number of cross-border M&As from 51.5 per cent in the 1990s to 42.0 per cent between 2007 and 2014. However, this is largely accounted for by a significant decrease in the number of M&As to the eurozone economies, whereas the number of M&As to other EU nations has increased slightly. In terms of their share of the value, this fell only slightly from 45.0 per cent to 43.5 per cent, with similar declines for the eurozone economies and the rest of the EU. In 2007, the biggest completed cross-border M&A was the $98.3 billion purchase of the Dutch Bank ABN-AMRO by RFS Holdings, a consortium of the Royal Bank of Scotland, Santander and Fortis. This occurred just before the banking crisis, which put a huge strain on the finances of the acquiring companies and was a major contributing factor to RBS having to be bailed out by the UK government in October 2008.

Every year there are numerous high-value cross-border deals around the world, including the $25.1 billion purchase of International Power PLC by GDF Suez Energy in 2011 and an $18 billion acquisition of Grupo Modelo by AB-InBev in 2013.[2] The growth in large deals was a key factor contributing to the growth of M&A activity in 2014, with the highest number of big deals since 2008 at 223. A notable point is that of these deals, 173 took place in developed economies, representing 77 per cent of the total value. Another notable point is the target company's home nation – with US companies being the target in one-third of these large cross-border M&A deals. This was particularly true of companies from China, Hong Kong (China) and Singapore targeting US and UK companies, including GIC, Singapore's sovereign wealth fund's acquisition of IndCor Properties (United States) for $8.1 billion.[3]

M&A activity was high in all sectors in 2014, but particularly in chemicals and pharmaceutical industries and in telecommunications. These included the purchase of Merck, a consumer care business, by Bayer, a German company, for $14.2 billion, the purchase of Chrysler by Fiat for $3.65 billion and of SFR SA (France) by Altice SA (Luxembourg) for $23 billion.[4]

Growing importance of developing nations

The emergence of developing and transition (former communist) economies has had an impact in many areas and their growing importance in the share of cross-border M&As cannot be overstated. In 2014 alone, there was an increase in the value of cross-border M&As where the acquired company was in developing and transition economies, of 16 and 66 per cent respectively.

Furthermore, companies based in developing economies are taking a greater role in cross-border M&As and have been focused on deals that involve companies from developed nations that are based in developing economies. Approximately 50 per cent of acquisitions from developing nations are accounted for by this type of M&A. Notable deals are outlined by the World Investment Report 2015:

> In 2014, MNEs continued to acquire firms and other assets owned by developed-country MNEs in host developing economies. For example, MMG South America Management Co Ltd (Hong Kong, China) acquired Xstrata Peru – a foreign affiliate of Glencore/Xstrata (Switzerland) for $7 billion, and Emirates Telecommunications Corp (United Arab Emirates) bought a 53 per cent stake of Itissalat Al Maghrib SA – a foreign affiliate of Vivendi (France) – for $5.7 billion.[5]

The trend of developing nations taking a greater share of the number and value of deals is likely to continue, although this may vary by type of industry. For example, in 2014, while the overall share of cross-border M&As involving developing countries rose, their share of M&As in manufacturing fell.

 Are the motives for merger likely to be different in a recession from in a period of rapid economic growth?

---

[2] *World Investment Report 2014*, Annex Tables, UNCTAD (September 2014).
[3] *World Investment Report 2015*, UNCTAD (June 2015), p. 11.

[4] Ibid. p. 10.
[5] Ibid. p. 11.

Wal-Mart or of Jaguar by Ford). They can also engage in an international strategic alliance (for example, the joint venture in 2006 between Finland's Nokia and Japan's Sanyo to produce mobile phones for the North American market or the 2014 alliance between Sony and Panasonic).

We need also to distinguish between horizontal, vertical or conglomerate expansion.

- *Horizontally integrated multinational.* This type of multinational seeks to produce essentially the same product in different countries (but perhaps with some variations in product specification to suit the needs and

tastes of the local market). The primary objective of this strategy is to achieve growth by expanding into new markets, as shown by cell C in the Growth Vector Matrix on page 67.

Definition

Horizontally integrated multinational A multinational that produces the same product in many different countries.

■ *Vertically integrated multinational*. In this case, the multinational undertakes the various stages of production in different countries. Thus in some countries it will go backwards into the business's supply chain to the components or raw materials stages, and in others it will go forwards into the product's assembly or distribution. Oil companies such as Shell and Exxon Mobil (Esso) are good examples of vertically integrated multinationals, undertaking in a global operation the extraction of crude oil, controlling its transportation, refining it and producing by-products, and controlling the retail sale of petrol and other oil products. The principal motive behind such a growth strategy is to be able to exert greater control over costs and reduce the uncertainty of the business environment.

■ *Conglomerate multinational*. Such multinationals produce a range of different products in different countries. By this process of diversification, conglomerate multinationals look to spread risks, and maximise returns through the careful buying of overseas assets. Unilever is a good example of a conglomerate multinational. It employs over 172 000 people in over 190 countries, producing various food, home care and personal care products, which are sold in more than 170 countries. It has around 400 brands, 13 of which generate sales in excess of €1 billion a year. These brands include Wall's and Ben & Jerry's ice cream; Knorr soups; Bovril and Marmite; Bertolli pasta sauces; Hellmann's mayonnaise; Lipton and PG Tips tea; Flora, Blue Band and Rama margarines and spreads; Signal toothpaste; Domestos, Cif, Omo, Persil and Comfort; Timotei, TRESemmé and SunSilk shampoos; VO5, Toni and Guy and Brylcreem hair products; Vaseline, Dove, Simple and Lux soaps; Pond's skin care products; Impulse, Lynx, Sure and Brut fragrances and antiperspirants.

We do also see joint ventures being formed by multinationals for projects where risks and development costs are high. This is particularly true for large MNCs. A good example is the decision by Sony and Panasonic in 2014 to join forces with Innovation Network Corporation of Japan (INCJ) and Japan Display Inc. (JDI) to set up a new company, JOLED Inc., to develop and produce organic LED (OLED) displays for tablets and laptops.

As noted at the beginning of the chapter, MNCs are a diverse group of enterprises and we can distinguish between their different motives for going abroad. Some MNCs use

their multinational base primarily as a means of reducing costs (vertically integrated multinationals), whereas others use it primarily to achieve growth (horizontal and conglomerate multinationals). Let us now consider how, by going multinational, such goals might be achieved.

Going global to reduce costs

The costs and availability of labour and other resources. Nations, like individuals, are not equally endowed with resources. Some nations are rich in labour, some in capital and some in raw materials. In general, the more plentiful a resource, the lower will be its cost. Multinationals take advantage of this. For example, they might locate labour-intensive activities, such as an assembly plant, in low-wage developing countries, but complex R&D operations in countries with the necessary technology and skilled labour. It is factors such as this which give MNCs a competitive advantage over purely national firms.

Cost differences between countries are ruthlessly exploited by Nike, the American sportswear manufacturer. An example is given in a Portland Business Journal article, which looks at the cost of making a pair of sneakers (trainers!).[1] Nike has organised itself globally such that it can respond rapidly to changing cost conditions in its international subsidiaries. Its product development operations are carried out in the USA, but all of its production operations are subcontracted out to over 40 overseas locations, mostly in South and South-East Asia. If wage rates, and hence costs, rise in one host country, then production is simply transferred to a lower-cost subsidiary. Another example is Gap Inc., which is examined in Case Study A.1 on the book's website.

> ### Pause for thought
>
> 1. Before reading on, try to identify ways in which locating production overseas might help to reduce costs.
> 2. Identify some of the potential strengths and weaknesses of businesses having their value chains located in a variety of different countries.

As businesses relocate many dimensions of their value chain, the structure and organisation of the business takes on a web-like appearance, with its various operations being spread throughout the world. The key thing for a company's headquarters is having the information about their costs and the costs of its subsidiaries, so that production can simply follow the movements in market forces.

The quality of inputs. The location of multinational operations does not depend simply on wages and other input

> ### Definitions
>
> **Vertically integrated multinational** A multinational that undertakes the various stages of production for a given product in different countries.
>
> **Conglomerate multinational** A multinational that produces different products in different countries.

---

[1] Matthew Kish, 'The cost breakdown of a $100 pair of sneakers', *Threads and Laces: Portland Business Journal* (19 December 2014).

prices; it also depends on the *quality* of resources. For example, a country might have a highly skilled or highly industrious workforce, and it is this, rather than simple wage rates, that attracts multinational investment. The issue here is still largely one of costs. Highly skilled workers might cost more to employ *per hour*, but if their productivity is higher, they might well cost less to employ *per unit of output*. Take the case of Nike again. Product innovation and research, along with marketing and promotion, are all undertaken in the USA, which has a cost advantage in these areas, not through lower wage rates, but through experience and skills.

If a country has both lower-priced resources and high-quality resources, it will be very attractive to multinational investors. In recent years, the UK government has sought to attract multinational investment through its lower labour costs and more flexible employment conditions than those of its European rivals, while still having a relatively highly trained labour force compared with those in developing countries. However, as the relocation of many call-centre and IT jobs to developing countries shows, such advantages are disappearing fast in many sectors. Though here it is worth noting that, due to many customer complaints, a number of large companies are bringing their call centres back to the UK, including BT, Santander and EE.

Entrepreneurial and managerial skills. Managers in MNCs are often more innovative in the way they do business and organise the value chain than managers of domestic firms. In some cases, this is essential. With the arrival of Japanese multinationals in the UK, it became instantly apparent that Japanese managers conducted business in a very different way from their British counterparts. The most fundamental difference concerned working practices, such as the use of quality circles. Japanese MNCs quickly established themselves as among the most efficient and productive businesses in the UK (see section 8.5 on the flexible firm) and this made it necessary for UK firms to respond.

Cost reductions through 'learning by doing'. This is where skills and productivity improve with experience. Such learning effects apply not only to workers in production, sales, distribution, etc., but also to managers, who learn to develop more efficient forms of organisation. When a firm expands globally, there may be more scope for learning by doing. For example, if a firm employs low-cost labour in developing countries, initially the lower cost per worker will, to some extent, be offset by lower productivity. As learning by doing takes place and productivity increases, these initial small cost advantages may become much more substantial.

Economies of scale. By increasing the scale of its operation, and by each plant in each country specialising in a particular part of the value chain, the multinational may be able to gain substantial economies of scale.

MNCs are likely to invest heavily in R&D in an attempt to maintain their global competitiveness. The global scale of their operations allows them to spread the costs of this R&D over a large output (i.e. the R&D has a low average fixed cost). MNCs, therefore, are often world leaders in process innovation and product development.

Reducing transactions costs. By setting up an overseas subsidiary (as opposed merely to exporting to that country), the MNC can save on the transactions costs of arranging a contract with an overseas import agent or with a firm in the host country to make the product under licence. Many firms go through a sequence from exporting to overseas investment. Nissan, for example, exported its cars to the UK using local motor vehicle retailers to distribute them prior to establishing a greenfield manufacturing site in the North East of England in 1984. Toyota and Honda entered the UK in the same way.

Transport costs. A business locating production overseas would be able to reduce transport costs if those overseas plants served local or regional markets, or used local raw materials.

Government policies. One of the biggest cost advantages concerns the avoidance of tariffs (customs duties). If a country imposes tariffs on imports, then, by locating within that country (i.e. behind the 'tariff wall'), the MNC gains a competitive advantage over its rivals which are attempting to import their products from outside the country, and which are thus having to pay the tariff. MNCs may, therefore, be able to pass their cost savings on to consumers in the form of lower prices, or maintain prices and increase their profit margins. These, in turn, could be used for R&D. Since the UK has voted to exit the EU, the tariff negotiations for trade with EU countries are of paramount importance for businesses located in the UK and we may see some firms thinking about the location of their business in light of this.

Costs might also be reduced as a result of various government incentives to attract inward investment. Examples include: favourable tax rates, substantial depreciation allowances and the provision of subsidised premises. Such cost-cutting incentives may help to reduce the fixed costs of the investment and hence reduce its risk. A fairly recent case in the UK saw a potential investor offered financial incentives valued at £37 000 per employee to locate production in an area of Wales!

In highly competitive global markets, even small cost savings might mean the difference between success and failure. Thus MNCs will be constantly searching for ways of minimising costs and locating production where the greatest advantage might be gained.

Going global to access new markets

International markets can offer businesses massive new opportunities for growth and expansion. Such markets would be particularly attractive to a business where domestic growth opportunities are limited as a result of either the maturity of the market or shifting consumer tastes. The global financial crisis affected many developed countries particularly harshly and, as a consequence, developing countries saw an increase in the FDI from investors in both developed and developing countries. The more buoyant economic conditions in many of these nations presented investors with an opportunity to access new markets and take advantage of more stable economic circumstances. In addition to the possibility of extra sales, expanding into new markets offers other advantages:

Spreading risks. One of the main advantages of a larger and more diverse market is to spread risks. The firm is no longer tied to the specific market conditions of one particular country or region. As such, falling sales in one region of the global economy might be effectively offset by increased sales elsewhere. We have seen this in the brewery industry and particularly in a range of German and Japanese businesses, including Toyota and Honda. This strategy was successful as companies were able to sustain their profitability despite slumps in key markets.

Exploiting competitive advantages in new markets. The multinational's superior technology, superior-quality products

---

BOX 7.2 ATTRACTING FOREIGN INVESTORS

An indication of change

In the past, UNCTAD has published both an FDI Attraction Index and an FDI Potential Index, which gave different measures of the relative attractiveness of different countries for FDI. As you will see throughout this chapter, the pattern of FDI flows has been changing and we are seeing increasing amounts of investment in emerging and developing economies. Since 2013, the Milken Institute has published a Global Opportunity Index, which considers the key factors that make a nation an attractive location for multinational investment. As we continue to see the pattern of FDI flows change, this index provides some interesting insights into just some of the factors making it happen.

The Global Opportunity Index

The Global Opportunity Index (GOI) ranks nations according to their attractiveness to foreign investors and so provides useful information to both companies and countries. For companies it provides information on which countries have the most potential, with low costs, good protection for business, strong economic performance and good returns. For countries it provides guidance as to how they can implement government policy in the most effective way to attract more investment. This is particularly important given falling communications and transport costs, so that more locations are becoming feasible for investors.

In 2015, the GOI ranked 136 nations and to do this, it used 61 variables across four key categories. Each category has various subcomponents and all are measured on a scale of 0 to 10, with 10 being the best scenario. The categories are:

1. *Economic fundamentals:* this measures the extent to which a country's macroeconomic environment is conducive to FDI. A value of 10 indicates very strong economic fundamentals.
2. *Ease of doing business:* this measures the explicit and implicit costs associated with business operations, with 10 indicating very low costs of doing business in a country.
3. *Quality of regulations/regulatory barriers to investment:* this assesses the effectiveness of policy making and enforcement in a country and the extent to which any laws and regulations restrict the free flow of trade and investment. A value of 10 indicates efficient enforcement of policies and minimal barriers to capital flows.
4. *Rule of law:* this considers the country's legal system and the extent to which it protects investors and property rights to enhance business investment. A value of 10 indicates commitment to the rule of law.

These four categories and their subcomponents are used to rank nations and together this gives the Global Opportunity Index. Clearly, as government policy is implemented and economic and political circumstances change, the rankings will also change.

The Milken Institute has found 'a robust relationship between the GOI and foreign direct investment; the higher the score, the greater the inflows'. According to this research, 57 per cent of the variation in FDI per capita is explained by the index. The Institute finds that 'each one-unit increase in the index is associated with a 42 per cent increase in FDI per capita'.

The rankings

The four categories represent important areas for foreign investors, as they provide information about the ease with which business can be conducted and the costs of doing it.

Clearly, things like tax rates will be important, as well as the costs of starting up a business and enforcing contracts. These items are included as subcomponents in the cost of doing business.

The size and quality of the human and physical capital will also be important, as will the country's current economic performance. Is demand increasing; is employment high; is the nation open to trade?

Legal factors will also be important, such as the justice system and the effectiveness of law enforcement and protection, together with the degree of transparency, corruption and the amount and type of regulation. Bureaucracy can slow down business decisions and in the fast-changing business environment, this can make the difference between success and failure.

All of these factors contribute towards the nation's economic fundamentals and any company will want to invest in a country with strong economic performance, as this can help to reduce uncertainty.

Over the past six years, there has been a relative decline in investment into more developed economies and a relative increase into emerging nations (see Figure 7.1 on page 163). Some of this has been driven by the financial crisis, which affected the developed world more significantly. But government policy in many developing nations has led to some major reforms which have made these countries more attractive to foreign investors.

and more effective marketing may allow it to compete particularly effectively in markets that, up until now, have been dominated by domestic producers.

Learning from experience in diverse markets. Successful businesses will learn from their global operations, copying or amending production techniques, organisation, marketing, etc. from one country to another as appropriate. In other words, they can draw lessons from experiences in one country for use in another.

Increasingly, it seems that the globalisation of business is like a game of competitive leapfrog, with businesses having to look overseas in order to maintain their competitive position in respect to their rivals. A fiercely competitive global environment, in which small cost differences or design improvements can mean the difference between business success and failure, ensures that strategic thinking within a global context is high on the business agenda.

The 2015 rankings are shown in the table below, which includes the top 10 nations and a selection of others.

Each of the four categories is given equal weight and so, as you can see from the rankings, it is possible for a country to make up for weaknesses in one area.

New Zealand is a good example here. It is a developed nation, but perhaps a nation on the periphery, given its location. Its economic fundamentals are very weak, at just 4.95, which is a similar level to Costa Rica, Georgia, Jordan and Lebanon. However, it makes up for this in attracting foreign investment through its leading scores in Quality of Regulations and particularly Rule of Law, giving it 4th place in the GOI ranking.

We can look at other nations, particularly developing ones, where their institutions are relatively weak and yet their economic performance is much stronger, often being seen as faster-growing economies, perhaps with more opportunities.

The top movers and shakers

The Index is by no means perfect and clearly companies will place different values on each of the four categories. For some countries, an abundance of natural resources is a serious draw for investors. For others, these natural endowments are in scarce supply, but perhaps other investors might be attracted by a highly skilled workforce or the existing location of other technology firms, with which they can share research, etc.

Global Opportunity Index ranking 2015

Country	Rank	Composite Score	Economic Fundamentals	Ease of doing Business	Quality of Regulations	Rule of Law
Singapore	1	8.70	7.64	8.78	9.20	9.20
Hong Kong	2	8.47	7.86	8.52	8.30	9.20
Finland	3	7.88	6.09	8.31	9.30	7.80
New Zealand	4	7.81	4.95	8.21	8.50	9.60
Sweden	5	7.79	6.77	7.68	8.60	8.10
Canada	6	7.73	6.14	8.00	8.00	8.80
Norway	7	7.64	5.64	7.84	8.80	8.30
UK	7	7.64	6.54	7.52	7.60	8.90
Ireland	9	7.61	6.50	7.94	7.20	8.80
Malaysia	10	7.57	7.32	7.68	7.20	8.80
Germany	18	7.14	6.18	7.78	7.60	7.00
USA	18	7.14	6.45	7.42	6.30	8.40
China	52	5.85	6.32	5.79	6.30	5.00
Mexico	69	5.34	5.27	5.89	5.50	4.70
Russia	81	5.01	6.27	6.47	4.30	3.00
India	83	4.90	4.00	4.21	4.60	6.80
Nigeria	116	3.87	2.59	4.21	4.10	4.60
Guinea	136	2.88	1.86	4.05	3.30	2.30

Source: Based on *Global Opportunity Index*, The Milken Institute (2015), Table 1, pp. 11–14

▶

The GOI allows the rankings to be adjusted depending on what is important to a particular country or company. If a foreign investor is more concerned about the country's economic performance, it can increase this weighting, reduce the others and find a new ranking. As such, this index can be tailored somewhat to the needs of an individual investor.

The worldwide pattern of FDI flows shows the emergence of the developing world and while high-tech firms and those engaged in R&D continue to invest in the developed nations, Africa and Asia are gaining a greater share. The Global Opportunity Index also confirms this. Since the inaugural report in 2013, the five countries which have made the biggest gains in the GOI rankings are:

1. The Ivory Coast: point change = 0.80; percentage change = 26.5
2. Burundi: point change = 0.74; percentage change = 34.4
3. Philippines: point change = 0.74; percentage change = 18.5
4. Ecuador: point change = 0.58; percentage change = 14.6
5. Bosnia and Herzegovina: point change = 4.07; percentage change = 14.0.

Progress in attracting FDI has undoubtedly been made, especially by developing and transition economies which have generally moved up the rankings in terms of being attractive locations for foreign investors, but the top spots are still dominated by the developed world and the bottom is comprised of developing nations, largely those in Africa. There is clearly a long way to go for this region to become as attractive as the developed world.

1. Which countries do you think have made the most progress since the financial crisis and which countries have fallen down the rankings? Explain your answer.
2. What measures might a country adopt to improve its attractiveness to foreign investors?

The product life cycle and the multinational

By shifting production overseas at a particular point in the product's life cycle, the business is able to reduce costs and maintain competitiveness. The product life cycle hypothesis was discussed in section 5.6 (page 128). However, it is worth reviewing its elements here in order to identify how an MNC, by altering the geographical production of a good, might extend its profitability.

A product's life cycle can be split into four phases: launch, growth, maturity and decline. These were shown in Figure 5.11 (page 128).

The launch phase. This will tend to see the new product developed and produced in the same economy and then exported to the rest of the world. At this stage of the product's life cycle, the novelty of the product and the monopoly position of the producer enable the business to charge high prices and make high profits.

The growth phase. As the market begins to grow, other producers will seek to copy or imitate the new product. Hence supply increases and prices begin to fall. In order to maintain competitiveness, the business will look to reduce costs, and at this stage might consider shifting production overseas to lower-cost production centres.

Maturity. At the early stage of maturity, the business is still looking to sell its product in the markets of the developed economies. Thus it may still be happy to locate some of its plants in such economies. As the original market becomes increasingly saturated, however, the MNC will seek to expand into markets abroad which are at an earlier stage of development. Part of this expansion will be by the MNC simply exporting to more of these economies, but increasingly it will involve relocating its production there too.

Maturity and decline. By the time the original markets are fully mature and moving into decline, the only way to extend the product's life may be to cut costs and sell the product in the markets of developing countries. The location of production may shift once again, this time to even lower-cost countries. By this stage, the country in which the product was developed will almost certainly be a net importer (if there is a market left for the product), but it may well be importing the product from a subsidiary of the same company that produced it within that country in the first place! Thus the product life cycle model explains how firms might first export and then engage in FDI. It explains how firms transfer production to different locations to reduce costs and enable profits to be made from a product that could have become unprofitable if its production had continued from its original production base.

RECAP

1. Why businesses go multinational depends largely on the nature of their business and their corporate strategy. Two of the major reasons are (a) reducing costs by locating production where inputs are cheaper and/or more productive; (b) accessing markets in other countries in order to achieve growth in sales.

2. MNC investment is often governed by the product life cycle. In this theory, a business will shift production around the world, seeking to reduce costs and extend a given product's life. The phases of a product's life will be conducted in different countries. As the product nears maturity and competition grows, reducing costs to maintain competitiveness will force businesses to locate production in low-cost markets, such as developing economies.

BOX 7.3   GROCERS GO GLOBAL

International expertise plus local knowledge – a winning combination?

In Carrefour's Chinese stores, you will see a fresh snake counter alongside the fish department! Wal-Mart boasts that in its Chinese stores you can find local delicacies such as whole roasted pigs and live frogs. Are fresh snakes and live frogs what's needed to succeed in China? It would seem so. Global companies thinking local, customising themselves to each market, is increasingly seen as the key to success in Asia and elsewhere around the world.

The expansion of European and American supermarkets into countries around the world has been underway for a number of years. Driven by stagnant markets at home with limited growth opportunities, the major players, such as Wal-Mart from the USA, Carrefour and Casino from France, Tesco in the UK, Ahold from Holland and Metro from Germany, have been looking to expand their overseas operations – but with mixed success.

In recent times, Asia has been the market's growth sector, with China a particular attraction. In the five years to 2013, the Chinese supermarket sector grew at an average annual rate of 12.3 per cent, although the rate has slowed slightly since. Other countries have also seen foreign retailers moving in. Tesco entered the Thai market in 1998. Tesco Lotus, the company's regional subsidiary, is now the country's number one retailer. In 2015 it had over 1700 stores employing more than 50 000 people. Carrefour and Wal-Mart have also opened hundreds of new outlets within the region over the past few years.

The advantages that international retailers have over their domestic competitors are expertise in systems, distribution, the range of products and merchandising. However, given the distinctive nature of markets within Asia, businesses must learn to adapt to local conditions. Joint ventures and local knowledge are seen as the key ingredients to success.

Facing up to the big boys

With the rapid expansion of hypermarkets throughout Asia, the retail landscape is undergoing revolutionary change. With a wide range of products all under one roof, from groceries to pharmaceuticals to white goods, and at cut-rate prices, local neighbourhood stores stand little chance in the competitive battle. 'Mom and pop operations have no economies of scale.'[1] As well as local retailers, local suppliers are also facing a squeeze on profits, as hypermarkets demand lower prices and use their buying power as leverage.

Such has been the dramatic impact these stores have had upon the retail and grocery sector that a number of Asian economies, such as Malaysia and Thailand, have introduced restrictions on the building of new outlets.

China, one of the toughest markets to enter, had restricted foreign companies to joint venture arrangements until 2004.

Tesco's answer to these restrictions was to go into 50:50 partnership with Taiwanese food supplier Ting Hsin. Initially, the stores were not the Tesco supermarkets with which we're familiar, with an orange colour scheme and few brands that the average British shopper would recognise. Since 2006, however, Tesco increased its stake to 90 per cent and with this came the familiar Tesco branding. Since 2004, there has been considerable expansion by global retailers in China. By mid-2015, Carrefour, the biggest international retailer in the Chinese market, had over 230 hypermarkets, having opened 11 more in 2014 and expected to open a further 15 hypermarkets in 2015.[2]

However, the expansion into China and other Asian markets has not been without difficulties for global retailers. Tesco entered the traditionally closed market of Japan in 2003 and by 2010 it had opened 128 stores, employing 3604 people. However, Tesco decided to leave Japan in 2012, after nine years in the market.[3] In 2014, Carrefour announced that it was leaving India, less than four years after opening its first store in the country, blaming underperformance, due, in part, to being required to make infrastructure investment and source many of its products locally.[4]

Even in markets like China, the pace of expansion is tending to slow. In May 2014, Tesco completed the establishment of a joint venture with state-run China Resources Enterprise (CRE).[5] This left Tesco owning 20 per cent of the business and CRE 80 per cent. The venture brought together Tesco's 131 stores in China with CRE's nearly 3000 outlets.

With relatively slower economic growth in China and complex local market conditions, Tesco, Carrefour and Wal-Mart did begin to pull back on their global expansions and although they are continuing, it is at a slower rate. Philip Clarke, Tesco's CEO, said about China:

> It's more of a marathon than a sprint. Many retailers putting down more space in the market; few seeing that translate into profitable growth.[6]

A Bloomberg industry analyst added:

> The rate of same-store sales increases is not what they [chains] were expecting it to be. The rate of addition of capacity has probably exceeded the growth of the market.[7]

 What are the advantages and disadvantages to developing countries of the expansion of global supermarket chains?

---

[1] 'Attack of the superstore', *Time Magazine* (11 April 2002).

[2] Wang Zhuoqiong, 'Carrefour to open 15 new hypermarkets in China', *China Daily* (3 June 2015).

[3] 'Tesco to leave Japanese market after nine years', *BBC News* (18 June 2012).

[4] 'Carrefour to exit India Business', *BBC News* (8 July 2014).

[5] 'Tesco completes the establishment of Joint Venture with CRE', *Tesco News Release* (29 May 2014).

[6] 'Tesco stumbles with Wal-Mart as China shoppers buy local', *Bloomberg* (19 October 2012).

[7] Ibid.

7.3 PROBLEMS FACING MULTINATIONALS

In the vast majority of cases, businesses go multinational for sound business and economic reasons, which we have outlined above. However, multinational corporations may face a number of problems resulting from their geographical expansion:

- *Language barriers.* The problem of working in different languages is a barrier that the MNC must overcome. English is widely spoken throughout the business world, especially in developed countries, thus the extent of the language barrier may depend on the characteristics of the host country and how common a language English actually is. Further, if a UK MNC tends to employ expatriates, communication will be more difficult and local staff may feel alienated and thus be less productive.

- *Selling and marketing in foreign markets.* Strategies that work at home might fail overseas, given wide social and cultural differences. Many US multinationals, such as McDonald's and Coca-Cola, are frequently accused of imposing American values in the design and promotion of their products, irrespective of the country and its culture. This can lead to resentment and hostility in the host country, which may ultimately backfire on the MNC.

- *Attitudes of host governments.* Governments will often try to get the best possible deal for their country from multinationals. This could result in governments insisting on part ownership in the subsidiary (either by themselves or by domestic firms), or tight rules and regulations governing the MNC's behaviour, or harsh tax regimes. In response, the MNC can always threaten to locate elsewhere.

- *Communication and co-ordination between subsidiaries.* Diseconomies of scale may result from an expanding global business. Lines of communication become longer and more complex, especially when language is an issue. These problems are likely to increase in line with the attempted level of control exerted by the parent company, i.e. the more the parent company attempts to conduct business as though the subsidiaries were regional branches. Multinational organisational structures where international subsidiaries operate largely independently of the parent company will tend to minimise such problems.

Within any global strategy there will be a degree of economic and political risk. However, as MNCs look to invest more in developing economies or emerging markets such as China, this risk will increase, as there are more and more uncertainties. However, it is often within emerging markets that the greatest returns are achieved. It is essentially this trade-off between potential returns and risk that a firm needs to consider in its strategic decisions (see Box 7.4, page 176).

A global business will need a strategy for effectively embracing foreign cultures and traditions in its working practices, and for devising an efficient global supply chain. Some businesses may be more suited to deal with such global issues than others.

The global strategy trade-off

A firm's drive to reduce costs and enhance profitability by embracing a global strategy is tempered by one critical consideration – the need to meet the very different demands of customers in foreign markets. To minimise costs, a firm may seek to standardise its product and its operations throughout the world. However, to meet foreign buyers' needs and respond to local market conditions, a firm may be required to differentiate both its product and its operations, such as marketing. In such cases, customisation will *add* to costs and generate a degree of duplication within the business. If a business is required to respond to local market conditions in many different markets, it might be faced with significantly higher costs. But if it fails to take into account the uniqueness of the market in which it wishes to sell, it may lose market share.

The trade-off between the cost reduction and local responsiveness can be a key strategic consideration for a firm to take into account when selling or producing overseas. As a general rule we will tend to find that cost pressures will be greatest in those markets where price is the principal competitive weapon. Where product differentiation is high, and attributes such as quality or some other non-price factor predominate within the competitive process, local responsiveness will tend to shape business thinking. In other words, cost considerations will tend to be secondary.

RECAP

1. Although becoming an MNC is largely advantageous to the business, there can be problems with language barriers, selling and marketing in foreign markets, attitudes of the host state and the communication and co-ordination of global business activities.

2. An MNC will often find a trade-off between producing a standardised product in order to cut costs and producing a customised product in order to take account of local demand conditions.

FDI is more likely to occur if a nation has buoyant economic growth, large market size, high disposable income, an appropriate demographic mix, low inflation, low taxation, few restrictive regulations on business, a good transport network, an excellent education system, a significant research culture, etc. In highly competitive global markets, such factors may make the difference between success and failure.

Advantages

Host governments are always on the look-out to attract foreign direct investment, and are prepared to put up considerable finance and make significant concessions, such as tax breaks, to attract overseas business. So what benefits do MNCs bring to the economy?

Employment

If MNC investment is in new plants (as opposed to taking over an existing company) this will generate employment. Most countries attempt to entice MNCs to depressed regions where investment is low and unemployment is high. Often these will be regions where a major industry has closed (e.g. the coal mining regions of South Wales). The employment that MNCs create is both direct, in the form of people employed in the new production facility, and indirect, through the impact that the MNC has on the local economy. This might be the consequence of establishing a new supply network, or simply the result of the increase in local incomes and expenditure, and hence the stimulus to local business.

It is possible, however, that jobs created in one region of a country by a new MNC venture, with its superior technology and working practices, might cause a business to fold elsewhere, thus leading to increased unemployment in that region.

> ### Pause for thought
>
> *Why might the size of these regional 'knock-on effects' of inward investment be difficult to estimate?*

The balance of payments

A country's balance of payments is likely to improve on a number of counts as a result of inward MNC investment (we look at the balance of payments in detail in section 13.1). First, the investment will represent a direct flow of capital into the country. Second, and perhaps more importantly (especially in the long term), MNC investment is likely to result in both *import substitution* and export promotion. Import substitution will occur as products, previously purchased as imports, are now produced domestically. Export promotion will be enhanced as many multinationals use their new production facilities as export platforms. For example, many Japanese MNCs invest in the UK in order to gain access to the European Union. Concerns about whether leaving the EU would discourage such inward investment was one of the issues raised both during the referendum campaign on whether the UK should remain in or leave the EU and after the Brexit vote.

The beneficial effect on the balance of payments, however, will be offset to the extent that profits earned from the investment are repatriated to the parent country, and to the extent that the exports of the MNC displace the exports of domestic producers.

Technology transfer

Technology transfer refers to the benefits gained by domestic producers from the technology imported by the MNC. Such benefits can occur in a number of ways. The most common is where domestic producers copy the production technology and working practices of the MNC. This is referred to as the 'demonstration effect' and has occurred widely in the UK, as British businesses have attempted to emulate many of the practices brought into the country by Japanese multinationals.

In addition to copying best practice, technology might also be transferred through the training of workers. When workers move jobs from the MNC to other firms in the industry, or to other industrial sectors, they take their newly acquired technical knowledge and skills with them.

Taxation

MNCs, like domestic producers, are required to pay tax and therefore contribute to public finances. Given the highly profitable nature of many MNCs, the level of tax revenue raised from this source could be highly significant.

Disadvantages

Thus far we have focused on the positive effects resulting from multinational investment. However, multinational investment may not always be beneficial in either the short or the long term.

Uncertainty. MNCs are often 'footloose', meaning that they can simply close down their operations in foreign countries and

> ### Definitions
>
> **Import substitution** The replacement of imports by domestically produced goods or services.
>
> **Technology transfer** Where a host state benefits from the new technology that an MNC brings with its investment.

BOX 7.4	INVESTING IN CHINA

Riding the dragon

'China is amazing. It is capitalism, but at an unprecedented speed.' 'The talent of Chinese software engineers is unbelievable. I can't believe how effective they are.' (Bill Gates, Chairman, Microsoft)

'If your business isn't making money in China, it probably wouldn't make money anywhere else.' (Carlos Ghosn, President, Nissan Motor Company)[1]

On the basis of several indicators, China's economic performance is extraordinary. From 1990 to 2015, annual economic growth averaged just under 10 per cent, with weaker figures since 2011 bringing the figure down slightly. The quantity of its exports of goods and services grew by an average of over 15 per cent (in real terms) (see chart (a)). In 2004 it overtook Japan to become the world's third largest exporter (after Germany and the USA) and by 2010 it had overtaken Germany to become the world's largest exporter. In terms of the domestic purchasing power of its national income, China is the world's second biggest economy after the USA, or third if the eurozone is taken as a single economy.

As the economy and exports have boomed, so foreign investment has flooded into the country. In 1990 foreign direct investment (FDI) into China at current prices was $3.4 billion. By 2008, the figure had risen to over $108.3 billion in current prices and although it then fell to $95 billion the following year, it recovered from 2010 to stand at $128.5 billion in 2014 (see chart (b)).

China's attraction for foreign investors

China became the world's largest recipient of FDI in 2014, but why are foreign investors so attracted to this emerging economy? Is it simply that the economy has been growing so rapidly relative to other developed and developing nations? Clearly that is part of the attraction, but it is more than that. For a start, the Chinese economy is huge. With a population of 1.39 billion and an estimated GDP of $12 trillion in 2015,

China represents a massive potential market. The government has also invested heavily in improving the country's transport, power and communications infrastructure, all of which are crucial to any company looking to invest.

What is more, much of the growth in income in the Chinese economy is concentrated in the hands of the middle classes. The definition of this group does vary significantly, but here we define it as those earning between $9000 and $34 000 a year in 2010 prices. In 2000, just 4 per cent of urban Chinese households were within this bracket, but by 2012, that figure had grown to 68 per cent. Research by McKinsey&Company suggests that more than 75 per cent of China's urban consumers will fall into this bracket by 2022.[2] The report states:

> In the decade ahead, the middle class's continued expansion will be powered by labour-market and policy initiatives that push wages up, financial reforms that stimulate employment and income growth, and the rising role of private enterprise, which should encourage productivity and help more income accrue to households. Should all this play out as expected, urban-household income will at least double by 2022.[3]

As more Chinese consumers move into and up the rungs of the middle class, and with relatively few holding investments, consumer spending by this group is increasing rapidly, driven by a very income-elastic demand. Sales of electrical goods, furniture, cars and fashion clothing are all growing rapidly and executives believe that this will continue, together with significant increases in the consumption of services, in particular within education. Not only foreign manufacturers, but foreign retailers too are taking advantage of this (see Box 7.3).

But it is not just the growing domestic Chinese market that attracts foreign investors. They are also attracted by the opportunity to manufacture products at low cost for export. Despite the growth in investment in more high-end

---

[1] 'Is China a goldmine or minefield?', *BBC News Online* (19 February 2004).

[2] *Mapping China's middle class*, McKinsey&Company (June 2013).
[3] Ibid.

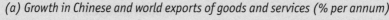

(a) Growth in Chinese and world exports of goods and services (% per annum)

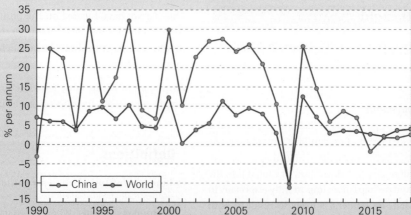

Note: Figures for 2016 to 2018 are based on IMF forecasts.
Source: Based on data in *UNCTAD Stat* and *World Economic Outlook* (IMF, October 2016).

manufactured products, China is still a key location for low-cost production. However, the types of products have begun to change, with Chinese factories taking more of the high-tech market share and moving up the value chain. Analysis by Kee and Tang in 2015 suggests that key factors in this change since 2000 are:

> structural transformation fused by trade and FDI liberalisation . . . such liberalisation encouraged intermediate input products in China to expand their product varieties, similar to what has been found in India . . . and in Bangladesh.[4]

The implication of this is that exporting Chinese companies have moved from using imported inputs to domestically produced inputs – but low-cost production still remains.

> China has moved up the 'value chain' and become a land of two economies. The sweatshops are still there, giving employment to millions of desperately poor migrant workers. But more and more companies become cutting edge and leapfrog foreign rivals. Whether games consoles, DVD recorders or flat-screen monitors, Chinese factories are grabbing high-tech market share.[5]

Despite past strong economic data, concerns of an economic slowdown in China have emerged and this has been reflected in 'unprecedented capital outflows' in the latter part of 2015 and early 2016, together with falling asset prices. To counter this, China has taken steps to loosen restrictions on inward foreign investment, particularly into onshore stock and bond markets and has tried to deflect talks of a major currency depreciation. However, according to the World Investment Report 2015, global corporate executives still view China as the best investment location in the world, closely followed by the USA.

Problems for foreign companies

In 2001, China joined the World Trade Organization (WTO). Many hoped that this would see the rapid dismantling of trade barriers and a wholesale deregulation of the economy. However, initially China became more selective in the investments that it approved, having concerns about asset stripping and job losses being implemented by Western managers.[6]

From 2006, a series of regulations were imposed on certain kinds of foreign investment into China, including rules that required the Ministry of Commerce to approve all deals involving national or economic security and the naming of seven sectors by the government over which it would retain 'absolute control'. However, the lack of clarity of the new legislation proved problematic for foreign businesspeople.

> One British businessman, who declined to be identified, cited the vagueness of China's definition of these sectors as a big hindrance. He said: 'The two letters IT embrace everything. There is a sense that liberalisation is going nowhere – and maybe even backwards. You never know when a new policy is going to be handed down.'[7]

On 13 April 2010, new guidelines for foreign investment in China were released by China's State Council, including: (1) foreign investment more welcome in foreign sectors; (2) new policies with a geographic focus; (3) more open domestic capital markets; and (4) improved and streamlined operational incentives.

> These new guidelines . . . encourage foreign funds to flow into high-end manufacturing, hi-tech and eco-friendly sectors and to the Central and Western areas of the nation. The guidelines restrict investment into environmentally unsound projects and in sectors suffering from overcapacity.

> Multinational companies will be encouraged to establish regional headquarters, R&D centers, financial management centers and other critical management and operational centers in China.

---

[4] Hiau Looi Kee and Heiwai Tang, 'How has China moved-up the global value chains?', *Let's talk development blog*, World Bank (11 January 2016).
[5] Pranab Bardhan, 'The slowing of two economic giants', *New York Times* (14 July 2013).

[6] Jane Macartney, 'New protectionism puts obstacles in the path of foreign investors', *The Times* (12 February 2007), © The Times/The Sun/nisyndication.com
[7] Ibid.

(b) Foreign direct investment inflows to China (in current prices)

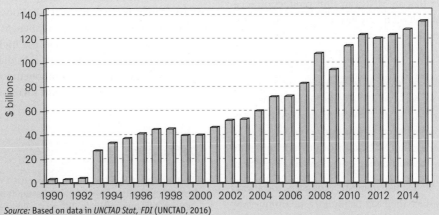

Source: Based on data in *UNCTAD Stat, FDI* (UNCTAD, 2016)

The approval procedures for foreign investment will be streamlined and the scope of approval and authorization will be reduced.

Through these new guidelines, China reiterates its support for foreign investment and this could be a response to some complaints that China was reversing its foreign investment policies ... These guidelines widen market access to foreign investors and better direct the inflow of foreign capital while also improving China's global competitiveness and promoting more efficient foreign investment into economically vital areas.[8]

Barriers for overseas investors looking to purchase publicly traded securities in mainland exchanges were lowered in 2012 as a means of encouraging further investment in China.[9] More recently, further loosening of restrictions on foreign investment in stock and bond markets have been implemented. Furthermore, in October 2016 the Chinese currency, the renminbi (RMB), was added to the basket of currencies that forms the IMF's Special Drawing Right (SDR) (joining the US dollar, the euro, the Japanese yen and the pound sterling). This may well help the economy's financial integration with the rest of the world and its economic and political stability, which, in turn, may prove attractive for foreign investors.

Other challenges facing China in attracting foreign investment over the coming years will be the rebalancing of the Chinese economy, as the government tries to move it towards a more consumption- and services-based economy, rather than an export- and investment-based economy. There are concerns that this will mean short-run growth, but that the economy will suffer in the long run and this may deter potential investors. John Zhu from HSBC noted that 'Pushing the economy along those paths too soon would be dangerous'.[10]

So it seems that a careful balancing act is needed by the Chinese government if the predictions of UNCTAD are to materialise and the Chinese economy will continue to be the most attractive place for foreign investment in the years to come.

1. *In what ways might a booming Chinese economy benefit the rest of the world?*
2. *Should multinational companies be cautious about investing in China?*

---

[8] Xu Ping, 'China reaffirms support for foreign investment', King & Wood Mallesons (19 April 2010).
[9] See 'China lowers entry barriers for overseas investors', *Bloomberg* (21 June 2012).
[10] 'China economic growth slowest in 25 years', *BBC News* (19 January 2016).

---

move if opportunities present themselves elsewhere. This is especially likely with older plants which would need updating if the MNC were to remain, or with plants that can be easily sold without too much loss. Also, during the maturity and decline stage of the product life cycle, cost-cutting may be essential and the MNC may move production to even lower-cost countries. The ability to close down its business operations and shift production, while being a distinct economic advantage to the MNC, is a prime concern facing the host nation. If a country has a large foreign multinational sector within the economy, it will become very vulnerable to such footloose activity, and face great uncertainty in the long term. It may thus be forced to offer the multinational 'perks' (e.g. grants, special tax relief or specific facilities) in order to persuade it to remain. These perks are clearly costly to the taxpayer.

Control. The fact that an MNC can shift production locations not only gives it economic flexibility, but enables it to exert various controls over the host country. This is particularly so in many developing countries, where MNCs are not only major employers but in many cases the principal wealth creators. Thus attempts by the host state, for example, to improve worker safety or impose pollution controls may be against what the MNC sees as its own best interests. It might thus oppose such measures or even threaten to withdraw from the country if such measures are not modified or dropped. The host nation is in a very weak position.

Transfer pricing. MNCs, like domestic producers, are always attempting to reduce their tax liabilities. One unique way that an MNC can do this is through a process known as *transfer pricing*, which refers to the price a business charges itself for transferring partly finished products from one division of the company to another. By manipulating this internal pricing system, the MNC can reduce its profits in countries with high rates of profit tax, and increase them in countries with low rates of profit tax.

For example, take a vertically integrated MNC where subsidiary A in one country supplies components to subsidiary B in another. The price at which the components are transferred between the two subsidiaries (the 'transfer price') will ultimately determine the costs and hence the levels of profit made in each country. Assume that in the country where subsidiary A is located, the level of corporation tax (the tax on company profits) is half that of the country where subsidiary B is located. If components are transferred from A to B at very high prices, then B's costs will rise and its profitability will fall. Conversely, A's profitability will rise. The MNC clearly benefits as more profit is taxed at the lower rather than the higher rate. Had it been the other way around, with subsidiary B facing the lower rate of tax, then the components would be transferred at a low price. This would increase subsidiary B's profits and reduce A's.

Definition

Transfer pricing The pricing system used within a business to transfer intermediate products between its various divisions, often in different countries.

The practice of transfer pricing was most starkly revealed in the Guardian newspaper in February 2009. Citing a paper that examined the flows of goods priced from US subsidiaries in Africa back to the USA, it stated that 'the public may be horrified to learn that companies have priced flash bulbs at $321.90 each, pillow cases at $909.29 each and a ton of sand at $1993.67, when the average world trade price was 66 cents, 62 cents and $11.20 respectively'.[2]

The environment. Many MNCs are accused of simply investing in countries to gain access to natural resources, which are subsequently extracted or used in a way that is not sensitive to the environment. Host nations, especially developing countries that are keen for investment, are frequently prepared to allow MNCs to do this. They often put more store on the short-run gains from the MNC's presence than on the long-run depletion of precious natural resources or damage to the environment. (We consider the environment in Chapter 9.) Governments, like many businesses, often have a very short-run focus; they are concerned more with their political survival (whether through the ballot box or through military force) than with the long-term interests of their people.

---

[2] Prem Sikka, 'Shifting profits across borders', *The Guardian* (12 February 2009).

Pause for thought

1. *What problems is a developing country likely to experience if it adopts a policy of restricting, or even preventing, access to its markets by multinational business?*
2. *To what extent is the relationship between host state and multinational a principal–agent one? What problems arise specifically from this relationship?*

RECAP

1. Host states find multinational investment advantageous in respect to employment creation, contributions to the balance of payments, the transfer of technology and the contribution to taxation.

2. They find it disadvantageous, however, in so far as it creates uncertainty; foreign business can control or manipulate the country or regions within it; tax payments can be avoided by transfer pricing; and MNCs might misuse the environment.

QUESTIONS

1. Using the FDI database in the statistics section of the UNCTAD website (UNCTADStat: http://unctadstat.unctad.org/EN/), find out what has happened to FDI flows over the past five years (a) worldwide; (b) to and from developed countries; (c) to and from developing countries; (d) to and from the UK. Explain any patterns that emerge.

2. What are the advantages and disadvantages to an economy, such as the UK, of having a large multinational sector?

3. How might the structure of a multinational differ depending on whether its objective of being multinational is to reduce costs or to grow?

4. Choose a multinational company and then, by using its website, assess its global strategy.

5. How might a business's strategy in the domestic and global economy be affected by the onset of recession?

6. If reducing costs is so important for many multinationals, why is it that they tend to locate production not in low-cost developing economies, but in economies within the developed world?

7. 'Going global, thinking local.' Explain this phrase, and identify the potential conflicts for a business in behaving in this way.

8. Explain the link between the life cycle of a product and multinational business.

9. Assess the advantages and disadvantages facing a host state when receiving MNC investment.

Labour and employment

Business issues covered in this chapter

- How are wage rates determined in a perfect labour market?
- What are the determinants of the demand and supply of labour and their respective elasticities?
- What forms of market power exist in the labour market and what determines the power of employers and labour?
- What effects do powerful employers and trade unions have on wages and employment?
- How has the minimum wage affected business and employment?
- What is meant by a 'flexible' labour market and how has increased flexibility affected working practices, employment and wages?
- How will various incentives affect the motivation and productivity of workers?
- Should senior executives be given large bonuses and stock options?
- What is the impact on the labour market and productivity of higher education?

In this chapter we consider how labour markets affect business. In particular, we will focus on the determination of wage rates in different types of market: ones where employers are wage takers, ones where they can choose the wage rate, and ones where wage rates are determined by a process of collective bargaining.

8.1 MARKET-DETERMINED WAGE RATES AND EMPLOYMENT

The labour market has undergone substantial changes in recent years. Advances in technology, changes in the pattern of output, a need to be competitive in international markets and various social changes have all contributed to changes in work practices and in the structure and composition of the workforce. Major changes in the UK are discussed in Case Study C.13 on the book's website.

When we consider wage rates, an obvious question is why do some people earn very high wages, whereas others,

who perhaps work just as hard, if not harder, earn much less? Why, for example, do top sportsmen and women get paid so much, but, perhaps more interestingly, why do only *some* of them get paid so much? Jamie Vardy, Sergio Ramos and Vincent Kompany are great footballers and earn very high wages. But have you ever wondered why they earn so much more than Lin Dan and Domagoj Duvnjak? Probably not. They are Chinese and Croatian and are seen as world greats in badminton and handball, respectively.

Economics allows us to develop a theory that explains why the greatest ever sportsman in one discipline can be paid so little relative to merely great sportsmen in other disciplines. You can read about the salaries of footballers and the revenues and costs of their clubs on the Sloman Economics News site in the blog, 'Why is it so difficult to make a profit? The problem of players' pay in the English Premier League'.

Perfect labour markets

Before we can answer such questions, we first need to consider how wages are determined and to do this we must make a similar distinction to that made in the theory of the firm: the distinction between perfect and imperfect markets. Although in practice few labour markets are totally perfect, many do at least approximate to it.

The key assumption of a perfect labour market is that everyone is a *wage taker*. In other words, neither employers nor employees have any economic power to affect wage rates. This situation is not uncommon. Small employers are likely to have to pay the 'going wage rate' to their employees, especially where the employee is of a clear category, such as an electrician, a bar worker, a secretary or a porter. As far as employees are concerned, being a wage taker means not being a member of a union and therefore not being able to use collective bargaining to push up the wage rate.

We assume also that there is perfect knowledge on the part of workers and employers and that there are no barriers that prevent the movement of labour. Therefore, workers are aware of available jobs and can move to new jobs and different parts of the country in response to higher wages, better working conditions, better promotion opportunities, etc. Likewise, employers know the type of workers that are available, how productive they are and how motivated. Finally, it is normally assumed that workers of a given category are identical in terms of productivity.

Wage rates and employment under perfect competition are determined by the interaction of the market demand and supply of labour. This is illustrated in Figure 8.1. The curves show the total number of hours workers would supply and the number of hours of labour firms would demand for each wage rate in a particular labour market. The equilibrium market wage rate is W_e, where demand equals supply. Equilibrium employment in terms of the total number of hours people are employed in the market is Q_e.

Generally it would be expected that the supply and demand curves slope the same way as in goods markets. The higher the wage paid for a certain type of job, the more workers will want to do that job. This gives an upward-sloping supply curve of labour. On the other hand, the higher the wage that employers have to pay, the less labour

Definition

Wage taker The wage rate is determined by market forces.

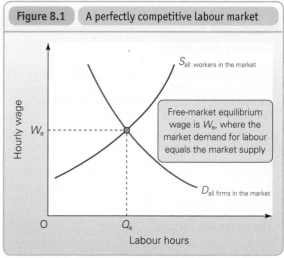

Figure 8.1 A perfectly competitive labour market

Free-market equilibrium wage is W_e, where the market demand for labour equals the market supply

they will want to employ. Either they will simply produce less output, or they will substitute other factors of production, like machinery, for labour. Thus the demand curve for labour slopes downwards.

We now turn to look at the supply and demand for labour in more detail.

The supply of labour

As we have seen, the supply of labour curve will typically be upward sloping. The *position* of the market supply curve of labour will depend on the number of people willing and able to do the job at each given wage rate. This depends on three things:

- the number of qualified people;
- the non-wage benefits or costs of the job, such as the pleasantness or otherwise of the working environment, job satisfaction or dissatisfaction, status, power, the degree of job security, holidays, perks and other fringe benefits;
- the wages and non-wage benefits in alternative jobs.

The wage rate is measured on the vertical axis, so a change in this variable will cause a movement along the supply curve. A change in any of these other three determinants will shift the whole curve.

Pause for thought

Which way will the supply curve shift if the wage rates in alternative jobs rise?

The elasticity of the market supply of labour

How *responsive* will the supply of labour be to a change in the wage rate? If the market wage rate goes up, will a lot more labour become available or only a little? It's not just a question of workers being *willing* to work, but also about them actually

---

BOX 8.1　**'TELECOMMUTERS'**

Growing flexibility

The increasing sophistication of information technology, with direct computer linking, broadband access to the Internet, mobile phones and Skype, has meant increased flexibility in the labour market.

Online recruitment agencies have developed and increasingly use social networking sites to help the matching process between workers and jobs. Use of the Internet is efficient both for workers, as there are more jobs in more industries open to them, and also for employers, as they face a greater choice of individuals and skills.

The electronic cottage

The development of the Internet has also meant that many people can now work from home. The number of these 'telecommuters' has grown steadily since the information technology revolution of the early 1980s.

According to Global Workplace Analytics, between 20 and 25 per cent of the US workforce work from home with some frequency and 3.7 million employees or 2.8 per cent of the workforce work from home at least half the time. Furthermore, there has been an increase in regular working from home since 2005 of 103 per cent, with growth of 5.6 per cent in the number of telecommuters between 2013 and 2014.[1]

In the UK, data from the ONS show that between January and March 2015, the percentage of people in employment who were working from home was 13.7 per cent, or 4.22 million of the 30.9 million people in work. This figure had increased from just 11.1 per cent in 1998.[2]

It has been found that where 'telecommuting networks' have been established, gains in productivity levels have been significant when compared with comparable office workers. Most studies indicate rises in productivity of over 35 per cent and at the same time a reduction in staff absenteeism. With fewer interruptions and less chatting with fellow workers,

less working time is lost. Add to this the stress-free environment, free from the strain of commuting, and the individual worker's performance is enhanced and workers are found to be more attentive. Evidence from China reinforces this, with a study that looked at over 12 000 workers at a Chinese travel agency and experimented by having 200 of these employees telecommute. The findings showed that those telecommuting took more calls, worked longer hours and had fewer sick days. By the end of the experiment, it was estimated that $2000 per employee would be saved every year by employees working at home and thus the option was offered to all workers across the firm.[3] In another study by O2 in Britain, the company's entire UK head office workforce (2500 people) were asked to work from home on 8 February 2012. Thirty-six per cent of them reported that they were more productive from home, with 52 per cent of the time saved commuting being spent working.[4]

With further savings in time, in the renting and maintenance of offices (often in high-cost inner city locations) and in heating and lighting costs, the economic arguments in favour of telecommuting seem very persuasive. What is more, concerns that managers lose control over their employees, and that the quality of work falls, appear unfounded. In fact the reverse seems to have occurred: the quality of work in many cases has improved.

These technological developments have been the equivalent of an increase in labour mobility. Work can be taken to the workers rather than the workers coming to the work. The effect is to reduce the premium that needs to be paid to workers in commercial centres, such as the City of London.

Then there are the broader gains to society. Telecommuting opens up the labour market to a wider group of workers who might find it difficult to leave the home – groups such as

---

[1] 'Latest telecommuting statistics', *Global Workplace Analytics* (January 2016).
[2] Update to 'Record proportion of people in employment are home workers', *Home workers rates and levels: Jan to Mar 2015*, ONS (8 April 2016).

[3] Nicholas Bloom, James Liang, John Roberts and Zhichun Jenny Ying, 'Does working from home work? Evidence from a Chinese Experiment', *CEP Discussion Paper No. 1194* (March 2013).
[4] 'O2 releases the results of the UK's biggest ever flexible working pilot', *The Blue* (3 April 2012).

---

being *able* to increase the supply of labour at the higher wage. This responsiveness (elasticity) depends on (a) the difficulties and costs of changing jobs and (b) the time period.

Another way of looking at the elasticity of supply of labour is in terms of the *mobility of labour*: the willingness and ability of labour to move to another job, whether in a different location (geographical mobility) or in a different

industry (occupational mobility). The mobility of labour (and hence the elasticity of supply of labour) will be higher when there are alternative jobs in the same location, when alternative jobs require similar skills and when people have good information about these jobs. It is also much higher in the long run, when people have the time to acquire new skills and when the education system has had time to adapt to the changing demands of industry.

Definition

Mobility of labour The ease with which labour can either shift between jobs (occupational mobility) or move to other parts of the country in search of work (geographical mobility).

The demand for labour: the marginal productivity theory

The market demand curve for labour will typically be downward sloping. To see why, let us examine the behaviour of a profit-maximising firm.

single parents and the disabled. This not only improves efficiency, as a better use is made of the full labour force, but enhances equity as well.

Also there are environmental gains, as fewer journeys to work means less traffic congestion and less pollution. The O2 study found that people spent 1000 fewer hours commuting – time that could have been spent working or in leisure – and this saved 2.2 tons of CO_2 emissions, the equivalent of some 42 000 miles of driving.

Global Workplace Analytics estimates that if those workers in the USA with jobs compatible with home working worked from home 50 per cent of the time, the total savings for the economy would be around $700 billion per year. This comprises business savings per person of $11 000; individual savings by the telecommuter of between $2000 and $7000 per year and 'greenhouse gas reduction [that] would be the equivalent of taking the entire New York State workforce permanently off the road'.[5]

Effects on workers

But do people working from home feel isolated? For many people, work is an important part of their social environment, providing them with an opportunity to meet others and to work as a team. Interestingly, in the Stanford study, only 50 per cent of those telecommuting said they would like to continue to do it, as they missed the social interactions of the office.

For those who are unable to leave the home, however, telecommuting may be the *only* means of earning a living: the choice of travelling to work may simply not be open to them. Furthermore, in the British study the telecommuters benefited from an additional 1000 hours of sleep and 14 per cent of them said that they saw more of their families.

However, telecommuters can be exploited. The Low Pay Commission has found that many homeworkers are paid well below the minimum wage because employers pay by the

amount of work done and underestimate the amount of time it takes to complete work.

International telecommuting

There is no reason, of course, why telecommuters cannot work in different countries. With the creation of transoceanic fibre-optical cable networks, international data transmission has become both faster and cheaper. Increasingly, therefore, companies in developed countries have employed relatively low-wage workers in the developing world to do data processing, telesales and various 'back-office' work – work that is often highly skilled. More than 500 multinational companies employ IT workers in Bangalore alone.

Some of the international teleworkers work in call centres; others work from their own homes. Increasingly, telecommuters in India are being provided with computers and broadband connection to enable them to do so.

> Call-centres of tomorrow will not be the ones operating from under a single roof. Instead, it will be a network of customer service agents (CSAs) working from their own homes miles away from each other . . . With all the push that the [Indian] government is giving to increase broadband penetration, this concept will trigger a revolution in the way call-centres of today operate.[6]

International telecommuting can be closer to home. Growing numbers of UK workers have moved to France or Spain, where property is much cheaper and, thanks to broadband, they can carry on their UK jobs from there. When they do have to come into the office, cheap travel by budget airlines makes that possible.

1. What effect is telecommuting likely to have on (a) trade union membership; (b) trade union power?
2. How are the developments referred to in this box likely to affect relative house prices between capital cities and the regions?

---

[5] 'Latest telecommuting statistics', *Global Workplace Analytics*.

[6] 'Telecommuting: the work-from-home option', *DQChannels of India* (18 February 2005).

The profit-maximising approach

How many workers will a profit-maximising firm want to employ? The firm will answer this question by weighing up the costs of employing extra labour against the benefits. It will use exactly the same principles as in deciding how much output to produce.

Pause for thought

What effect has the expansion of the EU, in particular the accession of the Central and Eastern European Countries (CEECs), had on the position and elasticity of the supply curve of various types of labour?

In the goods market, the firm will maximise profits where the marginal cost of an extra unit of *goods* produced equals the marginal revenue from selling it: $MC = MR$.

In the labour market, the firm will maximise profits where the marginal cost of employing an extra *worker* equals the marginal revenue that the worker's output earns for the firm: MC of labour $= MR$ of labour. To understand this, consider what would happen if they were not equal. If an extra worker adds more to a firm's revenue than to its costs, the firm's profits will increase if that extra worker is employed. But as more workers are employed, diminishing returns to labour will set in (see page 75). Each extra worker will produce less than the previous one, and thus earn less revenue for the firm. Eventually the marginal revenue from extra workers will fall to the level of their marginal cost. At that point the firm will stop employing extra workers. There are no additional profits to be gained. Profits are at a maximum.

Measuring the marginal cost and revenue of labour

Marginal cost of labour (MC$_L$). This is the extra cost of employing one more worker. Under perfect competition the firm is too small to affect the market wage. It faces a horizontal supply curve. In other words, it can employ as many workers as it chooses at the market wage rate. Thus the additional cost of employing one more person will simply be the wage rate: $MC_L = W$.

Marginal revenue of labour (MRP$_L$). The marginal revenue that the firm gains from employing one more worker is called the ***marginal revenue product of labour*** (MRP$_L$). The MRP$_L$ is found by multiplying two elements – the *marginal physical product* of labour (MPP$_L$) and the marginal revenue gained by selling one more unit of output (MR):

$$MRP_L = MPR_L \times MR$$

The MPP$_L$ is the extra output produced by the last worker. Thus if the last worker produces 100 tonnes of output per week (MPP$_L$), and if the firm can sell each unit for £2 (MR), then the worker's MRP is £200. This extra worker is adding £200 to the firm's revenue.

The profit-maximising level of employment for a firm

The MRP$_L$ curve is illustrated in Figure 8.2. As more workers are employed, there will come a point when diminishing returns set in (point *x*). Thereafter the MRP$_L$ curve slopes downwards. The figure also shows the MC$_L$ 'curve' at the current market wage W_e. Every worker is paid an identical wage and so the curve is horizontal, showing that the cost of employing each extra worker (MC$_L$) is the same, whether it is the 50th or the 500th worker.

Profits are maximised at an employment level of Q_e, where MC$_L$ (i.e. W) = MRP$_L$. Why? At levels of employment below Q_e, MRP$_L$ exceeds MC$_L$. The firm will increase profits

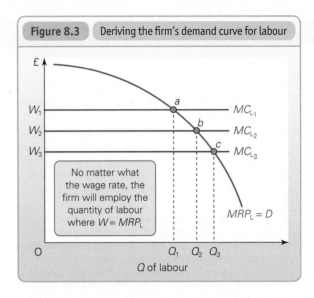

Figure 8.3 Deriving the firm's demand curve for labour

by employing more labour. At levels of employment above Q_e, MC$_L$ exceeds MRP$_L$. In this case the firm will increase profits by reducing employment.

Derivation of the firm's demand curve for labour

No matter what the wage rate is, if a firm is a profit-maximising employer of labour, the quantity of labour demanded will be found from the intersection of W (MC$_L$) and MRP$_L$ (see Figure 8.3). At a wage rate of W_1, Q_1 labour is demanded (point *a*); at W_2, Q_2 is demanded (point *b*); at W_3, Q_3 is demanded (point *c*).

Thus the MRP$_L$ curve shows the quantity of labour employed at each wage rate. But this is just what the demand curve for labour shows. Thus the MRP$_L$ curve is the demand curve for labour.

There are three determinants of the demand for labour:

- *The wage rate.* This determines the position *on* the demand curve. (Strictly speaking, we would refer here to the wage determining the 'quantity demanded' rather than the 'demand'.)
- *The productivity of labour (MPP$_L$).* This determines the position *of* the demand curve.
- *The demand for the good.* The higher the market demand for the good, the higher will be its market price, and hence the higher will be the MR, and thus the MRP$_L$. This too determines the position of the demand curve. It shows how the demand for labour (and other inputs) is a ***derived demand***, i.e. one derived from the demand for the good. For example, the higher the demand for houses, and hence the higher their price, the higher will be the demand for bricklayers.

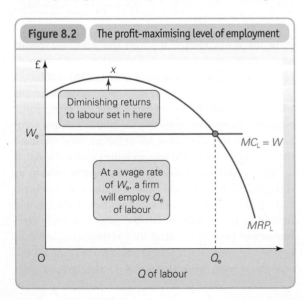

Figure 8.2 The profit-maximising level of employment

Definitions

Marginal revenue product of labour The extra revenue a firm earns from employing one more unit of labour.

Derived demand The demand for an input depends on the demand for the good that uses it.

A change in the wage rate is represented by a movement *along* the demand curve for labour. A change in the productivity of labour or in the demand for the good *shifts* the curve.

Market demand and its elasticity

For the same reason that the firm's demand for labour is downward sloping, so the whole market demand for labour will be downward sloping. At higher wage rates, firms in total will employ less labour. The *elasticity* of this market demand for labour (with respect to changes in the wage rate) depends on various factors. Elasticity will be greater:

The greater the price elasticity of demand for the good. If costs of production rise (e.g. a rise in wage rates), this will drive up the price of the good. If the market demand for the good is elastic, this rise in price will lead to a significant fall in sales and hence a bigger drop in the number of people employed.

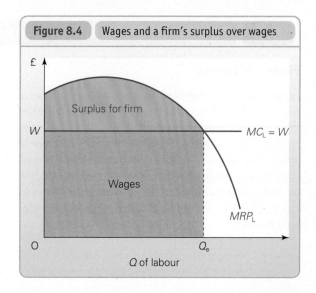

Figure 8.4 Wages and a firm's surplus over wages

Pause for thought

If the productivity of a group of workers rises by 10 per cent, will the wage rate they are paid also rise by 10 per cent? Explain why or why not.

The easier it is to substitute labour for other inputs and vice versa. If labour can be readily replaced by other inputs (e.g. machinery), then a rise in the wage rate will lead to a large reduction in labour as workers are replaced by these other inputs.

The greater the wage cost as a proportion of total costs. If wages are a large proportion of total costs and the wage rate rises, total costs will rise significantly; therefore production and sales will fall significantly, and so will the demand for labour.

The longer the time period. Given sufficient time, firms can respond to a rise in wage rates by reorganising their production processes. For example they could introduce robotic production lines.

Wages and profits under perfect competition

The wage rate (W) is determined by the interaction of demand and supply in the labour market. This will be equal to the value of the output that the last person produces (MRP_L).

Profits to the individual firm will arise from the fact that the MRP_L curve slopes downward (diminishing returns). Thus the last worker adds less to the revenue of firms than previous workers already employed.

If *all* workers in the firm receive a wage equal to the *MRP* of the *last* worker, everyone but the last worker will receive a wage *less* than their *MRP*. This excess of MRP_L over W of previous workers provides a surplus to the firm over its wages bill (see Figure 8.4). Part of this will be required for paying non-wage costs; part will be the profits for the firm.

Perfect competition between firms will ensure that profits are kept down to *normal* profits. If the surplus over wages is such that *supernormal* profits are made, new firms will enter the industry. As supply rises, the price of the good (and hence MRP_L) will fall, and as these new firms demand more labour, wages rates will be bid up, until only normal profits remain.

RECAP

1. Wages in a competitive labour market are determined by the interaction of demand and supply. The market supply of labour in any labour market is likely to be upward sloping.

2. The elasticity of labour supply will depend largely upon the geographical and occupational mobility of labour. The more readily labour can transfer between jobs and regions, the more elastic the supply of labour.

3. The demand for labour is traditionally assumed to be based upon labour's productivity. Marginal productivity theory assumes that the employer will demand labour up to the point where the cost of employing one additional worker (MC_L) is equal to the revenue earned from the output of that worker (MRP_L). The firm's demand curve for labour is its MRP_L curve.

4. The elasticity of demand for labour is determined by: the price elasticity of demand for the good that labour produces; the substitutability of labour for other factors; the proportion of wages to total costs; and time.

8.2 POWER IN THE LABOUR MARKET

Firms with power

In the real world, many firms have the power to influence wage rates: they are not wage takers. This is one of the major types of labour market 'imperfection'.

When a firm is the only employer of a particular type of labour, this situation is called a *monopsony*. Royal Mail used to be a monopsony employer of postal workers. Another example is when a factory is the only employer of certain types of labour in that district. It therefore has local monopsony power.

When there are just a few employers, this is called *oligopsony*. The big supermarkets are often considered to be oligopsonists, not because they are the only employers of a particular type of labour, but because they are the main buyers of certain products. Thus, they have significant power over farmers and other suppliers and can use that power to force down the prices they pay, thus cutting their costs.[1]

Monopsonists (and oligopsonists too) are 'wage setters', not 'wage takers'. Thus a large employer in a small town may have considerable power to resist wage increases or even to force wage rates down.

Such firms face an upward-sloping supply curve of labour. This is illustrated in Figure 8.5. If the firm wants to take on more labour, it will have to pay a higher wage rate to attract workers away from other industries. But conversely, by employing less labour it can get away with paying a lower wage rate.

The supply curve shows the wage that must be paid to attract a given quantity of labour. The wage it pays is the *average cost* to the firm of employing labour (AC_L): i.e. the cost per worker. The supply curve is also therefore the AC_L curve.

The *marginal* cost of employing one more worker (MC_L) will be above the wage (AC_L) (see Figure 8.5). The reason is that the wage rate has to be raised to attract extra workers. The MC_L will thus be the new higher wage paid to the new employee *plus* the small rise in the total wages bill for existing employees: after all, they will be paid the higher wage too.

The profit-maximising employment of labour would be at Q_1, where $MC_L = MRP_L$. The wage (found from the AC_L curve) would thus be W_1.

If this had been a perfectly competitive labour market, employment would have been at the higher level Q_2, with the wage rate at the higher level W_2, where $W = MRP_L$. What in effect the monopsonist is doing, therefore, is forcing the wage rate down by restricting the number of workers employed.

The role of trade unions

How can unions influence the determination of wages, and what might be the consequences of their actions?

The extent to which unions will succeed in pushing up wage rates depends on their power and militancy. It also depends on the power of firms to resist and on their ability to pay higher wages. In particular, the scope for unions to gain a better deal for their members depends on the sort of market in which the employers are producing.

Unions facing competitive employers

If the employers are producing in a highly competitive goods market, unions can raise wages only at the expense of employment. Firms are likely to be earning little more than normal profit. Thus if unions force up wages, the marginal firms will go bankrupt and leave the industry. Fewer workers will be employed. The fall in output will lead to higher prices. This will enable the remaining firms to pay a higher wage rate.

Figure 8.6 illustrates these effects. If unions force the wage rate up from W_1 to W_2, employment will fall from Q_1 to Q_2. There will be a surplus of people ($Q_3 - Q_2$) wishing to work in this industry for whom no jobs are available.

The union is in a doubly weak position. Not only will jobs be lost as a result of forcing up the wage rate, but also there is a danger that these unemployed people could undercut the union wage, unless the union can prevent firms employing non-unionised labour.

Definitions

Monopsony A market with a single buyer or employer.

Oligopsony A market with just a few buyers or employers.

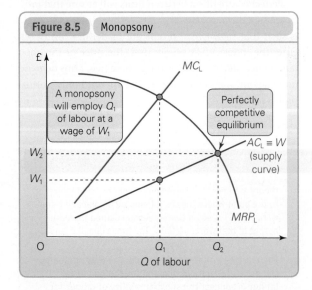

Figure 8.5 Monopsony

---

[1] Sarah Butler and Miles Brignall, 'Dairy farmers call for supermarket boycott as milk prices fall', *The Guardian* (6 August 2015).

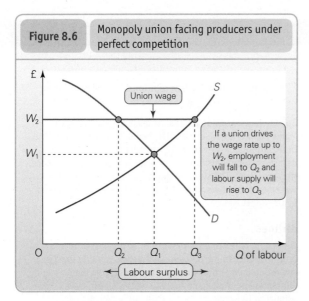

| Figure 8.6 | Monopoly union facing producers under perfect competition |

In a competitive market, then, the union is faced with the choice between wages and jobs. Its actions will depend on its objectives.

Wages can be increased without a reduction in the level of employment only if, as part of the bargain, the productivity of labour is increased. This is called a *productivity deal*. The *MRP* curve, and hence the demand curve in Figure 8.6, shifts to the right.

Pause for thought

At what wage rate in Figure 8.6 would employment be maximised: (a) W_1; (b) a wage rate above W_1; (c) a wage rate below W_1?

Bilateral monopoly

One interesting observation is that the largest and most powerful trade unions are often in industries where there are monopsonist or oligopsonist employers. In such cases, trade unions act as a countervailing power to the large employer. So, what happens when a union monopoly faces a monopsony employer? What will be the wage rate and level of employment? Unfortunately, economic theory cannot give a precise answer to these questions. There is no 'equilibrium' level as such. Ultimately, the wage rate and level of employment will depend on the relative bargaining strengths and skills of unions and management.

Strange as it may seem, unions may be in a stronger position to make substantial gains for their members when they are facing a powerful employer. There is often considerable scope for them to increase wage rates *without* this leading to a reduction in employment, or even for them to increase both the wage rate *and* employment. The reason is that if firms have power in the *goods* market too, and are making supernormal profit, then there is scope for a powerful union to redistribute some of these profits as wages.

The actual wage rate under bilateral monopoly is usually determined through a process of negotiation or 'collective bargaining'. The outcome of this bargaining will depend on a wide range of factors, which vary substantially from one industry or firm to another.

Collective bargaining

Sometimes when unions and management negotiate, *both* sides can gain from the resulting agreement. For example, the introduction of new technology may allow higher wages, improved working conditions and higher profits. Usually, however, one side's gain is the other's loss. Higher wages mean lower profits. Either way, both sides will want to gain the maximum for themselves.

The outcome of the negotiations will depend on the relative bargaining strengths of both sides. In bargaining there are various threats or promises that either side can make. For these to be effective, of course, the other side must believe that they will be carried out.

Union *threats* might include strike action, *picketing*, *working to rule* or refusing to co-operate with management, for example in the introduction of new technology. Alternatively, in return for higher wages or better working conditions, unions might *offer* no-strike agreements (or an informal promise not to take industrial action), increased productivity, reductions in the workforce or long-term deals over pay.

In response to, or in an attempt to prevent, industrial action, employers might *threaten* employees with plant closure, *lock-outs*, redundancies or the employment of non-union labour. Or they might *offer*, in return for lower wage increases, various 'perks' such as productivity bonuses, profit-sharing schemes, better working conditions, more overtime, better holidays or security of employment.

Industrial action imposes costs on both unions and firms. Unions lose pay; firms lose revenue. This is an example of a 'prisoners' dilemma game' (see pages 118–20). If played out, it will probably result in both sides losing. It is usually in both sides' interests, therefore, to settle by negotiation. Nevertheless, to gain the maximum advantage at the negotiations, each side must persuade the other that it will carry out its threats if pushed. In 1978–9, the UK experienced a period

Definitions

Productivity deal Where, in return for a wage increase, a union agrees to changes in working practices that will increase output per worker.

Picketing Where people on strike gather at the entrance to the firm and attempt to dissuade workers or delivery vehicles from entering.

Working to rule Workers do no more than they are supposed to, as set out in their job descriptions.

Lock-outs Union members are temporarily laid off until they are prepared to agree to the firm's conditions.

| BOX 8.2 | THE WINTER OF DISCONTENT |

The sequel?

In the winter of 1978/9 (dubbed the 'Winter of Discontent'), the UK economy almost ground to a halt when workers across the country went on strike. Miners, postal workers, bin-men, grave diggers, healthcare ancillaries, train and bus drivers, gas and electricity workers, lorry drivers for companies such as BP and Esso and workers at Ford all went on strike; there were even unofficial strikes by ambulance drivers. Although this occurred nearly 40 years ago, it looked as though lightning was about to strike for the second time in 2009 as the world economy plunged into a deep recession in the aftermath of the credit crunch.

There were fears that Britain was entering months of industrial unrest, as bus drivers, bin-men, airline and underground staff and firefighters followed the postal workers' lead and protested at changes to their pay, shift patterns and working conditions.

In the latter half of 2009 and early 2010, industrial action spread rapidly in the UK (and in other countries across the world). From bins to buses, and trains to planes, there was massive disruption, affecting everyone and reducing output at a vulnerable time for the country.

Postal services

Throughout 2009, members of the Communication Workers Union (CWU) held intermittent one-day strikes, and in October 2009 a national strike went ahead. The confrontation was concerned with pay, working conditions, a pension deficit and the introduction of modern efficient technology, which the CWU expected to lead to job losses and office closures. So, what were the effects?

- Post was delayed, with over 150 million undelivered letters and packets.
- Greetings cards companies had concerns that people would not send cards, affecting profitability at their busiest time.
- Households faced delays in paying bills and receiving payments.
- Businesses experienced delays in supplies, orders and customer service was affected.
- eBay traders had to delay sending packages.
- Businesses had to employ other delivery services, raising costs, cutting profits and causing lost customers.

Research by the London Chamber of Commerce suggested that the week of postal strikes cost London more than £500 million in lost business. The Chief Executive of the organisation said:

> Not being able to rely on a normal postal service forces companies to pay extra for couriers, delays consumer

spending, damages client relationships and plays havoc with a firm's cash flow.[1]

But the news was not all bad, at least not for the Royal Mail's competitors, such as TNT, Fedex and DHL. During the first 24 hours of the strike, TNT handled an extra 16 000 items, as companies looked for a substitute delivery service. However, even TNT suffered delays, as many of the bank statements and bills which they sorted were still delivered by the Royal Mail.

Airlines

While post failed to get from A to B, so did passengers, as talks with BA cabin crew over pay freezes, working practices and redundancies broke down. Strikes occurred over Christmas and then again in 2010, with those in March estimated to have cost BA approximately £45 million.[2]

The Spanish airline Iberia also experienced strikes over the renewal of contracts in 2009, which led to 400 flights being cancelled in two days, leaving thousands of passengers stranded. Pilots from India's Jet Airways held a five-day strike during September 2009, and Germany's Lufthansa had to cancel thousands of flights in early 2010, when 4000 pilots went on strike, with fears of foreign pilots being used to maintain the airline's profitability. Estimates suggest this cost the company some £21.9 million per day.

Airlines were severely hit by the recession, as holidays abroad became a luxury for cash-strapped consumers. While many airlines had other problems as well, lower revenues and profits meant that cost savings were needed, and so staff had to be cut. BA lost over £400 million in 2008, due to lower passenger numbers, and the resulting strike action imposed further costs.

The financial impact of these strikes not only included lost revenue, but the cost of hiring in planes and crew, as well as buying seats on rival carriers. The volcanic ash cloud from Iceland that grounded planes across northern Europe in April 2010 was a further blow to the airlines and cost them some £130 million per day.

Other problems

Over 800 drivers in Bolton, Bury and Wigan held numerous 24-hour strikes during 2009, because of disputes with First Bus over pay. At the same time, 1.5 million customers were affected when thousands of Underground workers went on

---

[1] Tom Sands, 'Postal strike costs London £500m', Parcel2Go.com (26 October 2009).
[2] 'BA strike: talks between airline and union resume', BBC News (7 April 2010).

---

known as 'The Winter of Discontent', when strikes took place simultaneously across a number of sectors. A blog on the Sloman Economics News site, 'The Winter of Discontent: the sequel?', considers concerns in 2009 that another bout of industrial action was about to occur (see Box 8.2).

Industrial action can also impose costs on the wider economy and society, as we have seen throughout the UK.

On the Sloman Economics News site, you will find blogs written about strikes and industrial action in posts entitled 'The Royal Mail', 'Quiet underground: busy overground', 'PCS vote to strike', 'A news blackout' and 'Turbulence in the air'.

In some cases, governments may become involved and can influence the outcome of collective bargaining, as we saw in the Winter of Discontent and also more recently in strike. Once again, these strikes cost businesses, as staff struggled to get to work, meaning lost hours, and as shoppers had problems getting to London, meaning lost sales.

Members of the National Union of Teachers and the National Association of Headteachers boycotted Sats tests in 2010, in part to 'protect their terms and conditions of employment', in particular regarding their working week and excessive workload.[3]

In Leeds, 92 per cent of refuse workers went on strike for several weeks, after refusing the council's offer relating to their working week and pay. Piles of rubbish built up, which, although not imposing direct costs on business, did adversely affect them. It was an 'external cost' imposed on consumers and business as it reduced the incentive to shop. We consider external costs in Chapter 9.

A trilogy or quadrilogy or . . .?

The 2009 strikes did not compare with The Winter of Discontent of 1978/9, but did still disrupt the lives of millions and cost the economy at a very bad time. With the election of the Coalition government and its 'austerity policies', many trade unions quickly began to mobilise. Public-sector unions were particularly vocal in response to cuts in their pay and a rise in the cost of their pensions. Further industrial action ensued, with the General Secretary of Unison saying in 2012:

> I think people have been pushed into a corner. They are moving into poverty . . . The threat is that if we can't move forward in negotiations to find a way through it then we will move to industrial action. There is no doubt whatsoever that we can create disputes throughout next year.[4]

In mid-2010, the Public and Commercial Services Union (PCS) threatened to re-launch strikes which had begun in March involving 200 000 civil servants, but which had been suspended for the election. In March 2013, the PCS voted to strike in response to job losses, changes in pensions and public-sector pay being frozen for two years for those earning above £21 000.

Further postal strikes occurred over the 2013 Easter weekend and again in the run-up to Christmas in 2014.[5] Baggage handlers at Stansted airport threatened to walk out following shift changes which could adversely affect their pay. This followed a four-day strike over the Jubilee weekend in June 2012.

Civil servants were called in to cover UK border control posts, which was the first time that the government recruited other members of the civil service to break a strike by immigration officials. Further strikes by a variety of airlines and air traffic controllers, in particular those in France, occurred throughout 2015[6] and again in 2016.[7]

In April 2016, there were strikes across the UK by junior doctors, protesting over a new contract in England. The government's plans to create a truly seven-day NHS (i.e. not just for emergencies), were proposed in 2012, but in 2014 talks had broken down, with the BMA claiming that the new contracts would make the NHS unsafe. With the help of ACAS, talks resumed in 2015, but no agreement was reached, with concerns remaining over pay and working practices. Instead, in November 2015, 98 per cent of junior doctors voted for a full strike and since then several strikes have been held.[8] With no agreement regarding the new contract, it is now due to be imposed on Junior Doctors from the summer of 2016, but legal challenges remain, both from the British Medical Association and by a campaign group, Just Health.

Despite the volume of industrial action we continue to observe, there has been growing recognition that employers and employees can learn from each other and with co-operation everyone can be made better off. However, negotiations often fail to resolve issues and industrial action, with its associated costs, results.

1. *Are strikes the best course of action for workers? In the cases outlined above, would you have advised any other responses by either side?*
2. *Which strike do you think was the most costly to (a) consumers, (b) businesses and (c) the economy? Explain.*
3. *Why might strains on public finances lead to continued industrial unrest?*

[3] Jessica Shepherd, 'Headteachers vote to boycott Sats test', *The Guardian* (16 April 2010).
[4] John Moylan, 'Trade union officials gather for TUC congress in Brighton', *BBC News* (9 September 2012).
[5] Chris Johnstone, 'Post Office workers set to stage one-day strike', *The Guardian* (6 December 2014).
[6] Simon Calder, 'French air-traffic strike: a formidable power to disrupt', *The Independent* (9 April 2015).
[7] 'Ryanair and EasyJet urge action over French strike', *BBC News* (21 March 2016).
[8] Nick Triggle, 'Junior doctors row: 98% vote in favour of strikes', *BBC News* (19 November 2015).

the junior doctors' strikes. There are also arbitration and conciliation services, which can be used to try to resolve conflicts. In the UK, the Advisory Conciliation and Arbitration Service (ACAS) conciliates in around 1000 disputes each year, roughly half of these involving pay-related issues. It also provides, on request by both sides, an arbitration service, where its findings will be binding.

The approach described so far has essentially been one of confrontation. The alternative is for both sides to concentrate on increasing the total net income of the firm by co-operating on ways to increase efficiency or the quality of the product. This approach is more likely when unions and management have built up an atmosphere of trust over time.

> **RECAP**
>
> 1. In an imperfect labour market, where a business has monopoly power in employing labour, it is known as a monopsonist. Such a firm will employ workers to the point where $MRP_L = MC_L$. Since the wage is below the MC_L, the monopsonist, other things being equal, will employ fewer workers at a lower wage than would be employed in a perfectly competitive labour market.
>
> 2. If a union has monopoly power, its power to raise wages will be limited if the employer operates in a highly competitive goods market. A rise in wage rates will force the employer to cut back on employment, unless there is a corresponding rise in productivity.
>
> 3. In a situation of bilateral monopoly (where a monopoly union faces a monopsony employer), the union may have considerable scope to raise wages above the monopsony level, without the employer wishing to reduce the level of employment. There is no unique equilibrium wage. The wage will depend on the outcome of a process of collective bargaining between union and management.

8.3 MINIMUM WAGES

Many countries have a statutory minimum wage that businesses must pay. Figure 8.7 shows the minimum wage rates in a number of countries in 2015. The red bars show real minimum hourly wage rates. These are adjusted for inflation and given in 2014 prices. They are also converted to US dollars at 'purchasing-power parity' exchange rates, which adjust the market exchange rate to reflect purchasing power: i.e. the exchange rates at which one dollar would be worth the same in purchasing power in each country. This allows more meaningful comparisons between countries. The blue bars show minimum hourly wage rates as a percentage of each country's median hourly wage rate for 2014.

Minimum wages in the UK

The UK introduced a minimum wage for adults of £3.60 in 1999. At the time, it was 47.0 and 36.8 per cent of the median and mean wage in the UK respectively.

Since then, the national minimum wage has been increased, in part because evidence indicated that the introduction of the minimum wage was having little effect on unemployment. As a result, it was raised faster than wages, to reach over 52 per cent of the median wage by 2008. By 2014, the minimum wage was 56.0 per cent of the median hourly wage for all workers and 49.4 per cent of that for

| **Figure 8.7** | Minimum hourly wages rates (2014/15) |

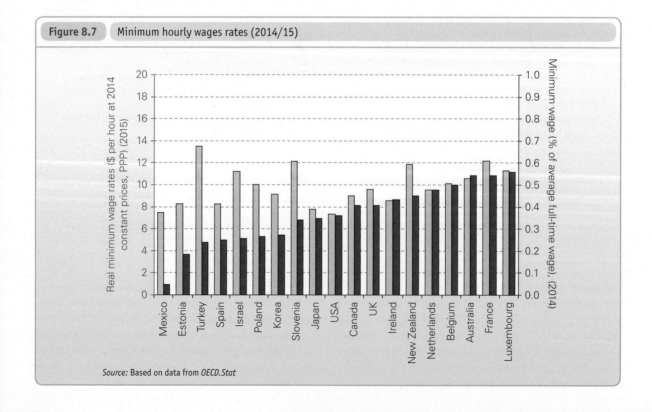

Source: Based on data from *OECD.Stat*

full-time workers. Yet many critics still argued that it was insufficient and was not a living wage.

In April 2016, the UK introduced a 'National Living Wage' (NLW) for those aged 25 and over, which was a little above the National Minimum Wage (NMW). From April 2017, the NLW is £7.50 per hour. For those aged 21–24 the NMW is £7.05; for those aged 18–20 it is £5.60 and for those aged 16–17 it is £4.05. Although the NLW is 45p above the NMW, critics argue that it does not represent a realistic 'living wage'. The NLW and NMW are adjusted annually in April. In 2016, the Living Wage Foundation suggested that workers in London required £9.75 per hour for accommodation, food and other necessities, while workers in other parts of the country needed £8.45 per hour. However, the government plans to increase the NLW each year to reach 60 per cent of the median wage of those aged 25 and over by 2020 (just under £9 in 2016 prices). You can read about the impact of the minimum wage in two articles on the Sloman Economics News site: 'An above-inflation rise in the NMW' and 'Effects of raising the minimum wage'.

This new National Living Wage has brought both praise and criticism. Some suggest that it is making significant progress towards paying workers a wage that they can live on, but others indicate that with this higher cost burden on companies, especially small ones, they will cut back on employment and there may be a negative effect on working conditions. There have been particular concerns raised about the provision of adult social care, where many care workers are paid on the minimum wage and where health and local authority budgets are stretched.

So, will paying a higher minimum wage erode profit for businesses and lead to a reduction in employment as they demand fewer workers? Supporters of a higher minimum wage argue that not only does it help to reduce poverty among the low paid, but also that it has little or no adverse effects on unemployment. Some go further. They argue that it can actually *increase* employment. Most economists argue that it depends on just how much the minimum wage is raised. Let us analyse the arguments.

Minimum wages in a competitive labour market

In a competitive labour market, workers will be hired up to the point where the marginal revenue product of labour (MRP_L), i.e. the demand for labour, is equal to the marginal cost of labour (MC_L), which gives the supply curve. The free-market equilibrium wage is W_1 in this particular industry and the level of employment is Q_1 (as shown in Figure 8.6 on page 187). A national minimum wage, set at W_2, will reduce the level of employment to Q_2 and increase the supply of labour to Q_3, thereby creating unemployment of the amount $Q_3 - Q_2$.

The level of unemployment created as a result of the national minimum wage will be determined not only by the level of the minimum wage, but also by the elasticity of labour demand and supply. The more elastic the demand and supply of labour, the bigger the unemployment effect will be. Evidence suggests that the demand for low-skilled

workers by any given employer is likely to be relatively wage sensitive. The most likely reason for this is that many of the goods or services produced by low-paid workers are very price sensitive, the firms frequently operating in very competitive markets, where there are many substitutes. If one firm alone raised its prices, to compensate for higher wage rates, it might well lose a considerable number of sales and hence reduce employment.

However, minimum wage legislation applies to *all* firms. If all the firms in an industry or sector put up their prices in response to higher wages, demand for any one firm would fall much less. Here the problem of consumers switching away from a firm's products, and hence of that firm being forced to reduce its workforce, would mainly only occur (a) if there were cheaper competitor products from abroad or (b) if other firms produced the products with more capital-intensive techniques, involving fewer workers to whom the minimum wage legislation applied.

Minimum wages and monopsony employers

In an imperfect labour market where the employer has some influence over rates of pay, the impact of the national minimum wage on levels of employment is even less clear-cut.

The situation is illustrated in Figure 8.8 (which is similar to Figure 8.5 on page 186). With no minimum wage, a monopsonistic employer will employ Q_1 workers: where the MC_L is equal to MRP_L. At this point the firm is maximising its return from the labour it employs. Remember that the MC_L curve lies above the supply of labour curve (AC_L), since the additional cost of employing one more unit of labour involves paying all existing employees the new wage. The wage rate paid by the monopsonist will be W_1.

If the minimum wage is set at W_2, the level of employment within the firm is likely to grow! Why should this be so? The reason is that the minimum wage cannot be bid down by the monopsonist cutting back on its workforce. The minimum

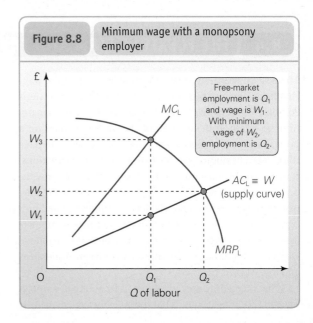

Figure 8.8 Minimum wage with a monopsony employer

Free-market employment is Q_1 and wage is W_1. With minimum wage of W_2, employment is Q_2.

wage rate is thus both the new AC_L and also the new MC_L; employers will thus choose to employ Q_2 workers, where MRP_L = (the new) MC_L. Thus the imposition of a minimum wage rate has *increased* the level of employment.

Clearly, if the minimum wage rate were very high then, other things being equal, the level of employment would fall. This would occur in Figure 8.8 if the minimum wage rate were above W_3. Employment would be below Q_1. But even this argument is not clear-cut, given that (a) a higher wage rate may increase labour productivity by improving worker motivation and (b) other firms, with which the firm might compete in the product market, will also be faced with paying the higher minimum wage rate. The resulting rise in prices is likely to shift the MRP_L curve to the right.

Pause for thought

If a rise in the minimum wage causes employers to substitute machines for workers, will this necessarily lead to higher unemployment?

On the other hand, to the extent that the imposition of a minimum wage rate reduces a firm's profits, this may lead it to cut down on investment, which may threaten long-term employment prospects.

Evidence on the effect of minimum wages

Evidence from the various countries suggests that modest increases in the minimum wage have had little effect upon employment. Employers have not responded by employing fewer workers. In the UK, after the introduction of the national minimum wage in 1999, unemployment rates actually fell up until about 2008, despite the minimum wage rising relative to both mean and median hourly wage rates. This, however, can be explained by a buoyant economy and increasing labour market flexibility (see section 8.4).

With the recession of 2009/10, however, many employers were claiming that it would be difficult to pay the minimum wage without reducing their workforce, given falling demand for their products and, in some cases, falling prices and revenue. And this would be made worse if the minimum wage were to rise substantially. Indeed, the minimum wage fell as a percentage of both median and mean hourly wage rates from 2007. The issue, then, seems to be how *high* the minimum wage can be set before unemployment begins to rise. With the significant increase in the living wage in the UK, it will be interesting to see if this has any discernible impact on unemployment. A lot will depend on the overall state of the economy and firms' profitability.

RECAP

1. Statutory minimum wage rates have been adopted in many countries.

2. In a perfect labour market, where employers are forced to accept the wage as determined by the market, any attempt to impose a minimum wage above this level will create unemployment. Amounts of additional unemployment are likely to be low, however, because the demand and supply of labour are relatively inelastic to changes in wage rates that apply to *all* firms.

3. In an imperfect labour market, where an employer has some monopsonistic power, the impact of a minimum wage is uncertain. The impact will depend largely upon how much workers are currently paid below their *MRP* and whether a higher wage encourages them to work more productively.

8.4 THE FLEXIBLE FIRM AND THE MARKET FOR LABOUR

The past 30 years have seen sweeping changes in the ways that firms organise their workforce. Three world recessions combined with rapid changes in technology have led many firms to question the wisdom of appointing workers on a permanent basis to specific jobs. Instead, they want to have the greatest flexibility possible to respond to new situations. If demand falls, they want to be able to 'shed' labour without facing large redundancy costs. If demand rises, they want rapid access to additional labour supplies. If technology changes, say with the introduction of new computerised processes, they want to have the flexibility to move workers around, or to take on new workers in some areas and lose workers in others.

What many firms seek, therefore, is flexibility in employing and allocating labour. What countries are experiencing is an increasingly flexible labour market, as workers and employment agencies respond to the new 'flexible firm'. More than half of all firms today are using flexible forms of work.

There are three main types of flexibility in the use of labour:

■ *Functional flexibility*. This is where an employer is able to transfer labour between different tasks within the production process. It contrasts with traditional forms of organisation where people were employed to do a

Definition

Functional flexibility Where employers can switch workers from job to job as requirements change.

specific job, and then stuck to it. A functionally flexible labour force will tend to be multi-skilled and relatively highly trained to enable them to move effectively between jobs, as needed.

■ *Numerical flexibility*. This is where the firm is able to adjust the size and composition of its workforce according to changing market conditions. To achieve this, the firm is likely to employ a large proportion of its labour on a part-time or casual basis, or even subcontract out specialist requirements, rather than employing such labour skills itself. Also, the changing nature of the family structure has increased the availability of part-time and casual workers, as women's participation in the workforce continues to grow.

■ *Financial flexibility*. This is where the firm has flexibility in its wage costs. In large part it is a result of functional and numerical flexibility. Financial flexibility can be achieved by rewarding individual effort and productivity rather than paying a given rate for a particular job. Such rates of pay are increasingly negotiated at the local level rather than being nationally set. The result is not only a widening of pay differentials between skilled and unskilled workers, but also growing differentials in pay between workers within the same industry but in different parts of the country.

Figure 8.9 shows how these three forms of flexibility are reflected in the organisation of a *flexible firm*, an organisation

quite different from that of the traditional firm. The most significant difference is that the labour force is segmented. The core group, drawn from the *primary labour market*, will be composed of *functionally* flexible workers, who have relatively secure employment and are generally on full-time permanent contracts. Such workers will be relatively well paid and receive wages reflecting their scarce skills.

The periphery, drawn from the *secondary labour market*, is more fragmented than the core, and can be subdivided into a first and a second peripheral group. The first peripheral group

---

Definitions

Numerical flexibility Where employers can change the size of their workforce as their labour requirements change.

Financial flexibility Where employers can vary their wage costs by changing the composition of their workforce or the terms on which workers are employed.

Flexible firm A firm that has the flexibility to respond to changing market conditions by changing the composition of its workforce.

Primary labour market The market for permanent full-time core workers.

Secondary labour market The market for peripheral workers, usually employed on a temporary or part-time basis, or a less secure 'permanent' basis.

| Figure 8.9 | The flexible firm |

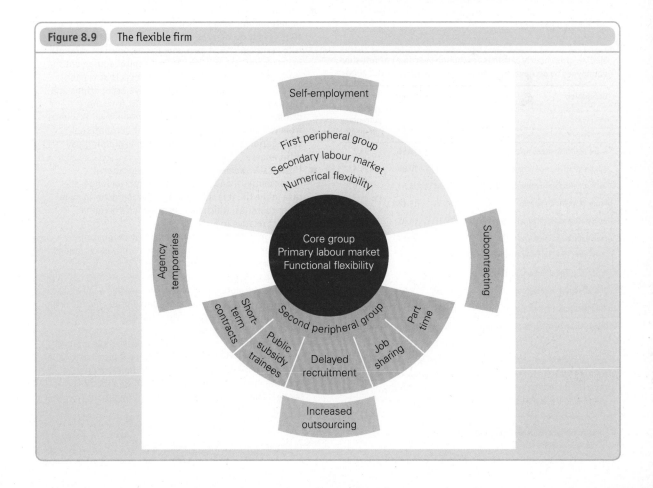

is composed of workers with a lower level of skill than those in the core, skills that tend to be general rather than firm-specific. Thus workers in the first peripheral group can usually be drawn from the external labour market. Such workers may be employed on full-time contracts, but they will generally face less secure employment than those workers in the core.

The business gains a greater level of numerical flexibility by drawing labour from the second peripheral group. Here workers are employed on a variety of short-term, part-time contracts, often through a recruitment agency. Some of these workers may be working from home, or online from another country, such as India, where wage rates are much lower. Workers in the second peripheral group have little job security.

As well as supplementing the level of labour in the first peripheral group, the second periphery can also provide high-level specialist skills that supplement the core. In this instance the business can subcontract or hire self-employed labour, minimising its commitment to such workers. The business thereby gains both functional and numerical flexibility simultaneously. An example is workers in the hotel industry, many of whom have little job security and who are on short-term or zero-hour contracts.[2]

---

[2] Margaret Deery and Leo K. Jago, 'The core and the periphery: an examination of the flexible workforce model in the hotel industry', *Centre for Hospitality and Tourism Research*, Victoria University, Melbourne (2002).

| BOX 8.3 | DOES GENDER INEQUALITY STILL EXIST? |

The pay gap between men and women

Women earn less than men in the UK and most other countries.

According to the Annual Survey of Hours and Earnings (ASHE) released by the ONS, the UK gender pay gap for median earnings of full-time employees in the UK was 9.4 per cent in 2014.[1] In other words, the median earnings for women was 9.4 per cent less than that for men. The gap has closed only slightly in recent years (e.g. it was 9.6 per cent in 2013), but this reflects a continuing downward trend: in 1970, women typically earned 37 per cent less than men and by 2000 it had fallen to 20 per cent.

Median gross hourly earnings (excluding overtime) of full-time employees by occupation, October–December 2015 (SOC 2000)

Occupation	Men	Women	Women's pay as a percentage of men's
Sales and customer services	8.99	8.60	95.7
Administrative and secretarial	11.50	10.86	94.4
Caring, leisure and other services	9.32	8.57	92.0
Professional occupations	20.70	18.42	89.0
Associate professional and technical	16.17	14.35	88.7
Elementary occupations	8.58	7.43	86.6
Managers, directors and senior officials	21.69	17.58	81.1
Process, plant and machine operatives	10.32	8.11	78.6
Skilled trades occupations	11.89	8.96	75.4
All employees	13.84	12.54	90.6

Source: Annual Survey of Hours and Earnings: 2015 Provisional Results, ONS (February 2016)

You might expect some earnings differential, as women tend to dominate the lower-paid occupations, but looking at the table, it is clear to see that even within occupations, inequality in pay still persists.

In the EU-28 as well, the gender pay gap persists, with women's gross hourly earnings being an average of 16.1 per cent below those of men. The variation of this gap between countries is significant, ranging from 2.9 per cent in Slovenia to 28.3 per cent in Estonia.[2]

Why does it persist?

- The marginal product of labour plays an important role in determining wages, as it is a key component of the *MRP*. It may be that the marginal productivity of women is lower than that of men, due to less physical strength or, more importantly, due to less capital equipment for every female worker. Evidence suggests that women tend to work in more labour-intensive occupations and thus we might expect males to benefit from more capital equipment and so be more productive. Evidence from the EU as a whole suggests that occupational segregation is a significant factor in explaining pay differences.
- Historically, women have had fewer educational opportunities than men and while this is no longer the case in the UK, it is still a highly relevant factor in many other countries, which reduces a woman's marginal product relative to a man's.
- Data suggest that women are less likely to join trade unions and tend to be in occupations with weaker unions. This means that men typically have greater bargaining power than women. Furthermore, a man's job has typically been seen as more 'important' than a woman's job and so women have tended to be less geographically mobile with more limited outside options and this acts to reduce women's bargaining power.
- Women are more likely to take breaks to have a family and to be part-time workers. Training is very costly and thus firms are often more willing to invest money in training men (who are more likely to be around for longer) than women and this pushes up men's marginal product.

---

[1] *Annual survey of hours and earnings: 2015 provisional results*, ONS (February 2016).

[2] *Gender pay gap statistics*, Eurostat (March 2016).

Pause for thought

How is the advent of flexible firms likely to alter the gender balance of employment and unemployment?

The Japanese model

The application of new flexible working patterns has become more prevalent in businesses in the UK and elsewhere in Europe and North America. In Japan, flexibility has been part of the business way of life for many years and was crucial in shaping the country's economic success in the 1970s and 1980s. In fact we now talk of a Japanese model of business organisation, which many of its competitors seek to emulate.

The model is based around four principles:

- *Total quality management (TQM).* This involves all employees working towards continuously improving all aspects of quality, both of the finished product and of methods of production.

- *Elimination of waste.* According to the 'just-in-time' (JIT) principle, businesses should take delivery of just sufficient quantities of raw materials and parts, at the right time and place. Stocks are kept to a minimum and hence the whole system of production runs with little, if any,

---

- Historically, women's pay has tended to be lower than men's and often it has little to do with differences in productivity. Equal pay legislation has had an effect, but gender discrimination in the labour market still persists.

Many of the above reasons for unequal pay might be viewed as rational, especially if they do lead to differences in marginal productivity. But what about the last point? Pure discrimination based on gender still exists. What are the effects?

Consider the wage rates set for men and women by a firm that has monopsony power and discriminates against women, despite the fact that both men and women have the same marginal productivity. By discriminating against women, the demand for women is lower than it otherwise would be. That is, the firm applies a negative discriminatory factor to the women's *MRP*, which acts to shift this curve to the left and thus pushes down their relative wage. It also reduces the number of women employed in equilibrium. This is a form of negative discrimination.

But what will happen to men's wages and the number of males employed by this firm? It might be that men's wages and the equilibrium number employed are left to be determined by their actual *MRP* and thus there is no positive discrimination. On the other hand, firms could apply economic discrimination in favour of men, thus adding a positive discriminatory factor to men's *MRP* curve (shifting it to the right), thereby pushing their wage up and employing more of them. This might have to be done if the firm requires a specific number of workers and by reducing the proportion of women (due to negative discrimination), the excess demand for workers must be made up by a relatively larger proportion of men. This positive discrimination makes the inequality between men's and women's pay and the number of workers employed even larger.

The glass ceiling

Although legislation has been passed to enforce equal pay, discrimination and prejudice still remain a concern, as does the number of women employed at the very top of the biggest

companies. In recent years, the UK government and others have taken an active role in trying to promote more women to the top jobs, such as in the boardrooms of FTSE 100 companies. The Davies Report set a target of 25 per cent of board members of FTSE 100 companies being occupied by women by 2015.[3] By March 2015, this figure had risen to 23.5 per cent, from a starting point of 12.5 per cent in 2011. Data from March 2016 show that the figure had reached 25.8 per cent.

The barriers to women being promoted to top jobs (known as the 'glass ceiling') are very difficult to legislate against. Businesses can simply claim that the 'better' person was promoted or that women do not put themselves forward. The Davies Report suggested various measures to increase the number of female board members, including discussions with company chairs on the issue, women on boards conferences, pressure from investors and requiring companies to report on their diversity policies.

Cranfield University continues to publish its Female FTSE Board report and this indicates the progress made in the UK, which now ranks as number five in Europe and the world in terms of female board membership. In 2015, a significant landmark was reached with the final all-male board, Glencore, appointing a woman and 41 of the FTSE 100 now having at least 25 per cent female board membership.[4]

There is still work to be done but, in Europe especially, the drive for greater diversity within the top boardrooms continues to gain momentum, with thoughts now turning to the diversity of women in these top roles.

1. *Drawing a diagram similar to Figure 8.5 on page 186, illustrate the effect of negative economic discrimination and positive economic discrimination.*
2. *What measures could governments introduce to increase the number of women getting the highest paid jobs?*

---

3 *Women on boards: the Davies Report*, GOV.UK (February 2011).
4 Professor Susan Vinnicombe CBE, Dr Elena Doldor, Dr Ruth Sealy, Dr Patricia Pryce, Caroline Turner, *The Female FTSE Board Report 2015*, Cranfield International Centre for Women Leaders (1 March 2015).

slack. For example, supermarkets today have smaller storerooms relative to the total shopping area than they did in the past, and take more frequent deliveries.

- *A belief in the superiority of teamwork.* Collective effort is a vital element in Japanese working practices. Teamwork is seen not only to enhance individual performance, but also to involve the individual in the running of the business and thus to create a sense of commitment.
- *Functional and numerical flexibility.* Both are seen as vital components in maintaining high levels of productivity.

The principles of this model are now widely accepted as being important in creating and maintaining a competitive business in a competitive marketplace.

Before the recession of the late 2000s, the UK had been one of the most successful countries in the EU in cutting unemployment and creating jobs. Much of this has been attributed to increased labour market flexibility. As a result, other EU countries, such as Italy and Germany, continue to seek to emulate many of the measures the UK has adopted.

RECAP

1. Changes in technology have had a massive impact upon the process of production and the experience of work. Labour markets and business organisations have become more flexible as a consequence.

2. There are three major forms of flexibility: functional, numerical and financial. The flexible firm incorporates these different forms of flexibility into its business operations.

3. It organises production around a core workforce, which it supplements with workers and skills drawn from a

periphery. Peripheral workers tend to hold general skills rather than firm-specific skills, and are employed on part-time and temporary contracts.

4. The application of the flexible firm model is closely mirrored in the practices of Japanese business. Commitments to improve quality, reduce waste, build teamwork and introduce flexible labour markets are seen as key components in the success of Japanese business organisation.

8.5 THE LABOUR MARKET AND INCENTIVES

Wages are a reward for labour. They are also, from a business perspective, a means of motivating the labour force. For example, the possibility of promotion to a post paying a higher wage can be a key incentive for employees to improve their performance. Another example is piece rates. This is where workers are paid according to the amount they produce. The more they produce, the higher their pay. Similarly a firm may pay commission to its sales force – as an incentive to sell more. Sometimes the firm will pay its senior executives bonuses related to company performance.

Because of the use of pay as a means of encouraging better performance by workers or management, firms will sometimes pay above the market rate. They pay what is known as an *efficiency wage rate*.

Efficiency wages

The *efficiency wage hypothesis* states that the productivity of workers rises as the wage rate rises. As a result, employers are frequently prepared to offer wage rates above the market-clearing level, attempting to balance increased wage costs against gains in productivity. But why may higher wage rates lead to higher productivity? There are three main explanations.

Less 'shirking'. In many jobs it is difficult to monitor the effort that individuals put into their work. In such cases

piece rates or commission may be impracticable. Workers may thus get away with shirking or careless behaviour.

The business could attempt to reduce shirking by imposing a series of sanctions, the most serious of which would be dismissal. The greater the wage rate currently received, the greater will be the cost to the individual of dismissal (the opportunity cost in terms of the salary forgone), and the less likely it is that workers will shirk. The business will benefit not only from the additional output, but also from a reduction in the costs of having to monitor workers' performance. As a consequence, the efficiency wage rate for the business will lie above the market-determined wage rate.

Reduced labour turnover. If workers receive on-the-job training or retraining, then to lose a worker once the training has been completed is a significant cost to the business, as it does not receive any of the benefits, yet incurs all of the costs. A few decades ago, workers tended to remain in the

---

Definitions

Efficiency wage rate The profit-maximising wage rate for the firm after taking into account the effects of wage rates on worker motivation, turnover and recruitment.

Efficiency wage hypothesis A hypothesis that states that a worker's productivity is linked to the wage they receive.

same job for much of their lives, but the labour market has changed, and it is now not unusual for workers to change jobs several times throughout their working life. As such, this issue of training has become more problematic. However, labour turnover, and hence its associated costs, can be reduced by paying a wage above the market-clearing rate. By paying such a wage, the business is seeking a degree of loyalty from its employees.

Morale. A simple reason for offering wage rates above the market-clearing level is to motivate the workforce – to create the feeling that the firm is a 'good' employer that cares about its employees. As a consequence, workers might be more industrious and more willing to accept the introduction of new technology (with the reorganisation that it involves).

> ### Pause for thought
>
> *Give some examples of things an employer could do to increase the morale of the workforce other than raising wages. How would you assess whether they were in the interests of the employer?*

The paying of efficiency wages above the market-clearing wage will depend upon the type of work involved. Workers who occupy skilled positions are likely to receive efficiency wages considerably above the market wage. This is especially true where the business has invested time in their training, which makes them costly to replace. By contrast, workers in unskilled positions, where shirking can be easily monitored, little training takes place and workers can be easily replaced, are unlikely to command an 'efficiency wage premium'. In such situations, rather than keeping wage rates high, the business will probably try to pay as little as possible and so the minimum wage legislation is likely to be important for such workers.

Principal–agent relationships in the labour market

The need to pay efficiency wages above the market rate is an example of the principal–agent problem (see pages 9–10). The worker, as an agent of the employer (the principal), is not necessarily going to act in the principal's interest.

At the time when people are interviewed for a job, they will clearly be keen to make a good impression on their potential employer and may promise all sorts of things. Once employed, however, a 'moral hazard' occurs (see pages 57–8) – workers will be tempted to take it easy. The principal (the firm) will therefore attempt to prevent this occurring. One solution, as we have seen, is to pay an efficiency wage. Another is to tighten up on job monitoring by managers. For example, regular performance appraisal could be instituted,

with sanctions imposed on workers who underperform. Such sanctions could range from support in the form of additional training to penalties in the form of closer monitoring, lost pay, lost bonuses or even dismissal. Another solution is to offer rewards for good performance in the form of bonuses or promotion.

In general, however, the poorer the information on the part of the principal (the greater the 'information asymmetry'), the more the employee will be able to get away with.

> ### Pause for thought
>
> *Does a moral hazard apply to employers as well as workers? If so, how might it affect employers' behaviour?*

There is also an 'adverse selection' problem for the employer (see pages 56–8). The most able workers are those most likely to leave for a better job elsewhere. The workers who elect to stay are likely to be the least able. To counter this problem, the employer might need to be willing to promote people to more senior posts to encourage them to stay.

Executive pay

There has been much resentment in recent years over the huge pay increases received by top managers, particularly since the start of the global financial crisis, as others saw their pay frozen. Up to the mid-1980s, the mean pay of US CEOs of top companies was some 30 times higher than that of production workers. By 2008, the figure had risen to 280 times. The gap then closed substantially following the financial crisis but has widened again as the US economy has recovered. By 2014, the gap had risen to over 300 per cent, with CEOs of top companies receiving an average of $16.3 million, while production workers received $53 200.

The picture is very similar in the UK, with the pay gap between CEOs and workers widening each year. Calculations from the High Pay Centre think-tank found that each year, by around the end of the second working day in January, the top CEOs in Britain have earned more than the average UK worker earns in the whole year. The data indicate that the average remuneration of CEOs of FTSE 100 companies in 2014 was £4.96 million: 182 times the earnings of the average full-time worker.[3] A report from the London School of Economics found the average pay for a UK CEO is around £1260 per hour and the increases show no sign of stopping.[4] Data from the High Pay Centre find that advertising company WPP's chief executive, Sir Martin Sorrell, was the highest paid CEO of the FTSE 100 in 2015, receiving £70.4 million in cash and shares.

---

[3] 'Fat Cat Tuesday 2016', *High Pay Centre* (4 January 2016).
[4] Cited in: Daniel Boffey, 'Pay for UK bosses is "absurdly high", top headhunters admit', *The Observer* (5 March 2016).

The nature of executive awards

For the top earners, salaries typically account for a relatively small percentage of their overall income. Incentives and bonuses often considerably outstrip basic salaries and it is increases in these aspects that has led to such significant increases in executive pay.

Although incentives and bonuses still take up around 74 per cent of an executive's total pay in the UK, this share has fallen slightly. Furthermore, in the UK between 2013 and 2014, the percentage of firms offering some form of payment through shares decreased from 86 per cent to 75 per cent. This effect echoes that in continental Europe, where that percentage has fallen from 45 per cent in 2007 to just 23 per cent in 2014.

Incentives are normally related to company performance, such as profit or turnover (revenue). Bonuses, however, are given retrospectively and are often unrelated to performance. They are often given even when the company is underperforming. One such example is BP, whose Chief Executive, Bob Dudley, received a 20 per cent pay rise to £13.9 million in 2016, despite the company's performance moving from a profit of $8.1 billion to a record loss of $5.2 billion and its share price falling by almost one-quarter over the year to 2016. On 14 April 2016, BP Chairman, Carl-Henric Svanberg, attempted to justify the pay of its Chief Executive saying:

> We have always judged executive performance not on the price of oil or bottom line profit but on measures that are clearly within management's control. And, from that perspective, the board has concluded that it has been an outstanding year. The pay reflects this.[5]

Despite the justification for the high pay even with such poor performance, this led to the biggest shareholder revolt in UK corporate history.

Shares and *share options* are an important part of many remuneration packages for top executives. These are normally given as a longer-term incentive. In the case of shares, these must be held for a period of time (say three years) before they can be cashed in. In the case of share options, the option is for the executive to buy shares at a price set when the option is granted, even though the current mar-

ket price might be considerably higher. The argument is that both shares and share options give the executive an incentive to ensure that the company performs well and its share price rises as a result. This can go some way to reducing the problem of moral hazard.

In recent years, bankers' bonuses have seen huge news coverage. In February 2010, Eric Daniels, the Chief Executive of Lloyds Banking Group was to be awarded a £2.3 million bonus, despite the bank making losses of some £7 billion. This bonus was turned down. However, in 2013, the new CEO appointed in March 2011, António Horta-Osório, was awarded a £1.5 million bonus for 2012, despite losses of £570 million – partly the result of having to compensate customers for the mis-selling of payment protection insurance (PPI). Bonuses across Lloyds Banking Group totalled £365 million, which was a fall of 3 per cent relative to those received in 2011. In 2014, following the bank's return to profit, António Horta-Osório's pay increased by more than 50 per cent.

The banking crisis was a prime example of executives receiving large bonuses, even when the company did badly. The argument is that the bonuses are used as an incentive to ensure that the best talent is attracted and remains at the company. There was, unsurprisingly, a significant public outcry against what were seen as totally undeserved rewards.

The years of such excessive bonuses and the public's response prompted action by the European Commission. From 1 January 2017, bankers' bonuses in the EU are capped at 100 per cent of annual salary. This can be increased to 200 per cent if 65 per cent of shareholders agree.

Furthermore, shareholders are able to oppose executive pay policy at the Annual General Meetings of the company. However, according to the High Pay Centre, across the FTSE 100, the average vote against pay awards was just 6.4 per cent.

Incentive effects?

So do these huge increases represent the necessary incentives and rewards for those leading industrial growth and taking risks? Or are they the result of market imperfections, where greedy executives can persuade complicit company boards of directors to give them what they want? Are they a sign of poor governance of industry and thus is the EU cap likely to have a positive effect?

> Extraordinary pay for great performance is fine, it is routinely said. But many executives have been paid a fortune for presiding over mediocrity. The Corporate Library, an American corporate-governance consultancy, last year [2006] identified 11 large and well known but poorly governed companies, including AT&T, Merck and Time Warner, where the chief executive had been paid at least $15m a year for two successive years even as the company's shares had underperformed. Robert Nardelli received a $210m pay-off when he lost his job earlier this month even though the shares of his company, Home Depot, fell slightly during his six years in charge. Carly

---

Definition

Share (or stock) options The right to buy shares in the future at a fixed price set today. When granted to senior executives as a reward they do not involve any outlay by the company. They act as an incentive, however, since the better the company performs, the more the market value of its shares is likely to rise above the option price and the more the executive stands to gain by exercising the option to buy shares at the fixed price and then sell them at the market price.

---

[5] *BBC 10 o'clock News* (14 April 2016).

BOX 8.4 EDUCATION, EARNINGS, PRODUCTIVITY AND TALENT

The return on a degree

Every year of education adds to an individual's human capital, but does an increase in that human capital actually cause an increase in productivity and, in turn, contribute towards the growth of the economy? There are two conflicting theories.

The human capital model suggests that education is causally related to higher productivity and hence to economic growth. Education is therefore an investment, which will not only boost individual earnings, but also create economic growth.

The signalling or screening hypothesis, however, sees education beyond a certain level not as a means of boosting productivity and growth, but as a filter – a means of signalling to employers who is the best person for the job. While there is a consensus that a basic level of education is essential for productivity and growth within a nation, there is less agreement about the role of higher education. So, why go to university?

According to the human capital model, a university degree boosts productivity and hence *MPP* and *MRP*, and by shifting the *MRP* curve to the right, with an upward-sloping supply of labour curve, it will push up the equilibrium wage rate.

There is significant evidence to support the higher lifetime earnings for individuals from obtaining a university degree.

In 2013, the Department for Business Innovation and Skills (BIS) found that the additional lifetime earnings from a degree, over not having a degree, were 28 per cent for men (or £168 000) and 53 per cent for women (or £252 000). Moreover, a 'good' degree was found to have further returns of £76 000 and £85 000 relative to a lower class degree for men and women respectively.[1]

A large-scale study by the IFS[2] published in April 2016, which looked at data from 2012/13, found that:

- Non-graduates are twice as likely to have no earnings as are graduates 10 years on, for all degree subjects and both genders.
- Half of non-graduate women had annual earnings below £8000 at age 30, whereas only a quarter of female graduates were earning less than this.
- Ten years after graduation, median earnings for males and females were £30 000 and £27 000, respectively. For non-graduates of the same age, median earnings were £22 000 and £18 000, respectively. (You might like to relate this to Box 8.3 when we considered the gender pay gap.)

One of the authors of this paper, Anna Vignoles said:

The research illustrates strongly that for most graduates, higher education leads to much better earnings than those earned by non-graduates, although students need to realise that their subject choice is important in determining how much of an earnings advantage they will have.

In terms of the subject studied, rates of return vary significantly. The IFS study found that in some subjects graduates earned no more on average than non-graduates, in particular those studying the Creative Arts. However, in other subjects such as Economics, Business, Medicine and Law, the median earnings in 2012/13 (10 years after graduation) were significantly higher than those for non-graduates. In particular, for Economics graduates, median earnings were second only to graduates in Medicine. And at the 90th percentile, Economics graduates had the highest earnings (£93 000 for women and £121 400 for men) of any subject by a significant margin. Medicine graduates at this percentile were the second highest earners, with women earning £68 000 and men £84 700 – though again here note the gender inequality for both subjects (see chart on page 200).

A report from Payscale looked at US data. It showed that back in 1972 graduates typically earned 20 per cent more than non-graduates. Since then this figure has increased to 70 per cent.[3]

The UK's productivity gap

Despite a higher education participation rate of 47 per cent for 2013/14 and a consistent participation rate above 40 per cent over the previous 10 years, the UK's productivity gap continues to lag behind other nations. The productivity gap measures differences in output per worker across nations, and data from the ONS[4] shows that the UK lags behind other members of the G7 and that the productivity gap has grown to its biggest level since 1991. Output per hour worked in the UK in 2014 was 18 percentage points below the average for the remaining six G7 nations, 30 percentage points below the USA and 36 percentage points below Germany (two percentage points more than in 2013). Part of the decline in UK productivity was due to the recession and the fact that the UK's productivity did not recover as fast as other Western nations, especially in manufacturing.

You might think that with so many students entering higher education, the UK would be a highly productive economy, but more important than the total number of students entering higher education, is the subjects they are studying and whether the economy itself is creating enough productive jobs. One of the causes of this productivity gap has been the creation of too many low-skilled and low-paid jobs, where productivity is at its lowest. According to data from the Chartered Institute of Personnel and Development, 58.8 per cent of graduates are taking jobs that are typically deemed as being non-graduate jobs.

Furthermore, criticism has been placed on consecutive governments for a lack of investment, too few innovations and ongoing problems of finance. In 2015 the then Chancellor, George Osborne, announced steps to address these issues, promising more long-term investment in infrastructure and the creation of better incentives for businesses. However, *The Government's Productivity Plan* was criticised for lacking clear goals and simply re-using existing government policies. The TUC General Secretary, Frances O'Grady said:

---

[1] 'The impact of university degrees on the lifecycle of earnings: some further analysis', *BIS Research Paper No. 112*, BIS (August 2013).
[2] 'What and where you study matter for graduate earnings – but so does parents' income', *IFS Press Release* (13 April 2016).

[3] Donald Armbrecht, 'Which degrees give the best financial return?', *World Economic Forum* (11 January 2016).
[4] 'Labour productivity: Oct to Dec 2015', *Statistical Bulletin*, ONS (7 April 2016).

▶

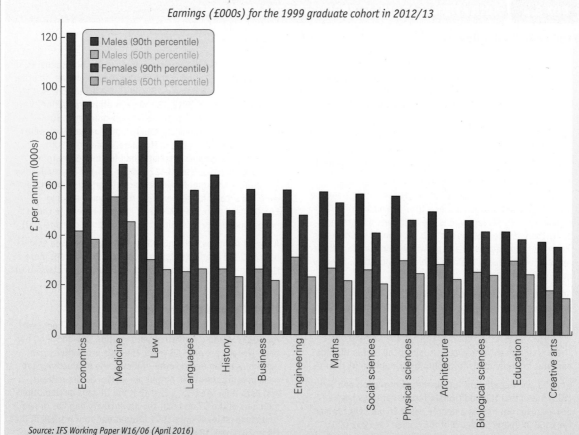

Earnings (£000s) for the 1999 graduate cohort in 2012/13

Legend:
- Males (90th percentile)
- Males (50th percentile)
- Females (90th percentile)
- Females (50th percentile)

£ per annum (000s)

Categories: Economics, Medicine, Law, Languages, History, Business, Engineering, Maths, Social sciences, Physical sciences, Architecture, Biological sciences, Education, Creative arts

Source: IFS Working Paper W16/06 (April 2016)

For all the good news on rising employment, the UK is still not creating enough quality jobs. The yawning productivity gap between us and other countries shows how much room there is for us to do better. The loss of middle-income jobs, in vital industries like steel, is holding the economy back and dragging down pay.[5]

[5] 'Productivity gap shows the UK needs to create more quality jobs, says TUC', *TUC* (18 February 2016).

The talent gap

Is part of the UK's productivity problem a result of the most talented graduates leaving the country, thus creating a talent gap? In the 2013 Global CEO Survey,[6] this was identified as a major concern and continues to be a key factor affecting many of the large companies.

[6] 'Dealing with disruption: adapting to survive and thrive', *16th Annual Global CEO Survey*, PwC (January 2013).

Fiorina, ejected from Hewlett-Packard almost $180m better off – including a severance payment of $21.6m – after a lacklustre tenure as chief executive, let it be known in her autobiography that money was not important to her. Not everyone believed her.[6]

As far as genuine incentive schemes are concerned, they may indeed encourage risk-taking and good performance. High remuneration may be necessary in some cases to attract the right talent and persuade them to stay. Generous bonuses for executives of poorly performing companies, however, clearly have the opposite effect – as do generous severance packages for executives leaving early.

Then there are the incentives for workers. If they feel that their senior managers' pay is unjustified, this can breed resentment and harm industrial relations.

Ultimately, businesses function with the blessing of workers, shareholders, customers and voters. If business leaders are universally seen as immoral and grasping, cynicism and mistrust will flourish and choke enterprise.[7]

An article from the Financial Times[8] provides some interesting insights on high pay and the extent to which changes in salary actually affect performance.

[7] Ibid.

[8] Andrew Hill, 'Bonuses are bad for bankers and even worse for banks', *Financial Times* (25 January 2016).

[6] 'In the money', *The Economist* (18 January 2007).

But it is not just in the UK where the talent gap is a cause for concern. With a declining working-age population, the talent pool is shrinking and concerns over a lack of talent in certain key industries, including IT and engineering, continues to grow. The former is of particular concern with cyber-crime increasing, and the UK's Cyber Security Strategy has identified this gap in skills as a 'key challenge'. A report states that:

> According to the government, the number of ICT and cybersecurity professionals in the UK has not increased in line with the growth of the Internet. This shortage of ICT skills hampers the UK's ability to protect itself in cyberspace and promote the use of the Internet both now and in the future.[7]

In the 2015 Talent Shortage Survey[8] by the ManPower Group, which covered 42 countries, 38 per cent of employers reported being unable to find the necessary talent they needed and that this was preventing them from meeting their business goals and client needs. Across the EU, the most common reason for the talent shortage is a lack of candidates with the necessary technical competencies. Other factors causing this problem include a lack of candidates with industry-specific professional qualifications or relevant skilled trades certifications, a lack of candidates in the job market and a shortage of candidates with relevant experience. According to the ManPower report:

> Developing the capabilities of existing staff, seeking out new recruitment channels and tapping into different labour pools are the most widely-used strategies for addressing talent shortages at the global level in 2015.

However, it was also found that companies themselves were not doing enough to address the talent shortages. The 19th Annual Global CEO Survey[9] finds that, despite companies understanding the importance of having the right talent, only 30 per cent of CEOs are changing their focus on skills and adaptability in their employees and only 4 per cent of CEOs are looking to change how they use technology to improve productivity through their use of workforce analytics.

A final concern for companies is not just about getting the right talent, but being able to keep it. One problem is that talented staff may be very ambitious and are likely to be more concerned with their own careers than the long-term interests of their employers. There is a 'moral hazard' here (see pages 57–8). The firm may invest a lot of time and expense in training talented workers, only to see them leave for another job. In other words, employing a person does not guarantee a commitment on their part to stay. Such people are often sought out by other companies, which may use 'head-hunting' agencies to find and recruit them. A job for life is no longer the norm and this can deter firms from providing sufficient training to their workers.

1. Draw a diagram showing the possible impact of a university education on an individual's earnings.
2. Do you think there is a problem of allocative efficiency with regards to the UK's productivity gap? Could online recruitment agencies help?
3. How would you attempt to measure the marginal productivity of a person hired for a specific talent?
4. Why might companies be wise to pay talented people more than the value of their marginal product?

---

[7] Jo Best, 'Skills shortage threatening UK cybersecurity "could last for 20 years"', *ZDNet* (12 February 2013).

[8] *2015 Talent Shortage Survey*, ManPower Group (May 2015).

[9] 'Redefining business success in a changing world', *19th Annual Global CEO Survey*, PwC (January 2016).

RECAP

1. The efficiency wage hypothesis states that a business is likely to pay a wage above the market-clearing rate in order to: reduce shirking; reduce labour turnover; and stimulate worker morale.

2. Employment is an example of a principal–agent relationship. Workers (the agents) may underperform as a result of lack of information on their performance by their employer (the principal). To combat this problem, employers may link pay more closely with output or monitor the performance of workers more closely.

3. Executive pay has risen much more rapidly than average pay. In addition to high salaries, many senior managers receive considerable bonuses, shares, share options and other perks. High pay may be necessary to act as an incentive for risk taking and to attract high calibre people. It is also often, however, a reflection of poor governance at the top of industry and in many cases is unrelated to performance.

QUESTIONS

1. If a firm faces a shortage of workers with very specific skills, it may decide to undertake the necessary training itself. If on the other hand it faces a shortage of unskilled workers it may well offer a small wage increase in order to obtain the extra labour. In the first case it is responding to an increase in demand for labour by attempting to shift the supply curve. In the second case it is merely allowing a movement along the supply curve. Use a demand and supply diagram to illustrate each case. Given that elasticity of supply is different in each case, do you think that these are the best policies for the firm to follow?

2. The wage rate a firm has to pay and the output it can produce varies with the number of workers as follows (all figures are hourly):

Number of workers	1	2	3	4	5	6	7	8
Wage rate (AC_L) (£)	3	4	5	6	7	8	9	10
Total output (TPP_L)	10	22	32	40	46	50	52	52

   Assume that output sells at £2 per unit.

   (a) Copy the table and add additional rows for TC_L, MC_L, TRP_L and MRP_L. Put the figures for MC_L and MRP_L in the spaces between the columns.
   (b) How many workers will the firm employ in order to maximise profits?
   (c) What will be its hourly wage bill at this level of employment?
   (d) How much hourly revenue will it earn at this level of employment?
   (e) Assuming that the firm faces other (fixed) costs of £30 per hour, how much hourly profit will it make?
   (f) Assume that the workers now form a union and that the firm agrees to pay the negotiated wage rate to all employees. What is the maximum to which the hourly wage rate could rise without causing the firm to try to reduce employment below that in (b) above? (See Figures 8.5 and 8.8.)
   (g) What would be the firm's hourly profit now?

3. For what types of reason does the marginal revenue product differ between workers in different jobs?

4. If, unlike a perfectly competitive employer, a monopsonist has to pay a higher wage to attract more workers, why, other things being equal, will a monopsonist pay a lower wage than a perfectly competitive employer?

5. The following are figures for a monopsonist employer:

Number of workers (1)	Wage rate (£)(2)	Total cost of labour (£)(3)	Marginal cost of labour (£)(4)	Marginal revenue product (£)(5)
1	100	100		
			110	230
2	105	210		
			120	240
3	110	230		
				240
4	115			
				230
5	120			
				210
6	125			
				190
7	130			
				170
8	135			
				150
9	140			
				130
10	145			

   Fill in the missing figures for columns (3) and (4). How many workers should the firm employ if it wishes to maximise profits?

6. To what extent could a trade union succeed in gaining a pay increase from an employer with no loss in employment?

7. Drawing on recent examples, consider the extent to which strike action is likely to help trade union members achieve their various aims.

8. Do any of the following contradict the theory that the demand for labour equals the marginal revenue product: wage scales related to length of service (incremental scales), nationally negotiated wage rates, discrimination, firms taking the lead from other firms in determining this year's pay increase?

9. What is the efficiency wage hypothesis? Explain what employers might gain from paying wages above the market-clearing level.

10. 'Statutory minimum wages will cause unemployment.' Is this so?

11. Identify the potential costs and benefits of the flexible firm to (a) employers and (b) employees.

12. How have changes in society, laws and technology affected the UK labour market?

13. Provide a case for and against high bonuses.

9 Chapter

Government, the firm and the market

Business issues covered in this chapter

- To what extent does business meet the interests of consumers and society in general?
- In what sense are perfect markets 'socially efficient' and why do most markets fail to achieve social efficiency?
- How do business ethics influence business behaviour?
- Is it in a business' interest to operate in a socially responsible manner?
- In what ways do governments intervene in markets and attempt to influence business behaviour?
- What forms do government environmental policies take, and how do they affect business?
- How does the government attempt to prevent both the abuse of monopoly power and collusion by oligopolists?
- How are privatised industries regulated and how has competition been increased in these industries?

Despite the fact that most countries today can be classified as 'market economies', governments nevertheless intervene substantially in the activities of business in order to protect the interests of consumers, workers or the environment.

Firms might collude to fix prices, use misleading advertising, create pollution, produce unsafe products, or use unacceptable employment practices. In such cases, government is expected to intervene to correct for the failings of the market system, e.g. by outlawing collusion, by establishing advertising standards, by taxing or otherwise penalising polluting firms, by imposing safety standards on firms' behaviour and products, or by protecting employment rights.

In this chapter we examine the ways in which markets might fail to protect people's interests, whether as consumers or simply as members of society. We also look at the different types of policy the government can adopt to correct these 'market failures'.

9.1 MARKET FAILURES

Markets and social objectives

One of the key arguments for government intervention in the behaviour of business is that, if left to its own devices, the private enterprise system will fail to achieve 'social efficiency'.

So what is meant by social efficiency? If the extra benefits to society – or *marginal social benefit* (*MSB*) – of producing more of any given good or service exceed the extra costs to society – or *marginal social cost* (*MSC*) – then it is said to be socially efficient to produce more. For example, if people's gains from having additional motorways exceed *all* the additional costs to society (both financial and non-financial) then it is socially efficient to construct more motorways.

If, however, the marginal social cost of producing more of any good or service exceeds the marginal social benefit, then it is socially efficient to produce less.

It follows that if the marginal social benefit of any activity is equal to the marginal social cost, then the current level is the optimum. To summarise, for *social efficiency* in the production of any good or service:

$MSB > MSC \rightarrow$ produce more
$MSB < MSC \rightarrow$ produce less
$MSB = MSC \rightarrow$ keep production at its current level

Similar rules apply to consumption. For example, if the marginal social benefit of consuming more of any good or service exceeds the marginal social cost, then society would benefit from more of the good being consumed.

 Social efficiency. This is achieved where no further net social gain can be made by producing more or less of a good. This will occur where marginal social benefit equals marginal social cost.

In the real world, the market rarely leads to social efficiency: the marginal social benefits from the production of most goods and services do not equal the marginal social costs. It is this failure of the market to allocate resources efficiently which gives governments the justification to intervene. In this section we examine why the free market fails to lead to social efficiency and what the government can do to rectify the situation.

Types of market failure

Externalities

Sometimes when businesses make production decisions, it is not just the firm and its consumers that are affected. For example, there may be impacts on the environment. Similarly, when we make consumption decisions, we can affect people other than ourselves.

These effects on other people, whether by firms or individuals are called *externalities*; they are the side effects or 'third-party' effects of production or consumption and can be either desirable or undesirable. Whenever other people are affected beneficially, there are said to be *external benefits*. Whenever other people are affected adversely, there are said to be *external costs*. If such externalities exist, the free market will not lead to social efficiency. (See, for example, the article 'Deforestation, soil erosion and chemical runoff sometimes the result of farming' from AG Week,[1] which looks at some of the externalities that arise from farming.)

In our analysis so far in this book, we have assumed there are no externalities and hence the costs and benefits to society are the same as the costs and benefits to the individual consumer or producer. However, when we introduce externalities, we now have to consider:

■ The *social cost*: comprised of the private cost faced by the firm(s) from the production of any good or service plus any externalities of production (positive or negative).

■ The *social benefit*: comprised of the private benefits enjoyed by consumers from the consumption of any good or service, plus any externalities of consumption (positive or negative).

 Externalities are spillover costs or benefits. Where these exist, even an otherwise perfect market will fail to achieve social efficiency.

Definitions

Marginal social benefit (*MSB*) The additional benefit gained by society of producing or consuming one more unit of a good.

Marginal social cost (*MSC*) The additional cost incurred by society of producing or consuming one more unit of a good.

Social efficiency Production and consumption at the point where $MSB = MSC$.

Externalities Costs or benefits of production or consumption experienced by society but not by the producers or consumers themselves. Sometimes referred to as 'spillover' or 'third-party' costs or benefits.

External benefits Benefits from production (or consumption) experienced by people other than the producer (or consumer).

External costs Costs of production (or consumption) borne by people other than the producer (or consumer).

Social cost Private cost plus externalities in production.

Social benefit Private benefit plus externalities in consumption.

---

[1] Harwood D. Schafer and Daryll E. Ray, 'Deforestation, soil erosion and chemical runoff sometimes the result of farming', *Agweek* (21 March 2016).

There are four different types of externality: (i) negative externalities in production; (ii) positive externalities in production; (iii) negative externalities in consumption and (iv) positive externalities in consumption.

When we think about externalities in production, we are considering a producer which imposes either costs or benefits on other parties and so in these cases there is a difference between the *marginal private cost to the producer* and the *marginal social cost* of production. If we have externalities in consumption, then a consumer imposes either costs or benefits on other parties and here we see a difference between the *marginal private benefit to the consumer* and the *marginal social benefit*.

Let's consider the first case above where a firm imposes an *external cost* during the production process. For simplicity, we assume that there are no externalities in consumption and that the firm is perfectly competitive and so it faces a horizontal demand curve (see section 4.4 on page 92).

External costs produced by business. Consider a chemical firm that dumps waste in a river or pollutes the air. Assuming this firm wants to maximise profits, it will produce where its marginal costs equals its marginal revenue (or price) at Q_1 in Figure 9.1. The market price (P) is what people buying the good are prepared to pay for one more unit of it (this is the marginal utility as we saw on pages 52–3) and it therefore reflects their *marginal private benefit* (*MPB*). As we have assumed no externalities from consumption, the marginal *private* benefit to consumers is the same as the marginal *social* benefit (*MSB*).

However, when the firm decides how much to produce, it considers the costs *it* incurs from producing an extra unit (e.g. raw materials, labour, etc.) and hence only considers its *marginal private costs* (*MPC*). But, in this case, when the firm produces each additional unit of output, the community bears additional costs, such as noise or air pollution and

these are the *external costs* (i.e. the *negative externality*). To find the marginal *social* cost we need to add together the marginal private and external costs. In this case, the marginal social cost (*MSC*) of chemical production exceeds the marginal private cost (*MC*): the difference is the *marginal external cost*. Diagrammatically, the *MSC* curve is above the *MC* curve. This is shown in Figure 9.1.

The socially optimum output would be Q_2, where P (i.e. *MSB*) = *MSC*. The firm, however, produces Q_1, as it is only concerned with the costs *it* incurs by producing. This output, however, is more than the optimum. Thus external costs lead to *overproduction* from society's point of view.

The problem of external costs arises in a free market economy because no one has legal ownership of the air or rivers and no one, therefore, can prevent or charge for their use as a dump for waste. Such a 'market' is missing. Control must, therefore, be left to the government or local authorities.

Other examples of firms producing external costs include extensive farming that destroys hedgerows and wildlife, acid rain caused by smoke from coal-fired power stations, nuclear waste from nuclear power stations and global warming from carbon emissions. In all of these cases, society bears some of the costs of production, but profit-maximising firms only consider their *private costs* and hence too much is produced. This means that the free market fails to lead to a socially efficient allocation of resources.

Other examples of externalities. Sometimes firms' actions *benefit* people other than consumers. An example is research and development. If other firms have access to the results of the research, then clearly the benefits extend beyond the firm that finances it. However, since the firm only receives the private benefits, it will conduct less than the optimal amount of research. What is the point in a firm conducting further research if many of the benefits simply go to other firms? Similarly, a forestry company planting new woodlands will not take into account the beneficial effect on the atmosphere, and hence it will plant less than the socially optimal number of trees.

Externalities occur in consumption too. For example, when people use their cars, other people suffer from their exhaust fumes, the added congestion, the noise, etc. These 'negative externalities' make the marginal social benefit of using cars less than the marginal private benefit (i.e. marginal utility to the car user). Other examples of negative externalities of consumption include noisy radios in public places, the smoke from cigarettes, and litter. The individuals doing these things have little incentive to consider the negative effects on others. A negative externality in consumption thus leads to over-consumption of the good or service and hence the free market fails to provide a socially optimal level of consumption.

Consumption externalities could be positive. For example, when people travel by train rather than by car, other people benefit from less congestion and exhaust fumes and fewer accidents on the roads. Thus the marginal social

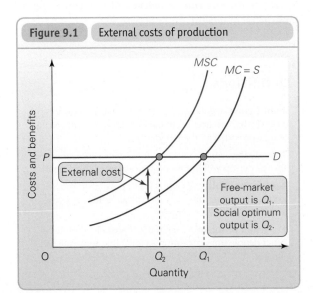

Figure 9.1 External costs of production

Costs and benefits

MSC

MC = S

P — — — *D*

External cost

Free-market output is Q_1.
Social optimum output is Q_2.

O Q_2 Q_1

Quantity

benefit of rail travel is greater than the marginal private benefit (i.e. the marginal utility to the rail passenger). Other examples of positive externalities of consumption include deodorants, vaccinations and attractive gardens in front of people's houses. For example, if one person is vaccinated against a disease, it not only benefits them, but also benefits others, who can no longer catch the disease from that person. In such cases, by not taking into account the effect on others, too little will be consumed.

To summarise, whenever there are external costs, there will be too much produced or consumed. Whenever there are external benefits, there will be too little produced or consumed. The market will not equate *MSB* and *MSC* and so it fails to provide the socially optimum level of output.

> ### Pause for thought
>
> *Give other examples of each of the four types of externality (external costs and benefits in both production and consumption). In each case, draw a diagram showing the difference between the marginal social and private cost and benefit curves.*

Public goods

There is a category of goods where the positive externalities are so great that the free market, whether perfect or imperfect, may not produce at all. They are called *public goods*. Examples include pavements, flood control dams, public drainage, public services such as the police and even government itself.

Public goods have two important characteristics: *non-rivalry* and *non-excludability*.

Non-rivalry. Rivalry occurs when one person's consumption of a good reduces the amount of it available for others. For example, if I consume a bar of chocolate, every chunk I eat reduces the amount of the chocolate bar left for you.

If, however, a good is perfectly *non-rivalrous*, then as I increase my consumption of the product, it has no impact on the ability of you or a 'rival' consumer to 'consume' the good. For example, imagine that you go outside and find that your neighbour is letting off fireworks. Your decision to watch (and enjoy) the fireworks does not reduce the amount of fireworks left for them to watch. The firework display is non-rivalrous – at least up to the point where people start getting in each other's way (as we shall see below).

> ### Pause for thought
>
> *Given our definition of public goods, can you now define a private good?*

In reality, many goods and services will be neither perfectly rivalrous nor non-rivalrous. In particular, a good may be non-rivalrous to begin with, but as additional people consume it (or the size of the population, N, gets bigger), rivalry may become a problem, due to the 'crowding effect'. You and a friend may be able to watch a video on your mobile phone, but if more and more people try to watch it with you, eventually crowding will become a problem, with some people prevented from seeing the video. There is now rivalry in consumption. The level of N at which crowding occurs will vary depending on the good or service in question. It may only take three or four people watching a mobile phone video on the same phone for this 'good' to become rivalrous, but there may have to be thousands or even millions of people watching a fireworks display before that 'good' becomes rivalrous in consumption.

Non-excludability. Excludability occurs when the supplier of a good can restrict who consumes it, usually by charging a price. Only those consumers who are prepared to pay that price will be able to have the good. For those goods already in the hands of consumers, excludability occurs when they can prevent other people benefiting too. In some cases, it is very easy to prevent people who have not purchased the good from benefiting from it – for example, goods consumed in your own home

However, there are some goods and services for which it is either too costly or simply not feasible to prevent people who have not paid for the good from enjoying the benefits of it. Such goods have the property of being *non-excludable*.

In some circumstances it may be theoretically possible to exclude non-payers but in reality the transaction costs involved are too great. For example, it may be very difficult to prevent anyone from fishing in the open ocean or enjoying the benefits of walking in a country park. If a good is non-excludable, consumers can get the benefits free and thus have no incentive to pay themselves. This is known as the *free-rider problem* and it is considered in more detail in Box 9.1.

> ### Definitions
>
> **Public good** A good or service which has the features of non-rivalry and non-excludability and as a result would not be provided by the free market.
>
> **Non-rivalry** Where the consumption of a good or service by one person will not prevent others from enjoying it.
>
> **Non-excludability** Where it is not possible to provide a good or service to one person without it thereby being available for others to enjoy.
>
> **Free-rider problem** When it is not possible to exclude other people from consuming a good that someone has bought.

BOX 9.1 THE PROBLEM OF FREE-RIDERS

A charitable solution?

Public goods present society with a problem, because of their inherent characteristics. Consider two individuals, Daniel and Emily, who are deciding whether or not to put on a firework display in their respective gardens and let's assume that these fireworks give them both utility. The nature of the firework display means that all those in the vicinity will all be able to enjoy it.

Now think about the decision of buying fireworks from Daniel's point of view. If he assumes that Emily will buy fireworks and put on a display, then Daniel has no incentive to also buy fireworks. Instead, he can benefit from Emily's display without having to pay for it. The same applies to Emily. This is the free-rider problem: no one has an incentive to contribute to the provision of a public good, because everyone assumes that others will contribute, meaning they can freely benefit.

This situation provides for some interesting analysis and is a useful application of game theory. The Nash equilibrium (see page 118) for both Daniel and Emily (under certain assumptions) is to free-ride. But, if everyone free-rides then in equilibrium, no one contributes and the public good (the firework display) would not be provided.

This is an example of the prisoners' dilemma: given that society benefits from the public good, everyone would actually be better off contributing (and there would be an explosive firework display!). But of course, without collaboration, no individual has any incentive to change their behaviour!

1. *Construct a pay-off matrix similar to that in Figure 5.5 (on page 118) showing a Nash equilibrium where neither player contributes. Explain why this situation could be improved.*

Encouraging provision

So, given that no firm or individual has a monetary incentive to provide a public good, how is it that they are still provided?

If the public were left to make voluntary contributions, we already know that there might be cases of free-riding. But, even if everyone agrees to contribute, there is another problem. All the contributors must agree on how much of the public good they want to be provided and how much they are willing to pay. Sometimes negotiation might have to take

place between the contributors to determine the optimal amount of the public good and their willingness to contribute. Here there may be a role for government provision, subsidisation and/or government intervention to enforce compulsory contributions, such as through taxation.

The role of charities

But is there another option that will encourage individuals to contribute to a public good without being forced into it? Charities have created an innovative way of doing this.

The motivations behind charitable donations vary, but often it is because of the 'warm glow'[1] we get from knowing that we have donated and that our donation will help someone else.

However, charitable donations suffer from free-riding. Many people are not concerned with how much they give individually, but more with how much society gives as a whole. If we see others donating, we know that they are contributing towards the objective of reducing poverty, helping fight diseases, or some other worthy cause, and thus we benefit from knowing that others are helping, without having to contribute ourselves. In other words, we can free-ride off other people's donations, making the good cause a public good. If this was how everyone thought, then charitable donations would be zero – we would end up in the prisoners' dilemma game where no one contributes.

To counter this, charities often frame their adverts in such a way that we see our donations as if they are going to a particular child/family or animal. By introducing the idea of 'sponsor a child', a private good emerges. Even though our contributions go to the wider public good of cutting poverty or saving rainforests, we have less of an incentive to free-ride, believing that we are helping a particular person, animal or even tree. By doing this, charities are able to avoid the prisoner's dilemma, which certainly does exist in society.

2. *If you see your donations to charity as a private good, explain whether there is any externality to giving to charity.*
3. *How does charitable giving become a public good?*

---

[1] James Andreoni, 'Impure altruism and donations to public goods: a theory of warm-glow giving', *Economic Journal*, vol. 100, no.401 (June 1990), pp. 464–77.

KEY IDEA 25 *The free-rider problem.* People are often unwilling to pay for things if they can make use of things other people have bought. This problem can lead to people not purchasing things which it would be to their benefit and that of other members of society to have.

When goods have these two features of non-rivalry and non-excludability, the free market will simply not provide them, as private firms would be unable to charge a price.

However, these goods often have large social benefits relative to private benefits: that is, large positive externalities.

This makes them socially desirable, but privately unprofitable. No one person would pay to have a pavement built along their street. The private benefit would be too small relative to the cost. And yet the social benefit to all the other people using the pavement will far outweigh the cost. But they have no incentive to pay for it, as they can simply *free ride* and use it for nothing.

As a result of this problem, we often see public goods provided by the government, or by a private firm subsidised by the government. Their provision will be financed through taxation and will significantly increase the utility of society.

(Note that not all goods and services produced by the public sector come into the category of public goods and services; thus education and health are publicly provided, but they *can* be, and indeed are, privately provided too.)

Market power

When there are no externalities, a perfect market will result in social efficiency. This can be seen from Figure 9.1. If there are no externalities, then the *MSC* and *MC* curves will be one and the same. Firms will produce where $MC (= MSC) = P$ $(= MSB)$: they will produce the socially optimal level of output. Note that $P = MSB$ since the price is equal to marginal utility (see pages 52–3). Marginal utility is the marginal private benefit that consumers gain, which, in the absence of externalities, will be the same as the *MSB*.

However, whenever markets are imperfect, whether as pure monopoly or monopsony or as some form of imperfect competition, the market will fail to equate *MSB* and *MSC*, even if there are no externalities.

Take the case of monopoly. A monopoly will produce less than the socially efficient output. This is illustrated in Figure 9.2. A monopoly faces a downward-sloping demand curve, and therefore marginal revenue is below average revenue (= P = *MSB*). Profits are maximised at an output of Q_1, where marginal revenue equals marginal cost (see Figure 5.2 on page 108). Assuming no externalities, the socially efficient output would be at the higher level of Q_2, where $MSB = MSC$.

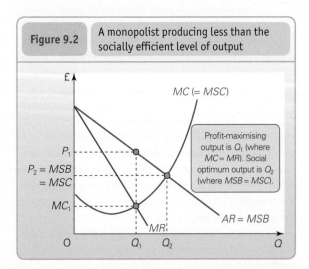

| Figure 9.2 | A monopolist producing less than the socially efficient level of output |

To summarise, firms with market power, if they are trying to maximise (or even increase) profit, will tend to set prices above the perfectly competitive level and thus reduce output below the socially efficient level.

Imperfect information

Markets can only operate efficiently if people have good knowledge of costs and benefits as they affect them. In the real world there is often a great deal of ignorance and uncertainty. Consumers are often ignorant of the properties of goods until they have bought them – by which time it is too late. This is especially relevant for larger consumer 'durables' that are purchased infrequently, such as washing machines or cars. Advertising may contribute to people's ignorance by misleading them as to the benefits of a good.

Firms are often ignorant of market opportunities, prices, costs, the productivity of labour (especially white-collar workers), the activity of rivals, etc.

Many economic decisions are based on expected future conditions. Since the future can never be known for certain, many decisions will be taken that later turn out to be wrong.

One particular type of imperfect information is when the different sides in an economic relationship have different amounts of information. This is known as 'asymmetric information' and (as we saw on pages 9–10) it is at the heart of the principal–agent problem.

Protecting people's interests

The government may feel that people need protecting from poor economic decisions that they make on their own behalf. It may feel that in a free market people will consume too many harmful things. Often such goods bring immediate benefits, whereas the costs happen in the future (e.g. eating unhealthy but tasty food or smoking). Thus if the government wants to discourage smoking, drinking and eating sugary products, it can put taxes on tobacco, alcohol (as discussed in the Sloman Economics News blog, 'A taxing pint of beer') and high-sugar products (as discussed in the blog, 'A sweet tax?'). In more extreme cases it could make various activities illegal, such as prostitution, certain types of gambling, and the sale and consumption of drugs.

Alternatively, the government may feel that people consume too little of things that are good for them, such as education, health care and sports facilities. Such goods are known as *merit goods*. The government could either provide them free or subsidise their production.

> ### Definition
>
> **Merit goods** Goods which the government feels that people will under-consume and which therefore ought to be subsidised or provided free.

RECAP

1. Social efficiency is achieved at the output where $MSC = MSB$ for each good and service. In practice, however, markets will fail to achieve social efficiency. This provides a justification for government intervention in the market.

2. Externalities are spillover costs or benefits. Whenever there are external costs, the market will (other things being equal) lead to a level of production and consumption above the socially efficient level. Whenever there are external benefits, the market will (other things being equal) lead to a level of production and consumption below the socially efficient level.

3. Public goods will not be provided by the market. The problem is that they have large social benefits relative to private benefits, and without government intervention it would not be possible to prevent people having a 'free ride', thereby making it unprofitable to supply.

4. Monopoly power will (other things being equal) lead to a level of output below the socially efficient level.

5. Ignorance and uncertainty may prevent people and firms from consuming or producing at the levels they would otherwise choose.

6. In a free market there may be inadequate provision for dependants and an inadequate output of merit goods.

9.2 BUSINESS ETHICS AND CORPORATE SOCIAL RESPONSIBILITY

It is often assumed that firms are simply concerned with maximising profits: that they are not concerned with broader issues of *corporate social responsibility*. In other words, firms tend to be more concerned with the interests of shareholders than they are about the interests of society. Indeed, many forms of market failure can be attributed directly to business practices that could not be classified as 'socially responsible': advertising campaigns that seek to misinform or in some way deceive the consumer; monopoly producers exploiting their monopoly position through charging excessively high prices; the conscious decision to ignore water and air pollution limits, knowing that the chances of being caught are slim.

Changing business attitudes?

To some extent, however, the role of modern business has changed, and society expects business to adhere to certain moral and social principles. Indeed, social responsibility is a key component in many companies' *business ethics*.

Modern businesses often see themselves as more than economic institutions, as they are actively involved in society's social, political and legal environments. As such, all businesses are responsible not only to their shareholders but to all *stakeholders*. Stakeholders are all those affected by the business's operations, not only shareholders, but workers, customers, suppliers, creditors and people living in the neighbourhood. Given the far-reaching environmental effects of many businesses, stakeholding might extend to the whole of society.

In many top corporations, *environmental scanning* is now an integral part of the planning process. This involves the business surveying changing social and political trends in order to remain in tune with consumer concerns. For example, product development programmes and business R&D strategies have increasingly focused on 'green' issues reflecting growing public awareness in this area. The more

successful a business is in linking its product or brand to the image of 'environmentally friendly', the more likely it is to enhance its sales or establish a measure of brand loyalty, and thereby to strengthen its competitive position.

Several companies have made great play of their social responsibility. In 2007, Marks & Spencer launched its 'Plan A': a five-year 100-point plan, which aimed 'to tackle some of the biggest challenges facing our business and our world' and involved work to combat 'climate change, reduce waste, safeguard natural resources, trade ethically and build a healthier nation'.[2]

Its commitments were extended in 2010 and within three years of the launch of the project, an annual net benefit of £105 million was delivered, through things such as resource efficiency. Since then, it has introduced Plan A 2020, with an ambition to become the world's most sustainable retailer.

In the very same week that M&S launched its original Plan A, Tesco unveiled its plans to cut carbon emissions from existing stores worldwide by at least 50 percent by

Definitions

Corporate social responsibility Where a business takes into account the interests and concerns of a community rather than just its shareholders.

Business ethics The values and principles that shape business behaviour.

Stakeholder An individual affected by the operations of a business.

Environmental scanning Where a business surveys social and political trends in order to take account of changes in its decision-making process.

---

[2] https://corporate.marksandspencer.com/plan-a

2020 and to make the reduction of its carbon footprint 'a central business driver'. It commissioned independent research to map the total carbon footprint of its activities across the world and introduced a carbon labelling system to encourage consumers to make greener choices and buy environmentally friendly products, with more special offers and more of such products in the value range.

In 2014/15, Tesco emitted 5.62 million tonnes of CO_2, representing a 4.3 per cent reduction in its net carbon intensity relative to the previous year and a 40.9 per cent reduction since the target was introduced in 2007.

More recently, Asda has launched its 'Wonky Veg Box',[3] as a means of cutting food waste, which is one of the ambitions of many of the leading supermarkets, including Tesco. This is considered in more detail in the blog, 'Do you mind if your vegetables are wonky?' on the Sloman Economics News site.

Pause for thought

Green taxes (e.g. on carbon emission) are designed to 'internalise' environmental externalities and thereby force firms to take such externalities into account in their decision making. Should such taxes be reduced for firms that adopt a more environmentally responsible approach?

Social responsibility and profitability

Consumers are increasingly favouring companies which are openly committed to sustainability and ethical practices. Firms hope that adopting such policies will enhance brand image and so strengthen loyalty, improve profitability and even help the firm in raising finance and attracting trading partners.

There are many awards available to recognise and promote social responsibility, including the 'Most admired companies' lists, such as those presented by *Management Today* in the UK and *Fortune* in America. Winning such awards has huge public relations and marketing potential, which can significantly contribute to a firm's socially responsible image.

Many studies have attempted to identify and evaluate the economic returns from social responsibility, including business growth rates, stock prices, sales and revenue. A survey by van Beurden and Gössling[4] evaluated the findings of 34 studies that considered the link between business ethics and enhanced profits. They concluded that 23 studies showed a positive link, nine suggested neutral effects or were inconclusive, and the remaining two suggested that there was a negative relationship.

The 2012 Co-operative's Ethical Consumer Markets Report showed that the value of funds invested by households in ethical financial products had risen from £6.5 billion in 2000 to £21.1 billion in 2011, an increase of 225 per cent. Consumer decisions are increasingly motivated by concerns over human rights, social justice, the environment or animal welfare. So-called 'ethical consumerism' increased from £13.5 billion in 2000 to £47.2 billion in 2012 and the report also indicated that the proportion of people who purchase a product at least once a year for ethical reasons rose from 27 per cent in 2000 to 42 per cent in 2012.[5]

The UK Ethical Markets Report 2015[6] found that ethical sales grew by 8 per cent over the previous year, with the overall value of the ethical market increasing from £35 billion to £38 billion. There was particular growth in electric, hybrid and other fuel-efficient cars and solar panels, growing by 40 per cent and 25 per cent respectively. The data clearly indicate that ethical consumption is growing, with consumers valuing environmental responsibility and active participation in the community when making purchasing decisions. Box 9.2 gives an example of a company that has built its reputation on being socially and environmentally responsible – The Body Shop.

Socially responsible companies also may find it easier to recruit and hold on to their employees. In a number of surveys of graduate employment intentions, students have claimed that they would be prepared to take a lower salary in order to work for a business with high ethical standards and a commitment to socially responsible business practices. An international survey in 2005 showed that 28 per cent of job seekers considered the ethical conduct and values of an employer to be an important factor in deciding whether to apply for work there.[7]

However, perhaps what is more important is the cost of not being socially responsible. Data from the Ethical Consumer Report show that more people are avoiding buying a product or service from a company with a poor ethical reputation, up from 44 per cent in 2000 to 50 per cent in 2012.[8] Gap received bad press coverage over the poor employment conditions in its factories in developing countries in the late 1990s and early 2000s (see Case Study A.1 on the book's website). There was a significant negative effect on its sales, which led to the company taking various actions and it is now regarded as one of the world's most ethical companies.

On 20 April 2010, there was a massive oil spill from the Deepwater Horizon rig in the Gulf of Mexico. This was blamed on poor safety standards and taking excessive risks with the environment. Before the final capping in August, some 4.9 million barrels of oil leaked into the Gulf of Mexico, causing immense environmental damage and destroying the livelihoods of people in the fishing and tourist industries.

---

[3] 'Asda's phenomenal Wonky Veg boxes coming to a store near you', *Asda News and Blogs* (18 February 2016).

[4] Peter van Beurden and Tobias Gössling, 'The worth of values – a literature review on the relation between corporate social and financial performance', *Journal of Business Ethics*, vol. 82, no. 2 (October 2008), pp. 407–24.

[5] The Ethical Consumer Markets Report (2012). Co-operative Bank.

[6] 'UK Ethical Markets Report (2015)', *Ethical Consumer*, Ethical Consumer Research Association Ltd (2016).

[7] 'What Makes a Great Employer?', MORI survey for Manpower (October 2005).

[8] *The Ethical Consumer Markets Report 2012*, Co-operative Bank (2013).

BOX 9.2	THE BODY SHOP

Is it 'worth it'?

The Body Shop was founded in 1976 and shot to fame in the 1980s. It stood for environmental awareness and an ethical approach to business. But its success had as much to do with what it sold as what it stood for. It sold natural cosmetics, Raspberry Ripple Bathing Bubbles and Chamomile Shampoo, products that were immensely popular with consumers.

Its profits increased from a little over £1 million in 1985 (€1.7 million) to approximately £65 million (€77.5 million) in 2012.[1] Although profits have since slipped, falling to €65.3 million in 2014 and €54.8 million in 2015, its profit growth in new markets over that same period was 12.4 per cent. Sales, meanwhile, grew even more dramatically, from £4.9 million in 1985 to approximately €967.2 million in 2015 (a 0.9 per cent fall on the previous year). However, first quarter growth for 2016 was 2.1 per cent higher compared to the same quarter in 2015.[2] In 2015, Body Shop International had over 3100 stores, operating in 61 countries, with its latest planned expansion into China.

What makes this success so remarkable is that The Body Shop did virtually no advertising. Its promotion stemmed largely from the activities and environmental campaigning of its founder Anita Roddick, and the company's uncompromising claims that it sold only 'green' products and conducted its business operations with high ethical standards. It actively supported green causes such as saving whales and protecting rainforests, and it refused to allow animal testing for its products. Perhaps most surprising in the world of big business was its high-profile initiative 'trade not aid', whereby it claimed to pay 'fair' prices for its ingredients, especially those supplied by people in developing countries, who were open to exploitation by large companies.

The growth strategy of The Body Shop focused on developing a distinctive and highly innovative product range, and at the same time identifying such products with major social issues of the day, such as the environment and animal rights.

Its initial expansion was based on a process of franchising:

> franchising. We didn't know what it was, but all these women came to us and said, if you can do this and you can't even read a balance sheet, then we can do it. I had a cabal of female friends all around Brighton, Hove and Chichester, and they started opening little units, all called The Body Shop. I just supplied them with gallons of products – we only had 19 different products, but we made it look like more as we sold them in five different sizes![3]

In 1984 the company went public. In the 1990s, however, sales growth was less rapid and in 1998 Anita Roddick stepped down as Chief Executive, but for a while she and her husband remained as co-chairs. In 2003 she was awarded a knighthood and became Dame Anita Roddick. Sales then grew rapidly from 2004 to 2006 from €553 million to €709 million.

Acquisition of The Body Shop by L'Oréal

A dramatic strategic event occurred in 2006 when The Body Shop was sold to the French cosmetics giant L'Oréal, which was 26 per cent owned by Nestlé. This resulted in the magazine *Ethical Consumer* downgrading The Body Shop's ethical rating from 11 out of 20 to a mere 2.5 and calling for a boycott of the company. Three weeks after the sale, the daily Brand Index recorded an 11 point drop in The Body Shop's consumer satisfaction rating from 25 to 14.

There were a number of reasons for this. L'Oréal's animal-testing policies conflicted with those of The Body Shop and L'Oréal had been accused of being involved in price fixing with other French perfume houses. L'Oréal's part-owner, Nestlé, had also been subject to various criticisms for ethical misconduct, including promoting formula milk to mothers with babies in poor countries rather than breast milk and using slave labour in cocoa farms in West Africa.

Anita Roddick, however, believed that, by taking over The Body Shop, L'Oréal would develop a more ethical approach to business and it did publicly recognise that it needed to develop its ethical and environmental policies. It adopted a new Code of Business Ethics in 2007 and has gained some external accreditation for its approach to sustainability and ethics. L'Oréal was ranked as one of the world's 100 most ethical companies by Ethisphere in 2007 and in 2016 it was again part of this list for the seventh time.

L'Oréal set itself three targets as part of its environmental strategy (2005–15), including a 50 per cent reduction in greenhouse gas emissions, water consumption and waste per finished product unit. It made a donation of $1.2 million to the US Environment Protection Agency to help bring an end to animal testing and in March 2013 it announced a 'total ban on the sale in Europe of any cosmetic product that was tested on animals or containing an ingredient that was tested on animals after this date'. It also promises that 'By 2020, we will innovate so that 100% of products have an environmental or social benefit.' Sadly, Anita Roddick died in 2007 and so has not been able to witness these changes.

L'Oréal has also looked to inject greater finance into the company, aimed at improving the marketing of products. In autumn 2006 a transactional website was launched and there have been greater press marketing campaigns. The Body Shop's latest commitment is its 'Enrich, not Exploit campaign', which aims at 'enriching our people, our products and our planet'. This commitment extends its emphasis never to test on animals and is also focused on biodiversity and resources and the fair treatment of its farmers and suppliers.[4]

1. *What assumptions has The Body Shop made about the 'rational consumer'?*
2. *How has The Body Shop's economic performance been affected by its attitudes towards ethical issues? (You could do an Internet search to find further evidence about its performance and the effects of its sale to L'Oréal.)*

---

[1] *Annual Results 2012*, L'Oréal Finance (February 2013).
[2] *Annual Results 2015*, L'Oréal Finance (February 2016).
[3] Anita Roddick interview, Startups.co.uk/6678842908657825127/anita-roddick.html

---

[4] See: www.thebodyshop.co.uk/commitment/index.aspx

It cost the owner, BP, some $3.5 billion in containment and clear-up operations, and $18.7 billion in legal claims, with a total cost of almost $54 billion. Further, its reputation plummeted in the USA, with motorists boycotting its gas stations. Its share price dropped from £628 in April 2010 to £296 in July. However, despite the adverse effect, BP remains the sixth largest multinational in the world (see Table 7.1 on page 161).

Despite the concern about cases like this, there are still many firms and consumers that care little about the social or natural environment. There is thus a strong case for government intervention to correct market failures.

RECAP

1. Sometimes firms are not aggressive profit maximisers but, instead, take a more socially responsible approach to business.

2. Evidence suggests that as the corporate responsibility of firms grows, economic performance is often enhanced through strengthened brand loyalty, higher sales and turnover, rising share prices, access to capital and higher employee retention.

3. Although there are growing numbers of consumers and businesses that are concerned with ethical and environmental issues, these still represent a niche market.

9.3 GOVERNMENT INTERVENTION IN THE MARKET

Given the various failures of the free market, what forms can government intervention take? There are several policy instruments that the government can use. At one extreme, it can totally replace the market by providing goods and services itself. At the other extreme, it can merely seek to persuade producers, consumers or workers to act differently. Between the two extremes the government has a number of instruments it can use to change the way markets operate. The major ones are taxes, subsidies, laws and regulatory bodies.

Taxes and subsidies

When there are market imperfections, social efficiency will not be achieved. Marginal social benefit (*MSB*) will not equal marginal social cost (*MSC*). A different level of output would be more desirable.

Taxes and subsidies can be used to correct these imperfections. Essentially the approach is to tax those goods or activities where the market produces too much, and subsidise those where the market produces too little.

Let's return to the chemical firm polluting the air as depicted in Figure 9.1 (on page 205). The pollution is costly to society, but the firm does not directly incur any of these costs, hence more than the social optimum is produced. However, by taxing the firm, the government increases the firm's marginal private cost (*MC*), moving this curve closer to the *MSC* curve and so makes the firm pay towards the cost of the pollution it causes. It internalises the externality, moving the profit-maximising output closer to the socially optimum output. If the tax is equal to the *full* amount of the marginal external cost, then the firm's private marginal cost becomes equal to the marginal social cost. In Figure 9.1, the firm will now maximise profits at Q_2, the socially optimal output.

In section 9.4 we examine how taxes and subsidies can be used to achieve various environmental and social goals.

Legislation and regulation

Laws are frequently used to correct market imperfections. Laws can be of three main types: those that prohibit or regulate behaviour that imposes external costs, those that prevent firms providing false or misleading information, and those that prevent or regulate monopolies and oligopolies.

The advantage of legal restrictions is that they are usually easy to understand and administer. Furthermore, it is often safer to make products illegal rather than merely imposing taxes. In cases where consumer information is very poor, legal intervention can also help to protect consumers from purchasing unsafe products. However, legal restrictions tend to be a rather blunt weapon. For example, imposing a legal limit on pollution levels leaves little incentive for firms to continue reducing their emissions once the target has been met.

Thus, rather than using legislation to ban or restrict various activities, a more 'subtle' approach can be adopted. This involves the use of various regulatory bodies. Having identified possible cases where action might be required (e.g. potential cases of pollution, misleading information or the abuse of monopoly power), the regulatory body may conduct an investigation, prepare a report containing its findings and recommendations and it might also have the power to enforce its decisions.

In the UK there are regulatory bodies for each of the major privatised utilities (see section 9.6). The Competition and Markets Authority provides the framework for UK competition policy and investigates and reports on suspected cases of anti-competitive practices and can order such firms to cease or modify these practices (see section 9.5).

Government provision

As we saw with public goods, such as street lights, private firms do not have an incentive to provide them, thus government may provide them itself, or pay private firms to do so. This may also occur with merit goods: neither education nor healthcare are public goods, yet in most countries they are provided by the government. In this way, the government ensures that individuals consume the 'right' amount of the good or service. This is especially important if consumers are unaware of how beneficial the good might be.

Another way in which governments may intervene to correct market failures is through the provision of information. By providing information about the negative effects of smoking or of eating certain foods, the government is trying to reduce the consumption of these goods to their social optimum. Information is also provided about schools, employment and prices to help consumers make more informed decisions and to provide a greater degree of certainty for firms.

RECAP

1. Governments intervene in markets in a number of ways. One is the use of taxes to curb production or subsidies to increase it.

2. Another is to use legislation or regulation to encourage or force businesses to behave in a more socially desirable way.

3. In some cases, the government or an agency may provide information to correct a market failure. However, if the market failure is so substantial, then the government may choose to intervene and provide the good itself.

9.4 ENVIRONMENTAL POLICY

Growing concerns over global warming, acid rain, the depletion of the ozone layer, industrial and domestic waste, traffic fumes and other forms of pollution have made the protection of the environment a major political and economic issue. As you can see from successive blogs on the Sloman Economics News site, worldwide action has been taken in the recent past to try to tackle global warming and climate change.[9] So what policy instruments are open to government?

Pause for thought

Why is the environment an economic issue?

Green taxes and subsidies

Increasingly, countries are introducing 'green' taxes in order to discourage pollution as goods are produced, consumed or disposed of.

Table 9.1 (page 214) shows the range of green taxes used around the world. OECD data from April 2016 shows that as a percentage of GDP, green tax revenues are highest in Slovenia at 4.23 per cent, with those in Scandinavia remaining consistently high, reflecting the strength of their environmental concerns. In 2014, they accounted for 4.11 per cent of GDP in Denmark, compared with just 0.72 per cent of GDP in the USA, the lowest of the major industrialised countries. The weighted average of the 34 OECD countries was 1.6 per cent.

In 2014, energy was the sector that generated the biggest tax revenues as a percentage of GDP across the OECD countries at 1.11 per cent, followed by motor vehicles and transport at 0.43 per cent. Fuel taxes are high in countries such as the UK and so, therefore, are green tax revenues, accounting for 2.31 per cent in 2014, although this figure has fallen with the growth in both more energy-efficient vehicles and electric cars.

Recently in the UK, we have seen the implementation of a 5p charge on plastic carrier bags, following similar charges in other countries.[10] Although this is not a tax and the revenue generated does not go to the government, it is a method being used to try to tackle over-use of plastic bags. You can find further details on the government website.[11]

Choosing the tax rate

The rule here is simple: to achieve the socially efficient output of a polluting activity, the government should impose a

---

[9] See the blogs: '20:20 climate vision?'; 'Wrong Climate at talks'; 'A changing climate at the White House'; 'The run-up to Copenhagen'; 'An Accord from discord - reflections on Copenhagen' and 'An historic agreement at the Paris Climate Change Conference'.

[10] See: *List by country; 'bag charges, taxes and bans'*, The Grocery Box Company Limited.

[11] www.gov.uk/government/publications/single-use-plastic-carrier-bags-why-were-introducing-the-charge/carrier-bags-why-theres-a-5p-charge

---

Table 9.1 Types of environmental taxes and charges

Motor fuels	Other goods	Air transport
Leaded/unleaded	Batteries	Noise charges
Diesel (quality differential)	Plastic carrier bags	Aviation fuels
Carbon/energy taxation	Glass containers	**Water**
Sulphur tax	Drink cans	Water charges
Other energy products	Tyres	Sewage charges
Carbon/energy tax	CFCs/halons	Water effluent charges
Sulphur tax or charge	Disposable razors/	Manure charges
NO_2 charge	cameras	**Direct tax provisions**
Methane charge	Lubricant oil charge	Tax relief on green investment
Agricultural inputs	Oil pollutant charge	Taxation on free company cars
Fertilisers	Solvents	Employer-paid commuting expenses
Pesticides	**Waste disposal**	taxable
Manure	Municipal waste charges	Employer-paid parking expenses
Vehicle-related taxation	Waste-disposal charges	taxable
Sales tax depends on car size	Hazardous waste charges	Commuter use of public transport tax
Road tax depends on car size	Landfill tax or charges	deductible
	Duties on waste water	

BOX 9.3 A STERN WARNING

It's much cheaper to act now on global warming than to wait

The analysis of global warming is not just for climate scientists. Economists have a major part to play in examining its causes and consequences and the possible solutions. And these solutions are likely to have a major impact on business.

Perhaps the most influential study of climate change in recent times has been the Stern Review. This was an independent review, commissioned by the UK Chancellor of the Exchequer, and headed by Sir Nicholas Stern, head of the Government Economic Service and former chief economist of the World Bank. Here was an economist using the methods of economics to analyse perhaps the most serious problem facing the world.

> Climate change presents a unique challenge for economics: it is the greatest and widest-ranging market failure ever seen. The economic analysis must therefore be global, deal with long time horizons, have the economics of risk and uncertainty at centre stage, and examine the possibility of major, non-marginal change. To meet these requirements, the Review draws on ideas and techniques from most of the important areas of economics, including many recent advances.[1]

First the bad news . . .

According to the Stern Report, if no action was taken, global temperatures would rise by some 2–3°C within 50 years. As a result the world economy would shrink by up to 20 per cent – and that would be just the average. The countries most seriously affected by floods, drought and crop failure could shrink by considerably more. These tend to be the poorest countries, least able to bear the costs of these changes.

Rising sea levels could displace some 200 million people; droughts could create tens or even hundreds of millions of 'climate refugees'. 'Ecosystems will be particularly vulnerable to climate change, with around 15–40 per cent of species potentially facing extinction after only 2°C of warming.' The Stern Report suggested that if CO_2 emissions are not reduced,

Greenhouse gas emissions in 2000, by source

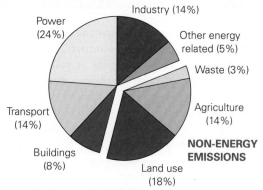

ENERGY EMISSIONS

Power (24%) · Industry (14%) · Other energy related (5%) · Waste (3%) · Agriculture (14%) · **NON-ENERGY EMISSIONS** · Land use (18%) · Buildings (8%) · Transport (14%)

Total emissions in 2000: 42 GtCO₂e.
Energy emissions are mostly CO_2 (some non-CO_2 in industry and other energy related).
Non-energy emissions are CO_2 (land use) and non-CO_2 (agriculture and waste).

the environmental impacts could lead to falls in GDP of between 5 and 20 per cent.

. . . Then the good

If action is taken now, these consequences could be averted – and at relatively low cost. According to the Stern Report, a sacrifice of just 1 per cent of global GDP (global income) could, if correctly targeted, be enough to stabilise greenhouse gases to an equivalent of 500–550 ppm of CO_2 – a level generally considered to be sustainable. However, in 2008 Lord Stern adjusted this estimate, saying that CO_2 levels needed to be reduced to 500 ppm and that the cost would be 2 per cent of global GDP per annum.[2]

---

[1] Stern Review: Executive Summary.

[2] W. R. Cline, 'Meeting the challenge of global warming', *Copenhagen Consensus Challenge Paper* (2004).

tax equal to the marginal external cost (or grant a subsidy equal to the marginal external benefit).

Consider again a chemical works that emits smoke from a chimney, imposing an external cost on others ($MSC > MC$) and polluting the atmosphere. This is illustrated in Figure 9.3 (page 216). For simplicity, it is assumed that the firm is a price taker. It produces Q_1 where $P = MC$ (its profit-maximising output), but takes no account of the external pollution costs it imposes on society. If the government imposes a tax on production equal to the marginal pollution cost, it will effectively 'internalise' the externality. The firm will have to pay an amount equal to the external cost it creates. The firm's MC curve thus shifts upwards to become the same as the MSC curve. It will therefore now maximise profits at Q_2, which is the socially optimum output where $MSB = MSC$.

Pause for thought

Assume that production by a firm has beneficial spillover effects, i.e. that there are positive externalities which have the effect of positioning the MSC curve below the MC curve. Illustrate this on a diagram similar to Figure 9.3 and show (a) the profit-maximising level of output; (b) the socially efficient level of output; (c) the optimum level of subsidy.

Advantages of taxes and subsidies

Many economists favour the tax/subsidy solution to market imperfections (especially the problem of externalities) because it still allows the market to operate. It forces firms to take on board the full social costs and benefits of their actions. It also has the flexibility of being adjustable according to the

To achieve this, action would need to be taken to cut emissions from their various sources (see the chart). This would involve a mixture of four things:

- Reducing consumer demand for emissions-intensive goods and services.
- Increased efficiency, which can save both money and emissions.
- Action on non-energy emissions, such as avoiding deforestation.
- Switching to lower-carbon technologies for power, heat and transport.

What policies did Sir Nicholas recommend to achieve these four objectives? Essentially the answer is to alter incentives. This could involve taxing polluting activities; subsidising green alternatives, including the development of green technology; establishing a price for carbon through trading carbon (see the section on tradable permits on pages 216–20) and regulating its production; and encouraging behavioural change through education, better labelling of products, imposing minimum standards for building and encouraging public debate.

We consider some of these alternatives in this section of the chapter.

Have we learned a lesson?

The Stern Report was produced over 10 years ago, but has progress been made? The international community has taken steps, as you can read about in the articles on the Sloman Economics News site (see footnote 9 on page 213). Furthermore, in 2014, the Intergovernmental Panel on Climate Change (IPCC) issued its Fifth Assessment Report (AR5),[3] which consisted of three working group reports looking at the physical science; the impacts, adaptation and vulnerability; and the mitigation of climate change, with economists playing a key role in the second and third reports.

Echoes of the Stern Report were evident in the impact report,[4] which explained the current effects of climate change across the world; the future risks from a changing climate, for which we are ill-prepared; and the opportunities that exist for us to take action now. Although adaptation is occurring, it is largely focused on reacting to past events rather than preparing for future changes. According to Chris Field, the Co-Chair of the second Impact Working Group:

Climate-change adaptation is not an exotic agenda that has never been tried. Governments, firms, and communities around the world are building experience with adaptation. This experience forms a starting point for bolder, more ambitious adaptations that will be important, as climate and society continue to change.

The opportunities for action were reiterated by the Mitigation Working Group, which published its own report,[5] including a summary for policymakers. Although it notes progress in policy development within countries at the sectoral level, it identifies a substantial time lag between the implementation of policies and the impact on the environment, noting that since 2008 emission growth has not yet deviated from the previous trend. Further, it reports that to make the necessary reductions in emissions, investment patterns will need to change significantly.

In this area and all others, international co-operation will be essential, as the effects of climate change do not recognise national boundaries. It is perhaps this that will create problems in the years ahead.

1. *Would it be in the interests of a business to reduce its carbon emissions if this involved it in increased costs?*
2. *How is the concept of 'opportunity cost' relevant in analysing the impact of business decisions on the environment?*
3. *The Stern Report was produced in 2006, but there has been a lack of progress. Why do you think progress has been so slow?*

[4] *Climate Change 2014: Impacts, adaptation, and vulnerability, from Working Group II of the IPCC* (IPCC, 2014).
[5] *Climate Change 2014: Mitigation from climate change, from Working Group III of the IPCC* (IPCC, 2014).

[3] *The Fifth Assessment Report (AR5)* (IPCC, 2014).

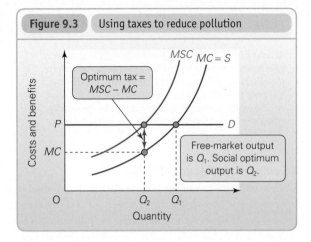

Figure 9.3   Using taxes to reduce pollution

Pause for thought

Why is it easier to use taxes and subsidies to tackle the problem of car exhaust pollution than to tackle the problem of peak-time traffic congestion in cities?

Laws and regulations

The traditional way of tackling pollution has been to set maximum permitted levels of emission or resource use, or minimum acceptable levels of environmental quality, and then to fine firms contravening these limits. Measures of this type are known as ***command-and-control (CAC) systems***. Clearly, there have to be inspectors to monitor the amount of pollution, and the fines have to be large enough to deter firms from exceeding the limit.

Virtually all countries have environmental regulations of one sort or another. For example, the EU has over 200 items of legislation covering areas such as air and water pollution, noise, the marketing and use of dangerous chemicals, waste management, the environmental impacts of new projects (such as power stations, roads and quarries), recycling, depletion of the ozone layer and global warming.

Assessing CAC systems. Given the uncertainty over the environmental impacts of pollutants, especially over the longer term, it is often better to play safe and set tough emissions standards. These could always be relaxed at a later stage if the effects turn out to be less damaging, but it might be too late to reverse damage if the effects turn out to be more serious. Taxes may be a more sophisticated means of reaching a socially efficient output, but CAC methods are usually more straightforward to devise, easier to understand by firms and easier to implement.

The weakness of command-and-control systems is that they fail to offer business any incentive to do better than the legally specified level. By contrast, with a pollution tax, the lower the pollution level, the less tax there will be to pay. There is thus a continuing incentive for businesses progressively to cut pollution levels and introduce cleaner technology.

magnitude of the problem. For example, the bigger the external costs of a firm's actions, the bigger the tax can be.

What is more, by taxing firms for polluting, they are encouraged to find cleaner ways of producing. The tax thus acts as an incentive over the longer run to reduce pollution: the more a firm can reduce its pollution, the more taxes it can save.

Likewise, when *good* practices are subsidised, firms have the incentive to adopt more good practices.

Disadvantages of taxes and subsidies

Infeasible to use different tax and subsidy rates. Each firm produces different levels and types of externality and operates under different degrees of imperfect competition. It would be expensive and administratively very difficult, if not impossible, to charge every offending firm its own particular tax rate (or grant every relevant firm its own particular rate of subsidy).

Lack of knowledge. Even if a government did decide to charge a tax equal to each offending firm's marginal external costs, it would still have the problem of measuring that cost. The damage from pollution is often extremely difficult to assess, especially the long-run damage. It is also difficult to apportion blame. For example, the damage to lakes and forests from acid rain has been a major concern since the beginning of the 1980s. But just how serious is that damage? What is its current monetary cost? How long lasting is the damage? What will be the position in 20 years? Just what and who are to blame? These are questions that cannot be answered precisely. It is thus impossible to fix the 'correct' pollution tax on, say, a particular coal-fired power station.

Despite these problems, it is nevertheless possible to charge firms by the amount of a particular emission. For example, firms could be charged for chimney smoke by so many parts per million of a given pollutant. Although it is difficult and potentially costly to 'fine-tune' such a system so that the charge reflects the precise number of people affected by the pollutant and by how much, it does go some way to internalising the externality.

Tradable permits

A policy measure that has grown in popularity in recent years is that of ***tradable permits***. This is a combination of

Definitions

Command-and-control (CAC) systems The use of laws or regulations backed up by inspections and penalties (such as fines) for non-compliance.

Tradable permits Each firm is given a permit to produce a given level of pollution. If less than the permitted amount is produced, the firm is given a credit. This can then be sold to another firm, allowing it to exceed its original limit. This is known as a 'cap and trade' scheme.

command-and-control and market-based systems. A maximum permitted level of emission is set for a given pollutant for a given factory, and the firm is given a permit to emit up to this amount. If it emits less than this amount, it is given a credit for the difference, which it can then use in another of its factories. Another option is to sell the credits to another firm. This firm can then pollute over its permitted level, by an amount equal to the credits. Thus the overall level of emissions is set by CAC methods, whereas their distribution is determined by the market.

Take the example of firms A and B, which are currently producing 12 units of a pollutant each. Now assume that a standard is set permitting them to produce only 10 units each. If firm A managed to reduce the pollutant to 8 units, it would be given a credit for 2 units. It could then sell this to firm B, enabling B to continue emitting 12 units. The effect would still be a total reduction of 4 units between the two firms. However, by allowing them to trade in pollution permits, pollution reduction can be concentrated in the firms where it can be achieved at lowest cost. In our example, if it cost firm B more to reduce its pollution than firm A, then the permits could be sold from A to B at a price that was profitable to both (i.e. at a price above the cost of emission reduction to A, but below the cost of emission reduction to B).

Pause for thought

To what extent will the introduction of tradable permits lead to a lower level of total pollution (as opposed to its redistribution)?

A similar principle can be used for using natural resources. Thus fish quotas could be assigned to fishing boats or fleets or countries. Any parts of these quotas not used could then be sold.

The EU carbon trading system
As part of its objective to reduce greenhouse gas emissions as set out in the Kyoto Protocol (see Case Study C.21 on the book's website), the EU launched a Carbon Emissions Trading System (ETS).

Phases I and II. From January 2005 until December 2007, governments across the EU allocated credits, known as EU allowances (EUAs), to approximately 12 000 industrial plants as part of Phase I of the scheme. These credits represented a limit for each company in terms of its emissions. Under the scheme, any company exceeding its allowance could purchase permits from other companies that managed to cut their emissions below their allowance. These 'greener' companies could therefore make a profit by selling their surplus credits and thus a trading system across Europe was created.

In January 2008, Phase II of the ETS began, whereby all existing allowances from Phase I became invalid. The same basic principles were in place, but now companies were able to use emission reductions in countries outside of the EU to offset their emissions within the EU.

Phase III. As Phase II was beginning, the European Commission published proposals for Phase III, commencing in January 2013 and with such a long lead-in time that companies had sufficient time to adapt their strategies and production techniques.

Lessons were learned from Phases I and II, with an initial move to an *EU-wide cap* on the volume of emissions and the total quantity of EUAs that would be issued, rather than the more decentralised, country-based allocation. Furthermore, while a proportion of EUAs *could* be auctioned in Phases I and II, very few actually were. Phase III moved towards the auctioning of EUAs, such that from 2013, most firms in the power sector have already had to purchase all of their allowances by auction. In other sectors, the average proportion of EUAs auctioned is expected to increase from 20 per cent in 2013 to 70 per cent by 2020.

The size of this EU-wide cap is being reduced by 1.74 per cent per year, so that total permitted emissions will be 21 per cent lower in 2020 than in 2005. The EU also proposes that they will be 43 per cent lower by 2030. This will require a larger annual reduction of 2.2 per cent from 2021, as discussed in the EU's 2030 framework for climate and energy policy.

As part of the EU 2020 Climate and Energy Package, a new directive came into force in 2013. A key aim is to have a more ambitious, certain and consistent approach to environmental regulation across the EU. A '20-20-20' package was agreed in December 2009 to tackle climate change, involving cutting greenhouse gases by 20 per cent by 2020 compared with 1990 levels, raising the use of renewable energy sources to 20 per cent of total energy usage and cutting energy consumption by 20 per cent. Many of the emissions reductions would be achieved by tighter caps under the ETS, with binding national targets for non-ETS sectors, such as agriculture, transport, buildings and services. However, over half of the reductions could be achieved by international carbon trading, where permits could be bought from abroad: e.g. under the Clean Development Mechanism of the Kyoto agreement.

Assessing the system of tradable permits
The main advantage of tradable permits is that they combine the simplicity of CAC methods with the benefits of achieving pollution reduction in the most efficient way. There is also the advantage that firms have a financial incentive to cut pollution. This might then make it easier for governments to impose tougher standards (i.e. impose lower permitted levels of emission).

There are, however, various problems with tradable permits. One is the possibility that trade will lead to pollution being concentrated in certain geographical areas. The equity of the allocation of allowances was a big concern in Phases I and II, especially when some countries were set tougher targets than others. However, this problem was addressed in Phase III with the EU-wide cap.

BOX 9.4 THE PROBLEM OF URBAN TRAFFIC CONGESTION

Does London have the answer?

Since the 1950s, there has been almost continuous growth in vehicle miles driven in most countries. In Great Britain, vehicle miles were over 10 times higher in 2015 than in 1949. Although the rate of traffic growth has been slowing over the past 20 years, and actually fell from 2007 to 2012, vehicle miles reached a peak of 317.8 billion in 2015.[1] With this increase in vehicle mileage, we have also seen an increase in road length of 6300 miles since 1994. However, this increase of 2.6 per cent does not come close to matching the growth in miles driven.[2] An obvious result has been increased traffic congestion.

A study from INRIX and the Centre for Economics and Business Research estimates that the annual cost of congestion in the UK will rise to £21 billion by 2030 – an increase of 63 per cent from 2013. It also finds that the cumulative cost of congestion to the UK economy in 2030 will be £307 billion (18 per cent of UK GDP in 2013), comprised of £191 billion of direct costs and £115 billion of indirect costs.[3]

Traffic congestion is a classic example of the problem of externalities. When people use their cars, not only do they incur private costs (petrol, wear and tear on the vehicle, tolls, the time taken to travel, etc.), but also they impose costs on other people. These external costs include the following:

Congestion costs: time. When a person uses a car, it adds to the congestion, slowing the traffic and increasing the journey time of other car users. The CBI found that in 2010, 19.2 seconds per mile were lost as a result of congestion and it expects this figure to increase to 32.3 seconds per mile by 2035.[4]

Congestion costs: monetary. Congestion increases fuel consumption and the costs of wear and tear. When a motorist adds to congestion, therefore, there are additional monetary costs imposed on other motorists. As it is, household expenditure on transport is already the largest category of spending, exceeding that on housing and power, recreation and culture, food and non-alcoholic drinks, and clothing and footwear. Average weekly household expenditure on transport in 2014 was £74.80, equating to 14 per cent of total expenditure. Out of this total figure, households spent £22.90 (30.6%) on petrol and diesel, £11.90 (15.9%) on repairs, services, parts and accessories, £23.80 (31.8%) on the purchase of new and second-hand cars and vans and £16.10 (21.5%) on train, bus and air fares.[5]

Environmental costs. Cars emit fumes and create noise, reducing the quality of the environment for pedestrians, other road users and especially those living along the road. Driving can cause accidents, a problem that increases as drivers become more impatient as a result of delays.

Exhaust gases cause long-term environmental damage and are one of the main causes of the greenhouse effect and of the increased acidity of lakes and rivers and the poisoning of forests. They can also cause long-term health problems (e.g. for asthma sufferers).

The socially efficient level of road usage

These externalities mean that road usage will be above the social optimum. This is illustrated in the diagram. Costs and benefits are shown on the vertical axis and are measured in money terms. Thus any non-monetary costs or benefits (such as time costs) must be given a monetary value. The horizontal axis measures road usage in terms of cars per minute passing a specified point on the road.

For simplicity it is assumed that there are no external benefits from car use and that therefore marginal private and marginal social benefits are the same. The *MSB* curve is shown as downward sloping. The reason for this is that different road users put a different value on any given journey. If the marginal (private) cost of making the journey were high, only those for whom the journey had a high marginal benefit would travel. If the marginal cost of making the journey fell, more people would make it, assuming the marginal cost was less than the marginal benefit. Thus the greater the number of cars, the lower the marginal benefit.

The marginal (private) cost curve (*MC*) is likely to be constant up to the level of traffic flow at which congestion begins to occur. This is shown as point *a* in the diagram. Beyond this point, marginal cost is likely to rise as time costs increase (i.e. journey times lengthen) and as fuel consumption rises.

The marginal *social* cost curve (*MSC*) is drawn above the marginal private cost curve. The vertical difference between the two represents the external costs. Up to point *b*, external costs are simply the environmental costs. Beyond point *b*, there are also external congestion costs, since additional road users slow down the journey of *other* road users. These external costs get progressively greater as traffic grinds to a halt.

The actual level of traffic flow will be at Q_1, where marginal private costs and benefits are equal (point *e*). The socially efficient level of traffic flow, however, will be at the lower level of Q_2 where marginal social costs and benefits are equal (point *d*). In other words, there will be an excessive level of road usage.

---

[1] *Provisional road traffic estimates, Great Britain: January 2015 to December 2015*, Department for Transport (11 February 2016).

[2] *Road lengths in Great Britain 2014*, Department for Transport (21 May 2015).

[3] 'Traffic congestion to cost the UK economy more than £300 billion over the next 16 years', *Press Release*, INRIX (14 October 2014).

[4] 'Infographic: UK road congestion – now and in 2035', *Bold Thinking: Roads report*, CBI (8 October 2012).

[5] *Family spending, 2015 edition*, ONS, Figure 1.1 (8 December 2015).

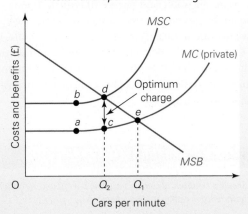

Actual and optimum road usage

So what can governments do to 'internalise' these externalities? To achieve a reduction in traffic to Q_2 the motorist should be charged an amount equal to d–c in the diagram. How can this be achieved? In practice this is difficult, given that congestion and its costs vary with location and the time of day. Also the external cost is hard to measure. One, albeit imperfect, solution is to impose charges on cars entering a 'congestion zone'. This solution is the one adopted in London.

Congestion charging in London

Car drivers must pay £11.50 per day to enter the inner London area (or 'congestion zone') any time between 7.00 and 18.00, Monday to Friday. Payment can be made by various means, including online, or by post, by phone or text, and at various shops and petrol stations. Payment can be in advance or up to midnight on the day of travel, or up to midnight on the following charging day for an extra £2.50. Alternatively, owners can register for auto-pay, being billed in arrears for all charges and receiving a £1 discount per day. Cars entering the congestion zone have their number plate recorded by camera and a computer check then leads to a fine of £130 being sent to those who have not paid (reduced to £65 for payment within 14 days).

The system was introduced in 2003 and the charging zone was extended in 2007. The initial effect was to reduce traffic in the zone by about 20 per cent and significantly increase the rate of traffic flow. Traffic in the zone has crept back somewhat since, but this is partly the result of a general increase in traffic. Transport for London has found that each day 80 000 fewer cars enter the original charging zone relative to 2002. The scheme does not address pollution directly, as the charge does not vary with the degree of congestion or the amount of time spent or distance travelled by a motorist within the zone.

Yet its simplicity makes it easy to understand and relatively cheap to operate.

However, it has led to an increase in electric and low emission cars (below 75g/km of CO_2) which are exempt from the congestion charge. Furthermore, London has a Low Emission Zone, covering most of Greater London, where heavy diesel vehicles must pay a charge of £500 or £1000 per day to enter the zone; and there are plans to introduce an Ultra Low Emission Zone in 2020, where all vehicles failing to meet low emission standards will be charged 24 hours per day. Such changes suggest a growing commitment to tackle both congestion and emission external costs within London's charging policy.

More sophisticated electronic road pricing

Other schemes attempt to relate directly the price charged to the motorist to the specific level of marginal external cost by varying charges according to the time of day. In Norway and parts of the USA, a relatively cheap road pricing system is in place, where traffic is forced into a single lane to register the car, but this does slow down traffic.

A more expensive and sophisticated Electronic Road Pricing (ERP) scheme operates in Singapore where cars are fitted with an in-vehicle unit (IU), where a rechargeable smart card is inserted containing pre-paid units. On specified roads, overhead gantries read the device and deduct units from the card. A sophisticated Global Navigation Satellite System is now being tested to remove the need for overhead gantries and vary the charge with the location, time of day, type of vehicle and the length of the congested road the driver has travelled on. In this way, road pricing directly relates charging to congestion.

Proposals to introduce a similar system in the UK have met with stiff opposition, especially from those who are forced to travel long distances or through congested areas simply to get to work.

Such charges do act as an incentive for people to reduce the amount they travel or to avoid peak times and put pressure on companies to use more flexible working times and to allow telecommuting (see Box 8.1 on page 182). However, unless there are feasible alternatives (fast, comfortable, reliable and affordable public transport), the demand for cars is going to remain highly price inelastic.

1. *Referring to a town or city with which you are familiar, consider what would be the most appropriate mix of policies to deal with its traffic congestion problems.*
2. *Explain how, by varying the charge to motorists according to the time of day or level of congestion, a socially optimal level of road use can be achieved.*

Finally, the system will lead to significant cuts in pollution only if the permitted levels are low. Once the system is in place, the government might then feel that the pressure is off to *reduce* the permitted levels. This was a major criticism of the EU's initial ETS. Between 2005 and 2007, carbon allowances were set far too high and so many firms had surplus credits, which pushed their price to a low level, reaching a minuscule €0.02 per tonne by the end of 2007, as discussed in the blog, 'The debate about cap and trade', on the Sloman Economics News site. This did reduce the pressure on 'dirty' firms to cut their emissions, as they could buy excess allowances so cheaply.

According to the Stern Report (see Box 9.3), carbon prices of $30 to $50 are necessary to stabilise levels of CO_2. The allowances were tightened in the second trading period (2008–12) and by mid-2008, carbon was trading at around €28 per tonne.

However, weak trading conditions during and after the recession caused the price to fall once more, as firms cut back on production. Despite the move to more auctioning of pollution permits, carbon prices have remained low, recording a 15 per cent drop in the first week of 2016 and a 23 per cent drop from the high in 2015 of €8.78 per tonne. This fall was in part due to Europe's weak economy and a boom in renewable and energy-efficient technology, but also due to speculation that further falls were likely. Such low prices are well below the price needed to stabilise levels of CO_2. They provide companies with little incentive to reduce emissions. There have thus been suggestions that some permits should be held back in Phase III to push carbon prices back up.

> ### Pause for thought
>
> *Should all emitters of carbon, including aircraft and agriculture, be included in carbon trading schemes?*

RECAP

1. There are three main types of environmental policy instrument: taxes and subsidies; command-and-control systems; tradable permits.

2. Taxes and subsidies have the advantages of 'internalising' externalities and of providing incentives to reduce external costs. The problem with using taxes and subsidies is in identifying the appropriate rates, since these will vary according to the environmental impact.

3. Command-and-control systems, such as making certain practices illegal or putting limits on discharges, are a less sophisticated alternative to taxes or subsidies. However, they may be preferable when the environmental costs of certain actions are unknown and it is wise to play safe.

4. Tradable permits are where firms are given permits to emit a certain level of pollution and then these can be traded. A firm that can relatively cheaply reduce its pollution below its permitted level can sell this credit to another firm which finds it more costly to do so. The ETS is the world's largest carbon trading scheme.

9.5 COMPETITION POLICY AND BUSINESS BEHAVIOUR

Competition, monopoly and the public interest

Most markets in the real world are imperfect, with firms having varying degrees of market power. But will this power be against the public interest? This question has been addressed by successive governments in framing legislation to deal with monopolies and oligopolies.

Market power enables firms to push up prices and make supernormal profit, thereby 'exploiting' the consumer. The fewer substitute products there are, the greater the firm's power and the higher prices will be relative to the costs of production. This is illustrated in Figure 9.4 (which is similar to Figure 5.2 on page 108).

The firm maximises profits at Q_1, where $MC = MR$. Profits are shown by the shaded area. The greater the firm's market power, the steeper will be the firm's AR and MR curves. The bigger will be the gap between price (point a) and marginal cost (point b). Remember that under perfect competition, price equals marginal cost (see Figure 4.4 on page 93). This is shown by point c, which is at a lower price and a higher output.

Although a lack of competition can result in higher prices and removes the incentive to become more efficient, market power is not necessarily a bad thing, as we saw in section 5.2. Economies of scale may allow a monopolist to charge a lower price than a more competitive firm; the threat of new competitors overcoming entry barriers may prevent firms from exploiting their position; and supernormal profits can provide funds for research and development or capital investment, potentially leading to new or innovative products.

Competition policy could seek to ban various structures or activities. For example, it could ban mergers leading to market share of more than a certain amount, or it could ban price-fixing arrangements between oligopolists. However, most countries prefer to adopt a more flexible approach and

Figure 9.4	Profit maximising under monopoly

(CMA), to replace the OFT and CC and take over any investigations. The aim was for a more streamlined process, with less duplication, speedier investigations, lower administration costs and more efficient resource allocation.

Some specific amendments have also been made to both restrictive practices and merger policy. These will be discussed in the following sections.

UK restrictive practices policy

The 2002 Enterprise Act made it a *criminal* offence to engage in cartel agreements (i.e. horizontal, rather than vertical, agreements between firms), irrespective of whether there are appreciable effects on competition. Convicted offenders may receive a prison sentence of up to five years and/or an unlimited fine. Prosecutions may be brought by the Serious Fraud Office or the CMA.

examine each case on its merits. Such an approach does not presume that the mere possession of power is against the public interest, but rather that certain uses of that power may be.

UK competition policy

Current UK policy is based on the 1998 Competition Act and the 2002 Enterprise Act, together with Part 3 of the 2013 Enterprise and Regulatory Reform Act. These Acts bring UK policy in line with EU competition policy (which is largely confined to firms trading between EU members).

The Competition Act has two key sets (or 'chapters') of prohibitions. Chapter I prohibits various collusive practices of oligopolies ('restrictive practices') (see pages 112–3). Chapter II prohibits various abuses of monopoly power. The Enterprise Act strengthened the Competition Act and introduced new measures for the control of mergers.

Under the two Acts, the body charged with ensuring that the prohibitions were carried out was the Office of Fair Trading (OFT). It could investigate any firm suspected of engaging in one or more prohibited practices, enter premises and request relevant documents. It could also require the firm to change its behaviour or cease its practices, with the option of imposing fines of up to 10 per cent of the firm's UK turnover.

The Competition Act also set up a Competition Commission (CC) to which the OFT could refer cases for further investigation. The CC would decide whether the structure of an industry or the practices of firms within it were detrimental to competition and impose the appropriate remedies. Appeals against decisions could be made to the Competition Appeal Tribunal (CAT), which continues as an independent body.

Following the outcome of a consultation on the links between competition and economic growth, the government introduced the 2013 Enterprise and Regulatory Reform Act. While retaining the principles and broad procedures of the 1998 and 2002 Acts, the 2013 Act set up a new unified body, the Competition and Markets Authority

Pause for thought

Are all such agreements necessarily against the interests of consumers?

But what practices constitute 'cartel agreements'? These involve one or more of the following agreements by firms: price fixing; limiting supply, perhaps by each firm agreeing to an output quota; sharing out markets by geographical area, type or size of customer or nature of outlet (e.g. bus companies agreeing not to run services in each other's areas); *collusive tendering* for a contract, where two or more firms put in a tender at secretly agreed (high) prices; or agreements between purchasers (e.g. supermarkets) to keep down prices paid to suppliers (e.g. farmers).

In the case of other types of agreement, the CMA has the discretion to decide, on a case-by-case basis, whether or not competition is appreciably restricted, and whether, therefore, they should be terminated or the firms should be exempted. Such cases include the following:

■ *Vertical price-fixing agreements.* These are price agreements between purchasing firms and their suppliers. An example of this is resale price maintenance. This is where a manufacturer or distributor sets the price for retailers to charge. It may well distribute a price list to retailers (e.g. a car manufacturer may distribute a price list to car showrooms). *Resale price maintenance* is a way of preventing

Definitions

Collusive tendering Where two or more firms secretly agree on the prices they will tender for a contract. These prices will be above those which would be put in under a genuinely competitive tendering process.

Resale price maintenance Where the manufacturer of a product (legally) insists that the product should be sold at a specified retail price.

competition between retailers driving down retail prices and ultimately the price they pay to the manufacturer. Both manufacturers and retailers, therefore, are likely to gain from resale price maintenance.

■ *Agreements to exchange information that could have the effect of reducing competition.* For example, if producers exchange information on their price intentions, it is a way of allowing price leadership (see page 113), a form of tacit collusion, to continue.

A problem with any policy to deal with collusion is the difficulty in rooting it out. When firms do all their deals 'behind closed doors' and are careful not to keep records or give clues, then collusion can be very hard to spot.

UK monopoly policy

Under the Chapter II prohibition of the 1998 Competition Act, it is illegal for a dominant firm to exercise its market power in such a way as to reduce competition. Any suspected case is investigated by the CMA, which uses a two-stage process in deciding whether an abuse has taken place.

The first stage is to establish whether a firm has a position of dominance. The firm does not literally have to be a monopoly. Rather 'dominance' normally involves the firm having at least a 40 per cent market share (national or local, whichever is appropriate), although this figure will vary from industry to industry. Also, dominance depends on the barriers to entry to new competitors. The higher the barriers to the entry of new firms, the less 'contestable' will be the market, and the more dominant a firm is likely to be for any given current market share.

If the firm *is* deemed to be dominant, the second stage involves the CMA deciding whether the firm's practices constitute an abuse of its position. Examples of such practices include:

■ *Charging excessively high prices.* These are prices above those that the firm would charge if it faced effective competition. One sign of excessively high prices is abnormally high rates of profit.
■ *Price discrimination.* This is regarded as an abuse only to the extent that the higher prices are excessive or the lower prices are used to exclude competitors.
■ *Predatory pricing.* This is where the price of a product is set at loss-making levels, so as to undercut competitors and drive them out of business. The firm uses profitable parts of its business to subsidise this loss making.
■ *Vertical restraints.* This is where a supplying firm imposes conditions on a purchasing firm (or vice versa). For example, a manufacturer may impose rules on retailers about displaying the product or the provision of after-

sales service, or it may refuse to supply certain outlets (e.g. perfume manufacturers refusing to supply discount chains, such as Superdrug).

The simple *existence* of any of these practices may not constitute an abuse. The CMA may carry out a detailed investigation to decide whether their *effect* is to restrict or distort competition. If this is found to be the case, the CMA decides what actions must be taken to remedy the situation.

UK merger policy

Merger policy is covered by the 2002 Enterprise Act. It seeks to prevent mergers that are likely to result in a substantial lessening of competition.

A merger or takeover will be investigated by the CMA if the target company has a turnover of £70 million or more, or if the merger results in the new company having a market share of 25 per cent or more.

One unusual aspect of UK policy is that there are no obligations on the participating firms to pre-notify the authorities about a merger that meets either of these two conditions. But, the CMA can still investigate such mergers, even after they have been completed and mergers themselves can be completed before they are officially cleared by the CMA. The risk here is that the 2013 Act gave the CMA more power to force companies to reverse any integration activities that were undertaken prior to an investigation. This would clearly impose significant costs on the business.

Any investigation involves the CMA conducting a preliminary or Phase 1 investigation (within 40 working days) to see whether competition is likely to be threatened. The CMA must then decide whether there is a significant chance that the merger would result in a substantial lessening of competition (SLC). If the CMA concludes that this might be the case, it begins Phase 2 of the process – a much more in-depth assessment. If no SLC issues are raised, the merger is allowed to go ahead, but the CMA can also require the merged firm to behave in certain ways in order to protect consumers' interests. In such cases, the CMA will then monitor the firm to ensure that it is abiding by any conditions.

In 2014/15, 68 per cent of merger cases were cleared unconditionally, 12 per cent were judged not to qualify and only six of the 83 Phase 1 cases (7 per cent) were referred for a Phase 2 investigation. An example of a referral for a Phase 2 investigation was BT Group plc's acquisition of EE Limited. However, approval was given for this merger in January 2016.

Complete prohibition of mergers has been relatively rare. In the 12 years to 2015/16, only 24 mergers were prohibited out of the 145 cases referred for Phase 2 investigation.

BOX 9.5 **FROM PAPER ENVELOPES TO CANNED MUSHROOMS: THE UMPIRE STRIKES BACK**

EU procedures for dealing with cartels

EU competition policy applies to companies operating in two or more EU countries. The policy is implemented by the European Commission, which has the power to levy substantial fines on companies found to be in breach of the legislation. In 2008, in order to simplify administrative processes and to reduce the number of cases going to the courts, new settlement procedures were introduced. If, on seeing the evidence against them, firms co-operated, then fines could be reduced by 10 per cent. Meanwhile, firms which have participated in a cartel but reveal details of its existence can be granted either immunity or further reductions in fines through a Leniency Notice.

Fixing prices at a mini-golf meeting

In September 2010, the European Commission began an investigation into the market for both standardised and customised paper envelopes in the EU. In December 2014, the Commission found Bong (of Sweden), GPV and Hamelin (of France), Mayer-Kuvert (of Germany) and Tompla (of Spain) guilty of participating in activities that restricted competition in this market. The meetings at which the details of the cartel arrangements were discussed were referred to by the participating firms as 'golf' or 'mini-golf' meetings!

The cartel arrangements directly affected the market for envelopes in Denmark, France, Germany, Norway, Sweden and the UK. The firms were judged to have been involved in the following restrictive practices that were in violation of Article 101:

- Allocating customers amongst members of the cartel.
- Agreeing on price increases.
- Co-ordinating responses to tenders initiated by major European customers.
- Exchanging commercially sensitive information on customers and sales volumes.

Details about the value of sales directly affected by the anti-competitive practices were made publicly available by the European Commission,[1] which is fairly rare, but this was considered to be an exceptional case, as the sales of envelopes affected by the cartel activities made up a large fraction of each firm's total turnover. Therefore the basic fines exceeded the 10 per cent cap on turnover normally set by the authorities. The fines were then reduced in a way that took account of (a) the value of affected sales for each firm as a proportion of their turnover and (b) the level of involvement in the restrictive practices.

Tompla, Hamelin and Mayer-Kuvert received reductions in their basic fines of 50, 25 and 10 per cent respectively. All five firms obtained an additional 10 per cent reduction for agreeing to the settlements and not taking their cases to court. Two firms also claimed that they were unable to pay the fine without getting into serious financial difficulties and were granted a further reduction. Affected sales, basic fines and final fines are summarised in the table.

Referring to this case, Commissioner Margrethe Vestager, in charge of competition policy said:

> Everybody uses envelopes. When cartelists raise the prices of everyday household objects they do so at the expense of millions of Europeans. The Commission's fight against cartels penalises such behaviour and also acts as a deterrent, protecting consumers from harm. On this case we have closed the envelope, sealed it and returned it to the sender with a clear message: don't cheat your customers, don't cartelise.[2]

1. What factors determine the likelihood that firms will collude to fix prices – despite the prospect of facing fines of up to 10 per cent of their annual global turnover?
2. Why might global cartels be harder to identify and eradicate than cartels located solely within the domestic economy? What problems does this raise for competition policy?

	Bong	GPV	Hamelin	Mayer-Kuvert	Tompla
Value of relevant sales (€m)	140.0	125.1	185.5	70.0	143.3
Basic fine (€m) (based on 15% of value of sales affected)	115.5	103.2	150.7	57.8	118.2
Final fine (€m)	3.118	1.651	4.996	4.991	4.729

[1] 'Cartel Procedure: Case AT.39780 – Envelopes', *European Commission* (10 December 2014).

[2] 'Antitrust: Commission fines five envelope producers over €19.4 million in cartel settlement', *European Commission Press Release* (11 December 2014).

RECAP

1. Competition policy in most countries recognises that monopolies, mergers and restrictive practices can bring both costs and benefits to the consumer. Generally, though, restrictive practices tend to be more damaging to consumers' interests than simple monopoly power or mergers.

2. UK legislation is covered by the 1998 Competition Act and 2002 Enterprise Act. The Competition and Markets Authority has replaced the Office of Fair Trading and Competition Commission and is now the unified body charged with ensuring that firms abide by the legislation.

3. Cartel agreements are a criminal offence and certain other types of collusive behaviour can be curtailed by the CMA if they are against the public interest.

4. The abuse of monopoly power by a dominant firm can also be prevented by the CMA. Such abuses include charging excessively high prices.

5. Mergers over a certain size are investigated by the CMA for a ruling as to whether they should be permitted.

9.6 THE REGULATION OF BUSINESS

Regulation and the privatised industries

In the late 1940s and early 1950s the Labour government *nationalised* many of the key transport, communications and power industries, such as the railways, freight transport, airlines, coal, gas, electricity and steel. The Thatcher and Major governments in the 1980s and early 1990s sold these industries to the private sector in a programme of *privatisation*. However, many of these privatised industries had considerable market power and so it was felt necessary to regulate their behaviour.

Regulation in practice

To some extent the behaviour of privatised industries may be governed by general monopoly and restrictive practice legislation. For example, in the UK privatised firms can be investigated by the Competition and Markets Authority (CMA).

In addition to this, there is a separate regulatory office to oversee the structure and behaviour of each of the privatised utilities. These regulators are as follows: the Office for Gas and Electricity Markets (Ofgem), the Office of Communications (Ofcom), the Office of Rail and Road (ORR) and the Office of Water Services (Ofwat). The regulators set terms under which the industries have to operate. For example, ORR sets the terms under which rail companies have access to the track and stations. The terms set by the regulator can be reviewed by negotiation between the regulator and the industry. If agreement cannot be reached, the CMA acts as an appeal court and its decision is binding.

The regulator for each industry also sets limits to the prices that certain parts of the industry can charge. These parts are those where there is little or no competition, e.g. the charges made to electricity and gas retailers by National Grid, the owner of the electricity grid and major gas pipelines.

The price-setting formulae are essentially of the '*RPI* minus *X*' variety. What this means is that the industries can raise their prices by the rate of increase in the retail price index (i.e. by the rate of inflation) *minus* a certain percentage (X) to take account of expected increases in efficiency.

Thus if the rate of inflation were 6 per cent, and if the regulator considered that the industry (or firm) could be expected to reduce its costs by 2 per cent ($X = 2$ per cent), then price rises would be capped at 4 per cent. The $RPI - X$ system is thus an example of *price-cap regulation*. The idea of this system of regulation is that it forces the industry to pass cost savings on to the consumer.

Pause for thought

If an industry regulator adopts an RPI – X formula for price regulation, is it desirable that the value of X should be adjusted as soon as cost conditions change?

Assessing the system of regulation in the UK

The system that has evolved in the UK has various advantages:

■ It is a discretionary system, with the regulator able to judge individual examples of the behaviour of the industry on their own merits. The regulator has a detailed knowledge of the industry which would not be available to government ministers or other bodies such as the CMA. The regulator could thus be argued to be in the best position to decide on whether the industry is acting in the public interest.

Definitions

Nationalised industries State-owned industries that produce goods or services that are sold in the market.

Privatisation Selling nationalised industries to the private sector. This may be through the public issue of shares, by a management buyout or by selling it to a private company.

Price-cap regulation Where the regulator puts a ceiling on the amount by which a firm can raise its price.

- The system is flexible, since it allows for the licence and price formula to be changed as circumstances change.
- The '*RPI* minus *X*' formula provides an incentive for the privatised firms to be as efficient as possible. If they can lower their costs by more than *X*, they will, in theory, be able to make larger profits and keep them. If on the other hand, they do not succeed in reducing costs sufficiently, they will make a loss. There is thus a continuing pressure on them to cut costs.

There are, however, some inherent problems with the way in which regulation operates in the UK:

- The '*RPI* minus *X*' formula was designed to provide an incentive for the firms to cut costs. But if *X* is set too low, the firm might make excessive profits. Frequently, regulators have underestimated the scope for cost reductions resulting from new technology and reorganisation, and have thus initially set *X* too low. As a result, instead of *X* remaining constant for a number of years, as intended, new higher values for *X* have been set after only one or two years. Alternatively, one-off price cuts have been ordered, as happened when the water companies were required by Ofwat to cut prices by an average of 10 per cent in 2000. In either case, the incentive for the industry to cut costs is reduced. What is the point of being more efficient if the regulator is merely going to insist on a higher value for *X* and thus take away the extra profits.
- Regulation is becoming increasingly complex. This makes it difficult for the industries to plan and may lead to a growth of 'short-termism'. One of the claimed advantages of privatisation was to give greater independence to the industries from short-term government interference, and allow them to plan for the longer term. In practice, one type of interference may have been replaced by another.
- As regulation becomes more detailed and complex and as the regulator becomes more and more involved in the detailed running of the industry, so managers and regulators will become increasingly involved in a game of strategy, each trying to outwit the other. Information will become distorted and time and energy will be wasted in playing this game of cat and mouse. This is an example of the principal–agent problem (see pages 9–10), where the agent (the company) is trying to avoid carrying out the wishes of the principal (the regulator).
- There is also the problem that as the regulator becomes more involved in the industry, they may be persuaded to see the managers' point of view and hence they could become less strict. This idea is known as *regulatory capture*. While it certainly remains a potential problem, commentators do not believe this has become an issue.

One way in which the dangers of ineffective or over-intrusive regulation can be avoided is to replace regulation with competition wherever this is possible. Indeed, one of the major concerns of the regulators has been to do just this. (See Case Studies C.25 and C.26 on the book's website for ways in which competition has been increased in the gas and electricity industries.)

Regulation versus competition

Where natural monopoly exists (see page 106), competition is impossible in a free market. Of course, the industry *could* be broken up by the government, with firms prohibited from owning more than a certain percentage of the industry. But this would lead to higher costs of production. Firms would be operating further back up a downward-sloping long-run average cost curve.

However, many parts of the privatised industries are not natural monopolies. Generally it is only the *grid* that is a natural monopoly. In the case of gas and water, it is the pipelines. It would be wasteful to duplicate these. In the case of electricity, it is the national grid and the local power lines. In the case of the railways, it is the track.

Other parts of these industries, however, have generally been opened up to competition (with the exception of water). Thus there are now many producers and sellers of electricity and gas. This is possible because they are given access, by law, to the national and local electricity grids and gas pipelines. The telecommunications market too has become more competitive with the growth of mobile phones and lines supplied by cable operators.

As competition has been introduced into these industries, so price-cap regulation has been progressively abandoned. For example, in 2006 Ofcom abandoned price control of BT and other phone companies over line rentals and phone charges. This was in response to the growth in competition from cable operators, mobile phones and free Internet calls from companies such as Skype via VoIP (voice Internet protocol).

Despite attempts to introduce competition into the privatised industries, they are still dominated by giant companies. Even if they are no longer strictly monopolies, they still have considerable market power and the scope for price leadership or other forms of oligopolistic collusion is great. Thus, although regulation through the price formula has been progressively abandoned as elements of competition have been introduced, the regulators have retained their role, namely preventing cases of collusion and the abuse of monopoly power. The companies, however, do have the right of appeal.

> ### Definition
>
> **Regulatory capture** Where the regulator is persuaded to operate in the industry's interests rather than those of the consumer.

RECAP

1. Regulation in the UK has involved setting up regulatory offices for the major privatised utilities. These generally operate informally, using negotiation and bargaining to persuade the industries to behave in the public interest.

2. As far as prices are concerned, parts of the industries are required to abide by an '*RPI* minus *X*' formula. This forces them to pass potential cost reductions on to the consumer. At the same time they are allowed to retain any additional profits gained from cost reductions greater than *X*. This provides them with an incentive to achieve even greater increases in efficiency.

3. Many parts of the privatised industries are not natural monopolies. In these parts, competition may be a more effective means of pursuing the public interest.

4. Various attempts have been made to make the privatised industries more competitive, often at the instigation of the regulator. Nevertheless, considerable market power remains in the hands of many privatised firms, and thus the need for regulation will continue.

QUESTIONS

1. Assume that a firm discharges waste into a river. As a result, the marginal social costs (*MSC*) are greater than the firm's marginal (private) costs (*MC*). The following table shows how *MC*, *MSC*, *AR* and *MR* vary with output.

Output	1	2	3	4	5	6	7	8
MC (£)	23	21	23	25	27	30	35	42
MSC (£)	35	34	38	42	46	52	60	72
TR (£)	60	102	138	168	195	219	238	252
AR (£)	60	51	46	42	39	36.5	34	31.5
MR (£)	60	42	36	30	27	24	19	14

   (a) How much will the firm produce if it seeks to maximise profits?
   (b) What is the socially efficient level of output (assuming no externalities on the demand side)?
   (c) How much is the marginal external cost at this level of output?
   (d) What size tax would be necessary for the firm to reduce its output to the socially efficient level?
   (e) Why is the tax less than the marginal externality?
   (f) Why might it be equitable to impose a lump-sum tax on this firm?
   (g) Why will a lump-sum tax not affect the firm's output (assuming that in the long run the firm can still make at least normal profit)?

2. Distinguish between publicly provided goods, public goods and merit goods.

3. Some roads could be regarded as a public good, but some could be provided by the market. Which types of road could be provided by the market? Why? Would it be a good idea?

4. Make a list of pieces of information a firm might want to know and consider whether it could buy the information and how reliable that information might be.

5. Why might it be better to ban certain activities that cause environmental damage rather than to tax them?

6. How suitable are legal restrictions in the following cases?

   (a) Ensuring adequate vehicle safety (e.g. tyres with sufficient tread or roadworthy vehicles).
   (b) Reducing traffic congestion.
   (c) Preventing the use of monopoly power.
   (d) Ensuring that mergers are in the public interest.
   (e) Ensuring that firms charge a price equal to marginal cost.

7. In what ways might business be socially responsible?

8. What economic costs and benefits might a business experience if it decided to adopt a more socially responsible position? How might such costs and benefits change over the longer term?

9. Using a demand and supply diagram, explain why carbon prices fell at the beginning of the Emissions Trading System (ETS), due to emissions allowances being too generous.

10. What problems are likely to arise in identifying which firms' practices are anti-competitive? Should the CMA take firms' assurances into account when deciding whether to grant an exemption?

11. If anti-monopoly legislation is effective enough, is there ever any need to prevent mergers from going ahead?

12. If two or more firms were charging similar prices, what types of evidence would you look for to prove that this was collusion rather than mere coincidence?

13. Should governments or regulators always attempt to eliminate the supernormal profits of monopolists/oligopolists?

14. Should regulators of utilities that have been privatised into several separate companies permit (a) horizontal mergers (within the industry); (b) vertical mergers; (c) mergers with firms in other related industries (e.g. gas and electricity suppliers)?

ADDITIONAL PART C CASE STUDIES ON THE *ECONOMICS AND THE BUSINESS ENVIRONMENT* WEBSITE (www.pearsoned.co.uk/sloman)

C.1 **B2B electronic marketplaces.** This case study examines the growth of firms trading with each other over the Internet (business to business or 'B2B') and considers the effects on competition.

C.2 **Measuring monopoly power.** This analyses how the degree of monopoly power possessed by a firm can be measured.

C.3 **X-inefficiency.** A type of inefficiency suffered by many large firms, resulting in a wasteful use of resources.

C.4 **Airline deregulation in the USA and Europe.** Whether the deregulation of various routes has led to more competition and lower prices.

C.5 **Bakeries: oligopoly or monopolistic competition.** A case study on the bread industry, showing that small-scale local bakeries can exist alongside giant national bakeries.

C.6 **Oligopoly in the brewing industry.** A case study showing how the UK brewing industry is becoming more concentrated.

C.7 **Cut throat competition.** An examination of the barriers to entry to the UK razor market.

C.8 **OPEC.** A case study examining OPEC's influence over oil prices from the early 1970s to the present day.

C.9 **Hybrid strategy.** Is it good for companies to use a mix of strategies?

C.10 **Stakeholder power.** An examination of the various stakeholders of a business and their influence on business behaviour.

C.11 **Logistics.** A case study of the use of the logistics industry by companies seeking to outsource their supply chain.

C.12 **Price discrimination in the cinema.** An illustration of why it may be in a cinema's interests to offer concessionary prices at off-peak times, but not at peak times.

C.13 **Peak-load pricing.** An example of price discrimination: charging more when it costs more to produce.

C.14 **How do UK companies set prices?** The findings of Bank of England and ECB surveys.

C.15 **Labour market trends.** This case study describes the changing patterns of employment in the UK, from the rise in service-sector employment and fall in manufacturing employment, to the rise in part-time working and a rise in female participation rates.

C.16 **The rise and decline of the labour movement.** A brief history of trade unions in the UK.

C.17 **How useful is marginal productivity theory?** How accurately does the theory describe employment decisions by firms?

C.18 **Profit sharing.** An examination of the case for and against profit sharing as a means of rewarding workers.

C.19 **Should health care provision be left to the market?** This identifies the market failures that would occur if health care provision were left to the free market.

C.20 **Corporate social responsibility.** An examination of social responsibility as a goal of firms and its effect on business performance.

C.21 **Technology and economic change.** How to get the benefits from technological advance.

C.22 **Can the market provide adequate protection for the environment?** This explains why markets generally fail to take into account environmental externalities.

C.23 **Green taxes.** Are they the perfect answer to the problem of pollution?

C.24 **Selling the environment.** The market-led solution of the Kyoto Protocol.

C.25 **Evaluating new road schemes.** The system used in the UK of assessing the costs and benefits of proposed new roads.

C.26 **Road pricing in Singapore.** A case study showing the methods Singapore has used to cut traffic congestion.

C.27 **Restricting car access to Athens.** A case study that examines how the Greeks have attempted to reduce local atmospheric pollution from road traffic.

C.28 **Environmental auditing.** Are businesses becoming greener? A growing number of firms are subjecting themselves to an 'environmental audit' to judge just how 'green' they are.

C.29 **Cartels set in concrete, steel and cardboard.** This examines some of the best-known Europe-wide cartels of recent years.

C.30 **Taking your vitamins at a price.** A case study showing how vitamin-producing companies were fined for price fixing.

C.31 **What price for peace of mind?** Exploiting monopoly power in the sale of extended warranties on electrical goods

C.32 **The right track to reform.** Reorganising the railways in the UK.

C.33 **Competition in the pipeline.** An examination of attempts to introduce competition into the gas industry in the UK.

C.34 **Selling power to the people.** Attempts to introduce competition into the UK electricity industry.

WEBSITES RELEVANT TO PART C

Numbers and sections refer to websites listed in the Web Appendix and hotlinked from this book's website at **www.pearsoned. co.uk/sloman/**

■ For news articles relevant to Part C, Google the Sloman Economics News site.

■ For general news on the microeconomic environment of business see websites in section A of the Web Appendix, and particularly A1–5, 7–9, 11, 12, 20–26, 35, 36. See also links to newspapers worldwide in A38, 39, 43 and 44 and the news search feature in Google at A41.

■ For student resources relevant to Part C, see section C, see sites C1–7, 9, 10, 14, 19.

■ For games and simulations relevant to Part C, see section D, and particularly sites D3, 6–9, 12–14, 16–20.

■ For sites that look at competition and market power, including competition policy, see section E, sites E4 and 10; and section G, sites G7 and 8. See also links in I7, 11 and 14. UK regulatory bodies can be found at sites E11, 15, 16, 18, 19, 22.

■ For information on stock markets, see sites F18 and A1, 3, 22–25; B27.

■ For data on SMEs, see the SME database in B3 or E10.

■ For information on pricing in the UK, see section E, and particularly site E10 and the sites of the regulators of the privatised industries: E15, 16, 19, 22.

■ For UK data on labour markets, see site B3 > Employment and Labour Market. For international labour market data see site H3 > Statistics and databases. Site I14 has links to various sources of data on various aspects of labour market.

■ Links to the TUC and Confederation of British Industry sites can be found in section E at E32 and 33.

■ For information on taxes and subsidies, see E30, 36; G13. For use of green taxes, see H5; G11; E2, 14. Site I14 has links to various sites from around the world looking at taxation.

■ For information on health and the economics of health care (Case Study C.19 on the website), see E8; H8.

■ For sites favouring the free market, see C17; E34. See also C18 for the development of ideas on the market and government intervention.

■ For the economics of the environment, see links in section I at sites I7, 11 and 14. For policy on the environment and transport, see section E for UK sites: E2, 7, 11, 14, 29 and 39; and section G for EU sites: G10, 11 and 19. See also H11.

The macroeconomic environment of business

The success of an individual business depends not only on its own particular market and its own particular decisions. It also depends on the whole macroeconomic environment in which it operates, including the international environment.

If the economy is booming, then individual businesses are likely to be more profitable than if the economy is in recession. It is thus important for businesses to understand the forces that affect the whole business climate.

One of these forces is the level of confidence, of both consumers and business. If business confidence is high, then firms are more likely to invest. Similarly, if consumer confidence is high, spending in the shops is likely to be high and this will increase business profitability. The result will be economic growth. If, however, people are predicting a recession, firms will hold off investing and consumer spending may well decline. This could tip the economy into recession.

In Chapter 10 we look at the various national forces affecting the performance of the economy.

Another key ingredient of the macroeconomic environment is government policy and the actions of the central bank (the Bank of England in the UK or the European Central Bank (ECB) in the eurozone). If the government raises taxes or the central bank raises interest rates this could impact directly on business profitability and on business confidence. We examine domestic macroeconomic policies in Chapter 11.

In the final two chapters we turn to the international macroeconomic environment. In Chapter 12 we look at the role of international trade. We see how countries and firms can gain from trade and why, despite this, governments sometimes choose to restrict trade.

Then in Chapter 13 we examine the flows of finance across international exchanges. We see how exchange rates are determined and how changes in exchange rates affect business. We study the euro and whether having a single currency for many EU countries benefits business. Finally, we look at attempts by governments worldwide to coordinate their macroeconomic policies.

The economy and business activity

Business issues covered in this chapter

- What are the main macroeconomic objectives and how do they conflict with each other?
- What determines the level of activity in the economy and hence the overall business climate?
- If a stimulus is given to the economy, what will be the effect on business output?
- Why do economies experience periods of boom followed by periods of recession? What determines the length and magnitude of these 'phases' of the business cycle?
- How are interest rates determined?
- What determines the supply of money in the economy and how does this affect interest rates?
- What are the causes of unemployment and how does unemployment relate to the level of business activity?
- What are the causes of inflation and how does inflation relate to the level of business activity?
- What are the costs of inflation and unemployment and to whom do they apply?

10.1 THE KEY MACROECONOMIC OBJECTIVES

There are several macroeconomic variables that governments seek to control. The macroeconomic environment will influence all aspects of businesses, including their markets, their costs and their potential profitability. We can group these macroeconomic elements into six key areas.

Economic growth. Governments aim to achieve economic growth over the long term. They will aim for a stable *rate of economic growth*, which avoids both short-term rapid growth that cannot be sustained and periods of recession. However, economies are unstable and growth rates will fluctuate, as is evident by recent history in both developed and developing nations.

Unemployment. Reducing unemployment is a key macroeconomic objective for government and we take a closer look at

it in section 10.6. It poses many costs for different groups across society, which is why it is such an important objective and we consider these costs in more detail in Box 10.4.

Inflation. This refers to a general rise in prices throughout the economy. The *rate of inflation* is the percentage increase in the level of prices over a 12-month period.

Definitions

Rate of economic growth The percentage increase in output over a 12-month period.

Rate of inflation The percentage increase in prices over a 12-month period.

Government policy aims to keep inflation low and stable, as this will aid economic decision making by creating a more certain economic environment. In fact, this has led many governments to adopt an inflation rate target and to delegate responsibility to its central bank for interventions in money markets to affect interest rates (we consider these interventions in section 11.2). A low and stable rate of inflation, in turn, affects the business climate and confidence and can help to encourage investment.

In recent years we have become used to low inflation rates, with some countries, particularly Japan, even experiencing falling prices, or deflation, as discussed in the blog on the Sloman Economics News site, 'Japan's deflation fears grow'. Despite slightly higher inflation rates in many countries in 2008 and again in 2010–11, they still remained low relative to the past, particularly the 1990s, when inflation rates in many developed countries rose into double figures. (It had been as high as 24 per cent in the UK in 1975.)[1] We consider inflation in more detail in section 10.7 and analyse the costs in Box 10.4.

The balance of payments. Governments aim to provide an environment in which exports can grow without an excessive growth in imports. They also aim to make the economy attractive to inward investment. In other words, they seek to create a climate in which the country's earnings of foreign currency at least match, or preferably exceed, the country's demand for foreign currency: they seek to achieve a favourable *balance of payments*.

The sale of exports and any other receipts earn foreign currency. The purchase of imports or any other payments abroad represent our demand for foreign currency. If we start to spend more foreign currency than we earn, one of two things must happen. Both are likely to be a problem:

■ *The balance of payments will go into deficit.* In other words, there will be a shortfall of foreign currencies. The government will therefore have to borrow money from abroad, or draw on its foreign currency reserves to make up the shortfall. This is a problem because, if it goes on for too long, overseas debts will mount, along with the interest that must be paid; and/or reserves will begin to run low.
■ *The exchange rate will fall.* The *exchange rate* is the rate at which one currency exchanges for another. For example, the exchange rate of the pound into the dollar might be £1 = $1.50. If the government does nothing to correct the balance of payments deficit, then the exchange rate must fall. A lower exchange rate (i.e. fewer dollars, yen, euros, etc. to the pound) will make UK goods cheaper to overseas buyers, and thus help to boost UK exports. A falling exchange rate is a problem, however, because it pushes up the price of imports and may fuel inflation.

Also, if the exchange rate fluctuates, this can cause great uncertainty for traders and can damage international trade and economic growth.

We consider the balance of payments and exchange rates in more detail in Chapter 13.

Financial well-being. It is increasingly recognised that the behaviour of individuals, businesses, governments and nations is affected by their financial well-being. If consumers and firms are worried about their financial well-being, they are likely to become more cautious: consumers may hold back on spending and try to reduce their debts; businesses may be more cautious about investing. If governments are concerned about government debt, they are likely to try to reduce spending and/or increase taxation.

Financial stability. A core aim of the government and the central bank is to ensure the stability of the financial system. After all, financial markets and institutions are an integral part of economies. Their well-being is crucial to the well-being of an economy.

Because of the global interconnectedness of financial institutions and markets, problems can spread globally like a contagion. The financial crisis of the late 2000s showed how financially distressed financial institutions can cause serious economic upheaval on a global scale. As we shall see in section 11.2, a major part of the global response to the financial crisis has been to try to ensure that financial institutions are more financially resilient. In particular, financial institutions should have more loss-absorbing capacity and therefore be better able to withstand 'shocks' and deteriorating macroeconomic conditions.

Government macroeconomic policy

From the above four issues we can identify six macroeconomic policy objectives that governments typically pursue:

■ High and stable economic growth.
■ Low unemployment.

Definitions

Balance of payments account A record of the country's transactions with the rest of the world. It shows the country's payments to or deposits in other countries (debits) and its receipts (credits) from other countries. It also shows the balance between these debits and credits under various headings.

Exchange rate The rate at which one national currency exchanges for another. The rate is expressed as the amount of one currency that is necessary to purchase *one unit* of another currency (e.g. $1.20 = £1).

---

[1] 'Inflation Great Britain 1975', *Inflation.EU: Worldwide Inflation Data.*

- Low and stable inflation.
- The avoidance of balance of payments deficits and excessive exchange rate fluctuations.
- The avoidance of excessively financially distressed sectors of the economy, including government.
- A stable financial system.

Unfortunately, these policy objectives may conflict. For example, a policy designed to accelerate the rate of economic growth may result in a higher rate of inflation; a balance of payments deficit and excessive borrowing. Governments are thus often faced with awkward policy choices. All the choices they make will impact on business.

RECAP

1. The macroeconomic environment of business is characterised by a series of inter-related macroeconomic variables. These include: economic growth, unemployment, inflation, the balance of payments, exchange rates, the financial well-being of households, businesses and governments, and the stability of the financial system.

2. Government macroeconomic policy seeks to influence these variables, e.g. to increase the rate of economic growth and reduce unemployment. However, the macroeconomic objectives of governments will often conflict with each other and so, to some extent, governments will have to prioritise.

10.2 BUSINESS ACTIVITY AND THE CIRCULAR FLOW OF INCOME

We now turn to the question of what determines the overall level of business activity. One of the most important determinants, at least in the short run, is the level of spending on firms' output. The more consumers spend, the more firms will want to produce in order to meet that consumer demand.

We use the term 'aggregate demand' (*AD*) to represent the total level of spending on the goods and services produced within the country over a given time period (normally a year). This spending consists of four elements: consumer spending on domestically produced goods and services (C_d), investment expenditure within the country by firms, whether on plant and equipment or on building up stocks (*I*), government spending on goods and services (such as health, education and transport) (*G*) and the expenditure by residents abroad on this country's exports (*X*). Thus:

$$AD = C_d + I + G + X$$

A small change you may sometimes see to the above equation is imports (*M*) being subtracted from exports. In the above equation, note that '*C*' has a subscript of 'd' showing that it is only domestic consumption being taken into account. That is, consumption of imports is already excluded. If C_d becomes just *C* (i.e. total consumption), then we must also subtract imports from the four components to ensure we are only considering the total spending in the domestic economy. The equation then becomes:

$$AD = C + I + G + X - M$$

The total annual output of goods and services on which aggregate demand is spent is called GDP, or 'gross domestic product'. As long as there is spare capacity in the economy, a rise in aggregate demand will stimulate firms to produce more. GDP will rise.

A simple way of understanding this process is to use a 'circular flow of income diagram'. This is shown in Figure 10.1.

In the diagram, the economy is divided into two major groups: *firms* and *households*. Each group has two roles. Firms are producers of goods and services; they are also the employers of labour. Households (the word we use for individuals) are the consumers of goods and services; they are also the suppliers of labour. In the diagram there is an inner flow and various outer flows of income between these two groups.

The inner flow, withdrawals and injections

The inner flow

Firms pay incomes to households in the form of wages and salaries. Some households also receive incomes from firms in the form of dividends on shares, or interest on loans or rent on property. Thus on the left-hand side of the diagram the money that flows directly from firms to households is simply household incomes.

Households, in turn, pay money to domestic firms when they *consume domestically produced goods and services* (C_d). This is shown on the right-hand side of the inner flow. There is thus a circular flow of payments from firms to households to firms and so on.

If households spend *all* their incomes on buying domestic goods and services, and if firms pay out *all* the income

---

Definition

Consumption of domestically produced goods and services (C_d) The direct flow of money payments from households to firms.

Figure 10.1 The circular flow of income

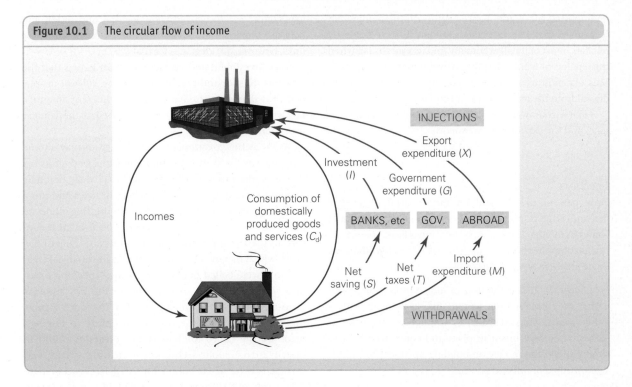

they receive from selling the goods and services back to domestic households in the form of wages, dividends, etc., and if the speed at which money flows around the system does not change, the flow will continue at the same level indefinitely. The money just goes round and round at the same speed and incomes remain unchanged.

In the real world, of course, it is not as simple as this. Not all income gets passed on round the inner flow; some is *withdrawn*. At the same time, incomes are *injected* into the flow from outside. Let us examine these withdrawals and injections.

Withdrawals

When households receive income, not all of it will be spent on domestic goods and services and hence there will be withdrawals from the inner flow. There are three forms of *withdrawals (W)* (or *leakages*, as they are sometimes called):

Net saving (S). Saving is income that households choose not to spend but to put aside for the future. Savings are normally deposited in financial institutions such as banks and building societies. This is shown in the bottom right of the diagram. Money flows from households to 'banks, etc.'. What we are seeking to measure here, however, is the net flow from households to the banking sector. We therefore have to subtract from saving any borrowing or drawing on past savings by households in order to get the *net* saving flow. Of course, if household borrowing exceeded saving, the net flow would be in the other direction; it would be negative.

Net taxes (T). When people pay taxes (to either central or local government), this represents a withdrawal of money

from the inner flow in much the same way as saving; only in this case people have no choice! Some taxes, such as income tax and employees' national insurance contributions, are paid out of household incomes. Others, such as VAT and excise duties, are paid out of consumer expenditure. Yet others, such as corporation tax, are paid out of firms' incomes before being received by households as dividends on shares. (For simplicity, however, we show taxes being withdrawn at just one point. It does not affect the argument.)

When, however, people receive *benefits* from the government, such as working tax credit, child benefit and pensions, the money flows the other way. Benefits are thus equivalent to a 'negative tax'. These benefits are known as *transfer payments*. They transfer money from one group of people (taxpayers) to others (the recipients).

In the model, 'net taxes' (*T*) represents the *net* flow to the government from households and firms. It consists of total taxes minus benefits.

Import expenditure (M). Not all consumption is of home-produced goods. Households spend some of their incomes

Definitions

Withdrawals (*W*) (or leakages) Incomes of households or firms that are not passed on round the inner flow. Withdrawals equal net saving (*S*) plus net taxes (*T*) plus import expenditure (*M*): $W = S + T + M$.

Transfer payments Moneys transferred from one person or group to another (e.g. from the government to individuals) without production taking place.

on imported goods and services. Although the money that consumers spend on such goods initially flows to domestic retailers, most of it will eventually find its way abroad when the retailers or wholesalers themselves import the products. This expenditure on imports constitutes the third withdrawal from the inner flow, as the money flows abroad.

Total withdrawals are simply the sum of net saving, net taxes and the expenditure on imports:

$$W = S + T + M$$

Injections

Only part of the demand for firms' output (aggregate demand) arises from consumers' expenditure. The remainder comes from other sources outside the inner flow. These additional components of spending are known as *injections (J)*. There are three types of injections:

Investment (I). This is the flow of money that firms spend which they obtain from various financial institutions – either past savings or loans, or through a new issue of shares. They may invest in plant and equipment or may simply spend the money on building up stocks of inputs, semi-finished or finished goods.

Government expenditure (G). When the government spends money on goods and services produced by firms, this counts as an injection. Examples of such government expenditure are spending on roads, hospitals and schools. (Note that government expenditure in this model does not include state benefits. These transfer payments, as we saw above, are the equivalent of negative taxes and have the effect of reducing the T component of withdrawals.)

Export expenditure (X). Money flows into the circular flow from abroad when residents abroad buy our exports of goods and services.

Total injections are thus the sum of investment, government expenditure and exports:

$$J = I + G + X$$

Aggregate demand, which is the total spending on output, is thus $C_d + J$.

The relationship between withdrawals and injections

There are indirect links between saving and investment via financial institutions, between taxation and government expenditure via the government (central and local), and between imports and exports via foreign countries. These links, however, do not guarantee that $S = I$ or $G = T$ or $M = X$.

Take investment and saving. The point here is that the decisions to save and invest are made by *different* people, and thus they plan to save and invest different amounts. Likewise the demand for imports may not equal the demand for exports.

As far as the government is concerned, it may choose not to make $T = G$. It may choose not to spend all its tax revenues and thus run a 'budget surplus' ($T > G$); or it may choose to spend more than it receives in taxes and run a 'budget deficit' ($G > T$), by borrowing or printing money to make up the difference. This issue has been of great concern in the UK and many other countries in the past few years, which had seen borrowing soar in the financial crisis as banks were bailed out and emergency spending measures were adopted by government. In the UK, austerity measures have been adopted since 2010 to reduce borrowing and bring down the deficit. According to forecasts made by the Office for Budget Responsibility (OBR) in March 2016,[2] public-sector net borrowing (PSNB) was expected to be £74.0 billion for 2015/16, equivalent to 3.9 per cent of GDP, down from £91.7 billion (or 5 per cent of GDP) in 2014/15 and £154.7 billion (or 10.3 per cent of GDP) in 2009/10

Thus, planned injections (J) may not equal planned withdrawals (W). But if they are not equal, what will be the consequences?

If injections exceed withdrawals, the level of expenditure will rise (the increase in spending from injections is greater than the reduction in spending from withdrawals). The extra spending will generate extra incomes. In other words, GDP will rise; there will be economic growth. This, as we shall see later in the chapter, will tend to reduce unemployment as firms take on more labour to meet the extra demand. It may, however, lead to a rise in inflation as the extra demand drives up the price of goods and services more rapidly than would have been the case.

If planned injections are *less* than planned withdrawals then the opposite of each of the above will occur. GDP will fall (there will be negative economic growth); unemployment will rise and inflation will fall.

> ### Pause for thought
>
> *If injections exceed withdrawals, will GDP go on rising indefinitely, or will a new equilibrium be reached? If so, explain how. (We answer this in the next section.)*

Changes in injections and withdrawals thus have a crucial effect on the whole macroeconomic environment in which businesses operate.

> ### Definition
>
> **Injections (J)** Expenditure on the production of domestic firms coming from outside the inner flow of the circular flow of income. Injections equal investment (I) plus government expenditure (G) plus expenditure on exports (X).

---

[2] *Public Finances Databank*, OBR (16 March 2016).

RECAP

1. Business activity is affected by the level of aggregate demand. Aggregate demand equals $C_d + I + G + X$ or $C + I + G + X - M$.

2. The circular flow of income model depicts the flows of money income and expenditure round the economy. The inner flow shows the direct flows between firms and households. Money flows from firms to households in the form of wages and other incomes, and back again as consumer expenditure on domestically produced goods and services.

3. Not all incomes get passed on directly round the inner flow. Some is withdrawn in the form of saving; some is paid in taxes; and some goes abroad as expenditure on imports.

4. Likewise, not all expenditure on domestic firms' products is by domestic consumers. Some is injected from outside the inner flow in the form of investment expenditure, government expenditure and expenditure on the country's exports.

5. Planned injections and withdrawals are unlikely to be the same.

6. If injections exceed withdrawals, GDP will rise. As a result unemployment will tend to fall and inflation will tend to rise. The reverse will happen if withdrawals exceed injections.

10.3 THE DETERMINATION OF BUSINESS ACTIVITY

We have seen that the relationship between planned injections and planned withdrawals determines whether GDP will rise or fall. But *by how much*?

Assume there is a rise in injections – say firms decide to invest more. Aggregate demand ($C_d + J$) will be higher. Firms will use more labour and other resources and thus pay out more incomes to households. Households will respond to this by consuming more and so firms will sell more.

Firms will respond to this by producing more, and thus using still more labour and other resources. Household incomes will rise again. Consumption and hence production will rise again, and so on. There will thus be a *multiplied* rise in GDP and employment. This is known as the *multiplier effect*.

The process, however, does not go on forever. Each time household incomes rise, households save more, pay more taxes and buy more imports. In other words, withdrawals rise. When withdrawals have risen to match the increase in injections, *equilibrium* will be achieved and GDP and employment will stop rising. The process can be summarised as follows:

$$J > W \rightarrow GDP \uparrow \rightarrow W \uparrow \text{ until } J = W$$

Similarly, an initial fall in injections (or rise in withdrawals) will lead to a multiplied fall in GDP and employment:

$$J < W \rightarrow GDP \downarrow \rightarrow W \downarrow \text{ until } J = W$$

Thus, equilibrium in the circular flow of income can be at *any* level of GDP and employment.

Definitions

Multiplier effect An initial increase in aggregate demand of £xm leads to an eventual rise in GDP that is greater than £xm.

Equilibrium GDP The level of GDP where injections equal withdrawals and where, therefore, there is no tendency for GDP to rise or fall.

Identifying the equilibrium level of GDP

Equilibrium can be shown on a 'Keynesian 45° line diagram'. This is named after the great economist, John Maynard Keynes (1883–1946) (see Case Study D.4 on the book's website). Keynes argued that GDP is determined by aggregate demand. A rise in aggregate demand will cause GDP to rise; a fall in aggregate demand will cause GDP to fall.

Equilibrium GDP can be at any level of capacity usage. If aggregate demand is buoyant, equilibrium GDP can be where businesses are operating at full capacity with full employment. If aggregate demand is low, however, equilibrium GDP can be at well below full capacity with high unemployment (i.e. a recession, as occurred in 2009). Keynes argued that it is important, therefore, for governments to manage the level of aggregate demand to avoid recessions.

Figure 10.2 plots various elements of the circular flow of income, such as consumption, withdrawals, injections and aggregate demand, against GDP (national income). Two continuous lines are shown. The 45° line out from the origin plots $C_d + W$ against GDP. It is a 45° line because by definition GDP = $C_d + W$. To understand this, consider what can happen to the income earned from GDP: either it must be spent on domestically produced goods (C_d) or it must be withdrawn from the circular flow – there is nothing else that can happen to it. Thus if GDP were £100 billion, then $C_d + W$ must also be £100 billion. If you draw a line such that whatever value is plotted on the horizontal axis (GDP) is also plotted on the vertical axis ($C_d + W$), the line will be at 45° (assuming that the axes are drawn to the same scale).

The other continuous line plots aggregate demand. In this diagram it is conventional to call it the 'aggregate expenditure line' (E). It consists of $C_d + J$, i.e. the total spending on domestic firms.

Figure 10.2 Equilibrium GDP

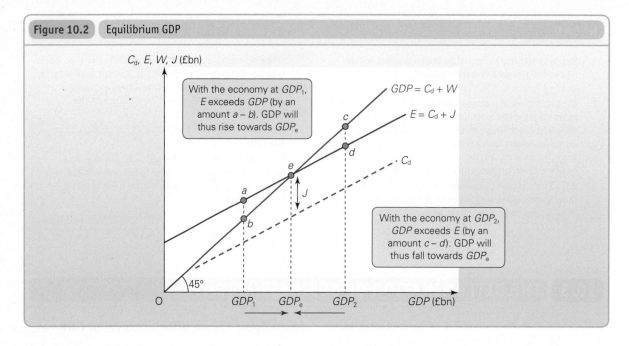

To show how this line is constructed, consider the dashed line. This shows C_d. It is flatter than the 45° line. The reason is that for any given rise in GDP, and hence people's incomes, only *part* will be spent on domestic products, while the remainder will be withdrawn, i.e. C_d rises less quickly than GDP. The E line consists of $C_d + J$. But we have assumed that J is constant with respect to changes in GDP. Thus the E line is simply the C_d line shifted upward by the amount of J.

If aggregate expenditure exceeded GDP, at say GDP_1, there would be excess demand in the economy (of $a - b$). In other words, people would be buying more than was currently being produced. Firms would thus find their stocks dwindling and would therefore increase their level of production. In doing so, they would employ more labour and other inputs. GDP would thus rise. As it did so, C_d and hence E would rise. There would be a movement up along the E line.

But because not all the extra incomes earned from the rise in GDP would be consumed (i.e. some would be withdrawn), expenditure would rise less quickly than income: the E line is flatter than the GDP line. As income rises towards GDP_e, the gap between the GDP and E lines gets smaller. Once point e is reached, $GDP = E$. There is then no further tendency for GDP to rise.

Pause for thought

Why is India likely to have a steeper E curve than Luxembourg?

If GDP exceeded aggregate expenditure, at say GDP_2, there would be insufficient demand for the goods and services currently being produced ($c - d$). Firms would find

their stocks of unsold goods building up. They would thus respond by producing less and employing fewer factors of production. GDP would thus fall and go on falling until GDP_e was reached.

The multiplier

As we have seen, when aggregate expenditure rises, this will cause a multiplied rise in GDP. The size of the *multiplier* is given by the letter k, where:

$$k = \Delta GDP/\Delta E$$

Thus, if aggregate expenditure rose by £10 million (ΔE) and as a result GDP rose by £30 million (ΔGDP), the multiplier would be 3. Figure 10.3 is drawn on the assumption that the multiplier is 3.

Assume in Figure 10.3 that aggregate expenditure rises by £20 billion, from E_1 to E_2. This could be caused by a rise in injections, or by a fall in withdrawals (and hence a rise in consumption of domestically produced goods) or by some combination of the two. Equilibrium GDP rises by £60 billion, from £100 billion to £160 billion (where the E_2 line crosses the GDP line).

Box 10.1 shows how the size of the multiplier can be calculated in advance.

Definition

The multiplier The number of times a rise in GDP (ΔGDP) is bigger than the initial rise in aggregate expenditure (ΔE) that caused it. Using the letter k to stand for the multiplier, the multiplier is defined as $k = \Delta GDP/\Delta E$.

Figure 10.3 The multiplier: a rise in aggregate expenditure

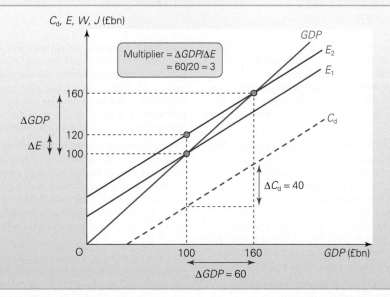

BOX 10.1

BOX 10.1   **DOING THE SUMS**

Calculating the size of the multiplier

What determines the size of the multiplier? The answer is that it depends on the 'marginal propensity to consume domestically produced goods' (mpc_d). The mpc_d is the proportion of any rise in GDP that is spent on domestically produced goods (i.e. the proportion that is not withdrawn):

$$mpc_d = \Delta C_d / \Delta GDP$$

So, if you are given £100, but choose to spend only £70 on home-produced goods, then only 70 per cent of the income you were given was spent on domestically produced goods. Some of the remaining £30 may be taken as taxation; you may choose to save part of it; or you might decide to spend it on imports. Either way, £30 is withdrawn from the circular flow of income. The proportion of the rise in income that is spent on domestically produced goods is:

$$mpc_d = \Delta C_d / \Delta GDP = £70/£100 = 7/10 = 0.7$$

In Figure 10.3, $mpc_d = \Delta C_d / \Delta GDP = £40bn/£60bn = \frac{2}{3}$ (i.e. the slope of the C_d line). The higher the mpc_d the greater the proportion of income generated from GDP that recirculates around the circular flow of income and thus generates extra output.

The *multiplier formula* is given by:

$$k = \frac{1}{1 - mpc_d}$$

In our example, with $mpc_d = \frac{2}{3}$

$$k = \frac{1}{1 - \frac{2}{3}} = \frac{1}{\frac{1}{3}} = 3$$

If the mpc_d were ¾, the multiplier would be 4. Thus the higher the mpc_d, the higher the multiplier. In the UK, the value of the mpc_d is between ⅓ and ½. This gives a value for the multiplier of between 1.5 and 2.

1. *Think of two reasons why a country might have a steep E line, and hence a high value for the multiplier.*
2. *Assume that 0.1 of any rise in income is saved, 0.2 goes in taxes and 0.1 is spent on imports. What is the mpc_d? What is the value of the multiplier?*
3. *The formula for the multiplier can also be written as $k = 1/mpw$. Why is this?*

Definition

Multiplier formula The formula for the multiplier is $k = 1/(1 - mpc_d)$.

BOX 10.2　THE ECONOMICS OF PLAYING HOST

Engines for growth?

Back in 1956, the *New York Times* reported on the Australian Olympics and the hope of its officials that the event might bring significant benefits, either with people settling in Australia or just doing more business. This has been the hope of many nations when bidding to host any number of big sporting events, such as the Olympics or the Football and Rugby World Cups.

Such events came to be regarded as 'economic engines', with winning a bid seen as a great victory, despite the huge costs associated with it. For example, American Football is a massive sporting event in the USA and in the 1994 Championship Game of Super Bowl XXVIII, an economic impact analysis by Humphrey estimated there would be 306 680 visitors per day. Each would spend $252 per day, leading to a direct impact of $77.3 million. With a multiplier of 2.148, this would lead to an indirect effect of $88.7 million and hence a total economic benefit of $166 million.[1]

In 2014, four US cities announced they were considering bidding to host the 2024 Olympics, with economic development as the justification. In Massachusetts, it was noted by a construction executive that a Boston Olympics could:

> catalyse and accelerate the economic-development and infrastructure improvements necessary to ensure that Massachusetts can compete globally now and in the future.[2]

Despite the assertions of many countries that hosting such an event is an engine for growth, there is relatively little evidence to support it and countries seem to be recognising this. Whereas 12 different cities bid for the 2004 Olympic Games, only five cities bid for the 2020 Games and only two were left in the race for the 2022 Winter Games, which eventually went to Beijing. Philip Porter from the University of South Florida commented:'The bottom line is, every time we've looked – dozens of scholars, dozens of times – we find no real change in economic activity.'[3]

However, for developing nations, it can be a signal to the rest of the world. This is the evidence found by a 2009 study by Andrew Rose, who noted that emerging economies hosting the Olympics benefit from an increase in trade. Yet it is not only the hosts that benefit. The research found that emerging nations that simply bid for the Olympics also experienced an increase in trade as a result of this signal – not because of any additional spending.[4] Perhaps here we have a method that delivers big benefits, without such big costs.

The macroeconomic impact

An obvious starting point in terms of estimating the macroeconomic effect of hosting a big sporting event is to look at the construction industry. Before the event, significant investment in stadiums, hotels, transport and general infrastructure is needed and this creates jobs for those involved in their construction, but also means that these workers use their incomes to buy other goods and services. This, in turn, increases aggregate demand, which creates further demand and so on. The multiplier begins to work and not just in the regions where such investment took place.

The multiplier will create knock-on effects throughout the national economy. The workers involved in the pre-event activities may also develop new skills during their training, which will be of long-term benefit. The investment in infrastructure will last for years and the regeneration of particular areas may bring in new businesses and home-owners, adding to the local multiplier effects.

During the event, there is also significant expenditure, including spending by visitors, spectators and the participants on everything from hotels and transport, to food and souvenirs, together with the inevitable expenditure on security. This then adds to the multiplier effect: higher expenditure generating higher incomes, generating higher consumption, generating higher incomes, and so on.

The London Olympics

A study commissioned by Lloyds Banking Group[5] provided a broad assessment of the impact of the London 2012 Olympic Games, before, during and after. Over a 12-year period, the study found that the London 2012 Olympics would generate a £16.5 billion contribution to GDP. The extra spending within the economy would create the equivalent of 267 000 additional person-years of employment between 2005 and 2017 and, of these jobs, 78 000 would be in the construction sector itself. The construction work was expected to generate significant multiplier effects totalling over £5 billion.

The report also indicated that 10 million UK and international residents would attend the 2012 Games and, purely because of the Olympics, a further 10.8 million tourist visits were expected between 2005 and 2017, generating a £2 billion contribution to UK GDP and supporting the equivalent of an additional 61 000 years of employment.

There were, however, concerns that London would take most of the benefits, with other regions in the UK contributing to the cost, but receiving few benefits. In a 2005 study[6] it was estimated that although there would be a direct gain to London's GDP of £5900 million over the period 2005–16, UK GDP as a whole would rise by only £1936 million. In other words, some of the gain to London would be at the expense of the rest of the UK as resources were diverted to London.

A post-games analysis[7] was conducted, finding that the Games would generate £28 billion to £41 billion in gross value added (GVA) and would create 618 000 to 893 000 years of

[1] V. A. Matheson, 'Economic multipliers and mega-event analysis', *Economics Department Working Paper No. 04-02* (June 2004).

[2] Binyamin Applebaum, 'Does hosting the Olympics actually pay off?', *The New York Times Magazine* (5 August 2014).

[3] Ibid.

[4] Ibid.

[5] *The economic impact of the London 2012 Olympic and Paralympic Games*, Oxford Economics, Commissioned by Lloyds Banking Group (July 2012).

[6] *Olympic Games impact study: final report*, PricewaterhouseCoopers (December 2005).

[7] *Post-Games evaluation; meta-evaluation of the impacts and legacy of the London 2012 Olympic Games and Paralympic Games*, Department for Culture, Media and Sport (July 2013).

employment by 2020. Further, the report stated: 'The economic benefits of this stimulus have been experienced by all regions and nations of the UK.' There was also a positive impact to the visitor economy, with a net boost of almost £600 million, excluding ticket sales, plus a net boost of over £360 million from domestic visitors.

The legacy of the Games is also expected to deliver significant health benefits, with more people participating in sport and leading more active and healthy lives. The brand of Britain was positively affected by the 2012 Olympics, with research indicating that 63 per cent of people who had seen coverage of the Olympics were more interested in visiting the country for a holiday. This led to a growth strategy for tourism from 2012 to 2020, which aims 'to attract 40 million overseas visitors (compared to 31 million in 2011) and to earn £31.5 billion from international tourism a year by 2020'.[8]

Problems of measuring the impact

It is difficult to estimate the overall *benefits* of any sporting event, in particular because although many do occur before and during the event, there are likely to be other benefits that occur in the long term. Many of these benefits may well be non-monetary and hence estimating their value is problematic.

The *costs* of hosting any event are easier to estimate, but they also tend to occur before or during the event. Hence, it can be a case of weighing up short-term costs against long-term benefits. These large up-front costs are perhaps causing fewer countries to bid for the honour of hosting key sporting events. Indeed, data and reports reviewing numerous such events indicate that the costs are nearly always under-estimated and rise quickly during the construction process.

The Brazil World Cup and Olympics

At the time of writing in May 2016, the Brazil Olympics is just round the corner and the Brazil World Cup is in the not so distant past (2014). So what is likely to be the net beneficial economic impact (i.e. economic benefits minus economic costs)?

The Brazil World Cup. As far as the World Cup is concerned, the net economic benefit, after adjusting for inflation, has been estimated at $11.9 billion for Japan and South Korea in 2002, $14.1 billion for Germany in 2006 and $5.6 billion for South Africa in 2010. Brazil's net economic benefit is estimated at somewhere between $3 billion and $14 billion, generating 3.63 million jobs per year and contributing an additional $8 billion in tax revenue.[9]

Many believe that emerging nations, such as Brazil, are keen to host such big sporting events as a means of showcasing their growing economic power and often pushing infrastructure projects through much more quickly, to the benefit of the nation. Such visibility is hoped to make them more attractive to foreign investors, who see significant investment going into infrastructure and expect the nation's prosperity to improve, creating greater incomes and demand.

However, there is an opportunity cost. The high spending needed on infrastructure, some of which will be obsolete after the event, can mean a reduction in spending on other public services, an increase in government borrowing or higher taxes. This was clearly a concern for the people of Brazil who went from a joyous nation when selected as the host of the World Cup, to a nation of protestors when the costs of the event became clear.[10] Looking back at the 2014 World Cup, it appears that it did little to help the Brazilian economy, possibly making poverty and inequality worse, increasing debt and delivering a lower than expected increase in the number of tourists.

In the run-up to a sporting event, the economic benefits are well-advertised, but the reports containing this analysis are typically commissioned or conducted by the relevant government – so positive figures are to be expected. However, critics of Brazil acting as host in the World Cup suggest that the cost of hosting the tournament was around $11.5 billion, with the cost of stadiums tripling to $3.68 billion. Furthermore, there were serious social costs, with estimates suggesting that every month, at least one construction worker died. This is similar to the data for Qatar, due to host the 2022 World Cup, where figures show one death of a worker every day.

The Brazil Olympics. For the 2016 Rio Olympics, similar problems are expected, with the costs outweighing the benefits. The original budget was $2.93 billion, but between January 2014 and May 2016, this had increased to $13.2 billion. Although it has been insisted by Brazilian officials that much of the funding is coming from private enterprise, the taxpayers will be the ones to fund much of the infrastructure development.

Furthermore, many individuals have been evicted from their homes, due to the need to free up land for Olympic projects. It is estimated that 3000 families in Rio have had to relocate because of this, with 67 000 people being evicted from their favelas (slums) since 2009 when Rio was selected as the 2016 Olympic host. One of the effects of the Olympics has been to force up the price of land and it is believed that after the Games are finished, luxury condos will be built in previously poor areas. Areas where the poor used to live will now only be available to the rich. One might argue, then, that the Olympics is doing a good thing for Brazil, by creating development in previously poor areas. But this hides the facts, with those who lived in the poorer areas simply being displaced and not benefiting from the economic development.

Happiness

The overall impact of any sporting event is always going to be difficult to estimate and it is likely that a final answer will only be known decades after the event, once the full multiplier and legacy benefits have materialised. By then, of course, it is too late if the positive economic impact is less than expected. However, one final benefit should be considered: something that is not always given the attention it deserves – happiness.

[8] *Delivering a Golden Legacy: a growth strategy for inbound tourism to Britain from 2012 to 2020*, Visit Britain (April 2013).

[9] Simon Chadwick, 'Hard evidence: what is the World Cup worth', *The Conversation* (4 June 2014).

[10] Mirele Matsuoka De Aragao, 'Economic impacts of the FIFA World Cup in developing countries', *Honors Theses*, Paper 2609, Lee Honors College, Western Michigan University (April 2015).

Research routinely indicates that sporting events create happiness and a 'feel-good' factor and that monetary benefits do arise from this boost in happiness. Business can benefit from better morale, especially if areas are available for its employees to watch events, though the impact on productivity and absenteeism is less certain! Euro 96 (UEFA European Football Championship), hosted by England, is estimated to have resulted in an average benefit to UK residents of £165 per head in terms of happiness. Referring to these non-monetary benefits, Victor Matheson, from the College of the Holy Cross in Massachusetts said:

> It's [hosting the Olympics or World Cup] like a wedding . . . It won't make you rich, but it may make you happy.[11]

<hr/>

[11] Applebaum, 'Does hosting the Olympics actually pay off?'

The big questions are then 'just how happy?' and 'how much does a nation value that happiness?'

1. *Give some examples of industries in the rest of the UK which could have benefited from increased expenditure in London.*
2. *When a nation hosts a big sporting event, there will be a multiplier effect. Why would the magnitude of the full multiplier effect on the whole economy be difficult to estimate?*
3. *Deciding whether hosting a big sporting event is worthwhile requires a full analysis of costs and benefits, including externalities. Identify some external costs and benefits from hosting the Olympics or the World Cup.*

RECAP

1. In the simple circular flow of income model, equilibrium national income (GDP) is where withdrawals equal injections: where $W = J$.

2. Equilibrium can be shown on a Keynesian 45° line diagram. Equilibrium is where GDP (shown by the 45° line) is equal to aggregate expenditure (E).

3. If there is an initial increase in aggregate expenditure (ΔE), which could result from an increase in injections or a reduction in withdrawals, there will be a multiplied rise in GDP. The multiplier is defined as $\Delta GDP/\Delta E$.

4. The size of the multiplier depends on the marginal propensity to consume domestically produced goods (mpc_d). The larger the mpc_d, the more will be spent each time incomes are generated round the circular flow, and thus the more will go round again as *additional* demand for domestic product. The multiplier formula is $1/1 - mpc_d$.

10.4 THE BUSINESS CYCLE

Economic growth tends to fluctuate. In some years there is a high rate of economic growth; the country experiences a boom. In other years, economic growth is low or even negative; the country experiences a *recession*, such as those in 2008/9 and 2011/12. This cycle of booms and recessions is known as the *business cycle* or *trade cycle*.

KEY IDEA 26

Economies suffer from inherent instability. As a result, economic growth and other macroeconomic indicators tend to fluctuate.

Definitions

Recession A period of falling GDP, i.e. of negative economic growth. Officially, a recession is where this occurs for two quarters or more.

Business cycle or trade cycle The periodic fluctuations of national output around its long-term trend.

The business cycle is illustrated in Figure 10.4. The first thing to note in the diagram is the ceiling to output. This is where all resources, including labour, are fully employed. This ceiling to output grows over time for two reasons:

- *Resources may increase.* This could be the result of an increase in the working population or as a result of investment in new plant and equipment, thus increasing the stock of capital.

- *Resources may become more productive.* The most likely reasons for this are technical progress and more efficient working practices. Both will lead to an increase in either the marginal product of labour or of capital, or both.

The diagram shows the cyclical fluctuations in actual output (GDP). Four 'phases' of the business cycle can be identified.

1. *The upturn.* In this phase, a stagnant economy begins to recover and growth in GDP resumes. Business confidence begins to grow.

2. *The expansion.* During this phase, there is rapid economic growth; the economy is booming. Rapid growth

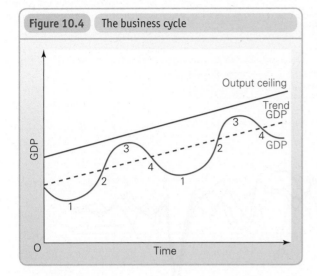

Figure 10.4 The business cycle

in consumer demand creates a climate of business confidence and firms respond by producing more, investing more and employing more people. The economy moves closer to the ceiling to output.

3. *The peaking-out.* During this phase, growth slows down or even ceases. Business confidence wanes.
4. *The slowdown, recession or slump.* During this phase, there is little or no growth or even a decline in output. Increasing slack develops in the economy as many businesses produce less and hold off from investing.

The third (dashed) line shows the trend of GDP over time (i.e. ignoring the cyclical fluctuations around the trend). If the average level of capacity that is unutilised stays constant from one cycle to another, then the trend line will have the same slope as the output ceiling line. If, however, the average level of capacity that is unutilised falls from one peak to the next, then the gap between the trend line and the full capacity line will become narrower. The trend line will have a steeper slope than the capacity output line.

Pause for thought

Will the ceiling to output be in any way affected by the short-run rate of growth of GDP? If so, how?

The business cycle in practice

The business cycle illustrated in Figure 10.4 is a 'stylised' cycle. It is nice and smooth and regular. Drawing it this way allows us to make a clear distinction between each of the four phases. In practice, however, business cycles are highly irregular. They are irregular in two ways:

The length of the phases. Some booms and recessions are short-lived, lasting only a few months or so. Others are much longer, lasting perhaps three or four years. We saw a deep recession in 2008–9, which was closely followed by

another recession (2011/12) with the intermediate economic upturn only short-lived. This is known as a double-dip recession, and at the beginning of 2013 there were concerns that this would become a triple-dip recession, although this was narrowly avoided, with growth of 0.3 per cent in the three months to March 2013. This meant that output had fallen for just one quarter, not the two necessary for it to qualify as a 'recession'.

The magnitude of the phases. Sometimes in phase 2 there is a very high rate of economic growth, perhaps 4 per cent per annum or more. On other occasions in phase 2, growth is much gentler. Sometimes in phase 4 there is a recession, with an actual decline in output (e.g. in the early 1980s, the early 1990s and late 2000s). On other occasions, phase 4 is merely a 'pause', with growth simply slowing down (e.g. in the early 2000s).

Nevertheless, despite the irregularity of the fluctuations, cycles are still clearly discernible, especially if we plot *growth* on the vertical axis rather than the *level* of output. This is done in Figure 10.5, which shows the business cycles in selected industrial economies from 1970 to 2020.

Causes of cyclical fluctuations

Why does the business cycle occur and what determines the length and magnitude of the phases of the cycle? To understand this we need to know why aggregate demand fluctuates. As we have seen, it is changes in aggregate demand that determine short-run economic growth. There are three questions we need to answer.

■ What causes aggregate demand to change in the first place?
■ Why do the effects of changes in aggregate demand persist? In other words, why do booms and recessions last for a period of time.
■ Why do booms and recessions come to an end? What determines the turning points?

What causes aggregate demand to change in the first place?

Anything that affects one or more of the four components of aggregate demand (C_d, I, G or X) could be the reason for a change in GDP. For example, an increase in business confidence could increase investment; an increase in consumer confidence could increase consumption. A cut in interest rates may encourage increased business and consumer borrowing, and hence an increase in investment and consumption. A cut in taxes will increase consumption, as consumers have more 'disposable' income. A rise in government expenditure will directly increase aggregate demand. A change in conditions abroad, or a change in the exchange rate, will affect imports and exports. (We examine these external factors in Chapter 13.)

Some of these factors, such as taxes and government expenditure, can be directly controlled by the government.

Figure 10.5	Growth rates in selected industrialised economies

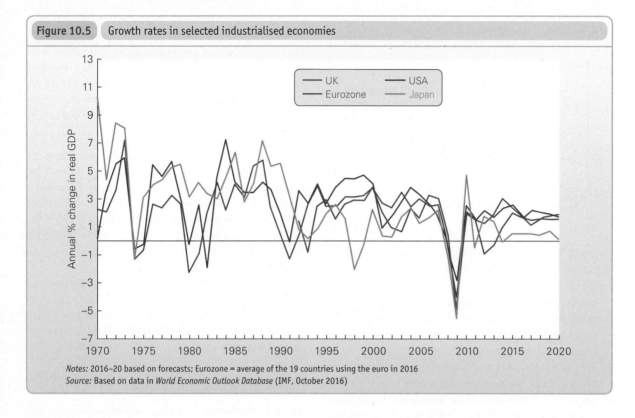

Notes: 2016–20 based on forecasts; Eurozone = average of the 19 countries using the euro in 2016
Source: Based on data in *World Economic Outlook Database* (IMF, October 2016)

In other words, government policy can be directed at controlling aggregate demand and hence the course of the business cycle. We call this 'demand management policy' – again we will look at this in the next chapter.

Why do booms and recessions persist for a period of time?

Time lags. It takes time for changes in aggregate demand to be fully reflected in changes in GDP and employment. The multiplier process takes time. Moreover, consumers, firms and government may not all respond immediately to new situations. Their responses are spread out over a period of time.

'Bandwagon' effects. Once the economy starts expanding, expectations become buoyant. People think ahead and adjust their expenditure behaviour; they consume and invest more *now*. Likewise in a recession a mood of pessimism may set in. The effect is cumulative.

One crucial effect here is called the *accelerator*. A rise in injections will cause a multiplied rise in GDP. But this rise in GDP will in turn cause a rise in investment, as firms seek to expand capacity to meet the extra demand. This compounds

Definition

Accelerator The level of investment depends on the rate of increase in consumer demand, and as a result is subject to substantial fluctuations. Increases in investment via the accelerator can compound the multiplier effect.

the increase in demand, as investment is itself an injection into the circular flow. This is the accelerator. The increased investment then causes a further multiplied rise in income. This then causes a further accelerator effect, a further multiplier effect, and so on.

Pause for thought

Under what circumstances would you expect a rise in national income to cause a large accelerator effect?

Why do booms and recessions come to an end? What determines the turning points?

Ceilings and floors. Actual output can go on growing more rapidly as long as there is slack in the economy. As full employment is approached, however, and as more and more firms reach full capacity, so a ceiling to output is reached.

At the other extreme, there is a basic minimum level of consumption that people tend to maintain. During a recession, people may not buy much in the way of luxury and durable goods, but they will continue to buy food and other basic goods. There is thus a floor to consumption.

The industries supplying these basic goods will need to maintain their level of replacement investment. Also there will always be some minimum investment demand as firms, in order to survive competition, need to install the latest equipment (such as computer hardware). There is thus a floor to investment too.

BOX 10.3 BUSINESS EXPECTATIONS AND THEIR EFFECT ON INVESTMENT

Recent European experience

Investment is highly volatile. It is subject to far more violent swings than GDP. This can be seen in chart (a), which shows growth in GDP and growth in investment from 1985 to 2017 for the 15 countries which have been members of the EU since before its expansion in 2004. The maximum annual growth in GDP was 4.2 per cent (in 1988) and the maximum fall was 4.7 per cent (in 2009). By contrast, the maximum annual growth in investment was 8.3 per cent (again in 1988) and the maximum fall was 13.0 per cent (again in 2009). The differences were even greater for individual EU countries.

These figures are consistent with the accelerator theory, which argues that the level of investment depends on the *rate of change* of GDP and hence of consumer demand. A relatively small percentage change in GDP can give a much bigger percentage change in investment.

Another factor affecting investment is the degree of business optimism. While this is partly determined by current rates of economic growth, there are many other factors that can affect the business climate. These include world political events (such as a war or a US election), national and international macroeconomic policies and shocks to the world economy (such as oil price changes or a banking crisis). Of course, to the extent that these other factors affect confidence, which in turn affects investment, so they will affect economic growth.

In the boom years of the late 1980s, business optimism was widespread throughout Europe. Investment was

correspondingly high, and with it there was a high rate of economic growth.

Surveys of European business expectations in the early 1990s, however, told a very different story. Pessimism was rife. Europe was in the grip of a recession. Growth slowed right down and output actually fell in 1993. Along with this decline in growth and deteriorating levels of business and consumer confidence, there was a significant fall in investment.

The industrial confidence indicator for the EU as a whole is plotted in chart (b). The indicator shows the percentage excess of confident over pessimistic replies to business questionnaires; a negative figure means that there was a higher percentage of pessimistic responses. You can see that the indicator was strongly negative in 1993. After 1993, pessimism began to decrease, and by the last quarter of 1994 the EU industrial confidence indicator became positive.

Between 1995 and 2000, the industrial confidence indicator swung between positive and negative values. These swings were similar in direction to those in the rate of economic growth. For example, both the rate of growth and the confidence indicator rose in 1997/8 and 2000 and fell in 1996.

Then, in 2001, with the world economy slowing down and the 11 September attack on the World Trade Center in New York, industrial confidence plummeted, and so did investment. Investment actually fell in 2002. Then as the European

(a) EU-15 growth in GDP and business investment: 1985–2017

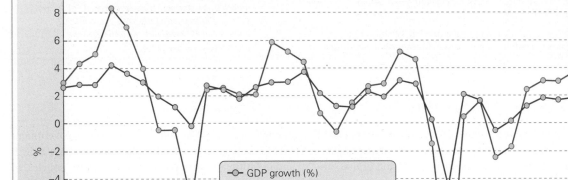

Note: EU-15 refers to the 15 member countries of the EU prior to its expansion in 2004; Figures for 2016 and 2017 based on forecasts
Source: AMECO Database (European Commission, 2016)

▶

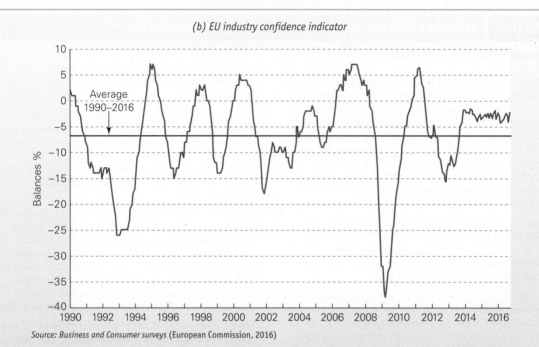

(b) EU industry confidence indicator

Source: Business and Consumer surveys (European Commission, 2016)

economy slowly recovered, with growth rates edging upwards, so confidence grew, as did the rate of investment. By the mid-2000s, economic growth was strong and confidence was high.

Then, with the banking crisis and credit crunch of 2008, so confidence plummeted; banks were less willing to lend and businesses were cautious about investing. Economies throughout Europe and many other parts of the world plunged into recession. However, with action by governments to stimulate economies, including cuts in interest rates and increased government spending, so European economies began to pull out of recession and confidence began to recover.

A downward trend re-emerged at the beginning of 2011, in part due to continuing problems in Greece and the eurozone.

Confidence in the EU once again began to deteriorate, although the fall was by no means as severe as that in 2008. Since 2014, confidence has been better than in previous years, but negative figures still remain. With uncertainty due to the UK vote to exit Europe, industrial confidence in the EU may suffer further.

1. *How is the existence of surveys of business confidence likely to affect firms' expectations and actions?*
2. *Why, if the growth in output slows down (but is still positive), is investment likely to fall (i.e. a negative growth in investment)? If you look at chart (a) you will see that this happened from 1991–3, and in 2002, 2008–9 and 2012–16. (See the sections on the accelerator on pages 242–4.)*

Echo effects. Durable consumer goods and capital equipment may last several years, but eventually they will need replacing. The necessary replacement of goods and capital purchased in a previous boom may help to bring a recession to an end.

The accelerator. For investment to continue rising, consumer demand must rise at a *faster and faster* rate. After all, firms invest to meet *extra* demand. They will therefore only invest more than the last period if the extra demand is more than in the last period, i.e. if the growth rate is *increasing*. If this does not happen, investment will fall back and the boom will break.

Random shocks. National or international political, social or natural events can affect the mood and attitudes of firms, governments and consumers, and thus affect aggregate demand.

Changes in government policy. In a boom, a government may become most worried by unsustainably high growth and inflation and thus pursue contractionary policies. In a recession, it may become most worried by unemployment and lack of growth and thus pursue expansionary policies, as it did to some extent in 2008/9. These government policies, if successful, will bring about a turning point in the cycle.

Pause for thought

Why is it difficult to predict precisely when a recession will come to an end and the economy will start growing rapidly?

10.5 MONEY, INTEREST RATES AND BUSINESS ACTIVITY

Business and interest rates

The financial sector was badly affected by the 'credit crunch' and this illustrated just how important financial institutions are in affecting businesses and the wider macroeconomy. It also presented many important questions for governments, central banks and regulators across the world.

One important determinant of business activity is the rate of interest. If interest rates rise, it will be more expensive for businesses to borrow and the rate of return on their investments will need to be higher to cover these borrowing costs; this will curtail investment. Higher interest rates are a particular problem for businesses that have a high ratio of borrowing at variable interest rates to their total turnover. In such cases, not only will a rise in interest rates discourage investment, it may also make it difficult for the business to find the money to pay the interest – to 'service' its debt.

Higher interest rates make saving more profitable, but it will also make it more expensive for the general public to borrow. If interest rates rise, whether on personal loans, on credit cards or on mortgages, consumers may well cut back on their borrowing and spending. Aggregate demand will fall.

Interest rates are also seen as a 'barometer' of the future course of the economy. If the Bank of England raises interest rates, this may be taken as a sign that the economy will slow down, especially if it is expected that rates are likely to be raised again in the near future. Business confidence may fall and so too, therefore, may investment. However, it all depends on how the rise in interest rates is interpreted. If it is seen as a means of preventing excessive expansion of the economy and therefore allowing expansion to be sustained, albeit at a more moderate rate, this may actually encourage investment. Thus expectations and how people interpret various changes in the instruments of government policy are likely to have a crucial effect on the course of the economy.

But what determines interest rates? In a free market, interest rates are determined by the demand for and supply of money. In practice the free-market interest rate may not be the rate that the Bank of England wants, in which case it

will alter it. This process of altering interest rates by the country's central bank (i.e. the Bank of England in the UK) is known as 'monetary policy'. We examine monetary policy in the next chapter. Here we look at the determination of interest rates in a free market.

The meaning of money

Before going any further we must define precisely what we mean by 'money'. An easy task, surely! However, money is more than just notes and coins. In fact the main component of a country's money supply is not cash, but deposits in banks and other financial institutions. The bulk of the deposits appear merely as bookkeeping entries in the banks' accounts. People can access and use this money in their accounts through cheques, debit cards, standing orders, direct debits, etc. without the need for cash. Only a very small proportion of these deposits, therefore, needs to be kept by the banks in their safes or tills in the form of cash.

In UK official statistics, two main measures of money are used: a narrow measure, *cash in circulation*, and a broad measure, *M4*, which we are normally referring to when we talk about 'money supply'. This broad measure includes cash outside the banks plus *all* deposits in banks and building societies, whether in the form of cash or merely as bookkeeping entries. This has grown from around £26 billion in 1970 (50 per cent of annual GDP) to £2.1 trillion in March 2016 (around 120 per cent of annual GDP).

In the eurozone and most other countries the broad measure of money is known as *M3*, which includes bank deposits and a range of other assets that are relatively easy to redeem without loss.

The supply of money

Banks and the creation of credit

By far the largest element of broad money supply (M4 in the UK, M3 elsewhere) is bank deposits. It is not surprising then that banks play an absolutely crucial role in the monetary system. This was clearly evident between 2007 and 2009, when we saw the collapse of the banking sector directly contribute to the UK (and global) recession.

Banks are able to create additional money by increasing the amount of bank deposits. They do this by lending to people: granting people overdrafts or loans. When these loans are spent, the shops deposit the money in their bank accounts, or have it directly transferred when debit cards are swiped across their tills. Thus the additional loans granted by the banks have become deposits in the shops' bank accounts. These deposits can be used by banks as the basis for further loans. These in turn create further deposits and so on. The process is known as the 'creation of credit'.

Can this process go on indefinitely? The answer is no. Banks must keep a certain proportion of their deposits in the form of cash to meet the demands of their customers for cash. That is, your demands to make withdrawals from your bank account. Let us say that 10 per cent of a bank's deposits have to be in the form of cash, then non-cash deposits would account for the remaining 90 per cent. So if additional cash of £10 million were deposited in the banking system, banks would need to hold 10 per cent (£1 million) as cash, but could lend out the remaining £9 million. When this £9 million is spent in shops or businesses, they will deposit it into their bank accounts, such that bank deposits increase by an extra £9 million. Of this extra £9 million, only 10 per cent needs to be held in the form of cash (£0.9 million), while the remainder (£8.1 million) can be lent out. And so the process continues. In this example, banks could create non-cash deposits of an additional £90 million – but no more. Of the total new deposits of £100 million, cash would be 10 per cent and non-cash deposits would be 90 per cent.

This effect is known as the *bank (or deposits) multiplier*. In this simple example with a cash ratio of 1/10 (i.e. 10 per cent), the deposits multiplier is 10. An initial increase in deposits of £10 million allowed total deposits to rise by £100 million. In this simple world, therefore, the deposits multiplier is the inverse of the cash ratio (L).

Deposits multiplier = $1/L$

The creation of credit: the real world

In practice, the creation of credit is not as simple as this. First, while banks must have access to cash if their customers want it, banks can keep some of the money deposited in them in a form that can be readily converted into cash rather than holding it as cash itself. There are various short-term securities that banks hold for this purpose. These securities can be sold for cash at very short notice. Securities held for these purposes are known as 'near money' and, together with cash, form banks' 'liquid assets'. What banks have to look at, therefore, is the *liquidity ratio*, the ratio of liquid assets to total deposits.

Second, at certain times banks may decide that it is prudent to hold a bigger proportion of liquid assets. If Christmas or the summer holidays are approaching and people are likely to make bigger cash withdrawals, banks may decide to hold more liquid assets. In the wake of the banking crisis of 2008, where many of the banks' assets fell in value, banks chose to hold more liquid assets in an attempt to increase confidence. On the other hand, there may be an upsurge in consumer demand for credit. Banks may be very keen to grant additional loans and thus make more profits, even though they have acquired no additional cash or other liquid assets. Conversely, banks may want to make loans, but customers may not want to borrow, if they are concerned about the future and the repayments.

What causes the money supply to rise?

The money supply might rise as a result of banks responding to an increased demand for credit. They may be prepared to operate with a lower liquidity ratio to meet this demand. Indeed, with the increased use of credit and debit cards, we have seen a trend of banks increasingly choosing a lower liquidity ratio – at least until the banking crisis of 2008/9.

Another source of extra money is from abroad. Sometimes the Bank of England will choose to build up the foreign currency reserves. To do this it will buy foreign currencies on the foreign exchange market using sterling. When the recipients of this extra sterling deposit it in UK banks, or spend it on UK exports and the exporters deposit the money in UK banks, credit will be created on the basis of it, leading to a multiplied increase in money supply.

One of the main reasons for an increase in money supply is government borrowing. If the government spends more than it receives in tax revenues, it will have to borrow to make up the difference. This difference is known as the *public-sector net borrowing (PSNB)*. The government borrows by selling interest-bearing securities. These are of two main types: (a) short-term securities in the form of Treasury bills – these have a three-month period to maturity (i.e. the date on which the government pays back the loan); (b) longer-term securities in the form of bonds, also known as 'gilts' – these often have several years to maturity.

Such securities could be sold to the Bank of England. The money paid to the government is in effect being created by the Bank of England and when it finds its way to the banks, the banks can use it as the basis for credit creation. Similarly, if the government borrows through additional Treasury bills, and if these are purchased by the banking sector, there will be a multiplied expansion of credit. The banks will now have additional liquid assets (bills), which can be used as the basis for credit creation.

Since 2009/10, the Bank of England and other central banks have taken emergency measures to increase the supply of money, known as 'quantitative easing'. This has involved the Bank of England (and other central banks) buying existing bonds from banks and other financial institutions and thereby releasing new money into the banking system. It was hoped that this extra liquidity in the banking system would encourage banks to lend.[3] The credit crunch is considered in more detail in Box 11.3.

The demand for money

The demand for money refers to the desire to *hold* money; to keep your wealth in the form of money, rather than spending it on goods and services or using it to purchase financial assets such as bonds or shares. But why should people want to hold on to money, rather than spending it or buying

some sort of security such as bonds or shares? There are two main reasons.

The first is that people receive money only at intervals (e.g. weekly or monthly) and not continuously. They thus need to hold balances of money in cash or in current accounts ready for spending later in the week or month.

The second is as a form of saving and thus of storing wealth. Money in a bank account earns a relatively small, but safe rate of return and so has the advantage of carrying no risk. Some assets, such as company shares or bonds, may earn you more on average, but there is a chance that their price will fall. In other words, they are risky.

What determines the size of the demand for money?

What would cause the demand for money to rise? This would occur if people's incomes rose. The more you earn, the more money you are likely to hold in the bank or in cash. A rise in money ('nominal') incomes in a country can be caused either by a rise in real GDP (i.e. real output) or by a rise in prices, or some combination of the two.

The demand for money would also rise if people thought that share prices or the prices of other securities were likely to fall. In such circumstances, owning shares or other forms of securities may be seen as too risky. To avoid this risk, people will want to hold money instead. Some clever (or lucky) individuals anticipated the 2008 stock market decline (see Box 2.1). They sold shares and 'went liquid'.

The rate of interest. In terms of the operation of money markets, this is the most important determinant. It is related to the opportunity cost of holding money. The opportunity cost is the interest forgone by not holding higher interest-bearing assets, such as bonds or shares. Generally, if rates of interest rise, they will rise more on bonds and other securities than on bank accounts. The demand for money will thus fall as people switch to these alternative securities. The demand for money is thus inversely related to the rate of interest. This is illustrated in Figure 10.6.

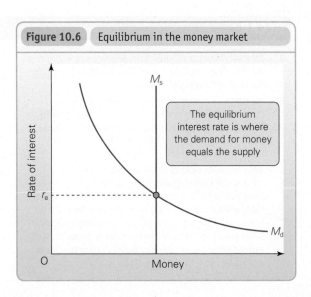

Figure 10.6   Equilibrium in the money market

The equilibrium interest rate is where the demand for money equals the supply

---

> ### Definition
>
> **Public-sector net cash borrowing (PSNB)** The (annual) deficit of the public sector (central government, local government and public corporations), and thus the amount that the public sector must borrow.

The equilibrium rate of interest

Equilibrium in the money market occurs when the demand for money (M_d) is equal to the supply of money (M_s). Figure 10.6 shows the demand for and supply of money plotted against the rate of interest. For simplicity, it is assumed that the supply of money is independent of interest rates, and is therefore drawn as a vertical straight line.[4]

The equilibrium rate of interest is r_e. But why? If the rate of interest were above r_e, people would have money balances surplus to their needs. They would use these to buy shares, bonds and other assets. This would drive up the price of these assets. But the price of assets is inversely related to interest rates. The higher the price of an asset (such as a government bond), the less will any given interest payment be as a percentage of its price (e.g. £10 as a percentage of £100 is 10 per cent, but as a percentage of £200, it is only 5 per cent). Thus a higher price of assets will correspond to lower interest rates.

As the rate of interest fell, so there would be a movement down along the M_s and M_d curves. The interest rate would go on falling until it reached r_e. Equilibrium would then be achieved.

---

[4] In practice, the supply-of-money curve is likely to be upward sloping. The reason is that a rise in aggregate demand will lead to an increased demand for money and hence a rise in interest rates. At the same time, banks are likely to respond to the rise in demand for money by creating more credit, thereby increasing the money supply. In other words, the higher interest rates correspond to an increased supply of money.

Similarly, if the rate of interest were below r_e, people would have insufficient money balances. They would sell securities, thus lowering their prices and raising the rate of interest until it reached r_e.

Causes of changes in interest rates

We saw above what would cause an increase in the supply of money. If money supply does increase, the M_s line will shift to the right in Figure 10.6. This will cause a fall in the rate of interest to the point where the new M_s line intersects with the M_d curve.

A change in interest rates will also occur if the demand for money changes (i.e. the M_d curve shifts). For example, a rise in incomes would lead to people wanting to hold larger money balances. This would shift the M_d curve to the right and drive up the rate of interest.

In practice, the Bank of England seeks to *control* the rate of interest. We see how it achieves this in the next chapter.

Effects of changes in interest rates

A reduction in interest rates (e.g. from a rise in money supply) will lead to a rise in investment and consumer spending as firms and consumers borrow more. This rise in aggregate demand will then lead to a multiplied rise in GDP. How much aggregate demand increases depends on (a) the elasticity of the demand-for-money curve – the steeper the M_d curve, the more interest rates will fall for any given rise in money supply; (b) the responsiveness of businesses and consumers to a change in interest rates – the more responsive they are, the bigger will be the rise in aggregate demand and hence the bigger the multiplied rise in GDP.

RECAP

1. Interest rates are an important determinant of business activity. They are determined by the interaction of the demand and supply of money.

2. Money in its narrow sense includes just cash in circulation. Money is normally defined more broadly, however, to include all bank deposits, not just those in the form of cash. M4 is the name given in the UK to this broader measure of the money supply.

3. Bank deposits expand through a process of credit creation. If banks' liquid assets increase, they can be used as a base for increasing loans. When the loans are redeposited in banks, they form the base for yet more loans, and thus a process of multiple credit expansion takes place. The ratio of the increase of deposits to an expansion of banks' liquidity base is called the 'bank multiplier'. It is the inverse of the liquidity ratio.

4. Money supply will rise if (a) banks respond to an increased demand for money by increasing credit without an increase in liquidity; (b) there is an inflow of money from abroad; (c) the government finances its borrowing by borrowing from the banking sector.

5. The demand for money is determined mainly by people's incomes, the risk attached to alternatives to money and the rate of interest (the opportunity cost of holding money). The higher the rate of interest, the lower the demand for money.

6. The equilibrium rate of interest is where the supply of money is equal to the demand. A rise in the rate of interest can be caused by an increased demand for money or a reduced supply.

10.6 UNEMPLOYMENT

Employment is determined in individual labour markets, as we saw in Chapter 8. In this section we look at the overall level of employment and unemployment in the economy. This depends in part on the level of business activity. When the economy is booming, employment will be high and unemployment low as businesses take on more labour to meet the extra demand.

Measuring unemployment

The unemployed are not simply those who do not have a job – we would not count a child as being unemployed! The usual definition that economists use for the *number unemployed* is: *those of working age who are without work, but who are available for work at current wage rates*. Unemployment can be expressed either as a number (e.g. 3 million) or as a percentage (e.g. 8 per cent). If the figure is to be expressed as a percentage, then it is a percentage of the total *labour force*. The labour force is defined as: *those in employment plus those unemployed*. Thus if 29 million people were employed and 2.5 million people were unemployed, the *unemployment rate* would be:

$$\frac{2.5}{29 + 2.5} = 7.94 \text{ per cent}$$

Two common measures of unemployment are used in official statistics. The first is *claimant unemployment*. This is simply a measure of all those in receipt of unemployment-related benefits. In the UK, claimants receive the 'jobseeker's allowance'.

The second measure is the *standardised unemployment rate*. Since 1998, this has been the main measure used by the UK government. It is the measure used by the International Labour Organisation (ILO) and the Organisation for Economic Co-operation and Development (OECD), two international organisations that publish unemployment statistics for many countries.

Definitions

Number unemployed (economist's definition) Those of working age, who are without work, but who are available for work at current wage rates.

Labour force The number employed plus the number unemployed.

Unemployment rate The number unemployed expressed as a percentage of the labour force.

Claimant unemployment Those in receipt of unemployment-related benefits.

Standardised unemployment rate The measure of the unemployment rate used by the ILO and OECD. The unemployed are defined as people of working age who are without work, available for work and actively seeking employment.

In this measure, the unemployed are defined as people of working age who are without work, available to start work within two weeks and *actively seeking employment* or waiting to take up an appointment. The figures are compiled from the results of national labour force surveys. In the UK the labour force survey is conducted quarterly.

But is the standardised unemployment rate likely to be higher or lower than the claimant unemployment rate? The standardised rate is likely to be higher to the extent that it includes people seeking work who are nevertheless not entitled to claim benefits, but lower to the extent that it excludes those who are claiming benefits and yet who are not actively seeking work. Clearly, the tougher the benefit regulations, the lower the claimant rate will be relative to the standardised rate. As an example, data from the ONS shows the standardised unemployment rate for those above 16 for the three months to February 2016 was 5.1 per cent (1.70 million people), whereas the claimant count for March 2016 recorded 0.73 million workers unemployed. You can find out more information about the differences in these measures of unemployment in an article from the Economic & Labour Market Review.[5]

Unemployment and the labour market

We now turn to the causes of unemployment. These causes fall into two broad categories: *equilibrium* unemployment and *disequilibrium* unemployment. To make clear the distinction between the two, it is necessary to look at how the labour market works.

Figure 10.7 shows the aggregate demand for labour and the aggregate supply of labour: that is, the total demand and

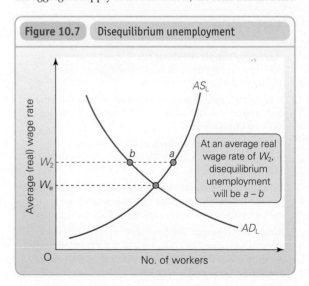

Figure 10.7 Disequilibrium unemployment

At an average real wage rate of W_2, disequilibrium unemployment will be $a - b$

---

[5] Gareth Clancy and Peter Stam, 'Explaining the difference between unemployment and the claimant count', *Economic & Labour Market Review*, vol. 4, no. 7, Office for National Statistics (July 2010).

supply of labour in the whole economy. The *real* average wage rate is plotted on the vertical axis. This is the average wage rate expressed in terms of its purchasing power: in other words, after taking inflation into account.

The *aggregate supply of labour curve* (AS_L) shows the number of workers *willing to accept jobs* at each wage rate. This curve is relatively inelastic, since the size of the workforce at any one time cannot change significantly. Nevertheless, it is not totally inelastic because (a) a higher wage rate will encourage some people to enter the labour market (e.g. parents raising children) and (b) the unemployed will be more willing to accept job offers rather than continuing to search for a better-paid job.

The *aggregate demand for labour curve* (AD_L) slopes downward. The higher the wage rate, the fewer workers firms will want to employ. They may decide to cut back on production, thereby reducing the number of workers they need, or the higher wage rate may encourage firms to economise on labour and to substitute other inputs for it.

The labour market is in equilibrium at a wage of W_e, where the demand for labour equals the supply. If the wage were above W_e, the labour market would be in a state of disequilibrium. At a wage rate of W_2, there is an excess supply of labour of $a - b$. This is called *disequilibrium unemployment*.

For disequilibrium unemployment to occur, two conditions must hold:

- The aggregate supply of labour must exceed the aggregate demand.
- There must be a 'stickiness' in wages. In other words, the wage rate must not immediately fall to W_e.

Even when the labour market *is* in equilibrium, however, not everyone looking for work will be employed. Some people will hold out, hoping to find a better job. The curve

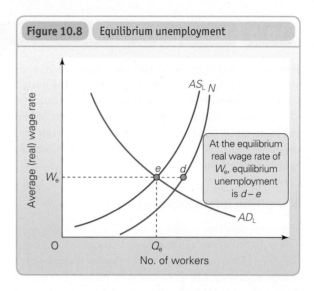

Figure 10.8 Equilibrium unemployment

At the equilibrium real wage rate of W_e, equilibrium unemployment is $d - e$

N in Figure 10.8 shows the total number in the labour force. The horizontal difference between it and the aggregate supply of labour curve (AS_L) represents the excess of people looking for work over those actually willing to accept jobs. Q_e represents the equilibrium level of employment and the distance $d - e$ represents the *equilibrium level of unemployment*. This is sometimes known as the *natural level of unemployment*. There are some interesting articles about this level of unemployment in the Sloman Economics News site blog, 'A full employment target'.

It is also important to note that, even if unemployment data show a low rate of unemployment, there may still be quite high *underemployment*. This is when workers would like to work more hours than they currently do. This is discussed in the blog, 'The State of the Labour Market in the UK'.

Types of disequilibrium unemployment

There are two main causes of disequilibrium unemployment.

Real-wage unemployment

Real-wage unemployment is where wages are set above the market-clearing level, for example at W_2 in Figure 10.7. This could be the result of either minimum wage legislation or the activities of trade unions. Excessive real wage rates were blamed by the Thatcher and Major governments for the high unemployment of the 1980s and early 1990s. The possibility of higher real-wage unemployment was also one of the reasons for their rejection of a national minimum wage.

Pause for thought

If this analysis is correct, namely that a reduction in wages will reduce the aggregate demand for goods, what assumption must we make about the relative proportions of wages and profits that are spent (given that a reduction in real wage rates will lead to a corresponding increase in rates of profit)? Is this a realistic assumption?

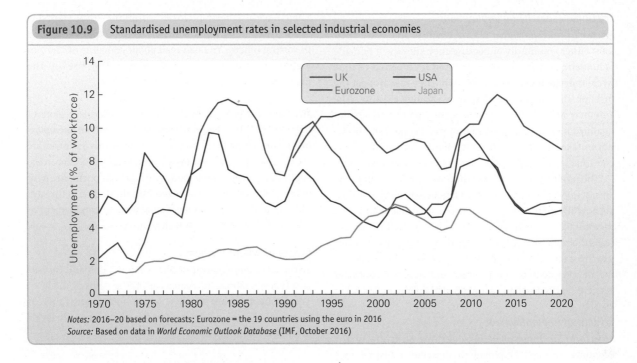

Figure 10.9 Standardised unemployment rates in selected industrial economies

Notes: 2016–20 based on forecasts; Eurozone = the 19 countries using the euro in 2016
Source: Based on data in *World Economic Outlook Database* (IMF, October 2016)

The solution to real-wage unemployment would seem to be a reduction in real wage rates. However, it may be very difficult to prevent unions pushing up wages, although this is now less of a problem in many countries. In the UK, part of this goes back to the Thatcher government, which curbed the power of trade unions, but more recently it is the process of globalisation and increased labour market flexibility which have reduced the ability of firms to concede to big pay rises. What is more, even if the government did succeed in reducing the average real wage rate, there would then be a problem of reduced consumer expenditure and hence a reduced demand for labour, with the result that unemployment might not fall at all!

Demand-deficient unemployment
Demand-deficient unemployment is associated with economic recessions. Many countries experienced a rise in unemployment in the recessions of 2008/9 and 2011/12.

As the economy moves into recession, consumer demand falls. Firms find that they are unable to sell their current level of output. For a time they may be prepared to build up stocks of unsold goods, but sooner or later they will start to cut back on production and cut back on the amount of labour they employ. In Figure 10.7 the AD_L curve shifts to the left. With real wages being 'sticky' downwards, the aggregate demand for labour is now less than the aggregate supply. Disequilibrium unemployment occurs. The deeper the recession becomes and the longer it lasts, the higher will demand-deficient unemployment become.

As the economy recovers and begins to grow again, so demand-deficient unemployment will start to fall. Because demand-deficient unemployment fluctuates with the business cycle, it is sometimes referred to as 'cyclical

unemployment'. Figure 10.9 shows the fluctuations in unemployment in various industrial economies. If you compare this figure with Figure 10.5, you can see how unemployment tends to rise in recessions and fall in booms.

Equilibrium unemployment

Looking at Figure 10.9, you can see how unemployment was higher in the 1980s and 1990s than in the 1970s. Much of the reason for this was the growth in equilibrium unemployment. Similarly, the lower unemployment in the early and mid-2000s across many developed nations (with the exception of Japan) was largely the result of a fall in equilibrium unemployment. This has been partly caused by more flexible labour markets, as we discussed in Chapter 8.

Although there may be overall *macro*economic equilibrium, with the *aggregate* demand for labour equal to the *aggregate* supply, and thus no disequilibrium unemployment, at a *micro*economic level supply and demand may not match. In other words, there may be vacancies in some parts of the economy, but an excess of labour (unemployment) in others. This is equilibrium unemployment. There are various types of equilibrium unemployment.

Definition

Demand-deficient (or cyclical) unemployment
Disequilibrium unemployment caused by a fall in aggregate demand with no corresponding fall in the real wage rate.

Frictional (search) unemployment

Frictional unemployment occurs when people leave their jobs, either voluntarily or because they are sacked or made redundant, and are then unemployed for a period of time while they are looking for a new job. They may not get the first job they apply for, despite a vacancy existing. The employer may continue searching, hoping to find a better qualified person. Likewise, unemployed people may choose not to take the first job they are offered. Instead they may continue searching, hoping that a better one will turn up.

The problem is that information is imperfect. Employers are not fully informed about what labour is available; workers are not fully informed about what jobs are available and what they entail. Both employers and workers, therefore, have to search: employers search for the right labour and workers search for the right jobs. The search process has been aided by the development of the Internet and online recruitment agencies, as discussed in Chapter 8, particularly in Box 8.1.

Structural unemployment

Structural unemployment is where the structure of the economy changes. Employment in some industries may expand while in others it contracts. There are two main reasons for this:

A change in the pattern of demand. Some industries experience declining demand. This may be due to a change in consumer tastes. Certain goods may go out of fashion. Or it may be due to competition from other industries. For example, consumer demand may shift away from coal and to other fuels. This will lead to structural unemployment in mining areas.

A change in the methods of production (technological unemployment). New techniques of production often allow the same level of output to be produced with fewer workers. This is known as 'labour-saving technical progress'. Unless output expands sufficiently to absorb the surplus labour, people will be made redundant. This creates *technological unemployment*. An example is the job losses in the banking industry caused by the increase in the number of cash machines and by the development of telephone and Internet banking. This is discussed in the blog, 'Job losses and labour mobility', on the Sloman Economics News site.

There have also been job losses within the Royal Mail, due to the new, modern and efficient technologies being used in sorting offices. You can read about concerns of technological unemployment in the blog, 'The rise of the machines'.

Structural unemployment often occurs in particular regions of the country. When it does, it is referred to as *regional unemployment*. This is most likely to occur when particular industries are concentrated in particular areas. For example, the decline in the South Wales coal mining industry led to high unemployment in the Welsh valleys and more recently, the decline in the steel industry in the UK has brought substantial unemployment to former 'steel towns', such as Redcar in Teesside.

Seasonal unemployment

Seasonal unemployment occurs when the demand for certain types of labour fluctuates with the seasons of the year. This problem is particularly severe in holiday areas such as Cornwall, where unemployment can reach very high levels in the winter months.

Definitions

Frictional (search) unemployment Unemployment that occurs as a result of imperfect information in the labour market. It often takes time for workers to find jobs (even though there are vacancies) and in the meantime they are unemployed.

Structural unemployment Unemployment that arises from changes in the pattern of demand or supply in the economy. People made redundant in one part of the economy cannot immediately take up jobs in other parts (even though there are vacancies).

Technological unemployment Structural unemployment that occurs as a result of the introduction of labour-saving technology.

Regional unemployment Structural unemployment occurring in specific regions of the country.

Seasonal unemployment Unemployment associated with industries or regions where the demand for labour is lower at certain times of the year.

RECAP

1. The two most common measures of unemployment are claimant unemployment (those claiming unemployment-related benefits) and ILO/OECD standardised unemployment (those available for work and actively seeking work or waiting to take up an appointment).

2. Unemployment can be divided into disequilibrium and equilibrium unemployment.

3. Disequilibrium unemployment occurs when the average real wage rate is above the level that will equate the aggregate demand and supply of labour. It can be caused by unions or government pushing up wages (real-wage unemployment) or by a fall in aggregate demand but a downward 'stickiness' in real wages (demand-deficient or cyclical unemployment).

4. Equilibrium unemployment occurs when there are people unable or unwilling to fill job vacancies. This may be due to poor information in the labour market and hence a time lag before people find suitable jobs (frictional unemployment), to a changing pattern of demand or supply in the economy and hence a mismatching of labour with jobs (structural unemployment – specific types being technological and regional unemployment), or to seasonal fluctuations in the demand for labour.

10.7 INFLATION

The rate of inflation measures the annual percentage increase in prices. The most commonly used measure of inflation is that of *consumer* prices. The UK government publishes a consumer prices index (CPI) each month, and the rate of inflation is the percentage increase in that index over the previous 12 months. Figure 10.10 shows the rates of inflation for various industrial economies from 1970 to 2020. As you can see, inflation was particularly severe between 1973 and 1983, and relatively low in the mid-1980s and in recent years.

If there is negative inflation (falling prices) we refer to this as 'deflation'. The Japanese economy suffered from deflation throughout much of the 2000s (see Figure 10.10) and prices fell in many other developed countries during the 2009 recession. Although inflation rose slightly in 2010 and 2011, it then fell and has remained below 2 per cent in most developed countries.

The rates of inflation are also given for the prices of other goods and services. For example, indices are published for commodity prices, food prices, house prices, import prices, prices after taking taxes into account, wages and so on. Their respective rates of inflation are simply their annual percentage increase.

When there is inflation, we have to be careful in assessing how much national output, consumption, wages, etc. are increasing. Take the case of GDP. GDP in year 2 may seem higher than in year 1, but this may be partly (or even wholly) the result of higher prices. Thus GDP in money terms may have risen by 5 per cent, but if inflation is 3 per cent, *real growth in GDP* will be only 2 per cent. In other words, the volume of output will be only 2 per cent higher.

> **KEY IDEA 27**
>
> *The distinction between real and nominal values.* Nominal figures are those using current prices, interest rates, etc. Real figures are figures corrected for inflation.

Before we proceed, a word of caution: be careful not to confuse a rise or fall in *inflation* with a rise or fall in *prices*. A rise in inflation means a *faster* increase in prices. A fall in inflation means a *slower* increase in prices (but still an increase as long as inflation is positive).

Aggregate demand and supply and the level of prices

The level of prices in the economy is determined by the interaction of aggregate demand and aggregate supply. The analysis is similar to that of demand and supply in individual markets (see Chapter 2), but there are some crucial differences. Figure 10.11 (page 256) shows aggregate demand and supply curves. Let us examine each in turn.

> **Definition**
>
> **Real growth values** Values of the rate of growth in GDP or any other variable after taking inflation into account. The real value of the growth in a variable equals its growth in money (or 'nominal') value minus the rate of inflation.

Figure 10.10	Inflation rates in selected industrial economies

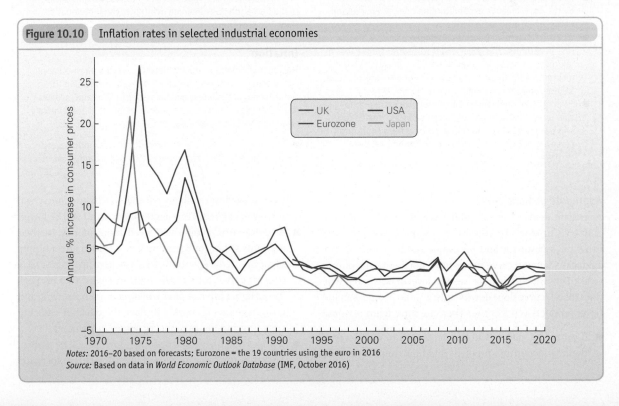

Notes: 2016–20 based on forecasts; Eurozone = the 19 countries using the euro in 2016
Source: Based on data in *World Economic Outlook Database* (IMF, October 2016)

BOX 10.4   INFLATION AND UNEMPLOYMENT: HOW COSTLY?

Do they really matter?

Unemployment and inflation are two key macroeconomic objectives and governments across the world place great importance on managing them. Indeed, the primary objective of many central banks is to keep inflation at a target level: 2 per cent in the UK ($+/-$ 1 per cent). When inflation rises (or falls) outside of its upper/lower bounds or when unemployment begins to creep up, newspaper headlines feed off these unfavourable trends; the opposition party questions the government's policies and business confidence and expectations begin to decline. So, why are rising rates of unemployment and inflation so costly and who is it that suffers?

Unemployment

The most obvious cost of unemployment is to the individual. Anyone who is unemployed will suffer a financial cost through lost earnings, which is measured as the difference between their previous wages and the unemployment benefits they receive. For many, there is an additional cost of unemployment that is non-monetary. If an individual becomes unemployed and finds it difficult to get another job, they may lose confidence in their abilities and their self-esteem is likely to fall.

In addition, unemployment will also impose costs on friends and family. If the unemployed individual was the only bread-winner in the household then an entire family could be pushed into poverty. Unemployment may also put a strain on personal relationships and evidence suggests that it can also lead to an increase in domestic violence and the separation of families.

While many aspects of the above two effects are non-monetary, there are numerous financial costs to the wider economy.

- The greater the number of unemployed, the greater will be the government's expenditure on unemployment and other out-of-work benefits.
- When an individual becomes unemployed and suffers a loss in earnings, the government will suffer from a loss in tax revenue, through lower income tax receipts, national insurance contributions and even lower VAT receipts, due to less consumer expenditure.
- High rates of unemployment will require extra public spending on benefit offices, social services, health care and even the police. These first three effects therefore place a greater burden on the government and the taxpayer.

- Unemployment represents a loss of output, as the economy is operating below its maximum potential. Resources are wasted and thus the economy is inefficient.
- The individual's loss in income will also affect other people. As an individual's income falls, their demand for goods and services will also tend to decline. Thus, they spend less money, so firms sell fewer goods. Profits may then decline and so could tax receipts. If the decline in sales is severe, workers may face a cut in pay (or smaller wage increases) or even lose their jobs. We described this type of unemployment as demand-deficient unemployment. The knock-on effects of operating below full employment can therefore be severe.
- The costs of long-term unemployment can be extremely high to both the individual and the economy. A lack of self-esteem and confidence in your ability is likely to become worse the longer you are unemployed. In severe cases, it can lead to health problems, which pose an additional cost to the government, through expenditure on healthcare. The longer an individual is without work, the more likely it is that they will lose their skills and thus become less suitable for new jobs. Alternatively, if they re-enter employment they are likely to require retraining and this could be a costly expenditure for a firm, which may deter the firm from hiring that worker.

Long-term involuntary unemployment is therefore a big economic and social problem, as de-motivated and unskilled workers are a drain on a country's resources. Keeping unemployment down and helping people back to work is therefore a key government policy. And it is not just to relieve the strain on the economy, but to provide help to the affected families, motivate the individuals and ensure that when a job does become available, the individual's skills are still there.

Inflation

The costs of inflation vary and depend crucially on whether or not people can correctly anticipate the rate of inflation. If we can correctly anticipate it and fully adjust prices and incomes to take it into account, then the costs of inflation are relatively small and are largely confined to the following two costs:

- Consumers have to adjust their idea of a fair price every time the inflation rate changes. The opportunity cost in

---

Aggregate demand curve

Aggregate demand is the total level of spending on the country's products by consumers, by the government, by firms on investment and by people residing abroad. The aggregate demand curve shows how much national output (real GDP) will be demanded at each level of prices. But why does the *AD* curve slope downwards: why do people demand fewer products as prices rise? There are three main reasons:

- If prices rise, people will be encouraged to buy fewer of their own country's products and more imports instead

(which are now relatively cheaper); also the country will sell fewer exports. Thus aggregate demand will be lower.
- As prices rise, people will need more money in their accounts to pay for their purchases. With a given supply of money in the economy, this will drive up interest rates (the M_d curve shifts to the right in Figure 10.6 on page 247). Higher interest rates will discourage borrowing and encourage saving. Both will have the effect of reducing spending and hence reducing aggregate demand.
- If prices rise, the value of people's savings will be eroded. They may thus save more (and spend less) to compensate.

terms of the time and energy taken to counter the effects of inflation are known as *shoe leather costs*.

■ Firms need to adjust their price labels, catalogues, menus, etc. These costs are known as *menu costs*.

However, people frequently make mistakes when predicting the rate of inflation and do not fully take it into account. The higher the rate of inflation, the more of a problem this becomes, as typically with higher inflation rates comes more volatile inflation rates. This then leads to further problems.

■ With high rates of inflation, domestically produced goods become relatively more expensive compared with those from abroad. Thus the country's exports become less competitive and we would expect to see a fall in their demand. At the same time, foreign goods become relatively cheaper and thus more imports are demanded. These two forces together will worsen the country's balance of payments. In response, the exchange rate must fall or interest rates must rise, which can lead to further problems, as discussed in Chapter 13.

■ Inflation can adversely affect the distribution of income by redistributing income away from those in the weakest bargaining positions and on fixed incomes towards those with the economic power to demand higher pay rates.

■ Some assets, such as property, rise in value with inflation and so high rates of inflation will also redistribute wealth to those with these assets and away from those with money in savings accounts that pay an interest rate below the rate of inflation.

■ As inflation rises, it typically fluctuates more and this creates uncertainty, which can be particularly costly for businesses. Firms find it more difficult to predict their own costs and revenues and those of their competitors. This may act to reduce their incentive to invest. If investment falls, then this might reduce aggregate demand and hence the rate of economic growth.

■ More resources will typically be needed, such as accountants and financial experts to help firms deal with the uncertainties created by high inflation.

■ If the increases in the price level enter the hundreds or thousands of per cent per year, this is known as *hyperinflation*. In such circumstances, the costs of inflation will increase significantly. As prices rise, workers will demand higher wage rates and as these push up costs of production, so workers will demand even higher wages to maintain their standard of living. A 'wage–price spiral'

can develop. In extreme cases, people stop saving and instead spend money as fast as possible or even stop using money as a means of exchange. In Zimbabwe between 2005 and 2008, inflation peaked at over 200 million per cent, as you can read in the blogs 'Fancy a hundred trillion dollar note?' and 'A remnant of hyperinflation in Zimbabwe' on the Sloman Economics News site.

Everything in moderation

Having some unemployment means that, if demand rises, there are spare resources to meet this demand. Furthermore, if workers voluntarily leave their job to find a new one, then it is reasonable to assume that the benefits of the new job will compensate for this temporary loss of income. This short-term unemployment creates a more flexible labour market that can only benefit the wider economy.

It is a similar story with inflation. The target rate is 2 per cent, but when inflation falls below 1 per cent, this is just as much a concern as when it rises above 3 per cent. Thus, 0 per cent inflation is not necessarily a good thing. The reason is that modest inflation allows relative wages and prices to change more easily to reflect changes in demand and supply. For example, given that many employers would find it difficult to cut nominal wage rates, by leaving them unchanged, *real* wages will fall by the rate of inflation. In other words, the purchasing power of a given wage rate will be eroded by the rate of inflation.

Deflation can be catastrophic for an economy. People will be reluctant to spend, believing that if they wait, goods will become cheaper. The result can be declining sales and profits, and rising unemployment and bankruptcy rates. Indeed, the Japanese economy was paralysed for over a decade by deflation, as discussed in the blogs, 'Japan's interesting monetary stance as deflation fears grow' and 'Japan's deflation fears grow (update)'.

Therefore, inflation and unemployment are not necessarily bad, as long as they are kept at manageable levels. With both of these objectives, as with many things, moderation is the key.

1. If you were in government, would you ever advocate zero unemployment?
2. Who are likely to be the winners and losers from inflation?

Pause for thought

Why are the three effects described above all substitution effects? Is there an income effect which can help to explain the shape of the aggregate demand curve?

Aggregate supply curve

The aggregate supply curve slopes upwards – at least in the short run. In other words, the higher the level of prices, the more will be produced. The reason is simple: provided that

input prices (and, in particular, wage rates) do not rise as rapidly as product prices, firms' profitability at each level of output will be higher than before. This will encourage them to produce more.

Equilibrium

The equilibrium price level will be where aggregate demand equals aggregate supply. To demonstrate this, consider what would happen if aggregate demand exceeded aggregate supply: e.g. at P_2 in Figure 10.11. The resulting shortages throughout the economy would drive up prices. This would

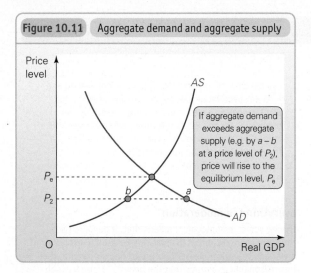

Figure 10.11 Aggregate demand and aggregate supply

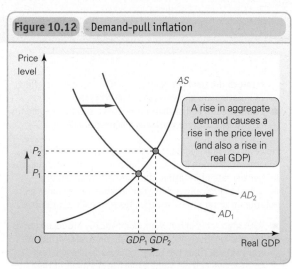

Figure 10.12 Demand-pull inflation

cause a movement up along both the *AD* and *AS* curves until *AD* = *AS* (at P_e).

Shifts in the AD or AS curves

If there is a change in the price level there will be a movement *along* the *AD* and *AS* curves. If any other determinant of *AD* or *AS* changes, the respective curve will shift. The analysis here is very similar to shifts and movements along demand and supply curves in individual markets (see pages 28–9 and 32).

The aggregate demand curve will shift if there is a change in any of its components – consumption of domestic products, investment, government expenditure or exports. Thus if the government decides to spend more, or if consumers spend more as a result of lower taxes, or if business confidence increases so that firms decide to invest more, the *AD* curve will shift to the right.

Similarly, the aggregate supply curve will shift to the right if there is a rise in labour productivity or in the stock of capital: i.e. if there is a rise in the capacity of the economy.

Causes of inflation

Demand-pull inflation

When the *AD* curve shifts to the right, output will rise and unemployment may fall as a result. However, at the same time, prices will rise. *Demand-pull inflation* is caused by continuing rises in aggregate demand. In Figure 10.12, the *AD* curve shifts to the right, and continues doing so. Firms will respond to the rise in aggregate demand partly by raising prices and partly by increasing output (there is a move upwards along the *AS* curve).

Just how much they raise prices depends on how much their costs rise as a result of increasing output. This in turn depends upon how close actual output is to the output ceiling (see Figure 10.4 on page 241). The less slack there is in the economy, the more will firms respond to a rise in demand by raising their prices (the steeper will be the *AS* curve).

Demand-pull inflation is typically associated with a booming economy. Many economists therefore argue that

it is the counterpart of demand-deficient unemployment. When the economy is in recession, demand-deficient unemployment will be high, but demand-pull inflation will be low. When, on the other hand, the economy is near the peak of the business cycle, demand-pull inflation will be high, but demand-deficient unemployment will be low.

Cost-push inflation

Cost-push inflation is associated with continuing rises in costs and hence continuing upward (leftward) shifts in the *AS* curve (see Figure 10.13). If firms face a rise in costs, they will respond partly by raising prices and passing the costs on to the consumer, and partly by cutting back on production (there is a movement back along the *AD* curve).

Definitions

Demand-pull inflation Inflation caused by persistent rises in aggregate demand.

Cost-push inflation Inflation caused by persistent rises in costs of production (independently of demand).

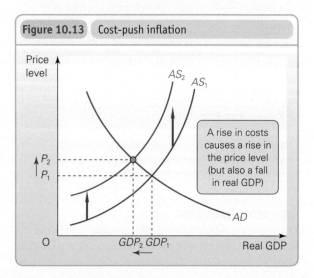

Figure 10.13 Cost-push inflation

Just how much firms raise prices and cut back on production depends on the shape of the aggregate demand curve. The less elastic the *AD* curve – in other words, the less consumers, firms and the government are prepared to cut back on real expenditure – the less sales will fall as a result of any price rise, and hence the more will firms be able to pass on the rise in their costs to consumers as higher prices.

The rise in costs may originate from a number of different sources, such as higher wages as a result of trade unions pushing up wages independently of the demand for labour, firms using their monopoly power to make bigger profits by pushing up prices independently of consumer demand, or import prices rising independently of the level of aggregate demand (e.g. OPEC putting up oil prices).

In all these cases, inflation occurs because one or more groups are exercising economic power. The problem is likely to get worse, therefore, if there is an increasing concentration of economic power over time (e.g. if firms or unions get bigger and bigger, and more monopolistic) or if groups become more militant.

Another cause of cost-push inflation is rising prices of various commodities – not just oil, but copper, aluminium, iron ore and other minerals – and also agricultural prices. The process of globalisation has helped to keep these cost-push pressures down, but with the growth in demand for raw materials and food from China and other rapidly developing economies, such as India and Brazil, rising costs became more of a problem, especially before the financial crisis and again from 2011 to 2014. This was especially true of oil, which increased in price from $51 per barrel in January 2007 to over $140 per barrel in July 2008 and then experienced a similar pattern when prices rose from $41 a barrel in January 2009 to $126 per barrel in May 2011 (see Box 2.4) and stayed at around this level until 2014.

Thus, what starts with a rise in aggregate demand in these countries (demand-pull inflation), becomes cost-push inflation for other countries having to pay higher prices for the commodities they import.

Part of the explanation for such low rates of inflation from 2014 has been falling costs of various commodities. For example, oil prices had fallen to $30 per barrel by January 2016, as we discussed in Box 2.4. It is also discussed in the blogs 'A crude indicator of the economy (Part 1)', 'A crude indicator of the economy (Part 2)' and 'The price of oil in 2015 and beyond' on the Sloman Economics News site.

Demand-pull and cost-push inflation together

Demand-pull and cost-push inflation can occur together, since wage and price rises can be caused both by increases in aggregate demand and by independent causes pushing up costs. Even when an inflationary process *starts* as either demand-pull or cost-push, it is often difficult to separate the two.

An initial cost-push inflation may encourage the government to expand aggregate demand to offset rises in unemployment. Alternatively, an initial demand-pull inflation may strengthen the power of certain groups, which then use this power to drive up costs. Either way, the result is likely to be continuing rightward shifts in the *AD* curve and upward shifts in the *AS* curve. Prices will carry on rising.

Expectations and inflation

Workers and firms take account of the *expected* rate of inflation when making decisions.

Imagine that a union and an employer are negotiating a wage increase. Let us assume that both sides expect a rate of inflation of 5 per cent. The union will be happy to receive a wage rise somewhat above 5 per cent. That way the members would be getting a *real* rise in incomes. The employers will be happy to pay a wage rise somewhat below 5 per cent. After all, they can put their price up by 5 per cent, knowing that their rivals will do approximately the same. The actual wage rise that the two sides agree on will thus be somewhere around 5 per cent.

Now let us assume that the expected rate of inflation is 10 per cent. Both sides will now negotiate around this benchmark, with the outcome being somewhere round about 10 per cent.

Thus the higher the expected rate of inflation, the higher will be the level of pay settlements and price rises, and hence the higher will be the resulting actual rate of inflation.

In recent years the importance of expectations in explaining the actual rate of inflation has been increasingly recognised by economists, and it has prompted them to discover just what determines people's expectations.

RECAP

1. Inflation is the annual percentage increase in prices.

2. Equilibrium in the economy occurs when aggregate demand equals aggregate supply. Prices will rise if there is a rightward shift in the aggregate demand curve or an upward (leftward) shift in the aggregate supply curve.

3. Demand-pull inflation occurs as a result of increases in aggregate demand. It is typically associated with a booming economy.

4. Cost-push inflation occurs when there are increases in the costs of production independent of rises in aggregate demand.

5. Expectations play a crucial role in determining the level of inflation. The higher people expect inflation to be, the higher it will be.

BOX 10.5 INFLATION OR DEFLATION

Where's the danger?

The spectre of deflation in the early 2000s

The first edition of this book in 2005 stated: 'Inflation no longer seems a serious worry in many developed economies. Instead, "deflation" (i.e. falling prices) has become a source of concern.'

One of the main reasons for this was dubbed the 'China price effect'. The rapid growth in cheap Chinese imports into developed countries was exerting downward pressure on prices. Furthermore, outsourcing of call-centre, back-office and IT work to developing countries has added to the downward pressure on wages. The Japanese economy experienced deflation in many years since the late 1990s (see Figure 10.10) and central banks, including the US Federal Reserve and the European Central Bank have continued to sound warnings that deflation is a real and present danger to their economies too.

Deflation can have a damaging effect on the economy. If consumers believe that prices will fall, they are likely to hold off buying certain goods, such as household furniture and equipment, hoping to get them cheaper later. This can dampen aggregate demand and reduce business profits and act as a brake on investment. Firms may cut staff in an attempt to reduce their own costs.

A return of inflation

The US and other OECD economies experienced rapid growth in the mid-2000s. Between 2004 and 2006, US economic growth averaged 3.8 per cent and the OECD countries averaged 3.1 per cent. These rates, however, were dwarfed by China and India, which experienced growth rates of 10.1 per cent and 8.4 per cent respectively over the same period.

The rapid growth in aggregate demand in many OECD countries put upward pressure on prices and wages but, unlike previously, the 'China price' effect was beginning to *reinforce* this upward pressure. As *The Economist* of 22 June 2006 stated:

> China's excessive growth is not only of domestic concern. With much of the world increasingly worried about inflation, questions arise about what an overheating Chinese economy could do to global prices . . . After being squeezed between rising input costs and falling factory-gate prices, China's manufacturers are starting to raise prices to rebuild margins – and getting away with it because both domestic demand and exports are still far stronger than they were two years ago. Add in higher domestic food and energy prices and surging labour costs, and the China price may soon be a good deal higher.[1]

By 2008, the growth in China, India and other rapidly developing countries was causing significant inflation in commodity prices (see the figures in Box 2.4).

However, with the onset of recession in mid-2008, inflation started to fall and the 'China effect' seemed to have gone away. Once more there seemed to be a spectre of deflation. By 2009, many people were asking themselves why they should buy now when, by delaying, they might be able to get an item more cheaply later on. The effect was to shift the *AD* curve leftward, forcing prices down even further and also creating further problems for economic growth.

But the worry about deflation was short-lived. As the world economy pulled out of recession and China resumed double-digit growth, so commodity and other prices began rising more rapidly. In the UK, inflation reached 5.2 per cent in the 12 months to September 2011. This figure was significantly higher than the Bank of England's 2 per cent target rate of inflation. Inflation did then move back towards its target level in 2012 and 2013.

Back to the spectre of deflation?

The period from 2010 saw a slight easing of global growth, falling from 5.4 per cent in 2010 to 3.1 per cent in 2015. China's growth slowed more dramatically, from 10.6 per cent in 2010 to 6.9 per cent in 2015. At the same time, investment in shale oils and in many other commodities increased their supply. Slowing demand and higher supply were reflected in falls in commodity prices. From April 2011 to January 2016, the all commodity price index fell from 201.9 to 83.05 – a fall of 59 per cent.

Falling commodity prices helped to moderate consumer price inflation rates. At the start of 2015, the annual rate of CPI inflation in the UK had fallen significantly to just 0 per cent and remained at around zero from several months (see the blog 'Fuelling the absence of inflation' on the Sloman Economics News site). Meanwhile, in the eurozone there was deflation at the beginning of 2015, as discussed in the blog, 'Eurozone: positive inflation', with the CPI inflation rate standing at –0.6 per cent. Although it hovered around zero for much of 2015, it was negative again in early 2016.

In the long term, whether the process of globalisation will have an inflationary or deflationary effect will depend on the balance of two opposing forces. Higher demand for commodities from the rapidly expanding developing countries will tend to push up prices. Increased global competition and the spread of technological advances, however, will tend to push down prices, or at least moderate their increase.

When the global economy is booming the first effect is likely to dominate. When the global economy is in recession or growing sluggishly, the second effect is likely to dominate.

1. *What long-term economic benefits might deflation generate for business and the economy in general?*
2. *Would an inflationary China price effect be an example of demand-pull or cost-push inflation?*

---

[1] From 'China's economy: exercising its pricing power', *The Economist* (22 June 2006).

QUESTIONS

1. What are the key macroeconomic objectives of government? Are there likely to be any conflicts between them?

2. The following table shows index numbers for real GDP (national output) for various countries (2010 = 100).

Using the formula $G = (GDP_t - GDP_{t-1})/GDP_{t-1} \times 100$ (where G is the rate of growth, GDP is the index number of output, t is any given year and $t - 1$ is the previous year):

	2010	2011	2012	2013	2014	2015	2016
USA	100.0	101.6	103.8	105.3	107.7	110.2	112.6
Japan	100.0	99.5	101.3	102.6	102.6	103.1	103.6
Germany	100.0	103.7	104.3	104.7	106.3	107.8	109.2
France	100.0	102.1	102.3	102.9	103.1	104.2	105.4
UK	100.0	102.0	103.2	105.3	108.2	110.4	112.3

Source: Based on data in World Economic Outlook database, IMF (April 2016)

(a) Work out the growth rate for each country for each year from 2011 to 2016.

(b) Plot the figures on a graph. Describe the pattern that emerges.

3. In terms of the UK circular flow of income, are the following net injections, net withdrawals or neither? If there is uncertainty, explain your assumptions.

(a) Firms are forced to take a cut in profits in order to give a pay rise.

(b) Firms spend money on research.

(c) The government increases personal tax allowances.

(d) The general public invests more money in building societies.

(e) UK investors earn higher dividends on overseas investments.

(f) The government purchases US military aircraft.

(g) People draw on their savings to finance holidays abroad.

(h) People draw on their savings to finance holidays in the UK.

(i) The government runs a budget deficit (spends more than it receives in tax revenues).

4. Assume that the multiplier has a value of 3. Now assume that the government decides to increase aggregate demand in an attempt to reduce unemployment. It raises government expenditure by £100 million with no increase in taxes. Firms, anticipating a rise in their sales, increase investment by £200 million, of which £50 million consists of purchases of foreign machinery. By how much will GDP rise? (Assume that nothing else changes.)

5. What factors could explain why some countries have a higher multiplier than others?

6. At what point of the business cycle is the country now? What do you predict will happen to growth over the next two years? On what basis do you make your prediction?

7. Why does a booming economy not carry on booming indefinitely? Why does an economy in recession pull out of that recession?

8. For what possible reasons may one country experience a persistently faster rate of economic growth than another?

9. Imagine that the banking system receives additional deposits of £100 million and that all the individual banks wish to retain their current liquidity ratio of 20 per cent.

(a) How much will banks choose to lend out initially?

(b) What will happen to banks' deposits when the money that is lent out is spent and the recipients of it deposit it in their bank accounts?

(c) How much of these latest deposits will be lent out by the banks?

(d) By how much will total deposits (liabilities) eventually have risen, assuming that none of the additional liquidity is held outside the banking sector?

(e) What is the size of the deposits multiplier?

10. What effects will the following have on the equilibrium rate of interest? (You should consider which way the demand and/or supply curves of money shift.)

(a) Banks find that they have a higher liquidity ratio than they need.

(b) A rise in incomes.

(c) A growing belief that interest rates will rise from their current level.

11. Would it be desirable to have zero unemployment?

12. Consider the most appropriate policy for tackling each of the different types of unemployment.

13. Under what circumstances will a reduction in unemployment be accompanied by (a) an increase in inflation; (b) a decrease in inflation? Explain your answer.

14. Imagine that you had to determine whether a particular period of inflation was demand-pull, or cost-push, or a combination of the two. What information would you require in order to conduct your analysis?

National macroeconomic policy

Business issues covered in this chapter

- What sorts of government macroeconomic policy are available to government and how will they affect business activity?
- What will be the impact on the economy and business of various fiscal policy measures?
- What determines the effectiveness of fiscal policy in smoothing out fluctuations in the economy?
- What fiscal rules are adopted by different governments and is following them always a good idea?
- What is the impact on the economy of monetary policy?
- How does monetary policy work in the UK and what is the role of the Bank of England?
- How do fiscal and monetary policy work in other countries, such as the eurozone?
- How does targeting inflation influence interest rates and hence business activity?
- Are there better rules for determining interest rates other than sticking to a simple inflation target?
- How can supply-side policy influence business and the economy?
- What types of supply-side policies can be pursued and what is their effectiveness?

A key influence on the macroeconomic environment of business is the government. Governments like to achieve economic success, including sustained and stable economic growth, low unemployment and low and stable inflation. To achieve these objectives, various types of policy are used. This chapter looks at the three main categories of macroeconomic policy.

The first is *fiscal policy*. This is where the government uses the balance of taxation (a withdrawal from the circular flow of income) and government expenditure (an injection) to influence the level of aggregate demand. If the economy is in recession, the government could increase government expenditure and/or cut taxes. This is called expansionary fiscal policy and the effect would be a higher level of aggregate demand and hence a multiplied rise in GDP and lower unemployment. If the economy was expanding too rapidly in a way that was unsustainable and hence inflation was rising, the government could do the reverse by using deflationary (or contractionary) fiscal policy: it could cut government expenditure and/or raise taxes. This would help to slow down the economy and dampen inflation.

Definitions

Fiscal policy Policy to affect aggregate demand by altering government expenditure and/or taxation.

The second type of policy is *monetary policy*. Here the government sets the framework of policy, which in many countries, including the UK, means setting a target for the rate of inflation. In the UK the rate is 2 per cent, as it is also in the eurozone. The central bank is then charged with adjusting interest rates to keep inflation on target.

These first two types of policy are referred to as *demand-side or demand management policies* as they seek to control the level of aggregate demand.

The third category of policy is *supply-side policy*. This seeks to control aggregate supply directly. For example, the government might seek ways of encouraging greater productivity through increased research and development or better training programmes. Or it might seek to improve the country's transport and communications infrastructure, for example by investing in the railways or building more roads. By increasing aggregate supply, the economy's capacity to produce expands.

The difference between demand-side and supply-side policies is illustrated in Figures 11.1(a) and (b). Both diagrams show an aggregate demand and an aggregate supply curve.

Demand-side policy seeks to shift the *AD* curve. This is illustrated in Figure 11.1(a). An expansionary fiscal or monetary policy would shift the *AD* curve to the right, say from AD_1 to AD_2. This will increase GDP (to GDP_2), thereby helping to reduce unemployment. On the other hand, it will result in higher prices: the price level will rise to P_2.

A contractionary fiscal or monetary policy would help to curb rightward shifts in the *AD* curve or even cause the curve to shift to the left. The policy could be used to tackle inflation, but it would run the risk of a reduction in the rate of growth of GDP, or even a recession, and higher unemployment.

Supply-side policy seeks to shift the *AS* curve to the right. If successful, it will lead to both higher GDP and employment and lower prices (or at least lower inflation). This is illustrated in Figure 11.1(b). A rightward shift in the aggregate supply curve from AS_1 to AS_2 results in a rise in GDP to GDP_2 and a fall in the price level to P_2.

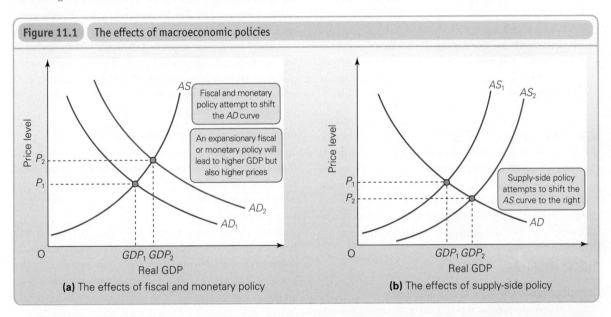

| Figure 11.1 | The effects of macroeconomic policies |

(a) The effects of fiscal and monetary policy

(b) The effects of supply-side policy

11.1 FISCAL POLICY

Fiscal policy can be used to perform two main functions:

■ *To prevent the occurrence of fundamental disequilibrium in the economy.* In other words, expansionary fiscal policy could be used to prevent a severe recession. Such a situation occurred in 2008/9 as governments around the world adopted 'stimulus packages' to prevent an even

Definitions

Monetary policy Policy to affect aggregate demand by central bank action to alter interest rates or money supply.

Demand-side or demand management policy Policy to affect aggregate demand (i.e. fiscal or monetary policy).

Supply-side policy Policy to affect aggregate supply directly.

deeper recession and mass unemployment, as discussed in the blogs on the Sloman Economics News site, 'Is there a plan B for the UK economy?' and 'The world economy'. Likewise, deflationary fiscal policy could be used to prevent excessive inflation, such as that experienced in many countries in the early 1970s.

- *To smooth out the fluctuations in the economy associated with the business cycle.* This would involve reducing government expenditure or raising taxes during the boom phase of the cycle. This would dampen down the expansion and prevent 'overheating' of the economy, with its attendant rising inflation. Conversely, with a slowing economy, the government should cut taxes or raise government expenditure in order to boost economic growth and prevent a rise in unemployment. Indeed, this was the action taken around the world from 2008 as countries attempted to tackle the recession that followed the banking crisis. For example, in the UK the government cut the rate of VAT from 17.5 to 15 per cent as a temporary measure. However, as we shall see, it is not always possible for expansionary policies to be used, especially if it is felt that the government has insufficient funds to finance them.

If these stabilisation policies are successful, they will amount merely to *fine-tuning*. Problems of excess or deficient demand will never be allowed to get severe. Any movement of aggregate demand away from a steady growth path will be immediately 'nipped in the bud'.

One final use of fiscal policy is to influence the capacity of the economy. While fiscal policy is a demand-side policy, it can be used to influence aggregate supply. Government spending could be directed towards infrastructure, or tax incentives could be given to businesses to encourage investment or to promote research and development. In so doing, the government can positively affect an economy's potential output and thus shift aggregate supply to the right.

Public finances

Central government deficits and surpluses

Since an expansionary fiscal policy involves raising government expenditure and/or lowering taxes, this has the effect of either increasing the *budget deficit* or reducing the *budget surplus*. A budget deficit in any one year is where central government's expenditure exceeds its revenue from taxation. A budget surplus is where tax revenues exceed central government expenditure.

With the exception of short periods in 1969–70, 1987–90 and 1998–2001, governments in the UK, like most governments around the world, have run budget deficits. These deficits soared in the recession of 2008/9 as tax revenues declined and as unemployment rose and with it the numbers receiving unemployment benefits, and also as governments boosted spending and/or cut taxes to stimulate the economy. This is clearly evident for the USA in the blog, 'Backing to the edge of the fiscal cliff' and from the series of

blogs regarding eurozone debt: 'Saving the eurozone? Saving the world?' (Parts A, B, C and D).

However, there has been a concerted effort by many governments around the world to reduce the size of their budget deficits. This was the number one economic priority of the Coalition government in the UK (2010–15) and the Conservative government (2015–20) has continued with this objective.

Some countries with large deficits have found it difficult to raise the necessary finance to fund debt and have had to seek international support. In 2010, Greece, with an annual budget deficit of 10.7 per cent of GDP and an accumulated national debt of 148 per cent of GDP, had to be bailed out by other eurozone countries and by the IMF with a loan of €110 billion. This proved insufficient and further bailouts were required, including €139 billion one year later and €86 billion in 2015, as you can read in the blogs, 'An end to Greek austerity?' and 'When the light at the end of the tunnel is yet another oncoming train'. The loans to Greece, however, came with tough conditions, most notably that the country would have to adopt strong austerity measures of cuts in government expenditure and tax increases. In 2015, the Greek people rejected these tough terms in a referendum. Despite this, very similar terms were eventually accepted by the Greek government. With too little debt relief, the crisis was set to continue.

Other countries requiring bailouts have included Ireland, Portugal, Spain and Cyprus: see the blog, 'Cyprus: one crisis ends; another begins'. The process of getting deficits and debts down has been painful and will continue to be so over the coming years for many countries.

Public-sector deficits and surpluses

To get a better view of the overall *stance of fiscal policy* – just how expansionary or contractionary it is – we would need to look at the deficit or surplus of the entire public sector: namely, central government, local government and public corporations.

If the public sector spends more than it earns, it will have to finance the deficit through borrowing: known as *public-sector net borrowing (PSNB)*. For example, if the public sector runs a deficit in the current year of, say, £1

> **Definitions**
>
> **Fine-tuning** The use of demand management policy (fiscal or monetary) to smooth out cyclical fluctuations in the economy.
>
> **Budget deficit** The excess of central government's spending over its tax receipts.
>
> **Budget surplus** The excess of central government's tax receipts over its spending.
>
> **Fiscal stance** How expansionary or contractionary fiscal policy is.
>
> **Public-sector net borrowing** The difference between the expenditures of the public sector and its receipts from taxation, the surpluses of public corporations and the sale of assets.

billion, then it will have to borrow £1 billion this year in order to finance it. The principal form of borrowing is through the sale of government bonds.

Deficits are shown as positive figures (the government must borrow). They add to the accumulated debts from the past. The accumulated debts of central and local government are known as the *general government debt*. If the public sector runs a *surplus* (a negative PSNB), then this will be used to *reduce* the general government debt.

Many developed nations averaged a deficit between the mid-1990s and 2007, though both their deficits and debts were smaller than they had been in the early 1990s. However, from 2008 to 2010, the average deficit increased for many countries and many have found it difficult to make significant reductions in deficits since. As a result, their general government debt has continued to rise, albeit at a slowing rate if their deficits have come down.

Figure 11.2 shows UK PSNB as a percentage of GDP from 1960 to 2015. Note the huge increase in the PSNB in 2009 as tax revenues fell in the recession and as the government attempted to reduce the depth of the recession by increasing expenditure. By 2009/10 the PSNB had reached £155 billion or 10.3 per cent of GDP

Then in subsequent years, the PSNB fell significantly. Part of the reason for this was attempts by the Coalition government to tackle the deficit. To achieve this, the government embarked on a series of spending cuts and tax rises. However, with economic growth significantly lower than hoped for, total public-sector spending fell by much less than planned, and by 2014/15 was still £92 billion (5.0 per cent of GDP). In response, the new Conservative government announced in 2015 that it planned to reduce the PSNB to below zero (i.e. a surplus) by 2019/20.

Pause for thought

If government is running a budget deficit, does this necessarily mean that GDP will increase?

The use of fiscal policy

Automatic fiscal stabilisers

To some extent, government expenditure and taxation will have the effect of *automatically* stabilising the economy. For example, as GDP rises, the amount of tax people pay automatically rises. This rise in withdrawals from the circular flow of income will help to dampen down the rise in GDP. This effect will be bigger if taxes are *progressive* (i.e. rise by a bigger percentage than GDP) as is the case with income tax in the UK.

Some government expenditure will have a similar effect. For example, total government expenditure on unemployment benefits will fall if rises in GDP cause a fall in unemployment. This again will have the effect of dampening the rise in GDP.

Discretionary fiscal policy

Automatic stabilisers cannot *prevent* fluctuations, they merely reduce their magnitude. If there is a fundamental

Definition

General government debt The accumulated central and local government deficits (less surpluses) over the years, i.e. the total amount owed by central and local government, both to domestic and overseas creditors.

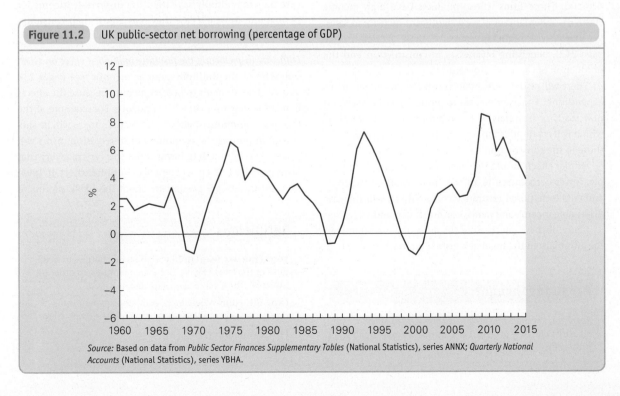

| Figure 11.2 | UK public-sector net borrowing (percentage of GDP) |

Source: Based on data from *Public Sector Finances Supplementary Tables* (National Statistics), series ANNX; *Quarterly National Accounts* (National Statistics), series YBHA.

disequilibrium in the economy or substantial fluctuations in GDP, these automatic stabilisers will not be enough. The government may thus choose to *alter* the level of government expenditure or the rates of taxation. This is known as *discretionary fiscal policy*.

If government expenditure on goods and services (roads, healthcare, education, etc.) is raised, this will create a full multiplied rise in GDP. The reason is that all the money gets spent and thus all of it goes to boosting aggregate demand.

Pause for thought

Why will the multiplier effect of government transfer payments, such as child benefit, pensions and social security benefits be less than the full multiplier effect from government expenditure on goods and services?

Cutting taxes (or increasing benefits), however, will have a smaller effect on GDP than raising government expenditure on goods and services by the same amount. The reason is that cutting taxes increases people's *disposable* incomes, of which only part will be spent. Part will be withdrawn into extra saving, imports and other taxes. In other words, not all the tax cuts will be passed on round the circular flow of income as extra expenditure. Thus if one-fifth of a cut in taxes is withdrawn and only four-fifths is spent, the tax multiplier will only be four-fifths as big as the government expenditure multiplier.

Expansionary fiscal policy will have indirect effects on virtually all firms, as aggregate demand will rise, which will increase GDP and this in turn means higher consumer demand. Those firms whose products have high income elasticity of demand may see a significant increase in sales. We may also see higher investment, via the accelerator (see page 242), benefiting businesses in construction and the production of capital equipment.

There will also be direct effects from higher government expenditure. For example, more money may be spent on new roads or hospitals or the refurbishment of premises, which will create additional work, income and spending for those in the construction and building industries.

Similar effects would also occur from tax cuts. For example, lower corporation taxes will increase after-tax profits and cuts in national insurance contributions will increase disposable income and hence consumer demand.

Many of these effects were the aims of governments in the aftermath of the financial crisis and recession.

Pause for thought

Apart from the industries mentioned above, what other industries are likely to benefit directly from an expansionary fiscal policy?

The effectiveness of fiscal policy

How successful will fiscal policy be? Will it be able to 'fine-tune' demand? Will it be able to achieve the level of GDP that the government would like it to achieve? Before changing government expenditure or taxation, the government will need to calculate the effect of any such change on GDP, employment and inflation. Predicting these effects, however, is often very unreliable.

Difficulty in predicting effects of changes in government expenditure. A rise in government expenditure of £*x* may lead to a rise in total injections (relative to withdrawals) that is smaller than £*x*. A major reason for this is a phenomenon known as *crowding out*. If the government relies on *pure fiscal policy* – that is, if it does not finance an increase in the budget deficit by increasing the money supply – it will have to borrow the money from individuals and firms. It will thus be competing with the private sector for finance and will have to offer higher interest rates. This will force the private sector also to offer higher interest rates, which may discourage firms from investing and individuals from buying on credit. Thus, government borrowing *crowds out* private borrowing. In the extreme case, the fall in consumption and investment may completely offset the rise in government expenditure, with the result that aggregate demand does not rise at all.

Difficulty in predicting effects of changes in taxes. A cut in taxes, by increasing people's disposable income, increases not only the amount they spend, but also the amount they save. The problem is that it is not easy to predict the relative size of these two increases. In part it will depend on whether people feel that the cut in tax is only temporary, in which case they may simply save the extra disposable income, or permanent, in which case they may adjust their consumption upwards.

Difficulty in predicting the resulting multiplied effect on GDP. The sizes of the multiplier and accelerator (see pages 236 and 242) are difficult to predict, mainly because the effects depend largely on people's confidence. For example, if the business community believes that a cut in taxes will be successful in pulling the economy out of recession, firms will invest. This will help to bring about the very recovery that firms predicted. There will be a big multiplier effect. If, however, businesses are pessimistic about the likely success of

---

Definitions

Discretionary fiscal policy Deliberate changes in tax rates or the level of government expenditure in order to influence the level of aggregate demand.

Crowding out Where increased public expenditure diverts money or resources away from the private sector.

Pure fiscal policy Fiscal policy which does not involve any change in money supply.

the policy, they are unlikely to invest. The economy may not recover. The credibility of the government and its policies may have a large influence here.

Another effect of confidence is on consumer spending and this directly affects the size of the multiplier. If people are confident about their future employment and that their incomes will grow, they are likely to spend more from any rise in income (and save less). The multiplier effect will be relatively large. If they are pessimistic, they will be likely to save more of any rise in income; the multiplier will be smaller. But it is difficult to predict these effects and thus how large the final multiplied rise in GDP will be.

Random shocks. Forecasts cannot take into account unpredictable events, such as the financial crisis, which, in hindsight, should have been predictable. Unfortunately, unpredictable events, such as a war, or a major industrial dispute, do occur and may seriously undermine the government's fiscal policy.

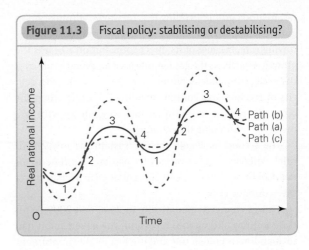

Figure 11.3 Fiscal policy: stabilising or destabilising?

> ### Pause for thought
>
> *Give some other examples of 'random shocks' that could undermine the government's fiscal policy.*

Problems of timing. Fiscal policy can involve considerable time lags. It may take time to recognise the nature of the problem before the government is willing or able to take action; tax or government expenditure changes take time to plan and implement – changes will have to wait until the next Budget to be announced and may come into effect some time later; the effects of such changes take time to work their way through the economy via the multiplier and accelerator.

If these time lags are long enough, fiscal policy could even be *de*stabilising. Expansionary policies taken to cure a recession may not take effect until the economy has *already* recovered and is experiencing a boom. Under these circumstances, expansionary policies are quite inappropriate; they simply worsen the problems of overheating. Similarly, deflationary (contractionary) policies taken to prevent excessive expansion may not take effect until the economy has already peaked and is plunging into recession. The deflationary policies only deepen the recession.

This problem is illustrated in Figure 11.3. Path (a) shows the course of the business cycle without government intervention. Ideally, with no time lags, the economy should be dampened in stage 2 and stimulated in stage 4. This would make the resulting course of the business cycle more like path (b), or even, if the policy were perfectly stabilising, a straight line. With the presence of time lags, however, deflationary policies taken in stage 2 may not come into effect until stage 4, and expansionary policies taken in stage 4 may not come into effect until stage 2. In this case the resulting course of the business cycle will be more like path

(c). Quite obviously, in these circumstances 'stabilising' fiscal policy actually makes the economy *less* stable.

Imperfect information. Although we have some idea about where the economy is in the business cycle, we can never be certain. The government may believe that the economy is at the very bottom, however, the economy could actually still be moving towards the bottom or even have entered the recovery phase. Government policy may, therefore, be based on inaccurate information about the economy's current position and again, we could see fiscal policy that has a *destabilising* effect. If the fluctuations in aggregate demand can be forecast, and if the lengths of the time lags are known, then all is not lost. At least the fiscal measures can be taken early and their delayed effects can be taken into account.

Fiscal rules

Given the problems of pursuing active fiscal policy, many governments had, until the recession of 2008/9, taken a much more passive approach. Instead of changing the policy as the economy changed, a rule was set for the level of public finances. This rule was then applied year after year, with taxes and government expenditure being planned to meet that rule. For example, a target could be set for the PSNB, with government expenditure and taxes being adjusted to keep the PSNB at or within its target level. Box 11.1 (page 268) looks at some examples of fiscal targets.

The UK's approach to fiscal policy

With Labour's election in 1997, two fiscal rules were introduced, which was very similar to the approach adopted within the eurozone, as set out in the Stability and Growth Pact (see Box 11.1). By following rules, fiscal policy as a means of adjusting aggregate demand had been largely abandoned.

The first rule was called the 'golden rule'. This committed the government to borrowing only to invest (e.g. in roads, hospitals and schools) over the economic cycle and not to fund current spending (e.g. on wages, administration and benefits). Investment was exempted from the zero borrowing rule, because of its direct contribution towards the growth of GDP. As the golden rule used an average rule over the cycle, automatic stabilisers were able to work, with deficits of receipts over current spending occurring when the economy was in recession or had sluggish growth as a means of stimulating the economy.

The second fiscal rule was its 'sustainable investment rule', whereby a target was set to maintain a *public-sector net debt* of no more than 40 per cent of GDP averaged over the economic cycle.

Things changed dramatically in 2008 and 2009. With the economy sliding into recession, the government had to abandon its golden rule and the sustainable investment rule. It argued that its 'immediate priority' was to support the economy, using discretionary fiscal policy to stimulate aggregate demand. VAT was cut from 17.5 per cent to 15 per cent for 13 months and £3 billion of capital spending on projects such as motorways, schools and new social housing was brought forward from 2010/11 to help the process.

Higher taxes and a rise in national insurance were used to pay for it, but public finances deteriorated, leading the Labour government to introduce a Fiscal Responsibility Bill, requiring governments to present to Parliament their fiscal plans to deliver sound public finances. The plan of the then Chancellor, Alistair Darling, was to halve the size of the deficit over the next Parliament.

As Figure 11.2 shows, public-sector borrowing continued to grow rapidly and when the Coalition government formed in 2010, facing one of the highest public-sector borrowing figures in the developed world (10.3 per cent of GDP), its fiscal priority was to bring public-sector borrowing down.

A 'fiscal mandate' was set, which included achieving a cyclically-adjusted current balance by 2015/16 – a balance of tax revenues and current (as opposed to investment) expenditure at the potential level of national income. This was essentially a return to Labour's golden rule. This was supplemented by a target for the ratio of public-sector debt to GDP to be falling by 2015/16. A discretionary 'consolidation package' was implemented with £99 billion of spending cuts by 2015/16 and tax increases of £23 billion. Spending cuts therefore accounted for 81 per cent of this consolidation package.

There were concerns about the contractionary fiscal policy and its impact on aggregate demand, when confidence was still low. It was feared that a resulting lack of economic growth could actually increase the level of government borrowing.

These problems were exacerbated by the crisis in the eurozone from 2011, with concerns over debt levels and the possibility of default. Growth and unemployment became worse across much of Europe and recovery in the USA remained modest, with conflict between a Republican House of Representatives in favour of fiscal restraint and a Democrat President looking to implement a growth package (see Case Study D.15 on the book's website). Growth rates in key emerging nations had slowed, cutting the UK's exports and with such low confidence and uncertainty, household and business spending was low. Aspects of the arguments over expansionary versus contractionary policy are considered in the blog 'A respectful debate over austerity versus stimulus' on the Sloman Economics News site.

Despite the severe cuts in the UK, including a reduction in departmental spending of £1.1 billion in 2013/14 and £1.2 billion in 2014/15, total public-sector spending fell by just 0.7 per cent between 2010/11 and 2014/15. Not only did the government fail to meet its targets, but the effects above did lead to lower than normal growth. Between 2010 and 2014, the average rate of growth was almost 1 percentage point below its long-term average at 1.7 per cent. However, in light of these 'external' events, the government insisted that 'significant progress' had been made.

The government faced pressure to relax its fiscal constraints, but argued that an expansionary fiscal policy would crowd out private-sector investment. In the Autumn Statement of 2014, at the end of the Coalition government, a new fiscal mandate and supplementary debt rule were published. These were contained in an updated Charter for Budget Responsibility which, since 2011, has set out before Parliament the government's objectives for fiscal policy and for managing the public debt.

The Charter was updated in October 2015 setting out a fiscal mandate, which requires a surplus on public-sector net borrowing by the end of 2019/20 and in each subsequent year. The supplementary target requires public-sector net debt to fall as a percentage of GDP in each year to 2019/20. Before changes in government policy, the Office for Budget Responsibility estimated that small deficits would be recorded in 2019/20 (£3.2 billion) and 2020/21 (£2.0 billion). However, policy within the 2016 Budget set out to raise £13.7 billion in 2019/20 and a further £13.1 billion in 2020/21, which, according to the OBR, means

> that the Government is more likely than not to meet its target on existing policy, but with a margin that is small in comparison with the uncertainty that surrounds our fiscal forecast at that horizon.

Table 11.1 shows the OBR's data on public-sector net borrowing from 2008 to 2015 and then includes the forecasts until 2021, with different probabilities, shown in 20 per cent probability bands, based on official forecast

---

Definition

Public-sector net debt The combined debt of the whole public sector: central government, local government, public corporations and any other public bodies.

Table 11.1	Public-sector net borrowing forecasts								
Percentile	10	20	30	40	50 (median)	60	70	80	90
2008–09					6.9				
2009–10					10.3				
2010–11					8.7				
2011–12					7.1				
2012–13					7.2				
2013–14					5.9				
2014–15					5.0				
2015–16	3.1	3.4	3.5	3.7	3.8	4.0	4.1	4.3	4.5
2016–17	1.0	1.6	2.1	2.5	2.9	3.2	3.6	4.1	4.7
2017–18	−1.0	0.0	0.7	1.3	1.9	2.5	3.2	4.0	5.2
2018–19	−2.0	−1.1	−0.3	0.3	1.0	1.7	2.5	3.5	4.8
2019–20	−3.5	−2.6	−1.9	−1.2	−0.5	0.3	1.1	2.2	3.6
2020–21	−3.6	−2.7	−1.9	−1.2	−0.5	0.3	1.2	2.3	4.0

Source: Economic and Fiscal Outlook, March 2016 (Office for Budget Responsibility)

errors from past data. As you can see, the forecasts are subject to significant uncertainty, which only grows as we look further into the future.

The data from Table 11.1 are then replicated in Figure 11.4, which shows a fan chart, with different shaded bands reflecting the probability of different outcomes occurring. The solid black line illustrates the OBR's median forecast and each successive pair of the lighter shaded areas around this median forecast shows 20 per cent probability bands. Thus public-sector net borrowing has a 90 per cent probability of being within the bands of the fan chart in each year.

Although the forecast suggests a falling PSNB, economic uncertainty continues to affect the global economy and meeting the new fiscal mandate will be dependent on both global demand and consumer and business confidence in the coming years.

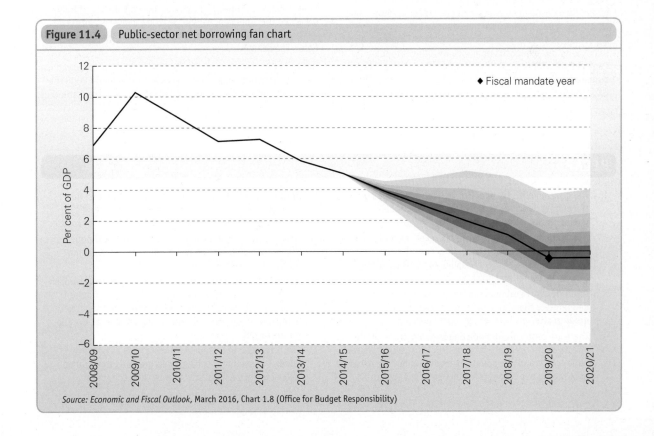

Figure 11.4 Public-sector net borrowing fan chart

Source: Economic and Fiscal Outlook, March 2016, Chart 1.8 (Office for Budget Responsibility)

BOX 11.1 THE FISCAL FRAMEWORK IN THE EUROZONE

Constraining the discretion over fiscal policy

If the government persistently runs a budget deficit, government debt will rise. If this debt rises faster than GDP, then it will account for a growing proportion of GDP. There is then likely to be an increasing problem of 'servicing' this debt, i.e. paying the interest on it. The government could find itself having to borrow more and more to meet the interest payments, and so government debt could rise faster still. As the government borrows more, it will have to pay higher interest rates to attract finance (unless this is offset by quantitative easing by the central bank: see pages 271 and 277–8). These higher interest rates may crowd out borrowing and hence investment by the private sector (see page 264).

The possibility of financial crowding out contributed towards many governments embarking on a strategy of fiscal consolidation during early 2010. But the recognition of this problem and the need for a fiscal framework had been shaping fiscal policy across Europe (and the USA) for some time. However, the financial crisis called into question how rigid any framework should be and hence how much discretion over fiscal policy national governments should have.

The EU Stability and Growth Pact

In June 1997, at the European Council in Amsterdam, the EU countries agreed on a Stability and Growth Pact (SGP). Under the Pact, which applied to countries adopting the euro, governments should seek to balance their budgets (or even aim for a surplus) averaged over the course of the business cycle. In addition, general government deficits should not exceed 3 per cent of GDP in any one year. A country's deficit was only permitted to exceed 3 per cent if its GDP had declined by at least 2 per cent (or 0.75 per cent with special permission from the Council of Ministers). Otherwise, countries with deficits exceeding 3 per cent were required to make deposits of money with the European Central Bank. These would then become fines if the excessive budget deficits were not eliminated within two years. The UK, however, was not legally bound by this procedure.

There were two main aims of targeting a zero budget deficit over the business cycle. The first was to allow automatic stabilisers to work without 'bumping into' the 3 per cent deficit ceiling in years when economies were slowing. The second was to allow a reduction in government debts as a proportion of GDP (assuming that GDP grew on average at around 2–3 per cent per year).

Keeping budget deficits within the 3 per cent ceiling?

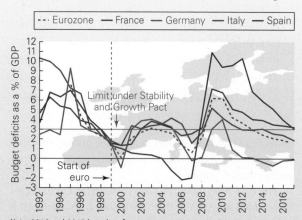

Note: 2016 and 2017 based on forecasts
Source: Based on data in *Statistical Annex to the European Economy* (European Commission).

From 2002, with slowing growth, Germany, France and Italy breached the 3 per cent ceiling. By 2007, however, after two years of relatively strong growth, deficits had been reduced well below the ceiling.

But then the credit crunch hit. As the EU economies slowed, so deficits rose. To combat the recession, in November 2008 the European Commission announced a €200 billion fiscal stimulus

RECAP

1. The government's fiscal policy will determine the size of the budget deficit or surplus and the size of the public-sector net borrowing (PSNB).

2. Automatic fiscal stabilisers are tax revenues that rise and benefits that fall as GDP rises. They have the effect of reducing the size of the multiplier and thus reducing cyclical upswings and downswings.

3. Discretionary fiscal policy is where the government deliberately changes taxes or government expenditure in order to alter the level of aggregate demand.

4. There are problems in predicting the magnitude of the effects of discretionary fiscal policy. Expansionary fiscal policy can crowd out private expenditure, but the extent of crowding out is hard to predict and depends on

business confidence. Also it is difficult to predict how people's spending will respond to changes in taxes. Various random shocks can knock fiscal policy off course.

5. There are various time lags involved with fiscal policy. If these are very long, the policy could be destabilising rather than stabilising.

6. Today many governments prefer a more passive approach towards fiscal policy. Targets are set for one or more measures of the public-sector finances, and then taxes and government expenditure are adjusted so as to keep to the target.

7. Nevertheless, in extreme circumstances, as occurred in 2008/9, governments have been prepared to abandon rules and give a fiscal stimulus to their economies.

plan, mainly in the form of increased public expenditure. €170 billion of the money would come from member governments and €30 billion from the EU, amounting to a total of 1.2 per cent of EU GDP. The money would be for a range of projects, such as job training, help to small businesses, developing green energy technologies and energy efficiency. Most member governments quickly followed, by announcing how their specific plans would accord with the overall plan.

The combination of the recession and the fiscal measures pushed most eurozone countries' budget deficits well above the 3 per cent ceiling (see the chart). The recession in EU countries deepened markedly in 2009, with GDP declining by 4.4 per cent in the eurozone as a whole, by 5.5 per cent in Italy, 5.1 per cent in Germany, 3.7 per cent in Spain and 3.1 per cent in France. As a result, the high budget deficits were not seen to breach SGP rules.

The Fiscal Compact

As the European economy began its recovery in 2010, there was tremendous pressure on member countries to begin reining in their deficits. The average eurozone deficit had risen to 6.2 per cent of GDP, and some countries' deficits were much higher. Indeed, with the Greek, Spanish and Irish deficits being 11.0, 9.6 and 29.3 per cent respectively, bringing the deficits back to the 3 per cent ceiling would be very painful. In these and other high-deficit countries, unemployment soared as a prolonged period of recession was experienced. As we saw on page 262, several countries required bailouts to allow them to pay debts that were maturing. To receive these bailouts, these countries had to agree to tough 'austerity policies', involving severe cuts in government expenditure and tax increases – which only deepened their recessions.

The SGP was now seen as needing reform. The result was an intense period of negotiation culminating in early 2012

with a new inter-governmental treaty to limit spending and borrowing. The treaty, known as the 'Fiscal Compact', requires that from January 2013 national governments not only abide by the excessive deficit procedure of the SGP but also keep structural deficits at no higher than 0.5 per cent of GDP. Structural deficits are that part of a deficit not directly related to the economic cycle and so would exist even if the economy were operating at its potential output.

In the cases of countries with a debt-to-GDP ratio significantly below 60 per cent, the structural deficit is permitted to reach 1 per cent of GDP. Finally, where the debt-to-GDP ratio exceeds 60 per cent, countries should, on average, reduce it by one-twentieth per year.

Where a national government is found by the European Court of Justice not to comply with the Fiscal Compact, the Court has the power to fine that country up to 0.1 per cent of GDP payable to the European Stability Mechanism (ESM). The ESM is a fund from which loans are provided to support a eurozone government in severe financing difficulty, or alternatively is used to purchase that country's bonds in the primary market.

Most member states have undertaken significant fiscal consolidation (i.e. deficit reduction) since 2011 and, according to the European Commission, the fiscal policy stance across the eurozone was broadly neutral in 2014 and 2015. Many commentators, however, have argued for an expansionary fiscal policy across the eurozone to stimulate economic growth.

1. *What effects will government investment expenditure have on general government deficits (a) in the short run; (b) in the long run?*
2. *If there is a danger of global recession, should governments loosen the strait-jacket of fiscal policy targets?*

11.2 MONETARY POLICY

The Bank of England's Monetary Policy Committee meets regularly to set Bank Rate. (Meetings were monthly up to 2016 and eight times per year from 2017.) Similarly, other central banks, such as the European Central Bank (ECB) and the Federal Reserve in the USA, meet regularly to set their rates, and in particular the rate at which they will lend to other banks. These central bank rates thus influence many other rates in the economy.

Before the onset of recession in 2009, central banks changed their interest rates fairly frequently as economic conditions changed. For several years from 2009, however, central banks kept their interest rates at historic lows in an attempt to revive their economies. This is illustrated in Figure 11.5.

But is monetary policy simply the setting of interest rates? In reality, it involves the central bank intervening in the money market to ensure that the interest rate that has been announced is also the *equilibrium* interest rate.

The policy setting

In framing its monetary policy, the government must decide on what the goals of the policy are. Is the aim simply to control inflation, or does the government wish also to affect output and employment, or does it want to control the exchange rate?

A decision also has to be made about who is to carry out the policy. There are three possible approaches here.

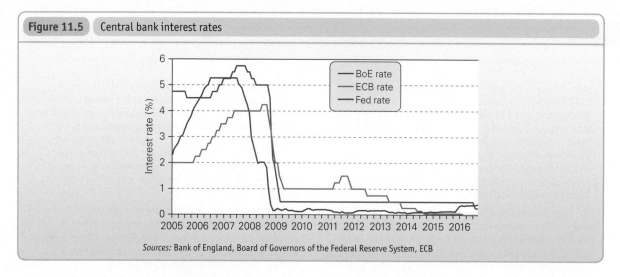

Figure 11.5 Central bank interest rates

Sources: Bank of England, Board of Governors of the Federal Reserve System, ECB

In the first, the government both sets the policy and decides the measures necessary to achieve it. Here the government would set the interest rate, with the central bank simply influencing money markets to achieve this rate. This occurred in the UK before 1997.

The second approach is for the government to set the policy *targets*, but for the central bank to be given independence in deciding interest rates. This is the approach adopted in the UK today. The government has set a target rate of inflation of 2 per cent for 24 months hence, but then the MPC is free to choose the rate of interest.

The third approach is for the central bank to be given independence not only in carrying out policy, but in setting the policy targets. The ECB, within the statutory objective of maintaining price stability over the medium term, decided on the target of keeping inflation below, but close, to 2 per cent over the medium term (see Box 11.2, page 275).

More and more countries have begun to use the second or third approach, with inflation targeting the most common policy objective. Part of the reasoning behind this is the apparent failure of discretionary macroeconomic policies, as they suffer from time lags and therefore can fail to straighten out the business cycle. But, why is inflation and not the money supply targeted?

Money supply targets were adopted by many countries in the 1980s, including the UK, but money supply targets proved very difficult to achieve. The money supply depends on the amount of credit banks create and this is difficult for the authorities to control. Furthermore, even if money supply is controlled, this does not necessarily mean that aggregate demand will be controlled; people may simply adjust the amount they hold in their bank accounts. The money supply is still targeted in some countries, although typically it is not the main target. Inflation, on the other hand, is the main target for macroeconomic policy, although some countries, such as the USA, in the light of the recession and slow recovery of recent years, began targeting other indicators, such as a maximum rate of unemployment.

Inflation targets have proved relatively easy to achieve – at least once they have been in place for a while. Initially there can be problems, especially if the actual rate of inflation is way above the target level. The high rates of interest necessary to bring inflation down can cause a recession. However, once inflation has been brought close to its target level, the objective is then to maintain it at that level and most countries have had success in doing this. Furthermore, success at meeting an inflation target seems to breed more success, as the policy and the government gain credibility. If inflation is on target, people expect inflation to remain on target and these expectations then help to keep inflation at the desired level.

With the persistent slow growth in many countries since the financial crisis, inflation has tended to be somewhat below target. But with interest rates close to zero, there has been little scope for further cuts in interest rates to bring inflation back up to target. Generally, however, inflation targeting has been moderately successful in keeping inflation close to target or a little below.

But this has created another potential problem. With worldwide inflation having fallen, and with global trade and competition helping to keep prices down, there is now less of a link between inflation and the business cycle. Booms no longer seem to generate the inflation they once did. Gearing interest rate policy to maintaining low inflation could still see economies experiencing unsustainable booms, followed by recession. Inflation may be controlled, but the business cycle may not be.

Implementing monetary policy

Inflation may be off target. Alternatively, the government (or central bank) may wish to alter its monetary policy (e.g. choose a new target). What can it do? There are two main approaches. The first is to alter the money supply; the second is to alter interest rates. These are illustrated in Figure 11.6, which shows the demand for and supply of money (this is similar to Figure 10.6 on page 247). With an initial supply of money of M_s the equilibrium interest rate is r_1.

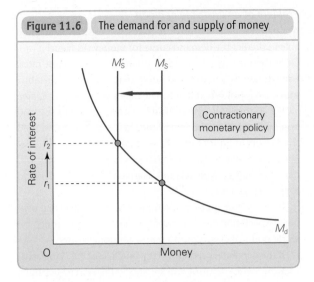

Figure 11.6 The demand for and supply of money

Assume that the central bank wants to tighten monetary policy in order to reduce inflation. It could (a) seek to shift the supply of money curve to the left, from M_s to M_s' (resulting in the equilibrium rate of interest rising from r_1 to r_2), (b) raise the interest rate directly from r_1 to r_2, and then manipulate the money supply to reduce it to M_s'.

Techniques to control the money supply

The main way that the central bank seeks to control the money supply is through *open-market operations*. This involves the sale or purchase by the central bank of government securities (bonds or bills; see pages 246–7) in the open market. These sales (or purchases) are *not* in response to changes in the public-sector deficit and are best understood, therefore, in the context of an unchanged deficit.

Pause for thought

Explain how open-market operations could be used to increase the money supply.

If the central bank wishes to *reduce* the money supply, it takes money from the banking system by selling more securities. When people buy these securities, they pay for them by drawing on their accounts in banks. Thus banks' balances with the central bank are reduced. If this brings bank reserves below their prudent liquidity ratio, banks will reduce advances. There will be a multiple contraction of credit and hence of money supply.

In 2008/9, the Bank of England wanted to *increase* the money supply. Here, through the process known as '*quantitative easing*' it used aggressive open-market operations to *buy* securities from the banking sector, thereby releasing new money into the banking system. The hope was that banks would use the new money as the basis for credit creation, with the extra lending stimulating consumer spending and investment and thereby helping recovery from the

recession. The measures taken in the UK, the eurozone and USA are discussed in more detail in Box 11.2 and you can read about the rather belated use of quantitative easing in the ECB in the blog, 'A seven-year emergency', on the Sloman Economics News site.

Techniques to control interest rates

The approach to monetary control today in most countries is to focus directly on interest rates. Normally an interest rate change will be announced, and then open-market operations will be conducted by the central bank to ensure that the money supply is adjusted so as to make the announced interest rate the *equilibrium* one. Let us assume that the central bank decides to raise interest rates. What does it do?

In general, it will seek to keep banks short of liquidity. This will happen automatically on any day when tax payments by banks' customers exceed the money they receive from government expenditure. This excess is effectively withdrawn from banks and ends up in the government's account at the central bank. Even when this does not occur, sales of government debt by the central bank (see above) will effectively keep the banking system short of liquidity.

How do banks acquire the necessary liquidity? The Bank of England (like other central banks) is willing to lend money to the banks on a short-term basis. It does this by entering into a *sale and repurchase ('repo') agreement* with the banks. This is an agreement whereby the banks sell some of their government bonds ('gilts') to the Bank of England on a temporary basis (normally two weeks), agreeing to buy them back again at the end of the period. The Bank of England is in effect giving a short-term loan to the banks and is thus tiding them over the period of liquidity shortage. In this role, the Bank of England is acting as *lender of last resort*, and ensures that the banks never run short of money.

Because banks frequently have to borrow from the Bank of England, it can use this to force through interest rate changes. The point is that the Bank of England can *choose the rate of interest to charge* (i.e. the repo rate). This will then have a knock-on effect on other interest rates throughout the banking system.

Definitions

Open-market operations The sale (or purchase) by the authorities of government securities in the open market in order to reduce (or increase) money supply.

Quantitative easing A deliberate attempt by the central bank to increase the money supply by buying large quantities of securities through open-market operations.

Sale and repurchase agreement (repo) An agreement between two financial institutions whereby one in effect borrows from another by selling some of its assets, agreeing to buy them back (repurchase them) at a fixed price and on a fixed date.

Lender of last resort The role of the central bank as the guarantor of sufficient liquidity in the monetary system.

The impact of monetary policy on business and the economy

Although interest rates are set by the central bank, they remain a key tool of macroeconomic policy, in particular because a change in interest rates can affect so many of the key components of aggregate demand and hence the government's objectives. An increase in interest rates will have the following effects:

■ It increases the return on saving and hence may discourage consumption, thus reducing aggregate demand.

■ It may discourage business investment and thereby reduce long-term economic growth.

■ It adds to the costs of production, to the costs of house purchase and generally to the cost of living, for example through higher mortgage repayments. Higher interest rates are thus cost inflationary.

■ It is politically unpopular, since the general public does not like paying higher interest rates on overdrafts, credit cards and mortgages.

As we shall see in the next chapter, high interest rates encourage inflows of money from abroad. This drives up the exchange rate, making domestically produced goods expensive relative to goods made abroad. This can be very damaging for export industries and industries competing with imports. Many firms in the UK suffered badly between 1997 and 2007 from a high exchange rate, caused partly by higher interest rates in the UK than in both the eurozone and, until 2006, in the USA.

A change in interest rates will therefore impact businesses, but by how much will the level of business activity and/or inflation be affected? This depends on the nature of the demand for loans. If this demand is (a) unresponsive to interest rate changes or (b) unstable because it is significantly affected by other determinants (such as anticipated income or foreign interest rates), then it will be very difficult to control by controlling the rate of interest.

Problem of an inelastic demand for loans

If the demand for loans is inelastic (i.e. a relatively steep M_d curve in Figure 11.6), any attempt to reduce demand will involve large rises in interest rates. The problem will be compounded if the demand curve shifts to the right, due, say, to a consumer spending boom. The effects described above will therefore be larger, such as a bigger decrease in business investment and hence a potentially larger dampening effect on long-term growth.

Evidence suggests that the demand for loans may indeed be quite inelastic. Especially in the short run, many firms and individuals simply cannot reduce their borrowing commitments. In fact, higher interest rates may force some people and firms to borrow *more* in order to finance the higher interest rate payments.

Problem of an unstable demand

Accurate monetary control requires the central bank to be able to predict the demand curve for money (in Figure 11.6). Only then can it set the appropriate level of interest rates. Unfortunately, the demand curve may shift unpredictably, making control very difficult. The major reason is *speculation*.

For example, if people think interest rates will rise and bond prices fall, in the meantime they will demand to hold their assets in liquid form. The demand for money will rise. Similarly, if people think exchange rates will rise, they will demand sterling while it is still relatively cheap. The demand for money will rise.

It is very difficult for the central bank to predict what people's expectations will be. Speculation depends so much on world political events, rumour and 'random shocks'.

If the demand curve shifts very much, and if it is inelastic, then monetary control will be very difficult. Furthermore, the central bank will have to make frequent and sizeable adjustments to interest rates. These fluctuations can be very damaging to business confidence and may discourage long-term investment.

The net result of an inelastic and unstable demand for money is that substantial interest rate changes may be necessary to bring about the required change in aggregate demand. An example occurred in 2008, when interest rates were cut drastically, first in the USA and then in the UK, the eurozone and most other countries. But, while this helped to reduce the decline in GDP, it was not enough to prevent recession.

> ### Pause for thought
>
> *Assume that the central bank announces a rise in interest rates and backs this up with open-market operations. What determines the size of the resulting fall in aggregate demand?*

Difficulties with choice of target

Assume that the government or central bank sets an inflation target. Should it then stick to that rate, come what may? Might not an extended period of relatively low inflation warrant a lower inflation target? The government must at least have the discretion to change the rules, even if only occasionally.

Then there is the question of whether success in achieving the target will bring success in achieving other macroeconomic objectives, such as low unemployment and stable economic growth. The problem is that something called *Goodhart's Law* is likely to apply. The law, named after

> ### Definition
>
> **Goodhart's Law** Controlling a symptom or indicator of a problem is unlikely to cure the problem; it will simply mean that what is being controlled now becomes a poor indicator of the problem.

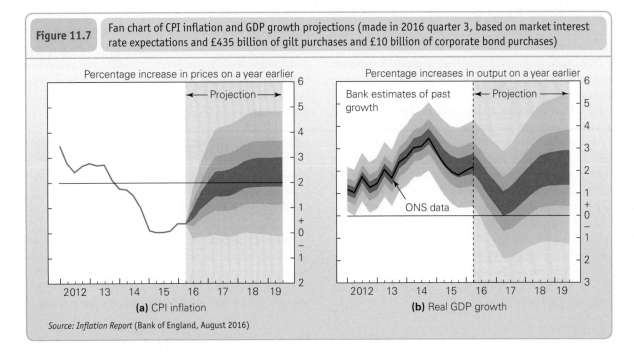

Figure 11.7 Fan chart of CPI inflation and GDP growth projections (made in 2016 quarter 3, based on market interest rate expectations and £435 billion of gilt purchases and £10 billion of corporate bond purchases)

(a) CPI inflation

(b) Real GDP growth

Source: Inflation Report (Bank of England, August 2016)

Charles Goodhart, formerly of the Bank of England, states that attempts to control an indicator of a problem may, as a result, make it cease to be a good indicator of the problem.

Targeting inflation may make it become a poor indicator of the state of the economy. If people believe that the central bank will be successful in achieving its inflation target, then those expectations will feed into their inflationary expectations, and not surprisingly the target will be met. But that target rate of inflation may now be consistent with both a buoyant and a depressed economy.

An example occurred in 2008, when there was a rapid slowdown in the economy and yet cost-push pressures from higher commodity prices pushed up the inflation rate. Simply targeting the current rate of inflation would have involved higher interest rates, which would have deepened the recession.

Thus, achieving the inflation target may not tackle the much more serious problem of creating stable economic growth and an environment which will therefore encourage long-term investment.

Use of a Taylor rule

For this reason, many economists have advocated the use of a *Taylor rule*,[1] rather than a simple inflation target. A Taylor rule takes two objectives into account – (1) inflation and (2) either economic growth or the rate of unemployment – and seeks to get the optimum degree of stability of the two. The degree of importance attached to each of the two objectives can be decided by the government or central bank. The central bank adjusts interest rates when either the rate of inflation diverges from its target or the rate of economic growth (or unemployment) diverges from its sustainable (or equilibrium) level.

Take the case where inflation is above its target level but economic growth is at the target level. The central bank following a Taylor rule will raise the rate of interest. It knows, however, that this will reduce economic growth. This, therefore, limits the amount that the central bank is prepared to raise the rate of interest. The more weight it attaches to stabilising inflation, the more it will raise the rate of interest. The more weight it attaches to maintaining stable economic growth, the less it will raise the rate of interest.

Thus, the central bank has to trade off inflation stability against stable economic growth. This is especially true in the eurozone, as the ECB's primary objective is to maintain price stability.

The Bank of England's approach

The Bank of England uses a rule that is apparently simpler than the Taylor rule, but in reality is more sophisticated. The Bank of England targets inflation alone; in this sense

---

[1] Named after John Taylor, from Stanford University, who proposed that for every 1 percent that GDP rises above sustainable GDP, real interest rates should be raised by 0.5 percentage point and for every 1 percent that inflation rises above its target level, real interest rates should be raised by 0.5 percentage point (i.e. nominal rates should be raised by 1.5 percentage points).

> **Definition**
>
> **Taylor rule** A rule adopted by a central bank for setting the rate of interest. It will raise the interest rate if (a) inflation is above target or (b) economic growth is above the sustainable level (or unemployment below the equilibrium rate). The rule states how much interest rates will be changed in each case. In other words, a relative weighting is attached to each of these two objectives.

the rule is simpler. But the inflation figure on which it bases its interest rate decisions is the *forecast* rate of inflation, not the current rate; in this sense it is more sophisticated.

The Bank of England publishes a quarterly Inflation Report, which contains the MPC's projections for inflation and real GDP growth for the next three years, assuming that interest rates follow market expectations. These projections are known as 'fan charts' and are shown in Figure 11.7.

In each case, the darkest central band represents 10 per cent likelihood, as do each of the eight subsequent pairs of lighter areas out from the central band. Thus inflation and GDP growth are considered to have 90 per cent probability of being within their respective fan. The bands get wider as the time horizon is extended, indicating increasing uncertainty about the outcome. Also, the less reliable are considered to be the forecasts by the MPC, the wider will be the fan. The dashed line indicates the two-year target point. Thus in quarter 3 of 2016, the 2 per cent inflation target was for quarter 3 of 2018.

These projections form the basis for the Monetary Policy Committee's deliberations. If the projected inflation in 24 months' time is off target, the MPC will change interest rates accordingly. The advantage of this is that it sends a very clear message to people that inflation *will* be kept under control. People will therefore be more likely to adjust their expectations accordingly and keep their borrowing in check.

> ### Pause for thought
>
> *If people believe that the central bank will be successful in keeping inflation on target, does it matter whether a simple inflation rule or a Taylor rule is used? Explain.*

Although projections are made for GDP growth, these are to help inform the forecast for inflation. GDP growth is not itself an explicit target.

Inflation targeting was introduced in the UK in 1992. For virtually all of the period from 1993 to 2007 inflation

---

BOX 11.2   THE CENTRAL BANKS OF THE USA AND THE EUROZONE

Managing the monetary system

The Federal Reserve

The Federal Reserve (or 'Fed') is the central bank in the USA, set up in 1913. Although it consists of 12 regional Federal Reserve Banks, it is the Federal Reserve Board in Washington that sets monetary policy and the Federal Open Market Committee (FOMC) that decides how to carry it out.

As is the case with many other central banks across the world, the Fed has independence from government. Its objectives include low inflation (2 per cent over the medium term), sustainable growth, low unemployment and moderate long-term interest rates. In these objectives, it is therefore different from the European Central Bank (ECB) and the Bank of England, which primarily target price stability. The problem in the Federal Reserve is that the various objectives often conflict with each other and when this happens, an assessment must be made as to which presents the most pressing problem.

If inflation is low, then monetary policy can be used to pursue other objectives, such as stimulating the economy. For example, if a recession is expected, the Fed may cut interest rates. Any increase in aggregate demand will push up prices, but if inflation is low, then this is unlikely to cause a problem. This was the case in 2001, where the rate was cut from 6 per cent in January to 1.75 per cent in December. The higher inflation is, the more problematic an expansionary monetary policy becomes, as any boost to aggregate demand will worsen inflationary pressures. However, this is not to say that high inflation precludes a loose monetary policy.

With the onset of the financial crisis in 2007/8, the Federal Reserve faced two problems. Not only was the economy

slowing, but inflation was rising. Any reduction in interest rates to boost the economy would therefore push up inflation, but any increase in interest rates to bring inflation under control would slow the economy even further. Prioritising was therefore crucial and, in this instance, the Fed focused on the slowdown in the economy and so cut interest rates several times. In August 2007, the rate was 5.25 per cent, but one year later it had fallen to 2 per cent, despite rising inflation. Inflation did then begin to fall and with the recession deepening, further rate cuts occurred, leaving interest rates between 0 and 0.25 per cent by December 2008 (see Figure 11.5 on page 270). They remained in this range, lower than both the Bank of England and, for most of the time, the ECB, until the Federal Reserve took the first step to return 'to normal' when it increased rates by one quarter of one per cent in December 2015.

The instruments used by the FOMC to carry out the monetary policy as set out by the Federal Reserve include:

- Open-market operations, whereby Treasury bills and government bonds are bought and sold. These enable the FOMC to change the money supply.
- A discount rate, known as the 'federal funds rate', which is the rate of interest at which the Fed is willing to lend to banks, thereby providing them with liquidity on which they can create credit.
- Variable minimum reserves, which determine the percentage of various assets which banks are legally required to hold in the form of non-interest-bearing reserves.

1. In what ways is the Fed's operation of monetary policy (a) similar to and (b) different from the Bank of England's?

diverged by no more than 1 percentage point from the target. Since then, with the turmoil of international commodity price fluctuations and recession, there has been a little more variation, but still small by historical standards. In the year to September 2011, inflation in the UK reached 5.2 per cent and in the year to February 2015, it reached 0 per cent, falling to –0.1 per cent in the years to April, September and October 2015.[2] Despite the relatively high rate of inflation in 2011, interest rates were not increased as this would have dampened aggregate demand and economic growth even further. The Bank of England argued that this was still consistent with targeting a 2 per cent inflation in 24 months' time as the low level of aggregate demand would have caused inflation to fall below 2 per cent if interest rates had been raised.

Following the Brexit vote in June 2016, there was a depreciation of sterling (see section 13.2) and economic

growth was forecast to slow. In August 2016, therefore, the Bank of England introduced a new set of stimulus measures, including a cut in Bank Rate from 0.5 per cent to 0.25 per cent and an increase in asset purchases under its quantitative easing programme from £375 billion to £445 billion (£435 billion of government bonds and £10 billion of corporate bonds). It also introduced a funding scheme for banks that provides loans to them from the Bank of England at ultra-low interest rates to encourage them to lend to customers, both households and businesses, with penalties if they do not.

Despite these measures, the Bank forecast that growth would fall, albeit less than it would have done, and that inflation would rise to 2.4 per cent in two years' time (see Figure 11.7). Although this would be slightly above the 2 per cent target, the MPC felt that this was an acceptable trade-off to help reduce the fall in growth. Inflation, it argued, would still return to the 2 per cent target, but over a somewhat longer period.

---

[2] See: Mehreen Khan, 'Britain remains stuck in deflation', *The Telegraph* (17 November 2015).

The European Central Bank

The European Central Bank (ECB) is based in Frankfurt and has the responsibility for operating monetary policy across the eurozone. In a similar way to the Federal Reserve, the ECB has overall control of monetary policy, but it is the role of the central banks of individual countries to issue currency and carry out the monetary policy set in Frankfurt. The target of monetary policy for the ECB is much more focused than that of the Federal Reserve, as its primary objective is a responsibility for achieving price stability across the eurozone. The medium-term target is for the weighted average inflation rate across all members of the eurozone to be below but close to 2 per cent.

Between 2005 and 2009, interest rates in the eurozone had been lower than those set in both the UK and USA. With the financial crisis and subsequent recession, both the Fed and the Bank of England began cutting their interest rates, but in July 2008, the ECB increased its rate to 4.25 per cent (the first increase in a year). The move was in response to higher inflation, which had reached 4 per cent in the eurozone. Although evidence showed growth in the eurozone to be decelerating, the primary objective of price stability was targeted. The increase, however, was short-lived, as by December 2008, with the eurozone entering a deep recession, interest rates stood at 2.5 per cent and by July 2012, they were just 0.75 per cent. They remained at this level until May 2013, when the ECB lowered them once more to a record low of 0.5 per cent, which matched the rate set by the Bank of England. But then, contrary to the central banks in the

UK and USA, the ECB reduced rates further to reach 0 per cent by March 2016.

The main tools used by the ECB in implementing its monetary policy include:

- Open-market operations in government bonds and other recognised assets, mainly in the form of repos to keep the ECB's desired interest rate at the equilibrium rate.
- Setting a minimum reserve ratio for eurozone banks of 2 per cent, primarily to prevent excessive lending. This was reduced to 1 per cent in January 2012 to help stimulate bank lending and was the first time that this tool had been used as part of an active monetary policy.

The operation of the Fed, ECB and Bank of England is similar in many ways, given their independence and use of interest rates to steer the economy. Central banks across the world responded in similar ways to the financial crisis, however, with a mixture of interest rate cuts and quantitative easing as we will discuss in Box 11.3.

2. *How does the ECB's operation of monetary policy differ from that in the UK?*

3. *Interest rates were cut in the eurozone, matching the rate in the UK, in May 2013 to help stimulate economic growth. Rates were then reduced further. How likely do you think it is that low rates of interest over such a sustained period of time will create growth?*

Using monetary policy

It is impossible to use monetary policy as a precise means of controlling aggregate demand. It is especially weak when it is pulling against the expectations of firms and consumers and when it is implemented too late. However, if the authorities operate a tight monetary policy firmly enough and long enough, they should eventually be able to reduce lending and aggregate demand. But there will inevitably be time lags and imprecision in the process.

An expansionary monetary policy is even less reliable. If the economy is in recession, no matter how low interest rates are driven, or however much the money supply is expanded, people cannot be forced to borrow if they do not wish to. Firms will not borrow to invest if they predict a

continuing recession. This was a serious problem in 2008/9. Despite substantial increases in the money supply by the central bank throughout 2009 as a means of encouraging banks to lend to each other and to customers, both firms and consumers were reluctant to borrow. There was too much uncertainty and confidence was low. As such, monetary policy struggled to stimulate aggregate demand.

A particular difficulty in using interest rate reductions to expand the economy arises if the repo rate is nearly zero but this is still not enough to stimulate the economy. The problem is that (nominal) interest rates cannot be negative, for clearly nobody would be willing to lend in these circumstances. Japan was in such a situation in the early 2000s. It was caught in what is known as the

---

| BOX 11.3 | THE CREDIT CRUNCH |

Causes and responses

Banks and other financial institutions want to make profits but, at the same time as pursuing this objective, they must also have sufficient funds to meet the day-to-day demands of their customers to withdraw money from their accounts. These two objectives often conflict, as the more liquid an asset, the less profitable it is likely to be and vice versa. For example, personal and business loans to customers are profitable to banks, but highly illiquid, as they are difficult to convert into cash without loss. On the other hand, keeping cash reserves in the bank will generate no profits, but they are completely liquid.

Banks must therefore hold a range of assets, with varying degrees of profitability and liquidity. It is this conflict which may have sown the seeds for the credit crunch that affected economies across the world.

Bank loans across the world had increased rapidly. Many of these loans were secured against property and were thus illiquid. However, there is a process by which banks can increase the liquidity of their balance sheets, and therefore expand the size of their illiquid assets, and many used this strategy prior to the credit crunch. The process is known as *securitisation*.

Securitisation is a form of financial engineering, where a financial institution pools some of its assets, such as residential mortgages, and sells them to an intermediary, known as a special purpose vehicle (SPV). The SPV, in purchasing these assets, gives the financial institution cash today, allowing them to make further advances. To finance their purchase, the SPV will issue bonds to investors (noteholders).

Securitisation grew rapidly in the UK and USA, especially among banks. Figures from the Bank of England show that the value of lending to individuals which was securitised increased from just over £0.8 billion in 1998 to £103.6 billion in 2008. Most of the securitised assets were in the form of residential mortgages.

Risks and the sub-prime market

The increase in securitisation up to 2008 highlights the strong demand among investors for these securities. The

attraction of these fixed-income products for the noteholders was the potential for higher returns than on (what were) similarly-rated products.

However, investors have no recourse should people with mortgages fall into arrears or, worse still, default on their mortgages. The securitisation of assets can therefore be highly risky for all those in the securitisation chain and consequently for the financial system as a whole.

The pooling of advances in itself *reduces* the cash-flow risk facing investors. However, there is a *moral hazard* problem here (see pages 57–8). The pooling of the risks may encourage lenders to lower their credit criteria by offering house purchasers higher income multiples (advances relative to annual household incomes) or higher loan-to-value ratios (advances relative to the price of housing).

Towards the end of 2006 the USA witnessed an increase in the number of defaults by households on residential mortgages. This was a particular problem in the *sub-prime market* – higher-risk households with poor credit ratings. Similarly, the number falling behind with their payments rose. This was on the back of rising interest rates. As long as house prices were rising, people could always sell their house to pay off their loan. But in 2006/7 US house prices were falling, forcing many people to default.

Definitions

Moral hazard The temptation to take more risks when you know that someone else will cover the risks if you get into difficulties. In the case of banks taking risks, the 'someone else' may be another bank, the central bank or the government.

Sub-prime debt Debt where there is a high risk of default by the borrower (e.g. mortgage holders who are on low incomes facing higher interest rates and falling house prices).

liquidity trap. The UK and many eurozone countries were in this position in the early 2010s. Despite record low interest rates and high levels of liquidity, borrowing and lending remained low, given worries about fiscal austerity and its dampening effects on economic growth. Paul Krugman discusses the liquidity trap in his *New York Times* blog.[3]

Despite these problems, changing interest rates can often be quite effective in the medium term. After all, they can be changed very rapidly. There are not the time lags of implementation that there are with fiscal policy. Indeed, since the early 1990s most governments or central banks in

OECD countries have used interest rate changes as the major means of keeping aggregate demand and inflation under control. Up until 2008, this policy had been successful. The question remains as to whether they can be successful again in managing the economy, once they have risen above their 'emergency' levels of near zero.

[3] Paul Krugman, 'Monetary policy in a liquidity trap', *The New York Times* (11 April 2013).

Definition

Liquidity trap When interest rates are at their floor and thus any further increases in money supply will not be spent but merely be held in bank accounts as people wait for the economy to recover and/or interest rates to rise.

These problems in the US sub-prime market were the catalyst for the liquidity problem that beset financial systems in 2007 and 2008. Where these assets were securitised, investors (largely other financial institutions) suffered from the contagion arising from arrears and defaults.

Securitisation also internationalised the contagion. Investors are global so that advances, such as a US family's residential mortgage, can cross national borders as part of a securitised asset. As the contagion spread globally, financial institutions across the world ended up having to write off debts. They thus saw their balance sheets deteriorate and this eventually led to the collapse in the demand for securitised assets.

Perhaps more important than this was the lack of trust between banks. Banks did not want to lend to each other, in case they were lending to a bank with worthless assets, meaning they were unlikely to repay any loan. Inter-bank lending therefore virtually dried up, as did liquidity. And so began the credit crunch, spreading rapidly from one nation to the next.

 1. *Does securitisation necessarily involve a moral hazard problem?*

How did the world respond?

With banks failing and confidence lacking, measures were introduced in many countries to provide stability for the financial system and to support ailing financial institutions. From summer 2007, central banks, including the US Federal Reserve and the Bank of England, became increasingly proactive in injecting liquidity into the financial system.

Then from late 2008, central banks cut interest rates so that by early 2009 they were virtually zero (see Figure 11.5 on page 270). Programmes of quantitative easing were adopted, first by the Fed, then by the Bank of England, then the Bank of Japan[1] and eventually in 2015 by the ECB.

[1] As we shall see in Box 11.4 (on page 280), the Bank of Japan had previously used quantitative easing in the early 2000s in an attempt to stimulate a stagnant economy.

US measures. In October 2008, a $700 billion rescue package was adopted for the struggling financial system in the USA, known as the *Troubled Asset Relief Program (TARP)*. The aim was to provide liquidity to the banking system. In addition, the Federal Reserve announced a planned purchase of $100 billion of corporate debt issued by government-sponsored financial enterprises and $500 billion of mortgage-backed securities.

With growth not increasing fast enough, a second round of quantitative easing ('QE2') was announced in November 2010, with the Fed buying $600 billion of Treasury securities by the end of quarter 2 of 2011. Then in September 2012 it launched QE3, saying that it would spend an additional $40 billion per month, which was then increased to $85 billion per month in December 2012. The Fed also announced that it would keep the federal funds rate near zero 'at least through 2015'.

Quantitative easing finally ended in October 2014, with the Fed having purchased a total of $3.5 trillion in assets.[2] With the US economy on a seemingly more stable footing, interest rates were finally increased in December 2015, after much speculation as to when the first rate rise would come.

 2. *How significant was the decision by Janet Yellen, Chair of the Federal Reserve, to raise interest rates and how might further rises by the Fed affect the global economy, given that many countries were (are) still in precarious positions?*

ECB measures. Various measures were taken in the eurozone, although these were not initially designed to increase money supply. A Securities Market Programme (SMP) began in May 2010 with the objective of supplying liquidity to the banking system. Under the programme, the ECB used existing funds to purchase various assets, including government bonds, from banks. Under SMP, the plan was for banks to buy them back at some point in the future (a form of repo).

[2] See: Jeff Kearns, 'The Fed eases off', *Bloomberg* (15 September 2015).

▶

Between December 2011 and February 2012, the ECB lent over €1 trillion to banks in the form of three-year loans at a mere 1 per cent rate of interest in return for a range of collateral. The hope was that the loans would help banks pay off maturing debt and allow banks to increase their lending. Also it was hoped that the banks would use the loans to buy government bonds, thereby easing the debt crisis in countries such as Greece, Portugal, Spain, Ireland and Italy. The reserve ratio (see Box 11.2) was also reduced in January 2012 from 2 per cent to 1 per cent, again with the objective of helping to alleviate some of the constraints on the volume of bank lending by financial institutions.

As concerns developed throughout 2012 about the future of the euro and the ability of countries such as Greece, Spain and Italy to remain in the monetary union and be able to borrow at affordable interest rates, a replacement for the SMP was announced. It would involve a more extensive programme of purchasing existing government bonds of countries in difficulty and so the scheme was designed to help troubled banks and troubled countries, rather than boosting the eurozone economy as a whole. The purchase of bonds was not time limited and the aim was to drive down these countries' interest rates and thereby make it cheaper to issue new bonds when old ones matured. These Outright Monetary Transactions (OMTs) were part of the ECB's strategy to do 'whatever it takes' to hold the single currency together.

With the eurozone still failing to achieve economic growth, the ECB announced that it was adopting a negative deposit rate (the rate paid to banks for overnight deposits in the ECB) and that it was embarking on a further series of targeted long-term refinancing operations so as to provide long-term loans to commercial banks at cheap rates until September 2018.

Eventually, in 2015, the ECB announced that it was introducing quantitative easing. This would be a large-scale programme whereby it would create new money to buy €60 billion of existing assets every month, mainly bonds of governments in the eurozone held largely by banks. This programme of asset purchases began in March 2015 and was set to continue until at least September 2016, bringing the total of asset purchased by that time to over €1.1 trillion.

However, the end of 2015 saw a divergence of monetary policy between the ECB and the Fed.[3] As the Fed raised rates and held off on any further quantitative easing, the ECB cut its deposit rate from –0.2 to –0.3 and announced a further extension of the €60 billion per month quantitative easing programme from September 2016 to March 2017, by which time the total would be €1.5 trillion. The deposit rate was further reduced to –0.4 per cent in March 2016, while the quantitative easing programme was increased to €80 billion per month (see the blog 'A seven-year emergency', on the Sloman Economics News site).

UK measures. With the onset of the credit crunch, various packages for generating liquidity were introduced, including a Credit Guarantee Scheme in late 2008, which made £250 billion available. This meant that if bank A lent to bank B and bank B then defaulted, the government would repay bank A. The guarantees were provided by HM Treasury for a fee

---

[3] Mohamed El-Erian, 'The Fed and the ECB: when monetary policy diverges', *The Guardian* (2 December 2015).

RECAP

1. The government or central bank can use monetary policy to restrict (or increase) the growth in aggregate demand by reducing (or increasing) money supply directly or by reducing (or increasing) the demand for money by raising (or lowering) interest rates.

2. The money supply can be reduced (increased) directly by using open-market operations. This involves the central bank selling (purchasing) more government securities and thereby reducing (increasing) banks' reserves when their customers pay for them from their bank accounts.

3. The current method of control in the UK involves the Bank of England's Monetary Policy Committee announcing the interest rate and then the Bank of England bringing this rate about by its operations in the repo market. It keeps banks short of liquidity, and then supplies them with liquidity through gilt repos at the chosen interest rate (gilt repo rate or 'Bank Rate'). This then has a knock-on effect on interest rates throughout the economy.

4. Higher interest rates, by reducing the demand for money, effectively also reduce the supply. However, with an inelastic demand for loans, interest rates may have to rise to very high levels in order to bring the required reduction in monetary growth.

5. Lower interest rates should stimulate the economy. However, if confidence by consumers and business is low, even interest rates approaching zero may be insufficient to achieve the required stimulus, as was seen in the years following the financial crisis of 2007–8.

6. Controlling aggregate demand through interest rates is made even more difficult by *fluctuations* in the demand for money. These fluctuations are made more severe by speculation against changes in interest rates, exchange rates, the rate of inflation, etc.

7. Nevertheless, controlling interest rates is a way of responding rapidly to changing forecasts, and can be an important signal to markets that inflation will be kept under control, especially when, as in the UK and the eurozone, there is a firm target for the rate of inflation.

8. Achieving inflation targets became increasingly easy in the 1990s and 2000s, but in the process inflation became increasingly less related to other key objectives, such as economic growth or unemployment.

9. Some economists advocate using a Taylor rule, which involves targeting a weighted average of inflation and economic growth.

10. The Bank of England bases its decisions on the forecast inflation rate in two years' time. It adjusts interest rates if this forecast rate of inflation diverges from 2 per cent.

payable each quarter and were designed to assist with the refinancing of maturing wholesale funding. This lending was crucial to kick-start the economy, build confidence and stimulate consumer spending. The Credit Guarantee Scheme came to an end in November 2012, suggesting that the financial system was returning to normality.

Northern Rock, Bradford and Bingley, the Royal Bank of Scotland and Lloyds Banking Group were just some of the UK financial institutions that were exposed during the financial crisis. In some cases, the government responded by making billions of pounds worth of extra capital available. The new capital was in the form of new shares owned by the government. So, essentially the government partially nationalised the financial institution in question.

Northern Rock was taken into full government ownership in February 2008. It was split into two companies and the bank, Northern Rock plc, was then sold to Virgin money for £747 million. In the case of both RBS and Lloyds Banking Group, the government (and thus the taxpayer) owns a substantial share, through the government injecting significant amounts of capital to save these failing banks.

Perhaps the most radical measure was a programme of *quantitative easing* under the Asset Purchase Facility (APF). This involved the Bank of England buying high-quality assets, mainly government bonds, from private institutions, such as pension funds, insurance companies and banks. These assets are purchased with newly created electronic money. The money, once deposited in banks, not only eases the liquidity position of banks but also becomes the basis for credit creation. The hope was that this would increase aggregate demand.

By 2013, four rounds of quantitative easing had taken place, beginning in March 2009 (£200 billion), October 2011 (£75 billion), February 2012 (£50 billion) and July 2012 (£50 billion), bringing the total to £375 billion, or 24 per cent of annual GDP.

The major problem with quantitative easing (QE), however, was that banks did not increase lending as much as had been hoped, preferring to retain a higher proportion of reserves in the Bank of England. The reason was partly a lack of willingness of banks to lend in an uncertain economic climate, and partly a lack of demand for loans from consumers and businesses, who also lacked confidence in the economy and sought to reduce their debts.

Much of the additional money from QE was used to purchase assets, rather than for consumption or investment. The result was that QE helped to push up asset prices, including house prices and share prices.

There was much speculation that soon after the Fed took the leap to raise interest rates, the Bank of England would follow suit. However, this did not happen, and following the Brexit vote on 23 June 2016, the Bank of England cut Bank Rate from 0.5 to 0.25 per cent and expanded its QE programme from £375 billion of asset purchases to £445 billion (see page 275).

3. *Why may supplying extra liquidity to banks not necessarily be successful in averting a slowdown in borrowing and spending?*

4. *Why is there a potential moral hazard in supporting failing banks? How could the terms of a bailout help to reduce this moral hazard?*

11.3 SUPPLY-SIDE POLICY

In considering economic policy up to this point we have focused our attention upon the demand side, where slow growth and unemployment are due to a lack of aggregate demand, and inflation is due to excessive aggregate demand. Many of the causes of these problems lie on the supply side, however, and as such require an alternative policy approach.

If successful, 'supply-side policies' will shift the aggregate supply curve to the right (see Figure 11.1(b) on page 261), thus increasing output for any given level of prices (or reducing the price level for any given level of output). Supply-side policies effectively increase an economy's capacity to produce; they may also raise the rate at which this potential output grows over time. These are policies, therefore, that can improve long-term economic growth.

Supply-side policies can take various forms. They can be 'market orientated' and focus on ways of 'freeing up' the market, such as encouraging private enterprise, risk taking and competition: policies that provide incentives and reward initiative, hard work and productivity. Alternatively, they can be interventionist in nature and focus on means of counteracting the deficiencies of the free market.

Either way, business leaders will be keen to have a supply-side policy that is favourable to them. This could be lower business taxes, improved education and training, a better transport and communications infrastructure or making regulation more 'light touch'. The Confederation of British Industry (and similar organisations in other countries), business pressure groups and also individual companies will seek to influence politicians in formulating supply-side policies. Frequently the argument is that 'business-friendly' policies will make the country more competitive.

Market-orientated supply-side policies

Radical market-orientated supply-side policies were first adopted in the early 1980s by the Thatcher government in the UK and the Reagan administration in the USA, but were subsequently copied by other right and centre-right governments around the world. The essence of this type of supply-side policy is to encourage and reward individual enterprise and initiative, and to reduce the role of government, to put more reliance on market forces and competition, and less on government intervention and regulation.

BOX 11.4 JAPAN'S VOLATILE PAST AND PRESENT

A sequence of downturns

1991–6

Throughout the 1980s, the Japanese economy was a picture of health, with an average growth rate of almost 4 per cent and a general government surplus. In the early 1990s, the growth rate plummeted to just 0.8 per cent in 1992 and 0.2 per cent in 1993.

Numerous stimulus packages were implemented, including tax cuts and spending increases of some 7 per cent per annum. The consequence was a general government deficit of over 5 per cent of GDP by 1996 and an increase in general government debt from 67.9 per cent of GDP in 1992 to 94.0 per cent of GDP by 1996. Yet the combined fiscal and monetary measures proved relatively ineffective, with significant growth only resuming in 1996.

> 1. *If government spending was rising and taxes were falling, why would aggregate demand not increase?*

1997–2007

When growth finally returned, external circumstances looked set to conspire against the recovering Japanese economy. Other Asian economies were performing poorly and a mood of pessimism quickly spread across the region, plunging the fragile Japanese economy back into recession. With government finances in a poor state (an average budget deficit of 5.2 per cent of GDP and general government debt of 117.2 per cent of GDP in the late 1990s), the economy moved into crisis and the government responded with another round of expansionary fiscal policy.

An initial ¥16 trillion (£80 billion) was injected into the economy in April 1998, followed by a further ¥18 trillion (£90 billion) 6 months later, which included both expenditure on public works projects and cuts in income and corporation tax.[1] Free shopping vouchers were also distributed to 35 million citizens worth ¥700 billion (£3.5 billion).

Yet the impact was rather muted. A key feature of the Japanese economy has been a high marginal propensity to save and with a pessimistic mood across the economy and uncertainty about job security, people responded to the tax cuts by simply saving more and used the vouchers to replace existing expenditure, allowing them to save the money they no longer needed.

The financial sector was in turmoil, with banks collapsing, and as Japanese businesses looked to cut costs, investment fell.

By the year 2000, the government's stimulus was beginning to have some effect, but the recovery was short-lived, as just a year later the economies of the USA and the EU were moving into recession. Demand from these economies began to fall and so did Japanese exports, returning the economy to its somewhat pessimistic state. Fiscal policy had already been used extensively to counter the two past downturns, such that the general government deficit was over 6 per cent of GDP and national debt was now over 140 per cent of GDP and both were rising. This meant that further spending rises or tax cuts were not possible.

As far as monetary policy was concerned, interest rates were practically zero and there was thus little scope for further interest rate cuts. In response to this dilemma, in 2001, in an attempt to stimulate bank lending, Japan introduced a variety of quantitative easing – the first in the world. Between 2001 and 2004, the Bank of Japan injected some ¥35 trillion (£178 billion) into banks.

From 2002 to 2007, economic growth returned, averaging 1.9 per cent per year, and the government deficit fell. Yet, despite inflation returning to positive numbers, consumer spending remained hesitant, with many people still choosing to save.

2008–12: from bad to worse

By 2008, general government debt was almost 192 per cent of GDP and as the financial crisis hit and the world economy slowed, the Japanese economy weakened once more, with its deepest recession seeing the economy shrink by 9.2 per cent between Q2 2008 and Q1 2009.

In response, Japan once more resorted to an expansionary fiscal policy. In August 2008, a ¥11.7 trillion (£56.8 billion) stimulus package was introduced, followed by a further ¥27 trillion (£170 billion) of extra government spending and tax cuts in early 2009.[2] Cash hand-outs[3] to households were made, in the hope that these would be spent, but by early 2009, GDP was rapidly falling in Japan[4] and around the world. Export-led growth had helped the economy back in the 1980s, but now export demand was low, in part due to the tough economic times in other countries, but also driven by an 11 per cent increase in the value of the yen, making its exports more expensive.

To make matters worse, a powerful earthquake centred off the eastern coast of Japan led to a devastating tsunami on 11 March 2011, causing massive loss of life and damage to the already weak economy.

---

[1] 'The economy rescue plan for Japan's economy', *BBC News* (12 November 1998).

[2] Justin McCurry, 'Japan helps small firms and families with bumper stimulus package', *The Guardian* (30 October 2008).

[3] 'Japan clears cash hand-out bill', *BBC News* (4 March 2009).

[4] Justin McCurry, 'Japanese economy shrinks at fastest rate in 35 years', *The Guardian* (16 February 2009).

Reducing government expenditure

The desire of many governments to cut government expenditure is not just to reduce the size of the public sector deficit and hence reduce the growth of money supply; it is also an essential ingredient of their supply-side strategy.

In most countries, the size of the public sector, relative to GDP, grew substantially between the 1950s and 1970s. A major aim of conservative-led governments throughout the world has been to reverse this trend. The public sector is portrayed as more bureaucratic and less efficient than the private sector. What is more, it is claimed that a growing proportion of public money has been spent on administration and other 'non-productive' activities, rather than on the direct provision of goods and services.

Before and after this event, various measures besides fiscal policy were used to combat the worsening economic situation, including intervention in the foreign exchange market, a £60 billion fund to enable Japanese firms to expand overseas and ¥15 trillion of support to the banking system, which was in much need of stability.

In August 2011, the Central Bank of Japan announced its intention to increase the size of its quantitative easing programme[5] to ¥50 trillion and this was expanded further to ¥80 trillion by September 2012.

2012 saw a return to growth, but as the year progressed and the world economic outlook deteriorated, the economic woes returned and the government was once again considering how to stimulate the economy. By this stage, general government debt was now 236.6 per cent of GDP, compared to an average figure of just 64.6 per cent of GDP in the 1980s, giving Japan the highest debt to GDP ratio in the developed world.

Abenomics: the three arrows of fiscal, monetary and supply-side policies

When Shinzo Abe came to office in December 2012, consistent growth in Japan had been virtually absent for two decades, except between 2003 and 2007, and the economy was on the verge of another downturn. Since 1992, Japan's growth had averaged only 0.8 per cent per annum. This compares with 1.3 per cent for Germany, 2.3 per cent for the UK, 2.6 per cent for the USA, 4.9 per cent for South Korea and 10.4 per cent for China over the same period.

Shinzo Abe developed a three-pronged approach to tackling low growth. These became known as the three arrows of 'Abenomics' (see the blog, 'Japan's three arrows', on the Sloman Economics News site). As far as fiscal policy is concerned, a package estimated at over $100 billion was implemented on large-scale infrastructure and investment projects. At the same time, Shinzo Abe set out a long-term plan for fiscal consolidation, once economic growth returned. In the short term, Japan was not expected to have any difficulty in financing the higher deficit, given that most of the borrowing was internal and denominated in yen.

In terms of monetary policy, the Bank of Japan undertook further quantitative easing. It also set an inflationary target of 2 per cent to try to encourage people to spend and not wait for prices to fall.

As far as supply-side measures were concerned, in addition to the new infrastructure expenditure, policies were adopted to encourage more women into work and new measures were introduced to deregulate goods, capital and labour markets.

Assessing Abenomics

Although there was success for inflation, which became positive, economic growth did not fare so well, with the economy contracting in quarters 2 and 3 of 2014. Part of the cause was a rise in sales tax in April 2014, planned by the previous government as a means of reducing the deficit and debt, which had by then reached 250 per cent of GDP. A further rise in the sales tax was due, but this was postponed to April 2017.

The economy experienced a short return to growth towards the end of 2014, but sustained economic growth once again remained elusive, with annual growth for 2014 at 0 per cent and annual growth for 2015 at just 0.4 per cent. Indeed, the economy's output in the fourth quarter of 2015 was actually 0.4 per cent lower than in the first quarter of 2008.

Since the mid-1990s, Japan has experienced six recessions and four of those have occurred since 2008. You can read about this volatility in the blog, 'Riding the Japanese rollercoaster'.

In October 2015 the Bank of Japan announced that it would accelerate the pace of quantitative easing.[6] This meant conducting open-market operations so that the monetary base would now increase annually by ¥80 trillion. It remained concerned about the pace of growth and more particularly that the downward pressure on inflation from falling commodity prices and the unwinding of the sales tax effect could result again in a 'deflationary mindset'. In January 2016, investors were surprised when the benchmark interest rate was cut below 0 per cent,[7] though some suggested it was simply evidence that the Japanese government had run out of options.

Fiscal policy has been at the heart of Japanese economic policy as it seeks the elusive target of sustained economic growth. Yet its recent past of averaging a recession every two years would suggest that sustainable growth is likely to remain elusive for some time, despite the policy of Abenomics focusing on a combination of fiscal, monetary and supply-side policies.

2. *If tax cuts are largely saved, should an expansionary fiscal policy be confined to increases in government spending?*
3. *What are Japans' three arrows and have they been successful?*

[5] Bank of Japan, 'Enhancement of monetary easing' (4 August 2011).

[6] Bank of Japan, 'Statement on monetary policy' (30 October 2015).
[7] 'Japan's economy contracts in fourth quarter', *BBC News* (15 February 2016).

Two things are needed, it is argued: (a) a more efficient use of resources within the public sector and (b) a reduction in the size of the public sector. This would allow private investment to increase with no overall rise in aggregate demand. Thus the supply-side benefits of higher investment could be achieved without the demand-side costs of higher inflation.

In practice, governments have found it very difficult to cut their expenditure relative to GDP. However, many countries were faced with trying to do this after the financial crisis and global economic slowdown of the late 2000s. Governments had to make difficult choices, particularly concerning the levels of services and the provision of infrastructure.

Tax cuts

Income tax cuts. Cutting the marginal rate of income tax was a major objective of the Thatcher and Major governments (1979–97) and the Blair government continued with this policy. By 2008, the standard and top rates were 20 per cent and 40 per cent respectively, reduced from 33 per cent and 83 per cent in 1979. By 2013, the basic rate was 20 per cent and a new top rate of income tax was in place at 45 per cent, having initially been set at 50 per cent. This top rate of income tax is for those earning in excess of £150 000, and was implemented largely as a means of plugging the deficit in public finances. You can read about the debate over the economic justification for this top rate of income tax in the blog, 'A 50p top tax rate: more or less money for the government?', on the Sloman Economics News site.

Cuts in the marginal rate of income tax are claimed to have many beneficial effects, e.g. people work longer hours; more people wish to work; people work more enthusiastically; unemployment falls; employment rises. The evidence regarding the truth of these claims, however, is less than certain.

For example, will people be prepared to work longer hours? On the one hand, each hour worked will be more valuable in terms of take-home pay, and thus people may be encouraged to work more and have less leisure time. This is a substitution effect (see page 26); people substitute work for leisure. On the other hand, a cut in income tax will make people better off, and therefore they may feel less need to do overtime than before. This is an income effect (see again page 26); they can afford to work less. The evidence on these two effects suggests that they just about cancel each other out. Anyway, for many people there is no such choice in the short run. There is no chance of doing overtime or working a shorter week. In the long run, there may be some flexibility in that people can change jobs.

Tax cuts for business and other investment incentives. A number of financial incentives can be given to encourage investment. Market-orientated policies seek to reduce the general level of taxation on profits, or to give greater tax relief to investment.

A cut in corporation tax (the tax on business profits) will increase after-tax profits. This will create more money for ploughing back into investment, and the higher after-tax return on investment will encourage more investment to take place. In 1983 the main rate of corporation tax in the UK stood at 52 per cent. A series of reductions have taken place since then, with the main rate having fallen to 20 per cent by 2015. The government hoped that such low rates would make the UK an attractive destination for business investment.

The danger of countries cutting taxes to make them more internationally competitive, however, is that it is a prisoners' dilemma game. Countries cannot all have lower taxes than each other! You may simply end up with global taxes being lower and governments receiving less tax revenue. Governments thus have to make a judgement as to whether or not cutting taxes will stimulate other countries to do the same.

However, there has been more global co-operation[4] over tax policy as countries seek to tackle large firms who have been able to avoid paying high tax bills, through both illegal means and various legal loopholes. Problems of tax evasion (illegal) and tax avoidance (legal) are not new, but we have seen some significant cases of both by some high profile firms, including Apple,[5] Starbucks,[6] Google[7] and Amazon.[8]

Reducing the power of labour

The argument here is that if labour costs to employers are reduced, their profits will probably rise. This could encourage and enable more investment and hence economic growth. If the monopoly power of labour is reduced, then cost-push inflation will also be reduced.

The Thatcher government took a number of measures to curtail the power of unions. These included the right of employees not to join unions, preventing workers taking action other than against their direct employers, and enforcing secret ballots on strike proposals. It set a lead in resisting strikes in the public sector.

As labour markets have become more flexible, with increased part-time working, zero-hour contracts and short-term contracts, and as the process of globalisation has exposed more companies to international competition, so this has further eroded the power of labour in many sectors of the economy (see section 8.4). In the aftermath of the recession of 2008–9, however, there was an increase in industrial action in many countries and this continued with the extensive government spending cuts designed to bring

---

4 Tracy McVeigh, 'Fury at corporate tax avoidance leads to call for a global response', *The Guardian*, (18 May 2013).
5 Luke Baker and Mark John, 'EU leaders look to end Apple-style tax avoidance schemes', *Reuters* (21 May 2013).
6 'Starbucks "paid just £8.6m UK tax in 14 years"', *BBC News* (16 October 2012).
7 'Google to pay UK £130m in back taxes', *The Telegraph* (22 January 2016).
8 Ian Griffiths, 'Amazon: £7bn sales; no UK corporation tax', *The Guardian* (4 April 2012).

down budget deficits (see Box 8.2 for the case of the UK) and the resulting rise in unemployment. In some countries, such as Greece and Spain, there have been major street protests and strikes.

Policies to encourage competition

If the government can encourage more competition, this should have the effect of increasing national output and reducing inflation. Four major types of policy have been pursued under this heading.

Privatisation. If privatisation simply involves the transfer of a natural monopoly to private hands (e.g. the water companies), the scope for increased competition is limited. However, where there is genuine scope for increased competition (e.g. in the supply of gas and electricity), privatisation can lead to increased efficiency, more consumer choice and lower prices.

Alternatively, privatisation can involve the introduction of private services into the public sector (e.g. private contractors providing cleaning services in hospitals, or refuse collection for local authorities). Private contractors may compete against each other for the franchise, thus driving down costs, but the quality of the service may then need monitoring.

Introducing market relationships into the public sector. This is where the government tries to get different departments or elements within a particular part of the public sector to 'trade' with each other, so as to encourage competition and efficiency. The most well-known examples are within education and health.

The process often involves 'devolved budgeting'. For example, in the UK, schools either can become 'academies' and then spend a centrally allocated grant as they choose, or, if they are still maintained by the local authority, they can also decide how to spend the budget allocated to them. The objective is to encourage them to become more efficient, cutting costs, thereby reducing the burden on either taxpayers or council-tax payers. However, one result is that schools have tended to appoint inexperienced (and hence cheaper) teachers rather than those who can bring the benefits of their years of teaching. Although this is a cost-saving approach, it could also be viewed as inefficient.

Another UK example is in the National Health Service. In 2003, the government introduced a system whereby hospitals could apply for 'foundation trust' status. If successful, they are given much greater financial autonomy in terms of purchasing, employment and investment decisions. Applications are judged by NHS Improvement, the independent health regulator, which also oversees and supports the operation of foundation trusts. By May 2016, there were 155 foundation trusts. Critics argue that funds have been diverted to foundation hospitals and away from the less well-performing hospitals where greater funding could help that performance. In the 2012 Health and Social Care Act, the government proposed that in due course all NHS hospitals become foundation trusts.

The Private Finance Initiative (PFI). This is where a private company, after a competitive tender, is contracted by a government department or local authority to finance and build a project, such as a new road or a prison. The government then pays the company to maintain and/or run it, or simply rents the assets from the company. The public sector thus becomes a purchaser of services rather than a direct provider itself.

The aim of these 'public–private partnerships' (PPPs) is to introduce competition (through the tendering process) and private-sector expertise into the provision of public services. It is hoped that the extra burden to the taxpayer of the private-sector profits will be more than offset by gains in efficiency. Critics, however, claim that PPPs have resulted in poorer quality of provision and that cost control has often been poor, resulting in a higher burden for the taxpayer in the long term. For example, in the NHS, over £2 billion per year is 'paid to private companies as part of an annual repayment fee for building and operating new hospitals as well as redeveloping old ones'.[9]

Free trade and capital movements. The opening up of international trade and investment is central to a market-orientated supply-side policy. One of the first measures of the Thatcher government (in October 1979) was to remove all controls on the purchase and sale of foreign currencies, thereby permitting the free inflow and outflow of capital, both long term and short term. Most other industrialised countries also removed or relaxed exchange controls during the 1980s and early 1990s.

The Single European Act of 1987, which came into force in 1993, was another example of international liberalisation (we examine this in section 12.4). It was designed to create a 'single market' in the EU: a market without barriers to the movement of goods, services, capital and labour. This has been largely achieved, although some restrictions on trade between members do still apply and the UK in particular has raised concerns regarding the free movement of labour. This is just one of the factors that led to the EU referendum.

Interventionist supply-side policy

As we have seen, supply-side policy is designed to increase potential output – the capacity of the economy to produce. Potential output depends on the quantity and quality (productivity) of inputs. This in turn depends to a large extent on investment – in education and training to increase labour productivity, in research and development, and in new capital.

But can investment be left to the market? Investment often involves risks. Firms may be unwilling to take those risks, since the costs of possible failure may be too high. When looked at nationally, however, the benefits of investment might well have substantially outweighed the costs, and thus

---

[9] Robert Mendick, Laura Donnelly and Ashley Kirk, 'The PFI hospitals costing NHS £2bn every year', *The Telegraph* (18 July 2015).

BOX 11.5 PRODUCTIVITY

A supply-side issue

Supply-side policies are those designed to increase the capacity of the economy. They focus on increasing either the quantity or productivity of inputs into production. In this box, we focus on productivity – of both labour and capital. The faster the growth in productivity, the faster is likely to be the country's rate of economic growth. Any government seeking to raise the long-term growth rate, therefore, must find ways of stimulating productivity growth.

On what does the growth of productivity depend? There are seven main determinants:

- Private investment in new physical capital (machinery and buildings) and in research and development (R&D).
- Public investment in education, R&D and infrastructure.
- Training and the development of labour skills.
- Innovation and the application of new technology.
- The organisation and management of inputs into production.
- The rate of entry of new firms into markets: generally such firms will have higher productivity than existing firms.
- The business environment in which firms operate. Is there competition over the quality and design of products? Is there competitive pressure to reduce costs?

 1. *Identify some policies a government could pursue to stimulate productivity growth through each of the above means.*

But what are the mechanisms whereby productivity growth feeds through into growth of the economy?

- The capacity of the economy to grow will increase as productivity improvements extend potential output.
- Productivity improvements will drive prices downwards, stimulating demand and actual growth.
- With high returns from their investment, investors might be prepared to embark upon new projects and enterprises, stimulating yet further productivity growth and higher output.

- As labour productivity rises, so wages are likely to rise. The higher wages will lead to higher consumption, and hence, via the multiplier and accelerator, to higher output and higher investment, thereby stimulating further advances in productivity.
- In the longer term, businesses experiencing higher productivity growth would expect their lower costs, and hence enhanced competitiveness, to allow them to gain greater market share. This will encourage further investment and productivity growth.

It is clear that the prosperity of a nation rests upon its ability to improve its productivity. The more successful it is in doing this, the greater will be its rate of economic growth.

Labour productivity

Chart (a) shows comparative labour productivity levels of various countries using GDP per hour worked. This measure is a better one than output per worker, which would give low figures for countries with many part-time workers and high figures for full-time workers who work very long hours but are not very efficient. GDP per hour worked is thus a good measure to gauge worker efficiency.

The chart shows that although productivity has increased in the UK, it is lower than all G7 nations, excluding Japan, and the average productivity of the eurozone.

Productivity growth has slowed in all nations since the financial crisis. The agency, the Conference Board, finds that in 2014, labour productivity growth in mature economies was 0.6 per cent, slightly down from 0.8 per cent in 2013.

Developing and emerging economies have fared better, with labour productivity growth of 3.3 per cent in 2013 and 3.4 per cent in 2014, but these growth rates are significantly lower than those experienced in the first few years from 2000. Despite these higher growth rates in labour productivity, actual productivity in emerging and developing economies remains considerably lower than that in developed economies and the average level for these countries was 19 per cent of the US level.

---

it would have been socially desirable for firms to have taken the risk. Successes would have outweighed failures.

Even when firms do wish to make such investments, they may find difficulties in raising finance. This can be a serious problem for small firms or start-up companies with no previous track record of investment.

Most developed countries have seen a decline in investment as a percentage of GDP, as Table 11.2 shows. The table also shows that the UK has had a lower level of investment relative to GDP than other industrialised countries.

Pause for thought

How can the UK's low level of investment relative to GDP be explained?

If the free market provides too little investment, there is a case for government intervention to boost investment. There are various approaches a government can take.

Funding research and development. There are potentially large externalities (benefits) from research and development (see page 205). Firms investing in developing and improving products, and especially firms engaged in more general scientific research, may produce results that provide benefits to many other firms. Thus the *social* rate of return on investment may be much higher than the private rate of return. Investment that is privately unprofitable for a firm may therefore still be economically desirable for the nation.

To increase a country's research and development, the government could fund universities or other research institutes through various grants, perhaps allocated by research

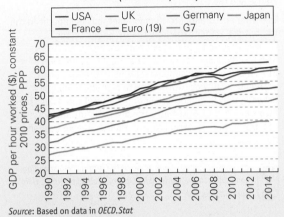

(a) Productivity in selected economies: GDP per hour worked ($ in 2010 prices)

Source: Based on data in OECD.Stat

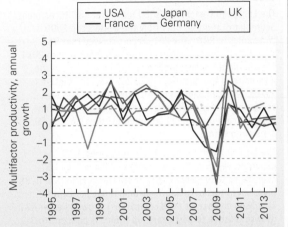

(b) Annual growth rate of multifactor productivity

Note: MFP: measured as that part of GDP growth that cannot be explained by growth in the *quantity* of labour and capital inputs.

Source: Based on data in *International Comparisons of Productivity* (National Statistics)

Capital productivity

Supply-side policies can also be used to affect capital: either to increase the quantity of a country's capital stock or to improve its quality by making each unit of capital more productive.

One way of capturing the growth in the productivity of both labour and capital together is to look at the growth in 'multifactor productivity' (MFP). This is the part of GDP growth that cannot be explained by growth in the *quantity* of labour or capital. Therefore it can be seen as a good indicator of technical progress. Chart (b) shows the annual growth in MFP for various economies.

The growth rate of multifactor productivity has been volatile, falling significantly across the world during the financial crisis and falling again as the world economy struggled to recover from 2011. According to the Conference Board, MFP has been around 0 per cent or even negative for the past few years for the world economy.[1] This compares with an average rate of over 1 per cent in the seven years leading up to the

[1] *Productivity Brief 2015*, The Conference Board (2015).

financial crisis. MFP figures show near zero or negative growth for the USA, the eurozone, Japan and also China.

These poor rates of productivity growth indicate a lack of technical progress, or at least a lack of incorporation of new techniques. This has significant implications for the ability of countries to continue to improve the living standards of their populations.

2. *Another way of measuring labour productivity is to use output per worker. Is this a better method of measuring labour productivity than GDP per hour worked? How might we explain differences in productivity between the nations shown in figure (a), especially if we use different means of measurement?*

3. *The productivity slowdown in the developed economies began before the financial crisis. What can explain this slowdown?*

Table 11.2	Gross fixed capital formation as a percentage of GDP, 1960–2017					
Year (average)	UK	Germany[a]	Japan	EU-15[b]	USA	Eurozone
1960–70	19.8	24.9	31.9	24.3	21.5	–
1971–80	22.3	22.5	32.7	24.2	22.3	–
1981–90	22.6	20.3	29.1	22.2	22.7	–
1991–2000	20.2	23.5	27.9	21.7	21.2	20.5
2001–10	17.9	19.8	22.3	21.3	21.3	22.3
2011–17	16.9	20.2	21.7	19.6	19.4	19.7

[a] West Germany prior to 1991
[b] The 15 members of the EU prior to the accession of ten new members in May 2004
Note: 2016–17 figures are forecasts

Source: Based on data in *European Economy Statistical Annex* (European Commission, 2016). Reproduced with permission

BOX 11.6 RESEARCH AND DEVELOPMENT

A target for supply-side policy

Global R&D

The European Commission's 'EU Industrial R&D Investment Scoreboard' analyses data from the world's top 2500 companies in R&D.[1] The 2015 report showed that R&D spending by these companies rose by 6.8 per cent in 2014, continuing the robust growth of R&D investment in the aftermath of the financial crisis. However, the picture is mixed, with companies in the EU responding less well compared to those in the USA. Of total R&D investment, 86.5 per cent occurred in four regions: the USA, the EU, Japan and China.

The largest share of these 2500 companies' R&D expenditure (over 38.2 per cent) in 2014 was by US companies (829 companies), where the growth rate in R&D investment was particularly strong at 8.1 per cent. EU-based companies (608 companies) showed better R&D growth relative to past years, up from 2.5 per cent to 3.3 per cent, taking a 28.1 per cent share of global R&D expenditure. China, where 301 of the 2500 companies are based, is now the third largest country by number of firms and here the growth rate of R&D investments increased by 23.6 per cent in 2014, largely driven by the IT hardware and software sector.

Japan has had a more difficult time, despite its companies being 'hardly affected by the crisis'. The earthquake and tsunami in 2011 had a significant impact, but since then, Japanese R&D investment has grown at an average rate of 2.6 per cent per annum.

R&D in the UK

Private-sector R&D is generally lower in the UK than in other major industrialised countries. This has meant that for many industries there has emerged a widening technological gap between the UK and its major competitors such as the USA and Germany. This, in turn, has led to a productivity gap between the UK and other G7 countries, with the exception of Japan. Although this gap was closing somewhat until 2008, since then it has widened (see Boxes 8.4 on page 199 and 11.5 on page 284).

R&D investment in the UK has seen growth in the pharmaceuticals and biotechnology sectors, as well as particularly strong growth in automobiles and parts, largely driven by Jaguar Land Rover. Despite growth in these areas, UK manufacturing firms as a whole have performed less well than many competitors in other countries and the UK remains a net importer of manufactured products, as it has been since 1983. These problems have led many economists to call for a much more active supply-side policy.

The government finances about one-third of UK R&D, but directs around 50 per cent of this funding to R&D in the defence, aerospace and nuclear power sectors. IT is another area that has received government support over the past 40 years, but it has been relatively small compared with Japan, France and the USA.

Tax relief and grants are common methods of support in the UK, but the amount spent by the UK public sector (universities and government and research councils) on R&D has remained fairly low, at around 0.55 per cent of GDP. This lower R&D support relative to the UK's main economic rivals has contributed to a productivity gap between the UK and other major developed countries (see Boxes 8.4 and 11.5: see also the blog, 'UK productivity: a constraint on long-term growth', on the Sloman Economics News site).

 UK-based companies are some of the largest R&D spending companies in the world. What, then, could explain the UK's poor R&D record?

The problem of comparatively low R&D expenditure has been recognised by successive UK governments, leading to various interventions, including:

- The creation of an Aerospace Technology Institute in 2013, with £2.1 billion of government R&D support over seven years.
- Tax relief for small, medium and large businesses as set out in the government's 'Corporate tax road map'[2] and £100 million in tax reliefs for creative and high-tech industries.
- A 'Patent Box' from April 2013, where a corporation tax rate of just 10 per cent applies to profits from the development and exploitation of patents. This is being phased in over a five-year period.
- R&D tax credits, whereby from April 2013, firms were able to apply for a credit of 10 per cent of their expenditure on R&D. This rate was increased in April 2015 to 11 per cent.

There have been concerns that the government, aiming to balance its budget, may swap R&D grants for loans and that this will further increase the productivity gap between the UK and other G7 nations. However, in the March 2016 Budget,[3] further measures were included to boost productivity, including a £6.7 billion package of cuts and reforms to business rates; a planned £15 million investment in the National Institute for Smart Data Innovation in Newcastle; £30 million investment for a 21st century nuclear manufacturing programme; construction of a £200 million new polar research vessel; grants of approximately £16 million both to Dyson, to support research into battery technology, and to aerospace research in the Midlands; and a £38 million grant, matched by industry, for collaborative R&D into low-emission vehicles.

[1] *The EU Industrial R&D Investment Scoreboard, 2015*, European Commission, IRI

[2] HM Treasury, *The corporate tax road map* (29 November 2010).
[3] HM Treasury, *Budget 2016: Policy Paper* (March 2016).

councils. Alternatively it could provide grants or tax relief to private firms to carry out R&D.

According to the OECD, R&D spending (both public and private) as a percentage of GDP for various countries include: Japan 3.6 per cent, Sweden 3.2 per cent, Germany 2.8 per cent; USA 2.7 per cent; France 2.3 per cent; and the UK just 1.7 per cent.[10] Box 11.6 examines research and development in various countries.

Direct provision. Improvements in infrastructure – such as a better motorway system – can be of direct benefit to industry. Alternatively, the government could provide factories or equipment to specific firms. The IMF, OECD and other international organisations have been calling for greater international expenditure on infrastructure as a way of increasing not only potential output but also aggregate demand.

Training. There are substantial external benefits from training. In other words, the benefits to the economy of trained labour extend beyond the firms undertaking the training when workers move to new jobs. The problem is that when this happens, the benefits are lost to the firm that provided the training. This, therefore, gives firms little incentive to invest heavily in training; hence the need for the government to step in.

The government may set up training schemes, or encourage educational institutions to make their courses more vocationally relevant, or introduce new vocational qualifications. Alternatively, the government could provide grants

or tax relief to firms which themselves provide training schemes. Well-targeted training can lead to substantial improvements in labour productivity. The UK invests little in training programmes compared with most of its industrial competitors.

Advice and persuasion. The government may engage in discussions with private firms in order to find ways to improve efficiency and innovation. It may bring firms together to exchange information, so as to co-ordinate their decisions and create a climate of greater certainty. It may bring firms and unions together to try to create greater industrial harmony.

Assistance to small firms. Various forms of advisory services, grants and tax concessions could be provided to stimulate investment by small companies. For example, in the UK small companies are given financial support for R&D expenditure through corporation tax relief. This means they can reduce the profits liable for tax by engaging in R&D. Support to small firms in the UK is examined in Case Study D.25 on the book's website.

Nationalisation. This is essentially the opposite of privatisation, whereby a private industry is taken into public ownership. Privatisation did become commonplace across many industrialised countries. However, with the credit crunch and the subsequent collapse of many financial institutions, some banks were taken into part or full public ownership. Therefore, nationalisation, perhaps just temporary, may be a suitable solution for rescuing vital industries suffering extreme market turbulence.

---

[10] 'GERD as a percentage of GDP', Main Science and Technology Indicators, OECD.

RECAP

1. Supply-side policies, if successful, will shift the aggregate supply curve to the right, and help to achieve faster economic growth without higher inflation.

2. Market-orientated supply-side policies aim to increase the rate of growth of aggregate supply and reduce the rate of unemployment by encouraging private enterprise and the freer play of market forces.

3. Reducing government expenditure as a proportion of GDP is a major element of such policies.

4. Tax cuts can be used to encourage more people to take up jobs, and people to work longer hours and more enthusiastically. The effects of tax cuts will depend on how people respond to incentives.

5. Various policies can be introduced to increase competition. These include privatisation, introducing market relationships into the public sector, and freer international trade and capital movements.

6. The UK has had a lower rate of investment than most other industrialised countries. This has contributed to a historically low rate of economic growth and imports of manufacture growing faster than exports. In response many argue for a more interventionist approach to supply-side policy.

7. Intervention can take the form of grants, supporting research and development, advice and persuasion, investing in training and the direct provision of infrastructure.

QUESTIONS

1. 'The existence of a budget deficit or a budget surplus tells us very little about the stance of fiscal policy.' Explain and discuss.

2. Adam Smith, the founder of modern economics, remarked in *The Wealth of Nations* (1776) concerning the balancing of budgets, 'What is prudence in the conduct of every private family can scarce be folly in that of a great kingdom.' What problems might there be if the government decided to follow a balanced budget approach to its spending?

3. Imagine you were called in by the government to advise on whether it should attempt to prevent cyclical fluctuations by the use of fiscal policy. What advice would you give and how would you justify the advice?

4. Why is it difficult to use fiscal policy to 'fine-tune' the economy?

5. When the Bank of England announces that it is putting down interest rates, how will it achieve this, given that interest rates are determined by demand and supply?

6. How does the Bank of England attempt to achieve the target rate of inflation of 2 per cent? What determines its likelihood of success in meeting the target?

7. To what extent did the Bank of England's Monetary Policy Committee and other central banks face a dilemma in 2008, when faced with rising inflation and the onset of recession?

8. What is meant by a Taylor rule? In what way is it a better rule for central banks to follow than one of adhering to a simple inflation target?

9. Under what circumstances would adherence to an inflation target lead to (a) more stable interest rates, (b) less stable interest rates, than pursuing discretionary demand management policy?

10. Define demand-side and supply-side policies. Are there any ways in which such policies are incompatible?

11. What types of tax cuts are likely to create the greatest (a) incentives, (b) disincentives to effort?

12. Imagine that you are asked to advise the government on ways of increasing investment in the economy. What advice would you give and why?

13. In what ways can interventionist industrial policy work with the market, rather than against it? What are the arguments for and against such policy?

The global trading environment

Business issues covered in this chapter

- ■ What are the benefits to countries and firms of international trade?
- ■ Which goods should a country export and which should it import?
- ■ What determines the competitiveness of a particular country and any given industry within it?
- ■ Why do countries sometimes try to restrict trade and protect their domestic industries?
- ■ What is the role of the World Trade Organization (WTO) in international trade?
- ■ What are preferential trading arrangements and what are their effects?
- ■ How has the 'single market' in the EU benefited its members?
- ■ Has the business environment in the EU become more competitive?
- ■ Why is the UK considering leaving the EU?
- ■ What benefits arise from the accession of new member states? Has the financial crisis affected the spread of these costs and benefits?

The macroeconomic environment of business extends beyond the domestic economy that we examined in the previous two chapters. Many firms are global in their reach, as we saw in Chapter 7. They are clearly affected not only by the economic situation at home, but also by the various countries in which they are based. For many, this means the global economy.

But even firms that are based solely in one country are still affected by the global macroeconomic situation. They may source some of their supplies from abroad, export some of their output or, as is the case with Tata Steel,[1] face competition from foreign firms. In other words, firms are locked into the global economy through the process of international trade.

Trading affects not only individual firms – it affects whole economies. Countries can become richer as a result of an open trading environment. Indeed, if we did not trade, items such as coffee, bananas and exotic fruits may not be available to us! We examine arguments for free trade in section 12.1.

Totally free trade, however, may bring problems to countries or to groups of people within those countries. Many people argue strongly for restrictions on trade. Textile workers see their jobs threatened by cheap imported cloth and the steel industry in developed countries is under threat from cheap Chinese exports. Car manufacturers worry about falling sales as customers switch to Japanese models or other East Asian ones. But are people justified in

---

[1] Sean Farrell, 'How the UK steel crisis unfolded' *The Guardian* (20 April 2016).

fearing international competition, or are they merely trying to protect some vested interest at the expense of everyone else? Section 12.2 examines the arguments for restricting trade.

If there are conflicting views as to whether we should have more or less trade, what has been happening on the world stage? Section 12.3 looks at the various moves towards making trade freer and at the obstacles that have been met.

A step on the road to freer trade is for countries to enter free-trade agreements with just a limited number of other countries. In section 12.4, we look at probably the world's most famous preferential trading system, the European Union and, in particular, at the development of a 'single European market'. Finally, we consider the growth of the European Union and the debate that surrounded first the referendum on the UK's continuing EU membership and then the nature and consequences of Brexit.

12.1 INTERNATIONAL TRADE

The growth of world trade

Since 1947, world trade has consistently grown faster than world GDP. This is illustrated in Figure 12.1. From 1955 to 2020 the average annual growth in world merchandise exports and GDP are expected to be around 6.1 per cent and 3.5 per cent respectively.

The chart also shows the significant negative impact of the global financial crisis at the end of the 2000s on both world output and, in particular, on the volume of exports. In 2009, worldwide merchandise exports fell by approximately 12 per cent in volume terms and their value declined by 23 per cent. This was the biggest contraction in global trade since World War II.

Since 2011, the growth of international trade has been slower, with the International Monetary Fund (IMF) forecasting an average growth rate between 2012 and 2020 of 3.3 per cent.

According to the World Trade Organization (WTO), numerous factors explain this slower growth, including political instability in the 'Arab Spring', leading to rising oil prices in 2010, followed by the earthquake in Japan and flooding in Thailand which shook global supply chains. The European debt crisis then added to uncertainty and with geo-political tensions intensifying from 2014, including the conflict between the Ukraine and Russia, world trade 'slowed to a crawl'. Forecasts of higher growth in the USA and eurozone failed to materialise and

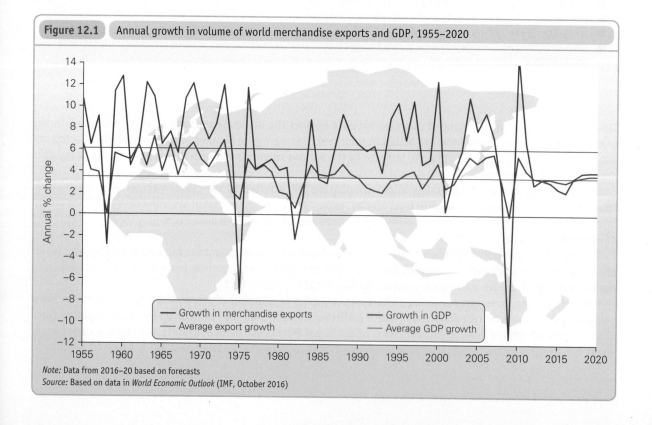

Figure 12.1 Annual growth in volume of world merchandise exports and GDP, 1955–2020

Legend:
— Growth in merchandise exports
— Average export growth
— Growth in GDP
— Average GDP growth

Note: Data from 2016–20 based on forecasts
Source: Based on data in *World Economic Outlook* (IMF, October 2016)

Figure 12.2	Share of world merchandise exports, by value (2015)

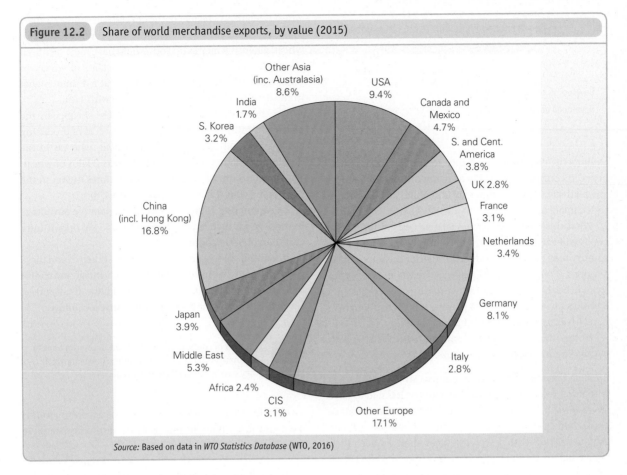

Source: Based on data in *WTO Statistics Database* (WTO, 2016)

throughout 2015 the growth rates in key emerging markets, such as China, Russia and Brazil, slowed. Finally, rising interest rates in the USA 'could have unpredictable knock-on effects in developing economies, stoking volatility in financial markets, exchange rates and investment flows'.[2]

All countries have been affected by these slower growth rates in trade and although, since the financial crisis, exports from developed nations have grown more slowly than exports from developing ones, the major industrial economies still dominate world trade (see Figure 12.2). In 2014, 56 per cent of global merchandise exports came from developed economies (down from 80 per cent in 1995 and 65 per cent in 2005).

China is the largest exporter with a 16.8 per cent share of world exports, followed by the USA with a 9.4 per cent share. The US remains the largest importer at 13.8 per cent of world imports, with China in second place at 13.4 per cent.

The top 10 nations account for a little over 50 per cent of all world trade and while the least developed nations have made progress from a 0.5 per cent share of world trade in 1995, in 2014 it still remained at only 1.1 per cent.

The advantages of trade

Specialisation as the basis for trade

Why do countries trade with each other and what do they gain from it? The reasons for international trade are really only an extension of the reasons for trade *within* a nation. Rather than people trying to be self-sufficient and doing everything for themselves, it makes sense to specialise.

Firms specialise in producing certain types of goods. This allows them to gain economies of scale and to exploit their entrepreneurial and management skills and the skills of their labour force.

Countries also specialise. They produce more than they need of certain goods (whether finished goods, raw materials or intermediate goods). What is not consumed domestically is exported. The revenues earned from the exports are used to import goods which are not produced in sufficient amounts at home. The same applies to various services, such as banking and tourism.

But which goods and services should a country specialise in? What should it export and what should it import? The answer is that it should specialise in those goods and services in which it has a *comparative advantage*.

The law of comparative advantage

Countries have different resources. They differ in population density, labour skills, climate, raw materials, capital

---

[2] World Trade Report 2015 (WTO).

Table 12.1		Production possibilities for two countries		
		Kilos of wheat		Metres of cloth
Developing country	Either	2	or	1
Developed country	Either	4	or	8

equipment, etc. Thus the ability to supply goods differs between countries, especially as many of these differences are relatively or even completely immobile, such as a country's climate or geography.

What this means is that the relative costs of producing goods will vary from country to country. For example, one country may be able to produce 1 fridge for the same cost as 6 tonnes of wheat or 3 MP4 players, whereas another country may be able to produce 1 fridge for the same cost as only 3 tonnes of wheat but 4 MP4 players. It is these differences in relative costs that form the basis of trade.

At this stage we need to distinguish between *absolute advantage* and *comparative advantage*.

Absolute advantage. When one country can produce a good with fewer resources than another country, it is said to have an *absolute advantage* in that good. If France can produce grapes with fewer resources than the UK, and the UK can produce barley with fewer resources than France, then France has an absolute advantage in grapes and the UK an absolute advantage in barley. Production and consumption of both grapes and barley will be maximised by each country specialising and then trading with the other country. Both will gain.

Comparative advantage. The above seems obvious, but trade between two countries can still be beneficial even if one country could produce all goods with fewer resources than the other, providing the relative efficiency with which goods can be produced differs between the two countries.

Take the case of a developed country that is absolutely more efficient than a developing country at producing both wheat and cloth. Assume that with a given amount of resources (labour, land and capital) the alternatives shown in Table 12.1 can be produced in each country.

Despite the developed country having an absolute advantage in both wheat and cloth, the developing country has a *comparative advantage* in wheat, and the developed country has a comparative advantage in cloth. This is because

Pause for thought

Draw up a table similar to Table 12.1, only this time assume that the figures are developing country: 6 wheat or 2 cloth; developed country: 8 wheat or 20 cloth. What are the opportunity cost ratios now? Which country should produce which good?

wheat is relatively cheaper in the developing country: only 1 metre of cloth has to be sacrificed to produce 2 kilos of wheat, whereas 8 metres of cloth would have to be sacrificed in the developed country to produce 4 kilos of wheat. In other words, the opportunity cost of wheat is 4 times higher in the developed country (8/4 compared with 1/2).

On the other hand, cloth is relatively cheaper in the developed country. Here the opportunity cost of producing 8 metres of cloth is only 4 kilos of wheat, whereas in the developing country 1 metre of cloth costs 2 kilos of wheat. Thus the opportunity cost of cloth is 4 times higher in the developing country (2/1 compared with 4/8).

To summarise, countries have a comparative advantage in those goods that can be produced at a lower opportunity cost than in other countries.

If countries are to gain from trade, they should export those goods in which they have a comparative advantage and import those goods in which they have a comparative disadvantage. Given this, we can state a *law of comparative advantage*.

 The Law of comparative advantage. Trade can benefit all countries if they specialise in the goods in which they have a comparative advantage.

But why do they gain if they specialise according to this law? And just what will that gain be? We consider these questions next.

The gains from trade based on comparative advantage

Before trade, unless markets are very imperfect, the prices of the two goods are likely to reflect their opportunity costs. For example, in Table 12.1, since the developing country can produce 2 kilos of wheat for 1 metre of cloth, the price of 2 kilos of wheat will roughly equal 1 metre of cloth.

Assume, then, that the pre-trade exchange ratios of wheat for cloth are as follows:

Developing country : 2 wheat for 1 cloth
Developed country : 1 wheat for 2 cloth (i.e. 4 for 8)

Definitions

Absolute advantage A country has an absolute advantage over another in the production of a good if it can produce it with fewer resources than the other country.

Comparative advantage A country has a comparative advantage over another in the production of a good if it can produce it at a lower opportunity cost, i.e. if it has to forgo less of other goods in order to produce it.

The law of comparative advantage Provided opportunity costs of various goods differ in two countries, both of them can gain from mutual trade if they specialise in producing (and exporting) those goods that have relatively low opportunity costs compared with the other country.

Both countries will now gain from trade, provided the exchange ratio is somewhere between 2:1 and 1:2. Assume, for the sake of argument, that it is 1:1. In other words, 1 unit of wheat trades internationally for 1 unit of cloth. How will each country gain?

The developing country gains by exporting wheat and importing cloth. At an exchange ratio of 1:1, it now only has to give up 1 kilo of wheat to obtain a metre of cloth, whereas before trade it had to give up 2 kilos of wheat.

The developed country gains by exporting cloth and importing wheat. Again at an exchange ratio of 1:1, it now only has to give up 1 metre of cloth to obtain a kilo of wheat, whereas before it had to give up 2 metres of cloth.

Pause for thought

Show how each country could gain from trade if the developing country could produce (before trade) 3 wheat for 1 cloth and the developed country could produce (before trade) 2 wheat for 5 cloth, and if the exchange ratio (with trade) was 1 wheat for 2 cloth. Would they both still gain if the exchange ratio was (a) 1 wheat for 1 cloth; (b) 1 wheat for 3 cloth?

Thus both countries have gained from trade.

The actual exchange ratios will depend on the relative prices of wheat and cloth after trade takes place. These prices will depend on total demand for and supply of the two goods. It may be that the trade exchange ratio is nearer to the pre-trade exchange ratio of one country than the other. Thus the gains to the two countries need not be equal.

Other gains from trade

Another major advantage from trade is the extra competition it brings. Competition from imports may stimulate greater efficiency at home, which could decrease a firm's costs. It could also prevent domestic monopolies/oligopolies from charging high prices. It may stimulate greater research and development and the more rapid adoption of new technology, which might enable faster growth, through the expansion of the supply side of the economy (see section 11.3). It may lead to a greater variety of products being made available to consumers. Finally, the extra price competition will help to keep inflation low.

Not all countries will have immediate comparative cost advantages. However, when they begin specialisation, possible cost savings from economies of scale may emerge. These benefits may then generate a comparative advantage. This reason for trading is particularly relevant for smaller nations, where trade can be essential to create a large enough market to support large-scale industries.

Pause for thought

If economies of scale and comparative cost advantages are not present, are there still benefits to be gained from trade?

The competitive advantage of nations

The theory of comparative advantage shows how countries can gain from trade, but why do countries have a comparative advantage in some goods rather than others?

One explanation is that it depends on the resources that countries have. If a country has plenty of land, then it makes sense to specialise in products that make use of this abundant resource. Thus Canada produces and exports wheat. If a country has a highly skilled workforce and an established research base, then it makes sense to specialise in high-tech products and export these. Thus Germany exports many highly sophisticated manufactured products. Many developing countries, by contrast, with plentiful but relatively low-skilled workers specialise in primary products or simple manufactured products that are labour-intensive.

In other words, countries should specialise in goods which make intensive use of their abundant resources. But this still does not give enough detail as to why countries specialise in the precise range of products that they do. Also, why do countries both export and import the same products? Why do many countries produce and export cars, but also import many cars too?

According to Porter,[3] there are four key determinants of why nations are highly competitive in certain products but less so in others. These are illustrated in a diagram which has become known as the 'Porter diamond' (see Figure 12.3).

Available resources. These include 'given' resources, such as raw materials, population and climate, but also specialised resources that have been developed by humans, such as the skills of the labour force, the amount and type of capital, the transport and communications infrastructure, and the science and technology base. These specialised resources vary

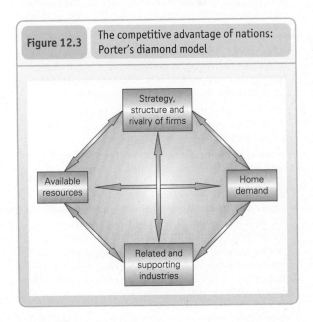

Figure 12.3 The competitive advantage of nations: Porter's diamond model

---

[3] Michael E. Porter, *The Competitive Advantage of Nations* (New York: The Free Press, 1998).

BOX 12.1 THE CHANGING FACE OF COMPARATIVE ADVANTAGE

What next for China?

Comparative advantage enables specialisation and trade and this can be one of the key factors that helps a country to grow and develop. China's emergence as an economic power is due to many things, but its ability to exploit its comparative advantage is certainly one such factor.

A country's comparative advantage often derives from its abundant resources and China used its abundance of cheap labour. With labour costs estimated to be between 60 and 90 per cent lower than in the USA, it was this that attracted many manufacturing companies to China, making a range of products using low- and moderately-skilled jobs.

According to the 2015 World Investment Report, China is now the world's largest recipient of FDI, growing 4 per cent from 2013 to stand at $129 billion. Lu Zheng, the Director of the Institute of Industrial Economics under the Chinese Academy of Social Sciences said that 'it [China's comparative advantage] will last at least two decades and play an important role in promoting China's economic growth'.

However, it is not just the quantity of labour that explained China's dominance in manufacturing. While many of its workers are low-skilled, many are educated. Furthermore, Paul Krugman notes another key factor:

> China's dominant role in the export of many labor-intensive manufactured goods surely reflects its combination of relatively abundant labor and relatively high manufacturing competence.[1]

It is unsurprising that companies would take advantage of lower costs of production and locate factories in China. But, while China has benefited from this, many developed nations have seen a decline in their manufactured exports. Countries like the UK and USA gradually adjusted and moved to exploit their comparative advantage in the services sector. They saw a comparative disadvantage emerge in manufactured items. This changing comparative advantage as a country develops is well-documented and could it be that China will soon begin to see its own comparative advantage change?

Rising labour costs. China's low labour costs are crucial, but these have been rising, as workers demand higher wages, shorter hours and more benefits. Data suggest that labour costs have been growing at some 20 per cent per year.

The first effect of this has been for some labour-intensive businesses to migrate towards inland China, where labour costs are lower.

However, in other cases the move has been more significant. With a comparative advantage in low-cost labour disappearing, some labour-intensive businesses have left China, moving to other nations which can boast cheap labour, such as Bangladesh, Cambodia, Indonesia and Vietnam. This is especially the case for companies specialising in the production of clothes and shoes.

But the story will not stop there. These industries require labour and as long as this remains the case, when a country begins to grow this will lead to higher wage demands, which in turn will raise costs. Production will shift once more.

Moving up the value chain

So, what does this mean for China? When the USA and Europe lost their comparative advantage in the production of manufactured products, they had to look elsewhere. They developed a comparative advantage in the production of products requiring highly skilled labour and increasingly specialised in the services sector. However, with rising costs in emerging economies, more manufacturing, especially of high-value products, is being returned to these developed nations.

Research from 2013 considers the iPhone and electronics manufacturing in terms of comparative advantage and the value chain. While the data on gross trade statistics confirm the decline of US competitiveness in this industry, the 'value-added trade statistics reveal the rising robustness of the United States' comparative advantage in electronics'. The suggestion is that, while China dominates in the sale of many finished exports, the simple sales data actually overstate China's productive capacity. Developed countries, such as the USA, the UK and Japan, often contribute to the value of the final products in terms of intellectual capital, design and technology.[2]

China will need to follow the pattern of the Western economies; its companies and workers will need to move up the value chain to find products that they can specialise in, which are not easily transferable to lower-wage countries.[3] This is no easy task, as moving up the value chain will involve entering into direct competition with countries that have had time to develop their comparative advantage.

> China's reliance on cheap labor has powered the country's economy to unprecedented heights. But China's manufacturing sector is running into problems these days: squeezed from one end by places with even lower labor costs, such as Laos and Vietnam, and yet struggling to move to higher ground making more advanced products because of competition from developed nations such as Germany and the United States.[4]

Despite the rising costs of production in China, it does have other factors that will ensure continued investment and production. In particular, the expansion of industrial clusters, such as Shenzhen, may help China to maintain its competitive advantage for many years.[5]

The changing nature of comparative advantage can cause problems for workers, businesses and countries, but benefits also emerge through greater competition, choice and innovation. The next few decades are likely to see some significant changes in the structure of industry in all countries.

 Why are countries likely to see their comparative advantage change as they develop?

[1] Paul Krugman, 'Increasing returns in a comparative advantage world', in Robert M. Stern, *Comparative Advantage, Growth, and the Gains from Trade and Globalization* (World Scientific 2011), Chapter 7, p. 45.

[2] Lauren Dai, 'The comparative advantage of nations: how global supply chains change our understanding of comparative advantage', *Harvard Political Review* (25 June 2013).

[3] Mohan Kompella, 'China, comparative advantage and moving up the value chain', *The Story of Business blog* (25 November 2012).

[4] Jia Lynn Yang, 'China's manufacturing sector must reinvent itself, if it's to survive', *The Washington Post* (23 November 2012).

[5] 'The Boomerang effect', *The Economist* (21 April 2012).

in detail from one country to another and give them a competitive advantage in very specific products. Once an industry has started to develop, this may attract further research and development, capital investment and training, all of which are very specific to that industry. This then further builds the country's competitive advantage in that industry. Thus, the highly developed engineering skills and equipment in Germany gives it a competitive advantage in producing well-engineered cars, as discussed in the blog, 'Made in Germany', on the Sloman Economics News site.

Demand conditions in the home market. The more discerning customers are within the country, the more this will drive the development of each firm's products and the more competitive the firm will then become in international markets. The demand for IT solutions within the USA drove the development of the software industry and gave companies such as Microsoft, Intel and Google an international advantage.

Strategy, structure and rivalry of firms. Competition between firms is not just in terms of price. Competitive rivalry extends to all aspects of business strategy, from product design, to marketing, to internal organisation, to production efficiency, to logistics, to after-sales support. The very particular competitive conditions within each industry can have a profound effect on the development of firms within that industry and determine whether or not they gain an international competitive advantage. Strategic investments and rivalry gave Japanese electronics companies an international competitive advantage.

Related and supporting industries. Firms are more likely to be successful internationally if there are well-developed supporting industries within the home economy. These may be industries providing specialist equipment or specialist consultancy, or they may simply be other parts of the main value chain, from suppliers of inputs to distributors of the firms' output. The more efficient this value chain, the greater the competitive advantage of firms within the industry.

 KEY IDEA 29

The competitive advantage of nations. The ability of countries to compete in the market for exports and with potential importers to their country. The competitiveness of any one industry depends on the availability and quality of resources, demand conditions at home in that industry, the strategies and rivalry of firms within the industry and the quality of supporting industries and infrastructure. It also depends on government policies, and there is also an element of chance.

As the arrows in Figure 12.3 show, the four determinants of competitive advantage are interlinked and influence each other. For example, the nature of related and supporting industries can influence a firm's strategic decision about whether to embark on a process of vertical integration or de-integration. Similarly, the nature of related and support-

ing industries depends on demand conditions in these industries and the availability of resources.

With each of the four determinants in Figure 12.3, competitive advantage can be stimulated by appropriate government supply-side policies, such as a supportive tax regime, investment in transport and communications infrastructure, investment in education and training, competition policy and sound macroeconomic management of the economy. Also chance often has a large part to play. For example, the pharmaceutical company that discovers a cure for AIDS or for various types of cancer will then have a significant competitive advantage.

> ## Pause for thought
>
> *Give two other examples of ways in which the determinants of competitive advantage are interlinked.*

The terms of trade

What price will our exports fetch abroad? What will we have to pay for imports? The answer to these questions is given by the *terms of trade*. The terms of trade are defined as:

$$\frac{\text{The average price of exports}}{\text{The average price of imports}}$$

expressed as an index, where prices are measured against a base year in which the terms of trade are assumed to be 100. Thus if the average price of exports relative to the average price of imports has risen by 20 per cent since the base year, the terms of trade will now be 120. If the terms of trade rise (export prices rising relative to import prices), they are said to have 'improved', since fewer exports now have to be sold to purchase any given quantity of imports. Changes in the terms of trade are caused by changes in the demand and supply of imports and exports and by changes in the exchange rate.

> ## Pause for thought
>
> *Assume that a developing country exports primary products whose demand on world markets is inelastic with respect to income. Assume also that it imports manufactured products whose demand in the country is elastic with respect to income. What is likely to happen to its terms of trade over the years as this country and other countries around the world experience economic growth?*

> ## Definition
>
> **Terms of trade** The price index of exports divided by the price index of imports and then expressed as a percentage. This means that the terms of trade will be 100 in the base year.

RECAP

1. Over many years, world trade has grown significantly faster than world GDP. However, in the recession of 2009, both output and world trade declined. Since then, world trade growth has been slower than before the financial crisis, but is still higher than world GDP growth. Developed countries export slightly more than developing countries, but the gap is closing and certain developing nations, such as China and India, have seen a rapid growth in trade.

2. Countries can gain from trade if they specialise in producing those goods in which they have a comparative advantage, i.e. those goods that can be produced at relatively lower opportunity costs.

3. If two countries trade, then, provided that the trade price ratio of exports and imports is between the pre-trade price ratios of these goods in the two countries, both countries can gain.

4. Trade can generate numerous benefits to firms and consumers, including promoting competition, cutting prices, increasing choice and acting as an engine for growth.

5. The terms of trade give the price of exports relative to the price of imports expressed as an index, where the base year is 100.

12.2 TRADE RESTRICTIONS

We have seen how trade can bring benefits to all countries. But when we look around the world, we still observe countries with barriers to trade. Their politicians know that trade involves costs as well as benefits.

In this section, we examine the arguments for restricting trade. Are people justified in fearing international competition, or are they merely trying to protect some vested interest at the expense of everyone else?

Types of restriction

If a country chooses to restrict trade, there are a number of protectionist measures open to it. Governments may:

- impose customs duties (or *tariffs*) on imports.
- restrict the amount of certain goods that can be imported ('quotas').
- subsidise domestic products to give them a price advantage over imports.
- impose administrative regulations designed to exclude imports, such as customs delays or excessive paperwork.
- favour domestic producers when purchasing equipment (e.g. defence equipment).

Governments may also favour domestic producers by subsidising their exports in a process known as *dumping*. The goods are 'dumped' at artificially low prices in the foreign market.

In looking at the costs and benefits of trade, the choice is not the stark one of whether to have free trade or no trade at all. Although countries may sometimes contemplate having completely free trade, typically they limit their trade. However, they certainly do not ban it altogether.

Arguments for restricting trade

The following are the main arguments that have been used to restrict trade.

The infant industry argument. Some industries in a country may be in their infancy but have a potential comparative advantage. This is particularly likely in developing countries. Such industries are too small yet to have gained economies of scale; their workers are inexperienced; there is a lack of back-up facilities – communications networks, specialist research and development, specialist suppliers, etc. – and they may have only limited access to finance for expansion. Without protection, these *infant industries* will not survive competition from abroad.

Pause for thought

How would you set about judging whether an industry had a genuine case for infant industry protection?

Protection from foreign competition, however, will allow them to expand and become more efficient. Once they have achieved a comparative advantage, the protection can then be removed to enable them to compete internationally. A risk here, however, is that the protectionist measure is not removed once the industry has become established and thus the incentive for efficiency may disappear.

To prevent 'dumping' and other unfair trade practices. A country may engage in dumping by subsidising its exports. The result

Definitions

Tariffs Taxes (customs duties) on imports. These could be a percentage of the value of the good (an 'ad valorem' tariff), or a fixed amount per unit (a 'specific' tariff).

Dumping Where exports are sold at prices below marginal cost – often as a result of government subsidies.

Infant industry An industry which has a potential comparative advantage, but which is, as yet, too underdeveloped to be able to realise this potential.

is that prices may no longer reflect comparative costs. Thus, the world would benefit from tariffs being imposed by importers to counteract the subsidy. An example is Chinese steel, which has been heavily subsidised and dumped on European and other markets. This has been a serious problem for European steel producers, which have found it virtually impossible to compete. A high-profile case was that of Tata Steel, which decided to pull out of the UK. The EU responded by imposing duties on various types of Chinese steel.[4]

Pause for thought

Does the consumer in the importing country gain or lose from dumping?

It can also be argued that there is a case for retaliating against countries which impose restrictions on your exports. In the short run, both countries are likely to be made worse off by a contraction in trade. But if the retaliation persuades the other country to remove its restrictions, it may have a longer-term benefit. In some cases, the mere threat of retaliation may be enough to persuade another country to remove its protection and here game theory can provide some useful insights (see section 5.4 on pages 117–22).

To prevent the establishment of a foreign-based monopoly. Competition from abroad could drive domestic producers out of business. The foreign company, now having a monopoly of the market, could charge high prices with a resulting misallocation of resources. The problem could be tackled either by restricting imports or by subsidising the domestic producer(s).

All the above arguments suggest that governments should adopt a 'strategic' approach to trade. **Strategic trade theory** argues that protecting certain industries allows a net gain in the long run from increased competition in the market (see Box 12.2).

To spread the risks of fluctuating markets. A highly specialised economy – Zambia with copper, Cuba with sugar – will be highly susceptible to world market fluctuations. Greater diversity and greater self-sufficiency, although maybe leading to less efficiency, can reduce these risks.

Definition

Strategic trade theory The theory that protecting/supporting certain industries can enable them to compete more effectively with large monopolistic rivals abroad. The effect of the protection is to increase long-run competition and may enable the protected firms to exploit a comparative advantage that they could not have done otherwise.

To reduce the influence of trade on consumer tastes. The assumption of fixed consumer tastes dictating the pattern of production through trade is false. Multinational companies through their advertising and other forms of sales promotion may influence consumer tastes. Many developing countries object to the insidious influence of Western consumerist values expounded by companies such as Coca-Cola and McDonald's.

To take account of externalities. Free trade will tend to reflect private costs. Both imports and exports, however, can involve externalities. The mining of many minerals for export may adversely affect the health of miners; the production of chemicals for export may involve pollution; the importation of juggernaut lorries may lead to structural damage to houses; shipping involves large amounts of CO_2 emissions (some 4–5 per cent of total world emissions).

The arguments considered so far are of general validity; restricting trade for such reasons could be of net benefit to the world. There are two other arguments, however, that are used by individual governments for restricting trade, where their country will gain, but at the expense of other countries, such that there will be a net loss to the world.

The first argument concerns taking advantage of market power in world trade. If a country, or a group of countries, has monopsony power in the purchase of imports (i.e. they are individually or collectively a very large economy, such as the USA or the EU), then they could gain by restricting imports so as to drive down their price. Similarly, if countries have monopoly power in the sale of some export (e.g. OPEC countries with oil), then they could gain by forcing up the price.

Pause for thought

What other reasons might cause a country (or more specifically its government) to restrict trade with another country?

The second argument concerns giving protection to declining industries. The human costs of sudden industrial closures can be very high. In such circumstances, temporary protection may be justified to allow the industry to decline more slowly, thus avoiding excessive structural unemployment. Such policies will be at the expense of the consumer, however, who will be denied access to cheaper foreign imports.

Problems with protection

Protection, by reducing the competitiveness or the number of imported goods, will tend to push up prices and restrict the choice of goods available. But apart from these direct

---

[4] Alan Tovey, 'Steel wars widen as Europe launches probe into claims China is subsidising producers', *The Telegraph* (13 May 2016).

BOX 12.2 STRATEGIC TRADE THEORY

The case of Airbus

Supporters of *strategic trade theory* hold that comparative advantage need not be the result of luck or circumstance, but may in fact be created by government. By diverting resources into selective industries, usually high tech and high skilled, a comparative advantage can be created through intervention.

An example of such intervention was the European aircraft industry, and in particular the creation of the European Airbus Consortium.

The Consortium was established in the late 1960s, its four members being Aérospatiale (France), British Aerospace (now BAE Systems) (UK), CASA (Spain) and DASA (Germany). The setting up of this consortium was seen as essential for the future of the European aircraft industry for three reasons:

■ To share high R&D costs
■ To generate economies of scale

■ To compete successfully with the market's major players in the USA – Boeing and McDonnell Douglas (which have since merged).

Airbus, although privately owned, was sponsored by government and received state aid, especially in its early years when the company failed to make a profit. Then, in 2000, the French, German and Spanish partners of the consortium merged to form the European Aeronautic Defence and Space Company (EADS), which had an 80 per cent share of Airbus (BAE Systems having the remaining 20 per cent share). Shortly afterwards, it was announced that enough orders had been secured for the planned new 550-seater A380 for production to go ahead. This new jumbo, which began its flights in April 2005, is a serious competitor to the long-established Boeing 747. In 2006, BAE Systems sold its 20 per cent stake in Airbus to EADS to

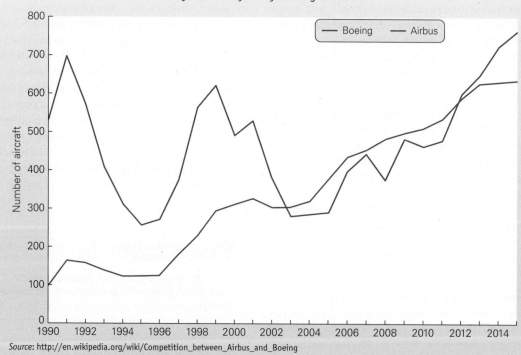

Yearly deliveries of aircraft: Boeing and Airbus

Source: http://en.wikipedia.org/wiki/Competition_between_Airbus_and_Boeing

costs to the consumer, there are several other problems. Some are a direct effect of the protection; others follow from the reactions of other nations.

Protection as 'second-best'. Many of the arguments for protection amount merely to arguments for some type of government intervention in the economy. Protection, however, may not be the best way of dealing with the problem, since protection may have undesirable side effects. There may be a more direct form of intervention that has no side effects.

In such a case, protection will be no more than a second-best solution.

For example, using tariffs to protect old, inefficient industries from foreign competition may help prevent unemployment in those parts of the economy, but the consumer will suffer from higher prices. A better solution would be to subsidise retraining and investment in those areas of the country in new efficient industries – industries with a comparative advantage. In this way, unemployment is avoided, but the consumer does not suffer.

concentrate on its core transatlantic defence and aerospace business.

Comparative performance

In 2003, Airbus, for the first time, sold more passenger aircraft than Boeing and this continued for some years.

Yet, despite Airbus's successes, by 2006 troubles were beginning to emerge. Although it continued to deliver more planes than Boeing, for the first time since 2000 it fell behind in terms of orders – 824, compared with 1044 for Boeing. Also, considerable delays (up to two years) and cost overruns were being experienced with the A380. With falling profitability and falling orders, in February 2007 Airbus announced plans to cut 10 000 jobs from its 57 000 workforce. The development of the A380 put significant financial strains on Airbus. Its launch was two and half years late and 50 per cent over budget, though it did provide competition to Boeing's 747-7 airliner.

Airbus continued to deliver more aircraft than Boeing until 2012, when Boeing once more returned to its leading position. It delivered more aircraft than Airbus in each of the years to 2015 and part of the problem for Airbus has been something of a déjà vu of the problems it faced with its A380. In 2014, Airbus launched its A350, a competitor for Boeing's 787 Dreamliner and 777 series, but once again delays led to cancelled orders and this was part of the explanation for sales lagging behind Boeing. Indeed, the gap in deliveries grew and in 2015 Boeing delivered 762 passenger aircrafts (an annual growth of 5.4 per cent), while Airbus delivered 635 passenger aircraft, representing an annual growth rate of just 0.95 per cent.

Smaller aircraft dominate the orders for both companies: in 2015, 77 per cent of orders for Airbus were for its A320 family of planes, while 65 per cent of Boeing's orders were for its single-aisle 737. Both figures have fallen over the past few years – in Boeing's case, driven by the growth in its 787 and in the case of Airbus, from the growth in its A330. As Airbus grew into a serious competitor, the Americans, and Boeing in particular, responded with accusations that Airbus is founded upon unfair trading practices and thus should not receive the level of government support that it does. (See Box 12.3, page 302, for more details.)

Airbus – support for strategic trade theory?

So does the experience of Airbus support the arguments of the strategic trade theorists? Essentially, two key benefits are claimed to flow from Airbus and its presence in the aircraft market: lower prices and economic spillovers.

■ Without Airbus the civil aircraft market would have been dominated by two American firms, Boeing and McDonnell Douglas (or possibly one, if the 1997 merger of Boeing and McDonnell Douglas had still gone ahead). Therefore the presence of Airbus would be expected to promote competition and thereby keep prices down. Studies in the 1980s and 1990s tended to support this view, suggesting that consumers have seen significant gains from lower prices. One survey estimated that without Airbus, commercial aircraft prices would have been 3.5 per cent higher than they currently are, and without both Airbus and McDonnell Douglas they would have been 15 per cent higher.

■ Economic spillovers from the Airbus Consortium, such as skills and technology developments, might be expected to benefit other industries. Findings are inconclusive on this point. It is clear, however, that although aggregate R&D in the whole aircraft industry has risen, so has the level of R&D duplication.

Although Boeing is back at the top of the market, it is clear that the growth of Airbus has been a good thing for competition, with both companies having to become more responsive to customer demand, which in turn benefits passengers. The strategic trade theory that was used to justify state aid, therefore, appears to have been largely vindicated, in creating a more competitive market.

1. In what other industries could the setting up of a consortium, backed by government aid, be justified as a means of exploiting a potential comparative advantage?
2. Is it only in industries that could be characterised as world oligopolies that strategic trade theory is relevant?

Retaliation. If the USA imposes restrictions on, say, imports from the EU, then the EU may impose restrictions on imports from the USA. Any gain to US firms competing with EU imports is offset by a loss to US exporters. What is more, US consumers suffer, since the benefits from comparative advantage have been lost.

The increased use of tariffs and other restrictions can lead to a trade war, with each country cutting back on imports from other countries. In the end, everyone loses. This is considered in the blog, 'Trade wars looming', on the Sloman Economics News site.

Protection may allow firms to remain inefficient. By removing or reducing foreign competition, firms' incentive to reduce costs may be reduced. Thus, if protection is being given to an infant industry, the government must ensure that the lack of competition does not prevent it 'growing up'. Protection should not be excessive and should be removed as soon as possible.

Bureaucracy. If a government is to avoid giving excessive protection to firms, it should examine each case carefully. This can lead to large administrative costs. It could also lead to corrupt officials accepting bribes from importers to give them favourable treatment.

RECAP

1. Reasons for restricting trade that have some validity in a world context include: the infant industry argument; the problem of dumping and other unfair trade practices; the danger of the establishment of a foreign-based monopoly; the need to spread the risks of fluctuating export prices; and the problems that free trade may adversely affect consumer tastes and may not take account of externalities.

2. Often, however, the arguments for restricting trade are in the context of one country benefiting even though other countries may lose more. Countries may intervene in trade in order to exploit their monopoly/monopsony power or to protect declining industries.

3. Even if government intervention to protect certain parts of the economy is desirable, restricting trade is unlikely to be a first-best solution to the problem, since it involves side-effect costs.

12.3 THE WORLD TRADING SYSTEM AND THE WTO

In 1947, 23 countries came together and signed the General Agreement on Tariffs and Trade (GATT). By November 2015 there were 162 members of its successor organisation, the World Trade Organization (WTO), which was formed in 1995. Between them, the members of the WTO account for 97.3 per cent of world trade. The aims of GATT, and now the WTO, are to liberalise trade.

WTO rules

The WTO requires its members to operate according to various rules. These include the following:

■ *Non-discrimination.* Under the 'most favoured nations clause', any trade concession that a country makes to one member must be granted to *all* signatories. The exception is free-trade areas and customs unions (such as the EU), where tariffs between members can be abolished, while still being maintained with the rest of the world.

■ *Reciprocity.* Any nation benefiting from a tariff reduction made by another country must reciprocate by making similar tariff reductions itself.

■ *The general prohibition of quotas.*

■ *Fair competition.* If unfair barriers are erected against a particular country, the WTO can sanction retaliatory action by that country. The country is not allowed, however, to take such action without permission.

■ *Binding tariffs.* Countries cannot raise existing tariffs without negotiating with their trading partners.

Unlike the GATT, the WTO has the power to impose sanctions on countries breaking trade agreements. If there are disputes between member nations, these will be settled by the WTO, and if an offending country continues to impose trade restrictions, permission can be granted for other countries to retaliate.

For example, in March 2002, the Bush administration imposed tariffs on steel imports into the USA in order to protect the ailing US steel industry (see Web Case D.28). The EU and other countries referred the case to the WTO, which in December 2003 ruled that they were illegal.[5] This ruling made it legitimate for the EU and other countries to impose retaliatory tariffs on US products. President Bush consequently announced that the steel tariffs would be abolished.

Pause for thought

Could US action to protect its steel industry from foreign competition be justified in terms of the interests of the USA as a whole (as opposed to the steel industry in particular)?

The greater power of the WTO has persuaded many countries to bring their disputes to it. From the time when the WTO replaced GATT in 1995 to May 2016, 507 disputes had been brought to the WTO (compared with 300 to GATT over the whole of its 48 years).

Trade rounds

Periodically, member countries have met to negotiate reductions in tariffs and other trade restrictions. There have been eight 'rounds' of such negotiations since the signing of GATT in 1947. The last major round to be completed was the Uruguay Round, which began in Uruguay in 1986, continued at meetings around the world and culminated in a deal being signed in April 1994. By that time, the average tariff on manufactured products was 4 per cent and falling. In 1947 the figure was nearly 40 per cent. The Uruguay Round agreement also involved a programme of phasing in substantial reductions in tariffs and other restrictions up to the year 2002 (see Case Study D.29 on the book's website).

Despite the reduction in tariffs, many countries have still tried to restrict trade by various other means, such as quotas

---

[5] Elizabeth Becker, 'U.S. tariffs on steel are illegal, World Trade Organization says', *New York Times* (11 November 2003).

and administrative barriers. Also, barriers have been particularly high on certain non-manufactures. Agricultural protection in particular has come in for sustained criticism by developing countries. High fixed prices and subsidies given to farmers in the EU, the USA and other developed countries mean that the industrialised world continues to export food to many developing countries which have a comparative advantage in food production! Farmers in developing countries often find it impossible to compete with subsidised food imports from the rich countries.

The most recent round of trade negotiations began in Doha, Qatar, in 2001. The negotiations have focused on both trade liberalisation and measures to encourage development of poorer countries. In particular, the Doha Development Agenda, as it is called, is concerned with measures to make trade fairer so that its benefits are spread more evenly around the world. This would involve improved access for developing countries to markets in the rich world. The Agenda is also concerned with the environmental impacts of trade and development.

The talks were originally scheduled for completion by January 2005, but this deadline has been extended numerous times, as agreements have failed to emerge.

The EU and USA blamed larger developing countries, such as Brazil and India, for being unwilling to make reductions in tariffs on manufactured and service-based imports. The developing countries, in turn, blamed the unwillingness of the developed countries, and especially the EU and the USA, to make sufficient cuts in agricultural protection. The EU blamed the USA for subsidising its farmers; the USA blamed the EU for high tariffs on imported food.

Pause for thought

How can game theory (see section 5.4) help us to understand the difficulty of getting countries to reach and then abide by trade agreements?

In Geneva 2008, the talks finally appeared to have broken down, despite the willingness of developing countries to reduce industrial tariffs and the EU and USA to cut tariffs and subsidies in agricultural sectors. The sticking point was agricultural protection for developing countries, which China and India wanted to be available as temporary measures should they be required. With the USA objecting to this, the talks collapsed, although commentators suggested that the lack of agreement was no significant loss, as complete trade liberalisation would only boost developing countries' GDP by 1 per cent. Tariffs were already at an all-time low, showing the extent of progress that had already

been made. But then with the 2008/9 recession, there were growing concerns that countries would introduce protectionist measures to support domestic industries. In the end, these concerns were unfounded.

There was a pledge at the G20 meeting in London in 2009 to complete the Doha round, followed by a report from an 'Experts Group' calling for 'one final push' to conclude the Doha Development Agenda.[6] Pascal Lamy, the Director-General in 2011, urged the WTO's members to 'think hard about the consequences of throwing away ten years of solid multilateral work'.[7]

In December 2013, agreement was reached on a range of issues at the WTO's Bali Ministerial Conference and these were adopted in November 2014 by the General Council. The agreement means a streamlining of trade to make it 'easier, faster and cheaper', with particular focus on the promotion of development, boosting the trade of the least developed countries and allowing developing countries more options for providing food security, as long as this does not distort international trade.

This was the first significant agreement of the round and goes some way to achieving around 25 per cent of the goals set for the Doha Round. Then in December 2015 at the Ministerial Conference in Nairobi, another historic agreement was made on various trade initiatives that should provide particular benefits to the WTO's poorest members. This 'Nairobi Package' contains six Ministerial Decisions on agriculture, cotton and issues related to least-developed countries, including a commitment to abolish export subsidies for farm exports. The Director-General said:

> Two years ago in Bali we did something that the WTO had never done before – we delivered major, multilaterally-negotiated outcomes . . . This week, here in Nairobi, we saw those same qualities at work. And today, once again, we delivered.[8]

These sentiments were echoed by the Chair of the Conference, Kenya's Cabinet Secretary for Foreign Affairs and International Trade, Amina Mohamed, who said that 'tough calls had to be made', but that in making them 'We have reaffirmed the central role of the WTO in international trade governance'.

While many issues remain outstanding, some progress has been made. However, many governments, including the USA, have indicated that this could well be the end of the road for the Doha Round (see the blog, 'Trade wars looming', on the Sloman Economics News site).

---

[6] *The Doha Round: setting a deadline, defining a final deal: Executive Summary*, WTO Experts Group (12 January 2011).

[7] *Documents from the negotiating chairs*, WTO (21 April 2011).

[8] 'WTO members secure "historic" Nairobi Package for Africa and the world', *WTO News Item* (19 December 2015).

BOX 12.3 | BEYOND BANANAS

EU/US trade disputes

Trade relations between the EU and USA have been strained for many years and it has been the role of the World Trade Organization, set up to manage trade and prevent disputes arising, to resolve the issues and restore order. The bad blood between the EU and USA started over bananas.

Bananas

The EU/US 'banana war',[1] which has now come to a conclusion, began in 1993 when the EU adopted a tariff and quota system that favoured banana producers in African, Caribbean and Pacific (ACP) countries, mostly ex-European colonies. Predictably, Latin American banana producers, owned by large American multinationals like Chiquita and Dole, took exception to this move. Latin American producers, with huge economies of scale, were able to produce bananas at considerably lower cost than producers in the ACP countries. But, faced with significant tariffs on entry into the EU market, their bananas became more expensive. Championed by the USA, the Latin American producers won the case at the WTO for removing the agreement.

The EU, however, failed to comply, arguing that the preferential access to EU markets for ACP producers was part of a general development strategy, known as the 'Lomé Convention', to support developing economies. Without preferential access, it was argued, ACP banana producers simply could not compete on world markets. As a European Commission document highlighted, 'The destruction of the Caribbean banana industry would provoke severe economic hardship and political instability in a region already struggling against deprivation.'[2]

As the EU refused to comply with the WTO ruling, the USA imposed $191 million worth of tariffs on EU exports in March 1999. After a series of battles over the issue at the WTO, the EU finally agreed in 2009 to reform its banana protocol and to cut tariffs on non-ACP bananas from $234 per tonne to $196 per tonne straight away and to $150 by 2016. In return, it would pay compensation to ACP nations.

Hormone-treated beef

Another equally contentious issue between the EU and USA involved a dispute over hormone-treated beef, which had been going on for a staggering 20 years.[3] In 1998, the WTO panel ruled against a ban by the EU on imports of hormone-treated beef from the USA and Canada. The ruling permitted the two countries to impose retaliatory sanctions on EU imports. After a process of arbitration, the values were set at $116.8 million for the USA and CDN$11.1 million for Canada.

Despite this, the EU continued to refuse to import any animal products, live or processed, that had received growth hormones. The ban was made on grounds of public health, and this remains the crux of the dispute.

Following an independent assessment of the risks to consumers of hormone-treated meat, which resulted in the EU banning certain hormones by its farmers, the EU argued that the sanctions should be lifted as it was no longer in breach of the WTO rules. In February 2005, a WTO panel was set up to consider the case.

In March 2008, the panel ruled the unilateral sanctions by the USA and Canada to be illegal, though it also stated that the EU hormones directive was not compatible with the WTO agreements on standards to protect the health of humans, plants and animals. Both sides appealed but the USA put in place a modified set of duties in January 2009.

However, in April 2009 the USA and EU resolved to work through the dispute: the EU would maintain its ban on hormone-treated beef, but the USA would start to remove its sanctions if the EU's duty-free import quotas of hormone-free beef increased significantly. The EU complied and in response the USA removed its import duties on all targeted European luxury foods.

Genetically modified (GM) foods

A more recent trade dispute, again in the field of public health, concerns the development of GM food.[4] GM strains of maize and soya have been available in the USA for many years, but the EU bans imports of such products, whether as seed or food. The US position is that EU consumers should be free to choose whether they have GM food or not. This, unsurprisingly, is rejected by the EU on the basis that GM

---

[1] www.wto.org/english/tratop_e/dispu_e/cases_e/ds27_e.htm
[2] 'EC fact sheet on Caribbean bananas and the WTO', EC Press Release, memo/97/28 (18 March 1997).

[3] www.wto.org/english/tratop_e/dispu_e/cases_e/ds26_e.htm
[4] www.wto.org/english/tratop_e/dispu_e/cases_e/ds291_e.htm

foods might contaminate the entire food supply once introduced. In July 2000, the EU decided to continue with its GM food ban indefinitely.

In response to a complaint to the WTO by the USA, Canada and Argentina, a panel was set up in March 2004 to consider the case. In 2006 the WTO concluded that the EU's GM ban was illegal because the risks shown by the scientific evidence did not warrant the ban. Accordingly, WTO rules should apply across EU member states. However, this did not prevent individual member states such as Austria, France, Germany, Greece, Hungary and Luxembourg banning GM maize produced by the US firm Monsanto. This led to the company mounting legal challenges in the French and German courts.

The ruling of the WTO Panel set a deadline of November 2007 for the EU to comply with its ruling, but this was extended by one year with no request for retaliation by Canada and Argentina. The USA, however, did request authorisation to retaliate, but subsequently reached an agreement with the EU to suspend the request made to the WTO.

Signs that the dispute was ending emerged in 2010, with GM crops being permitted to be grown under strict regulations throughout Europe. Barack Obama called for a free-trade agreement between the EU and USA, but despite the progress, GM crops do continue to be tightly regulated across Europe, including the requirement that products are clearly labelled.

Airbus

Another relatively recent example of an EU/US trade dispute concerns the Airbus Consortium[5] and EU industrial policy (an area which has been a bone of contention for the USA for many years). The issue concerns EU support given to the development of new aircraft, and especially the superjumbo, the A380. The Americans were unhappy with the loans and subsidies, claimed to be some $15 billion, which were provided by EU members to companies within the Airbus Consortium to develop the aircraft. (See Box 12.2 for more details on Airbus.) The American complaint was that such subsidies broke the WTO subsidy code and, as such, were unfair.

In October 2004, the USA requested the establishment of a WTO panel to consider the case. This provoked a counter-request by Airbus, claiming unfair subsidies of

[5] www.wto.org/english/tratop_e/dispu_e/cases_e/ds316_e.htm

$27.3 billion for Boeing by the US government since 1992. In July 2005, two panels were set up to deal with the two sets of allegations.

In March 2010, the WTO found Airbus guilty of using some illegal subsidies to win contracts through predatory pricing, but nevertheless dismissed most of Boeing's claims, as many of the subsidies were reimbursable at commercial rates of interest. However, some of the 'launch aid' for research and development was given at below market rates and hence did violate WTO rules. In May 2011, the WTO also ruled that some of the funding mechanisms used by Boeing were acting as illegal subsidies and must be repaid, totalling some $5.3 billion. Furthermore, an earlier ruling that European government launch aid was an 'unfair subsidy' was partly overturned.

The dispute continued with findings by the WTO reiterating the illegality of the subsidies received by Boeing, but confirming its earlier ruling in the case of Airbus regarding the loans it received. The WTO claimed that the subsidies received by Boeing cost Airbus $45 billion.

In April 2012, the USA announced its intention to implement the recommendations made by the Dispute Settlement Body, which was welcomed by the EU. However, later that year with no sign of the US implementing the recommendations, the EU requested permission from the WTO to impose countermeasures against the subsidy Boeing receives from the US government. Trade sanctions of up to $12 billion were requested by the EU, as the estimate of the cost resulting from the illegal subsidies given by the USA.

The dispute is far from over, with the EU making another complaint to the WTO regarding its earlier ruling that state subsidies for Boeing and other aerospace firms set to run until 2024 were illegal, yet they had been extended until 2040. The EU said that the extension scheme was worth $8.7 billion and represents 'the largest subsidy for the civil aerospace industry in US history'. In response, the WTO referred the complaint to a panel in April 2015. The saga continues.

 Why does the WTO appear to be so ineffective in resolving the disputes between the EU and USA?

| BOX 12.4 | PREFERENTIAL TRADING |

The development of trade blocs

The world economy has formed into a series of trade blocs, based upon regional groupings of countries. Such trade blocs are examples of *preferential trading arrangements*. These arrangements involve low or zero restrictions between the members, thus encouraging trade between them.

Trade restrictions remain, however, with the rest of the world. This causes complaints that members gain at the expense of the rest of the world. This can be a significant problem for developing nations looking to gain access to the most prosperous nations.

Types of preferential trading arrangement

There are three possible forms of such trading arrangements:

Free trade area. This is where member countries remove tariffs and quotas between themselves, but retain whatever restrictions *each member chooses* with non-member countries. Some provision will have to be made to prevent imports from outside coming into the area via the country with the lowest external tariff.

Customs union. This is like a free trade area, but in addition members must adopt *common* external tariffs and quotas with non-member countries.

Common market. This is where member countries operate as a *single* market. Like a customs union there are no tariffs and quotas between member countries and there are common external tariffs and quotas. But a full common market also includes the following features: a common system of taxation; a common system of laws and regulations governing production, employment and trade (e.g. competition law and trade union legislation); and the free movement of labour, capital and materials, and of goods and services (e.g. the freedom of workers from one member country to work in any other).

The effects of preferential trading

By joining a customs union (or free trade area), a country will find that its trade patterns change. Most of these changes are likely to be beneficial.

Definition

Preferential trading arrangements A trading arrangement whereby trade between the signatories is freer than trade with the rest of the world.

Countries will probably benefit from 'trade creation'. The removal of trade barriers allows greater specialisation according to comparative advantage. Instead of consumers having to pay high prices for domestically produced goods in which the country has a comparative disadvantage, the goods can now be obtained more cheaply from other members of the customs union. In return, the country can export to them goods in which it has a comparative advantage.

Other advantages from preferential trading include: competition from companies in other member states, which may stimulate efficiency and reduce monopoly power; economies of scale for firms which now have access to a bigger market; a more rapid spread of technology within the area; the bargaining power of the whole customs union with the rest of the world allowing member countries to gain better terms of trade; increased trade encouraging improvements in the infrastructure of the members of the union (better roads, railways, financial services, etc.).

There are some dangers, however, of customs unions. The first is that 'trade diversion' could take place. This is where countries that were previously importing from a low-cost country (which does not join the union), now buy from a higher cost country within the customs union, simply because there are no tariffs on this country's products and hence they can be purchased at a lower price, despite their higher cost of production.

Another danger is that resources may flow from the country to more efficient members of the customs union, or to the geographical centre of the union (so as to minimise transport costs). This can be a major problem for a *common market* (where there is free movement of labour and capital). The country could become a depressed 'region' of the community.

Finally, if integration creates co-operation, firms may be encouraged to collude with each other, in order to maintain high prices.

North American Free Trade Agreement (NAFTA)

Along with the EU, NAFTA is one of the two most powerful trading blocs in the world. It came into force in 1994 and consists of the USA, Canada and Mexico. These three countries have agreed to abolish tariffs between themselves in the hope that increased trade and co-operation will follow. Tariffs between the USA and Canada were phased out by 1999 and tariffs between all three countries were eliminated as of

RECAP

1. Most countries of the world are members of the WTO and in theory are in favour of moves towards freer trade.

2. The WTO can impose sanctions on countries not abiding by WTO rules.

3. There have been various 'rounds' of trade talks, originally under the auspices of GATT and more recently under the WTO. The Uruguay Round led to substantial reductions in tariffs and other trade restrictions.

4. The latest, the Doha Round, focuses on trade liberalisation and aims to spread the benefits of trade across developing countries. It has yet to be concluded, but progress has been made since 2013. There is some doubt, however, as to whether any further progress will be made and whether the round, therefore, is effectively over.

1 January 2008. Many non-tariff restrictions remain, although new ones are not permitted.

Of the three countries in NAFTA, Mexico potentially has the most to gain from the agreement. With easier access to US and Canadian markets, and the added attractiveness it now has to foreign investors, Mexico has become a thriving export economy that attracts sufficient foreign direct investment to finance its total current account deficit. However, as trade barriers have fallen, it has also faced increased competition from bigger and more efficient US and Canadian rivals.

Disputes do arise between the members. In 2009, for example, the USA reneged on a pilot scheme that would allow some Mexican trucks to travel over the US border. In response, Mexico imposed tariffs of up to 45 per cent on 90 US agricultural and industrial imports, ranging from strawberries and wine to cordless telephones.

NAFTA members hope that, with a market similar in size to the EU, they will be able to rival the EU's economic power in world trade. NAFTA is, however, at most only a free-trade area and not a common market. Unlike the EU, it does not seek to harmonise laws and regulations, except in very specific areas such as environmental management and labour standards. Member countries are permitted total legal independence, subject to the one proviso that they must treat firms of other member countries equally with their own firms – the principle of 'fair competition'. Nevertheless, NAFTA has encouraged a growth in trade between its members, most of which is trade creation rather than trade diversion.

Other countries may join in the future, so NAFTA may eventually develop into a Western Hemisphere free trade association. Leaders of 34 American countries have attempted to create a Free Trade Area of the Americas (FTAA), but little progress has been made.

Other trading agreements

APEC. Asia-Pacific Economic Co-operation (APEC) is a preferential trading area that was created in 1989 and it links 21 economies of the Pacific Rim, which together account for 57 per cent of the world's total output and 46 per cent of world trade. At the 1994 meeting of APEC leaders, it resolved to create a free-trade area across the Pacific by 2010 for the developed industrial countries and by 2020 for the rest.

This preferential trading area is by no means as advanced as NAFTA and is unlikely to move beyond a free-trade area. This is in part due to the fact that national interests differ significantly across the nations, as do the economic problems they face. Nevertheless, freer trade has brought economic benefits to the countries involved.

ASEAN. The Association of South-East Asian Nations (ASEAN) was formed in 1967 when six nations (Brunei, Indonesia, Malaysia, the Philippines, Singapore and Thailand) agreed to work towards an ASEAN Free Trade Area (AFTA). ASEAN now has 10 members (the new countries being Vietnam, Laos, Myanmar and Cambodia) with a population of 622 million people and is dedicated to increased economic co-operation within the region.

By 2010, virtually all tariffs between the six original members had been eliminated and both tariff and non-tariff barriers are falling quickly for both original and new members. The ASEAN Economic Community (AEC) was established in 2015, ahead of schedule, with the aim by 2025 to be 'highly integrated and cohesive; competitive, innovative and dynamic'.

ECOWAS. In Africa, the Economic Community of West African States (ECOWAS) has been attempting to create a common market between its 15 members. The West African franc is used in eight of the countries and another six plan to introduce a common currency, the eco. However, the launch of this has been delayed several times and it is now not expected until 2020. The ultimate goal is to combine the two currency areas and adopt a single currency for all member states.

There are also trading arrangements in Latin America and the Caribbean. Examples include the Latin American Integration Association (LAIA), the Andean Community, the Central American Integration System (SICA) and the Caribbean Community (CARICOM). In 1991, a Southern Common Market (MerCoSur) was formed, consisting of Argentina, Brazil, Paraguay and Uruguay. Venezuela joined in 2012. Most of MerCoSur's internal trade is free of tariffs and it also has a common external tariff.

1. *What factors will determine whether a country's joining a customs union will lead to trade creation or trade diversion?*
2. *Using the Internet, identify some other preferential trading arrangements around the world and their various features.*

12.4 THE EUROPEAN UNION AND THE SINGLE MARKET

In recognition of the benefits of free trade within the EU, the member countries signed the Single European Act in 1986. This sought to dismantle all barriers to internal trade within the EU by 1993, and create a genuine 'single market'. Although tariffs between member states had long been abolished, there were all sorts of non-tariff barriers, such as high taxes on wine by non-

wine-producing countries, special regulations designed to favour domestic producers, governments giving contracts to domestic producers (e.g. for defence equipment), and so on.

Most of the barriers were removed by 1993, and by the mid-1990s it was clear that the single market was bringing substantial benefits. In 2012, the European Commission published *20 Years of the European Single Market*, noting the following:

> EU27 GDP in 2008 was 2.13 per cent or €233 billion higher than it would have been if the Single Market had not been launched in 1992. In 2008 alone, this amounted to an average of €500 extra in income per person in the EU27. The gains come from the Single Market programme, liberalisation in network industries such as energy and telecommunication, and the enlargement of the EU to 27 member countries.

Although the size of the gains from the single market are difficult to quantify, the following are some of the main benefits:

Trade creation. The expansion of trade within the EU has reduced both prices and costs, as countries have been able to exploit their comparative advantage. Member countries have specialised further in those goods and services that they can produce at a relatively lower opportunity cost.

Reduction in the direct costs of barriers. This category includes administrative costs, border delays and technical regulations. Their abolition or harmonisation has led to substantial cost savings, shorter delivery times and a larger choice of suppliers.

Economies of scale. With industries based on a Europe-wide scale, many firms can now be large enough, and their plants large enough, to gain the full potential economies of scale. Yet the whole European market is large enough for there still to be adequate competition. Such gains have varied from industry to industry, depending on the minimum efficient scale of a plant or firm (see Box 4.4 on page 88). Economies of scale have also been gained from mergers and other forms of industrial restructuring.

Greater competition. Increased competition between firms has led to lower costs, lower prices and a wider range of products available to consumers. This has been particularly so in newly liberalised service sectors such as transport, financial services, telecommunications and broadcasting. In the long run, greater competition can stimulate greater innovation, the greater flow of technical information and the rationalisation of production.

Pause for thought

In what ways would competition be 'unfair' if VAT rates differed widely between member states?

The economic evidence was backed up by the perceptions of business. Firms from across the range of industries felt that the single market project had removed a series of obstacles to trade within the EU and had increased market opportunities.

Despite these gains, the single market has not received a universal welcome within the EU. Its critics argue that, in a Europe of oligopolies, unequal ownership of resources, rapidly changing technologies and industrial practices, and factor immobility, the removal of internal barriers to trade has merely exaggerated the problems of inequality and economic power. More specifically, the following criticisms are made:

Radical economic change is costly. Substantial economic change is necessary to achieve the full economies of scale and efficiency gains from a single European market. These changes necessarily involve redundancies – from bankruptcies, takeovers, rationalisation and the introduction of new technology. The severity of this 'structural' and 'technological' unemployment (see section 10.6) depends on (a) the pace of economic change and (b) the mobility of labour – both occupational and geographical. Clearly, the more integrated markets become across the EU, the lower will be the costs of future change.

Adverse regional effects. Firms are likely to locate as near as possible to the 'centre of gravity' of their markets and sources of supply. If, before barriers are removed, a firm's prime market was the UK, it might well have located in the Midlands or the North of England. If, however, with barriers now removed, its market has become Europe as a whole, it may choose to locate in the South of England or in France, Germany or the Benelux countries instead. The creation of a single European market thus tends to attract capital and jobs away from the edges of the Union and towards its geographical centre.

In an ideal market situation, areas like Cornwall, the south of Italy or Portugal and now parts of eastern Europe should attract resources from other parts of the Union. They are relatively depressed areas, thus wage rates and land prices are lower. The resulting lower industrial costs should encourage firms to move into those areas. In practice, however, as capital and labour (and especially young and skilled workers) leave the extremities of the Union, so these regions are likely to become more depressed. If, as a result, their infrastructure is neglected, they then become even less attractive to new investment.

The development of monopoly/oligopoly power. The free movement of capital can encourage the development of giant 'Euro-firms' with substantial economic power. Indeed, recent years have seen some very large European mergers. This can lead to higher, not lower prices and less choice for the consumer. It all depends on just how effective competition is, and how effective EU competition policy is in preventing monopolistic and collusive practices.

Trade diversion. It is possible that the internal market has actually diverted trade from those countries with lower costs to those with higher costs. Countries may have been importing from a low-cost country, but if this country does not join the union, then its imports may now become more expensive, because of the tariff. Trade may therefore be diverted away from this country to another country within the union, but as no tariff is imposed on these intra-union imports, they can be purchased at a lower price, despite their higher costs of production.

Perhaps the biggest objection raised against the single European market is a political one: the loss of national sovereignty. Governments find it much more difficult to intervene at a microeconomic level in their own economies and this is just one of the arguments that was leading the debate over Britain's future within Europe in the run-up to the referendum, as we discuss in Box 12.5.

Completing the internal market

Despite the reduction in barriers, the internal market is still not 'complete'. In other words, various barriers to trade between member states still remain. What is more, national governments have continued to introduce new technical standards, several of which have had the effect of erecting new barriers to trade.

In 1997, an 'Internal Market Scoreboard' was established to monitor the progress in dismantling trade barriers. This is published every six months and shows the percentage of EU single market directives still to be transposed into national law (see Case Study D.36 on the book's website). To counteract new barriers, the EU periodically issues new directives. If this process is more rapid than that of the transposition of existing directives into national law, the transposition deficit increases.

In addition to giving each country's 'transposition deficit', the Scoreboard identifies the number of infringements of the internal market that have taken place. The hope is that the 'naming and shaming' of countries will encourage them to make more rapid progress towards totally free trade within the EU.

In 1997, the average transposition deficit of member countries was 6.3 per cent. By 1999, this had fallen to 3.5 per cent and by 2015, to just 0.7 per cent, slightly higher than the record breaking 0.5 per cent in November 2014.

In February 2013, Michel Barnier, the member of the European Commission responsible for the Internal Market Scoreboard, said: 'It [the Internal Market Scoreboard] has become a transparent and objective yardstick of Member States' performance, it is an instrument of peer pressure that shows to what extent the national administrations are efficient in transposing directives and enforcing single market rules; and finally, it attracts political attention to the need to enforce these rules.'

The target for the average transposition deficit is 1 per cent, so recent scores are well within this and not far from the new target of 0.5 per cent proposed by the European Commission. If this tougher target is adopted by the European Council, it is hoped that individual countries will make even greater improvements to achieve it. As of May 2015, 23 member states had achieved the 1 per cent target

and of these, 14 had achieved 0.5 per cent, suggesting that this proposed score is realistic.

> ### Pause for thought
>
> *If there have been clear benefits from the single market programme, why do individual member governments still try to erect barriers, such as new technical standards?*

The effect of the new member states

Given the very different nature of the economies of the new entrants to the EU since 2004 and their lower levels of GDP per head, the potential for gain from membership has been substantial. The gains come through additional trade, increased competition, technological transfer and inward investment, both from other EU countries and from outside the EU.

A study in 2004[9] concluded that Poland's GDP would rise by 3.4 per cent and Hungary's by almost 7 per cent. Real wages would rise, with those of unskilled workers rising faster than those of skilled workers, in accordance with these countries' comparative advantage. There would also be benefits for the existing 15 EU countries from increased trade and investment, as well as access to cheaper inputs to production, but these would be relatively minor in comparison to the gains to the new members.

A European Commission Report produced in April 2009, five years after the enlargement,[10] found that the expansion had been a win–win situation for both old and new members. There had been significant improvements in the standard of living in new member states and they had benefited from modernisation of their economies and more stabilised institutions and laws. In addition, enterprises in old member states had enjoyed opportunities for new investment and exports, and there had been an overall increase in trade and competition between the member states.

From 2004 until the credit crunch hit the EU, there was 1.5 per cent annual growth in employment in new members and a solid 1 per cent growth in job creation in old members, silencing arguments that the enlargement would lead to unemployment in the western EU economies. Income per capita in the new members increased from 40 per cent of the old members' average in 1999 to 52 per cent in 2008 and their average growth rate rose from 3.5 per cent between 1999 and 2003 to 5.5 per cent between 2004 and 2008. While higher growth levels in new member states were expected, there were fears that this would be at the expense of the old members. However, data suggests that annual growth for the old members averaged around 2.2 per cent in both periods; so adverse affects were not seen.

---

[9] Maryla Maliszewska, *EU enlargement: benefits of the single market expansion for current and new member states*, Centrum Analiz Spoleczno-Ekonomicznych (January 2004).

[10] 'Five years of an enlarged EU – economic achievements and challenges', *European Economy 1 2009* (Commission of the European Communities).

| BOX 12.5 | THE EU REFERENDUM DEBATE AND THE AFTERMATH OF THE BREXIT VOTE |

The economic arguments and consequences

On 23 June 2016, the UK held a referendum on whether to remain a member of the EU. By a majority of 51.9 per cent to 48.1 per cent of the 72.1 per cent of the electorate who voted, Britain voted to leave the EU.

In the run-up to the vote there was heated debate on the merits and costs of membership and of leaving ('Brexit'). Although many of the arguments were concerned with sovereignty, security and other political factors, many of the arguments centred on whether there would be a net *economic* gain from either remaining or leaving.

Forecasting the economic impact of the decision, however, was difficult. First, the effects of either remaining or leaving were likely to be very different in the long run from the short run, and long-run forecasts are highly unreliable as the economy is likely to be affected by so many unpredictable events – few people, for example, predicted the financial crisis of 2007–8.

Second, the effects of leaving depend on the nature of any future trading relationships with the EU. Various possibilities were suggested, including 'the Norwegian model',[1] where Britain leaves the EU, but joins the European Economic Area, giving access to the single market, but removing regulation in some key areas, such as fisheries and home affairs. Another possibility is 'the Swiss model',[2] where the UK would negotiate trade deals on an individual basis, or 'the Turkish model',[3] where the UK forms a customs union with the EU. At the extreme, the UK could make a complete break from the EU and simply use its membership of the WTO to make trade agreements.

Views of economists

In a poll of 100 economists for the Financial Times,[4] 'almost three-quarters thought leaving the EU would damage the country's medium-term outlook, nine times more than the 8 per cent who thought the country would benefit from leaving'. Most feared damage to financial markets in the UK and to inward foreign direct investment.

Despite the barrage of pessimistic forecasts by economists about a British exit, there was a group of eight economists in favour of Brexit.[5] They claimed that leaving the EU would lead to a stronger economy, with higher GDP, a faster growth in real wages, lower unemployment and a smaller gap between imports and exports. The main argument to support the claims was that the UK would be more able to pursue trade creation freed from various EU rules and regulations.

Then, less than four weeks before the vote, a poll of economists[6] who were members of the Royal Economic Society and the Society of Business Economists came out

strongly in favour of continued membership of the EU. Of the 639 respondents, 72 per cent thought that the most likely impact of Brexit on UK real GDP would be negative over the next 10 to 20 years; and 88 per cent thought the impact on GDP would be negative in the next five years.

> Of those stating that a negative impact on GDP in the next 5 years would be most likely, a majority cited loss of access to the single market (67%) and increased uncertainty leading to reduced investment (66%).

Views of organisations

National and international organisations were generally in favour of remaining in the EU.

The Treasury found that each household would be poorer after 15 years if there were a vote to leave (see the blog, 'Brexit costs', on the Sloman Economics News site for details of the analysis). It distinguished between three new relationships with the EU. With a Norwegian-type deal, households would be £2600 worse off each year; a Swiss deal would lead to a £4300 annual loss of GDP per household and a complete exit would create a household loss per annum of £5200. It found that tax receipts would be lower and that the overall benefit to the UK of being in the EU, relative to another arrangement, would be between 3.4 per cent and 9.5 per cent of GDP, depending on the exact 'new deal'.[7]

The Bank of England warned of the dangers of Brexit.[8] The Governor, Mark Carney, argued that Brexit would be likely to result in lower growth – possibly a recession – increased unemployment, a fall in the exchange rate and higher prices. Greater economic uncertainty would damage investment.

The Treasury and Bank of England were supported in their analysis by various international organisations. The OECD suggested that Brexit would be like a tax, pushing up the costs and weakening the economy. Its analysis indicated that by 2020, GDP would be at least 3 per cent lower than it otherwise would have been, making households £2200 worse off. By 2030, these figures would be 5 per cent and £3200. It continues that:

> In the longer term, structural impacts would take hold through the channels of capital, immigration and lower technical progress. In particular, labour productivity would be held back by a drop in foreign direct investment and a smaller pool of skills. The extent of forgone GDP would increase over time . . . The effects would be even larger in a more pessimistic scenario and remain negative even in the optimistic scenario.[9]

The IMF also warned of the dangers of Brexit.[10] Its Managing Director, Christine Lagarde, indicated that a leave vote could lead to a stock market crash, falling house prices, rising

[1] Damien Gayle, 'The Norway option: what is it and what does it mean for Britain?', *The Guardian* (28 October 2015).

[2] Sabine Jenni, 'Is the Swiss model a Brexit solution?', *The UK in a changing Europe*, Kings College London (23 March 2016).

[3] 'Turkey', *Countries and Regions*, EC Trade Directorate.

[4] Chris Giles and Emily Cadman, 'Economists' forecasts: Brexit would damage growth?', *Financial Times* (3 January 2016).

[5] www.economistsforbrexit.co.uk/

[6] 'Economists' views on Brexit', Ipsos MORI polls (28 May 2016).

[7] HM Treasury, *EU Referendum: HM Treasury analysis key facts* (18 April 2016).

[8] Katie Allen, 'Brexit could lead to recession, says Bank of England', *The Guardian* (12 May 2016).

[9] OECD, *The economic consequences of Brexit: a taxing decision* (25 April 2016).

[10] Phillip Inman, 'Brexit would prompt stock market and house price crash, says IMF', *The Guardian* (13 May 2016).

inflation, unemployment and send the economy into recession, possibly even depressing long-term growth.

> Markets may anticipate such adverse economic effects. This could entail sharp drops in equity and house prices, increased borrowing costs for households and businesses, and even a sudden stop of investment inflows into key sectors such as commercial real estate and finance . . . The UK's record-high current account deficit and attendant reliance on external financing exacerbates these risks. Such market reactions could sharply contract economic activity, further depressing asset prices in a self-reinforcing cycle.

The pessimistic views about the effects of Brexit were supported by the Centre for Economic Performance, which predicted a reduction in GDP of between 6.3 per cent and 9.5 per cent, though with a potential for a loss of only 2.2 per cent of GDP.[11]

Open Europe, a think tank, provided a more nuanced assessment. In a best-case scenario, under which the UK manages to enter into favourable trade arrangements with the EU and the rest of the world, while pursuing large-scale deregulation at home, the UK could be better off by 1.6 per cent of GDP a year by 2030. The Remain campaign suggested that such trade arrangements would be unlikely, as the UK would not be allowed a 'pick and mix' approach that leads to a better deal for Britain than that for Germany or France. The same think tank however, offers another scenario, saying:

> A far more realistic range is between a 0.8 per cent permanent loss to GDP in 2030 and a 0.6 per cent permanent gain in GDP in 2030, in scenarios where Britain mixes policy approaches.[12]

Views of business leaders

A report for the CBI conducted by PricewaterhouseCoopers[13] analysed the effects of Brexit under two different trade scenarios – a free-trade agreement (FTA) negotiated with the EU and no trade agreement, where trade defaults to being conducted under WTO rules. It estimated that total UK GDP in 2020 could be between around 3 per cent and 5.5 per cent lower under the FTA and WTO scenarios respectively than if the UK remained in the EU. In the light of the report, the CBI argued that Brexit could cost the UK economy £100 billion by 2020, lead to nearly 1 million job losses and would leave the average household between £2100 and £3700 worse off. Not surprisingly, the CBI supported the UK remaining in the EU.

The CBI's stance was also supported by individual business leaders, suggesting that a downturn would result from a British exit and UK competitiveness would be hurt. Mark Dorsett, Director of Caterpillar, commented on UK membership as being 'fundamental to our business interests'

and James Quincey, President and Chief Operating Officer of Coca-Cola said 'as a business and for the Coca-Cola company and . . . many business, the principal issue will be the tremendous uncertainty that it will cause'.[14]

On the other side of the arguments, in May 2016, 300 business leaders wrote a letter in support of Brexit, outlining the adverse effect that EU membership has on British competitiveness because of rules and regulations.[15] Those 'signing up' to this letter included Peter Goldstein, a founder of Superdrug, and David Sismey, a MD of Goldman Sachs. Outside the EU, they maintained, British business would be free to grow faster, expand into new markets and create more jobs.

Clearly, Brexit will affect different industries in different ways. Much of the economic impact on them will depend on the extent to which they will still be governed by the rules of the single market and how any new trade deals will affect their export opportunities.

The impact of the Brexit vote

The short-run effects. The effects of the decision to leave the EU will take many months to become clear. In the short term, there were two major effects.

The first was a depreciation of sterling directly following the vote. The pound fell sharply as soon as the results of the referendum became clear. By the end of the day it had depreciated by 7.9 per cent against the dollar and 6.0 per cent against the euro. By early October, it had fallen by 16.0 per cent against the dollar and 14.7 per cent against the euro compared with directly before the referendum. A lower pound will make imports more expensive and hence will drive up prices and reduce the real value of sterling (see the blog, 'Sterling's slide', on the Sloman Economics News site). On the other hand, it will make exports cheaper and act as a boost to exports.

The second was the effect on confidence of both consumers and businesses. Several indicators, such as the EU's Business and Consumer Surveys, the Business Confidence Monitor of the Institute of Chartered Accountants for England and Wales (ICAEW) and the Markit/CIPS purchasing managers' index (PMI), showed a steep fall in confidence. A fall in consumer confidence discourages consumption of durables and other big-ticket items. A fall in business confidence discourages investment. However, confidence about the short-term situation quickly recovered and the UK economy performed well over 2016 as a whole.

The initial adverse effects were offset somewhat by a loosening of monetary policy. In August, the Bank of England cut Bank Rate from 0.5 per cent to 0.25 per cent and launched a further round of quantitative easing. They were also lessened by the new Conservative chancellor, Philip Hammond, deciding to postpone the previously planned reduction in public-sector borrowing.

[11] Swati Dhingra, Gianmarco Ottaviano and Thomas Sampson, 'Should we stay or should we go? The economic consequences of leaving the EU', *Centre for Economic Performance*, LSE (March 2015).

[12] Open Europe, *What if. . .? The consequences, challenges and opportunities facing Britain outside the EU* (23 March 2015).

[13] *Leaving the EU: Implications for the UK economy*, PwC for the CBI (2 March 2016).

[14] Gonzalo Viña, 'US businesses warn of Brexit's impact on UK investment', *Financial Times* (21 April 2016).

[15] Peter Dominczak, 'EU referendum: more than 300 business leaders back a Brexit', *The Telegraph* (15 May 2016).

Long-term effects. There will be long-term effects on *potential* output of any cutback in investment in the short term. Just how much potential output will be affected depends on how confidence and investment are affected over the months following the vote to leave, and how much the government invests in infrastructure.

Other long-term effects will depend on the outcome of negotiations about future relations between the UK and the EU. The greater the trade barriers between the UK and the EU, the more trade and inward investment will be discouraged.

But the more successful the UK's trade negotiations with other countries are, the less the UK's economy will suffer from Brexit.

1. *Use an aggregate demand and aggregate supply diagram to explain many economists' predictions that, with Brexit, the Bank of England would have to choose between tackling either inflation or unemployment.*
2. *How is Brexit likely to affect house prices?*
3. *Why has the Brexit vote caused the pound to fall?*

The financial crisis and aftermath caused problems for all countries in the EU, but a particular problem for some new members stemmed from previously easy access to finance. This had led to 'rapid and unchecked domestic credit growth, fuelled by foreign borrowing'.[11]

Problems of significant borrowing, however, were not limited to the new member states, with countries such as Greece, Spain and the UK suffering from severe budget deficits, as discussed in section 11.1. Indeed, the sovereign debt crisis in the EU adversely affected all member states, as did the lack of economic recovery in this region and in the global economy.

Looking at a variety of economic indicators, there are significant differences between member states, both within the EU15 (members prior to 2004) and the wider EU28. For example, data from the IMF indicate that in 2015, Ireland, the Czech Republic, Sweden and Poland grew by approximately 7.8, 4.2, 4.1 and 3.6 per cent, whereas Greece shrunk by 0.2 per cent, while Austria, Finland, France and Estonia grew by only 0.9, 0.4, 1.1 and 1.1 per cent respectively.

Meanwhile, unemployment rates range from a low of 4.3 per cent in Norway to a high of 25 and 22 per cent in Greece and Spain. The recovery of the region has been mixed, with the eurozone debt crisis continuing to create uncertainty. However, for 2016, growth in the EU is expected to be at its highest level since 2007.[12]

The future growth of the EU will depend on many factors, including the ability of governments to manage the sovereign debt crisis, whether confidence returns to the financial sector and on the effects of the UK leaving the EU (see Box 12.5).

Pause for thought

Why may the new members of the EU have the most to gain from the single market, but also the most to lose?

---

[11] Ibid.

[12] See Andrew Sentence, 'Europe is looking up – some good news to start 2016', *The Telegraph*, (1 January 2016).

RECAP

1. The Single European Act of 1986 sought to sweep away various administrative restrictions to free trade in the EU and to establish a genuine free market by 1993.

2. Benefits from completing the internal market have included trade creation, cost savings from no longer having to administer barriers, economies of scale for firms now able to operate on a Europe-wide scale, and greater competition leading to reduced costs and prices, greater flows of technical information and more innovation.

3. Critics of the single market point to the costs of radical changes in industrial structure, the attraction of capital away from the periphery of the EU to its geographical centre, possible problems of market power with the development of giant 'Euro-firms' and the political cost of lost national sovereignty.

4. New members have gained substantially from free trade within the EU. There have also been gains to existing member states.

5. Significant differences exist between members of the EU in terms of their economic performance and uncertainty remains as to how these economies will fare as the region starts to move out of recession.

QUESTIONS

1. Imagine that two countries, Richland and Poorland, can produce just two goods, computers and coal. Assume that for a given amount of land and capital, the output of these two products requires the following constant amounts of labour:

	Richland	Poorland
1 computer	2	4
100 tonnes of coal	4	5

Assume that each country has 20 million workers.

(a) If there is no trade, and in each country 12 million workers produce computers and 8 million workers produce coal, how many computers and tonnes of coal will each country produce? What will be the total production of each product?

(b) What is the opportunity cost of a computer in (i) Richland; (ii) Poorland?

(c) What is the opportunity cost of 100 tonnes of coal in (i) Richland; (ii) Poorland?

(d) Which country has a comparative advantage in which product?

(e) Assuming that price equals marginal cost, which of the following would represent possible exchange ratios?

   (i)   1 computer for 40 tonnes of coal;

   (ii)   2 computers for 140 tonnes of coal;

   (iii) 1 computer for 100 tonnes of coal;

   (iv) 1 computer for 60 tonnes of coal;

   (v)   4 computers for 360 tonnes of coal.

(f) Assume that trade now takes place and that 1 computer exchanges for 65 tonnes of coal. Both countries specialise completely in the product in which they have a comparative advantage. How much does each country produce of its respective product?

(g) The country producing computers sells 6 million domestically. How many does it export to the other country?

(h) How much coal does the other country consume?

2. Why doesn't the USA specialise as much as General Motors or Texaco? Why doesn't the UK specialise as much as Unilever? Is the answer to these questions similar to the answer to the questions, 'Why doesn't the USA specialise as much as Luxembourg?' and 'Why doesn't Unilever specialise as much as the local florist?'

3. To what extent are the arguments for countries specialising and then trading with each other the same as those for individuals specialising in doing the jobs to which they are relatively well suited?

4. The following are four items that are traded internationally: wheat, computers, textiles, insurance. In which one of the four is each of the following most likely to have a comparative advantage: India, the UK, Canada, Japan? Give reasons for your answer.

5. It is often argued that if the market fails to develop infant industries, then this is an argument for government intervention, but not necessarily in the form of restricting imports. In what *other* ways could infant industries be given government support?

6. Does the consumer in the importing country gain or lose from dumping? (Consider both the short run and the long run.)

7. What is fallacious about the following two arguments? Is there any truth in either?

(a) 'Imports should be reduced because money is going abroad which would be better spent at home.'

(b) 'We should protect our industries from being undercut by imports produced using cheap labour.'

8. Go through each of the arguments for restricting trade and provide a counter-argument for not restricting trade.

9. If countries are so keen to reduce the barriers to trade, why do many countries frequently attempt to erect barriers?

10. If rich countries stand to gain substantially from freer trade, why have they been so reluctant to reduce the levels of protection for agriculture?

11. Why is it difficult to estimate the magnitude of the benefits of completing the internal market of the EU?

12. Look through the costs and benefits that we identified from the single European market. Do the same costs and benefits arise from a substantially enlarged EU?

13. How did the financial crisis of 2008–9 and the subsequent economic downturn affect the costs and benefits of the latest EU enlargement?

The global financial environment

Business issues covered in this chapter

- What is meant by 'the balance of payments' and how do trade and financial movements affect it?
- How are exchange rates determined and what are the implications for business of changes in the exchange rate?
- How do governments and/or central banks seek to influence the exchange rate and what are the implications for other macroeconomic policies and for business?
- How do the vast flows of finance around the world affect business and the countries in which they are located?
- What are the advantages and disadvantages of the euro for members of the eurozone and for businesses inside and outside the eurozone?
- How do the major economies of the world seek to co-ordinate their policies and what difficulties arise in the process?
- What are the causes and effects on business of currency speculation?
- To what extent does the world gain or lose from the process of the globalisation of business?

When countries sell exports, there is an inflow of money into the economy. When they buy imports, there is an outflow. In this chapter we examine these international financial flows and their implications for business. With an increasingly interdependent world, these financial flows have a significant effect on economic performance.

But such flows are not just from trade. Inward investment leads to an inflow of money, as do deposits of money in this country made by people abroad. Outward investment and deposits of money abroad from people in this country result in an outflow of money.

All these inflows and outflows of money to and from a country are recorded in the 'balance of payments'. We examine this process in section 13.1.

Trade and investment are also influenced by the rates of exchange between currencies. Rates of exchange, in turn, are influenced by the demand and supply of currencies resulting from trade and investment. We will see what causes exchange rate fluctuations – a major cause of concern for many businesses – and how central banks can attempt to reduce these fluctuations. Section 13.2 looks at exchange rates.

The remaining sections look at various aspects of global finance: how global financial flows affect the world economy; whether the global financial environment can be managed; and how the EU has sought to achieve greater financial stability through the adoption of the euro by many of its members. Finally, by way of a postscript, we ask whether this whole process of economic globalisation with greater and greater economic and financial interdependence has been a 'good thing'.

13.1 THE BALANCE OF PAYMENTS

A country's balance of payments account records all the flows of money between residents of that country and the rest of the world. Receipts of money from abroad are regarded as credits and are entered in the accounts with a positive sign. Outflows of money from the country are regarded as debits and are entered with a negative sign.

The balance of payments account

There are three main parts of the balance of payments account: the current account, the capital account and the financial account. We shall look at each part in turn, and take the UK as an example. Table 13.1 gives a summary of the UK balance of payments for 2015.

The current account

The *current account* records (a) payments for exports (+) and imports (−) of goods and services, plus (b) incomes flowing into (+) and out of (−) the country (wages, profits, dividends on shares), plus (c) net transfers of money into (+) and out of (−) the country (e.g. money sent from Greece to a Greek student studying in the UK is an inflow of money and so would be a credit item on the UK balance of payments).

The *current account balance* is the overall balance of all these. A current account surplus is where credits exceed debits. A current account deficit is where debits exceed credits.

If you want to look purely at the balance of imports and exports (i.e. just item (a) above), this is given as the *balance of trade*. If exports exceed imports, there is a balance of trade surplus; if imports exceed exports, there is a balance of trade deficit.

The capital account

The *capital account* records the flows of funds, into the country (+/credits) and out of the country (−/debits), associated with the acquisition or disposal of fixed assets (e.g. land), the transfer of funds by migrants, and the payment of grants by the government for overseas projects and the receipt of EU money for capital projects (until the UK leaves the EU).

The financial account

The *financial account* of the balance of payments records cross-border changes in the holding of shares, property, bank deposits and loans, government securities, etc. In other words, unlike the current account, which is concerned with money incomes, the financial account is concerned with the flows of money for the purchase and sale of assets.

Some of these flows are for long-term investment. This can involve the acquisition of buildings and equipment (direct investment) or paper assets such as shares (portfolio investment).

Some of the flows involve the short-term deposit of money in bank accounts. Such short-term monetary flows

---

Table 13.1	UK balance of payments, 2015	
CURRENT ACCOUNT	**£m**	**% of GDP**
Balance on trade in goods and services (exports minus imports)	−36 673	−1.96
Net income flows (wages and investment income)	−34 775	−1.86
Net current transfers (government and private)	−24 779	−1.33
Balance on current account	−96 227	−5.16
CAPITAL ACCOUNT		
Net capital transfers	−1 101	−0.06
Balance on capital account	−1 101	−0.06
FINANCIAL ACCOUNT		
Direct investment	+66 092	+3.54
Portfolio investment	+269 272	+14.44
Other investment (mainly short-term flows)	−253 584	−13.60
Financial derivatives (net)	+33 078	+1.77
Reserves	−21 079	−1.13
Balance on financial account	+93 779	+5.03
Net errors and omissions	+3 549	+0.19
Total	0	0

Source: Balance of Payments: Oct to Dec and annual 2015, Office for National Statistics (March 2016)

Definitions

Current account of the balance of payments The record of a country's imports and exports of goods and services, plus incomes and transfers of money to and from abroad.

Current account balance The balance on trade in goods and services plus net incomes and current transfers, i.e. the sum of the credits on the current account minus the sum of the debits.

Balance of trade Exports of goods and services minus imports of goods and services.

Capital account of the balance of payments The record of transfers of capital to and from abroad.

Financial account of the balance of payments The record of the flows of money into and out of the country for the purpose of investment or as deposits in banks and other financial institutions.

are common between international financial centres, to take advantage of differences in countries' interest rates and changes in exchange rates. We saw the importance of this aspect of the financial account in the late 2000s, when there was massive disinvestment by non-UK residents in financial assets with UK financial institutions. Largely due to this, the UK's balance of 'other investment' deteriorated from a deficit of around £24 billion in 2006 to a deficit of some £222 billion in 2008. It then improved over the next few years, and as Table 13.1 shows, it was in significant surplus in 2015.

Anything that involves an acquisition of assets in this country by overseas residents (e.g. foreign companies investing in the UK) represents an inflow of money and is thus a credit (+) item. Any acquisition of assets abroad by UK residents (e.g. UK companies investing abroad) represents a debit (−) item.

Pause for thought

Where would interest payments on short-term foreign deposits in UK banks be entered on the balance of payments account?

Flows to and from the reserves

The UK, like all other countries, holds reserves of gold and foreign currencies. From time to time the Bank of England (acting as the government's agent) might release some of these reserves to purchase sterling on the foreign exchange market. It would do so as a means of supporting the rate of exchange (as we shall see in the next section). Drawing on reserves represents a credit item in the balance of payments account: money drawn from the reserves represents an inflow to the balance of payments (albeit an outflow from the reserves account). The reserves can thus be used to support a deficit elsewhere in the balance of payments.

Conversely, if there is a surplus elsewhere in the balance of payments, the Bank of England could use it to build up the reserves. Building up the reserves counts as a debit item in the balance of payments, since it represents an outflow from it (to the reserves).

Does the balance of payments balance?

When all the components of the balance of payments account are taken together, the balance of payments should exactly balance: credits should equal debits. As we shall see in section 13.2, if they were not equal, the rate of exchange would have to adjust until they were, or the government would have to intervene to make them equal.

When the statistics are compiled, however, a number of errors are likely to occur. As a result there will not be a balance. The main reason for the errors is that the statistics are obtained from a number of sources, and there are often delays before items are recorded and sometimes omissions too. To

'correct' for this, a *net errors and omissions* item is included in the accounts. This ensures that there will be an exact balance.

Does a deficit matter?

If the balance of payments must always balance, then in what sense does the balance of payments matter? The answer is that the individual accounts will not necessarily balance. The UK has traditionally imported more than it has exported. The resulting deficit on the current account has thus had to be financed by an equal and opposite surplus on the capital-plus-financial accounts. In other words, the UK has had to borrow from abroad or sell assets abroad to finance the excess of imports over exports. This has meant that it has had to have higher interest rates in order to attract deposits from overseas and have an increased ownership of domestic assets by residents abroad.

Higher interest rates can have a long-term dampening effect on the economy, by discouraging borrowing and investment. Inward direct investment, on the other hand, although resulting in increased overseas ownership of assets in the UK, will have the effect of stimulating output and employment.

Figure 13.1 shows the current account balances of the UK, the USA and Japan as a proportion of their GDP.

The UK in most years has had a current account deficit. This deficit, however, has fluctuated with the business cycle. In times of rapid economic growth relative to other countries, expenditure on imports rises rapidly relative to exports and the current account goes deeper into deficit. You can see this in the late 1980s and late 1990s. In times of recession, the current account improves, as it did in the early 1980s, the early 1990s and then again from 2008 to 2010, though less markedly. You can also see the effect of oil on the current account. In the late 1970s as North Sea oil was coming on stream, so the current account went into surplus. As oil exports declined in the early 2000s, so this contributed to a deepening of the deficit. In 2015, the UK's current account deficit as a percentage of GDP at current prices was the largest since records began at 5.2 per cent.

The current accounts of the USA and Japan are an approximate mirror image of each other as many of Japan's exports are imported by the USA. Much of Japan's current account surplus is then invested in the USA as direct investment, the acquisition of paper assets, such as shares (portfolio investment), or simply as deposits in US financial institutions. One reflection of this imbalance has been generally much higher interest rates in the USA than in Japan – at least until the financial crisis.

Definition

Net errors and omissions A statistical adjustment to ensure that the two sides of the balance of payments account balance. It is necessary because of errors in compiling the statistics.

| Figure 13.1 | Current account balance as % of GDP: 1970–2017 |

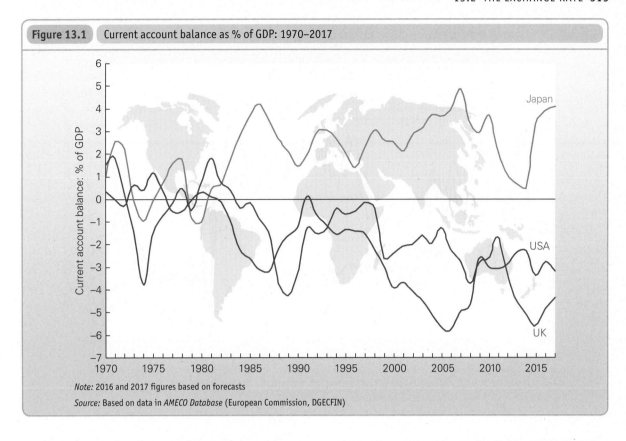

Note: 2016 and 2017 figures based on forecasts

Source: Based on data in *AMECO Database* (European Commission, DGECFIN)

Another consequence of the high US current account deficit is that most of it is paid in US dollars. This increases the supply of dollars in the world banking system, much of it on short-term deposit. These deposits can be rapidly transferred from one country to another, wherever interest rates are higher or where speculators anticipate a rise in the exchange rate (see next section). As we shall see, this movement of 'hot money' tends to lead to considerable instability in exchange rates.

RECAP

1. The balance of payments account records all payments to and receipts from other countries. The current account records payments for imports and exports, plus incomes and transfers of money to and from abroad. The capital account records all transfers of capital to and from abroad. The financial account records inflows and outflows of money for investment and as deposits in banks and other financial institutions. It also includes dealings in the country's foreign exchange reserves.

2. The whole account must balance, but surpluses or deficits can be recorded on any specific part of the account. Thus the current account could be in deficit but it would have to be matched by an equal and opposite capital plus financial account surplus.

3. The UK has traditionally had a current account deficit, but this does tend to fluctuate with the business cycle.

4. The US and Japanese current accounts are somewhat of a mirror image of each other. One result of large and persistent US deficits has been an increase in 'hot money', which has aggravated exchange rate instability.

13.2 THE EXCHANGE RATE

An exchange rate is the rate at which one currency trades for another on the foreign exchange market.

If you want to go abroad, you will need to exchange your pounds for euros, dollars, Swiss francs or whatever. To do this you might go to a bank. The bank will quote you that day's exchange rates: e.g. €1.25 to the pound, or $1.50 to the pound. It is similar for firms. If an importer wants to buy, say, some machinery from Japan, it will require yen to pay the Japanese supplier. It will thus ask the foreign exchange section of a bank to quote it a rate of exchange of the pound into yen. Similarly, if you want to buy some foreign stocks and shares, or if companies based in the UK

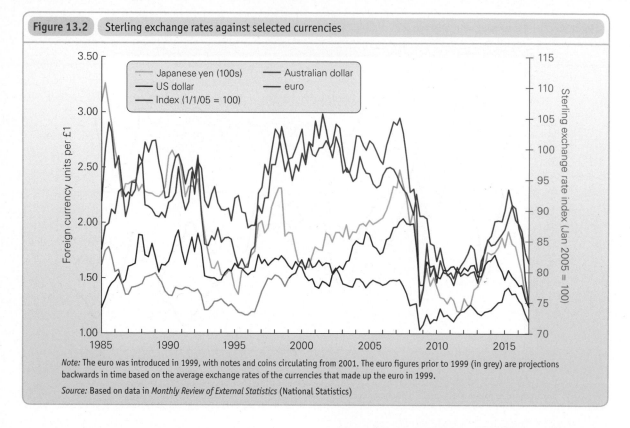

Figure 13.2 Sterling exchange rates against selected currencies

Note: The euro was introduced in 1999, with notes and coins circulating from 2001. The euro figures prior to 1999 (in grey) are projections backwards in time based on the average exchange rates of the currencies that made up the euro in 1999.

Source: Based on data in *Monthly Review of External Statistics* (National Statistics)

want to invest abroad, sterling will have to be exchanged for the appropriate foreign currency.

Likewise, if Americans want to come on holiday to the UK or to buy UK assets, or American firms want to import UK goods or to invest in the UK, they will require sterling. They will be quoted an exchange rate for the pound in the USA: say, £1 = $1.50. This means that they will have to pay $1.50 to obtain £1 worth of UK goods or assets.

Exchange rates are quoted between each of the major currencies of the world. These exchange rates are constantly changing. Minute by minute, dealers in the foreign exchange dealing rooms of the banks are adjusting the rates of exchange by buying and selling different currencies.

One of the problems, however, in assessing what is happening to a particular currency is that its rate of exchange may rise against some currencies (weak currencies) and fall against others (strong currencies). In order to gain an overall picture of its fluctuations, it is best to look at a weighted average exchange rate against all other currencies. This is known as the *exchange rate index*. The weight given to each currency in the index depends on the proportion of transactions done with that country.

Definition

Exchange rate index A weighted average exchange rate expressed as an index, where the value of the index is 100 in a given base year. The weights of the different currencies in the index add up to 1.

Pause for thought

How did the pound 'fare' compared with the dollar and the yen from 1985 to 2016? What about the euro since it began circulating? What conclusions can be drawn about the relative movements of these currencies?

Figure 13.2 shows the average quarterly exchange rates between the pound and various currencies since 1985. It also shows the average quarterly sterling exchange rate index over the same period based on January 2005 = 100.

The determination of the rate of exchange in a free market

In a free foreign exchange market, the rate of exchange is determined by demand and supply. Thus the sterling exchange rate is determined by the demand and supply of pounds. This is illustrated in Figure 13.3.

For simplicity, assume that there are just two countries, the UK and the USA. When UK importers wish to buy goods from the USA, or when UK residents wish to invest in the USA, they will supply pounds on the foreign exchange market in order to obtain dollars. In other words, they will go to banks or other foreign exchange dealers to buy dollars in exchange for pounds. The higher the exchange rate, the more dollars they will obtain for their pounds. This will effectively make American goods cheaper to buy and investment more profitable. Thus the higher the exchange rate,

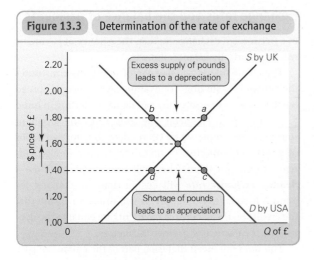

Figure 13.3 Determination of the rate of exchange

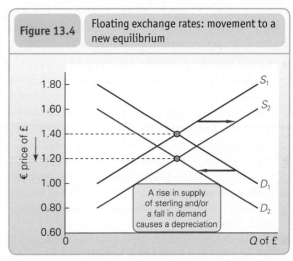

Figure 13.4 Floating exchange rates: movement to a new equilibrium

the more pounds will be supplied. The supply curve of pounds therefore typically slopes upwards.

When US residents wish to purchase UK goods or to invest in the UK, they will require pounds. They demand pounds by selling dollars on the foreign exchange market. In other words, they will go to banks or other foreign exchange dealers to buy pounds in exchange for dollars. The lower the dollar price of the pound (the exchange rate), the cheaper it will be for them to obtain UK goods and assets, and hence the more pounds they are likely to demand. The demand curve for pounds, therefore, typically slopes downwards.

The equilibrium exchange rate is where the demand for pounds equals the supply. In Figure 13.3 this is at an exchange rate of £1 = $1.60. But what is the mechanism that equates demand and supply?

If the current exchange rate were above the equilibrium, the supply of pounds being offered to the banks would exceed the demand. For example, in Figure 13.3, if the exchange rate were $1.80, there would be an excess supply of pounds of $a – b$. Banks would not have enough dollars to exchange for all these pounds. But the banks make money by exchanging currency, not by holding on to it. They would thus lower the exchange rate in order to encourage a greater demand for pounds and reduce the excessive supply. They would continue lowering the rate until demand equalled supply.

Similarly, if the rate were below the equilibrium, say at $1.40, there would be a shortage of pounds of $c – d$. The banks would find themselves with too few pounds to meet all the demand. At the same time, they would have an excess supply of dollars. The banks would thus raise the exchange rate until demand equalled supply.

In practice, the process of reaching equilibrium is extremely rapid. The foreign exchange dealers in the banks are continually adjusting the rate as new customers make new demands for currencies. What is more, the banks have to watch each other's actions closely. They are constantly in competition with each other and thus have to keep their rates in line. The dealers receive minute-by-minute updates on their computer screens of the rates being offered around the world.

Shifts in the currency demand and supply curves

Any shift in the demand or supply curves will cause the exchange rate to change. This is illustrated in Figure 13.4, which this time shows the euro/sterling exchange rate. If the demand and supply curves shift from D_1 and S_1 to D_2 and S_2 respectively, the exchange rate will fall from €1.40 to €1.20. A fall in the exchange rate is called a *depreciation*. A rise in the exchange rate is called an *appreciation*.

A depreciation will make imports more expensive as foreign currencies cost more in domestic currency terms. For example, in February 2016, research showed that the price of roses for Valentine's Day in the UK would be approximately 6 per cent more expensive compared to February 2015 because of the fall in the sterling exchange rate, which meant that flower imports were more expensive.[1] Conversely, an appreciation will make imports cheaper.

On the other hand, a depreciation will tend to make exports cheaper abroad in foreign currency terms and an appreciation will make them more expensive. Exporters thus tend to benefit from a depreciation as it makes their products more competitive abroad.

You can read about changes in sterling exchange rates before and after the Brexit vote in June 2016 in three blogs, 'Brexit fears', 'Falling sterling – bad for some; good for others' and 'Sterling's slide', on the Sloman Economics News site.

Definitions

Depreciation A fall in the free-market exchange rate of the domestic currency with foreign currencies.

Appreciation A rise in the free-market exchange rate of the domestic currency with foreign currencies.

---

[1] 'Valentine's Day roses will cost more in the UK this year . . . due to FX rates', *LeapRate* (13 February 2016).

Causes of shifts in currency demand and supply. But why should the demand and supply curves shift? The following are the major possible causes of a depreciation:

- *A fall in domestic interest rates.* UK rates would now be less competitive for savers and other depositors. More UK residents would be likely to deposit their money abroad, thus requiring foreign currency (the supply of sterling would rise), and fewer people abroad would deposit their money in the UK (the demand for sterling would fall).

- *Higher inflation in the domestic economy than abroad.* UK exports will become less competitive. The demand for sterling will fall. At the same time, imports will become relatively cheaper for UK consumers. The supply of sterling will rise.

- *A rise in domestic incomes relative to incomes abroad.* If UK incomes rise, the demand for imports, and hence the supply of sterling, will rise. If incomes in other countries fall, the demand for UK exports, and hence the demand for sterling, will fall.

- *Relative investment prospects improving abroad.* If investment prospects become brighter abroad than in the UK, perhaps because of better incentives abroad, or because of uncertainty over key things, such as the effects of Brexit or worries about an impending recession in the UK, again the demand for sterling will fall and the supply of sterling will rise.

- *Speculation that the exchange rate will fall.* If businesses involved in importing and exporting, and also banks and other foreign exchange dealers, think that the exchange rate is about to fall, they will sell pounds now before the rate does fall. The supply of sterling will thus rise. People planning to buy sterling will wait until the rate does fall. In the meantime, the demand for sterling will fall.

Pause for thought

Go through each of the listed causes for shifts in the demand for and supply of sterling and consider what would cause an appreciation of the pound.

Exchange rates and the balance of payments

In a free foreign exchange market, the balance of payments will automatically balance. But why?

The credit side of the balance of payments constitutes the demand for sterling. For example, when people abroad buy UK exports or assets they will demand sterling in order to pay for them. The debit side constitutes the supply of sterling. For example, when UK residents buy foreign goods or assets, the importers of them will require foreign currency to pay for them. They will thus supply pounds. A *floating exchange rate* will ensure that the demand for pounds is equal to the supply. It will thus also ensure that the credits on the balance of payments are equal to the debits; that the balance of payments balances.

This does not mean that each part of the balance of payments account will separately balance, but simply that any current account deficit must be matched by a capital-plus-financial account surplus and vice versa, as discussed in the blog, 'Influences on the UK current account'.

For example, suppose initially that each part of the balance of payments did separately balance. Then let us assume that interest rates rise. This will encourage larger short-term financial inflows as people abroad are attracted to deposit money in the UK; the demand for sterling would shift to the right (e.g. from D_2 to D_1 in Figure 13.4). It will also cause smaller short-term financial outflows as UK residents keep more of their money in the country; the supply of sterling shifts to the left (e.g. from S_2 to S_1 in Figure 13.4). The financial account will go into surplus. The exchange rate will appreciate.

Definitions

Floating exchange rate When the government does not intervene in the foreign exchange markets, but simply allows the exchange rate to be freely determined by demand and supply.

BOX 13.1   THE IMPORTANCE OF INTERNATIONAL FINANCIAL MOVEMENTS

How a current account deficit can coincide with an appreciating exchange rate

Since the early 1970s, most of the major economies of the world have operated with floating exchange rates. The opportunities that this gives for speculative gain have led to a huge increase in short-term international financial movements. Vast amounts of moneys transfer from country to country in search of higher interest rates or a currency that is likely to appreciate. This can have a bizarre effect on exchange rates.

If a country pursues an expansionary fiscal policy (i.e. cutting taxes and/or raising government expenditure), the current account will tend to go into deficit as extra imports are 'sucked in'. What effect will this have on exchange rates? You might think that the answer is obvious: the higher demand for imports will create an extra supply of domestic currency on the foreign exchange market and hence drive down the exchange rate.

In fact the opposite is likely. The higher interest rates resulting from the higher domestic demand can lead to a massive inflow of short-term finance. The financial account can thus move sharply into surplus. This is likely to outweigh the current account deficit and cause an appreciation of the exchange rate.

Exchange rate movements, especially in the short term, are largely brought about by changes on the financial rather than the current account.

 Why do high international financial mobility and an absence of exchange controls severely limit a country's ability to choose its interest rate?

As the exchange rate rises, this causes imports to be cheaper and exports to be more expensive. The current account will move into deficit. There is a movement up along the new demand and supply curves until a new equilibrium is reached. At this point, any financial account surplus is matched by an equal current (plus capital) account deficit.

Managing the exchange rate

The government or central bank may be unwilling to let the country's currency float freely. Frequent shifts in the demand and supply curves would cause frequent changes in the exchange rate. This, in turn, might cause uncertainty for businesses, which might curtail their trade and investment.

Assume, for example, that the Bank of England believes that an exchange rate of €1.40 to the pound is approximately the long-term equilibrium rate. Short-term leftward shifts in the demand for sterling and rightward shifts in the supply, however, are causing the exchange rate to fall below this level (see Figure 13.4). What can be done to keep the rate at €1.40?

Using reserves. The Bank of England can sell gold and foreign currencies from the reserves to buy pounds. This will shift the demand for sterling back to the right. The problem here is that countries' reserves are limited. If people are convinced that the sterling exchange rate will fall, there will be massive selling of pounds. It is unlikely that using the reserves to buy pounds will be adequate to stem the fall.

Borrowing from abroad. The government can negotiate a foreign currency loan from other countries or from an international agency such as the International Monetary Fund. The Bank of England can then use these monies to buy pounds on the foreign exchange market, thus again shifting the demand for sterling back to the right.

Raising interest rates. If the Bank of England raises interest rates, it will encourage people to deposit money in the UK and encourage UK residents to keep their money in the country. The demand for sterling will increase and the supply of sterling will decrease.

This is likely to be more effective than the other two measures, but using interest rates to control the exchange rate may conflict with using interest rates to target inflation.

Advantages of managed exchange rates
Surveys reveal that most businesspeople prefer relatively stable exchange rates, if not totally fixed then with minimum fluctuations. The following arguments are used to justify this preference.

Certainty. With stable exchange rates, international trade and investment become much less risky, since profits are not affected by violent movements in the exchange rate.

Assume a firm correctly forecasts that its product will sell in the USA for $1.50. It costs 80p to produce. If the rate of exchange is stable at £1 = $1.50, each unit will earn £1 and hence make a 20p profit. If, however, the rate of exchange

fluctuated, these profits could be wiped out. If, say, the rate appreciated to £1 = $2, and if units continued to sell for $1.50, they would now earn only 75p each, and hence make a 5p loss.

Little or no speculation. If people believe that the exchange rate will remain constant there is nothing to be gained from speculating. For example, between 1999 and 2001, when the old currencies of the eurozone countries were still used, but were totally fixed to the euro, there was no speculation that the German mark, say, would change in value against the French franc or the Dutch guilder.

With a totally free-floating exchange rate, by contrast, given that large amounts of short-term deposits are internationally 'footloose', speculation can be highly destabilising in the short run. If people think that the exchange rate will fall, then they will sell the currency, and this will cause the exchange rate to fall even further.

There is a problem with managed exchange rates, however, if speculators believe that the managed rate is not an equilibrium rate. If, for example, they believe that there will have to be a devaluation, speculation may become unstoppable and force the government to devalue. If the government delays doing so, it could cost the central bank a huge amount in attempting to support the currency.

Disadvantages of managed exchange rates
Exchange rate policy may conflict with the interests of domestic business and the economy as a whole. Managing the exchange rate will almost inevitably involve using interest rates for that purpose. But this may conflict with other macroeconomic objectives. For example, a depreciating exchange rate may force the central bank to raise interest rates to arrest the fall. But this may discourage business investment. This in turn will lower firms' profits in the long term and reduce the country's long-term rate of economic growth, potentially causing an increase in unemployment.

Also, if the economy is already in a recession, the higher interest rates could deepen the recession by making borrowing more expensive and thus reducing aggregate demand. In other words, the rate of interest that is suitable for the exchange rate may be unsuitable for the rest of the economy. You cannot use one instrument (the rate of interest) to control multiple targets (the exchange rate, growth, the rate of inflation etc.) if these objectives require a different rate of interest.

Under a free-floating rate, by contrast, the central bank can choose whatever rate of interest is necessary to meet domestic objectives, such as achieving a target rate of inflation. The exchange rate will simply adjust to the new rate of interest – a rise in interest rates causing an appreciation, a fall causing a depreciation. We saw this in the UK economy, where it was necessary to cut interest rates to 0.5 per cent in a bid to stimulate aggregate demand and tackle the recession, and this caused the value of sterling to fall.

Inability to adjust to shocks. Sometimes, it will prove impossible to maintain the exchange rate at the desired level.

BOX 13.2   EXCHANGE RATE FLUCTUATIONS AND THE PLIGHT OF SMEs

Small businesses and the perils of international trade

As if trading internationally wasn't hard enough for small businesses! It's bad enough trying to compete with large multinational corporations with all their international connections, trying to find a niche market or to offer some specialist service, perhaps, indeed, to multinationals themselves. What makes things doubly difficult for small business are the fluctuations in exchange rates.

In 2002, when asked to identify the main financial factor causing problems for SMEs, easily topping the list was the high exchange rate of sterling against the euro. Nearly half of the firms in the sample, 47 per cent, said this was very problematic for their business. In addition, more than a quarter responded to the survey by saying it was quite problematic.

The survey figure indicated that when sterling is strong against Europe's single currency, it is a problem for more than seven in ten SMEs. For those who sometimes argue that the SME community is less concerned about sterling's strength than its bigger brothers, this survey shows that is far

from being the case. SMEs suffer from a strong pound, but as we shall see, a weak pound can also be problematic.

'It is certainly the case that this is a problem for us, not just sterling against the euro but also against the dollar', said Bruno Kilshaw, managing director of London-based Sortex, which manufactures colour-sorting equipment for the agriculture and food-processing industries.

> We export 95 per cent of our production and would like to operate on the basis of euro and dollar price lists but often that is impossible because it would squeeze our margins too much.

> We would love to quote in customers' own currency but often we have to quote in sterling and convert at the time of the contract. It is both the high level of sterling and the instability that give us problems. If there was at least stability, we would be happier.[1]

---

[1] www.themanufacturer.com/content_detail.html?contents_id=2653&t=manufacturer&header=reports

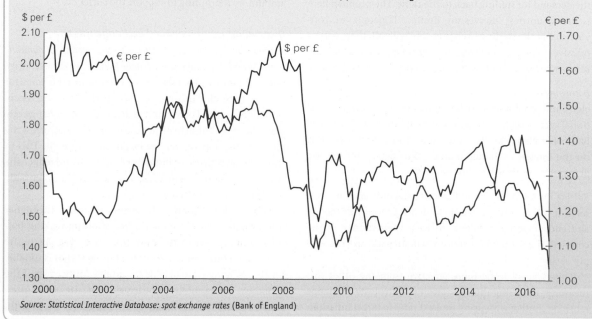

Fluctuations in the euro/pound and dollar/pound exchange rates

Source: Statistical Interactive Database: spot exchange rates (Bank of England)

For example, a sudden increase in oil prices can have a large effect on the balance of payments. Oil-importing countries may find that the downward pressure on their exchange rate is too strong to contain.

Pause for thought

If speculators on average gain from their speculation, who loses?

Speculation. If speculators believe that the central bank cannot prevent the exchange rate falling (or rising), speculation is likely to be massive. The speculation will bring about the very fall (or rise) in the exchange rate that the speculators anticipated and may well cause the exchange rate to overshoot its longer-run equilibrium rate. At times of international currency turmoil (see Box 13.3), such speculation can be enormous. Worldwide, over a trillion dollars on average passes daily across the foreign exchanges, greatly in excess of countries' foreign exchange reserves!

In October 2000, the exchange rate was £1 = €1.70 (see the chart). In other words, UK exporters had to sell €1.70 worth of exports to the eurozone in order to earn £1. From 2002, sterling began to depreciate significantly against the euro. By mid-2003, the rate was around £1 = €1.43. While this was good news for exporters, it was bad news for importers, who had to pay more in sterling to purchase things priced in euros. Many SMEs rely on key imported components. A rise in their price may force them to pass this on to their customers, making them less competitive with firms that are less reliant on imported components.

But just as sterling was depreciating against the euro, it was appreciating against the dollar (see the chart). In June 2001, the exchange rate was £1 = $1.41. By February 2004, it was £1 = $1.86. Then, despite dipping as low as $1.73 in November 2005, in November 2007 it reached $2.07. Thus, if an SME was importing inputs from the eurozone and then exporting to the USA, they found they were being squeezed in both directions.

Then in 2008, the pound plummeted. This might have seemed like a golden opportunity for exporters. But with many export markets in recession, SMEs typically preferred to keep foreign currency prices much the same and use the lower exchange rate to boost their earnings in sterling – earnings that for many were taking a battering in the recession at home.

As the UK economy began its weak recovery, sterling did appreciate against the dollar, reaching $1.60 in November 2010, again causing problems for exports to the USA. The sterling–euro exchange rate remained weaker, fluctuating between €1.09 and €1.20 from early 2009 to 2012. During this time, there were periods when the sterling exchange rate against the dollar and euro diverged. Sterling appreciated against the dollar from late 2010 to early 2011, but at the same time sterling was falling against the euro (though not considerably).

Between 2010 and 2013, the sterling exchange rate, while still fluctuating, did become slightly more stable and this helped to create a degree of certainty for traders. However, from mid-way through 2013, sterling began to appreciate against the dollar and also against the euro, though less quickly. It reached a peak against the dollar in July 2014 of over $1.70, but then fell, largely driven by uncertainty over the EU referendum, and in April 2016 was down to $1.43, similar to the rate in 2008.

While the pound was falling against the dollar, it continued to strengthen against the euro, reaching €1.41 in November 2015. However, with the EU referendum growing nearer and uncertainty surrounding the UK's future within the EU, the pound did begin to fall against the euro at the start of 2016. With the Brexit vote in June 2016, sterling depreciated significantly. As we saw on page 309, within just over three months of the referendum, it had fallen by 16.0 per cent against the dollar and 14.7 per cent against the euro (see the blog, 'Sterling slides', on the Sloman Economics News site).

For SMEs in particular any change in the exchange rate can have considerable effects on business performance and can force such firms to restrict their market size by focusing on domestic sales. Research by Héricourt and Poncet in 2012 found that firms cut back on the quantity of their exports to countries with higher exchange rate volatility and that this effect was more pronounced for those firms that were more financially vulnerable – often likely to be SMEs.[2]

The uncertainty surrounding the outcome of the EU referendum, and then the outcome of the Brexit negotiations, led to more volatility for sterling against the euro, with small things causing changes in both directions on any given day. An Ipsos Mori poll showing 55 per cent of voters supporting the remain campaign boosted the pound, while a few days later, it fell once more with warnings from the Bank of England of future monetary easing, in part driven by the uncertainty over the 'in–out' referendum. Then after the referendum, there was considerable volatility according to people's expectations about the likely nature of the Brexit deal. For example, when, at the beginning of October 2016, the government signified that it might favour 'hard Brexit', as opposed to seeking to remain in the European Single Market, the pound fell by around 5 per cent against the euro and 6 per cent against the dollar in just a week.

 Are SMEs likely to find it easier or harder than large multinational companies to switch the source of their supplies from countries where the pound has depreciated to ones where it has appreciated?

2 Jérôme Héricourt and Sandra Poncet, 'Exchange rate volatility, financial constraints and trade: empirical evidence from Chinese firms', *FIW Working Paper*, No. 112 (March 2013).

China is one country where intervention to affect the exchange rate has occurred. Worried about a slowing economy, in mid-August 2015 the Chinese central bank, the People's Bank of China, devalued its currency (the yuan) by just under 3 per cent. The aim was to help exports and stimulate aggregate demand. It also adopted other measures that put downward pressure on the exchange rate, such as lower interest rates and quantitative easing. By January 2016, the yuan had fallen by a total of 5.8 per cent since before the August devaluation. You can read about the Chinese action in the blogs, 'What a devalued yuan means to the rest of the world' and 'Chinese monetary policy' on the Sloman Economics News site.

Exchange rates in practice

Most countries today have a relatively free exchange rate. Nevertheless, the problems of instability that this can bring are well recognised, and thus many countries seek to regulate or manage their exchange rate.

BOX 13.3   THE EURO/DOLLAR SEESAW

What is the impact on business?

For periods of time, world currency markets can be quite peaceful, with only modest changes in exchange rates. But with the ability to move vast sums of money very rapidly from one part of the world to another and from one currency to another, speculators can suddenly turn this relatively peaceful world into one of extreme turmoil, which can be very damaging for business.

In this box we examine the huge swings of the euro against the dollar since the euro's launch in 1999.

First the down . . .

On 1 January 1999, the euro was launched and exchanged for $1.16. By October 2000 the euro had fallen to $0.85. What was the cause of this 27 per cent depreciation? The main one was the growing fear that inflationary pressures were increasing in the USA and that the Federal Reserve Bank would have to raise interest rates. At the same time, the eurozone economy was growing only slowly and inflation was well below the 2 per cent ceiling set by the ECB. There was thus pressure on the ECB to cut interest rates.

The speculators were not wrong. As the diagram shows, US interest rates rose, and ECB interest rates initially fell, and when eventually they did rise (in October 1999), the gap between US and ECB interest rates soon widened again.

In addition to the differences in interest rates, a lack of confidence in the recovery of the eurozone economy and continued confidence in the US economy encouraged investment to flow to the USA. This inflow of finance (and lack of inflow to the eurozone) further pushed up the dollar relative to the euro.

The low value of the euro meant a high value of the pound (and other currencies) relative to the euro. This made it very difficult for companies outside of the eurozone to export to eurozone countries and also for those competing with imports from the eurozone (which had been made cheaper by the fall in the euro).

In October 2000, with the euro trading at around 85¢, the ECB plus the US Federal Reserve Bank, the Bank of England and the Japanese central bank all intervened on the foreign exchange market to buy euros. This arrested the fall, and helped to restore confidence in the currency. People were more willing to hold euros, knowing that central banks would support it.

Fluctuations between the euro and the dollar

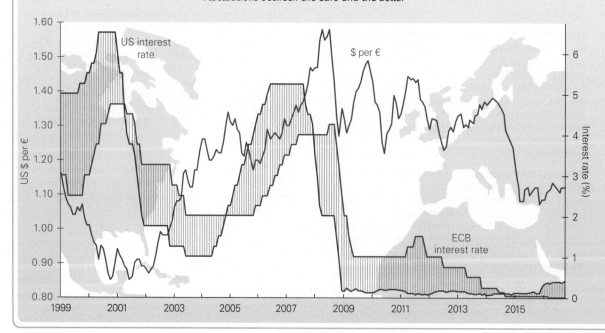

There have been many attempts to regulate exchange rates since 1945. By far the most successful was the Bretton Woods system, which was adopted worldwide from the end of World War II until 1971. This was a form of *adjustable peg* exchange rate, where countries pegged (i.e. fixed) their exchange rate to the US dollar, but could re-peg it at a lower or higher level (a *devaluation* or *revaluation* of their exchange rate) if there was a

persistent and substantial balance of payments deficit or surplus.

With growing world inflation and instability from the mid-1960s, it became more and more difficult to maintain fixed exchange rates, and the growing likelihood of devaluations and revaluations fuelled speculation. The system was abandoned in the early 1970s. What followed was a period of managed exchange rates. Under this system, exchange

. . . Then the up

The position completely changed in 2001. With the US economy slowing rapidly and fears of an impending recession, the Federal Reserve Bank reduced interest rates 11 times during the year, from 6.5 per cent at the beginning of the year to 1.75 per cent at the end (see the chart). Although the ECB also cut interest rates, the cuts were relatively modest, from 4.75 at the beginning of the year to 3.25 at the end. With eurozone interest rates now considerably above US rates, the euro began to rise.

In addition, a massive deficit on the US balance of payments current account, and a budget deficit nearing 4 per cent of GDP, led to investors pulling out of the USA. One estimate suggests that European investors alone sold $70 billion of US assets during 2002. The result was a massive depreciation of the dollar and appreciation of the euro, so that by December 2004 the exchange rate had risen to $1.36, a 60 per cent appreciation since June 2001!

In 2004–5, with the US economy growing strongly again, the Fed raised interest rates several times, from 1 per cent in early 2004 to 5.25 by June 2006. The ECB kept interest rates constant at 2 per cent until early 2006. The result was that the euro depreciated against the dollar in 2005. But then the rise of the euro began again as US growth slowed and eurozone growth rose and people anticipated a narrowing of the gap between US and eurozone interest rates.

As we saw in Box 13.3, the Fed cut interest rates significantly over a 16-month period from August 2007 to December 2008 to stave off recession. The ECB, in contrast, kept the eurozone rate at around 4 per cent. As a result, short-term finance flooded into the eurozone and the euro appreciated again, from $1.37 in mid-2007 to $1.58 in mid-2008.

. . . Then down again in a series of steps

Eventually, in September 2008, with the eurozone on the edge of recession and predictions that the ECB would cut interest rates, the euro at last began to fall. It continued to do so as the ECB cut rates. However, with monetary policy in the eurozone remaining tighter than in the USA, the euro began to rise again, only falling once more at the end of 2009 and into 2010 as US growth accelerated and speculators anticipated a tightening of US monetary policy.

Growing worries in 2010 about the level of government deficits and debt in various eurozone countries, such as Greece, Portugal, Spain, Italy and Ireland contributed to speculation and thus growing volatility of the euro. Throughout the first part of 2010, investors became increasingly reluctant to hold the euro, as fears of debt default mounted. As such, the euro fell substantially from $1.44 in January 2010 to $1.19 in June. This was a 17 per cent depreciation.

Then, as support was promised by the ECB and IMF to Greece in return for deficit reduction policies, and similar support could be made available to other eurozone countries with severe deficits, fears subsided and the euro rose again. By the end of October 2010, the euro was trading at $1.39. In April 2011, the euro increased to a high of $1.44.

Then began a dramatic fall in the euro as concerns grew over the eurozone's sluggish recovery and continuing high debt levels. Speculators thus believed that eurozone interest rates would have to continue falling. The ECB cut the main interest rate from 1.5 per cent in October 2011 in a series of steps to 0.05 per cent by September 2014.

With the ECB reducing interest rates and people increasingly predicting the introduction of quantitative easing (QE), the euro depreciated during 2014. Between March and December 2014 it depreciated by 11 per cent against the dollar, while the euro exchange rate index depreciated by 4 per cent. With the announced programme of QE being somewhat larger than markets expected, in the week following the announcement in January 2015, the euro fell a further 2.3 per cent against the dollar, and the euro exchange rate index also fell by 2.3 per cent. The result was that the euro was trading at its lowest level against the US dollar since April 2003 (see the blogs, 'The ECB takes the plunge at last' and 'Currency wars – a zero-sum game?' on the Sloman Economics News site).

With the long-awaited rise in US interest rates in December 2015 and a fall in the main EU rate to zero per cent in March 2016 and an increase in the ECB's quantitative easing programme, the euro remained weak against the dollar, as the chart shows.

The euro's short history shows that interest rate volatility and divergences in interest rates between the USA and the eurozone have been a major factor in exchange rate volatility between the euro and the dollar – itself a cause of uncertainty in international trade and finance. However, more recently concerns over the fiscal health of national eurozone governments have played a particularly important role in explaining fluctuations in the euro.

 Find out what has happened to the euro/dollar exchange rate over the past 12 months. (You can find the data on the Bank of England's Statistical Interactive Database). Explain why the exchange rate has moved the way it has.

---

rates are not pegged but allowed to float. However, central banks intervene from time to time to prevent excessive exchange rate fluctuations. This system largely continues to this day.

A further example of a managed exchange rate was in the form of the Exchange Rate Mechanism (ERM), which was the forerunner to the euro. Member countries' currencies were allowed to fluctuate against each other only within specified bands. We return to consider the ERM in more detail in section 13.4.

The problem of sovereign risk

Uncertainty over exchange rates creates problems for businesses that trade or invest internationally. This is part of the broader problem of *sovereign risk*. These are the risks associated with locating in or dealing with a particular country. For example, there is the risk that a country may raise business taxes or that its central bank may raise interest rates. Its government might impose new stricter regulatory controls that favour domestic firms, or impose stricter competition or environmental policies. There is a risk that the exchange rate may move adversely or that exchange controls may be imposed. In extreme cases, governments may appropriate a firm's assets or prevent it from trading.

The greater the perceived level of sovereign risk of a particular country, the less willing will firms be to trade with it or locate there. Countries are thus under pressure to create a more favourable environment for business and reduce sovereign risk.

> ## Pause for thought
>
> *Will the pressure on governments to reduce sovereign risk always lead to better outcomes for the citizens of that country?*

> ## Definitions
>
> **Adjustable peg** A system whereby exchange rates are fixed for a period of time, but may be devalued (or revalued) if a deficit (or surplus) becomes substantial.
>
> **Devaluation** Where the government or central bank re-pegs the exchange rate at a lower level.
>
> **Revaluation** Where the government or central bank re-pegs the exchange rate at a higher level.
>
> **Sovereign risk (for business)** The risk that a foreign country's government or central bank will make its policies less favourable. Such policies could involve changes in interest rates or tax regimes, the imposition of foreign exchange controls, or even defaulting on loans or the appropriation of a business's assets.

RECAP

1. The rate of exchange is the rate at which one currency exchanges for another. Rates of exchange are determined by demand and supply in the foreign exchange market. Demand for the domestic currency consists of all the credit items in the balance of payments account. Supply consists of all the debit items.

2. The exchange rate will depreciate (fall) if the demand for the domestic currency falls or the supply increases. These shifts can be caused by a fall in domestic interest rates, higher inflation in the domestic economy than abroad, a rise in domestic incomes relative to incomes abroad, relative investment prospects improving abroad, or the belief by speculators that the exchange rate will fall. The opposite in each case would cause an appreciation (rise).

3. The government can attempt to prevent the rate of exchange from falling by central bank purchases of the domestic currency in the foreign exchange market, either by selling foreign currency reserves or by using foreign loans. Alternatively, the central bank can raise interest rates. The reverse actions can be taken to prevent the rate from rising.

4. Managed exchange rates bring the advantage of greater certainty for the business community, which encourages trade and foreign investment. Also, if successful, they reduce speculation.

5. They bring the disadvantages of not being able to use interest rate changes to meet objectives other than a stable exchange rate, the difficulty in responding to shocks and the danger that speculation will be encouraged if speculators believe that the current exchange rate cannot be maintained.

6. There have been various attempts to manage exchange rates, without them being totally fixed. One example was the Bretton Woods system: a system of pegged exchange rates, but where devaluations or revaluations were allowed from time to time. Another was the ERM, which was the forerunner to the euro. Member countries' currencies were allowed to fluctuate against each other within a band.

7. Businesses face sovereign risk when investing in or trading with other countries. These risks relate to unforeseen exchange rate or interest rate movements, or adverse government policies.

13.3 THE GROWTH OF GLOBAL FINANCIAL FLOWS

Financial interdependence

We live in a highly interdependent world, where every country is affected by the economic performance and government policy of other countries. This was illustrated when the sub-prime market in the USA collapsed and spread like a contagion to cause a worldwide recession.

International trade has grown rapidly for many years (see Figure 12.1 on page 290), but international financial flows have grown much more rapidly. Each day, trillions of dollars of assets are traded across the foreign exchanges. It was estimated that during 2015, an average of $5.32 trillion of assets were being traded daily across the foreign exchanges (this compares with $5.87 trillion in 2014 and $5.30 trillion in 2013).[2] Many of the transactions are short-term financial flows, moving to where interest rates are most favourable or to currencies where the exchange rate is likely to appreciate. Countries have thus become increasingly financially dependent on each other.

Assume that the Federal Reserve Bank, worried about rising inflation, decides to raise interest rates. What will be the effect on business in America's trading partners? There are three major effects.

■ If aggregate demand in America falls, so will its expenditure on imports from firms abroad, thus directly affecting businesses exporting to the USA. With a decline in their exports, aggregate demand in these other countries falls.
■ The higher interest rate in the USA will tend to drive up interest rates in other countries. This will depress investment. Again, aggregate demand will tend to fall in these countries.
■ The higher interest rate will attract an inflow of funds from other countries. This will cause the dollar to appreciate relative to other currencies. This will make these other countries' exports to the USA more competitive and imports from the USA relatively more expensive. This will result in an improvement in the current account of the USA's trading partners: their exports rise and imports fall. This represents a rise in aggregate demand in these countries – the opposite from the first two effects.

There is a simple conclusion from the above analysis. The larger the financial flows, the more will interest rate changes in one country affect the economies of other countries; the greater will be the financial interdependence.

Pause for thought

What will be the effect on the UK economy if the European Central Bank cuts interest rates?

The impact of capital flows

Large movements of capital into and out of countries can have serious consequences for business. Some of these capital flows are for direct investment; some are for buying shares and other financial assets; some are simply short-term speculative deposits. The global supply of dollars available for such purposes has grown by some 18 per cent per year since the early 2000s. One of the main reasons for this has been the huge current account deficits of the USA. This has led to vast outflows of dollars from the USA into the world economy as Americans have effectively paid for their deficit by creating more dollars.

Capital inflows. Capital flows will be attracted to countries where investment prospects are good or for speculative purposes. When they are, the financial account of the balance of payments will improve, causing the exchange rate to appreciate. This appreciation, if set to continue, will attract further capital inflows in anticipation of a speculative gain from a rising exchange rate. As demand for the domestic currency increases, this will push the exchange rate even higher. Domestic currency will be worth more in dollars and other currencies. In other words, a dollar will buy less of the country's currency.

This will make it harder for firms to export. If exports are priced in foreign currency (e.g. dollars), firms must accept less domestic currency; if exports are priced in the domestic currency, the dollar price must rise. At the same time, imports will be cheaper. This makes it harder for domestic business to compete with imports.

For example, in 2006, capital inflows into the Thai economy pushed up the value of the Thai baht by 16 per cent. As Thai businesses struggled to compete, the Bank of Thailand imposed taxes on inward portfolio investment. But this was not the solution. Share prices fell dramatically, and the tax was hastily withdrawn.

So is the answer to cut interest rates? This would reduce capital inflows and help curb the appreciation of the currency. But it would create another problem. The lower interest rates would encourage more borrowing and hence higher credit growth and higher inflation.

Thus, large capital inflows leave countries with an uncomfortable choice: either allow the exchange rate to appreciate, thereby damaging business competitiveness, or cut interest rates, thereby causing higher inflation, which could also damage business competitiveness.

Capital outflows. Just as vast amounts of capital can flow into countries, so they can flow out too. The problem especially concerns money on short-term deposit. If a country's exchange rate is likely to fall, speculators will sell the currency before it does fall. This will then bring about the very depreciation that was anticipated. Such depreciation is likely if the currency had initially appreciated above its long-term equilibrium rate.

From the second half of 2014 and throughout 2015, China experienced significant capital outflows, as expectations of a depreciation of the yuan grew. In 2015 alone there were capital outflows of around $1 trillion.[3] In June 2014, China's reserves had reached a record high of $3.99 trillion, but then started to fall as the central bank drew on them to arrest the downward pressure on the exchange rate. They dropped by $513 billion in 2014 and $300 billion in 2015. However, the need for intervention in 2016 diminished as the exchange rate recovered.[4]

---

[2] Jeff Patterson, 'Global FX on the decline, migration to electronic venues unfolds', *Finance Magnates* (24 May 2016).

[3] 'China capital outflows rise to estimated $1 trillion in 2015', *Bloomberg* (25 January 2016).

[4] Gabriel Wildau, 'China capital outflows persist despite FX reserves rebound', *Financial Times* (9 May 2016).

Capital controls

Excessive capital flows, whether inward or outward, can be highly destabilising for exchange rates. This makes it very difficult for businesses to plan and can rapidly turn a profitable business into a loss-making one. The result is to undermine confidence in long-term investment. And the problem is getting worse as the supply of dollars and other international currencies continues to grow faster than international trade.

So what can be done? Many commentators have called for capital controls. The aim of such controls is not to prevent capital flows. After all, capital flows are an important source of financing investment. The aim is to prevent short-term speculative flows, based on rumour or herd instinct rather than on economic fundamentals.

Types of control

In what ways, then, can movements of short-term capital be controlled?

Quantitative controls. Here the authorities would restrict the amount of foreign exchange dealing that could take place. Perhaps financial institutions would be allowed to exchange only a certain percentage of their assets. Developed countries and most developing countries have rejected this approach, however, since it is seen to be far too anti-market.

Alternatively, certain types of inflow could be restricted. China, for example, restricts portfolio capital inflows. This has held down its exchange rate, thereby increasing its competitiveness. But this, in turn, has reduced the competitiveness of other countries in Asia and around the world.

A Tobin tax. This is named after James Tobin, who in 1972 advocated the imposition of a small tax of 0.1 to 0.5 per cent on all foreign exchange transactions, or on just capital and financial account transactions.[5] This would discourage destabilising speculation (by making it more expensive) and would thus impose some 'friction' in foreign exchange markets, making them less volatile.

In November 2001, the French National Assembly became the first national legislature to incorporate into law a Tobin tax of up to 0.1 per cent. This was followed by Belgium in 2002. In the wake of the 2007/8 banking crisis and the highly risky financial dealings that had led to the crisis, more countries have seriously considered introducing Tobin taxes. These, however, would be on speculative financial transactions generally and not just on foreign exchange transactions.

In September 2011, a proposal was made by the European Commission for an EU financial transaction tax to be implemented across the members of the EU by 2014. However, this faced stiff opposition, particularly from non-eurozone nations, including the UK. The UK government argued that the resulting decline in trades would reduce profits for financial institutions, which are a major part of the UK economy.

In October 2012, 11 of the 17 eurozone countries agreed to adopt a harmonised financial transactions tax at rates of 0.1 per cent on trading in bonds and shares and 0.01 per cent on trading in derivatives. It was approved by the European Parliament in December 2012 and by the Council of the European Union in January 2013, but concerns over tax and legal issues delayed its implementation. In December 2015, 10 of the countries (excluding Estonia) agreed on some aspects of the tax, with plans for the remaining details to be agreed by the middle of 2016.[6] You can read about the initial discussions of this type of Tobin Tax in the blog, 'Rolling out a Tobin tax', on the Sloman Economics News site.

Non-interest-bearing deposits. Here a certain percentage of inflows of finance would have to be deposited with the central bank in a non-interest-bearing account for a set period of time. Chile in the late 1990s used such a system. It required that 30 per cent of all inflows be deposited with Chile's central bank for a year. This clearly amounted to a considerable tax (i.e. in terms of interest sacrificed) and had the effect of discouraging short-term speculative flows. The problem was that it meant that interest rates in Chile had to be higher in order to attract finance.

South Korea operates a similar system and in December 2006 it raised the amount that banks must deposit with the central bank in an attempt to stem speculative capital inflows.

RECAP

1. Countries are increasingly financially interdependent. Changes in interest rates in one country will affect capital flows to and from other countries, and hence their exchange rates, interest rates and GDP. The credit crunch in the late 2000s and sovereign debt crisis in the eurozone are prime examples of this growing interdependence.

2. Capital flows have grown substantially in recent years and can be highly destabilising to an economy. Capital inflows can cause an appreciation, reducing a country's competitiveness.

3. If capital flows could be constrained, however, exchange rates could be stabilised somewhat. Forms of control include: quantitative controls, a tax on exchange transactions (a Tobin tax) and non-interest-bearing deposits with the central bank of a certain percentage of capital inflows.

---

[5] James Tobin, 'A proposal for international monetary reform', *The Eastern Economic Journal*, vol. 4, no. 3–4 (1978), pp. 153–9.

[6] Jan Strupczewski, 'Ten EU countries agree on aspects of a financial-transaction tax', *Reuters* (8 December 2015).

Although countries around the world generally operate a system of floating exchange rates, small countries sometimes peg their exchange rates to the dollar or other major currencies. Also, on a regional basis, there have been attempts to create greater exchange rate stability by countries pegging their exchange rates to each other.

Such a system was introduced in Europe in 1979 as the forerunner of the adoption of the euro. The name given to the EU system was the *exchange rate mechanism (ERM)*. The majority of the EU countries at the time were members. The UK initially chose not to join the ERM, but eventually did so in 1990.

The ERM

Under the ERM, each currency was given a central exchange rate with each of the other member currencies in a grid. However, fluctuations were allowed from the central rate within specified bands. For most countries these bands were set at $\pm 2\frac{1}{4}$ per cent. The central rates could be adjusted from time to time by agreement, thus making the ERM an adjustable peg system (see pages 323–4). All the currencies floated jointly with currencies outside the ERM.

In a system of pegged exchange rates, such as the ERM, countries should harmonise their policies to avoid excessive currency misalignments and hence the need for large devaluations or revaluations. There should be a convergence of their economies – they should be at a similar point on the business cycle and have similar inflation rates and interest rates.

Shortly after the UK joined the ERM in 1990, strains began to show. The reunification of Germany involved considerable reconstruction in the eastern part of the country. Financing this reconstruction was causing a growing budget deficit. The Bundesbank (the German central bank) thus felt obliged to maintain high interest rates in order to keep inflation in check. At the same time, the UK was experiencing a massive current account deficit (partly the result of entering the ERM at what many commentators argued was too high an exchange rate). It was thus obliged to raise interest rates in order to protect the pound, despite the fact that the economy was sliding rapidly into recession. The French franc and Italian lira were also perceived to be overvalued, and there were the first signs of worries as to whether their exchange rates within the ERM could be retained.

Definition

ERM (the exchange rate mechanism) A semi-fixed system whereby participating EU countries allowed fluctuations against each other's currencies only within agreed bands. Collectively they floated freely against all other currencies.

The US had cut interest rates to stimulate the economy and capital flowed from there to Germany, taking advantage of the higher interest rates. This pushed up the value of the German mark and the other ERM currencies.

In September 1992, things reached crisis point. On 'Black Wednesday' (16 September), the UK and Italy were forced to suspend their membership of the ERM; the pound and the lira were floated and depreciated substantially. The following year, in an attempt to rescue the ERM for the remaining countries, EU finance ministers agreed to adopt very wide ± 15 per cent bands.

The old ERM appeared to be at an end. The new ± 15 per cent bands hardly seemed like a 'pegged' system at all. However, the ERM did not die. Within months, the members were again managing to keep fluctuations within a very narrow range (for most of the time, within $\pm 2\frac{1}{4}$ per cent). The scene was being set for the abandonment of separate currencies and the adoption of a single currency: the euro.

Pause for thought

Under what circumstances may a currency bloc like the ERM (a) help to prevent speculation; (b) aggravate the problem of speculation?

With a single currency there can be no exchange rate fluctuations between the member states, any more than there can be fluctuations between the Californian and New York dollar, or between the English, Scottish and Welsh pound.

Birth of the euro

The Maastricht Treaty was signed in February 1992 and it set out the timetable for the adoption of a single currency in Europe. Before joining the currency union, member states had to meet five convergence criteria, to ensure that the economies of the potential members had sufficiently converged. They were:

■ Inflation: should be no more than 1½ per cent above the average inflation rate of the three countries in the EU with the lowest inflation.

■ Interest rates: the rate on long-term government bonds should be no more than 2 per cent above the average of the three countries with the lowest inflation.

■ Budget deficit: should be no more than 3 per cent of GDP.

■ General government debt: should be no more than 60 per cent of GDP.

■ Exchange rates: the currency should have been within the normal ERM bands for at least two years with no realignments or excessive intervention.

In March 1998, the European Commission ruled that 11 of the 15 member states were eligible to proceed to EMU in January 1999. Their economies were deemed to be sufficiently converged in terms of interest rates, inflation rates and government deficits and debt. The UK and Denmark were to exercise their 'opt out', negotiated at Maastricht back in 1992, and Sweden and Greece failed to meet one or more of the convergence criteria.

The euro finally came into being in January 1999 (although notes and coins did not circulate until January 2002). Greece joined the euro in 2001, Slovenia in 2007, Cyprus and Malta in 2008, Slovakia in 2009, Estonia in 2011, followed by Latvia and Lithuania in 2014 and 2015 respectively, making a total of 19 countries using the euro.

With a single currency, countries must have a single central bank (the European Central Bank for the eurozone) and a common monetary policy, involving common interest rates for all member countries. Such a system is known as *economic and monetary union (EMU)*.

Business and the euro

The adoption of the euro has had a profound effect on business, both within the eurozone and outside it. There are significant advantages in terms of greater certainty and greater inward investment, but also various costs in terms of reduced flexibility for governments in managing their economies.

Advantages of a single currency

Elimination of the costs of converting currencies. With separate currencies in each of the EU countries, costs were incurred each time one currency was exchanged into another. The elimination of these costs was, however, probably the least important benefit from the single currency. The European Commission estimated that the effect was to increase the GDP of the countries concerned by an average of only 0.4 per cent. The gains to countries like the UK, which have well-developed financial markets, would be even smaller.

Increased competition and efficiency. Not only has the single currency eliminated the need to convert one currency into another (a barrier to competition), but it has brought more transparency in pricing, and has put greater downward pressure on prices in high-cost firms and countries. This, of course, does not necessarily favour business, which might

> ### Definition
>
> **Economic and monetary union (EMU)** Where countries adopt a single currency and a single monetary policy. It might also involve other common policies, such as fiscal and supply-side policies.

find its profits squeezed, but it generally benefits consumers. Although there has been some price convergence across the eurozone, it has not been as extensive as many thought it would be.

Elimination of exchange rate uncertainty (between the members). The removal of exchange rate uncertainty has helped to encourage trade between the eurozone countries. Perhaps more importantly, it has encouraged investment by firms that trade between these countries, given the greater certainty in calculating costs and revenues from such trade.

In times of economic uncertainty, such as the credit crunch of 2008, exchange rate volatility between currencies can be high, as we saw with the experience of sterling. This volatility creates uncertainty, which leads to problems for both trade and investment. However, if the UK had adopted the euro, the uncertainty for the UK in its trade with eurozone countries would have been eliminated. Furthermore, had the eurozone countries not adopted the euro, the degree of banking turmoil they experienced in 2008 and 2009 may have been even more severe.

Increased inward investment. Investment from the rest of the world is attracted to a eurozone of over 330 million inhabitants, where there is no fear of internal currency movements. By contrast, the UK, by not joining, initially found that inward investment was diverted away to countries within the eurozone. From 1990 to 1998, the UK's share of inward investment to EU countries was nearly 20.4 per cent, but it fell to 12.5 per cent by 2003. From then until 2005, however, its share increased substantially to 35 per cent, as the UK economy grew more strongly than other major economies in the EU. But this was relatively short-lived, with the volatility of sterling acting as a deterrent to investment in the UK and its share fell to 10.4 per cent in 2011. With the UK's economy growing more rapidly than other members of the EU, its share of inward investment has increased, averaging around 20 per cent of EU inward investment since 2012.

Lower inflation and interest rates. A single monetary policy forces convergence in inflation rates (just as inflation rates are very similar between the different regions within a country). With the ECB being independent from short-term political manipulation, this has resulted in a lower average inflation rate in the eurozone countries. This, in turn, has helped to convince markets that the euro will be strong relative to other currencies. The result is lower long-term rates of interest. This, in turn, further encourages investment in the eurozone countries, both by member states and by the rest of the world.

Opposition to EMU

There are, however, many criticisms levelled at the monetary union. Many 'Eurosceptics' see it as a surrender of national, political and economic sovereignty.

Furthermore, a single currency reduces a country's ability to steer its own economy. It cannot adjust its exchange rate with other member countries and it cannot determine its own interest rates.

Inability to adjust exchange rates between members. This is a particular problem if a country finds that its economy is at all out of harmony with the rest of the Union. For example, if countries such as Italy, Greece and Spain have higher endemic rates of inflation (due, say, to greater cost-push pressures), then how are they to make their goods competitive with the rest of the Union? With separate currencies these countries could allow their currencies to depreciate, thus increasing competitiveness. Indeed, throughout 2008, sterling depreciated and this helped to make UK exports more competitive, thereby boosting aggregate demand and helping to soften the recession. With a single currency, however, they could become depressed 'regions' of Europe, with rising unemployment and all the other regional problems of depressed regions within a country. There is some evidence to suggest that this has occurred.

Pause for thought

How might multiplier effects (see page 236) lead to prosperous regions becoming more prosperous and less prosperous regions falling even further behind?

The answer given by proponents of EMU is that it is better to tackle the problem of high inflation or unemployment in such countries by the disciplines of competition from other eurozone countries than merely to feed that inflation by keeping separate currencies and allowing continued depreciation, with all the uncertainty that that brings. The critics of EMU, however, argue that cost differences, and hence unemployment, could persist.

Lack of separate monetary policies. Perhaps the most serious criticism is the loss of an independent monetary policy for individual member countries. This means that the same rate of interest must apply to all eurozone countries: the 'one size fits all' criticism. The trouble is that while one country might require a lower rate of interest in order to ward off recession (such as Portugal, Ireland and Greece in 2010–11), another might require a higher one to prevent inflation. Furthermore, some countries may be more sensitive to interest changes than others, hence the optimal change in interest rates for one country may represent too much or too little of a change in another. The greater the divergence between economies within the eurozone, the greater this problem becomes.

The problem of asymmetric shocks. A further problem for members of a single currency occurs in adjusting to a shock when that shock affects members to differing degrees. These are known as *asymmetric shocks*. For example, the banking crisis affected the UK more severely than other countries, given that London is a global financial centre.

This problem, however, should not be overstated. Divergences between economies are often the result of a lack of harmony between countries in their demand-management policies, thus closer integration and co-ordination between members can help to overcome this criticism. For the monetary union, there is clearly no problem with an integrated monetary policy, as that is one of the 'conditions' of membership. In terms of fiscal policy, there is some integration, partly through the Stability and Growth Pact. However, the Pact was not rigidly enforced and the rules allowed for discretion, such that with the recession in the late 2000s, deficits and debt rose sharply in the member states (see figure in Box 11.1 on page 268). It is perhaps this factor which has helped fuel the problem of asymmetric shocks.

Subsequently, efforts have been made to change the framework within which national governments make their fiscal choices (see Box 11.1). It is hoped that with common fiscal rules, as well as free trade, divergences between economies and thus the problem of asymmetric shocks will diminish over time.

However, even when shocks are uniformly felt in the member states there is still the problem that policies adopted centrally will have different impacts on each country. For example, in the UK, a large proportion of borrowing is at variable interest rates. In Germany, by contrast, much is at fixed rates. Thus if the UK adopted the euro and the ECB were to raise interest rates, the contractionary effects would be felt disproportionately in the UK. Of course, were this balance to change – and there is some evidence that types of borrowing are becoming more uniform across the EU – this problem would diminish.

When the euro was first discussed, the UK Labour government specified five convergence criteria that would have to be met before it would put the question of UK adoption of the euro to the electorate in a referendum. These are examined in Case Study D.45 on the book's website. The problem for economists is that the issue of monetary union is a very emotive one, especially when it comes to national sovereignty.

The debate over the euro in the UK went away, but it was replaced with debate over EU membership itself (see Box 12.5). As with the euro debate, the debate about EU membership and the effects of Brexit are emotive subjects and we have seen that a calm assessment of the arguments is difficult.

Definition

Asymmetric shocks Shocks (such as an oil price increase or a recession in another part of the world) that have different-sized effects on different industries, regions or countries.

RECAP

1. One means of achieving greater currency stability is for a group of countries to peg their internal exchange rates and yet float jointly with the rest of the world. The exchange rate mechanism of the EU (ERM) was an example. This was seen as an important first stage on the road to complete economic and monetary union (EMU) in the EU.

2. The euro was born on 1 January 1999 with euro notes and coins introduced in 2002. There are now 19 countries using the euro.

3. The advantages claimed for EMU are that it eliminates the costs of converting currencies and the uncertainties

associated with possible changes in former inter-EU exchange rates. This encourages more investment, both inward and by domestic firms, and greater trade between EU countries.

4. Critics, however, claim that the loss of independence in policy making might make adjustment to domestic economic problems more difficult, especially when these problems diverge from those of other members. A single monetary policy is claimed to be inappropriate for dealing with asymmetric shocks.

13.5 INTERNATIONAL ECONOMIC POLICY: MANAGING THE GLOBAL ECONOMY

Attempts to co-ordinate global business activity

There is an old saying: 'If America sneezes, the rest of the world catches a cold' and some have now extended this to include China in addition to America. Viruses of a similar nature regularly infect the world economy. A dramatic example was the global banking crisis of 2007–8. What started largely as a problem of risky mortgage loans in the USA ('sub-prime' mortgages) rapidly became a global banking crisis, necessitating a global policy response. This began in October 2008 when governments across the world initially injected some $2 trillion of extra capital into banks.

For many years now the leaders of the seven or eight major industrialised countries – the USA, Japan, Germany, France, the UK, Italy, Canada and sometimes Russia – have met once a year (and more frequently if felt necessary) at an economic summit conference. More recently there have been similar meetings of the much broader G20 group, which also includes major developing countries, such as China and India.

Top of the agenda in many of these meetings has been how to achieve a *harmonisation* of economic policies between nations to allow worldwide economic growth without major currency fluctuations. In other words, it is important that all the major countries are pursuing consistent policies aimed at common international goals.

But how can policy harmonisation be achieved? If there are significant domestic differences between the major economies, there is likely to be conflict, not harmony. For example, if one group of countries, say the USA and Japan, are worried about tackling recession, they may be unwilling to respond to demands from other countries for fiscal restraint to tackle the problem of large public sector deficits and debts. What is more, speculators, seeing differences between countries, are likely to exaggerate them by their actions, causing large changes in exchange rates.

The G8/G20 countries have therefore sought to achieve greater *convergence of their economies*. However, although convergence may be a goal of policy, in practice it has proved elusive.

Because of a lack of convergence, there are serious difficulties in achieving international policy harmonisation:

- Countries' budget deficits and accumulated government debts differ substantially as a proportion of their GDP. This puts very different pressures on the interest rates necessary to service these debts. In 2015, the ratio of the total stock of general government debt to annual GDP stood at 91 per cent in the UK, compared with 38 per cent for Australia, 69 per cent for Germany 87 per cent for Canada, 97 per cent for France and 246 per cent for Japan.

- Harmonising rates of monetary growth or inflation targets would involve letting interest rates fluctuate with the

Definition

International harmonisation of economic policies Where countries attempt to co-ordinate their macroeconomic policies so as to achieve common goals.

Definition

Convergence of economies When countries achieve similar levels of growth, inflation, budget deficits as a percentage of GDP, balance of payments, etc.

demand for money. Without convergence in the demand for money, interest rate fluctuations could be severe.

■ Harmonising interest rates would involve abandoning money, inflation or exchange rate targets (unless interest rate 'harmonisation' meant adjusting interest rates so as to maintain money or inflation targets or a given exchange rate).

■ Countries have different internal structural relationships. A lack of convergence here means that countries with higher endemic cost inflation would require higher interest rates and higher unemployment if international inflation rates were to be harmonised, or higher inflation if interest rates were to be harmonised.

■ Countries have different rates of productivity increase, product development, investment and market penetration. A lack of convergence here means that the growth in exports (relative to imports) will differ for any given level of inflation or growth.

■ Countries may be very unwilling to change their domestic policies to fall into line with other countries. They may prefer the other countries to fall into line with them!

If any one of the four – interest rates, growth rates, inflation rates or current account balance of payments – could be harmonised across countries, it is likely that the other three would then not be harmonised.

> ### Pause for thought
>
> *If total convergence were achieved, would harmonisation of policies follow automatically?*

Total convergence and thus total harmonisation may not be possible. Nevertheless, most governments favour some movement in that direction; some is better than none.

The problem of speculation

One important lesson of recent years is that concerted speculation has become virtually unstoppable. This was made clear by the expulsion of the UK and Italy from the ERM in 1992, a dramatic fall of the Mexican peso and a rise of the yen in 1995, the collapse of various South-East Asian currencies (see Case Study D.33 on the book's website) and the Russian rouble in 1997–8 and the collapse of the Argentinean peso in 2002 (see Case Study D.44), the fall in the pound in 2008 and the fall of the euro in 2010 and in 2014–15. In comparison with the vast amounts of short-term finance flowing across the foreign exchanges each day, the reserves of central banks seem trivial.

If there is a consensus in the markets that a currency will depreciate, there is little that central banks can do. For example, if there were a 50 per cent chance of a 10 per cent depreciation in the next week, then selling that currency now would yield an 'expected' return of just over 5 per cent for the week (i.e. 50 per cent of 10 per cent), equivalent to more than 5000 per cent at an annual rate!

For this reason, many commentators have argued that there are only two types of exchange rate system that can work over the long term. The first is a completely free-floating exchange rate, with no attempt by the central bank to support the exchange rate. With no intervention, there is no problem of a shortage of reserves!

BOX 13.4   A WORLDWIDE EPIDEMIC

Global answers to global problems?

We don't have to look far to see how much economic and financial interdependence affects our daily lives. As you walk down the street to the supermarket, many of the passing cars originate overseas or perhaps were built here by foreign-owned companies. You look up and the plane flying overhead is taking passengers to every corner of the world for both business and pleasure. As you enter the supermarket you see an array of goods from all over the world. Clearly, interdependence through trade connects economies. Recent decades have helped to demonstrate just how interdependent financial systems and financial institutions have become. Financial products have a passport to travel and they do!

Growth rates across the world have tended to converge. This is consistent with the idea of an international business cycle. The implication of this is that countries will tend to share common problems and concerns at the same time. At one time, the most pressing problem may be world inflationary pressures; at another time, it may be a world recession. Increasing economic and financial interdependence means that problems in one part of the world rapidly spread to other

parts. Just look at what happened when the US sub-prime mortgage market collapsed in 2007–8. America's illness turned into the world's flu!

But who should dish out the medicine? How potent can the medicine of national governments be in isolation? What role is there for co-ordinated monetary and fiscal policies and does it require stronger international institutions to deal with world problems?

Iceland's cold

The decline in output in Iceland in 2009–10, at nearly 11 per cent, was especially stark. The country had been especially badly hit by the global financial crisis.

An aggressive strategy of credit expansion had seen the liabilities of the three largest Icelandic banks rise from 100 per cent of GDP in 2004 to over 1000 per cent by 2008. Some of the funds from this expansion came from the inter-bank market but also from deposits overseas in subsidiaries of these banks in the Nordic countries and the UK. When the

▶

credit crunch hit, they found it increasingly difficult to roll over loans on the inter-bank market. What is more, the sheer scale of the banks' expansion made it virtually impossible for Iceland's central bank to guarantee repayments of the loans.

The result was that four of its largest banks were nationalised and run by Iceland's Financial Supervisory Authority.

In November 2008, the International Monetary Fund's executive board approved a $2.1 billion loan to Iceland to support an economic recovery programme. An initial payment of $827 million was made with subsequent payments to be spread over time, subject to IMF quarterly reviews of the recovery programme.

In August 2011 the bailout support officially ended and in early 2012 Iceland began repaying the bailout debt. Its strong recovery and sound policies enabled it to repay all of its Nordic loans and much of the IMF loan, while still retaining adequate foreign exchange reserves – a success story for IMF intervention.

A Greek tragedy

Greece had been struggling with the burden of a huge budget deficit for some years and with the credit crunch of 2008 its general government deficit soared, reaching 15.6 per cent of GDP in 2009. This was over five times higher than EU rules allow. The annual cost of servicing the debt was about 11.6 per cent of GDP and in early 2010 the government estimated that it would need to borrow €53 billion to cover budget shortfalls. Greece, like many other countries, was also experiencing rising unemployment and, by 2010, the rate had increased to over 12.5 per cent.

Austerity measures, as part of an IMF and EU rescue package aimed to reduce this deficit to less than 3 per cent of GDP by 2014. This would be achieved through a variety of spending cuts and tax rises and was the price that Greece had to pay to receive a bailout package worth €240 billion. This comprised an initial loan of €110 billion agreed in May 2010 and a further €130 billion agreed in October 2011. However, the

costs of the austerity measures in terms of disposable income and unemployment were high and there were widespread strikes by public-sector workers. By 2014, the budget deficit had fallen to 3.6 per cent of GDP, not far off the target of 3 per cent. By 2015, however, it had risen to 7.2 per cent.

The period from 2012 to 2014 saw the unemployment rate consistently around 25 per cent and the country operating with a negative output gap estimated at around 10 per cent of potential GDP. By 2014, real GDP per capita was 24 per cent lower than it had been in 2008.

Inevitably, the period saw bouts of social unrest and widespread strikes by public-sector workers. In January 2015, the anti-austerity party Syriza won Greece's general election and committed to renegotiating the terms of the bailout and to reversing the cuts in public services. However, throughout 2015 and 2016, austerity packages were implemented to enable the Greek economy to receive further bailouts. Despite the political environment turning on the once loved Syriza, Greece had to continue showing that it was meeting the promises it made to the EU and IMF in order to continue receiving bailouts.

The debt crisis, however, has not just been confined to Greece. Spain, Cyprus, Portugal, Ireland, the UK and the USA are just some of the countries struggling with high debts. 2013 saw Cyprus reach an agreement with the EU and the IMF over a €10 billion bailout for the island's banking system, while in 2010, Ireland agreed to a rescue package of up to €10 billion.

IMF to the rescue?

The IMF has been a common feature of the news since the financial crisis, in particular with the rescue packages it has financed, along with the EU, for countries like Greece, Cyprus and Ireland. But what is the IMF? And what does it do?

It is a 'specialised agency' of the United Nations and is financed by its 189 member countries (as of 2016). The role of the IMF is to ensure macroeconomic stability – such as in

The second is to share a common currency with other countries – to join a common currency area, such as the eurozone, and let the common currency float freely. The country would give up independence in its monetary policy, but at least there would be no problem of exchange rate

instability within the currency area. A similar alternative is to adopt a major currency of another country, such as the US dollar or the euro. Many smaller states have done this. For example, Kosovo and Montenegro have adopted the euro and Ecuador has adopted the US dollar.

RECAP

1. Currency fluctuations can be lessened if countries harmonise their economic policies. Ideally this would involve achieving common growth rates, inflation rates, balance of payments (as a percentage of GDP) and interest rates. The attempt to harmonise one of these goals, however, may bring conflicts with one of the other goals.

2. Leaders of the G8 or G20 countries meet regularly to discuss ways of harmonising their policies. Usually,

however, domestic issues are more important to the leaders than international ones, and frequently they pursue policies that are not in the interests of the other countries.

3. Many economists argue that, with the huge flows of short-term finance across the foreign exchanges, governments are forced to adopt one of two extreme forms of exchange rate regime: free floating or being a member of a currency union.

the Iceland case – and to foster global growth. It also works with developing nations to alleviate poverty and to achieve economic stability. To do this it provides countries with loans.

The IMF has not been without controversy, however. Conditions attached to loans have often been very harsh, especially for some of the most indebted developing countries.

The global economic and financial crisis provided the IMF with a challenge: which countries to support with a limited budget? For instance, at the same time as its agreement with Iceland, the IMF was approving a loan of $15.7 billion to Hungary, a member country of the European Union since 2004, which was struggling to meet external debt obligations and finance its general government deficit (3.4 per cent of GDP in 2008). Another country receiving support was Latvia, the EU country with the sharpest rate of economic decline in 2009 (13.1 per cent). From the start of the crisis in 2007 to 2016, the IMF committed well over $700 billion in financing to member countries, with a significant amount going to developed economies, especially within the EU.

Following crisis talks with finance ministers in Europe in May 2010, the IMF set aside €250 billion to support eurozone countries that were in financial difficulty. This was part of a €750 billion package made up by contributions from the eurozone countries themselves (€440 billion) and EU funds from all 27 members under the European Financial Stabilisation Mechanism (EFSM).

In October 2010 the EU agreed to establish a more permanent funding mechanism for eurozone countries in financial difficulties, known as the European Stability Mechanism (ESM). The Mechanism became operational in 2013 and transferred the first tranche of financial assistance to Cyprus. The IMF is a crucial stakeholder in the funding mechanism, both in committing funds but also in assessing, alongside the European Commission and the European Central Bank, the financial position of any country requesting help. This assessment includes possible 'macroeconomic adjustment programmes' for countries in receipt of funds.

Strengthening the IMF

World leaders meeting as part of the G20 in London in April 2009 announced the need to strengthen global financial institutions. They agreed that the resources available to the IMF should be trebled to $750 billion. They also agreed that the IMF would work with a new Financial Stability Board (FSB), made up, among others, of the G20 countries and the European Commission, so as to help in identifying potential economic and financial risks. Essentially, the G20 countries were looking for a better 'early warning system' to meet some of the challenges of an increasingly interdependent world.

However, the ongoing financial problems facing governments, particularly in the eurozone, led the international community in April 2012 to pledge a further increase of $430 billion in resources for the IMF. This was on top of countries' quotas.

All members of the IMF have a quota, which is a system that helps determine members' subscriptions, their voting power and their access to financing. Under the 14th General Quota Review in 2010, various conditions were agreed to increase members' subscriptions. These conditions were met on 26 January 2016 and this will double the total quota of all members to around $658 billion from approximately $329 billion. The intention is to create a credible 'firewall' to contain future financial crises.

A new quota formula is also likely, as a review of the existing formula was completed in January 2013. However, the reforms set out in this report have yet to be implemented and hence the 15th General Quota Review has been postponed until the implementation is complete.

 Do you see any problems arising from a strengthening of global economic and financial institutions?

We have come across many aspects of globalisation throughout this text, from the operation of international commodity markets (Chapter 2), to global fashions (Chapter 3), to the growth of multinational companies (Chapter 7), to the growth of international trade and financial flows (Chapter 12 and this chapter). Here we reflect on this process and ask whether the world benefits from this growing interdependence.

The supporters

Supporters of globalisation argue that it has massive potential to benefit the entire global economy. With freer trade, greater FDI and greater competition, countries and businesses within them are encouraged to think, plan and act globally. Technology spreads faster; countries specialise in particular products and processes and thereby exploit their core competitive advantages.

Both rich and poor, it is argued, benefit from such a process. Politically, globalisation brings us closer together. Political ties help stabilise relationships and offer the opportunity for countries to discuss their differences. However imperfect the current global political system might be, the alternative of independent nations is seen as potentially far worse. The globalisation of culture is also seen as beneficial, as a world of experience is opened, whether in respect to our holiday destinations, or the food we eat, or the music we listen to, or the TV programmes we watch.

Supporters of globalisation recognise that not all countries benefit equally from globalisation; those that have wealth will, as always, possess more opportunity to benefit from the globalisation process, whether from lower prices, global political agreements or cultural experience. However, long term, supporters of globalisation see it as ultimately being for the benefit of all – rich and poor alike.

The critics

Critics of globalisation argue that it contributes to growing inequality and further impoverishes poor nations. As an economic philosophy, globalisation allows multinational corporations, based largely in the USA, Europe and Japan, to exploit their dominant position in foreign markets. Without effective competition in these markets such companies are able to pursue profit with few constraints.

By 'exploiting' low-wage labour, companies are able to compete more effectively on world markets. As competitive pressures intensify and companies seek to cut costs further, this can put downward pressure on such wages – something that workers will find difficulty in resisting, given the monopsony power of multinational employers.

In political terms, critics of globalisation see the world being dominated by big business. Many multinational companies have a turnover larger than the GDP of whole countries, as we saw in Table 7.1 (on page 161). This gives them huge power in their dealings with such countries and in imposing conditions on them, whether in terms of generous tax regimes, privileged access to markets or limited rights for workers. Multinationals also put pressure on their home governments in America, Europe or Japan to promote their interests in their dealings with other countries, thereby heightening the dominance of rich countries over the poor.

Critics are no less damning of the cultural aspects of globalisation. They see the world dominated by multinational brands, western fashion, music and TV. Rather than globalisation fostering a mix of cultural expression, critics suggest that cultural differences are being replaced by the dominant (American or Western) culture of the day.

The above views represent the extremes, and to a greater or lesser degree both have elements of truth in them. The impact of globalisation on different groups is not even, and never will be. However, to suggest that 'big business rules' is also an exaggeration. Clearly big business is influential, but it is a question of degree. Influence will invariably fluctuate over time, between events, and between and within countries.

The momentum within the global economy had been for barriers to come down, but the financial crisis showed just how dangerous interdependence can be. Despite this danger, countries are likely to become increasingly open. In many global markets, competition rather than monopoly power is becoming the dominant force. This is having profound effects on both multinational business and the peoples of the world.

RECAP

1. Supporters of globalisation point to its potential to lead to faster growth and greater efficiency through trade, competition and investment. It also has the potential to draw the world closer together politically.

2. Critics of globalisation argue that it contributes to growing inequality and further impoverishes poor nations. It also erodes national cultures and can have adverse environmental consequences.

QUESTIONS

1. The following are the items in the UK's 2014 balance of payments:

	£ billions
Exports of goods	293.7
Imports of goods	416.9
Exports of services	219.7
Imports of services	130.9
Net income flows	−32.9
Net current transfers	−25.2
Net capital transfers	−0.4
Direct investment	+81.6
Portfolio investment	+114.7
Other financial flows	−88.2
Reserves	−7.1

   Calculate the following: (a) the balance on trade in goods; (b) the balance on trade in goods and services; (c) the balance of payments on current account; (d) the financial account balance; (e) the total current plus capital plus financial account balance; (f) net errors and omissions.

   Compare your answers with the UK's 2015 balance of payments, which can be found in Table 13.1. What changes took place between 2014 and 2015?

2. Assume that there is a free-floating exchange rate. Will the following cause the exchange rate to appreciate or depreciate? In each case you should consider whether there is a shift in the demand or supply curves of sterling (or both) and which way the curve(s) shift(s).

   (a) More video recorders are imported from Japan.
   Demand curve *shifts left/shifts right/does not shift*.
   Supply curve *shifts left/shifts right/does not shift*.
   Exchange rate *appreciates/depreciates*.

   (b) UK interest rates rise relative to those abroad.
   Demand curve *shifts left/shifts right/does not shift*.
   Supply curve *shifts left/shifts right/does not shift*.
   Exchange rate *appreciates/depreciates*.

   (c) The UK experiences a higher rate of inflation than other countries.
   Demand curve *shifts left/shifts right/does not shift*.
   Supply curve *shifts left/shifts right/does not shift*.
   Exchange rate *appreciates/depreciates*.

   (d) Speculators believe that the rate of exchange will appreciate.
   Demand curve *shifts left/shifts right/does not shift*.
   Supply curve *shifts left/shifts right/does not shift*.
   Exchange rate *appreciates/depreciates*.

3. What is the relationship between the balance of payments and the rate of exchange?

4. Consider the argument that in the modern world of large-scale short-term international financial movements, the ability of individual countries to affect their exchange rate is very limited.

5. Why may capital inflows damage the international competitiveness of a country's businesses?

6. What adverse effects on the domestic economy may follow from (a) a depreciation of the exchange rate and (b) an appreciation of the exchange rate?

7. What are the causes of exchange-rate volatility? Have these problems become greater or lesser in the past 15 years? Explain why.

8. Did the exchange rate difficulties experienced by countries under the ERM strengthen or weaken the arguments for progressing to a single European currency?

9. By what means would a depressed country in an economic union with a single currency be able to recover? Would the market provide a satisfactory solution or would (union) government intervention be necessary and, if so, what form would the intervention take?

10. Assume that just some of the members of a common market like the EU adopt full economic and monetary union, including a common currency. What are the advantages and disadvantages to those members joining the full EMU and to those not joining?

11. What are the economic (as opposed to political) difficulties in achieving an international harmonisation of economic policies so as to avoid damaging currency fluctuations?

12. To what extent can international negotiations over economic policy be seen as a game of strategy? Are there any parallels between the behaviour of countries and the behaviour of oligopolies?

13. Who are the winners and losers from globalisation?

ADDITIONAL PART D CASE STUDIES ON THE *ESSENTIAL ECONOMICS FOR BUSINESS* WEBSITE (www.pearsoned.co.uk/sloman)

D.1 Output gaps. A way of measuring how far actual output falls short of long-term trend output.

D.2 The costs of economic growth. Why economic growth may not be an unmixed blessing.

D.3 Comparing national income statistics. The importance of taking the purchasing power of local currencies into account.

D.4 John Maynard Keynes (1883–1946). A profile of the great economist.

D.5 The phases of the business cycle. A demand-side analysis of the factors contributing to each of the four phases.

D.6 The attributes of money. What makes something, such as metal, paper or electronic records, suitable as money?

D.7 UK monetary aggregates. This examines the various measures of money supply in the UK using both UK and eurozone monetary aggregates.

D.8 Changes in the banking industry. This case study looks at mergers and diversification in the banking industry.

D.9 Bailing out the banks. An overview of the concerted efforts made to rescue the banking system in the crisis of 2007–9.

D.10 Credit and the business cycle. This case traces cycles in the growth of credit and relates them to the business cycle. It also looks at some of the implications of the growth in credit.

D.11 Technology and unemployment. Does technological progress destroy jobs?

D.12 The national debt. This explores the question of whether it matters if a country has a high national debt.

D.13 Trends in public expenditure. This case examines attempts to control public expenditure in the UK and relates them to the crowding-out debate.

D.14 The crowding-out effect. The circumstances in which an increase in public expenditure can replace private expenditure.

D.15 Discretionary fiscal policy in Japan. How the Japanese government used fiscal policy on various occasions throughout the 1990s and 2000s in an attempt to bring the economy out of recession.

D.16 The operation of monetary policy in the UK. What practical steps does the Bank of England take to ensure that the market rate of interest is its own chosen rate?

D.17 Monetary policy in the eurozone. This looks at how interest rates are set in the eurozone and what rules govern the behaviour of the European Central Bank.

D.18 Central banking and monetary policy in the USA. This case examines how the Fed conducts monetary policy.

D.19 Should central banks be independent of government? An examination of the arguments for and against independent central banks.

D.20 The modern approach to industrial policy. This looks at changes in the approach to industrial policy around the world.

D.21 Productivity performance and the UK economy. A detailed examination of how the UK's productivity compares with that in other countries.

D.22 Assessing PFI. Has this been the perfect solution to funding investment for the public sector without raising taxes?

D.23 Assistance to small firms in the UK. An examination of current government measures to assist small firms.

D.24 Fallacious arguments for restricting trade. Some of the more common mistaken arguments for protection.

D.25 Free trade and the environment. Do whales, the rainforests and the atmosphere gain from free trade?

D.26 The Transnationality Index. An index designed to capture how globally orientated businesses are.

D.27 The Uruguay Round. An examination of the negotiations that led to substantial cuts in trade barriers.

D.28 The Battle of Seattle. This looks at the protests against the WTO at Seattle in November 1999 and considers the arguments for and against the free trade policies of the WTO.

D.29 The World Trade Organization. This looks at the various opportunities and threats posed by this major international organisation.

D.30 Assessing NAFTA. Who are the winners and losers from the North American Free Trade Agreement?

D.31 Steel barriers. The use by the USA of tariff protection for its steel industry and the effects of threats of retaliation by the EU.

D.32 The Internal Market Scoreboard. Keeping a tally on progress to a true single market in the EU.

D.33 Brexit. This case study expands the arguments of Box 12.5 by looking at some of the wider arguments over the costs and benefits of the UK leaving the EU.

D.34 The UK's balance of payments deficit. An examination of the UK's persistent trade and current account deficits.

D.35 Dealing in foreign exchange. The operation of international currency markets.

D.36 Using interest rates to control both aggregate demand and the exchange rate. A problem of one instrument and two targets.

D.37 The importance of international financial movements. How a current account deficit can coincide with an appreciating exchange rate.

D.38 Making sense of the financial balances on the balance of payments. An examination of the three main components of the financial account.

D.39 Argentina in crisis. An examination of the collapse of the Argentinean economy in 2001/2.

D.40 Attempts at harmonisation. A look at the meetings of the G7 economies where they attempt to come to agreement on means of achieving stable and sustained worldwide economic growth.

D.41 Oil prices. What is their effect on the world economy?

D.42 Optimal currency areas. What's the best size for a single currency area such as the eurozone?

WEBSITES RELEVANT TO PART D

Numbers and sections refer to websites listed in the Web Appendix and hotlinked from this book's website at **www.pearsoned.co.uk/sloman/**

- For news articles relevant to Part D, Google the Sloman Economics News site.

- For general news on macroeconomic issues, both national and international, see websites in section A, and particularly A1–5, 7–9. See also links to newspapers worldwide in A38, 39, 43 and 44 and the news search feature in Google at A41.

- For general news on money, banking and interest rates, see again websites in section A, particularly A20–23, 25, 26, 36.

- For macroeconomic data, see links in section B and particularly B1; also see B4, 12 and 35. For UK data, see B2, 3, 5 and 34. For EU data, see section G and particularly G1 > The Statistical Annex and AMECO; see also B38, 39 and 47. For US data, see B15 and 25 and the Data section of B17. For international data, see B15, 21, 24, 31, 33, 35. For links to data sets, see B1, 4, 28, 33, 35; I14.

- For data on UK unemployment, see section B and particularly B3, 1. National Statistics > the fourth link at the top, Employment and Labour Market. For International data on unemployment, see B1 (sites 7–10); see also sites G1 > The Statistical Annex and AMECO and H3.

- For monetary and financial data (including data for money supply and interest rates), see section F and particularly F2. Note that you can link to central banks worldwide from site F17. See also the links in B1.

- For information on UK fiscal policy and government borrowing, see section E, sites E18, 30, 36. See also news sites A1–8 at Budget time. For fiscal policy in the eurozone, see General Government Data in G1 and also G13.

- For monetary policy, see section F. For the UK, see site F1; for the eurozone, see F5 and 6; for the USA, see F8; for other countries, see the respective central banks sites in section F.

- For inflation targeting in the UK and the eurozone, see section F and particularly sites F1 and 6 and 11.

- For the current approach to UK supply-side policy, see sites in section E and particularly the latest Budget Report (e.g. sections on productivity and training) at site E30. See also sites E5 and 9. For European policy, see section G and particularly sites G5, 7, 9, 12, 14, 19. For support for a market-orientated approach to supply-side policy see C17 and E34. For information on training in the UK and Europe, see section E, sites E5 and 10; and section G, sites G5 and 14. For information on the support for small business in the UK see site E38.

- For general news on business in the international environment, see section A, and particularly A1–5, 7–9, 20, 23, 24, 25, 35, 36. See also links to newspapers worldwide in A38, 39, 43 and 44, and the news search feature in Google at A41.

- For international data on imports and exports, see section B, site B1. See also site H16 > *Documents, Data and Resources* > Statistics and site H2 > UNCTADStat. See also trade data in B31 and 35.

- For international data on balance of payments, see World Economic Outlook in H4 and OECD Economic Outlook in B21. For other sources, see B33.

- For international data on foreign direct investment (FDI), see H2 > UNCTADStat.

- For UK data on trade and the balance of payments, see B3 > *Business, Industry and Trade* > International Trade, and *Economy* > Balance of Payments; see also B34. For EU data, see G1 > *Economic Databases and Indicators* > AMECO and Statistical Annex of European Economy.

- For exchange rates, see F2 > Statistical Interactive Database; you can then choose the currencies and the dates to customise an Excel file. See also A1, 3; B34, 45; F2, 6, 8.

- For discussion papers on trade and the balance of payments, see section H, sites H4 and 7.

- For trade disputes, see H16.

- For information on NAFTA and other preferential trading arrangements, see section H, sites H20–23.

- For various pressure groups critical of the effects of free trade and globalisation, see section H, sites H11, 13, 14.

- For student resources relevant to Part D, see section C, sites C1–7, 9, 10, 19 and 21.

Web appendix

All the following websites can be accessed from the home page of this book's own website (www.pearsoned.co.uk/sloman). When you enter the site, click on **Hotlinks** button. You will find all the following sites listed. Click on the one you want and the 'hotlink' will take you straight to it.

The sections and numbers below refer to the ones used in the web references at the end of each Part of the text. Thus if the reference were to A21, this would refer to the Moneyextra site.

A General news sources

As the title of this section implies, websites here can be used for finding material on current news issues or tapping into news archives. Most archives are offered free of charge. However, some do require you to register. As well as key UK and American sources, you will also notice some slightly different places from where you can get your news, such as the St Petersburg Times and Kyodo News (from Japan). Check out site numbers 38. *MyRefdesk*, 43. *Guardian World News Guide* and 44. *Online Newspapers* for links to newspapers across the world. Try searching for an article on a particular topic by using site number 41. *Google News Search*.

1. BBC news
2. The Economist
3. The Financial Times
4. The Guardian
5. The Independent
6. ITN
7. The Observer
8. The Telegraph
9. Aljazeera
10. The New York Times
11. Fortune
12. Time Magazine
13. The Washington Post
14. Moscow Times (English)
15. St Petersburg Times (English)
16. Straits Times
17. New Straits Times
18. The Scotsman
19. The Herald
20. Euromoney
21. Moneyextra
22. Market News International
23. Bloomberg Businessweek
24. International Business Times
25. CNN Money
26. Wall Street Journal
27. Asia News Network
28. allAfrica.com
29. Greek News Sources (English)
30. Kyodo News: Japan (English)
31. Euronews
32. The Australian
33. Sydney Morning Herald
34. Japan Times
35. Reuters
36. Bloomberg
37. David Smith's Economics UK.com
38. Refdesk (links to a whole range of news sources)
39. Newspapers and Magazines on the World Wide Web
40. Yahoo News Search
41. Google News Search
42. ABYZ News Links
43. Guardian World News Guide
44. Onlinenewspapers

B Sources of economic and business data

Using websites to find up-to-date data is of immense value to the economist. The data sources below offer you a range of specialist and non-specialist data information. Universities have free access to MIMAS (site 12) and UK Data Service (site 35), which are huge databases of stat-istics. Site 34 in this set, the Treasury Pocket Data Bank, is a very useful source of key UK and world statistics, and is updated monthly. It downloads as an Excel file. The Economics Network's *Economic data freely available online* (site 1) gives links to various sections in 39 UK and international sites.

1. Economics Network gateway to economic data
2. Biz/ed Gateway to economic and company data
3. National Statistics
4. Data Archive (Essex)
5. Bank of England Statistical Database
6. Economic Resources (About)
7. Nationwide House Prices Site
8. House Web (data on housing market)

9. Economist global house price data
10. Halifax House Price Index
11. House price indices from ONS
12. Manchester Information and Associated Services (MIMAS)
13. Economist economic and financial indicators
14. FT market data
15. Economagic
16. Groningen Growth and Development Centre
17. AEAweb: Resources for economists on the Internet (RFE): data
18. Joseph Rowntree Foundation
19. Intute: Economics resources (archive site)
20. Energy Information Administration
21. OECD Statistics (StatExtracts)
22. CIA world statistics site (World Factbook)
23. UN Millennium Country Profiles
24. World Bank statistics
25. Federal Reserve Bank of St Louis, US Economic Datasets (FRED)
26. Ministry of Economy Trade and Industry (Japan)
27. Financial data from Yahoo
28. DataMarket
29. Index Mundi
30. Oanda Currency Converter
31. World Economic Outlook Database (IMF)
32. Telegraph shares and markets
33. OFFSTATS links to data sets
34. Treasury Pocket Data Bank (source of UK and world economic data)
35. UK Data Service (incorporating ESDS)
36. BBC News, market data
37. NationMaster
38. Statistical Annex of the European Economy
39. Business and Consumer Surveys (all EU countries)
40. Gapminder
41. WebEc economics Data
42. WTO International Trade Statistics database
43. UNCTAD trade, investment and development statistics (UNCTADstat)
44. London Metal Exchange
45. Bank for International Settlements, global nominal and real effective exchange rate indices
46. EconStats from EconomyWatch
47. AMECO database

C Sites for students and teachers of economics

The following websites offer useful ideas and resources to those who are studying or teaching economics. It is worth browsing through some just to see what is on offer. Try out the first four sites, for starters. The *Internet for Economists* (site 8) is a very helpful tutorial for economics students on making best use of the Internet for studying the subject.

1. The Economics Network
2. Biz/ed
3. Ecedweb
4. Studying Economics
5. Economics and Business Education Association
6. Tutor2U
7. Council for Economic Education
8. Internet for Economics (tutorial on using the Web)
9. Econoclass: Resources for economics teachers
10. Teaching resources for economists (RFE)
11. METAL – Mathematics for Economics: enhancing Teaching And Learning
12. Federal Reserve Bank of San Francisco: Economics Education
13. Excel in Economics Teaching
14. WebEc resources
15. Dr. T's EconLinks: Teaching Resources
16. Online Opinion (Economics)
17. The Idea Channel
18. History of Economic Thought
19. Resources For Economists on the Internet (RFE)
20. Classroom Expernomics
21. Bank of England education resources
22. Why Study Economics?
23. Economic Classroom Experiments
24. Veconlab: Charles Holt's classroom experiments
25. Embedding Threshold Concepts
26. MIT Open Courseware in Economics

D Economic models and simulations

Economic modelling is an important aspect of economic analysis. There are a number of sites that offer access to a model for you to use, e.g. Virtual economy (where you can play being Chancellor of the Exchequer). Using such models can be a useful way of finding out how economic theory works within an environment that claims to reflect reality.

1. Virtual economy
2. Virtual factory
3. Virtual Learning Arcade
4. About.com Economics
5. Classic Economic Models
6. Economics Network Handbook, chapter on simulations, games and role-play
7. Classroom Experiments, Internet Experiments, and Internet Simulations
8. Simulations
9. Experimental economics: Wikipedia
10. Software available on the Economics Network site
11. RFE Software
12. Virtual Worlds
13. Veconlab: Charles Holt's classroom experiments
14. EconPort
15. Denise Hazlett's Classroom Experiments in Macroeconomics
16. Games Economists Play
17. Finance and Economics Experimental Laboratory at Exeter (FEELE)

18. Classroom Expernomics
19. The Economics Network's Guide to Classroom Experiments and Games
20. Economic Classroom Experiments (Wikiversity)

E UK Government and UK Organisations' sites

If you want to see what a government department is up to, then look no further than the list below. Government departments' websites are an excellent source of information and data. They are particularly good at offering information on current legislation and policy initiatives.

1. Gateway site (GOV.UK)
2. Department for Communities and Local Government
3. Prime Minister's Office
4. Competition Commission
5. Department for Education
6. Department for International Development
7. Department for Transport
8. Department of Health
9. Department for Work and Pensions
10. Department for Business, Innovation and Skills
11. Environment Agency
12. Department of Energy and Climate Change
13. Low Pay Commission
14. Department for Environment, Food and Rural Affairs (DEFRA)
15. Office of Communications (Ofcom)
16. Office of Gas and Electricity Markets (Ofgem)
17. Official Documents OnLine
18. Office of Fair Trading (OFT)
19. Office of Rail Regulation (ORR)
20. The Takeover Panel
21. Sustainable Development Commission
22. OFWAT
23. National Statistics (NS)
24. National Statistics Datasets and Reference Tables
25. HM Revenue and Customs
26. UK Intellectual Property Office
27. Parliament website
28. Scottish Government
29. Scottish Environment Protection Agency
30. HM Treasury
31. Equality and Human Rights Commission
32. Trades Union Congress (TUC)
33. Confederation of British Industry
34. Adam Smith Institute
35. Chatham House
36. Institute for Fiscal Studies
37. Advertising Standards Authority
38. Businesses and Self-employed
39. Campaign for Better Transport
40. New Economics Foundation

F Sources of monetary and financial data

As the title suggests, here is a list of useful websites for finding information on financial matters. You will see that the list comprises mainly central banks, both within Europe and further afield.

1. Bank of England
2. Bank of England Monetary and Financial Statistics
3. Banque de France (in English)
4. Bundesbank (German central bank) (in English)
5. Central Bank of Ireland
6. European Central Bank
7. Eurostat
8. US Federal Reserve Bank
9. Netherlands Central Bank (in English)
10. Bank of Japan (in English)
11. Reserve Bank of Australia
12. Bank Negara Malaysia (in English)
13. Monetary Authority of Singapore
14. Bank of Canada
15. National Bank of Denmark (in English)
16. Reserve Bank of India
17. Links to central banks from the Bank for International Settlements
18. The London Stock Exchange

G European Union and related sources

For information on European issues, the following is a wide range of useful sites. The sites maintained by the European Union are an excellent source of information and are provided free of charge.

1. Economic and Financial Affairs (EC DG)
2. European Central Bank
3. EU official website
4. Eurostat
5. Employment, Social Affairs and Inclusion (EC DG)
6. Booklets on the EU
7. Enterprise and Industry (EC DG)
8. Competition (EC DG)
9. Agriculture and Rural Development (EC DC)
10. Energy and Transport (EC DG)
11. Environment (EC DG)
12. Regional Policy (EC DG)
13. Taxation and Customs Union (EC DG)
14. Education and Culture (EC DG)
15. European Patent Office
16. European Commission
17. European Parliament
18. European Council
19. Mobility and Transport (EC DG)
20. Trade (EC DG)
21. Internal Market and Services (EC DG)

H International organisations

This section casts its net beyond Europe and lists the web addresses of the main international organisations in the global economy. You will notice that some sites are run by charities, such as Oxfam, while others represent organisations set up to manage international affairs, such as the International Monetary Fund and the United Nations.

1. Food and Agriculture Organisation
2. United National Conference on Trade and Development (UNCTAD)
3. International Labour Organization (ILO)
4. International Monetary Fund (IMF)
5. Organisation for Economic Cooperation and Development (OECD)
6. OPEC
7. World Bank
8. World Health Organization
9. United Nations
10. United Nations Industrial Development Organisation
11. Friends of the Earth
12. Institute of International Finance
13. Oxfam
14. Christian Aid (reports on development issues)
15. European Bank for Reconstruction and Development (EBRD)
16. World Trade Organization (WTO)
17. United Nations Development Programme
18. UNICEF
19. EURODAD – European Network on Debt and Development
20. NAFTA
21. South American free trade areas
22. ASEAN
23. APEC

I Economics search and link sites

If you are having difficulty finding what you want from the list of sites above, the following sites offer links to other sites and are a very useful resource when you are looking for something a little bit more specialist. Once again, it is worth having a look at what these sites have to offer in order to judge their usefulness.

1. Gateway for UK official sites
2. Alta Plana
3. Data Archive Search
4. Inomics (search engine for economics information)
5. RePEc bibliographic database
6. Estima: Links to economics resources sites
7. Intute: Social Sciences (Economics) (archive site)
8. WebEc
9. One World (link to economic development sites)
10. Economic development sites (list) from OneWorld.net
11. DMOZ Open Directory: Economics
12. Web links for economists from the Economics Network
13. Yahoo's links to economic data
14. OFFSTATS links to data sets
15. Excite Economics links
16. Internet Resources for Economists
17. National Association of Business Economics links
18. Resources for Economists on the Internet
19. UK university economics departments
20. Economics education links
21. Development Gateway Foundation
22. Find the Best

J Internet search engines

The following search engines have been found to be useful.

1. Google
2. Bing
3. Whoosh UK
4. Excite
5. Infoseek
6. Search.com
7. MSN
8. Economics Search Engine from RFE
9. Yahoo
10. Ask
11. Kartoo
12. Blinkx (for videos and audio podcasts)

Key ideas

1. **The principal–agent problem.** Where people (principals), as a result of a lack of knowledge (asymmetric information), cannot ensure that their best interests are served by their agents. Agents may take advantage of this situation to the disadvantage of the principals. **(See page 9.)**

2. **The behaviour and performance of firms is affected by the business environment.** The business environment includes social/cultural (S), technological (T), economic (E), ethical (E), political (P), legal (L) and environmental (E) factors. The mnemonic STEEPLE can be used to remember these. **(See page 11.)**

3. **Opportunity cost.** The Opportunity cost of something is what you give up to get it/do it. In other words, it is cost measured in terms of the best alternative forgone. **(See page 20.)**

4. **Rational decision making involves weighing up the marginal benefit and marginal cost of any activity.** If the marginal benefit exceeds the marginal cost, it is rational to do the activity (or to do more of it). If the marginal cost exceeds the marginal benefit, it is rational not to do it (or to do less of it). **(See page 21.)**

5. **People respond to incentives, such as changes in prices or wages.** It is important, therefore, that incentives are appropriate and have the desired effect. **(See page 25.)**

6. **Changes in demand or supply cause markets to adjust.** Whenever such changes occur, the resulting 'disequilibrium' will bring an automatic change in prices, thereby restoring equilibrium (i.e. a balance of demand and supply). **(See page 26.)**

7. **People's actions are influenced by their expectations.** People respond not just to what is happening now (such as a change in price), but to what they anticipate will happen in the future. **(See page 28.)**

8. **Partial analysis: other things remaining equal (*ceteris paribus*).** In economics it is common to look at just one determinant of a variable such as demand or supply and see what happens when the determinant changes. For example, if price is taken as the determinant of demand, we can see what happens to quantity demanded as price changes. In the meantime we have to assume that other determinants remain unchanged. This is known as the 'other things being equal' assumption (or, using the Latin, the 'ceteris paribus' assumption). Once we have seen how our chosen determinant affects our variable, we can then see what happens when another determinant changes, and then another, and so on. **(See page 28.)**

9. **Equilibrium is the point where conflicting interests are balanced.** Only at this point is the amount that demanders are willing to purchase the same as the amount that suppliers are willing to supply. It is a point which will be automatically reached in a free market through the operation of the price mechanism. **(See page 33.)**

10. **Elasticity.** The responsiveness of one variable (e.g. demand) to a change in another (e.g. price). This concept is fundamental to understanding how markets work. The more elastic variables are, the more responsive is the market to changing circumstances. **(See page 37.)**

11. **The principle of diminishing marginal utility.** As you consume more of a product, and thus become more satisfied, so your desire for additional units of it will decline. **(See page 52.)**

12. **Adverse selection.** Where information is imperfect, high-risk/poor-quality groups will be attracted to profitable market opportunities to the disadvantage of the average buyer (or seller). **(See page 56.)**

13. **Moral hazard.** Following a deal, if there are information asymmetries (see page 9), it is likely that one party will engage in problematic (immoral and/or hazardous) behaviour to the detriment of the other. In other words, lack of information by one party to the deal may result in the deal not being honoured by the other party. **(See page 57.)**

14. **The law of diminishing marginal returns.** When increasing amounts of a variable input are used with a given amount of a fixed input, there will come a point when each extra unit of the variable input will produce less extra output than the previous unit. **(See page 75.)**

15. **Sunk costs and the 'bygones' principle** states that sunk (fixed) costs should be ignored when deciding whether to produce or sell more or less of a product. Only variable costs should be taken into account. **(See page 77.)**

16. **Transactions costs.** The costs associated with exchanging products. For buyers it is the costs over and above the price of the product. For sellers it is the costs over

and above the costs of production. Transactions costs include search costs, contract costs, monitoring and enforcement costs, and transport and handling costs. **(See page 86.)**

17. **Market power benefits the powerful at the expense of others.** When firms have market power over prices, they can use this to raise prices and profits above the perfectly competitive level. Other things being equal, the firm will gain at the expense of the consumer. Similarly, if consumers or workers have market power they can use this to their own benefit. **(See page 103.)**

18. **People often think and behave strategically.** How you think others will respond to your actions is likely to influence your own behaviour. Firms, for example, when considering a price or product change will often take into account the likely reactions of their rivals. **(See page 112.)**

19. **Nash equilibrium.** The position resulting from everyone making their optimal decision based on their assumptions about their rivals' decisions. Such an outcome, however, is unlikely to maximise the collective benefit. Nevertheless, without collusion in this 'game', whether open or tacit, there is no incentive to move from this position. **(See page 118.)**

20. **Competitive advantage.** The various factors that enable a firm to compete more effectively with its rivals. These can be supply-side factors, such as superior technology, better organisation, or greater power or efficiency in sourcing its supplies – resulting in lower costs; or they could be demand-side ones, such as producing a superior or better-value product in the eyes of consumers, or being more conveniently located – resulting in higher and/or less elastic demand. **(See page 134.)**

21. **Core competencies.** The areas of specialised expertise within a business that underpin its competitive advantage over its rivals. These competencies could be in production technologies or organisation, in relationships with suppliers, in the nature and specifications of the product, or in the firm's ability to innovate and develop its products and brand image. **(See page 140.)**

22. **Efficient capital markets.** Capital markets are efficient when the prices of shares accurately reflect information about companies' current and expected future performance. **(See page 154.)**

23. **Social efficiency.** This is achieved where no further net social gain can be made by producing more or less of a good. This will occur where marginal social benefit equals marginal social cost. **(See page 204.)**

24. **Externalities are spillover costs or benefits.** Where these exist, even an otherwise perfect market will fail to achieve social efficiency. **(See page 204.)**

25. **The free-rider problem.** People are often unwilling to pay for things if they can make use of things other people have bought. This problem can lead to people not purchasing things which it would be to their benefit and that of other members of society to have. **(See page 207.)**

26. **Economies suffer from inherent instability.** As a result, economic growth and other macroeconomic indicators tend to fluctuate. **(See page 240.)**

27. **The distinction between real and nominal values.** Nominal figures are those using current prices, interest rates, etc. Real figures are figures corrected for inflation. **(See page 253.)**

28. **The law of comparative advantage.** Provided opportunity costs of various goods differ in two countries, both of them can gain from mutual trade if they specialise in producing (and exporting) those goods that have relatively low opportunity costs compared with the other country. **(See page 292.)**

29. **The competitive advantage of nations.** The ability of countries to compete in the market for exports and with potential importers to their country. The competitiveness of any one industry depends on the availability and quality of resources, demand conditions at home in that industry, the strategies and rivalry of firms within the industry and the quality of supporting industries and infrastructure. It also depends on government policies, and there is also an element of chance. **(See page 295.)**

Glossary

Absolute advantage   A country has an absolute advantage over another in the production of a good if it can produce it with fewer resources than the other country.

Accelerator   The level of investment depends on the rate of increase in consumer demand, and as a result is subject to substantial fluctuations. Increases in investment via the accelerator can compound the multiplier effect.

Adjustable peg   A system whereby exchange rates are fixed for a period of time, but may be devalued (or revalued) if a deficit (or surplus) becomes substantial.

Adverse selection   Where information is imperfect, high-risk/poor-quality groups will be attracted to profitable market opportunities to the disadvantage of the average buyer (or seller).

Aggregate demand for labour curve   A curve showing the total demand for labour in the economy at different average real wage rates.

Aggregate supply of labour curve   A curve showing the total number of people willing and able to work at different average real wage rates.

Appreciation   A rise in the free-market exchange rate of the domestic currency with foreign currencies.

Asymmetric information   A situation in which one party in an economic relationship knows more than another.

Asymmetric shocks   Shocks (such as an oil price increase or a recession in another part of the world) that have different-sized effects on different industries, regions or countries.

Average cost or mark-up pricing   Where firms set the price by adding a profit mark-up to average costs.

Average fixed cost (*AFC*)   Total fixed cost per unit of output: $AFC = TFC/Q$.

Average revenue   Total revenue per unit of output. When all output is sold at the same price, average revenue will be the same as price: $AR = TR/Q = P$.

Average (total) cost (*AC*)   Total cost (fixed plus variable) per unit of output: $AC = TC/Q = AFC + AVC$.

Average variable cost (*AVC*)   Total variable cost per unit of output: $AVC = TVC/Q$.

Backward integration   Where a firm expands backwards down the supply chain to earlier stages of production.

Balance of payments account   A record of the country's transactions with the rest of the world. It shows the country's payments to or deposits in other countries (debits)
and its receipts (credits) from other countries. It also shows the balance between these debits and credits under various headings.

Balance of payments on current account   The balance on trade in goods and services plus net incomes and current transfers, i.e. the sum of the credits on the current account minus the sum of the debits.

Balance of trade   Exports of goods and services minus imports of goods and services.

Bank (or deposits) multiplier   The number of times greater the expansion of bank deposits is than the additional liquidity in banks that caused it: I/L (the inverse of the liquidity ratio).

Barometric forecasting   A technique used to predict future economic trends based upon analysing patterns of time-series data.

Behavioural theories of the firm   Theories that attempt to predict the actions of firms by studying the behaviour of various groups or people within the firm and their interactions under conditions of potentially conflicting interests.

Bounded rationality   When the ability to make rational decisions is limited by lack of information or the time necessary to obtain such information.

Budget deficit   The excess of central government's spending over its tax receipts.

Budget surplus   The excess of central government's tax receipts over its spending.

Buffer stocks   Stocks of a product used to stabilise its price. In years of abundance, the stocks are built up. In years of low supply, stocks are released onto the market.

Business cycle or trade cycle   The periodic fluctuations of national output around its long-term trend.

Business ethics   The values and principles that shape business behaviour.

Capital account of the balance of payments   The record of transfers of capital to and from abroad.

Cartel   A formal collusive agreement.

Cash in circulation   The measure of narrow money in the UK. This is all cash outside the Bank of England: in banks, in people's purses and wallets, in businesses' safes and tills, in government departments, etc.

Change in demand   The term used for a shift in the demand curve. It occurs when a determinant of demand *other* than price changes.

Change in supply The term used for a shift in the supply curve. It occurs when a determinant other than price changes.

Change in the quantity demanded The term used for a movement along the demand curve to a new point. It occurs when there is a change in price.

Change in the quantity supplied The term used for a movement along the supply curve to a new point. It occurs when there is a change in price.

Claimant unemployment Those in receipt of unemployment-related benefits.

Collusive oligopoly When oligopolists agree (formally or informally) to limit competition between themselves. They may set output quotas, fix prices, limit product promotion or development, or agree not to 'poach' each other's markets.

Collusive tendering Where two or more firms secretly agree on the prices they will tender for a contract. These prices will be above those which would be put in under a genuinely competitive tendering process.

Command-and-control (CAC) systems The use of laws or regulations backed up by inspections and penalties (such as fines) for non-compliance.

Comparative advantage A country has a comparative advantage over another in the production of a good if it can produce it at a lower opportunity cost, i.e. if it has to forgo less of other goods in order to produce it.

Competition for corporate control The competition for the control of companies through takeovers.

Competitive advantage The various factors, such as lower costs or a better product, that give a firm an advantage over its rivals.

Competitive advantage of nations The various factors that enable the industries in a particular country to compete more effectively with those in other countries.

Complementary goods A pair of goods consumed together. As the price of one goes up, the demand for both goods will fall.

Complementors Firms producing complementary goods (products that are used together).

Conglomerate merger Where two firms in different industries merge.

Conglomerate multinational A multinational that produces different products in different countries.

Consortium Where two or more firms work together on a specific project and create a separate company to run the project.

Consumer durable A consumer good that lasts a period of time, during which the consumer can continue gaining utility from it.

Consumer surplus The difference between how much a consumer is willing to pay for a good and how much they actually pay for it.

Consumption The act of using goods and services to satisfy wants. This will normally involve purchasing the goods and services.

Consumption of domestically produced goods and services (C_d) The direct flow of money payments from households to firms.

Convergence of economies When countries achieve similar levels of growth, inflation, budget deficits as a percentage of GDP, balance of payments, etc.

Core competencies The key skills of a business that underpin its competitive advantage.

Corporate social responsibility Where a business takes into account the interests and concerns of a community rather than just its shareholders.

Cost-push inflation Inflation caused by persistent rises in costs of production (independently of demand).

Credible threat (or promise) One that is believable to rivals because it is in the threatener's interests to carry it out.

Cross-price elasticity of demand The responsiveness of demand for one good to a change in the price of another: the proportionate change in demand for one good divided by the proportionate change in price of the other.

Crowding out Where increased public expenditure diverts money or resources away from the private sector.

Current account balance The balance on trade in goods and services plus net incomes and current transfers, i.e. the sum of the credits on the current account minus the sum of the debits.

Current account of the balance of payments The record of a country's imports and exports of goods and services, plus incomes and transfers of money to and from abroad.

Decision tree (or game tree) A diagram showing the sequence of possible decisions by competitor firms and the outcome of each combination of decisions.

Deindustrialisation The decline in the contribution to production of the manufacturing sector of the economy.

Demand curve A graph showing the relationship between the price of a good and the quantity of the good demanded over a given time period. Price is measured on the vertical axis; quantity demanded is measured on the horizontal axis. A demand curve can be for an individual consumer or a group of consumers, or more usually for the whole market.

Demand-deficient or cyclical unemployment Disequilibrium unemployment caused by a fall in aggregate demand with no corresponding fall in the real wage rate.

Demand-pull inflation Inflation caused by persistent rises in aggregate demand.

Demand schedule for an individual A table showing the different quantities of a good that a person is willing and able to buy at various prices over a given period of time.

Demand-side or demand management policy Policy to affect aggregate demand (i.e. fiscal or monetary policy).

Depreciation A fall in the free-market exchange rate of the domestic currency with foreign currencies.

Derived demand The demand for a factor of production depends on the demand for the good that uses it.

Devaluation Where the government or central bank re-pegs the exchange rate at a lower level.

Discretionary fiscal policy Deliberate changes in tax rates or the level of government expenditure in order to influence the level of aggregate demand.

Diseconomies of scale Where costs per unit of output increase as the scale of production increases.

Disequilibrium unemployment Unemployment resulting from real wages in the economy being above the equilibrium level.

Diversification A business growth strategy in which a business expands into new markets outside of its current interests.

Dominant strategy game Where the firm will choose the same strategy no matter what assumption it makes about its rivals' behaviour.

Downsizing Where a business reorganises and reduces its size, especially in respect to levels of employment, in order to cut costs.

Dumping Where exports are sold at prices below marginal cost – often as a result of government subsidy.

Economic and monetary union (EMU) Where countries adopt a single currency and a single monetary policy. It might also involve other common policies, such as fiscal and supply-side policies.

Economic growth The rise in GDP. The rate of economic growth is the percentage increase in GDP over a 12-month period.

Economies of scale When increasing the scale of production leads to a lower cost per unit of output.

Economies of scope When increasing the range of products produced by a firm reduces the cost of producing each one.

Efficiency wage hypothesis A hypothesis that states that a worker's productivity is linked to the wage he or she receives.

Efficiency wage rate The profit-maximising wage rate for the firm after taking into account the effects of wage rates on worker motivation, turnover and recruitment.

Efficient (capital) market hypothesis The hypothesis that new information about a company's current or future performance will be quickly and accurately reflected in its share price.

Elastic demand If demand is (price) elastic, then any change in price will cause the quantity demanded to change proportionately more. (Ignoring the negative sign) it will have a value greater than 1.

EMU (see Economic and monetary union).

Environmental scanning Where a business surveys social and political trends in order to take account of changes in its decision-making process.

Equilibrium A position of balance. A position from which there is no inherent tendency to move away.

Equilibrium GDP The level of GDP where injections equal withdrawals and where, therefore, there is no tendency for GDP to rise or fall.

Equilibrium price The price where the quantity demanded equals the quantity supplied; the price where there is no shortage or surplus.

Equilibrium ('natural') unemployment The difference between those who would like employment at the current wage rate and those willing and able to take a job.

ERM (the exchange rate mechanism) A semi-fixed system whereby participating EU countries allowed fluctuations against each other's currencies only within agreed bands. Collectively they floated freely against all other currencies.

Exchange rate The rate at which one national currency exchanges for another. The rate is expressed as the amount of one currency that is necessary to purchase *one unit* of another currency (e.g. €1.20 = £1).

Exchange rate index A weighted average exchange rate expressed as an index, where the value of the index is 100 in a given base year. The weights of the different currencies in the index add up to 1.

Explicit costs The payments to outside suppliers of inputs.

External benefits Benefits from production (or consumption) experienced by people other than the producer (or consumer).

External costs Costs of production (or consumption) borne by people other than the producer (or consumer).

External diseconomies of scale Where a firm's costs per unit of output increase as the size of the whole industry increases.

External economies of scale Where a firm's costs per unit of output decrease as the size of the whole industry grows.

External expansion Where business growth is achieved by merging with or taking over businesses within a market or industry.

Externalities Costs or benefits of production or consumption experienced by society but not by the producers or consumers themselves. Sometimes referred to as 'spillover' or 'third-party' costs or benefits.

Financial account of the balance of payments The record of the flows of money into and out of the country for the purpose of investment or as deposits in bank and other financial institutions.

Financial flexibility Where employers can vary their wage costs by changing the composition of their workforce or the terms on which workers are employed.

Fine-tuning The use of demand management policy (fiscal or monetary) to smooth out cyclical fluctuations in the economy.

First-mover advantage When a firm gains from being the first to take action.

Fiscal policy Policy to affect aggregate demand by altering government expenditure and/or taxation.

Fiscal stance How expansionary or contractionary fiscal policy is.

Fixed costs Total costs that do not vary with the amount of output produced.

Fixed input An input that cannot be increased in supply within a given time period.

Flat organisation One in which technology enables senior managers to communicate directly with those lower in the organisational structure. Middle managers are bypassed.

Flexible firm A firm that has the flexibility to respond to changing market conditions by changing the composition of its workforce.

Floating exchange rate When the government does not intervene in the foreign exchange markets, but simply allows the exchange rate to be freely determined by demand and supply.

Forward integration Where a firm expands forward up the supply chain towards the sale of the finished product.

Franchise A formal agreement whereby a company uses another company to produce or sell some or all of its product.

Free market One in which there is an absence of government intervention. Individual producers and consumers are free to make their own economic decisions.

Free-rider problem When it is not possible to exclude other people from consuming a good that someone has bought.

Frictional (search) unemployment Unemployment that occurs as a result of imperfect information in the labour market. It often takes time for workers to find jobs (even though there are vacancies) and in the meantime they are unemployed.

Functional flexibility Where employers can switch workers from job to job as requirements change.

Game theory (or the theory of games) The study of alternative strategies that oligopolists may choose to adopt, depending on their assumptions about their rivals' behaviour.

General government debt The accumulated central and local government deficits (less surpluses) over the years, i.e. the total amount owed by central and local government, both to domestic and overseas creditors.

Globalisation The process whereby the economies of the world are becoming increasingly integrated.

Goodhart's Law Controlling a symptom or indicator of a problem is unlikely to cure the problem; it will simply mean that what is being controlled now becomes a poor indicator of the problem.

Goods in joint supply These are two goods where the production of more of one leads to the production of more of the other.

Gross domestic product (GDP) The value of output produced within the country over a 12-month period.

Growth maximisation An alternative theory which assumes that managers seek to maximise the growth in sales revenue (or the capital value of the firm) over time.

Growth vector matrix A means by which a business might assess its product/market strategy.

Harmonisation (international) of economic policies Where countries attempt to co-ordinate their macroeconomic policies so as to achieve common goals.

Heuristics People's use of strategies that draw on simple lessons from past experience when they are faced with similar, although not identical, choices.

Historic costs The original amount the firm paid for inputs it now owns.

H-form or holding company A business organisation in which the parent company holds interests in a number of other companies or subsidiaries.

Horizontally integrated multinational A multinational that produces the same product in many different countries.

Horizontal merger Where two firms in the same industry at the same stage of the production process merge.

Imperfect competition The collective name for monopolistic competition and oligopoly.

Implicit costs Costs which do not involve a direct payment of money to a third party, but which nevertheless involve a sacrifice of some alternative.

Import substitution The replacement of imports by domestically produced goods or services.

Income effect The effect of a change in price on quantity demanded arising from the consumer becoming better or worse off as a result of the price change.

Income elasticity of demand The responsiveness of demand to a change in consumer incomes: the proportionate change in demand divided by the proportionate change in income.

Independent risks Where two risky events are unconnected. The occurrence of one will not affect the likelihood of the occurrence of the other.

Indivisibilities The impossibility of dividing an input into smaller units.

Industrial sector A grouping of industries producing similar products or services.

Industry A group of firms producing a particular product or service.

Industry's infrastructure The network of supply agents, communications, skills, training facilities, distribution channels, specialised financial services, etc. that support a particular industry.

Inelastic demand If demand is (price) inelastic, then any change will cause the quantity demanded to change by a proportionately smaller amount. (Ignoring the negative sign) it will have a value less than 1.

Infant industry An industry which has a potential comparative advantage, but which is as yet too underdeveloped to be able to realise this potential.

Inferior goods Goods whose demand falls as people's incomes rise. Such goods have a negative income elasticity of demand.

Information asymmetry A situation in which one party in an economic relationship knows more than another.

Injections (J) Expenditure on the production of domestic firms coming from outside the inner flow of the circular flow of income. Injections equal investment (*I*) plus government expenditure (*G*) plus expenditure on exports (*X*).

Interdependence (under oligopoly) One of the two key features of oligopoly. Each firm will be affected by its rivals' decisions. Likewise its decisions will affect its rivals. Firms recognise this interdependence. This recognition will affect their decisions.

Internal expansion Where a business adds to its productive capacity by adding to existing or by building new plant.

International harmonisation of economic policies Where countries attempt to co-ordinate their macroeconomic policies so as to achieve common goals.

Inter-temporal pricing This occurs where different groups have different price elasticities of demand for a product at different points in time.

Joint-stock company A company where ownership is distributed between shareholders.

Joint venture Where two or more firms set up and jointly own a new independent firm.

Just-in-time methods Where a firm purchases supplies and produces both components and finished products as they are required. This minimises stock holding and its associated costs.

Kinked demand theory The theory that oligopolists face a demand curve that is kinked at the current price: demand being significantly more elastic above the current price than below. The effect of this is to create a situation of price stability.

Labour force The number employed plus the number unemployed.

Law of comparative advantage Trade can benefit all countries if they specialise in the goods in which they have a comparative advantage.

Law of demand The quantity of a good demanded per period of time will fall as the price rises and rise as the price falls, other things being equal (*ceteris paribus*).

Law of diminishing (marginal) returns When one or more inputs are held fixed, there will come a point beyond which the extra output from additional units of the variable input will diminish.

Law of large numbers The larger the number of events of a particular type, the more predictable will be their average outcome.

Leading indicators Indicators that help predict future trends in the economy.

Lender of last resort The role of the central bank as the guarantor of sufficient liquidity in the monetary system.

Licensing Where the owner of a patented product allows another firm to produce it for a fee.

Limited liability Where the liability of the owners for the debts of a company is limited to the amount they have invested in it.

Liquidity ratio The ratio of liquid assets (cash and assets that can be readily converted to cash) to total deposits.

Liquidity trap When interest rates are at their floor and thus any further increases in money supply will not be spent but merely be held in bank accounts as people wait for the economy to recover and/or interest rates to rise.

Lock-outs Union members are temporarily laid off until they are prepared to agree to the firm's conditions.

Logistics The business of managing and handling inputs to and outputs from a firm.

Long run The period of time long enough for all inputs to be varied.

Long run under perfect competition The period of time which is long enough for new firms to enter the industry.

Long-run average cost curve A curve that shows how average cost varies with output on the assumption that all factors are variable.

Loss-leader A product whose price is cut by a business in order to attract custom.

M0 Cash plus banks' balances with the Bank of England. Note that this definition of narrow money is no longer used (see cash in circulation for the current measure of narrow money).

M3 (in eurozone and elsewhere) Cash outside the banks, bank deposits and various other assets that can be relatively easily turned into cash without loss.

M4 (in UK) Cash outside the banks plus all bank and building society deposits (including cash).

M-form business organisation One in which the business is organised into separate departments, such that responsibility for the day-to-day management of the enterprise is separated from the formulation of the business's strategic plan.

Marginal benefits The additional benefits of doing a little bit more (or *1 unit* more if a unit can be measured) of an activity.

Marginal cost (*MC*) The cost of producing one more unit of output: $MC = \Delta TC/\Delta Q$.

Marginal costs The additional cost of doing a little bit more (or *1 unit* more if a unit can be measured) of an activity.

Marginal revenue (MR) The extra revenue gained by selling one or more unit per time period: $MR = \Delta TR/\Delta Q$.

Marginal revenue product of labour The extra revenue a firm earns from employing one more unit of labour.

Marginal social benefit (*MSB*) The additional benefit gained by society of producing or consuming one more unit of a good.

Marginal social cost (*MSC*) The additional cost incurred by society of producing or consuming one more unit of a good.

Marginal utility (*MU*) The extra satisfaction gained from consuming one extra unit of a good within a given time period.

Market The interaction between buyers and sellers.

Market clearing A market clears when supply matches demand, leaving no shortage or surplus.

Market demand schedule A table showing the different total quantities of a good that consumers are willing and able to buy at various prices over a given period of time.

Market experiments Information gathered about consumers under artificial or simulated conditions. A method used widely in assessing the effects of advertising on consumers.

Market niche A part of a market (or new market) that has not been filled by an existing brand or business.

Market surveys Information gathered about consumers, usually via a questionnaire, that attempts to enhance the business's understanding of consumer behaviour.

Marketing mix The mix of product, price, place (distribution) and promotion that will determine a business's marketing strategy.

Maximum price A price ceiling set by the government or some other agency. The price is not allowed to rise above this level (although it is allowed to fall below it).

Merger The outcome of a mutual agreement made by two firms to combine their business activities.

Merit goods Goods which the government feels that people will underconsume and which therefore ought to be subsidised or provided free.

Minimum price A price floor set by the government or some other agency. The price is not allowed to fall below this level (although it is allowed to rise above it).

Mobility of labour The ease with which labour can either shift between jobs (occupational mobility) or move to other parts of the country in search of work (geographical mobility).

Monetary policy Policy to affect aggregate demand by central bank action to alter interest rates or money supply.

Monopolistic competition A market structure where, like perfect competition, there are many firms and freedom of entry into the industry, but where each firm produces a differentiated product and thus has some control over its price.

Monopoly A market structure where there is only one firm in the industry.

Monopsony A market with a single buyer or employer.

Moral hazard Following a deal, if there are information asymmetries, it is likely that one party will engage in problematic (immoral and/or hazardous) behaviour to the detriment of the other. In other words, lack of information by one party to the deal may result in the deal not being honoured by the other party.

Multinational corporations Businesses that either own or control foreign subsidiaries in more than one country.

Multiplier The number of times a rise in GDP (ΔGDP) is bigger than the initial rise in aggregate expenditure (ΔE) that caused it. Using the letter k to stand for the multiplier, the multiplier is defined as $k = \Delta GDP/\Delta E$.

Multiplier effect An initial increase in aggregate demand of £xm leads to an eventual rise in GDP that is greater than £xm.

Multiplier formula The formula for the multiplier is $k = 1/(1 - mpc_d)$.

Nash equilibrium The position resulting from everyone making their optimal decision based on their assump-

tions about their rivals' decisions. Without collusion, there is no incentive to move from this position.

Nationalised industries State-owned industries that produce goods or services that are sold in the market.

Natural monopoly A situation where long-run average costs would be lower if an industry were under monopoly than if it were shared between two or more competitors.

Net errors and omissions A statistical adjustment to ensure that the two sides of the balance of payments account balance. It is necessary because of errors in compiling the statistics.

Network An informal arrangement between businesses to work together towards some common goal.

Network economies The benefits to consumers of having a network of other people using the same product or service.

Non-collusive oligopoly When oligopolists have no agreement between themselves – formal, informal or tacit.

Non-excludability Where it is not possible to provide a good or service to one person without it thereby being available for others to enjoy.

Non-price competition Competition in terms of product promotion (advertising, packaging, etc.) or product development.

Non-rivalry Where the consumption of a good or service by one person will not prevent others from enjoying it.

Normal goods Goods whose demand increases as consumer incomes increase. They have a positive income elasticity of demand. Luxury goods will have a higher income elasticity of demand than more basic goods.

Normal profit The opportunity cost of being in business. It consists of the interest that could be earned on a riskless asset, plus a return for risk taking in this particular industry. It is counted as a cost of production.

Number unemployed (economist's definition) Those of working age, who are without work, but who are available for work at current wage rates.

Numerical flexibility Where employers can change the size of their workforce as their labour requirements change.

Observations of market behaviour Information gathered about consumers from the day-to-day activities of the business within the market.

Oligopoly A market structure where there are few enough firms to enable barriers to be erected against the entry of new firms.

Oligopsony A market with just a few buyers or employers.

Open-market operations The sale (or purchase) by the authorities of government securities in the open market in order to reduce (or increase) money supply.

Opportunity cost The cost of any activity measured in terms of the best alternative forgone.

Organisational slack When managers allow spare capacity to exist, thereby enabling them to respond more easily to changed circumstances.

Overheads   Costs arising from the general running of an organisation, and only indirectly related to the level of output.

Peak-load pricing   The practice of charging higher prices at times when demand is highest because the demand of many consumers (e.g. commuters) is less elastic and the constraints on capacity lead to higher marginal costs.

Perfectly competitive market   A market in which all producers and consumers of the product are price takers.

PEST (or STEEPLE) analysis   Where the political, economic, social and technological factors shaping a business environment are assessed by a business so as to devise future business strategy. STEEPLE analysis would also take into account ethical, legal and environmental factors.

Picketing   Where people on strike gather at the entrance to the firm and attempt to dissuade workers or delivery vehicles from entering.

Plant economies of scale   Economies of scale that arise because of the large size of the factory.

Preferential trading arrangements   A trading arrangement whereby trade between the signatories is freer than trade with the rest of the world.

Price-cap regulation   Where the regulator puts a ceiling on the amount by which a firm can raise its price.

Price discrimination   Where a firm sells the same product at different prices in different markets for reasons unrelated to costs.

Price elasticity of demand   A measure of the responsiveness of quantity demanded to a change in price.

Price elasticity of supply   The responsiveness of quantity supplied to a change in price: the proportionate change in quantity supplied divided by the proportionate change in price.

Price leadership   When firms (the followers) choose the same price as that set by one of the firms in the industry (the leader). The leader will normally be the largest firm.

Price mechanism   The system in a market economy whereby changes in price, in response to changes in demand and supply, have the effect of making demand equal to supply.

Price taker   A person or firm with no power to be able to influence the market price.

Primary labour market   The market for permanent full-time core workers.

Primary market in capital   Where shares are sold by the issuer of the shares (i.e. the firm) and where, therefore, finance is channelled directly from the purchasers (i.e. the shareholders) to the firm.

Primary production   The production and extraction of natural resources, plus agriculture.

Principal–agent problem   One where people (principals), as a result of lack of knowledge, cannot ensure that their best interests are served by their agents.

Prisoners' dilemma   Where two or more firms (or people), by attempting independently to choose the best strategy for whatever the other(s) are likely to do, end up in a worse position than if they had co-operated in the first place.

Privatisation   Selling nationalised industries to the private sector. This may be through the public issue of shares, by a management buyout or by selling it to a private company.

Product differentiation   Where a firm's product is in some way distinct from its rivals' products. In the context of growth strategies, this is where a business upgrades existing products or services so as to make them different from those of rival firms.

Production   The transformation of inputs into outputs by firms in order to earn profit (or meet some other objective).

Productivity deal   Where, in return for a wage increase, a union agrees to changes in working practices that will increase output per worker.

Profit-maximising rule   Profit is maximised where marginal revenue equals marginal cost.

Profit satisficing   Where decision makers in a firm aim for a target level of profit rather than the absolute maximum level.

Public good   A good or service which has the features of non-rivalry and non-excludability and as a result would not be provided by the free market.

Public-sector net cash requirement (PSNCR)   The (annual) deficit of the public sector (central government, local government and public corporations), and thus the amount that the public sector must borrow.

Public-sector net debt   The combined debt of the whole public sector: central government, local government, public corporations and any other public bodies.

Pure fiscal policy   Fiscal policy which does not involve any change in money supply.

Quantitative easing   A deliberate attempt by the central bank to increase the money supply by buying large quantities of securities through open-market operations.

Quantity demanded   The amount of a good that a consumer is willing and able to buy at a given price over a given period of time.

Quota (set by a cartel)   The output that a given member of a cartel is allowed to produce (production quota) or sell (sales quota).

Random walk   Where fluctuations in the value of a share away from its 'correct' value are random. When charted over time, these share price movements would appear like a 'random walk' – like the path of someone staggering along drunk!

Rate of economic growth   The percentage increase in output over a 12-month period.

Rate of inflation   The percentage increase in prices over a 12-month period.

Rational choices   Choices that involve weighing up the benefit of any activity against its opportunity cost.

Rational consumer behaviour   When consumers weigh up the marginal utility they expect to gain from a product they are considering purchasing against the product's price (i.e. the marginal cost to them). By buying more of a product whose marginal utility exceeds the price and buying less of a product whose price exceeds marginal utility, the consumer will maximise consumer surplus.

Rationalisation The reorganising of production (often after a merger) so as to cut out waste and duplication and generally to reduce costs.

Real growth values Values of the rate of growth in GDP or any other variable after taking inflation into account. The real value of the growth in a variable equals its growth in money (or 'nominal') value minus the rate of inflation.

Real-wage unemployment Disequilibrium unemployment caused by real wages being driven up above the market-clearing level.

Recession A period of falling GDP, i.e. of negative economic growth. Officially, a recession is where this occurs for two quarters or more.

Regional unemployment Structural unemployment occurring in specific regions of the country.

Regulatory capture Where the regulator is persuaded to operate in the industry's interests rather than those of the consumer.

Repeated or extensive-form games Where firms decide in turn in the light of what their rivals do. Such games thus involve two or more moves.

Replacement costs What the firm would have to pay to replace inputs it currently owns.

Resale price maintenance Where the manufacturer of a product (legally) insists that the product should be sold at a specified retail price.

Revaluation Where the government or central bank repegs the exchange rate at a higher level.

Risk This is when an outcome may or may not occur, but where the probability of its occurring is known.

Sale and repurchase agreement (repo) An agreement between two financial institutions whereby one in effect borrows from another by selling some of its assets, agreeing to buy them back (repurchase them) at a fixed price and on a fixed date.

Sales revenue maximisation An alternative theory of the firm which assumes that managers aim to maximise the firm's short-run total revenue.

Scarcity The excess of human wants over what can actually be produced to fulfil these wants.

Seasonal unemployment Unemployment associated with industries or regions where the demand for labour is lower at certain times of the year.

Secondary labour market The market for peripheral workers, usually employed on a temporary or part-time basis, or a less secure 'permanent' basis.

Secondary market in capital Where shareholders sell shares to others. This is thus a market in 'second-hand' shares.

Secondary production The production from manufacturing and construction sectors of the economy.

Self-fulfilling speculation The actions of speculators tend to cause the very effect that they had anticipated.

Share (or stock) options The right to buy shares in the future at a fixed price set today. When granted to senior executives as a reward they do not involve any outlay by the company. They act as an incentive, however, since the better the company performs, the more the market value of its shares is likely to rise above the option price and the more the executive stands to gain by exercising the option to buy shares at the fixed price and then selling them at the market price.

Short run The period of time over which at least one input is fixed.

Short-run shut-down point This is where the AR curve is tangential to the AVC curve. The firm can only just cover its variable costs. Any fall in revenue below this level will cause a profit-maximising firm to shut down immediately.

Short run under perfect competition The period during which there is too little time for new firms to enter the industry.

Short-termism Where firms and investors take decisions based on the likely short-term performance of a company, rather than on its long-term prospects. Firms may thus sacrifice long-term profits and growth for the sake of quick return.

Single-move or single-period or normal-form game Where each firm makes just one decision without at the time knowing the decision of the other.

Social benefit Private benefit plus externalities in consumption.

Social cost Private cost plus externalities in production.

Social efficiency Production and consumption at the point where $MSB = MSC$.

Sovereign risk (for business) The risk that a foreign country's government or central bank will make its policies less favourable. Such policies could involve changes in interest rates or tax regimes, the imposition of foreign exchange controls, or even defaulting on loans or the appropriation of a business's assets.

Specialisation and division of labour Where production is broken down into a number of simpler, more specialised tasks, thus allowing workers to acquire a high degree of efficiency.

Speculation This is where people make buying or selling decisions based on their anticipations of future prices.

Spreading risks (for an insurance company) The more policies an insurance company issues and the more independent the risks of claims from these policies are, the more predictable will be the number of claims.

Stakeholder An individual affected by the operations of a business.

Stakeholders (in a company) People who are affected by a company's activities and/or performance (customers, employees, owners, creditors, people living in the neighbourhood, etc.). They may or may not be in a position to take decisions, or influence decision taking, in the firm.

Standard Industrial Classification (SIC) The name given to the formal classification of firms into industries used by the government in order to collect data on business and industry trends.

Standardised unemployment rate The measure of the unemployment rate used by the ILO and OECD. The unemployed are defined as people of working age who are without work, available for work and actively seeking employment.

STEEPLE analysis Where the social, technological, economic, ethical, political, legal and environmental factors shaping a business environment are assessed by a business so as to devise future business strategy. (See also PEST analysis.)

Stock options (see **share options**).

Strategic alliance Where two firms work together, formally or informally, to achieve a mutually desirable goal.

Strategic management The management of the strategic long-term decisions and activities of the business.

Strategic trade theory The theory that protecting/supporting certain industries can enable them to compete more effectively with large monopolistic rivals abroad. The effect of the protection is to increase long-run competition and may enable the protected firms to exploit a comparative advantage that they could not have done otherwise.

Structural unemployment Unemployment that arises from changes in the pattern of demand or supply in the economy. People made redundant in one part of the economy cannot immediately take up jobs in other parts (even though there are vacancies).

Subcontracting Where a firm employs another firm to produce part of its output or some of its input(s).

Sub-prime debt Debt where there is a high risk of default by the borrower (e.g. mortgage holders who are on low incomes facing higher interest rates and falling house prices).

Substitute goods A pair of goods which are considered by consumers to be alternatives to each other. As the price of one goes up, the demand for the other rises.

Substitutes in supply These are two goods where an increased production of one means diverting resources away from producing the other.

Substitution effect The effect of a change in price on quantity demanded arising from the consumer switching to or from alternative (substitute) products.

Supernormal profit The excess of total profit above normal profit.

Supply chain The flow of inputs into a finished product from the raw materials stage, through manufacturing and distribution right through to the sale to the final consumer.

Supply curve A graph showing the relationship between the price of a good and the quantity of the good supplied over a given period of time.

Supply schedule A table showing the different quantities of a good that producers are willing and able to supply at various prices over a given time period. A supply schedule can be for an individual producer or group of producers, or for all producers (the market supply schedule).

Supply-side policy Policy to affect aggregate supply directly.

Tacit collusion When oligopolists take care not to engage in price cutting, excessive advertising or other forms of competition. There may be unwritten 'rules' of collusive behaviour such as price leadership.

Takeover (or acquisition) Where one business acquires another. A takeover may not necessarily involve mutual agreement between the two parties. In such cases, the takeover might be viewed as 'hostile'.

Takeover constraint The effect that the fear of being taken over has on a firm's willingness to undertake projects that reduce distributed profits.

Tapered vertical integration Where a firm is partially integrated with an earlier stage of production; where it produces *some* of an input itself and buys some from another firm.

Tariffs Taxes (customs duties) on imports. These could be a percentage of the value of the good (an 'ad valorem' tariff), or a fixed amount per unit (a 'specific' tariff).

Taylor rule A rule adopted by a central bank for setting the rate of interest. It will raise the interest rate if (a) inflation is above target or (b) economic growth is above the sustainable level (or unemployment below the equilibrium rate). The rule states how much interest rates will be changed in each case. In other words, a relative weighting is attached to each of these two objectives.

Technological unemployment Structural unemployment that occurs as a result of the introduction of labour-saving technology.

Technology transfer Where a host state benefits from the new technology that an MNC brings with its investment.

Terms of trade The price index of exports divided by the price index of imports and then expressed as a percentage. This means that the terms of trade will be 100 in the base year.

Tertiary production The production from the service sector of the economy.

Third-degree price discrimination When a firm divides consumers into different groups and charges a different price to consumers in the different groups, but the same price to all consumers within a group.

Tit-for-tat A strategy where you copy whatever your rival does. Thus if your rival cuts price, you will too. If your rival does not, neither will you.

Total consumer expenditure (TE) (per period) The price of the product multiplied by the quantity purchased: $TE = P \times Q$.

Total cost (TC) (per period) The sum of total fixed costs (TFC) and total variable costs (TVC): $TC = TFC + TVC$.

Total revenue (*TR*) (per period) The total amount received by firms from the sale of a product, before the deduction of taxes or any other costs. The price multiplied by the quantity sold: $TR = P \times Q$.

Total utility (*TU*) The total satisfaction a consumer gets from the consumption of all the units of a good consumed within a given time period.

Tradable permits Each firm is given a permit to produce a given level of pollution. If less than the permitted amount is produced, the firm is given a credit. This can then be sold to another firm, allowing it to exceed its original limit. This is known as a 'cap and trade' scheme.

Transactions costs The costs associated with exchanging products. For buyers it is the costs over and above the price of the product. For sellers it is the costs over and above the costs of production.

Transfer payments Moneys transferred from one person or group to another (e.g. from the government to individuals) without production taking place.

Transfer pricing The pricing system used within a business to transfer intermediate products between its various divisions, often in different countries.

U-form business organisation One in which the central organisation of the firm (the chief executive or a managerial team) is responsible both for the firm's day-to-day administration and for formulating its business strategy.

Uncertainty This is when an outcome may or may not occur and where its probability of occurring is not known.

Underemployment Where people would like to work more hours than they currently do – e.g. where part-time workers would like to work full time or more part-time hours.

Unemployment rate The number unemployed expressed as a percentage of the labour force.

Unit elasticity When the price elasticity of demand is unity, this is where quantity demanded changes by the same proportion as the price. Price elasticity is equal to –1.

Value chain The stages or activities that help to create product value.

Variable costs Total costs that do vary with the amount of output produced.

Variable input An input that can be increased in supply within a given time period.

Vertical integration A business growth strategy that involves expanding within an existing market, but at a different stage of production. Vertical integration can be 'forward', such as moving into distribution or retail, or 'backward', such as expanding into extracting raw materials or producing components.

Vertical merger Where two firms in the same industry at different stages in the production process merge.

Vertically integrated firm A firm that produces at more than one stage in the production and distribution of a product.

Vertically integrated multinational A multinational that undertakes the various stages of production for a given product in different countries.

Wage taker The wage rate is determined by market forces.

Withdrawals (*W*) (or leakages) Incomes of households or firms that are not passed on round the inner flow. Withdrawals equal net saving (*S*) plus net taxes (*T*) plus import expenditure (*M*): $W = S + T + M$.

Working to rule Workers do no more than they are supposed to, as set out in their job descriptions.

Index